FROM TEACHER THINKING TO TEACHERS AND TEACHING: THE EVOLUTION OF A RESEARCH COMMUNITY

ADVANCES IN RESEARCH ON TEACHING

Series Editor: Volumes 1–11: Jere Brophy

Volumes 12–18: Stefinee Pinnegar

Recent Volumes:

ADVANCES IN RESEARCH ON TEACHING   VOLUME 19

FROM TEACHER THINKING TO TEACHERS AND TEACHING: THE EVOLUTION OF A RESEARCH COMMUNITY

THIRTIETH ANNIVERSARY VOLUME OF THE INTERNATIONAL STUDY ASSOCIATION ON TEACHERS AND TEACHING

EDITED BY

CHERYL J. CRAIG
University of Houston, Houston, USA

PAULIEN C. MEIJER
Nijmegen University, Nijmegen, The Netherlands

JAN BROECKMANS
Hasselt University, Hasselt, Belgium

United Kingdom – North America – Japan
India – Malaysia – China

Emerald Group Publishing Limited
Howard House, Wagon Lane, Bingley BD16 1WA, UK

First edition 2013

Copyright © 2013 Emerald Group Publishing Limited

Reprints and permission service
Contact: permissions@emeraldinsight.com

British Library Cataloguing in Publication Data
A catalogue record for this book is available from the British Library.

ISBN: 978-1-78190-850-1
ISSN: 1479-3687 (Series)

ISOQAR certified
Management System,
awarded to Emerald
for adherence to
Environmental
standard
ISO 14001:2004.

Certificate Number 1985
ISO 14001

INVESTOR IN PEOPLE

CONTENTS

v

LIST OF CONTRIBUTORS

Beatrice Avalos	Centre for Advanced Research in Education, University of Chile, Chile
Douwe Beijaard	Eindhoven University of Technology, Eindhoven, The Netherlands
Amanda Berry	Leiden University, Leiden, The Netherlands
Sephora Boucenna	University of Namur, Namur, Belgium
Evelyne Charlier	University of Namur, Namur, Belgium
D. Jean Clandinin	University of Alberta, Edmonton, Canada
Christopher Day	University of Nottingham, Nottingham, UK
Freema Elbaz-Luwisch	University of Haifa, Haifa, Israel
Eila Estola	University of Oulu, Oulu, Finland
Zhuo Feng	Shenyang Normal University, Shenyang, China
Maria Assunção Flores	University of Minho, Braga, Portugal
David R. Goodwin	Missouri State University, Springfield, USA
Sigrun Gudmundsdottir	Deceased; formerly Department of Education, The University of Trondheim, Trondheim, Norway
Xiao Han	University of St. Thomas, Houston, TX, USA
Maher Hashweh	Birzeit University, Birzeit, Palestine
Jukka Husu	University of Turku, Turku, Finland

xi

Jayshri Kannan   Nagaland Board of School Education,
                                    Nagaland, India

Geert Kelchtermans   University of Leuven, Leuven, Belgium

Michael Kompf   Brock University, St. Catharines,
                                    Canada

Fred A. J. Korthagen   VU University, Utrecht,
                                    The Netherlands

Ora W. Y. Kwo   The University of Hong Kong, Hong
                                    Kong

Anneli Lauriala   University of Lapland, Rovaniemi,
                                    Finland

John Loughran   Monash University, Melbourne,
                                    Australia

Joost Lowyck   University of Leuven, Leuven, Belgium

Barica Marentič Požarnik   University of Ljubljana, Ljubljana,
                                    Slovenia

Maria Inês Marcondes   Pontifícia Universidade Católica do Rio
                                    de Janeiro, Brazil

Amanda McGraw   University of Ballarat, Ballarat, Australia

Paulien C. Meijer   Nijmegen University, Utrecht,
                                    The Netherlands

Cholpon Musaeva   English and Foreign Languages
                                    University, Hyderabad, India

Lily Orland-Barak   University of Haifa, Haifa, Israel

Samuel Ouma Oyoo   University of the Witwatersrand,
                                    Johannesburg, South Africa

Tara Ratnam   Independent ELT Consulant, India

Tom Russell   Queen's University, Kingston, Canada

Frances O'Connell Rust   University of Pennsylvania Graduate
                                    School of Education, Philadelphia,
                                    USA

Marjeta Šarić	University of Ljubljana, Ljubljana, Slovenia
Michael Schratz	University of Innsbruck, Innsbruck, Austria
Barbara Šteh	University of Ljubljana, Ljubljana, Slovenia
Carola Steinberg	University of the Witwatersrand, Johannesburg, South Africa
Leena Syrjälä	University of Oulu, Oulu, Finland
Edith Tabak	Levinsky College of Education, Tel-aviv, Israel
Kirsi Tirri	University of Helsinki, Helsinki, Finland
Auli Toom	University of Helsinki, Helsinki, Finland
Nico Verloop	Leiden University, Leiden, The Netherlands
Xiaohong Yang	Hangzhou Normal University, Hangzhou, China
Issa Danjun Ying	The Hong Kong Institute of Education, Hong Kong
Michal Zellermayer	Levinsky College of Education, Tel-aviv, Israel

FOREWORD

This volume, *From Teacher Thinking to Teachers and Teaching: The Evolution of a Research Community*, captures advances that have occurred in the thirty years that the International Study Association on Teachers and Teaching (ISATT) organization has been in existence (1983–2013). ISATT occupies an important place in educational history. It is the international birthplace of the paradigm shift that occurred in the field of education in the 1980s as well as the organization that helped transition the study of teacher thinking to the study of teachers and teaching in all of its complexities. ISATT, which began with a handful of members, now has a membership that hails from 45 countries. ISATT's near-global representation shows how the organization's reach has expanded over three decades.

This book is the cumulative effort of ISATT members dotted around the globe. Following the 2011 biennial meeting in Braga, Portugal, Paulien C. Meijer (chair) and Cheryl J. Craig (secretary) convened "a writing meeting" where the genesis of this book was discussed. From there, we divided ourselves into semi-autonomous regional groups, all of which would focus on ISATT's scholarship as it has developed through the years. This led to a second meeting that was held in Vancouver, Canada when many of us were there attending the American Educational Research Association (AERA) Meeting in April, 2012. On that occasion, our plans became solidified and each regional group found ways to contribute through featuring their own and others' scholarship. Also, Jan Broeckmans joined us as a third coeditor when he assumed the position of ISATT Treasurer.

From the outset, we planned to weave some historical work into the volume. These chapters were nominated by the regional editors in consultation with us and the authors of the works. A further principle that guided this book's development was our expressed desire to blend chapters written by early career scholars with those authored by accomplished scholars and invited guests. We also held gender equity closely in mind and included work of some of ISATT's past leadership, present national representatives and current executive committee members.

As editors, we (Cheryl J. Craig, Paulien C. Meijer, and Jan Broeckmans) wish to thank the many international researchers who contributed to this book endeavor. We especially want to recognize the regional editors because it is through their diligence that this volume was largely brought into being:

Europe 1
Bernadette Charlier, Educational Sciences Department, University of Fribourg, Fribourg, Switzerland
ISATT National Representative for Switzerland; Executive Committee Member

Isabel Rots, Department of Educational Studies, Ghent University, Ghent, Belgium

Europe 2
Anneli Lauriala, University of Lapland, Rovaniemi, Finland

Barbara Šteh, Faculty of Arts, University of Ljubljana, Ljubljana, Slovenia

Europe 3
Christopher Day, Past Chair, University of Nottingham, Nottingham, United Kingdom
Past Secretary; Editor-in-Chief, Teachers and Teaching: Theory and Practice

Maria Assunção Flores, University of Minho, Braga, Portugal

Middle East
Lily Orland-Barak, University of Haifa, Haifa, Israel
Book Editor, Teachers and Teaching: Theory and Practice

Freema Elbaz-Luwisch, University of Haifa, Haifa, Israel
Former Executive Committee Member

North America
Past Chair
Michael Kompf, Brock University, St Catharines, Canada

Frances O'Connell Rust, University of Pennsylvania, Graduate School of Education, USA

Asia Pacific
Issa Danjun Ying, The Hong Kong Institute of Education, Hong Kong.
ISATT National Representative for Hong Kong

Amanda McGraw, University of Ballarat, Ballarat, Australia

Amanda Berry, ICLON, Leiden University, Leiden, The Netherlands

New Regions

Tara Ratnam, Freelance Teacher Educator, Mysore, India
ISATT National Representative for India

Samuel Ouma Oyoo, School of Education, University of the Witwatersrand, Johannesburg, South Africa.
ISATT National Representative for South Africa [and larger Africa]; Executive Committee Member

David R. Goodwin, Missouri State University, Springfield, Missouri, USA

We furthermore wish to recognize four other individuals who worked tirelessly on this book project: Dr. Liping Wei and Gayle Curtis, Cheryl J. Craig's Research Assistants at the University of Houston; Daniela Hotolean, ISATT's Administrator and Dwaine Yeargin, Literacy Chair of Lanier Middle School in Houston, Texas who served as this volume's technical editor.

Without the near-herculean efforts of all of these people, this book would have not come to fruition. We salute each one of them for the contributions they made in both big and small ways.

As readers can imagine, figuring out how to characterize thirty years of history across 45 countries was a daunting task. While we knew we could not include everyone, we are hopeful that what we feature in this book is representative of our membership and the strands of research they pursue.

To this end, we have divided the volume into five parts for ease of reading:

I. The Origins of the International Study Association on Teachers and Teaching
II. Research Strands
III. Contemporary International Scholarship
IV. Advances in Teacher Education
V. Growth in Community

Lastly, we invite readers to accompany us on this journey into ISATT's past, present and imagined future. We hope that as you read along you will feel part of our research community's emergence and development. We know that the act of preparing this book served not only to capture ISATT's scholarly advances, but also concomitantly to continue to build international relationships around a shared purpose and project. On the occasion of ISATT's 30th Anniversary, we are delighted to honor ISATT's founding members as well as those who will help blaze trails for our study organization as it races toward a future that is yet unknown.

Cheryl J. Craig, Ph.D.
Secretary, ISATT

Paulien C. Meijer, Ph.D.
Chair, ISATT

Jan Broeckmans, Ph.D.
Treasurer, ISATT
Coeditors

PART I
THE ORIGINS OF THE INTERNATIONAL STUDY ASSOCIATION ON TEACHERS AND TEACHING

Over its distinguished 30 year history, ISATT transitioned from being the International Study Association on Teacher Thinking to the International Study Association on Teachers and Teaching. Three chapters trace this shift. Chapter 1, "The International Study Association on Teachers and Teaching (ISATT): Seeing Tracks and Making More" is contributed by The America's editors, Michael Kompf and Francis O'Connell Rust. Chapter 2, "The Origins of ISATT: An Idiosyncratic Perspective" is authored by ISATT's first chair, Joost Lowyck, and was solicited by European editor Isabel Rots. Chapter 3, "The Role of ISATT in the Professional Development of Barica Marentič Požarnik" is an interview that European editor Barbara Šteh conducted with her mentor, Barica Marentič Požarnik, who is now retired.

CHAPTER 1

THE INTERNATIONAL STUDY ASSOCIATION ON TEACHERS AND TEACHING (ISATT): SEEING TRACKS AND MAKING MORE

Michael Kompf and Frances O'Connell Rust

ABSTRACT

The first part of this chapter addresses the history and development of the International Study Association of Teachers and Teaching (ISATT) and its engagement with the global educational community. We provide an account of the context and background against which ISATT developed as well as information about the founders' orientations and the actions that led to ISATT's birth. The second part of the chapter uses patterns of topic focus as graphic indicators of the evolution of ISATT's research interests expressed through publication titles.

Keywords: ISATT; teacher organizations; international teacher organizations

From Teacher Thinking to Teachers and Teaching: The Evolution of a Research Community
Advances in Research on Teaching, Volume 19, 3–38
ISSN: 1479-3687/doi:10.1108/S1479-3687(2013)0000019004

PREAMBLE

Attaching a subtitle to papers, chapters and the like give authors an opportunity to further describe what readers can expect in the work that follows. A number of subtitles came to mind for this piece: *The Little Organisation that Grew*; or *A Funny Thing Happened on the Way to the Paradigm*; or perhaps *Setting Free the Scholars*. Of the many subtitle possibilities, *Seeing Tracks and Making More* seemed most appropriate. The back-story for this choice involves a situation recounted in the introduction to *Changing Research and Practice*,[1] a volume of selections from papers presented at the first North American ISATT conference held at Brock University in the summer of 1995.

Michael Kompf recalled a visit to his farm by Alan Brown during the following winter. Commenting on a visit with Maureen Pope, Alan wrote a concise note about a winter walk through the forest: 'We saw tracks and made more.' The still-fresh vision of walking through a snow-covered forest following deer and other tracks, obliterating some, sidestepping others and straying off remains; each of us made our own paths here and there that criss-crossed, converged and diverged. Later discussions of his note led to metaphorical forays about how the tracks and paths laid out by scholars were like footprints in the snow – temporary, often tentative but advisedly wary of the solid or not-so-solid footing that lies beneath.

ISATT has provided similar terrain for more than a few generations of scholars. Familiar paths are acknowledged and well-trodden with many layers of mind-prints. Educational explorers are encouraged to see tracks, make more and most importantly, to pay attention to the scenery that surrounds each step taken. Fond sentiment as expressed above is not maudlin because it has had and continues to have a necessary and vital place in any account of ISATT's origin and development. ISATT is a story about individuals, conversations and the emergence of a research community. No story of community is ever complete; community is a continuous and continual work in progress. Storied meanings change as the memories of participant members evolve, add, interpret and enrich authenticity with the individual colours of perspective and place. ISATT is an unfolding story of old friends, of those no longer with us, and those yet to find us. Most importantly ISATT is a story about freeing inquiry and providing a safe haven for ideas and discussions with tracks and paths that transcend geopolitical boundaries.

Our hope in this chapter is to convey a sense of the community that is ISATT by examining some of the tracks we have made and the further tracks we make possible. We appreciate the ambitious gravity of such a chore and can only ground it in available information and our own experiences with ISATT.[2]

We have been able to track down dusty copies of some conference proceedings and ISATT newsletters and have had the additional privilege of consulting with a number of founding and early members. However, the task of constructing a cohesive and accurate evolution of ISATT has been like trying to derive the plot and meaning of a film through a selection of still photos – taken from different perspectives. As some Aboriginal people object to having their photographs taken for fear of having their souls captured, we are wary of trying to capture the spirit of ISATT – but can write with certainty that it came about in times of discontent and change in how teacher education and education in general was thought about and practiced.

THE CONTEXT AND BACKGROUND OF ISATT'S DEVELOPMENT

Measuring the accomplishments and worth of those who taught teachers during the 1960s, 1970s and early 1980s had mostly to do with the scholarship and practice of teaching. A shift, perhaps most visible in North America but elsewhere as well, occurred in teacher education during those decades, as it moved from the simple certification provided by 'Normal' schools or 'Colleges' of education to the degree granting status provided by an academically accredited Faculty of Education associated with a university. However, unlike those faculties representing an academic discipline, Faculties of Education were regarded in many institutions as engaged in professional education, hence they did not share the same status as those in the arts and sciences, and recognition of their scholarly worth gradually transferred from within the university to professional associations and/or government legislation through which their students were certified for practice.

Teachers of the 1960s and 1970s found themselves between identities. While those who taught were regarded as members of the profession of teachers, the formal requisites of the status of 'professional' were argued as unmet. Professions have governing bodies with legislated rights to certify individuals with accredited training to practice in specific professions. Governing bodies of professions establish standards of practice and enforce regulations and disciplinary consequences as necessary. In Canada, Colleges of Teachers were established in various provinces (for example,

British Columbia in the late 1980s; Ontario in the late 1990s) with the intent of gaining recognition as a profession. While the back stories of this movement included debates over unionisation and collective bargaining rights as might be available to professions, the scholarship of teaching and learning began to shine too brightly to be ignored.

Looking back to those decades, writers such as Etzioni (1969) called teaching a 'semi-profession,' Glazer (1974) called it a 'minor profession,' and others, including Schön (1987) and Runté (1995), have since argued that a 'profession' only exists as a label. They argued that teachers are knowledge workers with personal and public responsibilities to be reflective practitioners accountable for the enterprise that education represented. Teachers were advised by such writers to stop worrying about trivial matters of status and focus on the deskilling and re-skilling of students.

During the 1970s and 1980s, as requirements by professional associations and/or government legislation framed undergraduate study as prerequisite for beginning teachers, a growing interest in further teacher education and specialised educational studies developed and was implemented in the establishment of graduate study programmes including the degrees of Master of Education (MEd) or Master of Arts in Teaching (MAT), Doctor of Education (EdD) and Doctor of Philosophy (PhD). These programmes were intended to produce professional educators who were teachers in a variety of subject areas depending on the level taught, and leaders of schools and school systems. In most, if not all, public education venues, a Master of Education degree became a minimal prerequisite for assuming school and district administrative positions such as Vice-Principal, Principal, Superintendent or Chancellor.

In many programmes of study, the MEd was accompanied by a research focus requiring a major research paper or thesis as an exit requirement. This meant that many teacher educators found themselves in pursuit of advanced degrees as a means of attaining the qualifications and skills required to meet academic and institutional expectations for supervision. As faculty expertise increased, the recognition of education as a definable discipline grew in the university, along with institutional expectations for ongoing relevant, important and meaningful research carried out in ways that reflected the terms and conditions of sister academic faculties and disciplines.

The 1960s, 1970s and 1980s can be fairly characterised as time during which a great many social changes occurred in politics, war, art, music, personal values, social issues and technology. Those of us who found maturity during those decades, or had it thrust upon us, faced head on the issues that separated us from those who had gone before. Baby-boomers were raised on a social diet of paradigm shift as modernity gave way to post-modernity, feminism raised questions about fundamental assumptions in theory, practice and representativeness and the civil rights movement brought matters of race and equality to the forefront of both social and educational agendas. Geopolitical shifts caused walls to crumble, nation-states to emerge from deserts and the dawning of a new sense of social justice that laid bare generations of unthinking assumptions marked by the multi-national global footprints of imperialism.

Issues of race, class, gender, religion and special learning needs and accommodations layered complexity on complexity for those who would provide new and practicing teachers with meaningful educational experiences and anticipations of vocational realisation. The generation of teacher educators who populated Faculties of Education during the 1960s, 1970s and 1980s carried with them, for the most part, an inherited factory model of teaching, learning and education in general. This 'traditional' approach was mainly grounded in a post-war legacy of methodologies and methods that focused on science, measurement and management. An empirical, mechanistic approach to schooling was defended as necessary to greet a booming population, rampant industrialisation and a growing need for consumer goods.[3]

The demand for workers with all ranges and levels of skills streamed learners, teachers and schools in directions determined by batteries of tests and measurements. Although well-intentioned from a social theory perspective, many facets of understanding education as a discipline were yet to be identified and investigated. As society shifted in response to growth and diversity, a concomitant shift occurred in the culture of teacher educators and in teaching culture as a whole. The movement from practice to inquiry elevated teaching from simple practice to theorising about practice regarding teaching and associated underlying activities in ways that legitimised teachers as producers of research and knowledge rather than mere recipients of information generated elsewhere. However, the movement was far from smooth, and led George Mouly (1978) to write:

> Actually teachers tend to be uneasy when dealing with research. Research seems to begin with the premise that common sense is not enough, that what teachers have always believed is 'as likely as not to be incorrect', that research is a painstakingly elaborate process beyond the capabilities of the average classroom teacher to do or even to read meaningfully. For many teachers, research is an entirely new experience, filled with elaborate technical procedures and specialized statistical terminologies and techniques, for which their undergraduate studies did not prepare them. In other

> words, the teacher is typically put in the position of being the 'recipient' of research, translated to him (sic) second-hand and often distorted in the process. To make matters worse, the inadequacies of published research in education are often such that the teacher must be cautious in what he accepts and rejects, but then this calls for him to be knowledgeable as to what is to be believed and what needs cautious interpretation. (p. 18)

Education, it seemed, was beginning to depart somewhat from the traditional scientific paradigms of research as deeper understandings of practice were better suited to the semantic implications of an 'inquiry' approach rather than the time and tradition-bound requisites of 'research.' While regarded by some as merely a subtle semantic twist, the differences between research and inquiry are important and have been discussed eloquently by Cordingley:

> Robinson (2003, p. 28) explores the overlap between the roles of practitioners and researchers and makes a powerful argument that good practice for practitioners requires them to conduct an ongoing inquiry into their individual and collective practice. Both [good research and good practice] require attitudes of openness, intellectual curiosity, and a willingness to step outside a frame of reference to see things in new ways. Most important of all is the ability to recognise that all research and all practice proceeds from a particular frame of reference.

> Robinson says that inquiry involves practitioners in examining the knowledge, skills, attitudes, and strategies that underpin their practice and in testing their assumptions. She adds that it should also be 'both scaffolded on the research findings of others and productive of new knowledge about their particular context'. (p. 29)

She argues that the development of teachers as researchers is a 'professional necessity.' Enhancement of the research role of teachers was central to sustainable school improvement, to effective teacher development, and, most important of all, to the professionalism of teachers.

Like Robinson, Reid (2004) and Cordingley (2003) identify a close relationship between inquiry and research. However, they are each careful to draw a distinction between the two. There are a number of characteristics of properly constituted research, including that it uses appropriate research methods and methodologies, builds upon the literature in the area being researched, is an accessible activity open to peer review, and that the knowledge that is produced is applicable to other researchers and research contexts. Sometimes inquiry may meet these requirements, often it will not (Reid, 2004, p. 8). Cordingley (2003) connected these ideas to practice:

> This does not mean that there is any less intellectual rigour involved in carrying out inquiry than in conducting research. The key difference is in the developmental aim

of practitioner inquiry and in the fact that it is not carried out with the intention, necessarily, of being made public. Removing the necessity to conform to the conventions for published research allows practitioners to focus on the complex task of interpreting evidence and research and applying the new knowledge to their practice. What role does conducting research play in your work? What role could or should it play? Not all teacher inquiry aims to produce evidence and understanding in a public form that can be tested and reviewed by others. Some teacher inquiry simply seeks to enhance the practice of the inquirer through the use of evidence...This kind of continuing professional development can accurately be described as evidence-based or informed practice. (p. 108)

Inquiry, then, draws on research methodologies and on published research but does not require practitioners to conform to strict research conventions. Some educators will, indeed, be researchers, but all of us should be inquirers into our professional practice. Such a stance was later brought home by 2001 ISATT keynote speaker John Elliott (1991) in *Action research for educational change* in which the acts of teaching were treated as research opportunities in and of themselves.

Once the epistemological and methodological doors opened, efforts to create a culture of inquiry took root, interrupting and advancing the cycles of social reproduction that characterised teacher training and the scholarship of teaching in previous generations. In those halcyon days, marked by creativity and experimentation, entry into the academy of teacher education and associated research activities was idealistically dependent more on dedication, intellect, gifted insight and a sense of vocation rather than the strategic, sometimes Machiavellian positioning and status-seeking activities often associated with mainstream academic culture. A cross-disciplinary debate was emerging over the merits and worth of quantitative and qualitative methods in social science research. The language and principles of critical social theorists was breaking through methodological walls, and borrowing liberally from anthropology and sociology, with occasional forays into narrative approaches.

By the early 1980s, Philip Jackson's (1968) *Life in classrooms* had become a standard inspiration for alternative inquiry approaches into what went on in teachers' minds, and spirits, as they prepared for, engaged with and reflected on events in and around their classroom practices. The *zeitgeist* was right for the birthing of alternative forums for inquiry into and treatment of teachers' lives, careers, thoughts and practices.

In Western Europe (mainly in The Netherlands, Germany and Belgium), Jackson's work was a significant source of inspiration as well for those who started to focus research on 'teacher thinking.' Other sources of inspiration played an important role as well. Shavelson and Stern's (1981) work in cognitive psychology connected information processing models of the learner with teacher's and decision making models. The Dutch educational psychologist Van Parreren[4] advocated action-oriented approaches based on, among others, the work of Russian scholars such as Vygotsky (1986) and *Gal'perin* (Haenen, 1996). The work of Frances Fuller (1969) on beginning teachers' concerns was also influential as was the large body of work from Walter Doyle on contextual factors in shaping teaching practice beginning in the 1960s. Doyle (2009) continues to contribute up to the present including a chapter in an edited book by ISATT member Theo Wubbels with colleagues Tartwijk and den Brok (in press).[5]

Those who founded ISATT in the early 1980s did so based on common interests in uncovering and studying the various aspects of teachers' thinking about teaching. Their interests signalled a departure from mainstream conceptual and methodological regard and treatment of significant topics with research importance in education.

ISATT'S FOUNDING AS THE INTERNATIONAL STUDY ASSOCIATION ON TEACHER THINKING

Rob Halkes was the initiator of ISATT. He observed in 1980 that a worldwide group of scholars were looking at and discussing ideas associated with teacher thinking. During a visit to Canada for the purposes of academic speaking engagements, Rob and John Olson (then teaching at Queen's University in Canada), discussed whether it would be a good idea to found a study association on the topic. Rob also met Alan Brown at The Ontario Institute for Studies in Education (OISE)[6] during that visit when he gave an address to faculty. According to Rob:

> As John agreed with the idea, I went on to send everyone I knew who was working in the field a letter to ask him or her thoughts on the idea. And if there was enough interest, I would invite them to have a symposium on the topic in which we would have a founding meeting. That was in 1982, in Tilburg. (Personal communication, 2012)

John Olson concurred:

> It was Rob Halkes, Chris Clark and myself who took steps to convene a conference committee led by Rob to hold the first meeting at Tilburg (in 1983). So we, and the committee, and those who came to the first conference ... might be considered the initiating group that founded ISATT. (Personal communication, 2012)

ISATT participants met again in Tilburg in 1984 with John Olson as the founding Chair. Alan Brown explained:

> ... at Tilburg 1 or 2 we did, in a plenary business session (all sessions were plenary), mention the concept of 'founder' status but resolved nothing excepting the thought, not voted upon, that everyone who showed for Tilburg 1 was part of ISATT's initiation.

Alan went on to say,

> No doubt about it, Halkes was the workhorse of ISATT's beginnings; he even paid some two thousand florins (roughly about $1000 USD) for that school-pencil logo (that is still in use). (Personal communication, 2012)

Michael Kompf was one of Alan Brown's PhD students at the time and can vividly recall the excitement Alan expressed on his return from Tilburg. The conference poster was framed and prominently displayed on Brown's office wall. The lure of attending the next meeting in Leuven was dangled with the condition that something interesting could be developed and presented. A buzz about this new group called ISATT circulated around OISE through Brown's network, at Queen's through John Olson's contacts and the connections of Antoinette Oberg at the University of Victoria (British Columbia, Canada). Similar buzzes occurred through the networks of Chris Clark (USA), Maureen Pope (UK). Halkes and Lowyck spread the word in Europe attracting others seeking something different in the academic work that characterised education.

Rob wrote in the introduction to the November 1985 (Number 003) ISATT Newsletter about that anticipated the 1986 meeting in Leuven:

> ISATT's activities are rapidly growing now. Since its initiation at the 1983 Symposium, people from all over the world have been registering for membership, and it is stimulating to see these to be active researchers in the field sometimes even with remarkable lists of publications. National committees of people representing ISATT in their respective countries have been formed in about fifteen countries.
>
> Of course, this is supported by the growing interest into the field of teacher thinking as may be seen in the number of research projects that are currently being conducted ... However, it is no easy field to be in. Researchers have been and are confronted with problems of all sorts, conceptual and methodological as was shown in the two conferences held. But there it was also revealed how endeavouring into the teacher's thinking perspective may render a new and more insightful view on teaching-learning processes for which the struggle with research problems is worth the effort. (p. 2)

Leuven was a transitional conference that propelled ISATT into an exclusive niche. Its meetings were attractive to many scholars as growing interest and understanding the nature of a global research agenda in education was increasingly valued as important and worthwhile. International comparative studies that went beyond the descriptive information provided by such organisations as The United Nations Organization for Education, Science and Culture (UNESCO) and into the idiosyncrasies of teacher thinking and teaching practice.

BECOMING AND BEING ISATT

In the November 1988 (Number 07) Newsletter, Rob wrote a 'personal note' that marked his departure from active involvement in ISATT:

> With the last conference (Leuven), ISATT entered a next stage in development. Having overcome limits of a starting association, it enjoys global acknowledgement and respect. Growing in membership too, it had found its place on earth, indeed ... this newsletter covers a lot of changes that have been made within ISATT at the conference. The main change, better – innovation, that we implemented, concerned the election of a new executive [Chair-Maureen Pope (UK), Secretary-Treasurer Chris Day (UK), Chris Clark (USA), Gunther Huber (West Germany), Antoinette Oberg (Canada), Naama Sabar (Israel)] ... This implies of course the goodbye to the former executive, the'founding' group that made a major step to begin with: Thank you Miriam Ben-Peretz, Rainer Bromme, Chris Clark, Joost Lowyck, John Olson, John Peters, Maureen Pope, Harm Tillema! Without you there would not have been an ISATT as it is now ... Special thanks must go to John Olson. He was the one that supported me at crucial times and, sometimes even against my willing, stimulated me to proceed with the very first activities for the further organisation of it. When I may be proud on being the 'founding member' of ISATT ... he is the cause for that ...

Rob continued:

> Due to my change of job, I knew that I had to resign from the secretarial office of ISATT. People who know me well, don't need to be told that I regret to do so. However, I do know at the same time that new spirit, enthusiasm and, most of all, energy is needed to bring ISATT to its next stage – a stage in which ISATT will be respected as a(n) international association of researchers who care most and know best about the teacher's profession, its skillful complexity and its practical pitfalls as well. With the new executive, chair and secretary the flame is burning sky-high again: a guarantee for the years to come. I wish to thank you all for having trusted me in the beginning endeavours of ISATT. It has become an important part of my life and I am pleased that I was allowed to do it. (pp. 4–5)

In the same newsletter Maureen Pope reported that:

> It was agreed that Rob Halkes be officially named as Founder of ISATT and would be co-opted on a permanent basis as consultant to the ISATT executive. (pp. 34–35)

With the departure of Rob Halkes, Maureen Pope's guiding hand as Chair led the organisation through periods of development and change.

ISATT's popularity grew slowly but surely leading to debates over whether or not new members should be recruited and increase numbers or whether membership should be contained and remain small enough to afford the collegial and congenial spirit that characterised meetings. National representatives for ISATT in 1988 (ISATT Newsletter 07) came from nineteen parts of the globe including: Australia, Austria, Belgium, Brazil, Canada, England, Finland, Federal Republic of Germany, Hong, Kong, Iceland, Israel, Mexico, The Netherlands, Portugal, Spain Sweden, Switzerland and the USA.

ISATT AND THE INTERNATIONAL STAGE OF INQUIRY

Several organisations of importance to educational researchers existed around the globe before, during and after ISATT's inception. For example, the Australian Council on Educational Research (ACER) has existed since 1930 for the purpose of promoting 'the advancement and diffusion of knowledge and understanding'. This organisation was initially funded through Carnegie grants for countries that were or had been members of the British Commonwealth. Founded in 1979, the Council of Australian Postgraduate Associations (CAPA) represents the research interests of much of Australia's academe.

A European conference founded in 1975 that was of increasing importance at the time, and still quite strong today, was the annual 'ORD' = '*Onderwijsresearchdagen*' or Educational Research Days organised by the Dutch (Netherlands) Educational Research Association. This organisation had and has strong Belgian (Flemish) participation to the extent that some conferences have been held in Flanders (Leuven, Antwerp, Ghent).

The European Educational Research Association (EERA) was founded in 1994 as a learned society specifically for the purposes of:

- encouraging collaboration amongst educational researchers in Europe
- promoting communication between educational researchers and international governmental organisations such as the EU, Council of Europe, OECD and UNESCO
- improving communication amongst educational research associations and institutes within Europe
- disseminating the findings of educational research and highlighting their contribution to policy and practice (http://www.eera-ecer.de/about/)

In North America, the premier conference for educators had for many years been the annual American Educational Research Association

(AERA). Attendees were mostly from the United States and included (but were not limited to) working academics sharing research findings, graduate students finding community and teacher practitioners reporting innovative practices. While most who attended AERA were American, educators from Canada, the UK and Europe could be found among presenters and participants.

In a similar vein, and slightly north, the Canadian Society for Studies in Education (CSSE) met annually as part of the broader Learned Congress offered annually for all disciplines and professions. CSSE, while open to international participants had a more national orientation and focus. According to Alan Brown:

> Canada's (research context) was somewhat more complex ... CSSE was/is itself an umbrella of a couple of dozen education disciplines (each running their own programmes) formed early in the 1970s to replace the very old Canadian Association of Professors of Education (CAPE) and corral together the now burgeoning number of separate associations, the first and most prominent of which was the Canadian Educational Researchers Association (CERA) which elected Alan Brown (a previous president of CAPE) as its first elected president. (Personal communication, 2012)

During the times in which the germ of ISATT was developing, AERA represented a culture of research that was a global crucible for the collegium. A paper presented at AERA was a desirable entry on any CV independent of whether the scholar was aspiring (new), perspiring (mid-career) or inspiring (aged and possibly wise). AERA endorsed a style of research methodology and methods, presentation dynamics, intellectual and social collegial interaction that sought to exemplify the conduct and rigour expected in that particular era of educational life in North America. A paper presented at nationally focussed conferences such as EERA or CSSE while academically significant did not convey the cachet of a presentation at AERA. However, that said, while Special Interest Groups (SIGS) did offer more focused discourse within AERA, these did not fully meet international scholars' needs for more intimate community and response, and thus the door was open for the growth of international organisations like ISATT.

The character of those times, as noted earlier, was beset with debate over the content, medium and process of scholarly production amidst contested methodological preferences and traditions. Colleagues described less than favourable critiques received at AERA as 'intellectual blood-letting' inflicted by scholars bent on either holding their traditional disciplinary course, or scoring points and reputation building – often at the expense of others. National gatherings seldom saw such encounters, perhaps erring on the side of characteristic politeness at the expense of critical debate.

John Olson added:

> At that time behaviorism – i.e., David Berliner – held a strong grip on research. Positivism led to critiques of work on teacher thinking as soft. Lee Shulman – teacher cognition – and Elliott Eisner – teaching as aesthetic performance (I think Elliott wanted to say moral but never got that far) – helped open the field at AERA for more nuanced studies of teacher thinking that were not positivistic. Mind you, I think ISATT was more advanced in its thinking about teaching than either of these perspectives. (Personal communication, 2012)

Scholars seeking more collegial, congenial and constructive encounters sought mid-ground where outside-the-box work and ideas in progress would not lead to either crucifixion or becoming encased in the concrete of practice. While those who envisioned ISATT were scholars in their own right who had 'made it' through crucible and concrete, their wish was for something more – something closer to a humanistic edge of inquiry in education. ISATT initiators and founders encouraged graduate students and colleagues to attend ISATT and experience an alternative culture of curiosity and inquiry and the difference that small, authentic gatherings could have.

Patterns of membership demographics roughly paralleled the venues of ISATT meetings, as the regional and institutional affiliation of the organisation's Chair at the time and the passions of national representatives created enduring and/or fleeting clusters of members. It seems that members became members in response to curiosity as well as the need for critical collegiality as shifting personal and professional interests marked the necessity for freer movement between and among fields of research and the renewal effects that such movement could have in fostering scholarly and intellectual adventure.

The 1986 meeting of ISATT (then, the International Study Association on Teacher Thinking) at the University of Leuven, Belgium marked the first full and formalised meeting of the organisation replete with keynote speakers and a wide array of paper presentations that were conducted in congenial, collegial and constructively critical ways. Participants at the Leuven meeting actualised the scholarly and social foundations on which ISATT rests.

Special acknowledgement is owed to Joost Lowyck not only for the guiding role he played in ISATT during the early years but for sowing the seeds of teacher thinking for many influential scholars. Jan Broeckmans explains:

> Since Joost was for me nothing less than a mentor in my Ph.D. time, my perception may be biased. In that perception, however, Joost did play an important role, maybe not in

the organisation of the first symposium and the organisation of the association, but as a source of inspiration to a number of researchers in the Netherlands and Belgium. The early work (usually Ph.D. research) of Harm Tillema, Douwe Beijaard (an assistant of John Peters at the time), Nico Verloop ... all had at least some conceptual link to Joost's Ph.D. dissertation – which was the first research study in our region to deal with teacher thinking. (Personal communication, 2012)

The mid-1980s can be characterised as a pre-cusp era of shifting discipline-based ideologies, methodologies, methods of inquiry and most importantly modes of dialogue and scholarly exchange between and among neophytes and veterans. The interpersonal contact and conduct that characterised plenary addresses, paper presentations and informal chats held at ISATT heralded new possibilities for the academy in which 'Why not?', What if?' and 'So what?' questions could be posed in ways that created potential for deeper thinking rather than the toxic dismissal and diminishment that, at that time, seemed to characterise many major gatherings of research in education.

The variety of characters, concerns and conundrums shared by this diverse group of academics from across the globe both illustrated diversity of practice and found deeper bonds in commonalities of how teaching was approached and thought about through anticipations, practices and reflections embedded in teachers' thinking. The focus on teacher thinking was initially supported through an emphasis on cognition. Much initial writing emanating from ISATT drew on cognitive psychology, for example, the work of personal construct psychologist George Kelly. Cross-pollinations between ISATT and the International Personal Construct Congress (IPCC) came about as many educators attended both meetings. Maureen Pope, Alan Brown, Miriam Ben-Peretz, Michael Kompf and others carried the ideas of Kelly's personal constructs into teacher thinking – and teacher thinking back to IPCC throughout the 1980s and early 1990s.

These alternative approaches to inquiry and understanding applied to teachers' lives and careers emerged as trends on the fringes of mainstream research interests during those times and, in retrospect, we can see that they anticipated shifts in meaning-making. The juxtaposition of collaborative efforts in research, cross-disciplinary studies and generational cusps among the professoriate distinguished the group. The spirit of inclusion, while not common in all academic disciplines, seemed to find early and firm roots in ISATT and supported what has become a hallmark conversation of the organisation, namely, a willingness to consider paradigmatic shifts in how teachers, teacher educators, administrators and learners think about teacher preparation and how it is understood.

Maureen Pope summarised:

> The current ISATT gatherings are much bigger than the early days when, for example, the first couple could get round a large boardroom table! ISATT has come a long way along the track and genuine friendships across the globe have materialised. Unlike many professional groups who gather at conferences the ISATT Community tends to be more collaborative than competitive- mirroring the approach one hopes will be reflected in teachers and teaching. (Personal communication, 2012)

ISATT BECOMES THE INTERNATIONAL STUDY ASSOCIATION ON TEACHERS AND TEACHING

Along with the increasing diversity of members and expansion of member interest and research direction, a name change was adopted in 1993 at members' meeting in Gothenburg when ISATT's name was changed from the International Study Association on *Teacher Thinking* to The International Study Association on *Teachers and Teaching*. The change reflected the membership's commitment to embracing inclusion of broader interests around level of study, educational venues and emergent technologies in learning and teaching. The latter name was debated by members and ratified by vote. Some objected and voiced concern that the shift to a broader mandate than the specific intent of 'Teacher Thinking' would cause ISATT to depart from or even lose its cognitive roots in specific areas of inquiry and methodology. Some were simply gratified that the acronym (and logo) would be preserved. During the meeting one member commented that 'it didn't matter what we called the organization,' what was most important was the work members carried out, how members' work was discussed and the safe place ISATT offered for intellectual discourse. Some members declined to participate following that change but others quickly filled in gaps in the ranks and subsequent meetings have shown much diversity of interest accommodated by the larger conceptual frame of *Teachers and Teaching*.

Organisations that work well have (un)even blends of organistic and mechanistic orientations, and members who exemplify those perspectives and preferences. The roots of the ISATT community are organistic in that collegial discussion and debate over ideas that are important, significant and meaningful are considered necessary, welcome, renewing and rewarding. This *gestalt* of ISATT meetings has been a primary observation of those who have attended over the years. ISATT has several cornerstone principles that account for its longevity: common interests, anticipatory thinking and inclusion.

Decisions about practices and policies are made on behalf of members by the Executive Committee except where consultation with and voting by members is carried out at general meetings held during conferences. Examples of democratic proceedings include the above-mentioned name change of ISATT, the duration of service by the Executive Committee, the terms and conditions of journal publications, providing travel subsidies to graduate students and the choice of conference venues.

ISATT GOVERNANCE

ISATT's organisational structure, function and values are articulated in a constitution initially formulated by the founding members. The constitution has been amended as necessary through motions and votes at members' meetings to reflect changing times and member needs. ISATT's structure consists of an executive committee elected by the membership comprising the positions of Chair, Secretary, Treasurer (or Secretary-Treasurer), Newsletter Editor, International Representatives Coordinator, Outreach Coordinator and members at large.

Of great significance is the role of Administrative Assistant that has been filled from 2002 to the present by Daniela Hotolean – or Danni as she is known to most members. This position acts as the narrow end of the funnel regarding membership status, newsletter co-ordination, website management, public relations and information flow between and among the executive and membership.

The role of ISATT Chair required a gentle hand on the organisational tiller as overall direction and destination were driven by expressed member needs. The remarkable democratic spirit allowed Chairs in consultation with Secretary and Treasurer to solicit, identify and act on member interests that stressed the importance of dialogue and the forward-looking distinctiveness embedded in the spirit of ISATT. Debates continued over the size to which ISATT should be allowed to grow, how recruitment practices were carried out, how to best embrace diverse methodological preferences and orientations, inclusion of higher education interests and, most importantly, expanding the international footprint promised by the name of the organisation.

Best recollections and consultations have led to the following chronology of ISATT Chairs elected during general meetings of ISATT held at each of the various conference host institutions. Note that a three-year gap exists between 1988 and 1991 as a meeting scheduled for Israel was cancelled and relocated one year later to Surrey UK for reasons related to political unrest.

Year	Host Institution	Country	Chair
1983	Tilburg	Netherlands	
1984	Tilburg	Netherlands	John Olson
1986	Leuven University	Belgium	Joost Lowyck
1988	Nottingham University	UK	Maureen Pope
1991	University of Surrey	UK	Maureen Pope
1993	Gothenburg University	Sweden	Gunnar Handal
1995	Brock University	Canada	John Olson
1997	IPN, Kiel	Germany	Marcella Kysilka
1999	St. Patrick's College, Dublin	Ireland	Michael Kompf
2001	University of the Algarve	Portugal	Ciaran Sugrue
2003	Leiden University	Netherlands	Michael Kompf
2005	ACU Sydney	Australia	Michael Kompf
2007	Brock University	Canada	Michael Kompf
2009	University of Lapland	Finland	Paulien Meijer
2011	University of Minho	Portugal	Paulien Meijer
2013	University of Ghent	Belgium	To be elected

ISATT AND THE INTERNET

Manfred Lang (Kiel University) ushered ISATT into the World Wide Web by hosting an ISATT web page as a sub-page in Kiel University's main system. Around 1999 the website 'isatt.org' was secured by Michael Kompf as a domain name that was hosted in Canada until 2007 but managed by Manfred at Kiel. With additional resources and personnel Manfred's important work and ISATT's presence on the internet transferred to Daniela Hotolean at the University of Reading and became firmly established as a forum for information, promotion of upcoming conferences and ISATT publications in addition to providing a members' area that facilitates sharing of research ideas.

CONFERENCES

Determination of conference venues became a more deliberative process over the years resulting in a set of criteria ultimately requiring a demonstration of institutional support, financial means, appropriate infrastructure elements for travel, meetings and accommodation, and such other aspects as might be required to host several hundred individuals. Presentations at the members' meeting end with a vote on venue. While subject to local custom, the host committee usually has a chair, sometimes a co-chair and an organising committee most often made up of willing colleagues and graduate student volunteers. An implicit goal of hosts has been that conference participants have all needs attended to from arrival to departure in order that full attention can be given to the professional and personal interaction such a gathering provides. Enduring thanks are owed to all hosting organisations for the amount of work, attentiveness and caring demonstrated over the years.

Conference organisers are given the mixed blessing of editing a book with a representative selection of papers presented. While editing can be an arduous task the implicit benefits of contributing to ISATT history and participation in the production and dissemination of knowledge have always been reward enough. Royalties earned by editors of ISATT publications are typically paid to ISATT by the publisher to assist student travel. Conference themes chosen by organisers at host institutions illustrate a consistency that acknowledges progress carefully crafted with phrasing that draws interest and attendance with ideas slightly ahead of their time. A typical gathering consists of a mixture of keynote addresses, member paper or poster presentations, book displays, and social and recreational opportunities capped by a banquet. Each venue has been able to showcase its cultural identity and distinctions in gracious and welcoming ways that seem to surpass preceding occasions. Overheard comments on opportunities for interaction with colleagues of all inclinations often include 'I had coffee with my bibliography.' While conferences are usually 'show and tell' opportunities where time and attention can be fully occupied with attending or presenting papers, posters, workshops and the like, the 'white spaces' between or after sessions and meetings at ISATT has provided opportunities for personal interactions. Conference hosts show hospitality in the extreme providing additional activities that showcase local flavour and attractions. Meetings are crowned with a Conference Dinner in venues chosen for enduring experiences and memories.

CONFERENCE THEMES AND KEYNOTES

1983 Tilburg, Netherlands – *Teacher thinking: A new perspective on persisting problems in education.* As noted above Alan Brown wrote that 'all sessions were plenary' In attendance, as listed in the table of contents in the resultant volume *Teacher thinking: A new perspective on persisting problems in education,* and discussion, initiators included, but may not be limited to:

Joost Lowyck	John Peters	John Olson	Rainer Bromme
Gunther L. Huber	Heinz Mandl	Christopher Day	James Calderhead
Richard L. Butt	Miriam Ben-Peretz	Maureen L. Pope	Eileen Scott
Staffan Larsson	D. Jean Clandinin	Rob Halkes	E. A. Rix
Rien Deykers	Angelika C. Wagner	Harm Tillema	Jan R. M. Gerris
Vincent A. M. Peters	Theo C. M. Bergen	Alan F. Brown	Jan Broeckmans
Hartmut Thiele			

1984 Tilburg, Netherlands – *Advances of research on teacher thinking.* No keynotes are indicated for this gathering. Assuming that all presented 'plenary' papers, the table of contents of *Advances of research on teacher thinking* (Ben Peretz, Bromme, & Halkes, 1986) contains full information too extensive to cite here.

1986 Leuven University, Belgium – *Teacher thinking and professional action*

Keynotes:	David C. Berliner	Rainer Bromme	Christopher M. Clark
	Günter L. Huber	Philip Jackson	Lee Shulman

1988 Nottingham University, UK – *Insights into teachers' thinking and practice*

Keynotes:	Joost Lowyck	Michael Eraut	Freema Elbaz
	Robert Burgess		

1991 University of Surrey, UK – *Research on teacher thinking: Towards understanding professional development*

Keynotes:	James Calderhead	Freema Elbaz	Sharon Feiman-Nemser
	Michael Huberman	Maureen Pope	Christopher Clark

1993 Gothenburg University, Sweden – *Teachers minds and actions: Research on teachers' thinking and practice*

Keynotes:	Kenneth M. Zeichner	Ference Marten	Yrjö Engeström
	Hans Joas		

1995 Brock University, Canada – *Changing research and practice: Teachers professionalism, identities and knowledge*

Keynotes:	Elliot Eisner	Ingrid Carlgren	Cecilia Reynolds
	D. Jean Clandinin	Ivor Goodson	

1997 IPN, Kiel, Germany – *Changing schools/changing practices: Perspectives on educational reform and teacher professionalism*
Keynotes: Ewald Terhart Marianne Horstkemper Max van Manen

Jean Rudduck Philip Jackson

1999 St. Patrick's College, Dublin, Ireland – *Developing teachers and teaching practice: International research perspectives*
Keynotes: Andy Hargreaves Milbrey W. McLaughlin Beatrice Avalos

2001 University of the Algarve, Portugal – *Connecting policy and practice: Challenges for teaching and learning in schools and universities*
Keynotes: Christopher Day John Elliott Judith Warren Little
Judith Sachs

2003 Leiden University Netherlands – *Teacher professional development in changing conditions*
Keynotes: Les Tickle John Loughran Kari Smith
Fred Korthagen D. Jean Clandinin

2004 Regional Conference Rzeszow, Poland – *Processes of globalization and teachers' profession: A cross cultural perspective*
Keynote: Michael Kompf

2005 ACU Sydney, Australia – *Making a difference: Challenges for teachers, teaching and teacher education*
Keynotes: Geert Kelchtermans Jennifer Gore Pam Grossman
Russell Bishop

2007 Brock University Canada – *Totems and taboos: Risk and relevance in research on teachers and teaching*
Keynotes: Kieran Egan Shannon Moore Joel Spring
Keith Trigwell

2009 University of Lapland, Finland – *Navigating in educational contexts: Identities and cultures in dialogue*
Keynotes: Liisa Keltikangas-Järvinen Paulien C. Meijer Maggi Savin-Baden

Freema Elbaz-Luwisch Michael Kompf

2010 ISATT symposium in Hong Kong, The 2nd East Asian International Conference on Teacher Education Research – *Teacher education for the future: International perspectives*

Symposium 1
Chair: Wendy Moran
Presenters: Penny Haworth, Paulien C. Meijer, Cheryl Craig
Discussants: Meher Rizvi, Ora Kwo

Symposium 2
Chair: Ora Kwo
Presenters: Paulien C. Meijer, Cheryl Craig
Discussants: Meher Rizvi, Annette La Grange, Tara Ratnam, Wendy Moran

2011 University of Minho Portugal – *Back to the future: Legacies, continuities and changes in educational policy, practice and research*

Keynotes:	António Nóvoa	Linda Darling-Hammond	João Formosinho
		Ciaran Sugrue	
	Flávia Vieira	Christopher Day	Geert Kelchtermans

2012 ISATT symposium in Hyderabad, India at the *Second International Conference for English Language Teacher Educators Assessing and Evaluating English Language Teacher Education Teaching and Learning*
Presenters/Speakers: Cheryl Craig and Tara Ratnam

2012 ISATT symposium in Kruger National Park, South Africa at the *ISTE 2012 International Conference On Mathematics, Science And Technology Education*
Presenters/Speakers: Cheryl Craig, Jan Broeckmans and Samuel Oyoo

2013 University of Ghent, Belgium – *Excellence of teachers? Practice, policy, research*

| **Keynotes:** | Amanda Berry | Sara Dexter | Diane Mayer |
| | Freddy Mortier | Michael Schratz | |

A word cloud of conference themes produced the image can be seen in Fig. 1 on the following page.

THE EXPRESSION OF ISATT RESEARCH INTERESTS

Books and Journals

The general research area of interest for the International Study Association on Teachers and Teaching (ISATT) was present even when ISATT was the acronym for the International Study Association on Teacher Thinking. *Teacher thinking* acknowledged the importance and significance of the pre-active, interactive and post-active dimensions of teachers' personal, practical and professional thinking about the events that defined life in and around

Fig. 1. Word Cloud of ISATT Conference Themes (1983–2013).

classrooms, schools and universities. The founders of ISATT came from a variety of disciplines within education, (i.e., science, technology, psychology, sociology and so on) and brought their curiosity about what did and could guide educators through not only understanding but conveying ways of knowing and thinking. The interconnections between what teachers did and who they were became a dual purpose lens for the examination of teaching and reflective practice.

The titles of journal articles published under the stewardship of ISATT were collected and assembled in yearly blocks and processed through the word cloud software available at tagxedo.com. Word clouds as produced by Tagxedo in some of the Figures in this chapter use word frequency to determine prominence in the resulting graphic. In other words, the more frequently a word appears in a block of text, the larger and more prominent it appears in the graphic. The word cloud graphic is meant to be taken at face value. These are the words we have used to title our published and presented works in given years. This is the language we use to describe our inquiry interests.[7]

As the word clouds are scanned, as one might flip through a stack of photographs, there is little surprise from consistently dominant words such as education, teachers, teaching, learning, students, classrooms, practises and research. Trends become visible as sub-themes; they wax and wane in prominence. Such themes as professionalism, reflection, development, mentoring, collaboration, culture, narrative, effectiveness, technology, reform and community are caught up in the ebb and flow of research focuses in the titles used to describe interests.

While arguable relationships exist between the interests represented by word cloud depictions and the bi-annual conference themes and the influence of article selections made by the editor and editorial board, it is clear that ISATT's interests have not only kept pace with global trends of educational research interests but have always led the field. The foundational similarities in word cloud depictions (see Fig. 5 for combined titles from 1995 to 2012) over the years speak to a consistency in ISATT interests while leaving space for inclusion of the anticipations of scholars whose thoughts, ideas and efforts had and have yet to hit the main stage of interest and inquiry.

While many options were discussed as to how best to approach the task of capturing the evolution of ISATT's research interests, none of the usual methods seemed able to picture the image of conceptual evolution we wished to convey. We were faced with a pre-TTTP collection of TATE issues as well as the online listings of TTTP issues representing many hundreds of articles.

A common interest in the use and intent of language and its defining relationship with culture led to several premises on which we eventually based our approach; to focus in on the langue used in the titles of meetings, presentations, journal articles, books and other publications. Our belief is that the research culture that gave and currently gives ISATT its *raison d'être* is in many ways characterised by the language used for description and discourse. Discourse during member interactions results in cross-influences evident in practice, meetings and print. The words used to convey interest and often underlying intent of inquiry are most evident in the word-bite provided by the title of a publication. Guides such as the American Psychological Association style guide have specific instructions as to the proper composition and framing of a title and its proper relations to the content that follows. We thus assumed that ISATT research interests could be captured by the language and specific words used in titles of journal articles.

Books (1985–1995)
ISATT initially provided a forum for discussion of works done, works in progress and going into ideas that were 'not quite ready for prime time'

perhaps drawn from what C. Wright Mills (1959) thought of as an idea file which contains possibilities for inquiry. All those who presented at Tilburg 1 (1983) had their work included in the volume:

> Halkes, R., & Olson, J. K. (Eds.). (1984). *Teacher thinking: A new perspective on persisting problems in education*. ISATT, Lisse: Swets and Zeitlinger.

Swets & Zeitlinger also published the collection of papers from Tilburg 2 (1984) as:

> Ben Peretz, M., Bromme, R., & Halkes, R. (Eds.). (1986). *Advances of research on teacher thinking*. ISATT, Lisse/Berwyn: Swets and Zeitlinger/Swets North America Inc.

The ideas, insights and directions of contributors to these volumes were of persisting use to an ever-increasing group of students and scholars interested in teacher thinking. Because, small initial publishing runs made these volumes rare, expanded re-publication with contributor commentaries was made in:

> Kompf, M., & Denicolo, P. M. (Eds.). (2003). *Teacher thinking twenty years on*. Lisse: Swets and Zeitlinger.

Following the 1986 meeting at Leuven University Lowyck and Clark edited a volume of selections from the proceedings from the conference thereby setting the subsequent pattern of post-conference publications:

> Lowyck, J., & Clark, C. M., (Eds.). (1989). *Teacher thinking and professional action*. Leuven, Belgium: Leuven University Press.

Like the first two volumes, this one had a small initial run. It was expanded and republished as:

> Denicolo, P. M., & Kompf M. (Eds.). (2005). *Teacher thinking and professional action*. New York, NY: Taylor and Francis.

Publications resulting from meetings held at the University of Nottingham, Surrey, Gothenberg and Brock were through Falmer Press resulting in:

> Day, C., Pope, M., & Denicolo, P. (Eds.). (1990). *Insights into teachers' thinking and practice*. London: Falmer Press.
>
> Day, C., Calderhead, J., & Denicolo, P. (Eds.). (1993). *Research on teacher thinking: Towards understanding professional development*. London: Falmer Press.
>
> Carlgren, I., Handal, G., & Vaage, S. (Eds.). (1994). *Teachers minds and actions: Research on teachers' thinking and practice*. London: Falmer Press.

Kompf, M., Boak, R. T., Bond, W. R., & Dworet, D. H. (Eds.). (1996). *Changing research and practice: Teachers professionalism, identities and knowledge.* London: Falmer Press.

Books compiled from subsequent conference presentations, while a main source and resource for educators and students and found various interested publishers between 1999 and 2005. For example:

Lang, M., Olson, J., Hansen, H., & Bunder, W. (Eds.). (1999). *Changing schools/ changing practices: Perspectives on educational reform and teacher professionalism.* Louvain, Belgium: Garant.

Sugrue, C., & Day. C. (Eds.). (2001). *Developing teachers and teaching practice: International research perspectives.* London: Routledge/Falmer Press.

Denicolo, P. M., & Kompf, M. (Eds.). (2005). *Connecting policy and practice: Challenges for teaching and learning in schools and Universities.* New York, NY: Taylor and Francis.

Beijaard, D., Meijer, P., Morine-Dershimer, G., & Tillema, H. (Eds.). (2005). *Teacher professional development in changing conditions.* Dordrect, The Netherlands: Springer.

Through connections made by Jude Butcher (ACU Australia), a new relationship was formed with Sense Publishers who have published recent volumes including:

Butcher, J., & McDonald, L. (2007). *Making a difference: Challenges for teachers, teaching and teacher education.* Rotterdam: Sense Publishers.

Kentel, J. A., & Short, A. (Eds.). (2008). *Totems and taboos: Risk and relevance in research on teachers and teaching.* Rotterdam: Sense Publishers.

Lauriala, A., Rajala, R., Ruokamo, H., & Ylitapio-Mantyla, O. (Eds.). (2011). *Navigating in educational contexts: Identities and cultures in dialogue.* Rotterdam: Sense Publishers.

Journal Issues (1985–1995)

Between 1985 and 1995, the research and writing of ISATT members appeared in a variety of sources including association newsletters and special theme issues based on ISATT member submissions of the Elsevier journal *Teaching and Teacher Education* (TATE).

In 1995, Taylor and Francis expressed an interest in publishing a regular journal supported by contributions of ISATT members and other writers with compatible fields of interest. The journal *Teachers and teaching: theory and practice* (TTTP) came into being with Christopher Day as executive editor supported by an editorial board comprised of ISATT members and an international panel of associate editors who act as referees. At Volume

17, TTTP's success is marked by gradual increases in issues per year to its current 2012 frequency of 6 per year.

As a sub-theme we examined 154 articles (studies, editorials, book reviews) by North American authors that appeared in the journal between 1999 and 2012. Our word clouds, developed by using the titles of articles for this period, showed education, teachers, teaching, research, students, and schools to be primary areas of focus. A deeper look obtained by reading through each of the abstracts offered a more full understanding of the word cloud categories. We found, for example, that teacher education, understood as the full range of pre-service and in-service education, has been a predominant focus of the journal: 58 articles were focused on pre-service education; 41 were focused on teacher professional development. Among these, there were 65 methodological studies, that is, studies that looked at ways in which to study teacher education and teaching. These ranged from looking at teacher research to studying teacher moves to the construction of video cases to developing analytic frameworks and more. There were 57 studies that focused on some aspect of classroom practice such as inquiry pedagogy, discussion, and critical thinking in math, science, social studies, and reading at the elementary and secondary levels.

Surprising to us was the appearance beginning in 2001 of a robust set of studies (21 in all) focused on educational policy and its implications for school reform and teacher education, and its impact on classroom practice and student learning. In most cases, these studies seemed to be in synch with or slightly ahead of policy-related studies being conducted across North America. While without a thorough study of the journal over the 1999–2012 period, we cannot make claims about the timing and impact of such work in the journal. However, the appearance of these studies in TTTP suggests to us that the journal may well be functioning as a means of keeping the international community informed that ISATT is alert to current trends in educational policy and research. It certainly made us want to step back and look even more closely at the journal contents relative to critical issues in education around the world – the focus of another study!

The word cloud presented in Fig. 2 summarises the article titles in our larger sample of TTTP issues from 1995 to 2012.

John Olson commented:

> During the last 30 years school systems have introduced systemic reforms – which aim to control all aspects of curriculum and teaching and have the intention of shaping teachers work to achieve externally mandated goals. These efforts often have undermined teacher professionalism by failing to recognize the complexities and sophistication of teacher

Fig. 2.   Word Cloud of TTTP Articles (1995–2012).

capabilities, ignoring the realities of school settings, and circumventing the contribution that teachers make to discourse about the goals of schooling. ISATT has inquired into and critiqued these trends by asking teachers to evaluate reform packages and policies, to explain their curricular and pedagogical commitments and by watching how life in classrooms unfolds in the process of change. By doing this ISATT researchers have provided the feedback needed to develop more nuanced approaches to change. Challenges remain. Efforts like *No Child Left Behind* and other top-down policies worldwide which are based on unreliable testing methods and regressive views of teacher expertise and narrow goals for education need to be studied in practice and the views and methods of teachers examined as they cope with trends to deskill them. The work of ISATT appears in a broad spectrum of scholarly journals not the least of which are those devoted to the study of curriculum and change. (Personal communication, 2012)

TRACKING AHEAD

Life can only be understood backwards, but must be lived forwards.

Søren Kierkegaard

Making sense of ISATT backwards is revealing and shows the ways in which many of the ambitious good intentions of the founders have been realised. As can be seen in the appended graphics, the language used to describe the work of members morphs from one word cloud to the next illustrating the flow of topics and concerns in ways that illustrate the shifting grounds of interest and anticipation.

The origins and early days of ISATT have essential characteristics that derived from constructivist philosophical roots with an underlay of critical thinking. Advocating, thinking about and studying educational life through a critical constructivist lens, especially during the years surrounding the formation of ISATT, carried with it the potential for a lonely and perhaps marginalised academic life. The 1970s were times during which possibilities for meaningful treatment of controversial topics and issues increased and gave rise to multiple forms of discourse and inquiry that reflected the nature of the topic rather than the standard fare of scientifically defensible research.

Such adventurous inquiry brought together elements of Max Weber's ideas of *Verstehen*[8] or an understanding methodology, George Kelly's (1955) anticipatory imperative and the dynamics of reflective thinking explored by Dewey (1933) and others. Further influences from Kuhn's (1962) explanation of shifting paradigms and increasing attention paid to the complex adaptive systems of what was called postmodernity formed the intellectual playground for ISATT members.

Anticipatory thought and practice requires a judicious mix of historical appreciation, and conceptual and methodological dexterity in order to embrace such questions as *What if?*, *So What?* and *What's Next?* Sometimes anticipatory thought is prescient with clues read backwards. By way of example, Chris Clark's early predisposition was demonstrated in his forward-looking 1978 reaction to a CBS News report that was critical of teachers:

> My suggestion for in-service teacher education is that we should find ways to put professional development into the hands of the teachers themselves. In-service training should be aimed at offering teachers the tools and concepts necessary for becoming researchers on their own teaching effectiveness. (p. 115)

While other expressions by other scholars in other places may be recounted by each reader, Clark, making such statements publicly was a signifier of what Malcolm Gladwell (2000) might call a road sign enroute to an 'academic tipping point' for the empowerment of teachers to inquire about their own practices. Clark's outing or orientation included many

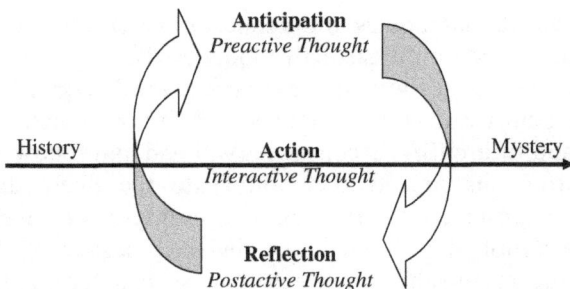

Fig. 3. Anticipation, Action and Reflection.

varied research undertakings and other writers and thinkers and eventually linked elements of what is depicted in Fig. 3 above, where teachers' anticipations and reflections turn around. These turn arounds happen in the moments of action between history and mystery on a path of preactive, interactive and postactive thinking about teaching actions in preparation and realisation of the continual flow of what defines 'next' moments as they become history and so on. Clark's contributions were and are significant as was his willingness to stand apart. He helped teacher thinking live its life forwards.

While the commonality of shared orientations about teaching, thinking and inquiry brought ISATT members together, the shifting social and educational needs of learners, teachers and teacher educators from technology and an ever-expanding range of social issues brought about diversification of focus. Methodological shifts occurred as a result of the quantitative-qualitative debate meeting unusual topics and circumstances for inquiry. However, passing a tipping point is a short journey and paths made are quickly over-trodden. On a topic-by-topic basis, ISATT has shown leadership in innovation, risk-taking and a somewhat adventurous nature in the affordances encouraged for exploration as evidenced by the contributions made to the various fields.

However, in spite of the gentle visual treatment the Tagxedo images provide, the language used to describe research interests says little about the manner, method and terms of engagement with those topics. Early ISATT contributors paid most attention to topics and ways of approaching them that arose through discontent and a felt need for engagement that departed from conventional approaches that fell short of resolution. Creating an alternative forum for engagement with, and expression of, intellectual and scholarly discontent may have seemed unreasonable to those invested in mainstream educational inquiry at the time. However, Shaw (1903) felt that all progress depended on unreasonable individuals.[9]

If the founders of ISATT were unreasonable in the diverging from what was acceptable in mainstream educational research, it is reasonable to anticipate that current and future ISATT colleagues will find and follow unreasonable and adventurous, inquiry as they anticipate the likely discontents in educational circumstances for the next ten, twenty-five or even fifty years. Such an expectation does seem to be the main legacy of the founders. Discharging the responsibilities attached to such a legacy, however, has become somewhat more intricate and complicated than it might have been thirty years ago (see Fig. 4 for Tagxedo depicting issues wanting attention).

Significant shifts have occurred pertaining to *who* learners are, *why* they participate in education, *what* learners and teachers think about, as well as *how, where* and from *whom* educational services are provided. For many learners in Western countries, higher education is a taken-for-granted necessity available to those who can afford the cost or are willing to face long-term debt. Alternative forms and formats for the delivery of educational services have provided a response and resource for learners with needs for economic or geographic accommodation. Disappointingly, in

Fig. 4.   Issues Wanting Attention.

concert with the global need for further education, the undereducated in developed and developing countries have become lucrative playgrounds for entrepreneurial institutions. Completion rates shown by the Organisation for Economic Co-operation and Development (OECD, 2012) indicate effectiveness through overall upward movement.

The *why* of learning has shifted from Dewey's ideas of education as an end unto itself to education as a commodity that is aggressively promoted and branded means to the end of increased consumptive capacity. *What* is studied has become less important than the employment potential to which successful completion may lead. Academic disciplines that attract funding through research or innovation also attract students with the lure of lucrative future earnings, which attracts funding which in turn ... and on.

The *How* of learning has become flexible, on-demand and ubiquitous. Online degrees, diplomas, certificates and training are too numerous to count and vary by quality, transferability, usefulness, cost and comprehensiveness – all with *caveat emptor* attached. Decline in quality as a consequent response to increased demands of and for students was anticipated some time ago (i.e., Ashworth, 1979; Cameron, 1983) but tended to focus on institutional dynamics rather than implications for learners and educators. Questions regarding performance decline as change with changing times and needs or deficits wanting attention have led to marvellously misguided educational reforms seemingly rooted in ground jointly tilled by educational legislators and those who control the various mediums of educational content, format and delivery (Knight, 2008; Kohn, 2004; Noble, 2001).

Information and communications technology (ICT) has brought with it a fundamental alteration in basic cognitive processes and knowledge production. Few would argue that the bio-neuro-socio-psychological implications of ICT-based education, whether formal, semi-formal or informal, are different than face-to-face exchanges, hard copy versus screen-based print medium, chalkboard versus PowerPoint slide, Wikipedia, YouTube, Google, Ted Talks and lectern-less learning.

Education as product, trade good or competitive institutional market share objective, has reformulated the very terms and conditions of learning, teaching and the provision of educational services and faces the danger of becoming a hollow purchase that feeds into downward spiralling benchmarks fed by media-driven performance indicated standards of practice – endorsed and advertised when favourable; dismissed as irrelevant when less than favourable.

The massification of educational purpose and practice has left disillusioned learners and teachers as casualties on the intellectual roadside with formal education complete and meaningful understandings of what learning truly means mainly untouched. Of great concern as well are the academics such generational miscues produce. The collegium, academy and intelligentsia seem somewhat shallow and turned inward with *What's in it for me?* questions posed as a prelude to commitments of tasks related to learner benefit. The research agenda that undergirded inquiry *back in the day* has been translated into fiscal terms of grants, patents and ownership.

Teaching has transformed from vocation to career in part seduced by the label and trappings of *professional* and *profession*. The domain in head and heart that once defined vocation seems filled with roles, rights and responsibilities that have less to do with direct student learning and more to do with management, marketing, control, power and the terms and conditions of work. Renewing the literacy of adventurous and unreasonable inquiry is an ongoing task for ISATT and its members; if you are not on the edge, you are taking up space.

NOTES

1. The theme and title *Changing Research and Practice* was later noted as having an unfortunate acronym.
2. Kompf became a member in 1986; Rust in 2001.
3. The current growing emphasis on the fields of Science, Technology, Engineering and Mathematics (STEM) harkens back to these times in a variety of interesting ways.
4. Carel Frederik van Parreren (1920–1991) was Professor of Psychology at the University of Utrecht.
5. Thanks to Jan Broeckmans for these connections.
6. OISE later became the University of Toronto's graduate school in education.
7. See appendix for word clouds derived from TTTP journal article titles which capture the conference themes and book titles for those years.
8. See Elwell (1996) for thorough treatment.
9. 'The reasonable man adapts himself to the world; the unreasonable one persists in trying to adapt the world to himself. Therefore all progress depends on the unreasonable man.' from *Man and Superman 'Maxims for Revolutionists'*.

ACKNOWLEDGEMENTS

Acknowledgement and thanks are owed to Alan Brown, Chris Clark, Rob Halkes, Joost Lowyck, John Olson and Maureen Pope who were generous and thoughtful in reading portions of drafts and offering comments and corrections.

REFERENCES

Ashworth, K. H. (1979). *American higher education in decline.* College Station, TX: Texas A & M University Press.

Cameron, K. (1983). Strategic responses to conditions of decline: Higher education and the private sector. *The Journal of Higher Education, 54*(4), 359–380.

Clark, C. M. (1978). Reactions of a researcher on teaching to 'Is anyone out there learning?' A CBS News report card on American public education. *The High School Journal, 62*(3), 114–115. Retrieved from http://www.jstor.org/stable/40365409. Accessed on December 8, 2012.

Cordingley, P. (2003). Research and evidence-based practice: Focusing on practice and practitioners. In L. Anderson & N. Bennett (Eds.), *Evidence-informed policy and practice in educational leadership and management.* Milton Keynes, UK: Open University. Retrieved from http://instep.net.nz/Inquiry-and-evidence-based-practice/Inquiry-based-practice/Inquiry-vs-research. Accessed on November 24, 2012.

Dewey, J. (1933). *How we think: A restatement of the relation of reflective thinking to the educative process* (Rev. ed.). Boston, MA: D. C. Heath.

Doyle, W. (2009). Situated practice: A reflection on person-centered classroom management. *Theory into Practice, 48*(2), 68–73.

Doyle, W. (in press). The teacher and the curriculum: From document to performance. In T. Wubbels, J. van Tartwijk, P. den Brok & J. Levy (Eds.), *Interpersonal relationships in education.* Rotterdam, The Netherlands: Sense Publishers.

Elliot, J. (1991). *Action research for educational change.* Milton Keynes, UK: Open University Press.

Elwell, F. (1996). Verstehen: The sociology of Max Weber. Retrieved from http://www.faculty.rsu.edu/~felwell/Theorists/Weber/Whome.htm. Accessed on June 1, 1999.

Etzioni, A. (1969). *The semi-professions and their organization.* New York, NY: The Free Press.

Fuller, F. F. (1969). A concern of teachers: A developmental conceptualization. *American Educational Research Journal, 6*(2), 207–226.

Gladwell, M. (2000). *The tipping point: How little things can make a big difference.* London, UK: Little Brown.

Glazer, N. (1974). The schools of the minor professions. *Minerva, XII*(3), 363.

Haenen, J. (1996). *Gal'perin: A psychologist in Vygotsky's footsteps.* Hauppauge, NY: Nova Science Publishers.

Jackson, P. (1968). *Life in classrooms.* New York, NY: Teachers College Press.

Kelly, G. (1955). *The psychology of personal constructs: A theory of personality.* New York, NY: W.W. Norton.

Knight, J. (2008). *Higher education in turmoil: The changing world of internationalization.* Rotterdam, The Netherlands: Sense Publishers.

Kohn, A. (2004). *What does it mean to be well-educated and more essays on standards, grading and other follies.* Boston, MA: Beacon Press.

Kuhn, T. S. (1962). *The structure of scientific revolutions.* Chicago, IL: University of Chicago Press.

Mouly, G. J. (1978). *Educational research: The art and science of inquiry.* Boston, MA: Allyn & Bacon.

Mills, C. W. (1959). *The sociological imagination.* London, UK: Oxford University Press.

Noble, D. (2001). *Digital diploma mills: The automation of higher education.* New York, NY: Monthly Review Press.

Organisation for Economic Co-operation and Development (OECD). (2012). *Education at a glance 2012: OECD indicators*. Paris, France: OECD Publishing.

Reid, A. (2004). *Towards a culture of inquiry in DECS*. Occasional Paper Series, No. 1. Adelaide, Australia: South Australian Department of Education and Children's Services.

Robinson, V. (2003). Teachers as researchers: A professional necessity? *Set: Research Information for Teachers, 1*, 27–29.

Runté, R. (1995). Is teaching a profession? In G. Taylor & R. Runté (Eds.), *Thinking about teaching: An introduction*. Toronto, Canada: Harcourt Brace.

Schön, D. (1987). *Educating the reflective practitioner*. San Francisco, CA: Jossey-Bass.

Shavelson, R. J., & Stern, P. (1981). Research on teachers' pedagogical thoughts, judgments, decisions, and behavior. *Review of Educational Research, 51*(4), 455–498.

Shaw, G. B. (1903). *Man and superman: Maxims for revolutionists*. Cambridge, MA: The University Press.

Vygotsky, L. S. (1986). *Thought and language* (revised and edited by Alex Kozulin). Cambridge, MA: The MIT Press.

APPENDIX: TAGXEDO WORD CLOUDS OF TTTP JOURNAL ARTICLES

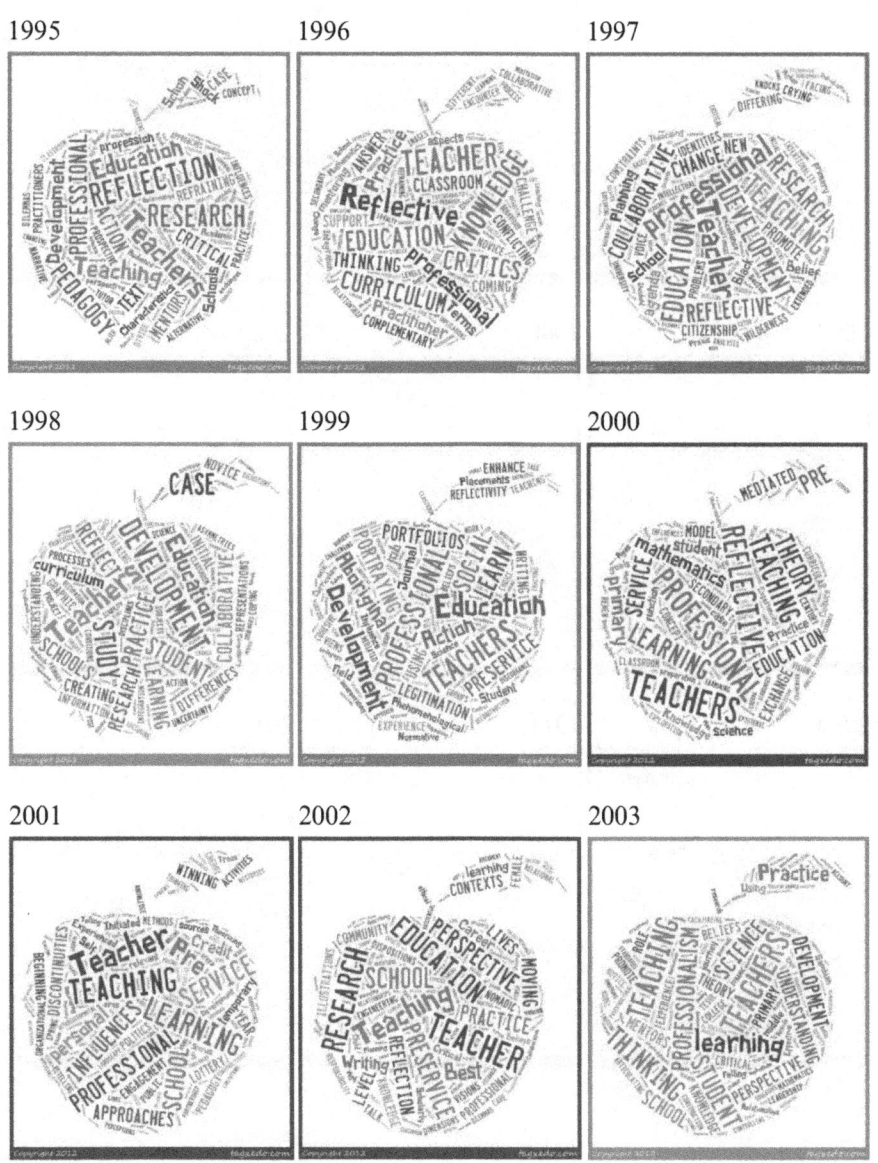

2004   2005   2006

2007   2008   2009

2010   2011   2012

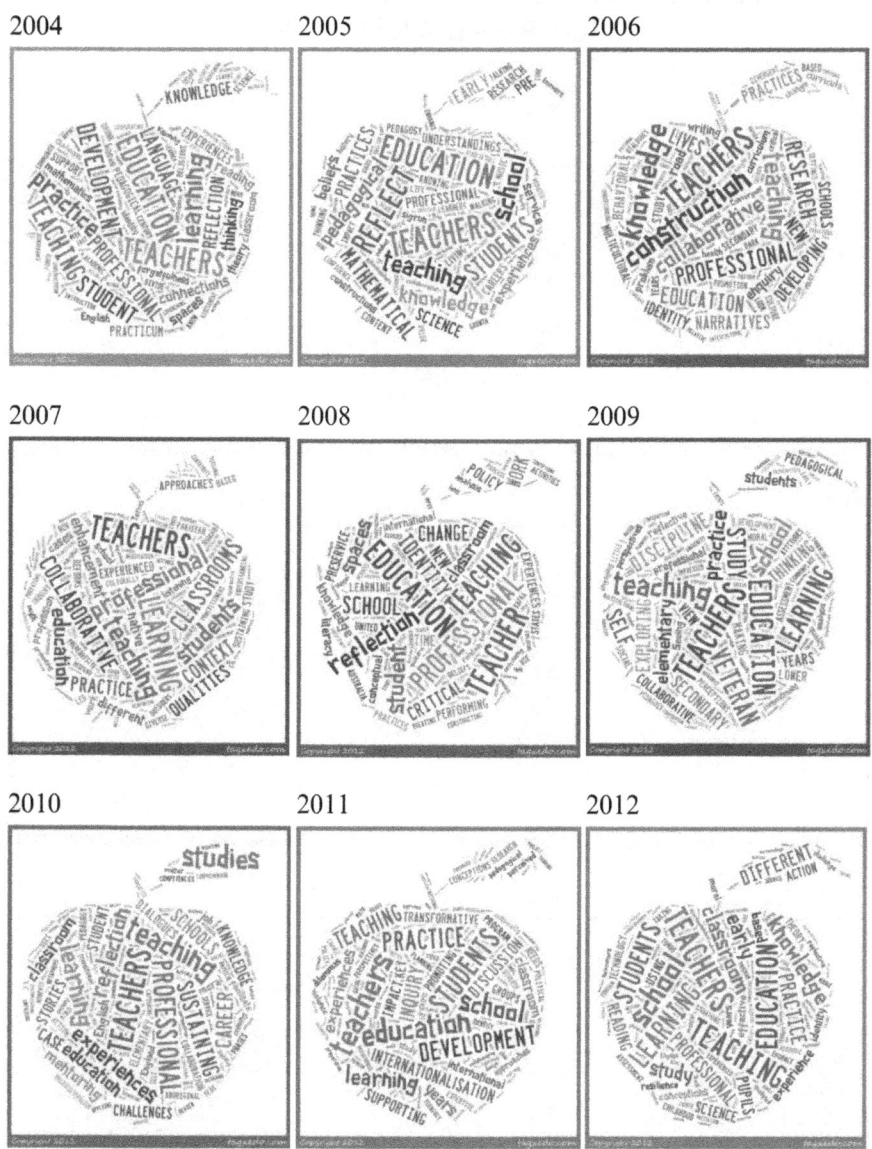

CHAPTER 2

THE ORIGINS OF ISATT: AN IDIOSYNCRATIC PERSPECTIVE

Joost Lowyck

ABSTRACT

This chapter presents a personal account of ISATT from the perspective of the first elected chair of the organization. In this work, the 1980s backdrop against which ISATT came into being is instantiated. Further to this, a panoramic view of the literature is offered and an "oral history" approach is used. To end, an archival document – a selection read at the 1988 biennial conference held near Sherwood Forest in Nottingham, England – pays tribute to Rob Halkes, the person who, with the assistance of key others, birthed the international study association which is now globally known as ISATT.

Keywords: Origins of ISATT; paradigm shift; research community; leadership

In this chapter, a personal account is given of the origins of ISATT, based on personal reminiscence and interpretation of context, as a kind of "oral history." Indeed, the foundation in 1983 of ISATT resulted from developments and challenges that were used as opportunities to build a new organization on teacher thinking, which eventually transitioned to a focus on teachers and teaching.

From Teacher Thinking to Teachers and Teaching: The Evolution of a Research Community
Advances in Research on Teaching, Volume 19, 39–49
ISSN: 1479-3687/doi:10.1108/S1479-3687(2013)0000019005

Developments in society and research can be described as successive waves (Toffler, 1980). Changes are initially almost imperceptible, gradually growing in importance to become the chief observable trend, and then eventually receding to be absorbed by new waves of change. In the days of test psychology, not teaching behavior but the teacher's personality was perceived as the paramount indicator of effectiveness since teaching is merely a by-product of teacher's personality (Getzels & Jackson, 1963). Results from correlations between teacher's characteristics and estimated teaching quality, however, indicated few valuable results as an influential American policy document indicated (Coleman et al., 1966). Outcomes of research tell little about the teaching profession since qualities such as being student-centered, friendly, enthusiastic, or psychologically stable apply to all occupations where interaction with (young) people is predominant. In addition, broad personality traits do not fit with elementary, discrete teaching behaviors since the unit of analysis highly differs.

Lack of clear research outcomes, together with the rise of behaviorism during the 1960s as the dominant psychological paradigm, shifted attention toward observable teaching behaviors that were correlated with learning results (Brophy & Good, 1986). In order to make teaching observable, the complex teaching activity is fragmented into elementary or discrete behaviors in line with the analytical paradigm advocated by Gage (1963). The basic question is which specific teaching behaviors (process variables) bring about learning gains in students (product variables). The so-called process–product research revealed powerful teaching characteristics, like clarity, variability, task orientation, criticism, indirectness, student's opportunity to learn, structuring comments, and use of different levels of questions and cognitive activities (Rosenshine & First, 1973). These discrete teaching behaviors were connected to, among others, classroom observation, interaction analysis, and micro-teaching as methods in teacher education. An exclusive focus on observable behaviors to define teaching effectiveness led nevertheless to a series of problems. First, a single set of teaching behaviors cannot account for learning outcomes in all subject-matter and for students from different socio-economic background or from all grades which makes process–product research "content-proof" and "pupil-proof." Second, almost all observational systems register traditional classroom teaching with emphasis on lecturing and question-answer cycles leaving individual or group work out of scope (Heath & Nielson, 1974) and rendering research endeavors "method-proof." Third, teaching is conceived of as a unidirectional activity of teachers neglecting any influence of the situation on the teacher as recognized by Doyle's mediating paradigm (Doyle, 1978) which makes research "situation-proof." Fourth, because emphasis is exclusively on observable classroom behaviors, no information is provided on cognitive processes of teachers and students or on the complex cognitive processing of teachers during the planning, interactive, and post-interactive phase of teaching (Jackson, 1968) resulting in a "cognition-proof" approach of research.

Anglo-Saxon countries shifted interest from behaviorism to a cognitivist approach. This was influenced by the work of Newell and Simon (1972) and predecessors like Miller, Galanter, and Pribram (1960) with emphasis on individual's processing of information and problem-solving. In a similar vein, teaching became conceived as a kind of clinical information processing (National Institute for Education, 1975). This publication has been perceived as a canonization of the research that followed on cognitive processes in teaching (Clark & Peterson, 1976; Clark & Yinger, 1977; Lowyck, 1978; Peterson & Clark, 1979; Winne & Marx, 1977; Yinger, 1977). This cognitive approach was consistent with a view of teaching as a profession that calls for higher-order cognitive skills in order to cope with the complexities of the educational environment. It is a profession resembling the one of physicians, engineers, and architects with emphasis on judgment, problem-solving, and decision-making.

ISATT AT THE CROSSROADS OF MANY INFLUENCES

Internationalization of Research

In Europe during the late 1970s, internationalization aimed to position European research in a competing international community through global networking. Increased competition in Europe for students and resources forced universities to improve in specialized fields of research to enhance the quality of knowledge-rich institutions. This is why in different European countries internationalization of universities became a paramount issue. To reach that goal, and given the many cultures, languages, and traditions in Europe, English gradually became the lingua franca. It is an interesting observation that in the 1970s doctoral dissertations were monographs written in the local language and even the reference lists of the first publications of ISATT (Halkes & Olson, 1984a, 1984b; Ben-Peretz, Bromme, & Halkes, 1986) contained publications in German or Dutch while in later editions English was the common vernacular. This, however, could suggest that the English language equals internationalization which is not the case at all. Even English speaking countries had to broaden their scope and to recruit international academics. This concern, among others, caused British, Canadian, Australian, and North American publishers and universities to open their doors to international forums. The increasing internationalization of organizations like American Educational Research Association (AERA), the opening of journal Editorial Boards to international members, and the recruitment of an international public in research associations form examples of this wave of internationalization. Universities put increased emphasis on publishing in international peer-reviewed journals and membership on the Boards of International organizations was highly valued in terms of career development. It was little wonder that in this context, the Netherlands and Flanders stressed the importance of launching new research organizations. The European Association for Research on Learning and Instruction (EARLI) was founded in Leuven on December 1983 by E. De Corte (Flanders), D. Snow (USA), R. J. Simons (University of Brabant, the Netherlands), and H. Lodewijks (director of the Dutch Foundation of Educational research). The University of Brabant, the university to which Rob Halkes belonged, supported Rob's idea to found an international group of scholars in the field of teaching. Proof of this involvement is still visible in the upper left corner of the ISATT logo shown in Fig. 1.

The red triangle is the logo of the University of Brabant where ISATT was first conceived. In October 1983, during the first meeting in Tilburg, ISATT was officially founded by Alan Brown, Christopher Clark, Erik De Corte,

Fig. 1.   ISATT Logo.

Rob Halkes, and William Reid. I, at that time, was a content-driven background player who asked Erik De Corte to join the founding fathers of ISATT because of his international network and position.

My Way

After my master studies in educational sciences at Leuven University, and with a grant of the Volkswagen Foundation (VW Stiftung), I specialized in teacher education and technology at Ruprecht-Karls University and the Higher Teacher Training Institute (Pädagogische Hochschule) in Heidelberg. I used Closed Circuit Television (CCTV) for classroom observation and micro-teaching. The highly analytical, systematic, and research-based approach of teaching was in strong contrast to my student's memory of vague didactic principles deduced from philosophy and I became – be it for a short time – a protagonist of behaviorism in teacher education.

Back in Leuven as a doctoral assistant, I used micro-teaching as a method for training student teachers. Gradually, I experienced problems with the ambition of a simplified training model to cover teaching complexities. I first sought the solution to the narrow focus in extending micro-teaching as a training method with interaction analysis, case method, role playing, simulation, and self-confrontation. That solution for the limited focus was sought in a multi-method approach. Further refinement of an experimental research project to investigate whether, and to what degree, specific constituents of training methods (information, observation, exercise, feedback, and rehearsal) render teaching skills effectiveness, led to a more fundamental problem, namely the nature of teaching (Lowyck, 1980). This uneasiness with a mere behavioristic perspective originated from contact with cognitive psychology. Since the early 1970s, our Research Center at Leuven University organized several meetings in Neerpelt, a small Flemish town near the Dutch border, with Professor van Parreren, an outstanding Dutch psychologist, and his research team. We discussed the work of Russian cognitive psychologists, like Gal'perin, Leontjew, Vygotskij, and the early European cognitive psychologists, like Dunker and Selz. After a study visit of Erik De Corte to the USA where he met Glaser, Resnick, Salomon, Snow, and many others, the cognitive paradigm was enlarged and even Russian psychologists entered via the USA international community. Influenced by this cognitive paradigm, I refocused my research project on the cognitive variables of teaching as referred to in the title of my dissertation: *Process analysis of teaching: The study of cognitive variables in planning and teaching behavior of experienced teachers" Literature study and descriptive-empirical research* (Lowyck, 1978). The work, which was published in Dutch, was first welcomed by Dutch and Flemish researchers who joined the cognitive paradigm in teaching and teacher education, scholars like Theo Bergen, Jan Broeckmans, John Peters, Harm Tillema, Douwe Beijaard, Nico Verloop, and many others. It was in this context that I met Rob Halkes several times.

The Dream of Rob Halkes

While I mainly networked in the Dutch, Flemish, and German research contexts, Rob Halkes travelled the world. He went to Canada where he met John Olson, Alan Brown, Jean Clandinin, and Michael Connelly. In the USA he contacted Chris Clark and Walter Doyle; in the UK, Maureen Pope, William Reid, and Christopher Day; in Israel, Miriam Ben-Peretz; and in Germany, Rainer Bromme, Hartmut Thiele, and Günter Huber. It is amazing how a young beginning researcher succeeded in contacting so many well-known international scholars. Speculators from time-to-time have told me that this was due to the Dutch way of conferring master degrees: Drs. as in *doctorandus*. This Latin term means that someone is entitled to start a doctoral dissertation, while in English speaking countries, Rob Halkes was perceived to be the owner of more than one doctoral diploma: Doctor in plural.

During our talks and inspired by his many contacts, Rob Halkes proposed to launch an organization that focused on teacher's thinking, taking into account the many different approaches, models and theories I had never confronted before, such as the work on teacher's concerns (Fuller) and the personal construct theory of Kelly. His idea was to gather interested people in a first Symposium in 1983 at Tilburg. It was supported by the founding figures of ISATT who clearly defined the kind of association they wanted. An association means that people from different countries and domains of research interest interact in an open and supportive way, though it was recognized from its inception that the nature of the association needed further clarification. Would it be a research association like EARLI or AERA? Should it be restricted to "researchers" in a field that had hardly started to develop? The decision was made to build a "Study" association that houses scholars interested in understanding teacher cognition. Should, given the support of Dutch and Flemish universities, the focus be on a European organization or on an international one? The choice was to launch a genuine, autonomous international association with equal access from all countries and traditions. I remember the discussion we had with the EARLI people at their first 1985 conference in Leuven. They wanted to make ISATT a division of EARLI and to join efforts to broaden the scope of EARLI. Rob Halkes answered that we first needed to explore the viability of ISATT before making further decisions. At the 1986 ISATT Conference in Leuven, a substantial number of international scholars in the field of teacher thinking joined the conference and supported ISATT as an organization. With an attractive scholarly agenda and a relevant focus, the future of ISATT was guaranteed.

A great concern of Rob Halkes was the need to create and preserve the open character of ISATT, making it a haven for many approaches, visions, methodologies, and knowledge domains like sociology, pedagogy, and philosophy (Halkes & Olson, 1984a, 1984b). Moreover, in order to avoid a strictly theoretical conception of teacher thinking, the link between teacher cognition and classroom behavior was emphasized. This orientation is evident, for example, in an early publication, which stated that "... it may be appropriate to abandon a too narrow concept of teachers' cognitive processes in favor of a wide range of experience, beliefs, and knowledge which is pertinent beyond decision" (Ben-Peretz, Bromme, & Halkes, 1986, p. 3). This is why the title chosen for the 1986 conference was *Teacher thinking and professional action*. The aim was clearly to "avoid a further bifurcation of research on teaching" (Berliner, 1989; Lowyck & Clark, 1989; Denicolo & Kompf, 2005). It seemed at least intellectually honest to reflect upon the possible integration of different research paradigms and not to accept a priori the dichotomous nature of description and prescription, teaching and learning, process and product, teacher thinking and professional action (Lowyck & Clark, 1989, p. II). A side effect of this conference with its focus on the integration of different research paradigms was that some members of ISATT did not appreciate the dominance of North Americans in the invited keynote addresses. Indeed, discussions of research paradigms and more idiosyncratic accounts of teacher's cognition needed to be more calibrated, as Rob informed me after the conference.

Synergy

ISATT as an organization has been built on the intersection between many influences: societal, organizational, local, and individual. Looking back, it seems that there was a need to reorient research on teaching away from a strict behavioral perspective toward a more encompassing paradigm that takes into account the complexity of teaching as a profession. Through the vision of Rob Halkes and other founding members who joined him, developments in the field of education that were initially almost imperceptible were transformed into ideas, and these ideas and dreams, in turn, evolved into a visible, viable international association. This is my idiosyncratic account of how ISATT – what is currently known as the International Study Association on Teachers and Teaching – evolved.

Afterword: Medieval Reflections on ISATT, Nottingham, September 1988

This is a story that I [Joost Lowyck], the first chair of ISATT, told at the medieval banquet in Nottingham 1988 near Sherwood, the Country of Robin Hood. The story was my way to honor ISATT's real founder, Rob Halkes.

Thou, Oh Sheriff, almost almighty and Thou, Oh Sheriff's Ladie also almost almighty, and ye, Oh Maureen [Pope], second daughter of the Pope of Rome and called by him "me gentely, me lovely," and ye Christopher [Day], child of the Sun and the Light shortly called Day, and ye, friendes.

I [Joost Lowyck], the first chair of a brotherhood and sistership interested in looking at the inside of the cranes of illuminated teachers.

Thou, Oh Sheriff of Sherrywood, subdivided into the districts of dry Sherrywood, medium Sherrywood Amontillado, and cream Sherrywood, listen now to me tacite ideas, me covert thoughts, me implicite knowledge.

The Story is about Robin [Halkes] the Cleverly, the Smartie. Born during the year 1153 after Jesus Christ, the Holy and Almighty. He grew up and down in our dark ages which later on pitifully will be called the Middle Ages (I said dark ages because we don't have electricity, no gas, but candles and oil which produce a romantic light). He lived in the woods of Tilliburge, near the boundaries of Allemagna, better known by later people as Germany because Germans are living there.

I, also born – however a good decade earlier – I met Robin for the first of all times when both we were swimming in the Harbour of Amsterdam, the Centre of the evil and the devil. While swimming he asked me what I was doing. And I made explicite me ideas by raising me voice, slightly modified by some gurgle water tones: "I am looking" I said "I am looking for understanding what we could find in the cranes of human beings." After having taken some air, he answered very enthusiastically "Me too" and he breathed deeply trying to avoid to drown. That was how we first met followed by several meetings in our Low Countries.

I, when moving these days from Flanders over Bretagna in France to Bretagna in Britain and – thanks God – arriving after swimming through troubled waters of what – later on – will be called the Channel, I raise me voice. So, listen to me voice, giveth me voice.

Arrived at our first stop in Canterbury, looking for tales and some wines, we sitted together eating sheeps, birds and deers. "I" he said while raising his voice. I again gave him voice and wine. After having closed almost totally his mouth, he opened it again and, after this, he said "I had an experience as a boy whilest sitting in the woods of Tilliburge. I never understood what people said because they were using words that were too difficult and I thought by meself 'I shall ask the teacher.'"

However, due to the fact that, in this conversation, I had to remember the long sentence "I Shall Ask The Teacher" which was taking almost all of my short-term memory capacity, I used the abbreviation "ISATT." As ye all know, during dark ages the retention of 45 bits of information is the absolute maximum. This amount later on will be raised until 7 bits of information as researched by Norman the Greek.

Having finished the sheeps, birds and deers, we drank some white and red wine until shortage of wine as the ultimate stop rule in our flow diagram of information processing. Robin, the Cleverly, the Smartie (what later on will be called "intelligent" by intelligent people), knew that he was not the only one to have to ask the teacher. And we, trotting into the hospital – in later centuries and for the sake of saving memory capacity it will be called hotel, we agreed to geographically spread the problem. In our Low Countries, spreading a problem is more popular than solving it.

Robin in his missionary state, travelled in a journey fashion to the unknown world of Indians where he met his later clark, Christopher [Clark], and from there he travelled to Canada – both were countries that would be discovered some centuries later – and he met at Kingston the son of Ol: Johannes [John] Olson. And because Christopher and Johannes also experienced the problem of understanding difficult language, they advised Robin to walk around the world to both proclaim his worldwide, worthwhile message and recruit people by bringing them together to discuss the old medieval question about how I should ask the teacher.

And in 1183 from all over the world and even from the United states (later on called by Dvořák the "new world" and by Huxley "the brave new world") more than thirty people met at Tilliburge and buildeth ISATT, meaning the "I shall Ask The Teacher," later on firstly changed into "International Story on the Acquisition of Troublesome Terminology" and afterwards into "International Study Association of Teacher Thinking." This is undoubtedly the last change of title, I assume. And since then, they have the tendency to meet at some more times and places, like in Lovania, and Nottingham. This will be, God giveth, part of a never-ending Story.

REFERENCES

Ben-Peretz, M., Bromme, R., & Halkes, R. (Eds.). (1986). *Advances in research on teacher thinking.* Berwyn/Lisse: Swets & Zeitlinger.

Berliner, D. C. (1989). The place of process-product research in developing the agenda for research on teacher thinking. In J. Lowyck & C. M. Clark (Eds.), *Teacher thinking and professional action* (pp. 3–21). Leuven: Leuven University Press.

Brophy, J., & Good, T. (1986). Teacher behavior and student achievement. In M. C. Wittrock (Ed.), *Handbook of research on teaching* (3rd ed., pp. 328–375). New York, NY: Macmillan.

Clark, C. M., & Peterson, P. L. (1976). *Teacher stimulated recall of interactive decisions* (EDRS-ED, 124 555). Stanford, CA, Stanford University: Stanford Center for Research and Development in Teaching.

Clark, C. M., & Yinger, R. J. (1977). Research on teacher thinking. *Curriculum Inquiry, 7*(4), 279–394.

Coleman, J. S., Campbell, E. Q., Hobson, C. J., Mcartland, J., Mood, A. M., Weinfeld, F. D., & York, R. L. (1966). *Equality of educational opportunity.* Washington, DC: U.S. Government Printing Office.

Denicolo, P. M., & Kompf, M. (Eds.). (2005). *Teacher thinking and professional action.* London: Routledge.

Doyle, W. (1978). Paradigms for research on teacher effectiveness. In L. S. Shulman (Ed.), *Review of research on teaching* (Vol. 5, pp. 392–431). Itasca, IL: Peacock.

Gage, N. L. (1963). Paradigms for research on teaching. In N. L. Gage (Ed.), *Handbook of research on teaching* (pp. 94–141). Chicago, IL: Rand McNally.

Getzels, J. W., & Jackson, P. W. (1963). The teacher's personality and characteristics. In N. L. Gage (Ed.), *Handbook of research on teaching* (pp. 506–582). Chicago, IL: Rand McNally.

Halkes, R., & Olson, J. K. (1984a). Introduction. In R. Halkes & J. K Olson (Eds.), *Teacher thinking: A new perspective on persisting problems in education* (pp. 1–6). Lisse, Holland: Swets & Zeitlinger.

Halkes, R., & Olson, J. K. (Eds.). (1984b). *Teacher thinking: A new perspective on persisting problems in education.* Lisse, Holland: Swets & Zeitlinger.

Heath, R. W., & Nielson, M. A. (1974). The research basis for performance-based teacher education. *Review of Educational Research, 44*(4), 463–484.

Jackson, P. W. (1968). *Life in classrooms.* New York, NY: Holt, Rinehart & Winston.

Lowyck, J. (1978). *Procesanalyse van het onderwijsgedrag. Studie van de cognitieve variabelen in het voorbereidings- en uitvoeringsgedrag van ervaren leerkrachten. Literatuurstudie en decriptief-empirisch onderzoek (Process analysis of teaching. Study of cognitive variables in the planning and teaching behavior of experienced teachers. Literature study and descriptive-empirical research).* Doctoral thesis, KU Leuven, Leuven, Faculty of Psychology and Educational sciences.

Lowyck, J. (1980). *A process analysis of teaching* (EDRS-ED 190513). Leuven: Leuven University, Department of Educational Sciences.

Lowyck, J., & Clark, C. (Eds.). (1989). *Teacher thinking and professional action* (Studia Paedagogica). Leuven: Leuven University Press.

Miller, G. A., Galanter, E., & Pribram, K. H. (1960). *Plans and the structure of behavior.* New York, NY: Henry Holt.

National Institute for Education. (1975). *Teaching as clinical information processing.* Washington, DC: U.S. Department of Health, Education and Welfare.

Newell, A., & Simon, H. A. (1972). *Human problem solving.* Englewood Cliffs, NJ: Prentice Hall.

Peterson, P. L., & Clark, C. M. (1979). Teachers' reports of their cognitive processes during teaching. *American Educational Research Journal, 15*(4), 555–565.

Rosenshine, B., & First, N. (1973). The use of direct observation to study teaching. In R. M. Travers (Ed.), *Second handbook of research on teaching* (pp. 122–183). Chicago, IL: RandMcNally.

Toffler, A. (1980). *The third wave.* New York, NY: William Morrow.

Winne, P. H., & Marx, R. W. (1977). Reconceptualizing research on teaching. *Journal of Educational Psychology, 69*(6), 668–678.

Yinger, R. J. (1977). *A study of teacher planning: Description and theory development using ethnographic and information processing methods.* Unpublished doctoral dissertation, Michigan State University, East Lansing, MI.

CHAPTER 3

THE ROLE OF ISATT IN THE PROFESSIONAL DEVELOPMENT OF BARICA MARENTIČ POŽARNIK

Barica Marentič Požarnik and Barbara Šteh

ABSTRACT

In this chapter, the story of professional development of Barica Marentič Požarnik (Professor Emerita, University of Ljubljana, Slovenia) is shared in an interview conducted by Barbara Šteh. Central to the story is the impact of her participation in ISATT together with other influences (organisations, projects, conferences, individual contacts) on her professional activities and beliefs. Through the telling, the Slovenian context, particularly in the areas of initial teacher education, continuous professional development, curricular reform and research practice, becomes visible. At the end, some remaining issues are revealed.

Keywords: Origins of ISATT; key influences; research community; mentoring

From Teacher Thinking to Teachers and Teaching: The Evolution of a Research Community
Advances in Research on Teaching, Volume 19, 51–64
ISSN: 1479-3687/doi:10.1108/S1479-3687(2013)0000019006

How did your ISATT story start? What were the incentives to join the organisation and to come to the Dublin conference? Your expectations? Your first impressions?

My beginning trace to two things: attending the first ISATT conference – that was in Dublin in 1999, which was relatively late in my professional career – or embracing ideas, the philosophy of ISATT which started much earlier than that, in the 1980s. Let me just mention the idea of teacher's subjective theories and their importance in steering actions. I first met this idea in Huber and Mandl early writings (Mandl & Huber, 1982). In this regard, I was fortunate to be able to read German. Later I found out that Günter Huber whom I visited in Tübingen was among the founding members of ISATT. Relatively early I also embraced the model of teacher as reflective practitioner doing (action) research into his teaching as an important part of professional development. I got enthusiastic about those ideas, also in the early 1980s, under the influence of colleagues from Klagenfurt University (Universität für Bildungswissenschaften), which was within easy reach from my hometown. There, I had frequent contacts with Herbert Altrichter and also with John Elliott from the University of East Anglia who was with his team a guest lecturer on the topic of action research in 1982.

So I joined ISATT because its mission seemed to embody the important ideas I had been trying to understand, develop and make popular in our national context since the early 1980s. Especially the stress on teacher's thinking seemed to be 'the right thing' but there were still so many unknowns. I felt a certain dissatisfaction with the purely analytic quantitative methodology prevailing in my country [Slovenia] and so I was glad to discover that many ISATT researchers did not suppress the subjective, qualitative and unique in their work, that was, in fact, a part of their philosophy. In 1999, I decided, together with some other colleagues from Slovenia – with you, Barbara, we had a joint presentation (Marentič Požarnik & Šteh, 1999) – to attend the conference to get the opportunity of personal contacts with all those ideas and authors.

I was not disappointed; Dublin (1999) represented an important milestone in my professional development. From the first keynote address by Peter Woods, I had the feeling of 'coming home at last'. In my Dublin notebook, I can still find underlined in red words and phrases like: 'teachers at the heart of the reform', 'joy of learning', 'skills to improvise and optimise learning', 'magic of childhood', 'confidence in learners', 'humour' ,'spontaneity', 'learning as acculturation into creation of knowledge', 'learning as active enquiring', 'new ways of research that respect feelings and subjectivities', 'research that gives voice to teachers and pupils and increases teacher's power base', 'school-based research', 'respect for wisdom of practice', and 'practical knowledge'. As I was very interested in different conceptions of knowledge and their consequences, the model of 'knowledge for practice, of practice and in practice' by Milbrey Laughlin helped me a lot to organise my thinking, as well as Korthagen's differentiation between knowledge as phronesis and episteme. I was also inspired by Viveca Lindberg's (1999) study on contextual nature of teacher's conception of knowledge.

As already mentioned, not all the ideas were new to me, but what mattered was the opportunity of a genuine dialogue, of placing ideas into a broader framework and also of finding different solutions to problems, like how to make teachers aware of the dissonance between their real and ideal self, between ambitious general goals and everyday practice, and how to help them to bridge it.

In Dublin, I also enjoyed the open friendly atmosphere co-created by our Irish colleagues, which was a good basis for a free exchange of ideas during breaks and free time. Whenever I later listened to *The Parting Glass* sung by The Dubliners, it made me think of the emotion-laden interpretation of this song by our host at the farewell dinner in the Veterans' Hospital.

What contributed to maintaining the contact with the organisation and to visit further conferences (up to 2009)? Which important events, messages, discussions, meetings with colleagues etc., can you recall? Did your initial ideas change over time?

In the decade 1999–2009 I attended five biennial ISATT conferences. One important feature that attracted me was the consistency of epistemology, ethics, research methodology and practical activity, which were the characteristics of people attending ISATT conferences. As already mentioned, in Slovenia the objectivist analytical quantitative methodology was – and still is – prevalent in educational research and publications, mainly under the influence of psychology which is regarded as the measuring stick of what represents 'real science'. ISATT gave me the opportunity to make personal contact with authors that represented alternative epistemology and methodology, authors that embodied the unity of cognitive, emotional and ethical, theoretical and practical aspects in their work. I appreciated the possibility to discuss in vivo dilemmas and alternatives, to give voice to my feelings, doubts, also frustrations, to get support. Later, reading articles of authors I met during the conference was even more exciting, similar to a private discussion with them.

The contributions at ISATT conferences were, on one hand, very varied, but, on the other hand, had much in common. I admired the genuine interest of contributors to deepen the understanding of teachers' inner worlds and their respect for it. Instead of the usual way of trying to get 'the truth' by analysing hundreds of answers on questionnaires, I met with in-depth analyses of biographies, stories, narratives of small groups, sometimes of just one person.

Actually, I made a paradigm shift in my professional development quite early, in the 1980s; I also have tried for a long time to base my work on humanistic values, but I could not see clearly the connection between the two – between the cognitive and the ethical. So I welcomed the scheme of Patrikainen (1999) who created a conceptual space combining two qualitatively different conceptions of learning (behaviouristic and cognitivist) and knowledge (objectivist and constructivist). He managed to position the continuum of technocratic and humanistic conceptions of man in this space.

It seems that especially visual models scaffold my understanding. So, I was also deeply influenced by Korthagen's 'onion model' layers of teacher's professionalism, presented at the Leiden conference in 2003. It has helped me, among others, to clarify the much debated concept of teacher's competencies that some wanted to 'instrumentalise' in the course of Bologna reform of study programmes.

I found that also in other countries there was an increasing stress on external tests, standards, performativity, within an 'instrumentalist', technical agenda and I looked for answers on how to cope with it. How to deal with uncertainty and dilemmas caused by outside pressures and the complexity of professional life? The keynote by Geert Kelchtermans in 2005 made quite an impression on me, by his analysis of the 'performativity rules' and their consequences and by his acknowledging vulnerability and uncertainty as 'fundamental characteristic of education'. I was somehow relieved to realise that simply 'we have to live with it', with all those polarities and dilemmas. In this sense, I welcomed the role of narrative-biographical approach that was nearly nonexistent in our Slovenian environment, an approach that opposes attempts to reduce education to instrumental enterprise and unveils moral, political and especially emotional dimensions of teaching; I liked and later frequently used the terms 'emotional geography' and 'emotional politics' that I became introduced to in a symposium led by Hargreaves in Dublin (Hargreaves, 1999).

Already in Dublin I had learned about the use of selected autobiographies, life histories of student teachers as 'an opportunity to build bridges between the past and the future'. This approach was further developed by Dutch and Canadian colleagues who pointed out also the mutually supportive connection between action research and reflective practice. I felt and later discovered the power of good metaphors for describing teacher's role.

One of the problems that bothered me was how to make student teachers practical experiences more fruitful. Of course we used student observations of lessons of experienced teachers 'as models' for discussions of those observations, sometimes with only university tutor present! I was very impressed by the process described by Ruth Ethell (1999), in which students had the opportunity to observe not only video recordings of expert teachers' classroom practice and comment it, but also to examine the thinking process of those teachers, based on stimulated recall, that was also video recorded together with the lessons. Up until now, I never had the opportunity to replicate this process, but it helped me to develop the habit to 'reveal' to students and other participants of my courses and workshops, what was the basis of my different moves, teaching decisions, what dilemmas I had and how I tried to solve them. In Leiden (2003) I got confirmation for this in John Loughran's excellent keynote speech (Loughran, 2003). He mentioned the impact of good apprenticeship of observation, the role of modelling to students not only 'good teaching', but also our doubts, uncertainties and risk-taking – all that happens in our minds and 'behind the scene'.

When after a long time I am re-reading my conference notes, I realise that my own learning was not a linear process. I met certain ideas very early on and then they were 'forgotten' for many years, but remained in my thinking and searching for answers in a latent form, only to be resurrected much later, when the situation was ripe. One of those ideas was appreciating the key role of mentors at practice schools and how to support their professional development. The idea was there already in the 1980s, when I co-organised training for them, but it moved in the centre of my attention again in 2004–2005 in the frame of the project, Partnership of Faculties and Schools. Similarly the question of competences and professional development of (university) teacher educators was with me since the 1970s, as part of my interest to improve teaching and learning in higher education. It bothered me that very few university lecturers were aware of the fact that theoretical knowledge was useful only when it was connected to the concrete experiences and locally produced knowledge by (student) teachers. And very few were themselves examples of reflective practitioners. So I embraced the idea of a series of extensive workshops for teacher educators, starting in 1986, with the last one in 2001 (Marentič Požarnik, 1987). In many ways, attending ISATT conferences helped me to connect existing, sometimes contradictory ideas and to 'build bridges' between them.

What was the distinctive role of ISATT in shaping your professional beliefs in the context of other (previous and concurrent) influences – organisations, projects, conferences, individual contacts?
I graduated in psychology and education and started my professional career as an educational researcher in the 1960s when I was lucky enough to get the opportunity of longer study stays in Norway and in the USA, also in West Germany in the 1970s. The 'iron curtain' in former Yugoslavia was not too tight, especially not in Slovenia. My first research interest was learning strategies of secondary school students; later, I expanded it to learning of (student) teachers, as I started to ask myself about the impact and relevance of my lectures on psychology of learning for all those hundreds of students in the lecture hall.

In the 1980s, the contacts with the newly founded University for Educational Sciences in Klagenfurt became important for my professional development. The 1979 Klagenfurt conference of EARDHE (European Association for Research and Development in Higher Education) was a starting point of two decades of tight professional cooperation with a nonformal group of university staff developers from different European countries, known as 'Maidstone group'. With my colleague, we recently described this fascinating experience (Marentič Požarnik & Peeters, 2012). Thus, my interest in professional development of teachers expanded to teachers in higher education – a group that was not so much in the centre of ISATT interest, although I remember attending the symposium led by Michael Kompf with an ironic title 'The dark tower: Between Ivory and Babel' already in 1999. During two decades, I co-organised numerous workshops, seminars and summer schools for university teachers, inviting Maidstone colleagues to Slovenia, like Brigitte Berendt, Roy Cox, David Jaques and Lewis Elton (for more details, see also Marentič Požarnik, 2009).

The underlying philosophy of the 'Maidstone group' was similar to the one in ISATT. There was a respect for everything experiential, subjective, unique and qualitative, with a strong ethical background. We helped each other to deepen our understanding of how to support professional development of university staff, taking into account the specific context and also their existing 'subjective theories'. Actually, the regular Maidstone member Gunnar Handall, who I later met at ISATT in Dublin, was there with Per Lauvas, co-author of the pioneering book on the importance of subjective theories and teacher reflection (Handall & Lauvas, 1987).

In the 1980s and 1990s, I attended conferences of different associations, mostly of the Association of Teacher Education in Europe (starting in 1984 in Linz with the last one being in 2010 in Riga; in 2006 we organised it in Slovenia). Also ICEL (International Council of Experiential Learning) gave me an important impetus, although I attended two conferences only – in Auckland in 2000 that was preparatory for the one we hosted in Ljubljana in 2002. It was fascinating to see how they applied their humanistic ideology in the multicultural frame of Maori population. Also the two conferences of a smaller organisation, ISTE, International Society for Teacher Education, one in Prague in 1989 and the other at Brock University in 1997, emanated a similar 'humanistic' mission. I also enjoyed many sessions at ECER – European Conference for Educational Research (1998 in Ljubljana, 2000 in Edinburgh, 2004 in Rethymnon). As you remember, Barbara, we had quite a few joint presentations, some also treating the 'new' field of professional development of university teachers (Marentič Požarnik & Šteh, 2004).

It is difficult for me to 'disentangle' influences of different organisations and conferences and to say, what was the distinctive role of ISATT in my professional development, especially as the same colleagues with similar ideas and research findings appeared at conferences by different associations. For example, as national representative, I was invited by Paulien C. Meijer to contribute to an ISATT symposium at ECER in Edinburgh in 2000, on the topic, *How can research on teacher's practical knowledge contribute to teacher education?*

How did ISATT affect your teaching, mentoring, research and development activities? Your cooperation with colleagues? In what way did you change your thinking, your methods and approaches?
As already mentioned, it is difficult to clearly separate ISATT influences on my professional work from influences of other authors and organisations that held similar views. It was a gradual, cumulative process that affected profound changes in my teaching, writing and research.

I gradually embraced and developed ideas like the central role of teacher's subjective theories and reflection, experiential learning, professional identity of (secondary and tertiary) teachers and teacher educators, the model of school-based in-service training and teacher action research. For example, by reflecting on and researching my own teaching practice (as Loughran put it in his Leiden keynote address) I introduced quite a few changes. My main subject was educational psychology for (hundreds of) student teachers of languages, social science and humanities and a separate, more intensive course for students of education. I gradually reduced the amount of one-way lecturing and introduced different experiential group activities, student presentations with mutual evaluations and reflection, learning through discussion (LTD), writing of reflexive diaries and similar activities. I was encouraged by positive reactions by the students.

Longer experiential workshops I organised for smaller groups of school mentors, university teachers and teacher educators were even more satisfying and hopefully more effective. To live and work together for 3–4 days and to learn from each other was a remarkable experience for all concerned, although it is not easy to 'measure' the long-term impact on thinking and acting of such workshops (Marentič Požarnik & Puklek Levpušček, 2002).

ISATT conferences gave me the much needed support, confirmation and theoretical background of my attempts to foster 'collegial learning' of teacher educators for whom I organised annual semi-formal workshops since 1986 (Marentič Požarnik, 1987). I also managed to perform, together with my colleague, some qualitative research on the development of their professional identity (Marentič Požarnik & Valenčič Zuljan, 2001). John Loughran's keynote speech in Leiden (2003) especially confirmed my endeavours.

It was easier to cultivate those ideas with my master and doctoral students because we had the opportunity to work and discuss matters together for a longer time period. It is interesting to mention that Milena Valenčič Zuljan had the opportunity to discuss with Douwe Beijaard the topic of her dissertation, 'The Cognitive Model of Professional Development of Student Teachers' (1999) at an ISATT conference in Kiel in 1997. Also the ideas for your [Barbara Šteh's] dissertation, including encouragement to use elements of qualitative methodology, matured on ISATT conferences where we also presented some findings (Šteh Kure, 2000; Šteh & Marentič Požarnik, 2001).

As an example of a more direct influence of ISATT, I can mention the biographical method including the exercise on 'the river of professional development'. In 2000, I followed Maureen Pope's and Pamela Denicolo's invitation to engage in reflective activities on our own teaching that included also the drawing of the river and describing, how a friend would describe us. Later I used the method rather frequently in workshops with teachers and mentors to induce reflection on their professional identity and visions of future development (Marentič Požarnik, 2006a). Also Korthagen's 'onion model' which started to fascinate me at Leiden conference (2003) helped me to place the much debated concept of teacher's competencies in an appropriate frame and to realise the importance of teachers 'core identity'. In 2004, I initiated an international conference in Slovenia on constructivism in teaching and teacher education (Marentič Požarnik, 2004) that attracted contributions from numerous researchers, mainly teacher educators.

How were ISATT ideas (that you also tried to present in translations) received in the broader Slovenian context, especially in the areas of initial teacher education, continuous professional development and curricular reform? How did proponents of 'traditional' objectivist, quantitative methodology/ ideology respond?

I tried also to influence the broader framework of teacher education policy in Slovenia, through being a member of different councils and committees, being involved in the reform of teacher education programmes, and by pointing out that precondition for any successful school reform is the professionalisation of teacher education (Marentič Požarnik, 2000). The transition of entire teacher education to the university was a new challenge on how to find the right way on the 'winding path between the universitisation and professionalization' (Marentič Požarnik & Valenčič Zuljan, 2002). But the changes in conceptions of teachers are slower than systemic reforms (Šteh & Marentič Požarnik, 2005).

We did achieve some progress in the course of a two-year project 'Partnership of Faculties and Schools' in 2004 and 2005 (The results are presented in Peklaj, 2006), especially in stressing the crucial role of a well-organised practice in schools and of well-educated mentors (Marentič Požarnik, 2006b), but it was difficult to achieve a 'sustainability' of good practice developed during the project. The main agenda of school policymakers is still moving mainly in the direction of 'technical rationality' and performativity and the Bologna reform did not bring the improvements we hoped for.

I tried to 'give voice' to ISATT ideas in our environment not only in my research and writing, but also by way of translation. For example, I proposed that Laursen's paper on 'authentic teacher', presented at the Leiden 2003 conference be translated into Slovene (Laursen, 2003). It seemed to me that it presented a fairly holistic picture of what is meant by teacher excellence and it was well received by our teachers.

My next opportunity came in 2009 when it was my turn to propose articles to translate for our Slovene journal, *Vzgoja in izobraževanje (Education and instruction)* (Volume 4, 2009). I decided that this should be a number in the 'ISATT spirit' and I have chosen some typical theoretical and empirical papers to be translated (Ballet, Kelchtermans, & Loughran, 2006; Korthagen, 2005; Korthagen & Vasalos, 2008; Leat, Lofthouse, & Taverner, 2006;

Zellermayer & Tabak, 2006). I hoped that descriptions of good qualitative research, like Zellermayer and Tabak's, for instance, would serve as attractive examples to be followed.

But the question remains: To what extent do teachers and even teacher educators change their ideas and professional activities merely by reading papers and books? Is not 'real' new knowledge, as Tickle put it in his memorable plenary address in Leiden (Tickle, 2003) fashioned above all through conversation? So I used to include those articles as 'required pre-reading' for discussions in in-service seminars and training workshops on action research methodology for teachers, teacher educators and super-visors. Action research is still a rarity; the idea about what counts as 'real', respectable scientific research is deeply engrained and mainly limited to objectivist quantitative studies. The space for alternative methodologies (Marentič Požarnik, 2001) is widening very slowly. There is not strong enough preparation in preservice and in-service teacher education. The problem is – as I learned on ISATT conferences – that it is not only the methodology itself, but the whole ideology that goes with it. It is the positivist ideology of technical rationality, of quality to be achieved only by curricula with well-defined measurable standards, the transmission of 'objective' knowledge and external testing. And this ideology still guides the decisions of many leading experts and school policy makers in Slovenia.

Thus, ideas like 'from teaching to learning' (Marentič Požarnik, 2005), (social) constructivism, importance of subjective theories and practical knowledge, methods that lead to active learning, etc. are being simplified and opposed in different ways. Just one example: the idea I expressed in one of my writings that some goals can be achieved better by other strategies than transmission by lecturing was met with strong opposition. The firm conviction of a number of our university professors is that one-way lecturing represents the most important and indispensable part also in teacher education ... It is difficult to change as it seems to touch the very core of their identity.

The important role of ISATT has been – and hopefully is still will be in the future – to give, especially to the younger generation of Slovenian teacher educators and researchers, the much needed energy, self-confidence and endurance in their teaching, research and attempts to influence policy of teacher education. They still represent a small island in the sea of objectivist, quantitative, standard-based ideology, recently also supported by glorifica-tion of information communication technology, international comparisons of achievement and by economical constraints. The belief that qualitative methods are more time-consuming and do not provide objective results prevails.

Where is Slovenia now, for example, in improving the theory–practice relationship in initial teacher education, in empowering teachers? What challenges do you see in future development?
One of the problems is that the 'seeds' of Bologna reform of study programmes for teachers were sewn on traditional university ground. We did manage to put teacher education on the master level of Bologna, in a consecutive model (5 years of study) and we tried hard to give more space to the 'professional part' of curricula in the last two years (an equivalent of one study year or 60 credits). In this framework, the amount of required school practice was increased, although it is still not enough. But we still lack a unifying concept. The process of bringing teacher education into the academy (Marentič Požarnik & Valenčič Zuljan, 2002) meant that the responsibility for teacher education got dispersed to a number of institutions (e.g., one for educating teachers of mathematics and physics, another for biology, the third for languages and humanities...) with other priorities. Some of these institutions introduced a 3 + 2 years model, some 4 + 1, in maths they managed to introduce a 5-year unified study for teachers, etc.

Also, many teacher educators at the university have no experience in teaching at the level for which they are preparing students. There is not enough cooperation between universities and schools. Furthermore, the status of school mentors is not clear. Research, performed 'with teachers or for teachers' does not count for promotion in university teachers' career; what counts are articles in eminent foreign journals, mostly in the basic disciplines (like organic chemistry, social linguistics), not in pedagogy and teaching and teacher education sources. Hence, there are quite a few obstacles in introducing innovations and improvements in content and methods of teacher education. Nevertheless, usage of qualitative research methods in diploma theses is gradually gaining a more respectable status, thanks to my younger colleagues – ISATT participants.

The present political and economic moment is not favourable to deeper changes. In times of tightening public budgets, the whole attention is being directed to existential problems of how to finance the salaries of teachers. Also, the financing of the master level of reformed programmes (the additional year or two) is endangered. To make it worse, each new political regime tends to neglect good achievements and proposals of the previous ones.

Maybe the main challenge is that in those difficult times we do not 'forget' basic lessons we already learned about sources of teacher's professional development – deeper reflection, emotions and motivation, 'core identity' (Korthagen, 2005) and that we concentrate on attempts to foster real growth, not only superficial changes in formal frames or bureaucratic control of new programmes. I am a 'realistic optimist' and I hope that ISATT will continue to give us substantial professional and moral support.

REFERENCES

Ballet, K., Kelchtermans, K., & Loughran, J. (2006). Beyond intensification towards a scholarship of practice: Analysing changes in teachers' work lives. *Teachers and Teaching: Theory and Practice, 12*(2), 209–229.

Ethell, R. (1999, July). *Sharing expertise: Helping novices access the wisdom of expert teachers.* Paper presented at the 9th biennial meeting of the ISATT, Dublin, Ireland.

Handall, G., & Lauvas, P. (1987). *Promoting reflective teaching: Supervision for action.* Philadelphia: Open University press.

Hargreaves, A. (1999, July). *The emotional politics of teaching and teacher development: With implications for educational leadership.* Symposium conducted at the 9th biennial meeting of the ISATT, Dublin, Ireland.

Kelchtermans, G. (2005, July). *Professional commitment beyond contract: Teachers' self-understanding, vulnerability and reflection.* Keynote speech presented at the biennial meeting of the ISATT, Sydney, Australia.

Kompf, M., et al. (1999, July). *The dark tower: Between ivory and Babel.* Symposium conducted at the 9th biennial meeting of the ISATT, Dublin.

Korthagen, F. (2005). Practice, theory and person in life-long professional learning. In D. Beijaard, P. C. Meijer, G. Morine-Dershimer & H. Tillema (Eds.), *Teacher professional development in changing conditions* (pp. 79–94). Dordrecht: Springer.

Korthagen, F., & Vasalos, A. (2008, March). *"Quality from within"as the key to professional development.* Paper presented at the meeting of American Educational Research Association, New York, NY.

Laursen, P. F. (2003). Avtentični učitelj [The authentic teacher]. *Vzgoja in izobraževanje, 34*(6), 4–10.

Leat, D., Lofthouse, R., & Taverner, S. (2006). The road taken: Professional pathways in innovative curriculum development. *Teachers and Teaching: Theory and Practice, 12*(6), 33–49.

Lindberg, V. (1999, July). *Contexts for developing concepts of knowledge.* Paper presented at the 9th biennial meeting of the ISATT, Dublin.

Loughran, J. (2003, June). *Knowledge construction and learning to teach About teaching.* Keynote speech presented at the bi-annual meeting of the ISATT, Leiden, The Netherlands.

Mandl, H., & Huber, G. (1982). *Subjektive theorien von lehrern: Forschungsberichte 18.* Tübingen: DIFF.

Marentič Požarnik, B. (1987). A workshop in experiential learning as a means of "training the trainers" in integrative approach to teacher education. In *Lehrerbildung in Europa vor den Herausforderungen der 90er Jahre, Beiträge zum 12* (pp. 402–412). Congress ATEE.

Marentič Požarnik, B. (2000). Profesionalizacija izobraževanja učiteljev: nujna predpostavka uspešne prenove [Professionalization of teacher education: The necessary prerequisite of successful educational reform]. *Vzgoja in izobraževanje, 31*(4), 4–11.

Marentič Požarnik, B. (2001). Uspešna prenova terja enakopravnejši položaj "alternativne" raziskovalne paradigme in učitelja raziskovalca [For a successful school reform we need an equal status of the "alternative" research paradigm and teacher as researcher]. *Sodobna pedagogika, 52*(2), 64–80.

Marentič Požarnik, B. (Ed.). (2004). *Konstruktivizem v šoli in izobraževanje učiteljev [Constructivism in teaching and teacher education]*. Ljubljana: Center za pedagoško izobraževanje Filozofske fakultete.

Marentič Požarnik, B. (2005). Spreminjanje paradigme poučevanja in učenja ter njunega odnosa: eden temeljnih izzivov sodobnega izobraževanja [Changing the paradigm of teaching and learning and their relationship: A key challenge of contemporary education]. *Sodobna pedagogika, 56*(1), 58–74.

Marentič Požarnik, B. (2006a). Pripovedi, zgodbe, dnevniški in (avto)biografski zapiski: poti do boljšega razumevanja in razvijanja učiteljeve profesionalnosti [Narratives, stories, diaries and autobiographies: Ways to a better understanding and developing teacher's professionalism]. *Vzgoja in izobraževanje, 37*(5), 4–9.

Marentič Požarnik, B. (2006b). Seminarji za mentorje kot priložnost za razvijanje kompetenc in poglabljanje refleksije ob parterskem sodelovanju s fakultetnimi učitelji [Seminars for mentors as opportunity to develop competencies and deepen reflection in partnership with university staff]. In C. Peklaj (Ed.), *Teorija in praksa v izobraževanju učiteljev [Theory and practice in teacher education]* (pp. 45–52). Ljubljana: Univerza v Ljubljani, Filozofska fakulteta.

Marentič Požarnik, B. (2009). Improving the quality of teaching and learning in higher education through supporting professional development of teaching staff. *Napredak, 150*(3/4), 341–359.

Marentič Požarnik, B., & Peeters, O. (2012). The (hi)story of Maidstone meetings: An inspiring example of an informal learning community involving European academic developers in the 'pioneer' stage. *Higher Education Research Network Journal, 5*(special issue), 53–66.

Marentič Požarnik, B., & Puklek Levpušček, M. (2002). Perceptions of quality and changes in teaching and learning by participants of university staff development courses. *Psihološka obzorja, 11*(2), 71–79.

Marentič Požarnik, B., & Šteh, B. (1999, July). *Observations of teacher's and student's role in the context of secondary school curricular reform.* Paper presented at the 9th biennial meeting of the ISATT, Dublin, Ireland.

Marentič Požarnik, B., & Šteh, B. (2004, September). *Students' perceptions of teaching/learning situation as a trigger for reflection in staff development courses.* Paper presented at the European Conference on Educational Research, Rethymnon.

Marentič Požarnik, B., & Valenčič Zuljan, M. (2001). The role of experiential learning in teacher educators' professional development. In N. Benton & R. Benton (Eds.), *Te Rito o te Mātauranga: Selected papers from the seventh conference of the International Consortium for Experiential Learning* (Vol. 2, pp. 95–102). Aotearoa/New Zealand: University of Auckland.

Marentič Požarnik, B., & Valenčič Zuljan, M. (2002). The winding path between universitisation and professionalisation of teacher education: A case of Slovenia [Special Issue]. *Changes in Education of Teachers in Europe*, *3*(5), 195–210.

Patrikainen, R. (1999, July). *Conception of man, conception of knowledge and conception of learning in primary teacher's pedagogical thinking*. Paper presented at the 9th biennial meeting of the ISATT, Dublin, Ireland.

Peklaj, C. (Ed.). (2006). *Teorija in praksa v izobraževanju učiteljev [Theory and practice in teacher education]*. Ljubljana: Univerza v Ljubljani, Filozofska fakulteta.

Šteh, B., & Marentič Požarnik, B. (2001). What is actually happening in secondary classrooms: The rhetoric and reality of curricular reform. In *ISATT 10th Biennial Conference, Conference Programme & Book of Abstract: Connecting policy and practice: Challenges for teaching and learning in schools and universities* (p. 80). Faro, PT: University of Algarve, Campus de Gambelas.

Šteh, B., & Marentič Požarnik, B. (2005). Teachers' perception of their professional autonomy in the environment of systemic change. In D. Beijaard, P. C. Meijer, G. Morine-Dershimer & H. Tillema (Eds.), *Teacher professional development in changing conditions* (pp. 349–363). Dordrecht: Springer.

Šteh, B. (2000). *Kakovost učenja in poučevanja v okviru gimnazijskega programa*, (Doktorsko delo). *The quality of learning and teaching in the frame of the secondary school programme*. Doctoral dissertation. University of Ljubljana, Ljubljana.

Tickle, L. (2003, June). *The crucible in the classroom: A learning environment for teachers, or a site of crucifixion?* Keynote speech presented at the bi-annual meeting of the ISATT, Leiden, The Netherlands.

Valenčič Zuljan, M. (1999). *Kognitivni model poklicnega razvoja študentov bodočih učiteljev* (Doktorsko delo). *The cognitive model of professional development of student teachers*. Doctoral dissertation, University of Ljubljana, Ljubljana.

Zellermayer, M., & Tabak, E. (2006). Knowledge construction in a teachers' community of enquiry: A possible road map. *Teachers and Teaching: Theory and Practice*, *12*(1), 33–49.

PART II
RESEARCH STRANDS

Part II features research strands that ISATT members have pursued over time. While not exhaustive, the strands we have culled represent a sampling of key research themes. Teacher Knowledge is attended to in Chapters 4, 5, and 6. Chapter 4, an article authored by Canadian D. Jean Clandinin, is one of many historical pieces of research that sat at the forefront of the paradigm shift in education. It is titled "Personal Practical Knowledge: A Study of Teachers' Classroom Images." Clandinin's historical work is followed by Chapter 5, "From Teacher Knowledge to Teacher Learning in Community: Transformations of Theory and Practice," authored by The Middle East regional editors, Freema Elbaz-Luwisch (who also spearheaded the paradigm shift) and Lily Orland-Barak. This work shows the transition of teacher knowledge into inquiries into learning in communities. From there, we learn in Chapter 6 about "Pedagogical Content Knowledge: Twenty-Five Years Later," which is authored by Maher Hashweh from Palestine. This chapter was also commissioned by our Middle East editors.

Next in the lineup is another historical work written by Sigrun Gudmundsdottir, a deceased ISATT member. In Chapter 7, "Story-Maker, Story teller: Narrative Structures in Curriculum," she pushes Lee Shulman's pedagogical content knowledge conceptualization into the realm of narrative, a connection that the personal practical knowledge conceptualization birthed by D. Jean Clandinin (Chapter 4), Freema Elbaz-Luwisch (Chapter 5) and F. M. Connelly (their advisor) also made. After that, we have a second chapter on narrative, this time from Finland. Chapter 8, "Narrative Research: From the Margins to Being Heard" is authored by Leena Syrjälä and Eila Estola and was invited by European editor Anneli Lauriala.

Teacher Professional Development, Teacher Professional Identity, and The Moral Matters of Teaching are the research strands that follow. Beatrice Avalos from Chile characterizes "Teacher Professional Development in *Teaching and Teacher Education* from 2000–2010" in Chapter 9. Then, in chapter 10, Douwe Beijaard, Paulien C. Meijer, and Nico Verloop, focus on teacher identity in their work titled "The Emergence of Research on Teachers' Professional Identity: A Review of Literature from 1988 to 2000." We then move on Chapter 11, another Northern European chapter solicited by editor Anneli Lauriala. "The Moral Matters of Teaching: A Finnish Perspective" is the name of the piece and it is contributed by Kirsi Tirri, Auli Toom, and Jukka Husu.

Chapters 12 to 15 all deal in some way with two similar research themes, Teacher Reflection and Reflective Practice. Chapter 12 is authored by Fred A. J. Korthagen and it is titled "In Search of the Essence of a Good Teacher: Toward a More Holistic Approach in Teacher Education." Chapters 13 and 14 are reprint articles, both having to do with reflection. The first, Chapter 13, is authored by Ora W. Y. Kwo from Hong Kong and is titled "Reflective Classroom Practice: Case Studies of Hong Kong Student Teachers at Work." The second, Chapter 14 is titled "Teacher Education in Brazil" and was contributed by Maria Inês Marcondes of Brazil. Then, we come to Chapter 15, which is a chapter invited by European editor Bernadette Charlier. It is titled "Reflective Practice in the Teaching Profession: The Case of Training and Research Practices in the French Community in Belgium" and is authored by Sephora Boucenna and Evelyne Charlier.

Chapter 16 moves readers into the territory of educational leadership and the kind of leaders that are needed to support high quality teaching and learning. The work, which was invited by European editor Isabel Rots, is authored by Michael Schratz. Schratz served as a keynote speaker at the 30th Anniversary Conference in Ghent, Belgium.

The Lives of Teachers is the theme taken up in Chapters 17 and 18. In Chapter 17, Christopher Day, a European section editor and editor-in-chief of ISATT's official journal, *Teachers and Teaching: Theory and Practice*, centers full attention on the theme. Day's chapter is followed by Chapter 18, a reprint article authored by Geert Kelchtermans, also having to do with teachers' lives. Kelchtermans' work is titled "Who I Am in How I Teach is the Message: Self-Understanding, Vulnerability, and Reflection."

Section II on Research Strands sets the stage for Section III Contemporary International Scholarship, all of which have to do with teacher development, teacher identity, teachers' lives, the moral decision making of teachers and the influence of leadership.

CHAPTER 4

PERSONAL PRACTICAL KNOWLEDGE: A STUDY OF TEACHERS' CLASSROOM IMAGES [☆]

D. Jean Clandinin

ABSTRACT

Teachers develop and use a special kind of knowledge. This knowledge is neither theoretical, in the sense of theories of learning, teaching, and curriculum, nor merely practical, in the sense of knowing children. If either of these were the essential ingredient of what teachers know, then it would be easy to see that others have a better knowledge of both; academics with better knowledge of the theoretical and parents and others with better knowledge of the practical. A teacher's special knowledge is composed of both kinds of knowledge, blended by the personal background and characteristics of the teacher, and expressed by her in particular situations. The idea of "image" is one form of personal practical knowledge, the name given to this special practical knowledge of teachers (Clandinin, 1985; Connelly & Dienes, 1982). In this chapter I show how one teacher's image of the "classroom as home" embodies her

☆This article was first published in 1985, in *Curriculum Inquiry*, Volume 15, No. 4 (Winter, 1985), pp. 361–385. Reprinted with permission from Wiley.

From Teacher Thinking to Teachers and Teaching: The Evolution of a Research Community
Advances in Research on Teaching, Volume 19, 67–95
Copyright © 2013 Wiley
ISSN: 1479-3687/doi:10.1108/S1479-3687(2013)0000019007

personal and professional experience and how, in turn, the image is expressed in her classroom practices and in her practices in her personal life. Using a variety of classroom episodes gathered over two years with two teachers, I offer a theoretical outline of the experiential dimensions of an image and, in so doing, present image as a knowledge term which resides at the nexus of the theoretical, the practical, the objective, and the subjective.

Keywords: Image; personal practical knowledge

THEORETICAL PERSPECTIVE AND KEY TERMS

The theoretical perspective[1] of the research derives from the notion of personal practical knowledge with its concern for the development of a person-centered language and perspective for accounting for school practices. According to the perspective, actions are both the expression and origin of the personal knowledge of the actor. Thus, action is imbued with knowledge and knowledge with passion. Action and knowledge are united in the actor and the account of both is of an actor.

The phrase "personal practical knowledge" has been discussed in detail elsewhere (Connelly & Clandinin, 1984, 1985). The following is a brief summary of what is intended by the phrase. What is meant by "personal" as defining knowledge is that the knowledge so defined participates in, and is imbued with, all that goes to make up a person. It is knowledge which has arisen from circumstances, actions, and undergoings which themselves had affective content for the person in question. This use of "personal" draws attention to the individual local factor which helps to constitute the character, the past, and the future of any individual. By personal as defining knowledge, is meant that knowledge which can be discovered in both the actions of the person and, under some circumstances, by discourse or conversation.

By "knowledge" in the phrase "personal practical knowledge" is meant that body of convictions, conscious or unconscious, which have arisen from experience, intimate, social, and traditional, and which are expressed in a person's actions. The actions in question are all those acts that make up the practice of teaching including its planning and evaluation. "Personal practical knowledge" is knowledge which is imbued with all the experiences that make up a person's being. Its meaning is derived from, and understood in terms of, a person's experiential history, both professional and personal.

There are at least four kinds of studies which focus on what teachers know (Clandinin, 1983, 1986). One kind of study focuses on what teachers know of theory. For example, such studies provide accounts of all of the pieces of knowledge such as knowledge of philosophy, sociology, and psychology that teachers in general, or even a teacher in particular, might be shown to hold. A second kind looks at what teachers know in practice. Such research offers a catalogue of components of knowledge which teachers, in general, could be seen to hold. A third kind examines teacher epistemologies in terms of existing philosophical categories. Accounts of teacher knowledge in theoretical terms are thus given. Research on personal practical knowledge constitutes a fourth kind of study focused on what teachers know. The notion of personal practical knowledge is not of knowledge which is just content nor knowledge which is just structure. It is, rather, knowledge which is "a contextually relative exercise of capacities for imaginatively ordering our experience" (Johnson, 1984, p. 467).

It is assumed that knowledge so defined is not found in lists of the contents of teacher education textbooks, workshop outlines, or teacher task analysis. These matters, of course, all have their part but such lists, with their categories of concepts, theories, facts, tasks, properties, and skills, do not define a teacher's personal practical knowledge. These lists of objective and definable content are leavened by one's personal and practical experience, subsumed, as Polanyi would say, in one's "subsidiary aware-ness" (Polanyi, 1958, p. 88). It is this personal and existential matrix that makes up what a teacher "knows" about teaching. Where, then, is this knowledge found? Personal practical knowledge and, in particular, images are found in a person acting. Accordingly, the study of teachers' personal practical knowledge begins in the study of practice. Personal practical knowledge is revealed through interpretations of observed practices over time and is given biographical, personal meaning through reconstructions of the teacher's narratives of experience. Personal practical knowledge is, therefore, found in practice. It is knowledge which is experiential, embodied, and based on the narrative of experience.

Image

This chapter offers a conceptualization of teacher "image."[2] "Image" as a component of personal practical knowledge and as based on the narrative unity (Clandinin & Connelly, 1984; Connelly & Clandinin, 1985) of an individual's life is seen as a central construct for understanding teachers' knowledge. It is important that the notion of image as part of personal practical knowledge not be confused with the notion of image as a "concept" and as a propositional knowledge term. If a critic claimed this definition for my work, it could then be easily argued that the term "image" adds little of substance since standard views on the concept of image and of related events, concepts, and propositions treat the same thing, namely, a form of conceptual knowledge. And this criticism might be true if, after all, my interest was with propositions and concepts about practice. But this is not my interest. Lakoff and Johnson's (1980) work in philosophy follows similar interests to my own in research on teaching. They have developed an alternative account in which human experience and understanding, rather than objective truth, plays the central role. It is, as they say, "an experiential approach ... to questions of our everyday experience" (p. x). Johnson further argues that it is our images and deep metaphorical structures, as well as our concepts and propositions that constitute our practical knowledge ..." (Johnson, 1984, p. 467).

My interest is in the imaginative processes by which meaningful and useful patterns are generated in practice. Propositional knowledge in this domain refers only to concepts of, and their relations to, practice. But practice involves more than this. It involves the calling forth of images from a history, from a narrative of experience, so that the "image" is then available to guide us in making sense of future situations. Images are within experience and are not only in the logically defined words which specify their conceptual status. Accordingly, for my work, images are embodied and enacted. Their embodiment entails emotionality, morality, and aesthetics and it is these affective, personally felt and believed, meanings which engender enactments.

CURRICULAR SIGNIFICANCE OF THE STUDY

The curricular importance of conceptualizing personal practical knowledge derives from at least two avenues of thought. One relates to the widespread disenchantment with much thinking about curriculum implementation work (Fullan & Pomfret, 1977). In part, the implementation of curriculum innovations did not produce intended changes in classrooms because implementers inadequately accounted for teachers. Connelly and Ben-Peretz (1980) describe three roles teachers have been required to play in implementation. In all three roles, teachers are expected to facilitate someone else's intentions. This failure to understand the teacher as an active holder and user of personal practical knowledge helps explain the limited success of curriculum implementation. When the more vital teacher view is adopted, the importance of understanding teachers' personal practical knowledge is heightened and we are led to more adequate ideas of school reform.

The second reason for the study of personal practical knowledge relates to the popular belief that teachers as professionals do not possess a body of knowledge (Lortie, 1975). Consequently, teaching does not have the status of other professions. What knowledge teachers are thought to have is of a subject matter such as science or reading, not professional knowledge. By recognizing and conceptualizing teachers' personal practical knowledge, one way of enhancing their professional status is secured.

Methodology

The conception of personal practical knowledge is of knowledge as experiential, value-laden, purposeful, and oriented to practice. Personal practical knowledge is viewed as tentative, subject to change and transient, rather than something fixed, objective, and unchanging. These characteristics led to the use of dialectical research methods since it was felt that both the ongoing study and its results would be best pursued with a reflexive outlook between participant and researcher and between action and idea.

Personal practical knowledge as a concept embodies a dialectical view of theory and practice. In the dialectical view (McKeon, 1952), theory and practice are viewed as inseparable; practice is seen as theory in action. In this view theory is assumed to change and modify according to the shifting exigencies of the practical world. The essential task of the dialectical is to resolve oppositions in theory, oppositions in practice, and oppositions between theory and practice. Elbaz (1983), whose work is a forerunner of my own, can, for example, be seen to assume a dialectical relationship between theory and practice in her conception of practical knowledge where she has shown how the world of practice continually shapes the teacher's knowledge and, conversely, how the teacher herself structures the practical situation in accordance with her knowledge and her purposes. The present research is conceptualized dialectically both in the methodologies adopted in the relationships established with the two teachers and in the conception of personal practical knowledge offered.

The foregoing considerations gave rise to the use of qualitative methodologies in the study of image. In part, justification of the methodologies comes from the dialectical relationship that characterizes the interdependence of researcher and researched. As researcher, I cannot enter into a teacher's classroom as a neutral observer and try to give an account of her reality. Instead, I enter into the research process as a person with my own personal practical knowledge. My knowledge of teaching interacts with that of my participants. Inevitably, the data collected reflects my own participation in the classroom and my own personal practical knowledge colors the interpretations offered. The research process is, accordingly, an interactive, dialectical one characterized by Dwyer (1979) as "a particular form of social action that creates dialectical confrontations and produces intersubjective meaning" (p. 211). The meaning created in the process of working together in the classroom, of offering interpretations and of talking together, is a shared one. Neither teacher nor researcher emerges unchanged. In terms of narrative it is appropriate to view this process as the negotiation of two people's narrative unities.

The notion of narrative unity is borrowed from MacIntyre (1981) and is defined as a continuum within a person's experience which renders life experiences meaningful for the unity they achieve for the person. What we mean by unity is the union in a particular person in a particular place and time of all that he has been and undergone in the past and in the past of the tradition which helped to shape him. The notion of narrative unity is not merely a description of a person's history but a meaning-giving account, an interpretation, of one's history. We can see within the history of an individual a number of narrative unities. The notion of narrative unity allows us the possibility of imagining the living out of a narrative as well as the revision of ongoing narrative unities and the creation of new ones.

Intensive dialectical relationships with the two teachers were established over more than a year of participant observation and interviews. The study focused on these teachers in their classroom reality-coping with students, parents, other staff, the principal, and consultants and with program demands, for to understand the teachers' personal practical knowledge, one needs to understand how they work in their classroom milieu.

Two primary teachers, Aileen and Stephanie, participated in the study.[3] Aileen is an Early Childhood Education teacher with 12 years experience in kindergarten to Grade 3 classes. During the research period, she taught Junior and Senior kindergarten in a traditional elementary school and was the only teacher on the staff using what she calls a "play-based" approach to teaching. Aileen became interested in participating in the study when she was pursuing a graduate degree. Stephanie is an elementary school teacher with 12 years experience in two inner-city schools. During the research period she taught a split Grade 1 and 2 class in the first year and a Grade 1 class in the second. Stephanie agreed to participate in the study when her school was approached to participate in a large scale research project (Connelly & Clandinin, 1984).

Participant observation methodology was used in both classrooms. I worked in Stephanie's classroom for three half-days per week from April, 1981 to June, 1981 and from September, 1981 to February, 1982, and in Aileen's classroom for the equivalent of one full week in February and March, 1982.

In each classroom I took an active role as a teacher assistant and colleague. I became more deeply involved in Stephanie's class and took a more central role in planning sessions, in discussions of student progress, and in taking responsibility for class projects. (This chapter focuses primarily on Stephanie. For a full account of work with both teachers, see Clandinin, 1986.)

My involvement with students precluded note-taking during school visits. After leaving the school, usually the same day, events were reconstructed in anthropological style field notes. Dictaphone notes were made and entered into a Dec-10 mainframe computer using a Digital word processor. The principal topics on which notes were made were student activities, discussions with the teacher, observations of the teacher's activities, projects completed, the physical appearance of the classroom, and my own activities. My notes attempted to give a complete account, recording as much detail as could be remembered.

Two unstructured, open-ended interviews were held with each teacher: March and June, 1980 with Aileen and June, 1981 and January, 1982 with Stephanie. The second of each of the interviews were focused, in part, by the teachers' reactions to the narrative accounts discussed below. These interviews were taped and later transcribed and computer-entered. Transcripts were shared with the teachers to give them an opportunity to correct and modify the interview data.

Field note and interview data were initially divided into content units, coded by brief descriptive phrases. This initial interpretive process was enriched by a "theoretical memo" process (Glaser & Strauss, 1967), in which preliminary interpretations and comments on segments of the data were written as I analyzed field note and interview data. After initial analysis, the data, which now included raw data, descriptive phrases, and theoretical memos, were re-read in order to identify practices which seemed "minded"[4] by what I speculated were images.

Preliminary narrative accounts were prepared and shared with teachers. These accounts took the form of long letters from me to each participant.

The accounts not only provided feedback on my interpretation of classroom activities and interviews but also advanced tentative notions of image grounded in my interpretation of events. The accounts were designed to capture the personal practical knowledge of each teacher by detailing her images and their expression in minded practices in both classroom and interviews. These accounts also described my participation in the classroom and offered tentative ideas on the concept of image for consideration by the teachers.

The teachers responded to the narrative accounts in the second of the above-noted interviews (June, 1980 with Aileen and January, 1982 with Stephanie). Their responses provided insight into their imagery as it was embodied in their practice. These responses, combined with the ongoing participant observation work, led to the preparation of a second narrative account and a brief discussion with each participating teacher in November, 1982.

The essential outline of the notion of image presented in this chapter was developed in these four narrative accounts (two per teacher) and has, therefore, been discussed with each teacher. In this way, the reflexive dialectical methods that characterized the practical classroom research are replayed at the ideational level.

Thus, reflexivity is apparent at several levels in the study. There is, at one level, ongoing reflexivity between researcher and teacher participating in classroom practices. At another level, reflexivity marks the relationship between the interview and classroom participant observation data as transcript and field note material are read, given meaning, and re-read with new insights. Reflexivity also marks the relationship between the narrative accounts and the interview discussions that focus on the account. We can see, therefore, that as the methodology of the study is worked through, reflexive dialectical relationships are a recurring mark. There is a dialectical relationship between the concrete and the experiential on the one hand and the concrete and theoretical on the other as the methodology unfolds.

In sum, the key idea in this study is of image as an experiential construct. It is a term which reflexively links the person to her practice at one level and, at another level, offers the potential of making links between participant observation data on individual teachers with ideas about teachers in general. I came to understand Aileen and Stephanie's classroom practices in terms of their past experience as it could be seen to crystallize in the form of their imagery and as their imagery was embodied in their practice. Although the interpretations offered in the study are of two individual, distinctive persons, the structure of how and of what I can give an account is the same.

I give accounts, in general, of practices, experiences, images, and relationships while acknowledging the particular practices, experiences, images, and relationships of each individual. I talk about Stephanie and Aileen as individuals and also about teachers in general as persons whose experience is reconstructed in the form of images which are expressed in practice. In this way image relates individual participant observation data to teachers in general. Methodologically, then, image is both a practical and a theoretical term. It is a term designed to embody the dialectic of practice and of inquiry.

STEPHANIE'S IMAGE OF THE "CLASSROOM AS HOME"

We now turn to a conceptualization of the nature of image through an examination of what I call Stephanie's "classroom as home" image. Through the analysis, the dimensions of the construct of image become apparent.

As noted in the account of the methodology of the study, the notion of image developed through a cyclical sequence of participation observation, interview, and interpretation. My understanding of what I have termed Stephanie's image of classroom as home developed through such a process. The following account, abstracted from the July, 1982 narrative account written to Stephanie, provides a context for understanding the development of the particular image and the concept of image. The excerpt has been altered very slightly because of the changed audience. For example, in the first sentence, "our June, 1981 interview" is altered to read "the June, 1981 interview" and "you" is altered to read "Stephanie."

The Emerging Image of Classroom as Home

In the June, 1981 interview Stephanie explained working in the classroom as being something like "running a house." This statement was tentatively identified as an expression of an image which I labeled the "classroom as home" image. After the interview, I began to read the field notes in order to see how I might interpret the way Stephanie's classroom practices could be minded by such an image. I had problems offering an adequate interpretation in the first narrative account. In the January, 1982 interview,[5] Stephanie responded to my interpretation in the following ways:

Transcript Segment 1:

T. Right, that I refer to our class as our home as our house ...

I. Yes, yes, and ...

T. Yes, yes I think so.

I. Okay...

T. Yes especially with young children, and even older children, I mean. I don't even know how, I think I say things that slip out, as Freudian slips and I don't even know why, but you know deep down there's something back there, you picked up everything... (S.W.,2,61)

Transcript Segment 2:

T. Yes, I don't know, now don't ask me, now you're going back and want the Freudian reasoning for that but I don't know why it even comes out except that I, the closeness and, and, and ... I don't know. I don't see how you can, you can segregate, you know that's the big thing there which education always tried to do and it was there in all different parts of the bureaucracy I guess and it's separate, and this is what causes so many problems I think caused a lot of our problems, and the sixties came out of that, people were saying no ...

I. Uhhuh

T. no, you know, we want a more together life and not have this type of, of a segregation as it was ... to our, to our lifestyle ... (S.W.,2,62)

Transcript Segment 3:

T. You know but that idea of the home well it's a home. I mean, it's or a way, my idea of how a home should be, maybe that was a wrong word to use, maybe or a community, I should have just called it ...

I. Uhhuh T. but sure every little area ... I. A home is the way you like to think of, of this as being?

T. Of a home being, like when I say home this would be my idea, is a group of people interacting together and cooperating together ...

I. Uhhuh

T. so that's, that was why I used that term or you could even say minicommunity, I think would even be better in that sense cause we're all coming from different backgrounds but yah, I mean, I spend as much time here as I do in my own home and you, you know it should feel, I mean, I feel that you should feel comfortable here, you know which I do ... cause you know you want to just get out as soon as that bell goes, you've had it, its been a rough day or week, fine but I mean I think you have to have a feeling for a place because if not, I think it shows, it shows in your work, it shows how you work with the children, it shows in the children themselves, how they relate to each other you know ...

I. Uhhuh

T. and I, I've always been that way, and so this really I guess starts right back from my early years as the big thing was to get that sense of environment to me was very important. I didn't care that they learned one and one is two if they were at each other's throats daily cause you've got to live here, you know, and I just personally, I, I couldn't stand ... being the ... you know ... you know being there to stop fights and whatever, to live and work in that kind of atmosphere . . .

I. Uhhuh

T. so environment and atmosphere have always been very important to me because we're living here, it's a living, learning experience, a living area, it's not a dead room, this room comes alive as soon as we all come in here, you know ... it, it breathes again and lives again and that's how I see it and that's how I hope, really homes should have, should be, you know, interacting together. (S.W., 2, 64–65)

I realized as Stephanie spoke, in the interview, that I had not completely captured either the depth or the significance of the image as a part of her personal practical knowledge. The image as it now appeared seemed more powerful and important than merely an analogous comparison between running or managing a home and managing a classroom.

In the interview Stephanie indicated the classroom was "a home." Her classroom was her "idea of how a home should be," "a group of people interacting and cooperating together ...." She felt it "should feel comfortable there" and that "you have to have a feeling for the place because if not, I think it shows, it shows in your work, it shows in how you work with the children, it shows in the children themselves, how they relate to each other."

The image of "classroom as home" as it was expressed in the interviews and in the classroom subsumed various elements of the content of her personal practical knowledge. Knowledge of the instructional process; knowledge of herself as a teacher and person; and knowledge of appropriate subject matter for primary school were all captured by the image. The following three narrative fragments were seen as the embodiment and enactment of Stephanie's "classroom as home" image.

1. At the end of September, the class was being restructured to reduce the class size. Fifteen of the children were being sent to a new classroom. Stephanie wanted to make the last day a special one. She created a party setting much as one would in one's home when friends leave or move away. The following field notes record the event. Stephanie told me that because it would be the children's last day in the classroom, as a whole class, she wanted to do something special. She had brought her popcorn maker in and we were going to make popcorn. She also brought in her

camera and wanted to take pictures. Stephanie and I discussed the best way to serve the popcorn.

Stephanie initially suggested we let the students pass the popcorn as they worked at making it. However, as it turned out, this plan did not work as the students all wanted to gather around and watch the popcorn be made. Stephanie then suggested we just serve them family-style by handing the bins around as they were seated on the carpet. Family-style was Stephanie's way of describing it. (Field Notes, September 25, 1982)

2. A second series of events involving a unit on planting was also an expression of the "classroom as home" image. Stephanie had, very early in our work together, asked me to put together a unit on planting. As we worked on the unit and later in the summer and fall, she tried out her planting and growing skills at school and then took her newly acquired skills and knowledge home to put them to use. The following field note segments are a partial account of the events.

Stephanie found that Al, a Grade 5 teacher, does a lot of planting and growing in his classroom and she had been asking him a lot of questions about how to set things up. He gave her a geranium and said he would teach her how to make cuttings. Stephanie was quite amazed that the geranium she had, had grown from a cutting. Stephanie is also delighted because an avocado she has been trying to grow has finally started to grow. This is the first time Stephanie has been able to do this. (Field notes, May 8, 1981)

She commented that she was "very happy about how the beans were growing," and she was "excited about what we had been planting."
She had collected many more pots; she wanted to transplant some of the plants from the school to her garden; and she wondered about starting tomato plants. She said they had cleaned both their front and back yards and had taken out a tremendous amount of garbage. She wanted to have space to plant things. She filled an old bathtub on her front lawn for the first time in two years with geraniums. What we had done at school had really made her excited to get things done at home. (Field notes, May 20, 1981).

Later in October:

I forgot to mention earlier in the morning, before school started, her friend came over to the school with two pumpkins from their garden. We put the pumpkins under the language experience chart. Stephanie had left the earth on the pumpkins because she wanted to let the students know she had grown them.
(Field notes, October 26, 1981).

3. Stephanie's practices around the Hallowe'en celebration were an expression of Stephanie's image of "classroom as home." Her preparations for the event seemed to me to be reminiscent of how I get ready for a celebration in my own home. The box of Hallowe'en decorations, the displays to create atmosphere, and the culmination of the week of festivities in a party are presented in the following field note segments.

I arrived at the school at 8:30. I went right down to Stephanie's class. She was in the room, the door was open. I was immediately struck by how much had happened in the room over the weekend. The farm display at the back was set up, the pictures off the back wall were down, there were criss-crossed clotheslines hanging from the ceiling with Hallowe'en displays, the Hallowe'en words were up in the display and the front board displays were all arranged.
(Field notes, October 26, 1981).

She showed me some Hallowe'en pictures she wanted me to laminate that morning. She also wanted me to mark and file the work. When we were going through the Hallowe'en box digging out the pictures for laminating, she found some sample Hallowe'en books and decided she wanted to have the children make those. She needed one more pumpkin cut out and laminated. The pumpkin needed to have the word "mask" printed on it. The preparation of the Hallowe'en pictures seemed to be her first priority.
(Field notes, October 26, 1981).

After recess time I worked with the children on the baking of the pumpkin seeds. I came back down to the classroom about twenty-five to twelve and told Stephanie she should be on her way out to get more party supplies. Stephanie told me she didn't think there would be time for a story. When I arrived back in the classroom, several children were hanging balloons, Wallace's table was being covered with a black tablecloth made of crepe paper, Gail and another student were sorting apples for bobbing and there was much party activity going on. I tried hastening Stephanie out of the classroom by telling her she had to get back to take the pumpkin seeds out of the oven. She said she would do that on her way out of the school. She wanted all the books and boxes left stacked in the centre of the children's tables so the napkins could be handed around and so the children would have room at the tables. I told her I would have the children do that.
(Field notes, October 30, 1981).

The importance of the home center; the importance of baking and cooking; the amount of personal money spent in the classroom and the beautiful displays she used to create a warm homey atmosphere, also were expressions of the image of the "classroom as home."

The preceding section, taken from a narrative account, provides a sense of how my understanding of what I call Stephanie's image of classroom as home emerged through the research process. In the remainder of the chapter, I outline the dimensions of the classroom as home image. I explore first how the "classroom as home" image links Stephanie's personal life with her professional teaching life.

The Image as a Link between Stephanie's Educational and Personal Life

What I refer to as Stephanie's image of the "classroom as home" highlights the experiential link between a teacher's educational and personal private life. This image captures, in its origin and function, aspects of both spheres of Stephanie's life. Stephanie, in talking about her teaching, speaks of her classroom as a home, "You know about that idea of the home. Well it's a home. I mean ... my idea of how a home should be" (S.W., 2, 64).[6] In this verbal expression of the image, both personal private and educational aspects of her life are captured; the image draws together both the home and classroom. An examination of how the image provides this link between Stephanie's personal private and educational life through its origins in her experience is presented first.

Origins of the Image of "Classroom as Home"

The image has its origin in Stephanie's personal private life. She holds a view of herself as a child and as a student who was "always different" and who marched to "another beat" (S.W., 2, 38). She described her own school experiences as a "packaging" experience and felt that those who did not fit the package were "scattered by the side" by the educational system (S.W., 2, 13). She describes herself as one of the ones who didn't fit the package and was "left out" (S.W., 2, 13).

A sense emerged from the transcripts that she had experienced a home such as the home she wants to reconstruct in her classroom. It is a place where "people cooperate and interact together" (S.W., 2, 66). No clear sense of where or in what manner she participated in such a home emerged. She describes the emotional and social attributes of the imagined home as a place where people can interact and cooperate but where each person has his or her own space and where each is "free to march to their own drummer" (S.W., 2, 38). Two other aspects of the "home" were apparent: a home is to be full of treasured things and it is to be a "living area" (S.W., 2, 66). The "classroom as home" image is, thus, rooted in her personal school and home experiences. But the image also has its roots in her professional experience. In Teacher's College, she again felt out of step-out of step with the way student teachers were being taught, that is, as "mini-models where you had to model the style of the teacher" (S.W., 2, 56) and with what and how they were to teach. She saw herself as someone who reacted to this felt-pressure for conformity and "so," she says, "I came liberal" (S.W., 1, 45). The significance of this personal interpretation of her experience is that she felt a continuity of experience as her experience of public schooling was replayed as she entered professional life.

Not until Stephanie had her own class did she begin to feel "in step." She underwent what she called "a metamorphosis" (S.W., 2, 40) after she began teaching. In her classroom she was able to create a space in which she felt "in step." She spent then, as she continues to do now, long hours creating an environment in which she and her students could feel comfortable and cared for, in short, a home environment.

In its origin then, the image is rooted in four areas of Stephanie's experience: in her professional experience, "so this really I guess starts right back from my early years as the big thing was to get that sense of environment" (S.W., 2, 65); in her professional training, "that's the big thing there which education always tried to do and it was there in all different parts of the bureaucracy" (S.W., 2, 62); in her own school experience, "and I think it did a lot of harm in those years" (S.W., 2, 62); and in her private life, "like when I say home this would be my idea – a group of people interacting together and cooperating together" (S.W., 2, 62). These professional and personal origins are linked in Stephanie's classroom practices by the image of the "classroom as home."

This brief narrative account of Stephanie's personal and professional biography, as reconstructed in her personal knowledge of her classroom as a home, sets the stage for the reader to see how the personal and professional are linked both in Stephanie's personal and professional life. The following two instances illustrate how the image links her personal and professional life in practice.

The Planting Unit

The image was expressed in a number of classroom events recorded in my field notes. One instance detailed above in the narrative account, was the work on the planting unit. When Stephanie first asked me to work on the unit, I did not understand it as anything more than a science unit in the program. At the time I saw it more or less as a random choice and thought it could have been any other unit. However, I now see Stephanie's request as minded, in part, by the "class room as home" image. The link between her personal private life and her educational life is especially important in providing an understanding of how the image functions within her personal practical knowledge.

To many people and particularly to Stephanie, a home should have a garden or at least have growing things as part of it. Her emphasis on a "living" (S.W., 2, 66) component of the home image suggests that importance, as does her choice of her personal home, an old house she is renovating in an inner city neighborhood. To be able to grow things is important to Stephanie. Her interest in the planting and growing activities serves functions in both her personal and professional life.

On one side, the planting activities contribute to the "home in the classroom." The bean plants, the garden, the avocado, and the geranium, discussed briefly in the excerpt from the interpretive account, contributed to the home-like classroom environment. On the other side, the planting activities at school were a way for her to try out something for her personal life. With the success of our activities at school, Stephanie took her new-found skills home. As noted earlier in the narrative account, she planted her front yard bathtub with geraniums and, in her backyard, grew a garden complete with vegetables and pumpkins for Hallowe'en. The classroom "home" became a testing ground for her personal home.

Thus we see how the unity of the personal and professional in Stephanie's personal practical knowledge is expressed in both the personal and professional spheres of her life. Further, we see how the personal and the professional interact reflexively within the image of "classroom as home." The effect on both home and school of the image expressed in action is dramatic. Elements in both are transformed. On the school side, school subject matter is selected and organized in a particular way; the classroom atmosphere is changed; inner-city students are given new experiences; Stephanie sees herself as a resource to other teachers interested in planting; and she seeks out staff members who are interested in similar activities. On the personal side, her home life is enriched as new hobbies develop and the physical appearance of her personal environment is enhanced. This, in turn will, I speculate, affect such matters as her relationship with friends as she shows off her garden, and her interaction with neighbors as she works in her garden.

The Celebration of Cultural Holidays
The image is dramatically expressed in Stephanie's rhythm[7] of the school year. Stephanie responds in her practice to the cycle of major celebrations in mainstream Canadian society, events such as Hallowe'en, Christmas, and Easter, events celebrated by many people in their homes with family traditions and rituals.

Stephanie's image of the "classroom as home" is given meaning by her particular rhythms of teaching. Just as there are rhythms in our North American Christian home life[8] tied to cultural givens such as the work week and cultural holidays such as Christmas, Thanksgiving, and Easter, there are similar rhythms in Stephanie's classroom life. Rhythms serve to modulate an individual teacher's imagery and to moderate, smooth out, and make harmonious personal and social action. Stephanie's rhythm is one in which she expresses the rhythms of her culture at the same time as she accommodates the cultural holidays of others. The result is a harmonious living out of the school year in such a way that her own personal and cultural rhythms and those of her students find expression in her classroom.

The ways in which Stephanie approaches each celebration are expressions in part, of the "classroom as home" image. For example, in the narrative account noted above, we saw how at Hallowe'en she transformed the classroom. She devoted her weekend to decorating it; she made Hallowe'en activities a priority for both her own and my activities; and she rejected what I wanted to do, that is, read a story, in favor of making the room more home-like by setting up tables with tablecloths and napkins. The focus for the celebration moved from her private home to the classroom home.

Her classroom practices are ones of living out and knowing the classroom rhythmically and as a home. Because she knows the classroom in these ways, the celebration of Hallowe'en in the classroom is a way for Stephanie to make the children feel "at home" and to permit them to participate in her culturally influenced rhythms of the classroom.

These two expressions of the image – the planting unit and the celebration of cultural holidays – illustrate how the "classroom as home" image links Stephanie's personal private and professional life. As the image was expressed in action, new forms of expression were added. Stephanie's home, both in the classroom and in her personal home, became places where plants flourished. Stephanie's classroom became a place where her personal cultural holidays and those of her students could be celebrated.

Temporality and the Image of "Classroom as Home"

The expression of the image both in verbal communication and in classroom practices is always in the present. Its origins are in the past. As the image finds new forms of expression in practice, however, it reaches into the past and reorders both professional and personal private experiences. For example, one expression of the "classroom as home" image was in the baking and cooking activities Stephanie suggested I do with the children in the classroom. These activities constituted a new expression of the image. As a result of this expression of the image we might imagine Stephanie came to see earlier baking activities with students, for example, making potato latkes which she had done for the school Festival of Lights (Field notes, December 16, 1981), as important in creating a home atmosphere. Similarly, we might imagine that previous baking-related experiences in her personal private life were important in creating Stephanie's personal home.

Experiential images, therefore, have an historical character, both in their origin and in their reconstruction of past experiences, to meet the demands of a particular situation. But experiential images also have a future character. The image of home points the way to future expressions in both Stephanie's personal and professional life. For example, Stephanie told me in a conversation "that once you have taught kindergarten or been in the primary, any grade level within the primary is not too much of a challenge" (Field notes, September 10, 1981). If Stephanie were to teach in another grade or in another subject area such as English as a Second Language (an area into which she would like to move), the "classroom as home" image would find expression in new settings. In future situations in both her personal and professional life, the image would still be expressed in her practices. It would be marked by an emphasis on environment, her interactions with others, and the importance of creating a space where each participant would be free to "march to his or her own drummer."

In this temporal (past, present, and future) aspect of the image, insight is gained into how image as a knowledge component is related to the phenomenal world and to future knowledge. New situations are experienced from the perspective of the image as a part of personal practical knowledge. Teaching at a different level or in a different program area is interpreted from Stephanie's perspective of the "classroom as home" image. New situations in her personal life, such as planning for another holiday celebration, can also be interpreted as being experienced from the perspective of the image. New knowledge can be added as previous experience is reordered and shaped by expressions of the image. Hence, Stephanie gains knowledge of herself as a person able to successfully grow plants as a result of the expression of the "classroom as home" image in her school planting practices.

Emotional and Moral Dimensions of the Image of "Classroom as Home"

To understand the image of home as a link between Stephanie's personal private life and her educational life is an important step in understanding her teaching practice as an expression of her personal practical knowledge. Image as a form of personal practical knowledge is an embodied, experiential meaning complex and we understand Stephanie's image of home as a crystallization of her experience, experience in which emotions and morality are elements. Without an understanding of the moral and the emotional, this account remains lifeless and lacks the fire that characterizes her teaching.

The Emotional Dimension
The image of "classroom as home" is strongly held. As the image was expressed in our second interview, Stephanie tried to reject it. "you know, about that idea of the home. Well it's a home. I mean, my idea of how a home should be. Maybe that was a wrong word to use, maybe a community, I should have just called it ..." (S.W., 2, 64). But after briefly exploring the possibility of rejecting it, she returned to affirm the image of "classroom as home," as pointing to crucial ways in which she knows her teaching.

The words used to convey her meaning were ones which conveyed the image's emotional dimension. She talked about "the closeness" (S.W., 2, 62); the relational aspects, "interacting" and "cooperating" (S.W., 2, 64); and "the living" aspects of being with others (S.W., 2, 65). In her verbal expression of it, there seemed little doubt there was an emotional coloring to the image.

This coloring derives from the experiences that gave rise to the image. The experiences were emotional ones and this emotion is carried forward as part of the image. Dewey (1934, p. 42) describes emotion as "the moving and cementing force" in an experience. Emotion, says Dewey, "selects what is congruous and dyes what is selected with its color, thereby giving qualitative unity to materials externally disparate and dissimiliar." The experiences in which Stephanie's image of "classroom as home" are rooted, make real Dewey's view of emotion in experience. Emotion was evident in Stephanie's verbal expression of the experiences of her home, school, professional training, and teaching. She described her school experiences with words loaded with emotion, such as "bitter" (S.W., 2, 17), "terrible" (S.W., 2, 17), and as "desperately unhappy" (S.W., 2, 38). The "metamorphosis" (S.W., 2, 40) she underwent in her early years of teaching was described as allowing her "to get the confidence" (S.W., 2, 41) to "give of herself" (S.W., 2, 40).

The emotion within each of these early experiences is recollected by Stephanie and we sense how emotion has been, and continues to be, a "moving" and "cementing" force in the image of "classroom as home," an image central to her teaching. It is, perhaps, easiest to understand the emotional strength of the image when we consider its moral dimension. The two are so closely connected in experience that it is difficult to talk about one without the other. Stephanie does not "know" abstractly that a teaching act is good or bad; she feels it as such. It is their combination, their unity in the image, that contributes to the image as a "moving force" in practice.

The Moral Dimension
In Stephanie's verbal expression of the image, a sense of its moral coloring emerged. The image is not neutral; a classroom should be like a home and both classroom and home should have certain features. There is, then, in her verbal expression of the image a "should" and a "should not" character. A sense of the possibility of "better" or "worse" action emerges. For Stephanie the better action allowed her "to live here" (S.W., 2, 65) and "to treat people as individuals and humans" (S.W., 2, 63).

In its practical expression, a sense of the moral dimension of the image also emerged. For example, the party Stephanie held in her classroom to mark the departure of some of her students in September, 1981, noted above in the narrative account, is an expression of her "classroom as home" image. The party was an exceptional gesture, such as one might make to mark the departure of friends from one's home. In the expression of the image, there was a better and a worse way to acknowledge the students' departure. Stephanie could have chosen to act differently. We might, for example, imagine alternative expressions of the "classroom as home" image in this instance. But not to mark their departure by an expression appropriate to that of persons leaving her home would not have been the "right" thing for Stephanie to do.

The moral character of the image provides Stephanie with a judgmental standard for her practices. This standard is unique to Stephanie. When practices are discordant, the moral coloring of the image highlights the discordancy. In my work with Stephanie, this was most clearly evident when I took action, or attempted to take action, which conflicted with an expression of her imagery in practice. For example, I suggested that we have the children take home the growing bean plants when I felt the unit was complete. Stephanie resisted my suggestion as she felt the plants were continuing to add to the "classroom as home" environment (I.A.2). In its practical expression, environment was an important element of the image. A certain kind of environment "should" be created in the expression of the image. My interference created a discordant note and Stephanie acted to stop my plan.

As is the case with the emotional, the moral coloring of the image emerges from the experiences in which it has its origin and from her judgment of the experiences as "good" or "bad." Accordingly, the moral character of the "classroom as home" image emerges, in part, from Stephanie's judgment of her school experience as a "packaging experience" (S.W., 2, 13) in which she was hurt. The image takes on the moral shadings of her judgment of the experience as bad, and from this experience she derives a standard of judgment of her own practices. Similarly, her experiences of herself as a child who was marching to a different drummer; who failed to fit into the standard mold; and who eventually came to see herself as "slow" and not able to "see things properly in a perspective" (S.W., 2, 38) all contribute to the moral coloring of the "classroom as home" image. These experiences were negative and her judgment of them contributes to her standards of judgment for her practices.

In my final narrative account of Stephanie, I characterized her within a governing framework of relationships. The relationship theme illustrates how the moral coloring of Stephanie's "classroom as home" image emerges from its origins in her experiences of relationships with others and in her judgment of herself within those relationships. The experiences appear to be ones in which the particularly critical moral issue of hurting is involved. My account of Stephanie's experience parallels Gilligan's account of women's moral development. "It is," says Gilligan, "in their care and concern for others that women have both judged themselves and been judged." (1982, p. 165). The relationship context helps both to explain the moral vividness of the image, and how this image serves as a guide to Stephanie in her relations with students.

Gilligan highlights the importance of understanding women within a framework of relationships. To understand Stephanie's image of "classroom as home," the relationship aspects of the originating experiences and the resulting moral coloring of the image must be confronted. I noted above Stephanie's struggle in her early teaching experiences to see herself as a worthwhile person after her experiences in both school and professional training in which she saw herself as being hurt. Through what Stephanie termed her "metamorphosis" she came to see herself as a person worthy of care and as someone whom she considered it "moral" not to hurt. Her earlier experiences were seen by her as negative, and while she doesn't judge herself as wrong within her relationships, she now has a standard for judging herself in her relationships with others both in school and outside of it.

In sum, the image of "classroom as home" became a nucleus around which significant elements of her experience, complete with moral coloring, were attracted and shaped. The moral character of the "classroom as home" image derives from significant elements of her home, school, professional training, and teaching experiences. In the coalescence of Stephanie's experiences into the image, all life experiences, not only those from her personal private life nor only those from her educational professional life were attracted and drawn together to form her personal practical knowledge. Thus we see how the moral coloring of the image is grounded in her experiences and ultimately in how she judges herself within her relationships.

THE CONCEPT OF IMAGE SUMMARIZED

The concept of image is frequently used in the social science literature. However, my use of the concept is as a form of personal practical knowledge and the term assumes its meaning within the framework of personal practical knowledge. I do not view it as a therapeutic tool as, for example, it is used in the psychological literature (Assagioli, 1965; Progoff, 1975), nor as a standard for instructional purposes in the way Howard (1982) develops the notion for music instruction. Rather, image, in this research, is a kind of knowledge, embodied in a person and connected with the individual's past, present, and future. Image draws both the present and future into a personally meaningful nexus of experience focused on the immediate situation which called it forth. It reaches into the past, gathering up experiential threads meaningfully connected to the present. And it reaches intentionally into the future and creates new meaningfully connected threads as situations are experienced and new situations anticipated from the perspective of the image. Image is the glue that melds together a person's diverse experiences, both personal and professional. An image has emotional and moral dimensions and I have shown how these characteristics mark out the knowing contained in the expression of image in classroom and interview practices. In accordance with this view, action, and the personal knowledge embodied in it, is imbued with meaning-giving emotionality and morality. The concept of image, as developed in this study, emerges from the imaginative processes by which meaningful and useful patterns are generated in minded practice. Minded practice involves the emergence of images out of experience so images are then available as guides for the person to make sense of future situations.

In subsequent pages I turn to a general consideration of the origin and expression of images.

The Origin of Image in Experience

The central idea of the research is that teachers' classroom images grow out of their experience, both private and professional. They are a kind of coalescence of experience, with moral, emotional, and personal overtones reflecting the quality of the experiences in which they are based. Just as each image is specific to a particular teacher, the experiences in which the image is rooted, and the way it is related to that experience, are also specific to the teacher.

Some experiences have a "watershed" character and form vivid detailed visual images.[9] Aileen's image of a particular child's face is illustrative. She now views her experience with this particular child as a turning point in her teaching, frequently calling his face to mind when confronted with other children's problems. The image has a copy-sense impression. This child's face and Aileen's relationship to the child form the core experience around which the image has developed. Stephanie's image of her high school math experience is similarly rooted in one watershed experience. In her case, however, while the image is vividly emotional, it contains less visual detail.

Other images, equally powerful, are less directly linked to specific events in the teachers' lives. These images are formed from a coalescence of many diverse experiences over a long period of time. Their formation occurs in processes similar to those described by Dewey in his notion of the "continuity of experience" (1938) and by MacIntyre in his notion of the "narrative unity of life" (1981).

Some of the images linked to experience in this narrative sense assume a metaphorical quality. Aileen's image of "language is the key" is illustrative.

For Aileen, language is the central cognitive, substantive, and social theme around which her classroom is organized. This is seen in her play-based kindergarten program, justified by her in terms of children's language development; in her graduate level study in a combined Early Childhood and Language Education program; and in her tendency to equate children's cognitive development with their language development. Her phrase "language is the key" expresses metaphorically her deep sense of the importance of language in her teaching. Images of this kind take on the quality of Lakoff and Johnson's "experiential metaphors" (1980).

Other images exhibit the same quality as "language is the key" but retain more of the specifics associated with images connected to watershed experiences. Stephanie's image of "the classroom as home" is illustrative. Unlike Aileen, who often asserts that "language is the key," Stephanie only infrequently refers to the classroom as a home. Yet in the organization of classroom activities; in the interpersonal relationships she establishes with students; in the daily opening and closing class routines; and in her curriculum planning around annual cycles of school events, Stephanie is clearly living out her image of "classroom as home." The specificity of this image is seen in the organization of her own home life and in her cultural traditions. Images with this metaphoric quality have a "real analogy" sense like that described by Black (1962).

This study has not, of course, exhausted either the possible kinds of experiential images or their various possible experiential origins. Such an understanding will emerge from the results of long-term studies of images of more teachers than the two in this work. Furthermore, unraveling the historical antecedents to particular teacher images is a task that depends on the aspects of classroom experience in which one is interested. Gendlin (1962) puts the matter well when he reminds us of the many meanings an experience may have for a person. "Any experienced meaning," he writes, "will be differentiable into countless experienced meanings, each of which, because it is a meaning, will again be differentiable into countless meanings. Apart from this specification, it is always multiple. Experiencing is multiple, non-numerical." (Gendlin, 1962, p. 152). We may imagine, therefore, that the search for understanding of the experiential origins of images is rich in possibilities.

The Expression of Images

In earlier sections, we saw how the "classroom as home" image was expressed in Stephanie's classroom and in her home. In this section,

I distinguish between the verbal[10] expression of images and their expression in classroom practices. Logically, either form of expression may occur without the other. A teacher may, in her explanations of her teaching, express herself with images which may not be expressed in her classroom practices. Likewise, a teacher's classroom practices may be expressions of images that are not verbally expressed.

Perhaps because of the widespread and common use of interview methodologies for the study of classrooms, teachers' speech about themselves has often been equated with their practice. If there is a spoken report of a practice, there is a tendency to say that there is such a practice. But my study of teacher images in classroom and in interview practices leads me to view this matter more akin to that of Einstein when he wrote, "The words or the language do not seem to play any role in my mechanism of thought. The physical entities which seem to serve as elements in thoughts are certain signs and more or less clear images which can be voluntarily reproduced and combined ..." (Einstein in Hadamard, 1945, p. 142).

Einstein was speaking of a different situation and of images with different content but the translation of images into words seems remarkably like Stephanie's translation of the "classroom as home" image, with its disparate elements, into words in our interview. Stephanie struggled to give an adequate verbal expression. She tried one, rejected it, and settled on the classroom being a home. She chose to use a metaphor to capture the image. In her choice of metaphor she chose one with a public meaning. We often say a place is homelike or homey when we want to convey a notion of warmth or coziness. The verbal expression then, at one level, is a public one.

Hunt comes close to what I intend in his notion of "teachers as their own best theorists" (Hunt, 1976). A teachers' verbal expression of an image is essentially her theory, her explanation to others, of her practices. This, in general, is the relationship between the two modes of image expression that emerged in this study.

The Verbal Expression of Images
Some of the teachers' images were frequently expressed verbally, for example, Aileen's images of "language is the key" and of "myself as an island." Whenever discussion turned to the purposes of instruction or to her professional place within the school, she used these images to explain herself.

Other images were not expressed verbally as, for example, Stephanie's image of herself as "maker." She did, however, readily agree to the interpretation of her practice, which showed how she taught language arts through the making of books, pictures, and models. What I have called Stephanie's image of "making" is part of the image of "classroom as home," which is more deeply embedded in her life. Occasionally, Stephanie referred to the "classroom as a home" in her conversations and she occasionally discussed classroom management with the children in terms of what was proper to the running of a home.

Overall, the verbal expression of an image tends to function metaphorically in situations where the teacher is explaining herself to another. These verbal expressions of images represent "personal theories" of oneself. In this sense, verbally expressed images allow teachers to generalize on their experience and to offer theoretical accounts of what they do.

Expression of Images in Practice

Because a teacher's world is essentially one of action, they are not often called upon to verbally explain themselves and to put terms on their actions. Talking about what they do is not a necessary part of their practice. However, an interesting (and unanticipated) benefit of this study was the value teachers placed on the reflective opportunity to read and discuss interpretations of their work.

Since the central focus of the research was to understand practice, all of the images described were built up out of field notes made in classrooms. It was from reflection on practice that this study's concept of image grew. The images are essentially images of practice. In the two instances where my first insight into the images came verbally, that is, Aileen's "language is the key" and "myself as an island" images, I sought confirmation and expression of its meaning in classroom events.

The account of Stephanie's "maker" image, an image expressed only in practice, grew up out of repeated observations and was tested through discussions of the narrative accounts with Stephanie. At most, the verbal showed up in practice in Stephanie's student directions such as "show me" rather than "tell me." One of the implications of this method of studying images is that they are not merely mental constructs to be expressed; they are embodied in action. When we see practice, we see embodied images (Johnson, Personal communication, 1983).

CONCLUSION

There is a dialectic between the two purposes of the study: the practical understanding of the two teachers and the theoretical notions of personal practical knowledge, particularly image, as a language and perspective for inquiry. The theoretical ideas are based on the classroom data and, in turn, enrich our understanding of the teachers.

The conceptualization of image developed in this study contributes to a theoretical understanding of the nature of personal knowledge that differs from that usually thought of when we consider the problem of knowledge, a point well made by Polanyi (1958). Personal practical knowledge is an emotional and moral knowledge. It actively carries our being into inter-action with classroom events. Personal practical knowledge is, furthermore, intimately connected with the personal and professional narratives of our lives. It is not something which has an independent and objective standing apart from our personal histories. Readers have seen how the image of "classroom as home" originates in both the personal and professional spheres of Stephanie's life; binds the two together in a narrative unity; and are reflected back upon each as the image is expressed in Stephanie's home and school activities. Finally, it is evident from the discussion of the verbal and practical expressions of images that personal practical knowledge need not be clearly articulated and logically definable in order to exert a powerful influence in teachers' lives.

This research has at least two practical consequences. One is that with the concept of personal practical knowledge as a language and perspective for viewing school practices, we assume a stance which credits and values teachers' knowledge. A second is the formation of a different notion about the improvement of schools, a notion that builds on the personal practical knowledge of teachers by working with them rather than on or against them.

NOTES

1. I am indebted to Professor Joseph Schwab for his detailed comments and assistance in developing this introductory section.

2. Professors Elliot Eisner and Mark Johnson have aided my thinking on image. The one has encouraged my development of the study of imagination as a novel way of thinking about the practice of teaching and the other has encouraged me to reflect on the philosophical significance of an experiential conception of knowledge.

3. To protect the privacy of participants, pseudonyms are used throughout the chapter.

4. The use of the term minded was triggered by Jenning's (1982) notion of minded action in his discussion of religious ritual. In our work on personal practical knowledge (Connelly & Clandinin, 1984), we view teachers' practices as the embodi-ment and enactment of their personal practical knowledge. In my work on images,

I understood Stephanie's and Aileen's practices as the embodiment and enactment of their personal practical knowledge of which their imagery was a part. The concept of minded practice is used to capture this understanding.

5. The interview transcripts have been edited slightly to improve their readability.

6. Bracketed material refers to coded field note, interview, and narrative account material.

7. Rhythm is used in the commonplace sense of something recurring repetitively, perhaps cyclically, and which has an aesthetic quality as performed. Rhythms as part of personal practical knowledge serve to modulate an individual teacher's imagery and the narrative unities of which the imagery is a part (Clandinin & Connelly, 1984).

8. What we mean by the rhythms in our North American Christian home life are the patterns of events tied to Sunday designated as the Sabbath with shops and school closures, Monday designated as the first day of the work week, school and business closures for Christmas, Easter Sunday, Good Friday and so on.

9. The concept of a watershed experience is credited in my thinking to Professor James Britton who, in a personal discussion of image, described one of his images of what he termed a watershed experience in World War II. He described the image in vivid detail and credited the experience with being a profound influence in his personal knowledge.

10. Verbal is used in the conceptual sense of having to do with words, whether written or spoken, as opposed to ideas and actions.

ACKNOWLEDGMENTS

This work was supported by research grants from the Social Sciences and Humanities Research Council of Canada (Grant #410-80-0688-X1) and the United States National Institute of Education (Grant #NIE-G-81-0020).

REFERENCES

Assagioli, R. (1965). *Psychosynthesis*. Middlesex, England: Harmondsworth.
Black, M. (1962). *Models and metaphors*. Ithaca, NY: Cornell University Press.
Clandinin, D. J. (1983). *A conceptualization of image as a component of teacher personal practical knowledge*. Unpublished doctoral dissertation. University of Toronto, Canada.
Clandinin, D. J. (1985). Terms for inquiry into teacher thinking: The place of practical knowledge and the Elbaz case. *Journal of Curriculum Theorizing, 6*(2), 131–148.
Clandinin, D. J. (1986). *Classroom practices: Teacher images in action*. Barcombe Lewes: Falmer Press.
Clandinin, D. J., & Connelly, F. M. (1984, March). *Teachers personal practical knowledge: Calendars, cycles, habits and rhythms*. Paper presented at the Curriculum in the Making Conference, University of Haifa, Haifa.

Connelly, F. M., & Clandinin, D. J. (1984). Teachers' personal practical knowledge. In R. Halkaes & J. K. Olson (Eds.), *Teacher thinking: A new perspective on (persistent problems in) education.* Heirewig, Holland: Swets Publishing Service.

Connelly, F. M., & Clandinin, D. J. (1985). Personal practical knowledge and the modes of knowing: Relevance for teaching and learning. In E. Eisner (Ed.), *Learning and teaching the ways of knowing. NSSE Yearbook* (pp. 174–198). Chicago, IL: University of Chicago Press.

Connelly, F. M., & Ben-Peretz, M. (1980). Teachers' roles in the using and doing of research and curriculum development. *Journal of Curriculum Studies, 12,* 95–107.

Connelly, F. M., & Dienes, B. (1982). The teacher's role in curriculum planning: A case study. In K. Leithwood (Ed.), *Studies in curriculum decision-making* (pp. 183–198). Toronto: OISE Press.

Dewey, J. (1934). *Art as experience.* New York, NY: Capricorn Books.

Dewey, J. (1938). *Experience and education.* New York, NY: Collier Books.

Dwyer, K. (1979). The dialogic of ethnology. *Dialectical Anthropology, 4,* 205–224.

Elbaz, F. (1983). *Teacher thinking: A study of practical knowledge.* London: Croom Helm.

Fullan, M., & Pomfret, A. (1977). Research on curriculum and instruction. *Review of Educational Research, 47*(2), 335–397.

Gendlin, E. T. (1962). *Experiencing and the creation of meaning.* New York, NY: The Free Press of Gelcoe.

Gilligan, C. (1982). *In a different voice.* Cambridge, MA: Harvard University Press.

Glaser, B. G., & Strauss, A. L. (1967). *The discovery of grounded theory: Strategies for qualitative research.* Chicago, IL: Aldine Publishing Company.

Hadamard, J. (1945). *The psychology of invention in the mathematical field.* Princeton, NJ: Princeton University Press.

Howard, V. A. (1982). *Artistry: The work of artists.* Indianapolis, IN: Hackett Publishing Company.

Hunt, D. (1976). Teachers are psychologists, too: On the application of Psychology to Education. *Canadian Psychology Review, 17*(3), 210–218.

Jennings, T. W. (1982). On ritual knowledge. *Journal of Religion, 62*(2), 111–127.

Johnson, M. (1984). Review of Elbaz, Freema, Teacher thinking: A study of practical knowledge. *Curriculum Inquiry, 14*(4), 465–468.

Lakoff, G., & Johnson, M. (1980). *Metaphors we live by.* Chicago, IL: The University of Chicago Press.

Lortie, D. C. (1975). *Schoolteacher: A sociological study.* Chicago, IL: University of Chicago Press.

MacIntyre, A. (1981). *After virtue. A study in moral theory.* London: Gerald Duckworth & Co. Ltd.

McKeon, R. (1952). Philosophy and action. *Ethics, 62*(2), 79–100.

Polanyi, M. (1958). *Personal knowledge.* Chicago, IL: The University of Chicago Press.

Progoff, I. (1975). *At a journal workshop.* New York, NY: Dialogue House Library.

CHAPTER 5

FROM TEACHER KNOWLEDGE TO TEACHER LEARNING IN COMMUNITY: TRANSFORMATIONS OF THEORY AND PRACTICE

Freema Elbaz-Luwisch and Lily Orland-Barak

ABSTRACT

This chapter traces the development of teacher knowledge in the field of education from the 1970s onward. It pays attention to the conceptualizations of personal knowledge and personal practical knowledge and relates pedagogical content knowledge to the aforementioned concepts. It then moves on to the more expansive topic of teacher learning in community paying particular attention to dialogical and relational ways of knowing. The work covers intellectual ground that has been traveled and signals new areas where research is likely to be conducted.

Keywords: Teacher knowledge; teacher community; practical knowledge; personal practical knowledge; pedagogical content knowledge

From Teacher Thinking to Teachers and Teaching: The Evolution of a Research Community
Advances in Research on Teaching, Volume 19, 97–113
Copyright © 2013 by Emerald Group Publishing Limited
All rights of reproduction in any form reserved
ISSN: 1479-3687/doi:10.1108/S1479-3687(2013)0000019008

In this chapter we provide an overview and a critique of the path of development from conceptualizations of teacher *knowledge* toward a more dynamic understanding of teacher *learning in community*. As we do so, we reference our own work and that of our colleagues in Israel and elsewhere around the world, many of whom belong to the International Study Association of Teachers and Teaching (ISATT). We highlight changes and transformations that have taken place in how we conceive of teacher knowledge and teacher learning as the field embraces the future.

TEACHER KNOWLEDGE

Early research on teaching, up to about 1970, was shaped by research in psychology on the one hand and by the needs of policy on the other hand. There was a concern to map and examine teacher characteristics (Ryans, 1960), in order to identify the personality of the "good" teacher and understand why people entered the teaching profession, or left it; such research obviously was intended to enable selection of the "best" candidates for teacher education programs and for employment in school systems. Only a few studies looked at teaching from a more personal perspective, asking about the dilemmas faced by teachers, (Jersild, 1970) and about their inner lives (Abraham, 1972).

This early research, however, was criticized as being too vague to contribute to the understanding or improvement of teaching. Beginning in the 1960s, the "scientific study of the art of teaching" (Gage, 1978) invoked a process–product logic in order to study how teacher performance influenced student outcomes; this was primarily "knowledge *for* teaching" (Cochran-Smith & Lytle, 1998), formulated and developed by researchers and intended to be used by practitioners to improve teaching in classrooms. From the late 1970s onward, a lively debate ensued around the significance and usefulness of the process–product logic. The knowledge of teaching generated by this logic was challenged on many counts: it was suggested that extensive research had generated only weak correlations between teacher behavior and student outcomes, that the findings were not educationally useful, that lacking causal links, correlations were unable to explain *why* particular teacher behaviors were effective, and that such research did not take into account the context of teaching and the intentional nature of what teachers do (Bolster, 1983; Doyle, 1977; Fenstermacher, 1978; Garrison & Macmillan, 1984). Responding to critics, Gage and Needels (1989) defended the approach and sought to provide examples of work that in their view addressed many of the criticisms.

While these debates continued, it slowly became apparent that an alternative view was being formulated according to which teachers were understood to be thinkers, knowers, and holders of knowledge in their own right (Clandinin, 1985; Clark & Yinger, 1977; Elbaz, 1981). Gradually the polemic of criticism was left behind, and the research on teacher thinking and teacher knowledge earned a place for itself on its own merits within the study of teaching. The founding of ISATT in 1983 as the International Study Association on *Teacher Thinking* consolidated this new focus, highlighting work on teacher thinking and knowledge done from a range of theoretical and methodological perspectives. Some researchers drew on concepts and theories from cognitive psychology, while others conducted more experiential studies of teaching drawing on phenomenological and ethnographic methods. The elaboration of a naturalistic logic of inquiry (Lincoln & Guba, 1985), and the development of a wide range of qualitative methods for studying the *experience* of teaching, were essential to the legitimating of the new field, the "arrival" of which was clearly marked by two reviews that appeared in the 3rd *Handbook of Research on Teaching*, examining research on teachers' thought processes (Clark & Peterson, 1986) and on the cultures of teaching (Feiman-Nemser & Floden, 1986).

The notion of "teacher knowledge" had begun to appear in the literature on teaching in various guises during the 1970s, for example, in sociological studies of teaching (i.e., Esland, 1971; Keddie, 1971) and in an interview study of teachers' understandings of open education (Bussis, Chittenden, & Amarel, 1976). Building on these efforts, a case study conducted with one teacher of English language and literature in a Canadian school (Elbaz, 1981) sought to describe and conceptualize the knowledge that teachers hold and use in their work employing the term, "practical knowledge." Making no empirical claims about the quality or value of the knowledge possessed by teachers, this study began from an assumption that

> while teachers' knowledge may be largely unarticulated, teachers do have a broad range of knowledge which guides their work – knowledge of subject matter; of classroom organization and instructional techniques; of the structuring of learning experiences and curriculum content; of students' needs, abilities, and interests; of the social framework of the school and its surrounding community; and of their own strengths and shortcomings as teachers. This assumption ... constitutes a proposal that we begin to look at the work of teaching as the exercise of a particular kind of knowledge, for in doing their work, teachers confront all manner of tasks and problems, and they draw on a variety of sources of knowledge to help them to deal with these. (Elbaz, 1981, p. 47)

Based on a series of in-depth interviews with the teacher, Sarah, this study described her practical knowledge from several overlapping perspectives: content, orientation, and structure. The content of her knowledge was mapped in the areas of curriculum, subject matter, instruction, self and the social; the way that she held this knowledge was viewed in terms of a number of "orientations" (situational, social, personal, experiential and theoretical). Also, the structure of her knowledge was outlined in terms of three levels: rules of practice, practical principles, and images.

To illustrate the discussion of the structure of this teacher's knowledge, we can look at one aspect of Sarah's knowledge of instruction: her understanding of communication skills and practices (an essential element of the "learning course" she had developed together with colleagues). Her "rules of practice" in this area were expressed by a statement such as "I certainly try very hard to listen very actively to the kids, to paraphrase, to encourage them to paraphrase, and at most times to allow them to express their concerns without judging them." Underlying these rules is a practical principle that Sarah expressed in the statement that "students should be provided with a class atmosphere in which they are able to take risks and thereby come to communicate more openly." Finally, an image that captures Sarah's work with respect to communication was found in her comment that she wanted "to 'have a window onto the kids and what they're thinking,' and, in turn, she wanted her own window to be more open" (Elbaz, 1981, p. 62).

Although this study discussed the content of practical knowledge in terms of the essential areas of curriculum, subject matter, and instruction, adding to these the teacher's personal and social knowledge, it is fair to say that the teacher's knowledge of subject matter did not receive a prominent place in the overall analysis. This may have been due to the fact that the teacher studied had moved away from her original specialization as a teacher of English literature, to a focus on skill development in an innovative, teacher-developed program known as the "learning course." Similarly, Clandinin's (1985) work with two elementary school teachers focused particularly on imagery in the teachers' knowledge of practice; subject matter for teaching was not a prominent focus. In other work, Connelly and Clandinin (1986) do highlight the subject matter knowledge of two teachers, one in science and the other a language teacher; however, their concern is largely with how the teachers' work, including their approach to subject matter, gives expression to the "narrative unities" underlying and motivating their teaching, and not with whether or how they manage to teach their subject successfully.

Thus, it is not entirely surprising that Shulman (1986) referred to teachers' knowledge of their subject matter for teaching as a "missing paradigm" in the research on teaching. His critique gave rise to a significant development in the study of teacher knowledge with the conceptualization of "pedagogical content knowledge," the knowledge of subject matter for teaching that is developed largely through experience in the classroom. The Hashweh chapter elsewhere in this book tells the story of the development of this line of work in the study of science teaching and its ongoing contribution to the field over a twenty-five year period. His account testifies to the viability and fruitfulness of the concept of pedagogical content knowledge, which continues to be developed and to give rise to new knowledge of teaching in many areas.

Practical knowledge as conceptualized by Elbaz, Clandinin, and Connelly has also proven to be a conceptualization with broad applicability. A current research program exploring teachers' practical knowledge in China is described by Chen (2009) and also by other Chinese authors in this volume. Chen's account shows how a group of academics, working collaboratively with school-based teacher researchers, have been examining the practical knowledge of the teachers in a long-term study that has taken advantage of many approaches found in the literature, including narrative inquiry, reflection in action, Deweyan pragmatism, and social constructivism. These researchers view the teacher as a subject who is the owner of her knowledge, thus focusing attention on the personal side of practical knowledge, but they also look closely at the teaching of subject matter, and at the way the teachers' practical knowledge develops over time. Images, particularly those based in Chinese culture, are explored and used to describe the teachers' knowledge. For example, they highlight the notion of the "classroom eye," a "native concept used by some senior teachers in China," which refers to

an almost perfect learning atmosphere when students' prior knowledge and motivation to learn, teachers' passion for and tact of teaching, and the learning contents are all synchronized in a harmonious and rhythmic manner, which spins students learning into depths like the eye of a typhoon. (Chen, 2009, p. 105)

The image of the "classroom eye" highlights the central role of cultural understandings, local knowledge and discourse in shaping knowledge of teaching, and indeed, these were directions taken early on in the further development of the idea of teacher knowledge. However, it can hardly be contested that the central development in the area of teacher knowledge has been the "narrative turn."

Interviewing teachers, and paying attention to their stories of teaching but also to the stories of their lives and to their life histories (i.e., Ball & Goodson, 1985) became more common in studies of teaching during the 1980s. The recognition that this form of study was in effect a form of narrative inquiry is credited to Connelly and Clandinin whose work (i.e., Connelly & Clandinin, 1986) first began to search for "narrative unities" in teachers' accounts and to refer to the developing methodology of their work as "narrative method." In fact there do not seem to be many references to narrative in teaching prior to about 1988, but the use of the terms "narrative" and "story" in the study of teaching was growing, and seemed to burst on the scene at the Fourth ISATT Conference held in Nottingham in 1988. Many of the papers presented at that conference were based on teacher stories, interviews with practitioners and elaborations of teacher knowledge through narrative, while a keynote presentation by Elbaz-Luwisch (1988) explored the theme directly. The central importance of story and narrative for the study of teaching was elaborated by Connelly and Clandinin (1990) and by Elbaz-Luwisch (1991); in 1992, Kathy Carter's Division K Vice-Presidential Address at the Annual Meeting of the American Educational Research Association, also addressed the topic and was subsequently published (Carter, 1993).

As the scope and volume of narrative research on teaching grew, it became apparent that the connection between teacher knowledge and narrative inquiry was by no means accidental. Narrative inquirers examined teacher stories about their practice, as well as teachers' life stories into teaching; researchers chose to use "story" as the preferred unit of analysis for a number of good reasons. First, researchers showed that teachers' knowledge could be seen to have a narrative structure (Doyle, 1997). Second, the phenomenon of story was a powerful linking mechanism, joining theory and practice (Dewey, 1938), thought and action, and the personal and the professional in teachers' experience. Stories and narratives are told and written in context, thus highlighting the social, historical, and political dimensions of teachers' work and knowledge (Goodson, 1992; Kelchtermans & Ballet, 2002). Narrative also came to be a preferred method of inquiry in teacher education as well as generating a variety of formats for teacher development (Carter, 1993; Heikkinen, 1998; Johnson & Golombek, 2002).

The work of Sigrun Gudmundsdottir was influential in forging links between pedagogical content knowledge and practical knowledge research. Her study of the pedagogical content knowledge of social studies teachers had shown how the teachers' work was organized and shaped in distinctively narrative ways: the teachers developed their own materials for teaching organized around overarching "curriculum stories" that sometimes were told over the span of the entire school year, drawing together the required material to be covered under topics that were personally meaningful for the teachers and that enabled them to teach, for example, American history, in more convincing and compelling ways (Gudmundsdottir, 1991). Her work directly highlighted the "narrative nature of pedagogical content knowledge" (Gudmundsdottir, 1995). One of her influential articles (Gudmundsdottir, 1996) demonstrates how much of the research on teaching is shaped by narrative structures even when the chosen methodology does not invoke narrative ideas. Our familiarity with the story form, and with the kind of interpretation that we learn to use in making sense of stories and narratives, shapes our research often without our being aware of it, Gudmundsdottir argues.

It should be noted that lively discussion and debate continues around the validation of the knowledge of teaching (i.e., Barone, 2007; Conle, 2001; Polkinghorne, 2007; Spector-Mersel, 2010) as well as concerning the implications of this knowledge for policy (Griffiths & Macleod, 2008; Lyons, 2007). At the same time, ongoing narrative research on teaching continues to be concerned with the issue of teacher knowledge, but now conceives this in broader terms, looking at themes such as teachers' lives, voice, and identity (i.e., Estola, Erkkilä, & Syrjälä, 2003; Zembylas, 2003), the interaction between knowledge and context in teaching (i.e., Olson & Craig, 2001), change processes and reform in teaching (i.e., Craig, 2003), issues of diversity, multiculturalism and inclusive education (i.e., Li, Conle, & Elbaz-Luwisch, 2009; Moen, Nilssen, & Weidemann, 2007; Phillion, He, & Connelly, 2005), and the place of body and bodily knowledge in teaching (i.e., Estola & Elbaz-Luwisch, 2003). This diverse work has been reviewed in different venues (Day & Laneve, 2011; Elbaz-Luwisch, 2007, 2011). With the expansion of topics and contexts for study, the dynamic and changing nature of teacher knowledge has also become more prominent. This has led quite naturally to increasing interest in the development of teacher knowledge, teacher learning, and in particular, teacher learning in community. We now turn to examine these matters.

TEACHER LEARNING IN COMMUNITY

The dynamic and changing nature of teacher knowledge has, for the past two decades or so, led to a focus on community settings as contexts for constructing teacher knowledge and for fostering teacher development. This line of work extends the notion of teacher knowledge to a more complex view of teacher learning in community. It draws on Wenger's notion of "communities of practice" (CoP) (Wenger, 1998) and its application to diverse situations, such as classroom communities (i.e., Perrenet & Terwel, 1997; Seixas 1993), communities of teachers focused on disciplinary learning (i.e., Shulman & Sherin, 2004), the professional development of teachers (i.e., Cochran-Smith & Lytle, 1999; Griffiths, 2006), and the mentoring process (Carroll, 2005; Orland-Barak, 2005).

Influenced by global educational reforms toward privatization and high-stakes accountability of processes and outcomes, educational policy in many countries has, over the past few decades, moved toward decentralization alongside the standardization of the assessment of curriculum, teaching, learning and, most recently, teacher education programs. Paradoxically, or rather in response to the above controlling shifts, professional conversation frameworks for teacher learning in community are gradually being recognized as particularly valuable means for enhancing and sustaining a motivated professional community that can stand up to these pressures and challenges. Mostly, they are viewed as relevant and authentic spaces for participants to critically, collaboratively, and supportively create knowledge and examine their roles and practices as shaped by accountability systems and often competing political agendas of educational reforms (Orland-Barak, 2010). Despite differences in terms of content, design, processes, and expected outcomes across contexts, practices of professional conversation introduce a feminist narrative to communities of practice – one which imbues an ideology of diversity, values embodied knowledge and attends to the influence of structures of power (Griffiths, 1995). Such a narrative seems to operate as a social-professional backbone to assist participants in managing the external narrative of standardized outcomes to which they must respond in their work (Orland-Barak, 2009). In fostering collegiality and professional communication among teachers, the presence of a collaborative group in which positions can be argued and clarified and work can be shared, is thus, seen as critical to professional growth and to prospects for educational change (Craig, 2009; Craig & Deretchin, 2009).

Another important contribution of teacher knowledge development in a communal and collaborative inquiry setting, according to Cochran-Smith and Lytle (1999), is that it enables the teachers' "knowledge-of-practice" to evolve. The goal of such inquiry "is to provide the social and intellectual contexts in which teachers at all points along the professional life span can take critical perspectives on their own assumptions as well as [on] the theory and research of others and also jointly construct local knowledge that connects their work in schools to larger social and political issues" (Cochran-Smith & Lytle, 1999, p. 283). Thus, this extended area of research on teacher knowledge and teacher learning, speaks to the intellectual, personal, and professional development of teachers in community settings as well to the potential that such development holds for the improvement of schooling in the wider context. To this end, and as reflected in the chapter by Zellermayer and Tabak in this volume, recent trends in teacher education have moved away from transmission-oriented approaches and toward collaborative professional conversation models as powerful channels for supporting the construction of teacher professional knowledge in community (Feldman, 1999; Florio-Ruane, 1991; Florio-Ruane & Clark, 1993, Lewis & Ketter, 2002; Tillema & Orland-Barak, 2006). Theoretically, professional conversations forward a view of knowledge as constructed in social acts and as situated and enacted in social communities of practice. In this social constructivist view, teacher knowledge is defined as transactional, and as constructed in social practice and in conversation between persons (Lave & Wenger, 1991); thus professional conversations are conceived as social contexts for constructing and negotiating meanings, bringing practice under critical scrutiny, and for developing a professional discourse of practice (Clark, 2001). Professional conversations are also regarded as important for preparing professionals to undertake new roles within the same domain, such as the passage from teaching to mentoring, in the process of which new discourses of practice are acquired (Orland-Barak, 2002; Rust & Orland-Barak, 2001).

The dialogic view of teacher learning in community is represented in the ideas of Vygotsky (1962, 1978) and Wertsch (1991, 1998), whereby individual learning is considered to be mediated by social discourse. Views of learning as a dialogical process involving the social distribution of intelligence are also reflected in the work of Resnick (1991), Pea (1994), Perkins (1993) and others. These ideas are supported by the work of Wegerif and Mercer (2000), Rojas-Drummond (2000) and Rojas-Drummod, Perez, Velez, Gomez, and Mendoza (2003). Vygotsky's (1962, 1978) ideas on the primacy of language in the development of mental functioning and of mediated action are taken further by Wertsch (1991, 1998), who sees dialogism in community as central to the understanding of human action. Especially relevant to understanding social processes such as collaborative learning are Bakhtin's (1981) ideas of voice, utterance, interanimation, and ventriloquation. Bakhtin's special contribution to translinguistics, a field that has become known as discourse analysis, is his view that an utterance is never final and that it involves both the person who is doing the talking and the person being addressed. Each speaker's utterances come into contact, or interanimate, with the utterances of another because each person's voice also contains that of another, so that ventriloquation is always involved in spoken or written texts. This means that it is not possible to understand single utterances out of the context of the extended flow of speech communication. This is directly relevant to the analysis of knowledge development in social settings, where groups learn collaboratively via conversational interaction, precisely the type of setting in which professional conversations take place in communities of teacher learning.

Studies have also shed light on the conditions that sustain conversation frameworks and on their outcomes for teacher professional learning. We know, for example, that professional conversations can constitute significant opportunities for the development of interpersonal reasoning (Noddings, 1991) and for encouraging participants to develop new ideas (Pfeiffer, Featherstone, & Smith, 1993). They can also function as valuable spaces for public expression, for crossing boundaries, for authoring articles (Florio-Ruane, 1991), for articulating, analyzing, and framing dilemmas; and for solving pedagogical problems (Clark, 2001; Cochran-Smith & Lytle, 1991; Florio-Ruane 1991; Little, 1993; Olson & Craig, 2001).

Studies on professional conversations have also attended to the process and content of teachers' conversational learning (Bailey, 1996; Feldman, 1999). Lewis and Ketter (2002), adding a socio-cultural perspective to the study of the content and process of teachers' professional conversations, show how participants in their study group take up each other's genres, discourses and voices in talk about texts, to construct new understandings about their identities and their teaching. In the context of mentors' professional conversations, Orland-Barak's (2005) study shows that any one conversation can constitute various forms of dialogue, each of which is potentially valuable for examining either instrumental or conceptual aspects of professional practice (i.e., concrete burning issues, or differences and similarities across contexts of practice). The study also showed that some of these dialogues can provide opportunities for prompting and enhancing a discourse in which professionals expose, scrutinize, and contest deeply ingrained assumptions about their practice, stressing the active role of the facilitator, or "mentor of mentors."

Learning in community is referred to in the literature as a professional "discourse of practice," defined as the acts, values, ideologies, beliefs, identities, and local and professional languages that shape participants' professional identity and conceptions of their practice (Freeman, 1993; Gee,

1992; Miller-Marsh, 2002). Socio-culturally constituted, such professional discourse is grounded in and mediated by participants' past and present discourses, each carrying particular values and ideologies, and constantly playing out in the unconscious and implicit meanings that participants make of their experiences in conversation (Hicks, 1996). Professional conversations are thus seen as contexts for the construction of knowledge, generated and constituted by dialogue and conversation, and drawing on a view of learning and language as a social, communicative act.

THE ROAD TRAVELED

Our account thus far may suggest a linear development from the more specific and relatively bounded idea of teacher knowledge, in its different forms, toward an expanded view of teacher professionalism based on teachers' construction and enactment of their knowledge in the context of professional communities and through gradually developing discourses of practice. It is possible to construct a narrative of the development of research on teacher knowledge and teacher learning that highlights a linear progression. As educational history has shown, the idea of teacher knowledge was a sorely needed corrective to the view of teachers as the mere implementers of policy formulated by others. Once this idea became accepted, it promoted the kind of research that moved in close to observe and document the actual work of teaching, and from that point on many previously unnoticed phenomena came to the fore: teachers developing their own "craft knowledge," talking to one another, learning together, and dealing with a range of constraints. The notion that teachers both listened to and told what could be termed "sacred stories" and "cover stories" (Clandinin & Connelly, 1996), the conceptualization of communities of practice, and the development of professional discourse all follow directly from this point.

However, based on our years of experience conducting research, we suggest that a nonlinear narrative is more plausible. After all, diverse conceptualizations of teacher knowledge, teacher learning and development continue to exist, interact and thrive on the research landscape. Pedagogical content knowledge research continues to be productive, as well as blending in useful ways with the ideas of professional learning in community. Likewise, narrative research on teaching, sometimes with a focus on the work of individual teachers, continues to be pursued worldwide and to inform our understandings of the many dilemmas that confront teachers, and how they are sometimes limited in their practice by system-wide constraints and at other times respond in creative ways. Research on teacher learning also proceeds according to diverse perspectives, in response to new challenges and to take advantage of changing opportunities, as the range of contributions in an edited volume by Kwo (2010) makes evident. It seems important to emphasize that teachers still need to develop their own "craft knowledge" of teaching even when, as we might hope, they work within the setting of a supportive professional community.

Thus our account suggests a nonlinear portrayal, one where our understandings of teacher knowledge and teacher learning have developed in much the same way that Zellermayer and Tabak (2013) later tell us collaborative communities have formed, dispersed and reformed according to perceived needs, drawing on learnings from earlier stages and from diverse sources outside the particular community in dynamic, partly random sequences which can be described in terms of botanical metaphors (rhizomes, mycorrhizae) as well as in the metaphor of "knotwork." Interestingly, Li (2005) already drew on the metaphor of knotwork (grounded in her own Chinese cultural heritage) to account for the interactions, cultural learning and development that was generated by her own narrative inquiry with a diverse group of teachers. The metaphor highlights a creative, dynamic and responsive mode of working that adapts and often improvises the next steps – whether of the teacher or the researcher – in answer to perceived developments and needs arising in the field. Zellermayer and Tabak in their chapter later in this book speak of "the importance of being involved in a process of becoming in which there is no predetermined limit on what we may become or how we may engage with problems and create events" (2013). This statement describes, and hopefully will continue to describe, our approach to the themes of teacher knowledge and teacher learning.

REFERENCES

Abraham, A. (1972). *Le monde intérieure des enseignants*. Paris: Epi Editeurs.

Bailey, F. (1996). The role of collaborative dialogue in teacher education. In D. Freeman & J. G. Richards (Eds.), *Teacher learning in language teaching* (pp. 260–281). New York, NY: Cambridge University Press.

Bakhtin, M. (1981). *The dialogic imagination*. Austin, TX: University of Texas Press.

Ball, S. J., & Goodson, I. F. (1985). *Teachers' lives and careers*. London: Falmer Press.

Barone, T. (2007). A return to the gold standard? Questioning the future of narrative construction as educational research. *Qualitative Inquiry, 13*(4), 454–455.

Bolster, R. (1983). Towards a more effective model of research on teaching. *Harvard Educational Review, 53*, 239–265.

Bussis, A., Chittenden, E., & Amarel, M. (1976). *Beyond surface curriculum.* Boulder, CO: Westview Press.

Carroll, D. (2005). Learning through interactive talk: A school-based mentor teacher study group as a context for professional learning. *Teaching and Teacher Education, 21*(5), 457–473.

Carter, K. (1993). The place of story in the study of teaching and teacher education. *Educational Researcher, 22*, 5–12.

Chen, X. (2009). An inquiry into components of teachers' practical knowledge in Chinese schools. *Educational Studies in Japan, International Yearbook, 4,* 103–115.

Clandinin, D. J. (1985). Personal practical knowledge: A study of teachers' classroom images. *Curriculum Inquiry, 15*(4), 361–385.

Clandinin, D. J., & Connelly, F. M. (1996). Teachers' professional knowledge landscapes: Teacher stories, stories of teachers. School stories, stories of schools. *Educational Researcher, 25*(3), 24–30.

Clark, C. (2001). *Talking shop.* New York, NY: Teachers College Press, Columbia University.

Clark, C. M., & Peterson, P. L. (1986). Teachers' thought processes. In M. C. Wittrock (Ed.), *Handbook of research on teaching* (3rd ed., pp. 255–296). New York, NY: Macmillan.

Clark, C. M., & Yinger, R. (1977). Research on teacher thinking. *Curriculum Inquiry, 7*(4), 279–304.

Cochran-Smith, M., & Lytle, S. (1991). Research on teaching and teacher research: The issues that divide. *Educational Researcher, 19*(2), 2–10.

Cochran-Smith, M., & Lytle, S. (1999). Relationships of knowledge and practice: Teacher learning in communities. In A. Iran-Najad & C. Pearson (Eds.), *Review of research in education* (Vol. 24, pp. 249–305). Washington, DC: American Educational Research Association.

Conle, C. (2001). The rationality of narrative inquiry in research and professional development. *European Journal of Teacher Education, 24*(1), 21–33.

Connelly, F. M., & Clandinin, D. J. (1986). On narrative method, personal philosophy, and narrative unities in the story of teaching. *Journal of Research in Science Teaching, 23,* 293–310.

Connelly, F. M., & Clandinin, D. J. (1990). Stories of experience and narrative inquiry. *Educational Researcher, 19*(5), 2–14.

Craig, C. (2009). Research in the midst of organized school reform: Versions of teacher community in tension. *American Educational Research Journal, 46*(2), 598–619.

Craig, C. J. (2003). Characterizing the human experience of reform in an urban middle school context. *Journal of Curriculum Studies, 35*(5), 627–648.

Craig, C., & Deretchin, L. (Eds.). (2009). *Teacher learning in small group settings.* American Teacher Educators' Yearbook. Lanham, MD: Rowman & Littlefield.

Day, C., & Laneve, C. (Eds.). (2011). *Analysis of educational practices: A comparison of research models.* Brescia: Editrice La Scuola.

Dewey, J. (1938). *Experience and education.* New York, NY: Collier Books.

Doyle, W. (1977). Paradigms for research on teacher effectiveness. *Review of Research in Education, 5,* 163–198.

Doyle, W. (1997). Heard any really good stories lately? A critique of the critics of narrative in educational research. *Teaching and Teacher Education, 13*(1), 93–99. EARCH OYE.

Elbaz, F. (1981). The teacher's "practical knowledge": Report of a case study. *Curriculum Inquiry, 11*(1), 43–71.

Elbaz-Luwisch, F. (1988, July). *Knowledge and discourse: The evolution of research on teacher thinking*. Paper presented at the Conference of the International Study Association on Teacher Thinking, University of Nottingham, England.

Elbaz-Luwisch, F. (1991). Research on teacher's knowledge: The evolution of a discourse. *Journal of Curriculum Studies, 23*(1), 1–19.

Elbaz-Luwisch, F. (2007). Studying teachers' lives and experience: Narrative inquiry in K-12 teaching. In D. J. Clandinin (Ed.), *Handbook of narrative inquiry: Mapping a methodology* (pp. 357–382). Thousand Oaks, CA: Sage Publications.

Elbaz-Luwisch, F. (2011). The narrative study of teaching: ISATT and North American research on teaching. In C. Day & C. Laneve (Eds.), *Analysis of educational practices: A comparison of research models* (pp. 99–108). Brescia: Editrice La Scuola.

Esland, G. M. (1971). Teaching and learning as the organization of knowledge. In M. F. D. Young (Ed.), *Knowledge and control* (pp. 70–115). London: Collier-MacMillan.

Estola, E., & Elbaz-Luwisch, F. (2003). Teaching bodies at work. *Journal of Curriculum Studies, 35*, 1–23.

Estola, E., Erkkilä, R., & Syrjälä, L. (2003). A moral voice of vocation in teachers' narratives. *Teachers and Teaching: Theory and Practice, 9*(3), 239–256.

Feiman-Nemser, S., & Floden, R. (1986). The cultures of teaching. In M. C. Wittrock (Ed.), *Handbook of research on teaching* (3rd ed., pp. 505–526). New York, NY: Macmillan.

Feldman, A. (1999, April). *Conversational complexity*. Paper presented at the American Educational Research Association annual meeting, Montreal.

Fenstermacher, G. (1978). A philosophical consideration of recent research on teacher effectiveness. *Review of Research in Education, 6*, 157–185.

Florio-Ruane, S., & Clark, C. M. (1993, August). *Authentic conversation: A medium for research on teachers' knowledge and a context for professional development*. Paper presented at the International Study Association on Teacher Thinking meeting, Goteborg, Sweden.

Florio-Ruane, S. (1991). Conversation and narrative in collaborative research: An ethnography of the Written Literary Forum. In C. Witherell & N. Noddings (Eds.), *Stories lives tell: Narrative and dialogue in education* (pp. 234–256). New York, NY: Teachers College Press.

Freeman, D. (1993). Renaming experience/reconstructing practice. In D. Freeman & J. G. Richards (Eds.), *Teacher learning in language teaching* (pp. 221–242). New York, NY: Cambridge University Press.

Gage, N. L. (1978). *The scientific basis of the art of teaching*. New York, NY: Teachers College Press.

Gage, N. L., & Needels, M. C. (1989). Process-product research on teaching: A review of criticisms. *The Elementary School Journal, 89*(3), 253–300.

Garrison, J. W., & Macmillan, C. J. B. (1984). A philosophical critique of process-product research on teaching. *Educational Theory, 34*, 255–274.

Gee, J. (1992). *The social mind: Language, ideology and social practice*. New York, NY: Bergin & Garvey.

Goodson, I. F. (1992). Sponsoring the teacher's voice: Teachers' lives and teacher development. In A. Hargreaves, & M. Fullan (Eds.), *Understanding teacher development* (pp. 110-121). London: Cassell.

Griffiths, M. (1995). *Feminisms and the self: The web of identity*. London: Routledge.

Griffiths, M. (2006). The feminization of teaching and the practice of teaching: Threat or opportunity? *Educational Theory, 56*(4), 387–405.

Griffiths, M., & Macleod, G. (2008). Personal narratives and policy: Never the twain? *Journal of Philosophy of Education, 42*(1), 121–143.

Gudmundsdottir, S. (1995). The narrative nature of pedagogical content knowledge. In H. McEwan & K. Egan (Eds.), *Narrative in teaching, learning and research* (pp. 24–38). New York, NY: Teachers College Press.

Gudmundsdottir, S. (1996). The teller, the tale, and the one being told: The narrative nature of the research interview. *Curriculum Inquiry, 26*(3), 293–306.

Gudmundsdottir, S. (1991). Story-maker, story-teller: Narrative structures in curriculum. *Journal of Curriculum Studies, 23*(3), 207–218.

Heikkinen, H. (1998). Becoming yourself through narrative: Autobiographical approach in teacher education. In R. Erkkila, A. Willman & L. Syrjala (Eds.), *Promoting teachers' personal and professional growth* (pp. 111–131). Oulu: Oulu University Press.

Hicks, D. (1996). Discourse, learning, and teaching. In M. Apple (Ed.), *Review of research in education* (Vol. 21, pp. 49–95). Washington, DC: American Educational Research Association.

Jersild, A. T. (1970). *When teachers face themselves.* New York, NY: Teachers College Press.

Johnson, K. E., & Golombek, P. R. (Eds.). (2002). *Narrative inquiry as professional development.* New York: Cambridge University Press.

Keddie, N. (1971). Classroom knowledge. In M. F. D. Young (Ed.), *Knowledge and control* (pp. 133–160). London: Collier-MacMillan.

Kelchtermans, G., & Ballet, K. (2002). Micropolitics in teacher induction: A narrative-biographical study on teacher development. *Teaching & Teacher Education, 18*(1), 105–120.

Kwo, O. (Ed.). (2010). *Teachers as learners: Critical discourse on challenges and opportunities.* Hong Kong: Comparative Education Research Centre, U.H.K., & Springer.

Lave, J., & Wenger, E. (1991). *Situated learning: Legitimate peripheral participation.* Cambridge, UK: Cambridge University Press.

Lewis, C., & Ketter, J. (2002, April). *Learning as social interaction: Interdiscursivity in a teacher and researcher study group.* Paper presented at the annual meeting of the American Educational Research Association, New Orleans.

Li, X. (2005). A Tao of narrative: Dynamic splicing of teacher stories. *Curriculum Inquiry, 35*(3), 339–365.

Li, X., Conle, C., & Elbaz-Luwisch, F. (2009). *Shifting polarized positions: A Narrative approach in teacher education.* New York, NY: Peter Lang.

Lincoln, Y. S., & Guba, E. G. (1985). *Naturalistic inquiry.* Beverly Hills, CA: Sage.

Little, J. W. (1993). Teachers professional development in a climate of educational reform. *Educational Evaluation and Policy Analysis, 15*(2), 129–151.

Lyons, N. (2007). Narrative inquiry: What possible future influence on policy or practice? In D. J. Clandinin (Ed.), *Handbook of narrative inquiry: Mapping a methodology* (pp. 600–631). Thousand Oaks, CA: Sage Publications.

Miller-Marsh, M. (2002). The influence of discourses on the precarious nature of mentoring. *Reflective Practice, 3*, 103–115.

Moen, T., Nilssen, V., & Weidemann, N. (2007). An aspect of a teacher's inclusive educational practice: Scaffolding pupils through transitions. *Teachers and Teaching: Theory and Practice, 13*(3), 269–286.

Noddings, N. (1991). Stories in dialogue: Caring and interpersonal reasoning. In C. Witherell & N. Noddings (Eds.), *Stories lives tell: Narrative and dialogue in education* (pp. 157–170). New York: Teachers College Press.

Olson, M. R., & Craig, C. J. (2001). Opportunities and challenges in the development of teachers' knowledge: The development of narrative authority through knowledge communities. *Teaching & Teacher Education, 17*(6), 667–684.

Orland-Barak, L. (2002). What's in a case? What mentors' cases reveal about the practice of mentoring. *Journal of Curriculum Studies, 34*(4), 451–468.

Orland-Barak, L. (2005). Convergent, divergent and parallel dialogues in mentors' professional conversations. *Teachers and Teaching: Theory and Practice, 12*(1), 13–33.

Orland-Barak, L. (2009). Constructing practice through conversation in professional learning groups. In C. J. Craig & L. Deretchin (Eds.), *Teacher learning in small group settings: American Teacher Educators' Yearbook*. Lanham, MD: Rowman & Littlefield.

Orland-Barak, L. (2010). *Learning to mentor as praxis: Foundations for a curriculum in teacher education*. New York, NY: Springer.

Pea, R. D. (1994). Seeing what we build together: Distributed multimedia learning environments for transformative communications. *The Journal of the Learning Sciences, 3*(3), 285–299.

Perkins, D. N. (1993). Person-plus: A distributed view of thinking and learning. In G. Salomon (Ed.), *Distributed cognitions: Psychological and educational considerations* (pp. 88–110). Cambridge: Cambridge University Press.

Perrenet, J. C., & Terwel, J. (1997). Learning together in multicultural groups: A curriculum innovation. *Curriculum and Teaching, 12*(1), 31–44.

Pfeiffer, L., Featherstone, H., & Smith, S. P. (April, 1993). "Do you really mean all when you say all?" *A close look at the ecology of pushing in talk about mathematics teaching*. National Center for Research on Teacher Learning, Michigan State University, East Lansing, Michigan.

Phillion, J., He, M. F., & Connelly, F. M. (Eds.). (2005). *Multicultural education: Narrative and experiential approaches*. Thousand Oaks, CA: Sage Publications.

Polkinghorne, D. (2007). Validity issues in narrative research. *Qualitative Inquiry, 13*(40), 471–486.

Resnick, L. B. (1991). Shared cognition: Thinking as social practice. In L. B. Resnick, J. M. Levine & S. D. Teasley (Eds.), *Perspectives on socially shared cognition* (pp. 1–22). Washington, DC: American Psychological Association.

Rojas-Drummond, S. (2000). Guided participation, discourse and the construction of knowledge in Mexican classrooms. In H. Cowie & G. van der Aalsvoort (Eds.), *Social interaction in learning and instruction: The meaning of discourse for the construction of knowledge* (pp. 193–213). Amsterdam: Pergamon.

Rojas-Drummod, S., Perez, V., Velez, M., Gomez, L., & Mendoza, A. (2003). Talking for reasoning among Mexican primary school children. *Learning and Instruction, 13*(6), 653–670.

Rust, F. O., & Orland-Barak, L. (2001). Learning the discourse of teaching: Conversation as professional development. In C. M. Clark (Ed.), *Talking shop* (pp. 82–118). New York, NY: Teachers College Press.

Ryans, D. G. (1960). *Characteristics of teachers: Their description, comparison, and appraisal*. Washington, DC: American Council on Education.

Seixas, P. (1993). The community of inquiry as a basis for knowledge and learning: The case of history. *American Educational Research Journal, 30*(2), 305–324.

Shulman, L. (1986). Paradigms and research programs in the study of teaching: A contemporary perspective. In M. Wittrock (Ed.), *Handbook of research on teaching* (3rd ed., pp. 3–36). New York, NY: Macmillan.

Shulman, L. J., & Sherin, M. G. (2004). Fostering communities of teachers as learners: Disciplinary perspectives. *Journal of Curriculum Studies, 6*(2), 135–140.

Spector-Mersel, G. (2010). Narrative research: Time for a paradigm. *Narrative Inquiry, 20*(1), 205–225.

Tillema, H. H, & Orland-Barak, L. (2006). Constructing knowledge in professional conversations: The role of beliefs on knowledge and knowing. *Learning & Instruction, 16*(6), 1–17.

Vygotsky, L. S. (1962). *Thought and language*. London: John Wiley & Sons.

Vygotsky, L. S. (1978). *Mind in society: The development of higher psychological processes*. Cambridge, MA: Harvard University Press.

Wegerif, R., & Mercer, N. (2000). Language for thinking: A study of children solving reasoning test problems together. In H. Cowie & G. van der Aalsvoort (Eds.), *Social interaction in learning and instruction: The meaning of discourse for the construction of knowledge*. Amsterdam: Pergamon.

Wenger, E. (1998). *Communities of practice: Learning, meaning, and identity*. Cambridge: Cambridge University Press.

Wertsch, J. V. (1991). *Voices of the mind: A sociocultural approach to mediated action*. Cambridge, MA: Harvard University Press.

Wertsch, J. V. (1998). *Mind as action*. New York, NY: Oxford University Press.

Zellermayer, M., & Tabak, E. (2013). The sustainability and nonsustainability of a decade of change and continuity in teacher education. In C. J. Craig, P. C. Meijer & J. Broeckmans (Eds.), *From teacher thinking to teachers and teaching: The evolution of a research community* (Vol. 19, pp. 615–635). Bingley, UK: Emerald Group Publishing.

Zembylas, M. (2003). Emotions and teacher identity: A poststructural perspective. *Teachers and Teaching: Theory and Practice, 9*(3), 213–238.

CHAPTER 6

PEDAGOGICAL CONTENT KNOWLEDGE: TWENTY-FIVE YEARS LATER

Maher Hashweh

ABSTRACT

This chapter briefly reviews the research related to the construct of pedagogical content knowledge (PCK) over the past 25 years. Despite the remarkable implications of the PCK conceptualization, questions remain concerning the vagueness of the construct and the studies conducted on the PCK research line, questions which may lead to new developments in defining the nature of the conceptualization, its validity, and its utility. However, agreement exists concerning the need to portray specific cases of PCK of successful teaching. The work argues for a need to develop models of teacher learning and professional development that are subject matter specific. The chapter ends with a call for basing professional development on the conceptualization of PCK.

Keywords: Teacher knowledge; teacher beliefs; pedagogical content knowledge; teacher professional development

Nearly a quarter of a century has passed since Shulman (1986a, 1987) proposed the construct of pedagogical content knowledge, or PCK for short. In this chapter, I review developments concerning the construct and

From Teacher Thinking to Teachers and Teaching: The Evolution of a Research Community
Advances in Research on Teaching, Volume 19, 115–140
Copyright © 2013 by Emerald Group Publishing Limited
All rights of reproduction in any form reserved
ISSN: 1479-3687/doi:10.1108/S1479-3687(2013)0000019009

recent trends in research utilizing it. I point out recent agreement among many researchers on the need to describe concrete examples of topic-specific PCK, and draw on a previous paper (Hashweh, 2005) to describe my conceptualization of this topic-specific PCK. Finally, I argue for integrating two domains of research – topic-specific PCK and teacher learning and professional development. I contend this holds great promise for the development of research in both areas.

BACKGROUND AND SHULMAN'S CONCEPTUALIZATION

PCK was conceptualized by Lee Shulman (Shulman, 1986a, 1987) in the mid-1980s and drew attention to the importance of studying teacher knowledge. The first article that appeared was mainly about teacher knowledge of subject matter, the missing paradigm that Shulman identified in another article published in that same year (Shulman, 1986b). PCK was introduced as a subcategory of teacher content knowledge (the two other subcategories being subject matter content knowledge and curricular knowledge). Shulman argued that this knowledge, associated with "the most regularly taught topics in one's subject area" (Shulman, 1986b, p. 9), includes representations of knowledge (analogies, illustrations, examples, explanations, and demonstrations), and student learning difficulties and strategies to deal with them. According to the conceptualization, PCK: (a) is a subcategory of content knowledge; (b) is topic-specific; and (c) includes two further subcategories: knowledge of representations and of learning difficulties and strategies of overcoming them. While the topic-specificity of PCK was neglected by some researchers, the conceptualization of PCK as a subcategory of teacher content knowledge (as subject matter knowledge for teaching) was accepted.

In the 1987 article Shulman identified PCK as a category of the knowledge base of teachers, as one of seven categories that also included content knowledge, general pedagogical knowledge, curriculum knowledge, knowledge of learners and their characteristics, knowledge of educational contexts, and knowledge of educational ends, purposes and values. PCK was conceptualized as a category on its own, and not as a subcategory of content knowledge as conceptualized in the 1986 article.

In this second article, Shulman again emphasized the topic specificity of PCK, and, implicitly, how it develops as a result of interactions among different components, or categories, of teacher knowledge and beliefs.

However, by proposing PCK as one of seven categories of the knowledge base, and by neglecting the interactions among the other categories, the hierarchies that might exist between them, or the different forms or types of knowledge within each category, Shulman left the task of further developing the conceptualization of PCK to others. At a time when inquiry into teacher knowledge and beliefs was in its infancy, this was an important contribution. During the ensuing twenty-five years, we have witnessed different developments in the conceptualization of PCK, conceptualizations which will be described in a latter section of this chapter.

It is important to remember the intellectual backdrop against which the PCK construct was developed. During the decade prior to Shulman's introduction of the idea of PCK, the process–product paradigm guided the study of teaching, a research program which aimed to identify relations between teacher behavior (process) and student learning or achievement (product). The advent of cognitive psychology influenced researchers to focus on teacher planning or teacher thinking rather than behavior as the important "process." Models of teacher planning were proposed as a result of these investigations. Shulman's ground-breaking contribution pointed out that even these more cognitively based programs of research on teaching were still viewing teaching as a generic activity. Lee Shulman called attention to what he called the missing paradigm or program in research on teaching – the study of teaching of particular subject matter.

The construct of PCK was adopted, modified, or appropriated by numerous educationalists since 1986. Shulman's 1986 a article has been cited over 7,400 times while his 1987 article has been referenced over 7,500 times. The number of published articles annually on PCK continues to grow. The research utilizing PCK concentrated on different subject areas, with the highest number of researchers working in science and mathematics education.

PCK also has been used as a basis for designing pre-service teacher education programs and continuous professional development programs. Additionally, PCK has formed a framework for teacher assessment. For example, the National Board for Professional Teaching Standards in the USA certifies teachers by the content area and educational level at which the teacher works. Subject matter knowledge and knowledge of students, the two most important components of PCK, are clearly highlighted in this framework. The PCK construct has not only caught the interest of educationalists working at the school level; in higher education, the idea was well received because, as Shulman himself has pointed out, it shows that teaching, like research, is domain or discipline specific. However, despite the remarkable implications of the introduction of the PCK conceptualization, questions still remain about the construct and PCK research. These wonders and ponders have led to new developments in defining the nature of the construct, its validity, and its utility.

LATER DEVELOPMENTS (1980S–1990S)

A few years after Shulman unveiled the PCK construct, Gudmundsdottir (1990, 1995) expressed dissatisfaction with it. She made a case for introducing additional components to PCK, namely components related to the value-laden and narrative nature of teacher professional knowledge. The view that PCK has a component related to the teacher's beliefs about content or subject matter was not unique to Gudmundsdottir. Shulman and his colleagues also were awakening to this component, the teacher's orientation to subject matter (i.e., Grossman, Wilson, & Shulman, 1989). However, the distinctive contribution of Gudmundsdottir was her insistence on both the value-laden and narrative nature of PCK.

Other researchers proposed additional components of PCK. It was transformed from that special amalgam of subject matter and pedagogy that Shulman (1986a, 1987) described to a category of teacher knowledge that curiously seemed able to encompass all other categories of teacher knowledge and beliefs, such as knowledge of subject matter, orientations, student characteristics, aims and purposes, resources and pedagogy.

This trend to include new knowledge and beliefs components as subcategories of PCK continued well into the 1980s and 1990s. Grossman (1990) added two other components to PCK (in addition to the two identified by Shulman – representations, and student difficulties with topic): knowledge and beliefs about purposes, and knowledge of curriculum materials. These were components that Shulman originally considered separate categories of the knowledge base. Here we notice early inclusions of what were considered categories separate from PCK into PCK itself. Marks (1990) included knowledge of subject matter per se as part of PCK, while neglecting Grossman's inclusion of purposes. Closely related to this trend was the tendency of some researchers to view PCK as a category of teacher knowledge and beliefs that is not different in type from other categories. For example, they treat PCK as general theoretical knowledge just like subject matter knowledge.

Other researchers emphasized the influence of other categories of teacher knowledge and beliefs on PCK. An important contribution was made by Cochran, DeRuiter, and King (1993) when they emphasized that PCKg (pedagogical content knowing) is the "teacher's integrated understanding of four components of pedagogy, subject matter content, student characteristics, and the environmental context of learning" (p. 266). Fernandez-Balboa and Stieh (1995), while claiming that PCK had a generic nature, also asserted that PCK results from the integration of different knowledge components.

Additionally, PCK seemed to lose its most important characteristics, its topic specificity, and was regarded as a broad and general form of knowledge (Fernandez-Balboa & Stieh, 1995). If PCK, according to some researchers, had become that generic all-encompassing form of teacher knowledge and beliefs then, we do not need the term PCK. In short, it had become synonymous with teacher knowledge and beliefs, and even practices for some. On the other hand, many researchers have empirically examined teacher PCK and concluded it includes some or all of these components. It seemed, at the time, that an impasse regarding the nature of PCK and its utility as a theoretical construct had been reached.

RECENT TRENDS EMPHASIZING TOPIC-SPECIFIC PCK (LATE 1990S – NOW)

This was not the case. In contrast to the claim about the generic nature of PCK, Van Driel, Verloop, and De Vos (1998) emphasized the topic specificity of PCK. The authors wrote: "In our view, the value of PCK lies essentially in its relation with specific topics" (p. 691). They also presented the topic-specific PCK for teaching chemical equilibrium in Chemistry. More recently, Van Driel and Berry (2010) asserted that few topic-specific examples of PCK existed in the literature. The first study that had identified PCK (it was termed subject matter pedagogical knowledge) (Hashweh, 1985) conceptualized PCK as the topic-specific knowledge that the teacher develops and accumulates in relation to teaching that topic. The conceptualization of PCK proposed by Van Driel and Berry is very close to this original conceptualization.

A conceptualization of PCK that captures both its topic-specificity and its development as a result of interactions between other knowledge and beliefs categories was presented by Loughran, Milroy, Berry, Gunstone, and Mulhal (2001). Loughran, Berry, and Mulhall (2012) developed a method of identifying topic-specific PCK and portraying it in a way that is useful to teachers. For each science topic investigated, they developed a resource folio consisting of a content representation and what they termed as pedagogical and professional experience repertoire. The content representation has elements similar to Shulman's categories, for example, knowledge of the main ideas of the content of a topic, teaching strategies, and knowledge about students. This representation is connected to a set of narratives describing a number of teachers' experiences in teaching the topic. In this way, Gudmundsdottir's concern for the value-laden and narrative nature of PCK was addressed.

There seems to be agreement lately among scholars working in Australia, the Netherlands, and Palestine, among others, about the topic-specific nature of PCK and on the need to portray specific cases of PCK of successful teaching. Previously, I had proposed that we think of PCK as a set or repertoire of personal content-specific pedagogical constructions which teachers develop as a result of repeated planning, teaching and reflection on the teaching of the most regularly taught topics (Hashweh, 2005). These cases have components of both story-based and generalized event-based memories. Additionally, a specific pedagogical construction is a result of the interaction of the different knowledge categories in the teacher's mind (i.e., subject matter knowledge, aims and purposes, and knowledge of students), and has components which echo these general knowledge categories (i.e., content knowledge about forces and motion, the teacher's aims and purposes when teaching about forces and motion, and student specific difficulties and alternative conceptions about motion and forces). The approach allows for the identification, description, and representation of concrete cases, or pedagogical constructions, related to the successful teaching of important topics within specific domains. It also permits us to identify important features necessary to the teaching of a certain topic which are common among pedagogical constructions of different successful teachers. That is, the approach facilitates the portrayal of standard common professional practice in the teaching of specific topics while simultaneously legitimating the diversity in teaching approaches arising from individual teacher philosophies and constrains of contexts. Finally, the approach provides outcomes that are directly related to the improvement of practice.

Let us now turn to the detailed description of this conception. I propose the following definition of PCK which results from a re-conceptualization of the nature of PCK as originally proposed in Hashweh (1985) and Shulman (1986a, 1987), taking the results of major later studies and conceptualizations of PCK into consideration, appropriating new ideas about the structure of memory (Schank, 2000), and undertaking a reanalysis and presentation of the data in a previous study (Hashweh, 1985). PCK is the set or repertoire of private and personal content-specific general event-based as well as story-based pedagogical constructions that the experienced teacher has developed as a result of repeated planning, teaching, and reflection on the teaching of the most regularly taught topics. The following assertions are incorporated in this definition:

1. PCK represents personal and private knowledge.
2. PCK is a collection of basic units called teacher pedagogical constructions.
3. Teacher pedagogical constructions result mainly from planning, but also from the interactive and postactive phases of teaching.
4. Pedagogical constructions result from an inventive process that is influenced by the interaction of knowledge and beliefs from different categories.
5. Pedagogical constructions constitute both a generalized event-based and a story-based kind of memory.
6. Pedagogical constructions are topic specific.
7. Pedagogical constructions are (or should ideally be) labeled in multiple interesting ways that connect them to other categories and subcategories of teacher knowledge and beliefs.

Private Knowledge

The definition indicates, first of all, that what we are studying here is personal and private knowledge, rather than public and objective knowledge. We capture this knowledge by observing individual teachers at work and talking to them. We ask them to plan while thinking aloud, or ask them how they would respond to certain critical incidents that might occur in teaching a certain topic (i.e., Hashweh, 1985). Efforts by some researchers to capture and represent PCK, as well as teacher self reports, cases, and teacher research, can transform it into more public knowledge.

PCK as a Collection of Teacher Pedagogical Constructions

Second, the definition asserts that PCK is a group or collection of smaller knowledge entities or units that I called pedagogical constructions. The plural term "constructions" better indicates the conceptualization of PCK as a set of entities and not as one whole unit. To use an analogy from chemistry, each of these constructions is a molecule, but PCK is essentially a mixture of different molecules, and not a new compound (larger and more complex molecules). This is in contrast to the deep knowledge that a teacher might have of subject matter, where the knowledge is well organized and hierarchically ordered.

Teacher Pedagogical Constructions Develop through Experience

Third, these units are teacher intellectual and professional constructions. They comprise the knowledge that the experienced teacher builds and accumulates pertaining to the teaching of specific regularly taught topics, such as photosynthesis for the science teacher. I claim that they result initially, and most importantly, from teacher planning, which is essentially a design process (Yinger, 1977). When a teacher plans for teaching a topic, such as photosynthesis, he or she has to answer different questions. The teacher draws on many sources of knowledge for answering such questions. The most important of these sources are the other general categories of teacher knowledge and beliefs – knowledge of subject matter, of students, pedagogy, assessment, and other categories. The resulting plan is a construction, not as tangible as the end-product of an architectural design process, but a construction nonetheless.

These constructions are further developed as a result of interactive teaching and postactive reflection. A teacher might invent an analogy during interactive teaching when she realizes she needs one more representation to explain a certain concept. Or she might, upon reflecting on the last lesson, realize she needs a new analogy, and invent a new one or ask a more experienced colleague. These analogies are added to that teacher's pedagogical construction. If we develop the architectural design analogy further, these pedagogical constructions embody the implemented building, not just its plans. Finally, if we perceive pedagogical constructions as resulting from a design process, as solutions to ill-structured problems, we realize that diversity is a natural outcome – different teachers will come up with different inventive solutions to the problem of teaching a certain topic at a certain grade level.

Pedagogical Constructions are Influenced by the Interaction of Different Knowledge and Beliefs Categories

Fourth, and as mentioned earlier, the pedagogical constructions are largely the result of the interaction between different teacher knowledge and beliefs categories. Rich PCK does not result from deep knowledge in a single knowledge category. For instance, subject matter knowledge alone is not enough. Teachers who are able to detect student alternative conceptions in photosynthesis, and who have developed superior strategies for engaging these student prior ideas, are not only knowledgeable about photosynthesis; they also hold constructivist epistemological beliefs (Hashweh, 1985). In this regard, Gudmundsdottir (1990) was right; PCK has a value or beliefs components, but it also has a subject matter component, a purposes component, a pedagogy component, and other components. Teachers develop what some have called an amalgam of subject matter knowledge and pedagogy, and other categories as well, to teach particular topics. To pursue our chemical analogy further, each new pedagogical construction is a newly designed compound, a new molecule, that the teacher has designed using atoms from different elements at his or her disposal (the categories of knowledge and beliefs such as subject matter knowledge, general pedagogy, educational aims and purposes, etc.). As a result, it is not surprising that upon careful analysis we are able to identify the different original atoms in this new compound. This explains why researchers feel obliged to include in PCK some knowledge categories that others have conceptualized as separate knowledge categories. However, PCK is not part of other knowledge and beliefs categories, and certainly not a subset of the subject matter knowledge category. There is even indication that teachers themselves are cognizant of the difference. When one teacher was asked about what she knew about photosynthesis she gave a very detailed account of her subject matter knowledge. The researcher then asked if she could add more details, and she gave a detailed account of the knowledge associated with teaching photosynthesis (Hashweh, 1985).

Research on teacher planning flourished in the late 1970s to the 1980s of the last century (Clark & Peterson, 1986). It showed, among other things, that teacher planning is a nonlinear design process that usually starts with teacher thinking about subject matter, moves to teaching methodology, and then takes other factors into consideration. However, the models that were developed to describe teacher planning focused on processes and neglected content.

It is interesting to note that in our efforts to understand teacher knowledge and thinking we have focused on knowledge at the expense of thinking processes. An examination of the last two handbooks of research on teaching (Richardson, 2001; Wittrock, 1986) is revealing, and shows a shift from studying teacher thinking to studying teacher knowledge. To understand what PCK really is, we need to devote attention to its development, and studying teacher planning again, given the arsenal of theoretical and methodological tools that we now possess, might be a fruitful program.

The teacher planning literature of three decades ago focused on processes and neglected content. It was mainly concerned with elementary school teachers. Recently, there has been some renewed interest in the study of teacher planning. A recent study paid attention to subject matter knowledge and PCK in the planning of a secondary school teacher (McCutcheon & Milner, 2002). It showed that the teacher drew on his rich content knowledge in long-term pre-active planning to develop interconnected themes for his courses, and that this kind of planning was his major form of preparing to teach. In another study (Milner, 2003) it was found that PCK was a basis for teacher planning, but the study failed to study the development of PCK as a result of planning. Both studies call for a renewed interest in teacher planning. Also, research on PCK has in other ways failed to attend to teacher planning. The time is ripe for a renewed study of teacher planning, with an emphasis on the dialectical relations between teacher knowledge and beliefs and teacher planning.

To further clarify the assertion that pedagogical constructions result mainly from the interactions between different kinds, or categories, of teacher knowledge, and that they contain the traces of these original knowledge categories, Fig. 1 and Tables 1 and 2 show a model of a hypothetical science teacher's knowledge and beliefs. I use the term "hypothetical" because, although the model was partly inductively built using a reanalysis of the data from one of the six teachers studied in 1985 (Hashweh, 1985), the model is partly speculative because the original study did not aim to describe the full range of teacher knowledge and beliefs of the teacher. Its aim was to describe some categories, mainly teacher knowledge of subject matter, and teacher conceptions of learning, and their effects on teaching. Consequently, in Table 1 I hypothesized the existence of some general knowledge categories, such as knowledge of resources or knowledge of context, and developed the model proposed in an earlier study (Hashweh, 1985, pp. 329–330), using Shulman's (1986, 1987) conceptualizations and those of some of his students and colleagues. As a result, the model of teacher knowledge and beliefs, and of PCK in particular, that is presented in this study, while partly supported by Hashweh (1985) and consonant with studies of teacher knowledge and PCK, emphasizes the hypothesis-formation phase of educational inquiry, and should be more formally tested in the future.

The lines in Fig. 1 represent some of the possible interactions between the different knowledge categories, and the dialectical relationships between

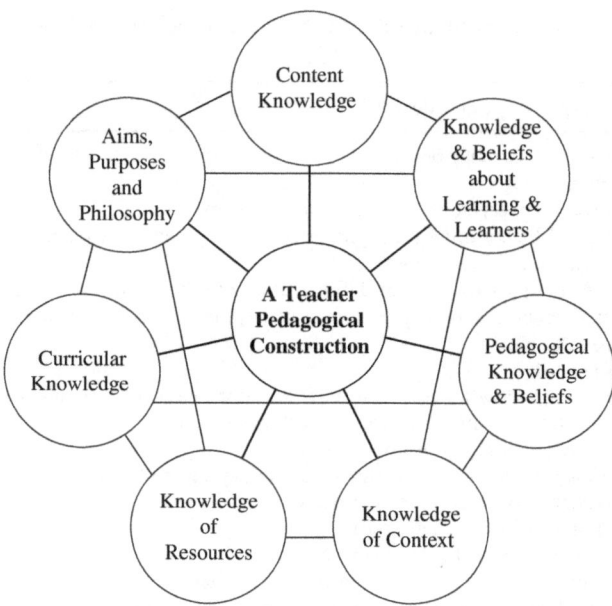

Fig. 1. A Model of a Science Teacher's Knowledge and Beliefs.

PCK, or Teacher Professional Construction (TPC) in particular, and the different knowledge categories. Table 1 should be viewed as a snapshot of the teacher's "conceptual ecology" (Strike & Posner, 1992) at a certain point in time. While the figure shows the interactionist view of these ecologies, it fails to show the developmental view of the ecologies. A TPC has a niche in a certain conceptual ecology; it is part of a web of interacting intellectual entities. While we have emphasized how the context or ecology affects the TPC, the TPC itself also affects the ecology. A teacher who has developed, perhaps implicitly, one or more TPCs that include anomalies to confront student misconceptions (in the photosynthesis and respiration TPCs, for example) may upon reflection on her practice generalize the strategy and store it as an explicit strategy in her general pedagogical knowledge category. Strike and Posner (1992), though discussing conceptual change in science students rather than teacher knowledge, expressed it well, "Our view ... must therefore be more dynamic and developmental, emphasizing the shifting patterns of mutual influence between the various components of an evolving conceptual ecology. We must say with Heraclitus that all is in flux. ... [I]t is difficult to step into the same conceptual ecology twice" (p. 163).

Table 1.   The Organization of a Science Teacher's Knowledge and
Beliefs.

Science Teacher Knowledge and Beliefs

Subject Matter Knowledge and Beliefs
  Substantive Knowledge
    Knowledge of concepts, principles, relations, topics
    Knowledge of higher-order principles or conceptual schemes (e.g., energy storage and
      release in chemical reactions)
    Knowledge of approaches, or of different ways of relating topics to other discipline
      "entities" (concepts, principles, topics, conceptual schemes) (e.g., a molecular/energy
      approach to biology)
  Syntactic Knowledge
    Knowledge of science process (control of variables, etc.) and scientific inquiry
      (identification of a problem, testing hypotheses, ...)
Aims, Purposes, and Philosophy of Education
  Beliefs about general aims of education (e.g., biology can be taught to develop good
    nutritional habits or to develop environmental awareness)
  Beliefs about aims of science education
Knowledge and Beliefs about Learning and Learners
  Conceptions of learning (e.g., social constructivist beliefs)
  Knowledge of student characteristics (experiences, abilities, interests, ...)
Pedagogical Knowledge and Beliefs
  Beliefs about importance of representations
  Knowledge of general lesson types (developmental lesson, lecture, demonstrations,
    laboratory, group work, ...)
  Knowledge of planning
  Knowledge of classroom management
Curricular Knowledge
  Vertical curricular knowledge (science curriculum in different grade levels)
  Horizontal curricular knowledge (curricula of different subjects in same grade level)
Knowledge of Resources
  Knowledge of available textbooks, films, equipment, etc ...
Knowledge of Context
  Knowledge of local educational system
  Knowledge of community
  Knowledge of particular students
Pedagogical Content Knowledge (see separate frame)

Examination of Tables 1 and 2 reveals how components of the general
knowledge categories are echoed, at a more concrete or a more local level, in
the TPCs. As previously mentioned, each of the two frames displays parts of
the knowledge of a hypothetical biology teacher, based on the findings in
Hashweh (1985). The data that was used in these two frames comes from a
biology teacher who was one of three biology teachers and three physics

Table 2. The Organization of Pedagogical Content Knowledge.

Pedagogical Content Knowledge

Photosynthesis Pedagogical Construction
   Subject matter
      Knowledge of photosynthesis details (input, output, dark, and light cycles, ...)
      Potential energy is stored in bonds in glucose molecules that are produced by
         photosynthesis
      Photosynthesis and respiration are related: the energy that is stored in the molecules in
         photosynthesis is released when these molecules are broken down in respiration
   Aims/purposes
      Relate photosynthesis to respiration, and use respiration to discuss nutritional value of
         breakfast for students
      Relate photosynthesis to production of oxygen by plankton in seas, and discuss effects of
         pollution
   Student characteristics
      Students think plants take their food from soil, that plants respire only at night, and
         photosynthesize only during the day
      Students do not know enough chemistry to understand photosynthesis
      Students have difficulties in understanding how ATP-ADP transformations occur, and
         the function of ATP in energy transfer
   Teaching photosynthesis
      Lesson types
         Developmental lesson on first day to teach ...
         Laboratory on second
         Worksheets, followed by revision and mini-lecture on third, etc...
      Explanations, representations and teaching strategies
         To emphasize that oxygen from photosynthesis comes mainly form the sea I use a film
           and the example of oxygen in the desert
         To explain ATP I use the shopping cart or the paper bag analogy
         To confront misconception of respiration only at night I show need for energy all the
           time
      Activities and assignments
         Activity of water plant to measure amount of oxygen produced by photosynthesis
         Examining Elodea cells under the microscope
      Assessment
         Questions that I use to assess understanding of function of photosynthesis, or to detect
           if they still believe plants take their food from soil
         Different versions of end-of-unit exam that I use
      Curriculum
         Relate to a previous unit on structure and function
         Prepare for a future unit on respiration
      Resources
         Knowledge of particular film about photosynthesis
         Handouts and worksheets I have previously developed about different aspect of
           photosynthesis
      Context
         Should finish this unit in two weeks
         Student X can bring Elodea plant
         Can relate this to study of local ecology
Respiration Pedagogical Construction
Structure and Function Pedagogical Construction

teachers who were studied. Each of the teachers was interviewed to assess his/her knowledge of subject-matter (one physics and one biology topic) using summary free recall, concept-map line labeling, and sorting tasks. The teachers' conceptions of learning were assessed using the clinical interview method. Each teacher's planning and simulated teaching of each of the two topics was appraised using think-aloud and critical-incidents techniques. Relations between some general knowledge categories presented in Table 1, and some subcategories of the Photosynthesis TPC, featured in Table 2, will be illustrated below using the biology teacher's data.

Table 2 gives some details of the Photosynthesis TPC, but it should be realized that PCK contains other TPCs, such as the Respiration TPC and the Structure and Function TPC. As can be seen, the Subject Knowledge and Beliefs category (Table 1) is echoed in the Photosynthesis TPC (Table 2). The teacher has a molecular/energy approach or orientation to her subject matter (It might be remembered that the BSCS produced three versions of their curriculum: molecular, ecological, and evolutionary versions). When assessing this teacher's knowledge of subject matter she emphasized the chemical and energy-related aspects of biological processes at the cellular level. This teacher's approach is reflected in her teaching of photosynthesis: She relates photosynthesis and respiration to emphasize this molecular/ energy approach. For her, it is important to emphasize that energy is needed to make complex molecules, that energy is released when complex molecules are broken down, and that chemical energy is stored in bonds. Consequently, she defined the function of photosynthesis at the molecular level: to trap energy in chemical bonds. None of the other teachers in the study described the function of photosynthesis at this level. The teacher's description of the photosynthesis process was also molecular: attaching molecules to one another and trapping energy in chemical bonds. She related cellular respiration to photosynthesis through the use of this molecular/energy approach. She described respiration as the process of breaking down the chemical bonds to liberate energy for cell activity. She also used the same approach to relate photosynthesis to food/nutrition, and emphasized the energy approach in discussing energy wastage in food chains.

The Subject Knowledge and Beliefs category is echoed in the Photo-synthesis TPC in a second way as well. The featured teacher clearly stated the theme at the beginning of her teaching: energy is released when complex molecules are broken apart and required when molecules are built. She changed the sequence of topics to start with energy release, or respiration, the first part of her theme. She explained how this released energy is transferred by ATP to other locations in the cell to be used in several cell processes. She compared respiration and fermentation, another energy releasing process. Finally, she asked about the origin of glucose (and the chemical energy in it) that is used in respiration. This led her to discuss photosynthesis as an energy-requiring process. She also stated that she would usually teach photosynthesis as the second topic in a unit on cell energy, the first unit of which would deal with the chemistry of life. Incidentally, here we notice the integration of the photosynthesis TPC with another general knowledge category – curricular knowledge.

The Subject Matter Knowledge and Beliefs category (in Table 1) is mirrored in the photosynthesis TPC (in Table 2) in yet a third way. The knowledge representations (examples, analogies, activities) that she uses also emphasize the molecular/energy approach to subject-matter. In the planning interview the teacher explained the function of respiration and the use of cell energy as follows:

> Sometimes the students don't understand what the cells need energy for. […] I say, "I am living in this house, OK? And somebody missed the turn on my street and ran their car through my wall. There's a big hole in my wall, in my house. […] What am I gonna have to do?" They say, "You're gonna have to get bricks, and you're gonna have to get wood, and you're gonna have to build a new wall." I say, "What does it take?" They say, "It takes energy." I say, We've got a cell here, and right here this membrane ruptures. What's the cell gonna do?" "The cell is gonna have to fix it." "What's the cell need to fix it?" "Oh, it needs proteins and it needs building blocks." I say, "What is it gonna have to do to hook one protein molecule to the next, to make them stick as one atom to the next?" "It needs energy." I say, "That's one of the things that you do cellular respiration for." (Hashweh, 1985, p. 243)

This teacher had developed a repertoire of analogies for use in teaching photosynthesis, most of them reflecting her molecular/energy orientation. She was aware of particular student difficulties (another important aspect of PCK) and had developed analogies to help students overcome these difficulties:

> If the students understand that ATP is an energy-carrying molecule; its job is to take the energy from the mitochondrion and take it to whatever part of the cell that needs that energy, then it just breaks apart and goes back and does it all over gain. And they say, "Don't you mean it's used up there?" And I say, "No, it just drops off the energy."

The general Aims and Purposes category for this teacher includes, as one of her aims for science teaching, the development of students' environmental awareness. She uses the photosynthesis topic (and probably other topics that she finds appropriate), to realize this aim, and allocated time to discuss the region's ecology.

The general Knowledge and Beliefs about Learning and Learners category (Table 1) is also echoed in the Photosynthesis TPC (Table 2).

The biology Teacher subscribed to what might be called a cognitive view of learning:

> I like to do what's called an overview. And I like to show them how this particular subject that we're dealing with ties into stuff that they already own, how it fits into stuff that they've learned about [...]. I help them fit it into their intellectual framework if possible. (Hashweh, 1985, p. 259)

The teacher thought it was crucial for students to express their ideas in class because she believed in the active role of the learner, and discussed the methods she used in class to allow this to occur. She also thought that students come to science classrooms with alternative conceptions of science phenomena. The corresponding TPC student characteristics category includes knowledge about the specific alternative conceptions that students hold, for example, that they think plants only photosynthesize but do not respire. The Teacher's TPC also shows she had developed a strategy that might be termed "applying science framework to situation" to confront this alternative conception. The teacher, when planning to teach respiration and photosynthesis, started by providing the larger scientific framework: how building complex molecules requires energy while breaking-up complex ones releases energy, and how energy is needed for vital cellular processes. Within this framework, the featured teacher showed that every cell needs to provide energy for these cellular processes or "it's dead meat." Respiration, she explained, was the mechanism for providing this energy. In summary, the highlighted teacher's strategy depended on showing that, from a scientific point of view, it is expected that all living cells, whether plant or animal cells, respire. The influence of conceptions of learning and the learners on the use of strategies that facilitate learning becomes clearer if we compare this teacher to another physics teacher in the same study who subscribed to a conceptual change view of learning and who used strategies that directly confronted students' alternative conceptions.

I have emphasized in this section how the interaction between different knowledge and beliefs categories affects PCK, and how we can find traces of the original general knowledge and beliefs categories in PCK or in a particular TPC. However, there are indications that the original beliefs, in particular, are not only part and parcel of PCK, but that certain beliefs are more favorable than others to the development of rich PCK. Hashweh (1985), using a qualitative approach, found that teachers holding construc-tivist beliefs about knowledge and learning are cognizant of their students' prior ideas and alternative conceptions related to a certain topic, while teachers holding empiricist beliefs were not aware of the students' characteristics related to the same topic. In a later study that employed a more quantitative approach (Hashweh, 1996), he reached a similar conclusion: teachers holding constructivist views have developed richer PCK compared to empiricist teachers. Masalmeh (1998) replicated these findings when studying secondary school chemistry teachers. It seems that, not only does PCK have a beliefs component, but that certain beliefs are more favorable than others to the development of rich PCK.

Pedagogical Constructions Have Components of Both Generalized Event-Based and Story-Based Memories

We should not be led to believe that the neat organization of knowledge represented in the figures really represents teachers' TPCs; this representation, extracted from teachers' responses to tasks that examined their planning using thinking-aloud and stimulated recall techniques, or that examined their teaching using the critical-incident technique, enforces an order on teacher knowledge for analytic purposes. It emphasizes the general event-based memory for TPCs. The concept of event-based memory proposed by Schank (2000) is similar to the familiar concept of semantic memory long used in cognitive psychology. It refers to the continuous updating and organization of our general knowledge base through experience. Teachers seem to develop a schema, or a script, that organizes and stores their memory for any single TPC. Restaurant goers develop restaurant scripts that describe their experience – it allows them to comprehend the series of events, to predict what will happen, and to exhibit the proper conduct. Similarly, a teacher who teaches a topic regularly develops a script that describes the typical sequence of events in teaching the material. Among other things, the teacher comes to know in advance what knowledge, alternative conceptions, and interests the typical student brings to the study of the topic, what difficulties he or she will face, and how best to engage these prior ideas and confront difficulties. He or she knows what knowledge representations to use, and how to use them.

In reality, however, teacher knowledge is more undifferentiated and has a narrative or story-based character as well. Schank (2000) has proposed that we disconnect events when we update our general knowledge categories (event-based memory); "actual experiences are constantly being broken up into their component pieces and are being added to general event memory bit by bit in different places [and] no coherent whole remains" (p. 122). In contrast, story-based memory allows us to remember events in sequence.

According to Shank, "story-based knowledge expresses our points of view
and philosophy of life and, as it comes from experience, is closer in spirit to
what psychologists have meant when they have spoken of episodic memory"
(Schank, 2000, p. 125). Analogies, examples, films, the purposes for using
them, and the way they are used are all intertwined in a narrative, a story
that the teacher remembers about teaching a certain topic. For example,
analogies and examples are not separated in the teacher's mind from the way
they are used in class. We have seen this previously when the biology teacher
talked about the analogies she uses – she described the analogy, the typical
exchange with her students when she uses it, and her feelings about it. The
teacher spotlighted earlier actually mentioned four analogies that she uses to
help her students understand the role of ATP and how it functions when
teaching photosynthesis (Hashweh, 1985). The description of the analogies,
and more generally the knowledge representations, their use, and the typical
conversation that takes place in class was common to all teachers in the
study, and not unique to this one. The following excerpt has to do with the
use of the first analogy.

> I do things very physically when I'm talking to them ... and when I'm talking about this
> I say, "OK, here's a carbon and here's a carbon. And how am I gonna get them
> together?" [She brings her fists together pretending she has to exert an effort to overcome
> the repulsion they have for each other]. They say, "You're gonna push them." I say,
> "OK, now what do I have here? I have a bond. OK, now could you come up here, please,
> could you break these two hands apart?" And the kids will go like this, and my hands
> will fly apart. And I say, "What just got released?" And they say, "Energy." (Hashweh,
> 1985, p. 292)

Teacher pedagogical constructions are cases of repeated experiences of
teaching a familiar topic. In my opinion (see Hashweh, 2004) they represent
an intertwining of knowledge categories that are usually conceived as
separate and contrasting – dualisms that emphasize sharp conceptual
distinctions with clear boundaries: theoretical versus practical knowledge,
declarative versus procedural knowledge, research versus narration, emotion versus cognition. Those of us who have listened to teachers narrate their
stories of professional practice have become skeptical about these dualisms.
If anything, teacher professional constructions reveal the importance of
border crossing, of intertwining the practical and the theoretical, emotion
and cognition, research or systematic investigations and narration. Recently,
Gudmundsdottir's (2001) use of the term narrative research challenges the
traditional distinction between research and narrative. Schank (2000) finds
limitations with the traditional episodic/semantic distinction in cognitive
psychology, and proposed the distinction I used above between story-based

memory and generalized event-based memory. Schank (2000), however, makes it clear that even this distinction does not always hold. In the case of a teacher pedagogical construction the teacher knows what preconceptions exist, and what anomalies can be used to confront them (generalized scripts) but he might also remember what happened the last time he used them with a specific student (story-based memory).

Pedagogical Constructions are Topic-Specific Cases, Yet Labeled in Multiple Interesting Ways

Assertions 6 and 7, taken together, portray a picture of each TPC as, first of all, being mainly connected in memory to a certain topic that the teacher regularly uses. This explains why some researchers considered PCK as a subcategory of subject matter knowledge. Each topic acts as an index or label that helps the teacher recall the associated TPC when required: photosynthesis is a label that triggers the photosynthesis TPC in memory.

However, the topic is just the surface feature of the TPC. There are other more interesting features of the TPC that allow it to be used in other situations. These are the labels exemplified by the relations between the TPC and other general categories of teacher knowledge and beliefs. A teacher might use the students' characteristics category, or, specifically, the alternative misconceptions subcategory, to remind him of specific misconceptions about photosynthesis – knowledge that is stored in the Photosynthesis TPC. The label in this case was student alternative conceptions, and not photosynthesis in the teacher's subject matter category. However, we should not be led to believe that there is a close one-to-one correspondence between each subcategory of a TPC and the corresponding general category of teacher knowledge for all teachers. There are probably many different interesting ways that teachers relate a TPC to other entities in their memory. This depends on how teachers label or index (Schank, 2000) their TPCs.

We can view the relations between a TPC and other knowledge and beliefs categories as representing relations in an event-based general memory and as representing relations in semantic memory. In the second case, they represent a logical relation; for instance, between the general pedagogical category (using anomalous examples to confront alternative conceptions) and a specific TPC (using a specific demonstration to show that only the tip of a plant's stem grows and not all the stem, for example).

On the other hand, when teachers store their TPC in a story-based manner then the key to using it in new novel situations, when there are no available scripts to use, is in labeling it in a clever manner. In this case, the teacher thinks analogically, from the concrete past experience to the new novel concrete situation. He or she has to remember a past precedent and see it as a precedent. As Schank (2000) suggests, to remember something someone would have to have cleverly labeled it in the first place. One way to do this is to reflect on the original experience, to mull over it, and to see it as a case of something, that is, to label it. Telling the story to others also is crucially important because it preserves it in memory as a single unit. Otherwise, the components of this event or story would be used to update our knowledge in other categories, and the unity of the event would be lost (see Schank, 2000, for a detailed treatment of this point). Consequently, we see that storing the TPC in a story-based manner is important since it allows us to use it in future novel situations. However, to store it as a story one has to label it and to inform others about it.

Whether a TPC is stored as general event-based (scripts or schemas), or as stories, the main determinant for its future use is its integration into the memory structure of the teacher, the organization of this memory, and the labeling of these TPC. Teachers use a TPC when it is well-connected to other memory entities, when it is labeled in multiple interesting ways.

OTHER RECENT TRENDS IN PCK RESEARCH

The conceptualization of PCK has guided scholars at my institution in documenting the PCK of some science and mathematics teachers about the teaching of specific topics (Adawi, 2008; Haddad, 2008; Hamdeh, 2008; Mrebei, 2007), and we have represented some topic-specific PCK as interactive electronic cases which we use in teacher education. We have found that even good teachers selected by the use of prior screening procedures (including questionnaires of epistemological beliefs and tests of subject matter knowledge) have pedagogical constructions which are lacking in some dimensions. The construction of a group topic-specific PCK, advocated by Loughran et al. (2012), can remedy this. Another solution is to use professional development to develop the PCK of the participating teachers, an approach that is further explicated later in this chapter.

Ball, Thames, and Phelps (2008) took a different route to investigating the nature of PCK. Paying closer attention to Shulman's categorization of PCK as a subcategory of teacher knowledge in his 1986 article, and less attention to the topic-specificity of PCK, the group identified "pure" subject matter knowledge in mathematics that is exclusive to the teaching of school mathematics. Taking a third route, other researchers, including Baumert et al. (2010), investigated the effect of well-developed teacher PCK on student achievement. We have investigated the relation between teacher PCK about density and student achievement and found modest correlations between the two (Habbas, 2009). This endeavor is needed since the conceptualization has tended to rely more on normative, rather than empirical, grounds. Additionally, it addresses the need to study teacher knowledge in its relations to student learning outcomes, that is, it constitutes a return to the process–product paradigm in research on teaching, albeit with a more sophisticated approach taking into consideration teacher and student cognition, on the one hand, and the domain specificity of teaching, on the other hand. These works continue the theoretical development, analytic clarification, and empirical testing of the construct which is taking place in the last decade.

TEACHER PROFESSIONAL DEVELOPMENT

Research on teacher professional development has a long history starting with the traditional top-down models of the 1970s to the new models based on teacher research and the building of teacher professional learning communities. The following table compares the two patterns of development (Table 3).

Consensus has been reached in the literature that professional development should provide opportunities for teachers to collaborate in

Table 3. Traditional and Modern Approaches of Professional Development.

Traditional Approach	Modern Approach
Externally imposed, obligatory	Internally motivated, voluntary
Emphasis on scientific/theoretical knowledge	Emphasis on practical knowledge
Focus on generic teaching methods	Focus on content and student learning
Funding external experts	Funding practitioners themselves
Teacher as technician	Teacher as professional
Development via learning products of research	Development via collaborative action research
Individual development	Community of learners
Disempowering teachers	Empowering teachers
One-shot workshops	Continuous development

professional communities (Borko, Jacobs, & Koellner, 2010). Additionally, models that describe teacher learning in different kinds of professional development programs have been proposed. Guskey (2002) proposed a linear model that starts with professional development activities affecting changes in teachers' classroom practices, which, in turn, affect changes in student learning outcomes, and, when the latter occurs, this leads to changes in teachers' beliefs and attitudes. L. Shulman and Shulman (2002) proposed a more interactive model that emphasizes learning from experience through reflection and which connects individual, community, and institutional levels of interaction. Other researchers have used models to describe the learning that occurs, such as the Kolb Cycle (concrete experience, reflective observation, abstract conceptualization, active experimentation), Shulmans' (2004) Table of Learning (engagement, understanding, action, reflection, judgment, commitment), Bell and Gilbert's (1996) model for science teachers in particular, or Clarke and Hollingsworth's (2002) cyclical model of reflection and enactment. Recent reviews of science teachers' professional development and learning (Simon & Campbell, 2012; Wallace & Loughran, 2012) also emphasize individual reflection, group deliberations and collaborations, interactions between teacher knowledge and beliefs, on the one hand, and teaching practices, on the other hand, and teacher research as keys to learning and development.

However, in spite of these developments in research on teacher learning and professional development, many researchers are dissatisfied with the current state of affairs. Feiman-Nemser (2008) has pointed to the need for more conceptual work on the content, mechanisms, and contexts of teacher learning, and "more thoughtful efforts to link teacher learning to meaningful student learning" (p. 704). Wilson and Berne (1999) stated that, in order to better understand teacher learning, we need to "weave together ideas of teacher learning, professional development, teacher knowledge and student learning – fields that have largely operated independent of one another" (p. 104). Vescio, Ross, and Adams (2008) have found that there is limited research evidence on the effects of teacher participation in professional learning communities.

In addition to this, in my opinion, research on teacher learning and development (as described in the models earlier) still views teacher learning as a generic activity and neglects the domain or discipline specificity of teacher learning and development. This is surprising in view of Shulman's call to study the teaching and learning of specific subject matter in the 1980s, and the contribution of this call to the development of the concept of PCK. The neglect of discipline specificity is also surprising in light of the recent dominance of socio-cultural theories of learning and teaching. A socio-cultural approach would emphasize the interactions between what teachers bring to a situation and what they encounter, including the contexts of teacher learning. Basing teacher professional development on an important component of what teachers bring, namely their PCK, would address the significant neglect of subject matter in models of teacher professional development.

There has been a call recently for basing professional development on PCK and a debate concerning how PCK could be used in professional development activities (Bausmith & Barry, 2011; Van Driel & Berry, 2012). The approach proposed here is closer to that of Van Driel and Berry in that it acknowledges the complexity of PCK and its development. Basing professional development on PCK would also have added advantages. It has been pointed out that previous models explained teacher learning and development generically using the construct of reflection as the main mechanism for learning from experience and from professional development activities. The concept of PCK would address the interactions between prior teacher knowledge of subject matter, orientation to subject matter knowledge and beliefs about knowledge and learning, among other components of what teachers bring, and teacher learning. Previous research which I (Hashweh, 1985, 1996) conducted indicates that teachers with specific characteristics (rich subject matter knowledge and constructivist epistemological beliefs) had higher aptitude to learn from experience and to develop richer PCK. In another article (Hashweh, 2003), I described the details of the interaction between prior knowledge, experience, and new knowledge for a science teacher. A similar approach is needed to model teacher learning and professional development while developing topic specific PCK, and this would be beneficial to both research domains – research in PCK and on teacher learning and professional development.

CONCLUSION

In this chapter I have reviewed developments in research based on the PCK conceptualization, and presented a view of PCK as a collection of Teacher Professional Constructions, a form of knowledge that preserves the planning and wisdom of practice that the teacher acquires when repeatedly teaching a certain topic and that simultaneously integrates this knowledge with the theoretical knowledge in Education. Viewing PCK as a collection of TPCs, and basing teacher professional development on sharing and enhancing participating teachers' TPCs should allow us to better investigate and model teacher learning and professional development and to better design these programs.

REFERENCES

Adawi, S. (2008). Mathematics teachers' pedagogical content knowledge of the algebra unit in grade eight: A case study. Unpublished master's thesis. Birzeit University, Birzeit, Palestine.

Ball, D. L., Thames, M. H., & Phelps, G. C. (2008). Content knowledge for teaching: What makes it special? *Journal of Teacher Education, 59*(5), 389–407.

Baumert, J., Kunter, M., Blum, W., Brunner, M., Voss, T., Jordan, A., ... Tsai, Y. (2010). Teachers' mathematical knowledge, cognitive activation in the classroom, and student progress. *American Educational Research Journal, 47*(1), 133–180.

Bausmith, J. M., & Barry, C. (2011). Revisiting professional learning communities to increase college readiness: The importance of pedagogical content knowledge. *Educational Researcher, 40*(4), 175–178.

Bell, B., & Gilbert, J. (1996). *Teacher development: A model from science education.* London: Routledge Falmer.

Borko, H., Jacobs, J., & Koellner, K. (2010). Contemporary approaches to teacher professional development. In B. McGraw, P. L. Peterson & E. Baker (Eds.), *International encyclopedia of education* (3rd ed., Vol. 7, pp. 548–556). Oxford: Elsevier.

Clark, C., & Peterson, P. (1986). Teachers' thought processes. In M. Wittrock (Ed.), *Handbook of research on teaching* (3rd ed., pp. 255–296). New York, NY: Macmillan.

Clarke, D., & Hollingsworth, H. (2002). Elaborating a model of teacher professional growth. *Teaching and Teacher education, 18*(8), 947–967.

Cochran, K., DeRuiter, J., & King, R. (1993). Pedagogical content knowing: An integrative model for teacher preparation. *Journal of Teacher Education, 44*(4), 263–271.

Feiman-Nemser, S. (2008). Teacher learning: How do teachers learn to teach? In M. Cochran-Smith, S. Feiman-Nemser & D. J. McIntyre (Eds.), *Handbook of research on teacher education* (3rd ed., pp. 697–705). New York, NY: Routledge.

Fernandez-Balboa, J-M., & Stieh, J. (1995). The generic nature of pedagogical content knowledge among college professors. *Teaching and Teacher Education, 11*(3), 293–306.

Grossman, P., Wilson, S., & Shulman, L. (1989). Teachers of substance: Subject matter knowledge for teaching. In M. Reynolds (Ed.), *Knowledge base for the beginning teacher* (pp. 23–36). New York, NY: Pergamon Press.

Grossman, P. L. (1990). *The making of a teacher: Teacher knowledge and teacher education.* New York, NY: Teachers College Press.

Gudmundsdottir, S. (1990). Values in pedagogical content knowledge. *Journal of Teacher Education, 41*(3), 44–52.

Gudmundsdottir, S. (1995). The narrative nature of pedagogical content knowledge. In H. McEwan & K. Egan (Eds.), *Narrative in teaching, learning and research* (pp. 24–38). New York, NY: Teachers College Press.

Gudmundsdottir, S. (2001). Narrative research on school practice. In V. Richardson (Ed.), *Handbook of research on teaching* (4th ed., pp. 226–240). Washington, DC: AERA.

Guskey, T. (2002). Professional development and teacher change. *Teachers and Teaching: Theory and Practice, 8*(3/4), 381–391.

Habbas, M. (2009). *Effects of teachers' PCK about density on student achievement in seventh grade.* Unpublished master's thesis. Birzeit University, Birzeit, Palestine.

Haddad, S. (2008). *Pedagogical content knowledge of science teachers about chemical reactions in grade eight: A case study.* Unpublished master's thesis. Birzeit University, Birzeit, Palestine.

Hamdeh, A. (2008). Science teachers' pedagogical content knowledge about teaching the wave motion unit in grade eight: A case study. Unpublished master's thesis. Birzeit University, Birzeit, Palestine.

Hashweh, M. (1985). *An exploratory study of teacher knowledge and teaching: The effects of science teachers' knowledge of their subject matter and their conceptions of learning on their teaching.* Unpublished doctoral dissertation. Stanford Graduate School of Education, Stanford, CA.

Hashweh, M. (1996). Effects of science teachers' beliefs in teaching. *Journal of Research in Science Teaching, 33*(1), 47–63.

Hashweh, M. (2004). Case writing as border-crossing: describing, understanding and promoting teacher change. *Teachers and Teaching: Theory and Practice, 10*(3), 244–246.

Hashweh, M. (2003). Teacher accommodative change. *Teaching and Teacher Education, 19,* 421–434.

Hashweh, M. (2005). Teacher pedagogical constructions: A reconfiguration of pedagogical content knowledge. *Teachers and Teaching: Theory and Practice, 11*(3), 273–292.

Loughran, J., Berry, A., & Mulhall, P. (2012). *Understanding and developing science pedagogical content knowledge* (2nd ed.). Rotterdam: Sense Publishers.

Loughran, J., Milroy, P., Berry, A., Gunstone, R., & Mulhal, P. (2001). Documenting science teachers' pedagogical content knowledge through PaP-eRs. *Research in Science Education, 31*(2), 289–307.

Marks, R. (1990). Pedagogical content knowledge: From a mathematical case to a modified conception. *Journal of Teacher Education, 41*(3), 3–11.

Masalmeh, J. (1998). *Effects of teachers' epistemological beliefs on their pedagogical content knowledge.* Unpublished master's thesis, Birzeit University, Birzeit, Palestine.

McCutcheon, G., & Milner, H. R. (2002). A contemporary study of teacher planning in a high school English class. *Teachers and Teaching: Theory and Practice, 8*(1), 81–94.

Milner, H. R. (2003). A case study of an African American English teacher's cultural comprehensive knowledge and self-reflective planning. *Journal of Curriculum and Supervision, 18*(2), 175–196.

Mrebei, W. (2007). *Mathematics teachers' pedagogical content knowledge of a geometry unit in grade eight: A case study.* Unpublished master's thesis. Birzeit University, Birzeit, Palestine.

Richardson, V. (Ed.). (2001). *Handbook of research on teaching* (4th ed.). Washington, DC: AERA.

Schank, R. (2000). *Tell me a story: Narrative and intelligence.* Evanston, IL: Northwestern University Press.

Shulman, L. (1986a). Those who understand: Knowledge growth in teaching. *Educational Researcher, 15*(2), 4–14.

Shulman, L. (1986b). Paradigms and research programs in the study of teaching: A contemporary perspective. In M. Wittrock (Ed.), *Handbook of research on teaching* (3rd ed.). New York: Macmillan.

Shulman, L. (1987). Knowledge and teaching: Foundations of the new reform. *Harvard Educational Review, 57*(1), 1–22.

Shulman, L. S. (2004). Making differences: A table of learning. *Change, 34*(6), 36–44.

Shulman, L., & Shulman, J. (2002). How and what teachers learn: A shifting perspective. *Journal of Curriculum Studies, 36*(2), 257–271.

Simon, S., & Campbell, S. (2012). Teacher learning and professional development in science education. In B. J. Fraser, K. G. Tobin & C. J. McRobbie (Eds.), *Second international handbook of science education* (pp. 307–321). Dordrecht: Springer.

Strike, K., & Posner, G. (1992). A revisionist theory of conceptual change. In R. Duschl & R. Hamilton (Eds.), *Philosophy of science, cognitive psychology, and educational theory and practice*. Albany, NY: State University of New York.

Van Driel, J., Verloop, N., & De Vos, W. (1998). Developing science teachers' pedagogical content knowledge. *Journal of Research in Science Teaching, 35*(6), 673–695.

Van Driel, J. H., & Berry, A. (2010). Pedagogical content knowledge. In B. McGraw, P. L. Peterson & E. Baker (Eds.), *International encyclopedia of education* (3rd ed., Vol. 7, pp. 656–661). Oxford: Elsevier.

Van Driel, J. H., & Berry, A. (2012). Teacher professional development focusing on pedagogical content knowledge. *Educational Researcher, 41*(1), 26–28.

Vescio, V., Ross, D., & Adams, A. (2008). A review of research on the impact of professional learning communities on teaching practice and student learning. *Teaching and Teacher education, 24*(1), 80–91.

Wallace, J., & Loughran, J. (2012). Science teacher learning. In B. J. Fraser, K. G. Tobin & C. J. McRobbie (Eds.), *Second international handbook of science education* (pp. 295–306). Dordrecht: Springer.

Wilson, S. M., & Berne, J. (1999). Teacher learning and the acquisition of professional knowledge: An examination of research on contemporary professional development. In A. Iran-Nejad & P. D. Pearson (Eds.), *Review of research in education* (Vol. 24, pp. 173–209). Washington, DC: American Educational Research Association.

Wittrock, M. (1986). *Handbook of research on teaching* (3rd ed.). New York, NY: Macmillan.

Yinger, R. (1977). *A study of teacher planning: Description and theory development using ethnographic and information processing methods*. Unpublished doctoral dissertation. Michigan State University, East Lansing.

CHAPTER 7

STORY-MAKER, STORYTELLER: NARRATIVE STRUCTURES IN CURRICULUM [*]

Sigrun Gudmundsdottir[†]

ABSTRACT

This chapter explains pedagogical content knowledge as a narrative way of knowing. It describes how narratives serve as a means of explaining that understanding to others. It discusses two San Francisco (California) high school teachers' use of narrative in teaching. It concludes that, because teaching is like writing a story, understanding teaching is like interpreting a story.

Keywords: High school students; pedagogical content knowledge; personal narratives; secondary education; story telling; teacher–student relationship; teaching methods; teaching styles

Classrooms are places where stories are told. Textbooks tell stories and teachers bring stories to tell, stories about the subject matter they teach, or curriculum stories. These stories are narratives that organize the curriculum

---

[*]This article was first published in 1991, *Journal of Curriculum Studies*, Vol. 23(3), p. 207–218. Reprinted with permission from the publisher, Taylor & Francis Ltd, www.tandfonline.com.
[†]Deceased

From Teacher Thinking to Teachers and Teaching: The Evolution of a Research Community
Advances in Research on Teaching, Volume 19, 141–156
Copyright © 2013 Taylor & Francis Ltd
All rights of reproduction in any form reserved
ISSN: 1479-3687/doi:10.1108/S1479-3687(2013)0000019010

and are communicated in the classroom throughout the school year. Curriculum stories also generate numerous shorter stories that teachers tell as explanations or illustrations of a larger idea. These stories are part of a narrative way of knowing that is basic to the ways in which human beings understand the world and communicate that understanding to others. In this chapter I explain pedagogical content knowledge as a narrative way of knowing, and describe how narratives serve as a way of explaining that understanding to others. I tell a story about the stories two history teachers have created about their subject matter, stories they tell their students. These two teachers are atypical in many ways, but they are the subject of this story because their stories and the way in which they use narrative in teaching serve to illuminate my thesis. The characters of my story are two experienced history teachers who teach history in a San Francisco Bay Area high school. They are master story-makers and storytellers. In fact, I have come to believe that their excellence as teachers is mostly due to the storied nature of their pedagogical content knowledge and the interesting stories they tell their students.

Narratives have recently emerged as an important unit of analysis among social scientists. Several publications mark this entrance of narratives on the scholarly scene, especially Bruner's (1986) *Actual Minds, Possible Worlds,* Polkinghorne's (1988) *Narrative Knowing and the Human Sciences* and Sarbin's (1986) *Narrative Psychology: The Storied Nature of Human Conduct.* In educational research, recent publications by Connelly and Clandinin (1986, 1990), Elbaz (1981, 1991) and McEwan (1990) demonstrate the growing interest among the educational research community in understanding this basic way of knowing and teaching.

Stories are part of our identity and our culture. We create stories about ourselves that we communicate in various ways to our colleagues. This self-narrative enables us to construe who we are and where we are heading in our lives. At the cultural level narratives give cohesion to shared beliefs. As members of a culture we are at the receiving end of all kinds of stories: verbal, written, or visual. Barthes (quoted by Polkinghorne, 1988, p. 14) observes that 'the narrative is present at all times, in all places, in all societies, the history of narrative begins with the history of mankind; there does not exist, and there never has existed a people without narratives'.

Stories are the result of a narrative way of knowing. Bruner (1986) suggests that there are two fundamental ways of knowing. One is the 'paradigmatic' way, the search for universal truth conditions. This way is primarily the province of the natural and physical sciences. The other fundamental way of perceiving and knowing about the world, according to

Bruner, is the 'narrative', which looks for particular connections between events. Narrative ordering makes individual events comprehensible by identifying the whole to which they contribute and the effect one has on another. Bruner (1986, p. 13) observes that the 'imaginative application of the narrative mode leads to good stories, gripping drama, believable (though not necessarily "true") historical accounts'.

STORIES MADE AND STORIES TOLD

I want to suggest that the narrative is many teachers' solution to a special teachers' problem; that is, translating 'knowing into telling' (Whyte, 1981). Teachers achieve this by activating two types of stories, curriculum stories and shorter stories, told as explanations and illustrations. The relationship between the curriculum stories and the shorter stories can be understood in terms of Jakobson's (1956) theory of the poetic function of language. Developing Saussure's ideas of *parole* and *langue,* Jakobson identified two axes functioning in poetic language: a vertical axis, which he calls the 'selective dimension', and a horizontal axis which he calls the 'combinative dimension'. In narratives, the combinative dimension moves the story along, and the selective dimension selects significant or important elements out of an unorganized or semi-organized experience. Even though Jakobson developed these concepts to explain the poetic function of language, they appear in all uses of language, including narratives (Hawkes, 1977). The curriculum story functions like the horizontal axis, providing continuity and structure to content throughout the school year; the shorter stories that are explanations, illustrations, or examples function like the vertical axis. The horizontal narrative selects significant short stories that can move the story line along.

Research on teaching and curriculum supports the idea that teachers use an organizing horizontal principle in the curriculum. Such an organizing principle has been called a 'major idea' (Yinger, 1977) and 'curriculum potential' (Ben-Peretz, 1975). These two conceptions are related to the curriculum story in that they recognize the fact that curriculum materials include far more ideas than the developers intended. The idea of a curriculum story, however, goes beyond identifying a potential or a major idea in the curriculum. It develops the organizing principles through the story schema.

Thus, the curriculum story is a narrative device that helps history teachers to unify theory, themes and specific events or facts into larger units. It has characters, it has a beginning, a middle, and an end, and is told through the curriculum throughout the school year. Curriculum theorists and teachers with an eye for the practical application of good ideas have advocated the use of stories for individual curriculum units (Egan, 1988, Marshall, 1963, Paley, 1981, 1990). A student teacher in social studies has been observed trying to impose meaning on a required curriculum that was essentially meaningless to him (Gudmundsdottir & Shulman, 1987). Meaning in the curriculum, according to the student teacher, was creating a narrative, a curriculum story for individual units. The motivation for the student teacher was that he did not agree with the freshman (grade 9) social-studies curriculum he was required to teach. His stories were his attempts to 'repair' the curriculum. He was trying to progress from a 'bad' story to one he felt was more complete and convincing. Being a cultural anthropologist, he found his convincing story by placing 'Man' at the centre of his narrative. His success in creating meaning in his curriculum was not a matter of being a storyteller. Instead, it was a matter of reorganizing content he knew well and adapting it to his story schema (Gudmundsdottir, 1990).

Not all stories take the full school year to develop. Teachers also tell shorter stories as examples, explanations, or illustrations – these are the vertical axes. The shorter stories are related to, or generated by, the curriculum stories teachers use. Excellent teachers have been reported using them effectively in the classroom (Tierney, 1988). Ball (in press) describes how an excellent experienced elementary teacher, Magdalene Lampert, taught multiplication through stories and illustrations generated by herself and her students. Jackson (1986) has a prominent place for stories and storytelling in his alternative outlook on teaching. The excellent teachers that are his exemplars as 'teacher-as-storyteller' are Socrates and Jesus, Joseph's son, from Nazareth. If these types of shorter stories are to serve their function, they need to relate to a larger whole, that is, the curriculum story.

Narratives are constructed through the story schema and reflection. The story schema is defined as 'a mental structure consisting of sets of expectations about the way in which stories proceed' (Mandler, 1984, p. 18). It identifies categories and relationships between categories (Robinson & Hawpe, 1986). Narrative thinking involves matching a problem, situation, or an idea to the story schema. It is a heuristic process, 'one which requires skill, judgement, and experience' (Robinson & Hawpe, 1986, p. 111).

The story schema is, in many ways, a natural choice for educators. Teachers know stories because we are all surrounded by stories from birth to the grave, and we need the narrative to understand, explain, and find meaning in experience (Early, 1982, Coles, 1989). The stories we hear throughout our lives are full of regularities that we have incorporated into a story schema used to organize experience (Mandler, 1984). The story schema is also practical because it helps us to remember. Mandler's (1984) studies show that a recall of stories one, two and three weeks later improved considerably from week one to two, and then only slightly declined in week three. The improved recall over time indicates, according to Mandler, that there is a story schema embedded in our mind and, with time, new information becomes more dependent upon this schema. In the classroom, this narrative way of organizing knowledge and remembering lends itself to story-making and story-telling, examples of which can be observed in teaching, especially among excellent experienced teachers.

Teachers are probably unaware of the curriculum stories they use – at least the experienced teachers in this study were unaware that they used this mode of organizing the curriculum. They discovered their curriculum stories only when they had to explain their curriculum to someone who had limited experience with US high schools. Teachers probably spend their entire careers developing their stories (short and long) as they encounter different kinds of courses and students. Unlike Athena, who leaped out of Zeus's head as a mature woman, curriculum stories take several years to develop, a process that will never end as long as the teachers continue to grow and develop professionally. Each year, teachers have the opportunity to modify and shape their stories to take into account new understanding or insight. Some aspects of each curriculum story are found to be successful and they may grow stronger. Others are not successful and they grow weaker or disappear altogether.

The stories teachers make and tell their students are not like traditional stories such as myths, legends, or fairy tales. Their content is the subject matter, and their structure is different from those traditional stories, yet including enough similarities to qualify as a story. Stein and Policastro (1983) have argued that no single structural definition can account for the wide range of compositions people accept as stories. They suggest that our story concept should consist of a prototype and its variants. This concept is the foundation for pedagogical content knowledge as a narrative way of knowing.

NARRATIVE KNOWING AND PEDAGOGICAL CONTENT KNOWLEDGE

Experienced teachers often have a unique understanding of the content they teach. Shulman (1987) calls this way of knowing 'pedagogical content knowledge'. It is a practical way of knowing, and like many practical ways of knowing it has a storied nature. Pedagogical content knowledge is, in Shulman's words, 'that special amalgam of pedagogy and content that is uniquely the province of teachers'. The 'amalgam of pedagogy and content' that Shulman refers to, has obviously been facilitated by practical teaching experience. Yet, teacher education has traditionally presented to student teachers (at the secondary level) content knowledge and pedagogy in separate units. They take methods courses and subject-matter courses to beef up their lack of content knowledge in the subjects they expect to teach.

Pedagogical content knowledge is the experienced teacher's way of knowing the subject matter. Even though this concept has captured the attention of researchers on both sides of the Atlantic, there are great gaps in our knowledge. There are several studies of novice teachers (Grossman, Wilson, & Shulman, 1989, Reynolds, Haymore, Ringstaff, & Grossman, 1988, Wilson, Shulman, & Richert, 1987) and fewer studies of experienced teachers who have taught for more than two decades (Gudmundsdottir, 1988, Leinhardt & Smith, 1985). The studies of novice teachers show them struggling with restructuring their content knowledge, trying to make it more 'pedagogical'. For example, drawing on his developing pedagogical content knowledge, one novice teacher is described as 'trying to come up with a story' (Gudmundsdottir & Shulman, 1987, Gudmundsdottir, 1990). His stories, however, last for only one unit. The following unit has a new story that has little or no connection with the previous one.

The studies of experienced, excellent teachers describe sophisticated pedagogical content knowledge. These teachers have developed a way of knowing that enables them to function effectively and efficiently in the classroom. The difference between the pedagogical content knowledge of promising novices and excellent, experienced teachers is striking, and raises important questions about how such teachers learned what they know. Since there are no longitudinal studies describing the 20-year-long march from novitiate to excellence, one can only speculate.

High-school teachers usually have one important starting point in their teaching career, the subject matter they studied in college. As Rashdall (1936, Vol. 3, p. 324) observed in his history of the medieval universities of Europe, disciplines are basically pedagogical structures. The disciplines as we know them today, according to Rashdall, came about because of the need to organize knowledge for teaching. Although educational researchers have chosen to ignore this, most teachers probably do not. For many novice teachers, the subject matter is what they start out with, for better or for worse (Grossman & Gudmundsdottir, 1987). If content knowledge and pedagogical knowledge integrate and create the more powerful and practical pedagogical content knowledge, novice teachers have a great deal to learn, especially in pedagogical knowledge. They learn on the job, trying things out and learning from other teachers, and if one considers the difference between novice teachers and experienced teachers, inexperienced teachers must learn a great deal.

Listening to other teachers' stories is one important way of such learning. The stories teachers tell each other about their practice have been called 'recipe knowledge' (Huberman, 1983). Such practical knowledge is not accepted uncritically; however, it has to 'undergo an intuitive test – how the message or product feels or fits – before it is tried out in the classroom' (Huberman, 1983, p. 484). One does not have to spend a long time in the teachers' lounge to hear them swap stories about 'what worked for me when I had Jimmy in my class'. These stories tend to be about cases, a case being a difficult child, a good class, mathematics materials, reading books, a topic, or group work. Case knowledge is characteristic of practitioners who work with people. Polkinghorne (1988, p. x) notes 'that practitioners work with narrative knowledge ... They work with case histories and use narrative explanations to understand why the people they work with behave the way they do'. Teachers are not the only practitioners who work with such case knowledge: lawyers and physicians do, as well as third-world midwives. The third-world midwives studied by Jordan (1989, p. 935) have a knowledge-base of case stories that are 'packages of situated knowledge, knowledge that is not known abstractly, but is called up as the characteristics of the situation require it'. Narratives, as I describe them below, are carriers of the 'core understanding' that teachers have of 'content' converted into vehicles for teaching.

CREATING NARRATIVES IN THE CLASSROOM

As I have already noted, my story is about two high-school social-studies teachers who teach in the same school in Northern California. This story serves to explain how I believe experienced teachers know their subject matter and how they use narratives in the classroom. The story focuses on the curriculum in one of the courses each of them taught. The teachers were interviewed five and six times, and observed teaching twenty and twenty-two times. Harry and David are considered to be excellent teachers by colleagues and students. After spending four intensive months in their classrooms,

I agree. They teach junior (grade 11) students US history. Harry teaches 'general track' students and David teaches Advanced Placement (AP) students.[1] They are veterans, having taught social studies for 37 and 28 years respectively.

Harry and David, and indeed almost all teachers, use textbooks. These texts tell stories that are not always accepted as valid by teachers. Harry and David have their own agenda for their curricula that often conflict with the textbooks they use. They consider their textbooks to be far from perfect; Harry calls his book 'bad history', and David claims he uses it like a 'dictionary'. Their stories are their attempts to transform an inadequate story into a more complete, compelling and convincing one. To create a better story they bring to class additional curriculum materials, and they apply their stories, curriculum stories, and the shorter stories, to this incomplete story.

David teaches a US history class. The curriculum in his class reflects the official AP programme. David's aim is to help his students pass the AP examination, and, at the same time, he wants to provide them with an experience that is equivalent to a college or university freshman (first-year) course. David had divided the curriculum into historical periods that reflect a traditional chronological organization. He structures the course content with stories. He tells four stories that all start with the Age of Jackson (1828–1836): *Women, Reform, Supreme Court Cases* and *Wars.* The stories cover the whole curriculum and are told throughout the school year. At different times, David calls upon the stories to explain and illuminate the topics he wants to cover.

One of David's stories, *Wars,* can serve as an example of how he uses stories. According to David, it is the most important story. Like all his stories, this one begins during the Age of Jackson. David's story *Wars* is a peace-activist's story. In this story, he explores the causes of wars and how war escalates from a local affair, as in America's nineteenth-century Civil War, to total destruction of life on earth. His story begins by exploring eight different interpretations for the causes of the Civil War. (David has in his private curriculum collection a photocopy of an article that presents eight different interpretations for the causes of this war.) He tells the students about the dramatic events leading to the Civil War. The characters are the politicians, the industrialists and common people whose lives were affected. The story is about a local war, the Civil War. This means that, while the Civil War was a devastating experience for many Americans, large parts of the country and the rest of the world were unaffected. He tells them about Antietem, the bloodiest battle of the war, non-military factors, and foreign policy. The characters are the common soldiers, the generals, the politicians, and women and children who suffered.

David's personal values as a peace activist influence his selection of events during the period he identifies as the Civil War. He covers only one battle with the class, and the idea he wants to highlight is that war is a bloody affair and people die. The day before, he prepares the students for discussion by handing out a pie chart showing American casualties on the battlefield in all the wars Americans have fought. The pie chart shows percentages, but it does not tell which wars the slices represent. The students' assignment is to figure that out. The following day, David opens the discussion of Antietam by focusing on the enormous casualties and the fact that neither side won this battle, a subtle and powerful message of a peace activist about the futility of war. During the next two periods, Reconstruction and Imperialism, the *Wars* story steps into the sidelines, only to make a grand appearance in the next three periods, the First World War, Intermission and the Second World War, where it becomes the story. Local war is now total war, and David brings back his eight interpretations for the causes of the Civil War and looks at the causes for the two World Wars. This time, the focus is on the role of propaganda in escalating and spreading conflict, so that now war means total war. The end of David's curriculum story is about the nuclear arms race, *Star Wars* and superpower potential to blow up the world. He tells them about the nuclear bomb, the Holocaust and the relocation of people during and after wars.

Harry is the second veteran teacher. His knowledge of US history is impressive. He majored in history and has a Master's degree in the subject. He teaches US history to a general track class. The curriculum covers the period from Columbus's discovery of the Americas to the present day. Like David's curriculum, it is a chronological progression that tends to emphasize political and economic history. The curriculum is divided into periods, some of which correspond to the textbook, but most of which are Harry's ideas.

Harry has developed four stories that he communicates through the curriculum: *The Growth of Opportunities, The Age of Discoveries, Clash of Cultures* and *Transformations of Cultures and Institutions*. Each story highlights different topics in the curriculum and connects them to similar ideas previously covered. One of Harry's stories, *Clash of Cultures,* serves as an example of the ways in which he uses his curriculum stories.

This story highlights events and ideas during several periods in the history of the USA. Initially, this is an important story since it highlights several topics during the first period covered in the course, colonial history. Among those topics highlighted during this period are the English settlers, their interactions with the native Americans, and how they eliminated the French in the New World. During the next period, the American Revolution, Americans entered into an armed conflict with their authority, the British, and this story focuses on several elements. The story about the clash of cultures becomes prominent again in the discussion of the Jacksonian era. The topics highlighted are manifest destiny, where white people came increasingly into conflict with the native Americans, the Industrial Revolution and the European immigrants that settled in the north who helped bring it about, and according to Harry, also at the same time, helped entrench slavery in the south.

To explain this last but important point about the entrenchment of slavery in the south, Harry selects an illustrative example that communicates it to the students in a meaningful way:

> Harry. ... Let me illustrate. Near the mouth of the Mississippi on the eastern shore, there is a city of Natchez ... There is a strange geographical location there [Harry draws a diagram on the board]. They raise a lot of cotton here and they bale it, the bales being huge big things, so they would haul that to the part of Natchez here at the top of the hill. Now, how would you get the bales down the hill?
>
> Student 1: You drop them.
>
> Harry: Right, they dropped them down a big slide. And they had people at the bottom of the slide who tried to take advantage of the momentum of the bales of cotton to roll them right on to the waiting ships. At one of these positions they had slaves, in one they had free immigrant labour. Which was which? ...

A discussion follows where students bring forward their suggestions and their reasons why. Eventually, they realize that the slaves were at the top of the hill because they were valuable property to their owners. Harry moves this momentum forward:

> Harry: ... So if you were a free person coming to America, are you likely to move to Natchez?

Both David and Harry use this kind of example extensively in their teaching. Sometimes they pull it out of their private collection and bring it to class; sometimes in class, as at the drop of a hat, they lunge into a story that 'explains it'. David's pie chart of dead soldiers and Harry's cotton bales rolling down a slide and crushing free immigrant labour, and Ronald Reagan and Walter Mondale debating on television are not 'just stories'. They are important stories because they provide access to a larger and more complex historical narrative-a fundamental aspect of Harry's and David's pedagogical content knowledge. Other important criteria in the selection process seem to be drama and people, since practically all their examples include people. Decades of teaching have shaped these examples and tailored them to the needs of different kinds of students, not unlike the fairy tales and legends of our past (Bettelheim, 1975).

DISCUSSION

Harry's and David's stories indicate a strong narrative element in their pedagogical content knowledge. This narrative element, however, is not available for examination. The knowledge structures that guide processing of information are procedural knowledge 'that works beyond awareness' (Mandler, 1984). Instead, we can examine the impressive results of the process, the stories Harry and David make and tell their students. Their stories show a great flexibility in their story schema.

Their stories cover a great deal of information told over a long period of time. They use props such as diagrams, as well as more traditional stories. Even though the use of props in story-making and story-telling is not a strong western tradition, non-western cultures use them extensively and very effectively (Pellowski, 1984). It seems that the unpredictable and complicated world of classrooms calls for unconventional story-making and story-telling, and a flexible story schema.

It is not enough to be a good storyteller, one has to know good stories to tell. Traditional storytellers learn their stories from others. Harry and David, however, have no such tradition to draw on. They have to make their own stories, and these stories indicate that there are powerful narrative elements in their pedagogical content knowledge, something that seems to distinguish them from novice teachers. Most of the events and people included in Harry's and David's curriculum stories are in the textbook, which they both consider bad or, at best, incomplete. Their curriculum stories are their attempts at making more complete or more meaningful stories, and since they use several stories, it is clear that they feel it takes more than one good story to account for the complexities in the history of their country.

A good story, according to Harry and David, has several important qualities. It is not only more complete and compelling than bad stories, it also provides the continuity in history that students often find problematic. A good story enables the teacher to make connections and help students detect relationships. It enables them to move back and forth in history, for example, between the Boston Tea Party and Reagan and Mondale on television, and between the battle of Antietam and the nuclear arms race. And finally, good stories also have to include the events and characters that have traditionally been considered important in US history.

The curriculum stories Harry and David have made and tell through the curriculum are set against the background of traditional periods in US history. It seems that the two teachers look at each historical period through different perspectives provided by the curriculum stories. Each story highlights and selects certain events in each historical period. In this way, the curriculum story functions like the horizontal axis that provides the continuity in the narrative (Jakobson, 1956). The events highlighted and selected become the subject of the stories the teachers tell as explanations or illustrations, such as the entrenchment of slavery during the Jacksonian era. Like the experienced teachers reported by Tierney (1988) and Ball (in press), Harry and David have a large reservoir of those explanations and illustrations. Some are planned, others surface spontaneously like improvisations in jazz (Yinger, 1987).

Each curriculum story includes events that are significant to its development and excludes those that are insignificant. Danto (1985, p. 133) describes four ways in which events can be significant. (1) An event has a pragmatic significance when the subject is of moral interest to the historian/ teacher, 'So that, in addition to writing what precisely happened, he hopes to be making a moral point'. Many of the explanations and illustrations David includes in the curriculum stories, especially his *Wars* story, are characterized by a distinct moral point of view, a perspective that highlights the horrors of war. (2) Events have theoretical significance if the historian/ teacher 'sees them standing in an evidential or illustrative relationship to some general theory he is concerned to establish or disestablish' (Danto, 1985, p. 133). Many of the illustrations and explanations Harry uses for his story are instrumental in showing how a theory works, like his story about the slaves and free immigrants in the city of Natchez on the Mississippi. (3) Events are selected because of their consequential significance. Most events have consequences, but not all are equally significant. The events included in a narrative such as the curriculum story are there because the historian/teacher has assigned consequential significance to them. This notion of significance, according to Danto, is basic to narratives. If an event has no significance to something that happens later in the story it does not belong in the narrative. A series of events without consequential significance is not a story. This element of narratives is central to all the curriculum stories Harry and David use. It is the component that enables them to establish continuity in history and link the past to the present. (4) Events also have *revelatory significance:* Danto (1985, pp. 134–135, emphasis in original) suggests that 'the relationship of a story to a body of evidence may, at a certain stage, be abductive. That is, on the basis of some set of records, we postulate a kind of story, and then go on to seek out further supporting evidence'. There were no obvious signs of Harry's using this approach. David, however, did try to show his students how theory is selective. He had his students try to interpret events during the Age of Jackson as if the Civil War never happened.

Even though David tends to emphasize the pragmatic approach to assigning significance to events, he does not do so at the exclusion of other approaches. Theoretical and consequential approaches also feature prominently in his curriculum stories. It is the same for Harry. He tends to focus on the theoretical significance of historical events, yet the moral side of issues and policies are always there ready to surface at the first opportunity. Furthermore, he is constantly reminding his students of the consequential side of history. He has them constructing time lines to show how one event leads to another. This polyperspective-taking enables both teachers to look at the many layers of meaning that are embedded in the interpretation of past events. There are no simple explanations and no simple solutions to historical problems in David's and Harry's classrooms. That is perhaps one of the many reasons why their stories are good.

CONCLUSIONS

Teaching, as I see it, is basically about the making of meaning. Teachers have to make meaning for themselves in the content they teach and they have to transform their private meaning into a form they feel students will understand. And to do this they need a knowledge-base: pedagogical content knowledge. I have tried to show in this chapter that the making of meaning for teachers involves the creation of narratives, curriculum stories and shorter stories. The narratives described in this chapter further indicate that there is an important narrative element in pedagogical content knowledge that enables teachers to create these narratives. I conclude by paraphrasing Polkinghorne (1988, p. 142), and suggest that teaching is like writing a story, and the understanding of teaching is like arriving at an interpretation of a story.

NOTE

1. Advanced Placement (AP) is a school-taught but externally examined programme of subject courses which, if successfully completed, gives US high-school students university credit.

ACKNOWLEDGEMENTS

The research reported in this chapter was conducted under a grant from the Spencer Foundation to Stanford University for The Knowledge Growth in a Profession project; Lee Shulman, Principal Investigator. The preparation of this chapter was made possible by a grant from Norges allmennvitenska-pelige forskningsrad (NAVF). The author would like to thank Freema Elbaz, Robert Donmoyer, Michael Huberman, Asmund Stromnes, Ian Westbury and Robert Yinger for their critical comments on earlier drafts of this chapter.

REFERENCES

Ball, D. (1991). Research on teaching mathematics: Making subject matter part of the equation. In J. E. Brophy (Ed.), *Teacher's knowledge as of subject matter as it relates to their teaching practice*. Advances in Research on Teaching (Vol. 2). Greenwich, CT: JAI Press.

Ben-Peretz, M. (1975). The concept of curriculum potential. *Curriculum Theory Network*, *5*(2), 151–159.

Bettelheim, B. (1975). *The uses of enchantment*. London, UK: Thames & Hudson.

Bruner, J. S. (1986). *Actual minds, possible worlds*. Cambridge, MA: Harvard University Press.

Coles, R. (1989). *The call of stories: Teaching and the moral imagination*. Boston, MA: Houghton Mifflin Company.

Connelly, F. M., & Clandinin, D. J. (1986). On narrative method, personal philosophy, and narrative units in the story of teaching. *Journal of Research in Science Teaching*, *23*(4), 293–310.

Connelly, F. M., & Clandinin, D. J. (1990). Stories of experience and narrative inquiry. *Educational Researcher*, *19*(4), 2–14.

Danto, A. (1985). *Narration and knowledge*. New York, NY: Columbia University Press.

Early, E. (1982). The logic of well being: Therapeutic narratives in Cairo, Egypt. *Social Science and Medicine*, *16*, 1491–1497.

Egan, K. (1988). *Teaching as storytelling: An alternative approach to teaching and curriculum in the elementary school*. London: Althouse Press.

Elbaz, F. (1981). Literature and curriculum: Toward a view of curriculum as discursive practice. *Curriculum Inquiry*, *11*(2), 105–122.

Elbaz, F. (1991). Knowledge and discourse: The evolution of research on teaching. *Journal of Curriculum Studies*, *2*(2), 1–19.

Fines, J. (1975). The narrative approach. *Teaching History*, *4*(11), 97–104.

Grossman, P., & Gudmundsdottir, S. (1987). *Teachers and texts: an expert/novice comparison in English*. Paper presented at the Annual Meeting of the American Educational Research Association, Washington, DC.

Grossman, P., Wilson, S., & Shulman, L. (1989). Teachers of substance: Subject matter knowledge for teaching. In M. Reynolds (Ed.), *Knowledge base for the beginning teacher* (pp. 23–36). Oxford, UK: Pergamon Press.

Gudmundsdottir, S. (1988). *Knowledge use among experienced use among experienced teachers: Four case studies of high school teaching*. Doctoral dissertation, Stanford University, Stanford, CA.

Gudmundsdottir, S. (1990). Curriculum stories. In C. Day, P. Denicolo & M. Pope (Eds.), *Insights into teachers' thinking and action*. Lewes, Sussex: Falmer Press.

Gudmundsdottir, S., & Shulman, L. S. (1987). Pedagogical content knowledge in social studies. *Scandinavian Journal of Educational Research*, *31*(2), 59–70.

Hannam, C. (1975). Do you tell stories? *Teaching History*, *4*, 47–49.

Hawkes, T. (1977). *Structuralism and Semiotics*. Berkeley CA: University of California Press.

Huberman, M. (1983). Recipes for busy kitchens: A situational analysis of routine knowledge use in schools. *Knowledge: Creation, Diffusion, Utilization*, *4*(4), 478–510.

Jackson, P. W. (1986). *The practice of teaching*. New York, NY: Teachers College Press.

Jakobson, R. (1956). *Fundamentals of language. Janua linguarium, series minor, I*. The Hague, Netherlands: Mouton.

Jordan, B. (1989). Cosmopolitan obstetrics: Some insights from the training of traditional midwives. *Social Science and Medicine*, *28*(9), 925–944.

Leinhardt, G., & Smith, D. (1985). Expertise in mathematics instruction: Subject matter knowledge. *Journal of Educational Psychology*, *77*(3), 247–271.

Mandler, J. (1984). *Stories, scripts, and scenes: Aspects of schema theory*. Hillsdale, NJ: Lawrence Erlbaum Associates.

Marshall, S. (1963). *An experiment in education*. Cambridge, MA: Cambridge University Press.

Mcewan, H. (1990). *Teaching acts: An unfinished story*. Paper presented at the 36th Annual Meeting of the Philosophy of Education Society, Miami, FL.

Paley, V. G. (1981). *Wally's stories*. Cambridge, MA: Harvard University Press.

Paley, V. G. (1990). *The boy who would be a helicopter*. Cambridge, MA: Harvard University Press.

Pellowski, A. (1984). *The story vine*. New York, NY: Macmillan.

Polkinghorne, D. E. (1988). *Narrative knowing and the human sciences*. Albany, NY: State University of New York Press.

Rashdall, H. (1936). *Universities of Europe in the Middle Ages* (Vol. 3). London: Oxford University Press.

Reynolds, A., Haymore, J., Ringstaff, C., & Grossman, P. (1988). Teachers and curricular materials: who is driving whom? *Curriculum Perspectives*, *8*(1), 22–29.

Robinson, J., & Hawpe, L. (1986). Narrative thinking as a heuristic process. In T. Sarbin (Ed.), *Narrative psychology: The storied nature of human conduct* (pp. 111–125). New York, NY: Praeger Special Studies.

Sarbin, T. (Ed.). (1986). *Narrative psychology: The storied nature of human conduct*. New York, NY: Praeger Special Studies.

Scholes, R. E., & Kellogg, R. (1966). *The nature of narrative*. New York, NY: Oxford University Press.

Shulman, L. S. (1987). Knowledge and teaching: Foundations of the new reform. *Harvard Educational Review*, *57*(1), 1–22.

Stein, N., & Policastro, M. (1983). The concept of a story: Comparison between children's and teachers' viewpoints. In H. Mandl, N. Stein & T. Trabasso (Eds.), *Learning and comprehension of text* (pp. 113–155). Hillsdale, NJ: Lawrence Erlbaum Associates.

Tierney, D. (1988). *How teachers explain things: Metaphoric representation of social studies concepts.* Paper presented at the annual meeting of the American Educational Research Association, New Orleans, LA.

Whyte, H. (1981). The value of narrativity in the representation of reality. In W. J. T. Mitchell (Ed.), *On narrative* (pp. 1–25). Chicago, IL: University of Chicago Press.

Wilson, S., Shulman, L., & Richert, A. (1987). '150 different ways' of knowing: Representations of knowledge in teaching. In J. Calderhead (Ed.), *Exploring teachers' thinking* (pp. 104–124). London, UK: Cassell.

Yinger, R. (1977). *A study of teacher planning: Description and theory development using ethnographic and information processing methods.* Doctoral dissertation, Michigan State University, East Lansing, MI.

Yinger, R. (1987). *By the seat of our pants: An inquiry into improvisation and teaching.* Paper presented at the annual meeting of the American Educational Research Association, Washington, DC.

CHAPTER 8

NARRATIVE RESEARCH: FROM THE MARGINS TO BEING HEARD

Leena Syrjälä and Eila Estola

ABSTRACT

This chapter traces the rise of narrative research as a method and form of inquiry in the field of education. While the work mainly focuses on the increased use of narrative in Finland, the fact of the matter is that the interpretative turn, which some call the narrative turn, has spread throughout the world and into almost every disciplinary area of study (medicine, law, religion, etc.). ISATT members internationally have played a key role in its development. The authors of this chapter claim that narrative not only instantiates people's knowledge, experiences, and situations but also changes their lives. They aver that this constitutes the transformational power of narrative research and forms the essence of why it is being drawn in from the margins and gaining acceptance in mainstream discourse and society.

Keywords: Narrative research; research method; paradigm shift; Finland

The Finnish school system and its teachers are well-regarded globally. Finland is the only Western nation to consistently rank alongside East Asian countries like Singapore and China (Shanghai). Educational policymakers

From Teacher Thinking to Teachers and Teaching: The Evolution of a Research Community
Advances in Research on Teaching, Volume 19, 157–173
ISSN: 1479-3687/doi:10.1108/S1479-3687(2013)0000019011

and researchers from many parts of the world are eager to meet Finnish teachers who are viewed as vital to the "PISA (Programme for International Student Assessment) miracle" (Sahlberg, 2011). Near the end of the 1980s, however, Finland's situation was quite different. During that time, educational research was more concerned with learning and new technology-oriented learning environments, while the role of the teachers was considered relatively insignificant. Despite this, we, as authors of this chapter, were more interested in the significance of individual teachers in developing their own work and their contributions to whole school milieus. We believed that school reforms can be better understood by examining the life narratives of individual teachers. Hence, we disregarded the old approaches, and enabled teachers and their stories to be heard. At the end of the day, we recognized that it is teachers who make reforms happen.

We first became interested in biographical research which was more popular in anthropology and religious sciences at the time. Back then, the examples and methods of narrative research were rather scarce in educational sciences. We had to pave our own way as biographical research, let alone narrative research, was not highly regarded in Finnish academia for years to come. Not until we met Sigrun Gudmundsdottir and Geert Kelchtermans at an ISATT conference in Kiel, Germany in 1997, did we form a clearer picture of narrative research in educational sciences, and the movement started to gain more worldwide prominence especially in ISATT circles. It was through Sigrun Gudmunsdottir that we learned of Freema Elbaz-Luwisch as well, whose publications of which we were already aware. These contacts gave us courage to continue with our teacher research, and formed the seeds of international collaboration that continue to this day. Sigrun Gudmundsdottir's early death was a serious personal and professional blow to our research group. Our contacts, mainly through ISATT associations, confirmed for us the importance of narrative research in understanding the significance of teachers' lives and work. We continued our research despite the fact it was often misunderstood in academia. Nevertheless, after acquiring an extensive data pool of teachers' life narratives, we received funding from the Academy of Finland to study them. Slowly our work earned a place in academia. Our experiences about the change in the status of narrative research are similar to the ones that researchers in different parts of the world have also observed. Elliot Mishler wrote in 2006 that "with surprising speed, the loosely defined field of narrative studies has moved from its early marginal status in the human sciences to a robust legitimacy" (p. iv). The 1997 special issue on the topic of narrative research carried in the journal *Teaching and Teacher Education* was a major step forward for the developing research niche. In that issue, Freema Elbaz-Luwisch (1997) asked in her article *Narrative research: Political issues and implications* what makes a good story and whose tastes and standards are authorized to make this judgment. Thus, questions about ethics and politics have helped frame the discussion of narrative research throughout the years. As narrative research has expanded in the sciences, Gabriela Spector-Mersel (2010) has argued that it is time to separate narrative research from other qualitative and interpretive research methods and begin to talk about a narrative paradigm. This kind of discussion proves that narrative research is here to stay. From our point of view, we believe multiple research approaches support one another. Narrative research can benefit from different methods, for instance, from ethnographic research, action research, and discursive research.

Presently, we see narrative research as a way to help us conceive of the world as we and others experience it. Along the lines of Spector-Mersel, narrative research involves certain commitments having to do with the ways of knowing, methodology, and the position of the researcher with respect to the inquiry and those being researched. In the next section, we discuss some commitments that are significant to discussions about narrative research and its ability to see and hear from those in the margins. Our methodological observations are founded on our studies where the narrators have been teachers and teacher students, or adults and small children in their respective contexts of two northern rural villages in Finland. Based on our research, we describe narrative research as (a) an ethically and politically motivated practice, (b) a multivoiced practice, and (c) an embodied practice. To conclude this chapter, we offer our views on narrative research and ponder what difference does the expansion of narrative research mean for teacher education and for those who are in the margins. In the best case scenario, the increase of participants in narrative research would make their own voices better heard, whether they be teachers, adults, or students in the two northern villages. At the same time, during our sessions with the participants, we have had to further question whose voices are actually being heard and on whose terms.

NARRATIVE RESEARCH AS AN ETHICALLY AND POLITICALLY MOTIVATED PRACTICE

One common principle of narrative research is to listen to those who have not typically been heard in research investigations. This interest has both driven and inspired narrative researchers from the very beginning. Questions like "What do teachers in the North think of themselves and of their work?", "What are their experiences?", "What about the children, students, and parents and their experiences?", and "What kind of stories do they have to tell about their lives?" have intrigued us and other researchers in the narrative field.

Freema Elbaz-Luwisch (1997) concluded that because personal documents are the main materials of narrative researchers, such documents invite reflection and provide possibilities to view things in different ways. Although reflection is not necessarily a political act, it can become so in the frame of narrative research since the conduct of narrative research has a tendency to "go against the grain" and challenge the dominance of more established modes of inquiry. If we challenge dominant modes of inquiry and listen to silent voices, ethical questions having to do with this different positioning automatically are raised.

We understand that the narrative research process is a moral practice (Syrjälä, Estola, Uitto, & Kaunisto, 2006). Because of the long research process in which participants have relatively close relationships with one another and the researcher(s), special attention must be paid to the nature of these mutual relations. Among other things the issues of trust, openness, and voluntariness must be discussed from the beginning of the research process. There are several questions that researchers face: For whom and with whom do we conduct our research? How do we best protect participants, whose anonymity is not always easy to mask? And what if the participants want to use their own names, what challenges might arise and for whom? That is why there is a continuous need for ethical sensitivity and consideration of the kind of questions that cannot be answered in advance of the study.

Ultimately, the quality of narrative research must be evaluated by using perspectives which are more relevant for the nature of narrative research than traditional concepts of reliability and validity. The alternative perspectives given by Heikkinen, Huttunen, Syrjälä, and Pesonen (2012) especially emphasize the ethical aspects (ethics and evocativeness). We have come to see in our own empirical research that traditional codes of ethics alone are not enough protection for those narrating their stories.

In our research that took place in a northern rural school, we faced many questions which made us consider our responsibilities as researchers. It seems that in narrative research developing relationships, taking responsibility for the "other," and emphasizing the uniqueness of both participants and situations are important.

Responsibility is the ethical principle that emphasizes that there are no general rules to ensure ethically good research, but researchers have to try to see the world from that particular perspective. In the village where our study took place, we had to face our own interests and likes and dislikes at the same time as we tried to see the world from the perspectives of the villagers. The people of the northern village were quick to remind us about our visitor status and we struggled to behave in an ethical manner. When we looked back at our experiences, we categorized three different dimensions of research responsibility. The first dimension was the responsibility for relationships. This had to do with being accepted by villagers and keeping trustful relationships throughout the research process (Hyry-Beihammer, Estola, & Syrjälä, 2012).

The second dimension concerns the responsibility for political intervention. We were invited to support the villagers in their efforts to keep their school open because the politicians of the municipality wanted to close it. We traveled to the village and participated in the meeting with the people inhabiting the villager and representatives from the school administration (For some of them, the meeting was their first visit to the village!). We focused on the pedagogical issues on why it is important to keep the school open. Specifically, we talked about place-conscious education (Gruenewald, 2003). In the end result, the school board decided that the school could remain open at least for one more school year. No one knows if our visit had any bearing on the decision. For us the decision meant that we were able to continue our in-depth work in the village.

The third dimension of research responsibility involves maintaining a democratic stance while presenting findings. Responsibilities include the question: To whom will this research study be disseminated through the publication process? There are no easy responses to these matters but they must be given careful consideration. The university demands that the results are published in referred international journals and doctoral dissertations and that is an expectation of our work to which we conform.

At the end of the project, we felt that we have research responsibilities toward the villagers who had given us their time, talked with us, and invited us into their homes, day care facilities, and schools. In order to give something back of human value, we have tried other forms of sharing different stages of our research in different media outlets such as local newspapers and local radio stations. We also engaged in a short public dialogue in a university forum. In addition, we organized a village meeting where we invited participants from both villages. We talked about our research and the villagers presented a small play and a panel discussion organized around the theme "prerequisites for life in a small northern village." As it often happens in research, we disappeared from the village and returned to our academic lives. We still are uneasy and feel that we should do something more. We plan to do more in the last year of the funded research project.

NARRATIVE RESEARCH AS A MULTIVOICED PRACTICE

From the beginning of our work, we have wanted to draw attention to those voices that have been more or less ignored. We started with teachers from the northern part of Finland and collected about 100 oral and written autobiographical stories. Reading teachers' stories opened our eyes that to voices which had silent. Because the public discussion about teaching has been so noisy, those quiet voices did not have the power to become heard. In the current climate, teachers are often told they are unprofessional, troublesome, and lazy and that teaching is full of problems. But in listening closely to these unheard voices, we encountered different stories, where teachers talked about sensitive matters like teaching as a calling (Hansen, 1995) and the love and hope that fueled teachers' continuation of their work (Estola, 2003; Estola, Erkkilä, & Syrjälä, 2003; Estola & Syrjälä, 2002).

Somehow we felt that it is not enough to read the contents of the stories. We invited teachers to meet personally with us and that was an eye-opening session. We discovered very clearly that teachers had many different stories to tell. We became more and more aware that "collecting stories" is a co-construction between researchers and research participants. The situation is the same with analysis and interpretation. We found out that teachers' stories often told about schools in different ways than what was reported earlier. For instance, the major school reform effort in Finland was communication of various voices: with silence, irony, submission, active resistance, and in a voice of possibility and opportunity (Estola & Syrjälä, 2002).

In her doctoral research in a small Sami village, Raija Erkkilä (2005) explored teachers' stories of their life and school work in Lapland. The autobiographical narrative of one of the Sami teachers distinctly indicated the significance of local knowledge for teachers' work. The focus of this autobiographical story did not involve only the teacher but also the community, the people, the place, and the culture of which the teacher felt a part.

In another study, a teacher by the name of Helena provided us the access to her professional written autobiography, observation, and discussion material and an extensive personal journal collection (Estola & Syrjälä, 2002). These three different forms of narratives proved how different ways of eliciting experience produce different kinds of reflection and open up different elements of teacher's work for interpretation and analysis. The autobiography was a multivoiced story of a teacher's identity revealed in three critical phases, all shaped by the moral horizon of love. The phases were to learn to love by being loved, to learn to love struggle, and recognize love as a struggle. Love turned out to be a certain way of working in relationship with children, including many emotions that ranged from hate to joy (see Ruddick, 1995). The diary was a window into the embodied experiences (Estola & Syrjälä, 2002) of teacher's work and observations, and interviews as research tools were more focused on pedagogy and changes in how Helena had personally organized the curriculum and integrated subjects into projects (Estola & Syrjälä, 2002). This case study taught us as researchers how love can be translated into teachers' practices in dynamic ways.

We do not only find individual teacher's stories interesting. In our research project with 11 female teachers, from early childhood teachers to vocational level teachers who met 16 times during a one-and-a-half year period, we had the opportunity to explore how teachers' stories emerged in interaction within peer group discussions. Listeners were crucial to the way stories ultimately were told. This co-construction process of narrative has also caused us to think about the meaning of telling and retelling stories (Connelly & Clandinin, 1990; Kaunisto, Estola, & Leiman, 2013). Telling and retelling can lead to different effects. The supportive and therapeutic impact of ongoing story work has often been reported. Teachers also mention how sharing stories has prompted them to see new ways of looking at their work and themselves. But there is also a danger that sharing stories can harm the participants. This is a caution researchers must keep in mind and reflect upon. The issue is especially sensitive if and when we want to make silent voices audible in public arenas.

Based on our findings, one of the challenges of teacher education is to develop ways of working whereby students can critically evaluate their autobiographical and personal knowledge. Student teachers construct their identities via a narrative process which is rooted in their own school experiences (Estola, 2003; Uitto, 2011). Studies have shown that pre-service teacher education is a critical period in which student teachers should have opportunities to reflect on their emerging teacher identities in order to make a difference in their educational practices (Korthagen, 2001). Teaching as a moral practice also requires future teachers to contemplate the moral aspects of their profession. Hope is one of the moral dimensions of teaching (Elbaz, 1992). In our research we found out that although student teachers consider hope as an important part of teaching, they concurrently felt that feeling a sense of hope was unrealistic (Estola, 2003). This inconsistency between what students considered as important and what kind of problems they encountered in realizing it made some student think about abandoning teaching and becoming teacher attrition statistics. The contradiction became concrete in questions of how a teacher creates trustful relationships with children under difficult work conditions (Estola, 2003). These results concur with other research which states that diverse relationships sit at the core of teachers' work. A key question of pre-service teacher education is how to manage differing agendas while maintaining a positive outlook.

Lately our interest has focused increasingly on peer group discussions. Our first project on this topic occurred between 2004 and 2006. A group of 11 female teachers met together 16 times during an 18 month project called INTO (Inspirational Narratives of Teaching as an Opportunity). The voluntary-peer group was established as a form of in-service teacher education in order to support teachers' coping and renewal at work. The teachers were employed in Finnish daycare centers, primary and secondary schools, and vocational institutions. Their ages ranged from approximately 30 to 60 years, and from beginning teachers to seasoned teachers, some of whom would soon be retiring from the profession.

The way the group worked was based on a narrative approach. Narrative ways of working used in the group included oral discussions, sharing of cases, drama presentations, and writing. The group provided the teachers with a reflective space to discuss their everyday life and experiences as teachers. Each group meeting had a particular theme which was agreed on by the teacher participants. Some examples of the themes were conflict in the workplace and changes in the nature of teacher's work. In all cases, the teachers were able to direct the course of the discussion. As an example of what transpired we present a short excerpt from a conversation between the 11 teachers in the group. We italicize sections of the discussion to which we wish to direct readers' attention.

Tina, who is a beginning teacher, started the discussion and other participants continued it.

Tina: I'm really worn-out with the curriculum at the moment because actually I feel I've been left alone ... at times. Then, you know, the attitude of teachers to revising curriculum and then there's me as a new person there in the front who doesn't know anything yet but tries to put it together and then everything falls down around me.

Elina, a participant in the group, responded:

This is really an awful situation that *I've also realized myself as a young teacher, you do the work.*

Later Airi, another participant: Yeah, *they trust that you will do it* – and it will be turned in by the deadline, so it is.

Maria: Yes. *But it is trust. Think about it in that way.*

The extract describes how the other participant supports Tina by telling her a similar experience from her life. The passage also shows how discussion can open a new way of looking at a difficult situation. In general, the results of the project indicated that beginning teachers experience emotional burdens from being alone. The micropolitical context of a school influences a beginning teacher's identity construction. Often, the school is illustrated as a place where beginning teachers work alone, feel pressure to succeed, and where there is no room to discuss feeling worn out, uncertain or incompetent. Such emotions can shape a part of teacher identity (see Kelctermans & Ballet, 2002).

Since many beginning teachers abandon their profession of choice during their first years at work (Heikkinen, Jokinen, & Tynjälä, 2012), solutions need to be reached as to how teacher attrition can be avoided. The Ministry of Education and Culture of Finland has financed a nationwide project of peer-group mentoring to support the professional development and lifelong learning of beginning teachers. The methods we developed in INTO group have also been applied in this national peer-group mentoring project. At the moment, the project has prepared mentors for all areas of Finland and at all levels of teaching including vocational schools. In the groups, teachers share their experiences, discuss problems, and support each other. The Finnish model differs from the traditional one in which one-to-one discussions are used (Heikkinen, Jokinen, & Tynjälä, 2012).

We have an additional example of the multivoicedness of stories that we wish to share. In the research project, *Life in Place*, we collected stories in two remote northern villages. "Mainstream" research conducted in the North has proven that Lapland is a miserable area where Finns experience health problems, unemployment, and rapid national migration from the rural areas to population centers. When listening to the villagers, the multivoicedness of stories invited us to broaden this view. Maija Lanas (2011) described how in the villagers' narratives the village was presented as the hub of the people's lives, dynamic even in quietude, and life in the villages was presented as an active choice. These stories, which can be called counter-narratives (Bamberg & Andrews, 2004), challenge the national representations that tend to arise from the discourse of social exclusion.

NARRATIVE RESEARCH AS AN EMBODIED PRACTICE

While conducting our research studies, we noted how embodiment is also present in stories. Despite the fact that teaching still mainly happens in classrooms where sitting and moving embodied figures are present, educational research has paid little attention to the embodied practices of teaching (Estola & Elbaz-Luwisch, 2003). Mark Johnson (1989) was one of the first who wrote about human experience as embodied. In teachers' stories, the body necessarily exists. It lives in routines (Leinhardt, Weidman, & Hammond, 1987) and rhythms (Clandinin & Connelly, 1986). It also is evident in teacher images (Weber & Mitchell, 1995) and part of their identities (Mitchell & Weber, 1999). Nevertheless, the postmodern philosophy has reduced bodies to discourses (Burkitt, 1999), whereas the Cartesian legacy has historically privileged the intellectual life of the mind while treating the body as debasing.

In their stories, teachers reference touching, moving, and spacio-temporal orientation; they speak of touching students' shoulders or walking around the classroom as an essential part of the dialogue between teachers and children. The body makes it possible to be in interaction with youth, and appropriate hugs and physical contact can be a significant part of teachers' educational practices. This was the case in Helena's story which we mentioned earlier in this chapter. Helena's diary was a manifestation of different ways of using one's body to express good emotions and attachment rather than using the body for punishment and order or paying attention only to the mind and reason (Estola & Syrjälä, 2002).

In another teacher's story, a Finnish language teacher Liisa wrote:

> The most difficult thing in this demanding job of teaching is the perpetual presence. You cannot hide your own being, feelings, and attitudes behind the subjects you are teaching. Every moment, no matter what kind of a phase of life you are living in, you have to be

there. You have to be present in just the very situation where learning takes place and where the developing individuals, your pupils, are watching you. At the same time they are modeling themselves by you and they also need guidance and encouragement. (Estola & Elbaz-Luwisch, 2003, p. 703)

Indeed, teaching and teacher identities are embedded in the body, since social and cultural norms and habits are performed through bodies. Teachers are remembered as persons who do something and look like something (Uitto & Estola, 2009). Thus, the way teachers concretely behave is the only way children can be in relationships with those who instruct them. This connects teaching to power relations and to emotions (Uitto & Syrjälä, 2008; Uitto, 2011). The way how schools and school days are organized also has concrete consequence for the embodied character of teaching.

Embodiment and the multimodality of telling became more apparent as we started our narrative child research. When we started to study small children in their everyday lives and considered matters relating to their well-being, we had to once again question what we meant by narrative. It was obvious that children who do not speak a word do not have narratives in the traditional sense. But do children have narratives in the absence of speech acts? We were supported by Ochs and Capps (2001) who pointed out that children's narratives are contextually embedded meaning-making processes rather than a finished product of a well-formed story (Ochs & Capps, 2001). We learned that young children's means of expressing and communicating their experiences are not restricted to their verbal language. In addition to words, children's narratives involve, for example, other linguistic means, emotional expressions, action, body language, play, and art (see Ahn & Filipenko, 2007; Engel, 2006; Puroila, Estola, & Syrjälä, 2012).

By observing young children and entering into discussions with them, we have come to understand the nature of children's narratives. Their characteristics include fragmentariness, multimodality, collaborative construction, and the complex relationship between personal narratives and the storied contexts within which the storytellers told them. Typically, these are small stories, episodes which can take only a minute or two and only a few words, if any. However, there are many other forms of narrating. In fact, it is the researcher who, in the end result, constructs a story based on those small incidents (Puroila et al., 2012).

The following example features a discussion in a children's group.

Anna, Maria, Laura, Lisa, and Timo – five four- to five-year-old children are drawing at a table in a kindergarten classroom. While drawing, they talk about the Christmas season, which is forthcoming. Suddenly Anna says:

Anna: Those who believe in Santa Claus, raise your hand!

Other children except Anna raise their hands.

Anna: I do not believe.

A fuss follows this comment. Other children begin to talk in unison (How come? Why? Santa Claus came to my home...).

Anna: Santa Claus is just a man who has dressed up in those clothes! My mama said that Santa does not exist.

Other children: How? Santa came to my home!

Anna (stressing the words with hands on hips): I cannot tell you because you will never believe me!

Timo: I will believe you!

Maria: Santa at least came to my house! But Anna, how come he can live for so long time? If he was born once again...

Timo: People cannot be born once again!

Maria: I don't know when Santa has his birthday.

Anna: How old is he and is he as old as a granddad (with laughter)?

The conversation about Santa Claus faded out. The children began to talk about other topics.

[Later in the afternoon]

Anna and Timo are drawing.

Anna: Last Christmas, Santa did not come to our home, but the Christmas before that he came.

Timo: Thus he must exist!

Anna: You are right! First I did not believe but now I believe in Santa. I write here that "Dear Santa" (sniggering), dear Santa, from Anna.

Anna begins to sing "Jingle bells, jingle bells ..."

The notion of the holistic and multimodal nature of young children's narratives has consequences for our research methodology. Rather than "asking children directly," we apply a methodology that encourages the exploration of the rich variation of children's expressions of their experiences as they unravel in young children's own terms. Thus, listening to children's narratives requires that researchers acquire knowledge in other ways than simply by listening to words. Narratives collected by intensive participant observation sessions are as significant as oral and written stories which we collected in our earlier projects. In the narration process, telling and listening are intertwined, and the narratives become more or less multivoiced.

CONCLUSION

For the past two decades, we have been listening, reading, and rewriting numerous stories lived and told, and relived and retold by teachers, stories which afterwards became part of our own lives as teacher educators. While we use different narrative and action methods in our teaching, we also have realized the power of telling stories. Students can relate to the stories told by their teachers while teachers simultaneously can ponder their own identities as teachers. The life stories of some teachers have even touched us personally. We have returned to these narratives over time, and they have contributed to the shaping of our own identities as researchers and teachers. We see the profession of a teacher educator first and foremost as moral action where narrative sensitivity is essential. Narrative research has emerged especially as a communicative and social action. The given story is constructed as an outcome of communication in a certain historical, social, psychological, and geographical context. The role of the researcher is central as his or her persona and one's own life story is always present in the making of a narrative. The cultural heritage of storytelling and the context where the narrative is constructed also reflect on storytelling.

Based on our research and field experiences, we would suggest that the narrative approach should be central to teacher education along the continuum (pre- and in-service stages of career). At the very least, this would require time and a safe environment where prospective and practicing teachers would build and rebuild the narrative of their professional identity. This, we argue, would deepen the individuals' understanding on the teaching profession and reflections on one's own teacher identity. Therefore, there should be room in the pre-service curriculum for collaborative and narrative identity work. This sort of an identity work should not be considered merely personal but it should also include critical reflection on what kind of teachers, schools, programs, and childhoods are being produced. It might be significant to collaboratively address counter-narratives to current teacher images. The stories teachers tell emphasize the importance of relationships, hope, and even calling, whereas the neoliberal agenda speaks of teacher accountability, efficiency, and costs.

Narrative research does not aim at predetermined change per se, even if the concept of a narrative includes a representation of a desired change. In this sense, narrative research differs from action research where change is the starting point of research. These two approaches have recently converged, and the idea of narrative action research has been conceptualized (Heikkinen et al., 2012). In narrative research, there is an opportunity for self-reflection on one's own work and actions. This, in turn, generates change, albeit in no preconceived manner. This became clear to us during our research on 11 female teachers who met for 18 months to collaboratively reflect on their work through narrative commingled with action research methods. The self-reflection which emerged spoke of how one feels emotionally drained from teaching. In these situations, mere reflection on decisions related to teaching situations is not enough. Rather, more reflection on more personal experiences is needed. Through the self-reflection process, one can become more aware of personal, familial, social, and school resources and life stories can lead to new perspectives on work. Thus, the self-reflection process can offer a more realistic view of one's professional options too (Kaunisto et al., 2013).

When focusing on personal stories, the idea that narratives are constructed in a certain historical, social, psychological, geographical, cultural, and political context must be taken in to account. Otherwise, the danger is that over time the stories will become static and start to merely reaffirm stuck practices. Narratives have multiple functions which the researcher needs to analyze carefully. Stories can connect one to the community but also destroy, stigmatize, or marginalize the narrator and the research participants. At the moment, we are interested in how narrative research can be used to reinterpret the phenomenon of marginalization as a process which is evident in some narrative practices (i.e., Gubrium & Holstein, 2009). Observing different narrative contexts in teacher education and in other educational communities is essential for their development.

Most of our research deals with the narrative identity work of both teacher developers and student teachers in their respective peer groups. Our preliminary understanding of teaching as being human relationships has furthermore become strengthened. Essential for our understanding is that teacher identity could be more clearly connected with feelings and moral questions. Previously we were interested in teachers' written or oral life stories. But at the moment we are interested in the construction of narratives in everyday discussions, through so called short narratives (Juzwik & Ives, 2010) which enables the communicative nature of narration to emerge.

We once again ask: Has narrative research managed to surface the voices of the marginalized? Without a doubt, more diverse and alternative narratives have been collected and presented, but whose voice is actually articulated remains unclear. On the other hand, the question of who is in the margins is complicit in producing the marginalized. Maybe we should also consider if being marginalized could actually be beneficial in some contexts. We might also say that narrative research is now an established research method in the academy with its own body of literature and set of research tool. However, narrative research is changing all the time and we think this is necessary to its survival.

To end, we have a question we posed and answered with and for each other.

Eila: Leena, I have a question for you? What would you say to beginning researchers who are interested in narrative research?

Leena: First thing I would say is to emphasize that narrative research means a commitment to narrative knowing. It is understanding narration as a meaning-making process which is always connected to time and the place in which stories are told. In my experience, narrative research is a learning process for all participants including researchers. We have been lucky because we have a strong research community, where we can work together with others.

Leena: And what about you, Eila? What would you say about narrative research?

Eila: I have various thoughts and experiences. Quite recently our article was criticized because it was not written according to the traditional structure. The reviewers suggested radical changes. However, a similar article structure was well received in another journal, which was more accommodating of narrative research. Positive feedback gives us energy to continue in narrative research. On the other hand, debate and critique are important to our scientific community; we do not have to be afraid of others' responses. They can promote our development as researchers. I would like to add that narrative research is almost the only way to reach human experience. We could say that experience comes to us through stories.

Leena: Although the focus of the whole research process is on the narratives, it is the researcher and his or her personal story which shapes the interpretations. Once again I would emphasize that researchers' ethical commitments are crucial in relation to how narrative research develops. We

172 LEENA SYRJÄLÄ AND EILA ESTOLA

could ask: "What kind of world do we want to build?" and "Is there a diversity of voices being heard and seen in our work?"

REFERENCES

Ahn, J., & Filipenko, M. (2007). Narrative, imaginary play, art, and self: Intersecting worlds. *Early Childhood Education Journal, 34*(4), 279–289. doi: 10.1007/s10643-006-0137-4

Bamberg, M., & Andrews, M. (2004). *Considering counter-narratives: Narrating, resisting, making sense.* Amsterdam: John Benjamins.

Burkitt, I. (1999). *Bodies of thought: Embodiment, identity and modernity.* London: Sage.

Clandinin, D. J., & Connelly, F. M. (1986). Rhythms of teaching: The narrative study of teachers' personal practical knowledge of classrooms. *Teaching and Teacher Education, 2*(4), 377–387.

Connelly, F. M., & Clandinin, D. J. (1990). Stories of experience and narrative inquiry. *Educational Researcher, 19*(5), 2–14.

Elbaz, F. (1992). Hope, attentiveness, and caring for difference: The moral voice in teaching. *Teaching and Teacher Education, 8*(5–6), 421–432.

Elbaz-Luwisch, F. (1997). Narrative research: Political issues and implications. *Teaching and Teacher Education, 13*(1), 75–84.

Engel, S. (2006). Narrative analysis of children's experience. In S. Greene & D. Hogan (Eds.), *Researching children's experience: Approaches and methods* (pp. 199–216). London: Sage.

Erkkilä, R. (2005). *Moniääninen paikka – opettajien kertomuksia elämästä ja koulutyöstä Lapissa.* Acta Universitatis Ouluensis E79. Oulu: Oulun yliopistopaino.

Estola, E. (2003). Hope as work – student teachers constructing their narrative identities. *Scandinavian Journal of Educational Research, 47*(2), 181–203.

Estola, E., & Elbaz-Luwisch, F. (2003). Teaching bodies at work. *Journal of Curriculum Studies, 35*(6), 697–718.

Estola, E., Erkkilä, R., & Syrjälä, L. (2003). A moral voice of vocation in teachers' narratives. *Teachers and Teaching: Theory and Practice, 9*(3), 239–256.

Estola, E., & Syrjälä, L. (2002). Love, body and change: A teacher's narrative reflections. *Reflective Practice, 3*(1), 53–69.

Gruenewald, D. (2003). Foundations of place: A multidisciplinary framework for place-conscious education. *American Educational Research Journal, 40*(3), 619–654.

Gubrium, J., & Holstein, J. (2009). *Analyzing narrative reality.* Los Angeles, CA: Sage.

Hansen, D. T. (1995). *The call to teach.* New York, NY: Teachers College Press.

Heikkinen, H. L. T., Huttunen, R., Syrjälä, L., & Pesonen, J. (2012). Action research and narrative inquiry: Five principles for validation revisited. *Educational Action Research, 20*(1), 5–21. doi: 10.1080/09650792.2012.647635

Heikkinen, H. L. T., Jokinen, H., & Tynjälä, P. (2012). Teacher education and development as lifelong and lifewide learning. In H. L. T. Heikkinen, H. Jokinen & P. Tynjälä (Eds.), *Peer-group mentoring for teacher development* (pp. 3–30). London: Routledge.

Hyry-Beihammer, E. K., Estola, E., & Syrjälä, L. (2012). Issues of responsibility when conducting research in a northern rural school. *International Journal of Qualitative Studies in Education.* doi:10.1080/09518398.2012.731538 (iFirst article).

Johnson, M. (1989). *The body in the mind: The bodily basics of meaning, imagination, and reason.* Chicago, IL: The University Chicago Press.

Juzwik, M. M., & Ives, D. (2010). Small stories as resources for performing teacher identity. *Narrative Inquiry, 20*(1), 37–61. doi: 10.1075/ni.20.1.03juz

Kaunisto, S. L., Estola, E., & Leiman, M. (2013). I've let myself get tired": One teacher's reflective process in a peer group. *Reflective Practice, 14*(3), 406–419. doi:10.1080/14623943.2013.767236

Kelchtermans, G., & Ballet, K. (2002). The micropolitics of teacher education: A narrative-biographical study of teacher socialization. *Teaching and Teacher Education, 18*(1), 105–120.

Korthagen, F. (2001). A reflection on reflection. In F. Korthagen, J. Kessels, B. Koster, B. Lagerwerf & T. Wubbels (Eds.), *Linking practice to theory: A pedagogy of realistic teacher education.* Mahwah, NJ: Lawrence Erlbaum.

Lanas, M. (2011). *Smashing potatoes: Challenging student agency as utterances.* Acta Universitatis Ouluensis E120. Tampere: Juvenes Print.

Leinhardt, G., Weidman, C., & Hammond, K. M. (1987). Introduction and integration of classroom routines by expert teachers. *Curriculum Inquiry, 17*(2), 135–176.

Mishler, E. (2006). Foreward. In F. Rapport & P. Wainwright (Eds.), *The self in health and illness: Patients, professionals and narrative identity* (pp. iv–vvii). Oxford: Radcliffe.

Mitchell, C., & Weber, S. (1999). *Reinventing ourselves as teachers: Beyond nostalgia.* London: Falmer Press.

Ochs, E., & Capps, L. (2001). *Living narratives.* Cambridge: Harvard University Press.

Puroila, A. M., Estola, E., & Syrjälä, L. (2012). Does Santa exist? Children's everyday narratives as dynamic meeting places in a day care centre context. *Early Child Development and Care, 182*(2), 191–206.

Ruddick, S. (1995). *Maternal thinking.* Towards a politics of peace. Boston, MA: Beacon Press.

Sahlberg, P. (2011). *Finnish lessons. What can the world learn from educational change in Finland?* New York, NY: Teachers College Columbia University.

Spector-Mersel, G. (2010). Narrative research: Time for a paradigm. *Narrative Inquiry, 20*(1), 204–224.

Syrjälä, L., Estola, E., Uitto, M., & Kaunisto, S. L. (2006). Kertomuksen tutkijan eettisiä haasteita [Ethical challenges in researching stories]. In J. Hallamaa, V. Launis, S. Lötjönen & I. Sorvali (Eds.), *Etiikkaa Ihmistieteille* (pp. 181–202). Helsinki: SKS.

Uitto, M. (2011). *Storied relationships: Students recall their teachers.* Acta Universitatis Ouluensis E122. Tampere: Juvenes Print.

Uitto, M., & Estola, E. (2009). Gender and emotions in relationships: A group of teachers recalling their own teachers. *Gender and Education, 21*(5), 517–530.

Uitto, M., & Syrjälä, L. (2008). Body, caring and power in teacher-pupil relationships: Encounters in former pupils' memories. *Scandinavian Journal of Educational Research, 52*(4), 355–371.

Weber, S., & Mitchell, C. (1995). *That's funny. You don't look like a teacher! Interrogating images and identity in popular culture.* London: Falmer Press.

CHAPTER 9

TEACHER PROFESSIONAL DEVELOPMENT IN *TEACHING AND TEACHER EDUCATION* FROM 2000–2010 ☆

Beatrice Avalos

ABSTRACT

A review of publications in teaching and teacher education over 10 years (2000–2010) on teacher professional development is the subject of this chapter. The first part synthesises production referred to learning, facilitation and collaboration, factors influencing professional development, effectiveness of professional development and issues around the themes. The second part selects from the production nine articles for closer examination. The chapter concludes by noting how the production brings out the complexities of teacher professional learning and how research and development have taken cognizance of these factors and provided food for optimism about their effects, although not yet about their sustainability in time.

Keyword: Teacher professional development

☆This article was first published in 2011, in the journal *Teaching and Teacher Education*, Volume 27, No. 1, pp. 10–20. Reprinted with permission from Elsevier.

From Teacher Thinking to Teachers and Teaching: The Evolution of a Research Community
Advances in Research on Teaching, Volume 19, 175–204
Copyright © 2013 Elsevier
All rights of reproduction in any form reserved
ISSN: 1479-3687/doi:10.1108/S1479-3687(2013)0000019012

INTRODUCTION

The professional development of teachers is studied and presented in the relevant literature in many different ways. But always at the core of such endeavours is the understanding that professional development is about teachers learning, learning how to learn and transforming their knowledge into practice for the benefit of their students' growth. Teacher professional learning is a complex process, which requires cognitive and emotional involvement of teachers individually and collectively, the capacity and willingness to examine where each one stands in terms of convictions and beliefs and the perusal and enactment of appropriate alternatives for improvement or change. All this occurs in particular educational policy environments or school cultures, some of which are more appropriate and conducive to learning than others. The instruments used to trigger development also depend on the objectives and needs of teachers as well as of their students. Thus, formal structures such as courses and workshops may serve some purposes, while involvement in the production of curricula, the discussion of assessment data or the sharing of strategies may serve other purposes. Not every form of professional development, even those with the greatest evidence of positive impact, is of itself relevant to all teachers. There is thus a constant need to study, experiment, discuss and reflect in dealing with teacher professional development on the interacting links and influences of the history and traditions of groups of teachers, the educational needs of their student populations, the expectations of their education systems, teachers' working conditions and the opportunities to learn that are open to them.

During the past 10 years a large number of articles published in *Teaching and Teacher Education* have reported on research and interventions designed for teachers, with teachers and by teachers aimed at their professional learning, with an eye on their impact on teacher and student changes. They cover different geographical regions and different research and development procedures. The first part of this chapter provides a bird's eye view of the content of these pieces, thematically organised in terms of their main emphases. The second part reviews more closely nine articles selected as being particularly illustrative of the thematic areas, and also representative of different geographic locations and contextual particularities.

THEMATIC EMPHASES OVER 10 YEARS (2000–2010)

The Scopus search machine (http://www.scopus.com.scopeesprx.elsevier.com/home.url) was used to retrieve a list of articles that included 'teacher professional development' in their key words to select 111 relevant ones and, by examining their abstracts or the entire article, to produce the classification presented in Table 1. While it might be artificial to classify journal articles according to a single thematic emphasis as usually they have more than one central focus, to do so seemed a sensible way of providing a synthetic overview of what was published over the period. In the rest of this first section then I briefly review the production under each one of the thematic areas.

Table 1. Professional Development Articles Published in *Teaching and Teacher Education* (2000–2010).

Thematic Area	Number of Articles	Geographical Location
Professional learning (general)	9	Canada (1), England (2), The Netherlands (2), South Africa (1), USA (3)
Reflection processes	11	Australia (1), Canada (1), England (1), Portugal (1), The Netherlands (1), USA (6)
Tools as learning instruments	10	Australia (1), Spain (1), Taiwan (1), USA (7)
Beginning teachers learning	13	Australia (1), Belgium (1), Canada (1), England (2), Hong Kong (1), Ireland (1), Norway (1) Scotland (1), The Netherlands (1), USA (3)
Mediations		
School–university partnership	11	Canada (2), Greece (1), USA (8)
Teacher co-learning	13	Canada (2), Hong Kong (1), Singapore (1), The Netherlands (2), USA (7)
Workplace learning	3	Japan (1), The Netherlands (1), USA (1)
Conditions and factors		
Macro conditions	10	South Africa (1), USA (9)
School cultures	6	Canada (1), England (2), USA (3)
Effectiveness of professional development		
Cognitions, beliefs and practices	10	Italy (1), New Zealand (1), Portugal (1, The Netherlands (2), USA (5)
Student learning and teacher satisfaction	7	Belgium (1), Canada (1), Israel (1), Switzerland (1), USA (3)
Specific areas and issues	8	Australia (1), Canada (1), Ireland (1), The Netherlands (1), USA (4)
Total articles	111	

Source: http://www.scopus.com.scopeesprx.elsevier.com/home.url

Professional Learning

These articles deal in general with how teachers learn and change by developing theory or applying theory to the discussion of teacher change (Clarke & Hollingsworth, 2002; Korthagen, 2004, 2010; Penlington, 2008; Snow-Gerono, 2008). They examine the personal processes that are involved in the various formats used for teacher learning, how teacher learning is researched and propose or discuss models of teacher professional learning (Castle, 2006; James & McCormick, 2009; Mushayikwa & Lubben, 2009; Olson & Craig, 2001). The main emphasis of these studies is to understand the processes whereby teachers change. While some are centred on conceptual analysis, others describe the approach with both qualitative and quantitative research examples.

Within this broad area of professional learning, there are three specific groups that stand out in terms of the number of articles they contain. Articles that deal with reflection and narratives form one group. A second one centres on the role of different tools in professional learning, especially technological ones and a considerable number focus on beginning teacher learning.

Reflection Processes

The assumption in articles dealing with teacher reflection is that analysis of needs, problems, change processes, feelings of efficacy and beliefs are all factors that contribute to teacher professional development, be it through enhanced cognitions or new or improved practices. Reflection is discussed and used in research in several ways. The studies in this decade centre primarily on reflection as an instrument for change and on the various ways in which reflection can be developed. A group explicitly considers the contribution to reflection of narrative methods such as storytelling (e.g. about Professional Development School experiences) and the construction of stories within professional development activities (Breault, 2010; Day & Leitch, 2001; Doecke, Brown, & Loughran, 2000; Jenlink & Kinnuncan-Welsch, 2001; Shank, 2006). Narrative accounts serve also to unveil the role of emotions in change. Other articles consider the importance for reflection of involvement in research, and more practically the opportunity offered by self-assessment tools or reflective school portfolios as triggers for change (Burbank & Kauchak, 2003; Craig, 2003; Reis-Jorge, 2007; Romano, 2006; Ross & Bruce, 2007; Runhaar, Sanders, & Yang, 2010).

Tools as Learning Instruments

Several articles deal with uses of technology in professional development. For example, discourse and content analysis serve to study teacher discussions of videos in video clubs, online forums, online video case discussions, as well as the use of classroom video for teaching and learning (Borko, Jacobs, Eiteljorg, & Pittman, 2008; De la Torre Cruz & Casanova Arias, 2007; Hou, Sung, & Chang, 2009; Koc, Peker, & Osmanoglu, 2009; Kucan, Palincsar, Khasnabis, & Chang, 2009; Prestridge, 2010; Sherin & Han, 2004; Van Es & Sherin, 2008; Warren Little, 2002). One article in particular proposes a 'model-hypertextual function to consider teachers' thinking, practice, and development in the use of technology' (Schussler, Poole, Whitlock, & Evertson, 2007).

Beginning Teachers

Beginning to teach is now well recognised around the world as a particular and complex stage of teacher learning (OECD, 2005). Thus, a large number of papers examine various aspects related to mentoring, induction as well as comparisons between novice and experienced teachers. An extensive review of international literature on mentoring (Hobson, Ashby, Malderez, & Tomlinson, 2009) looks at the process in terms of benefits, costs, needs and suggestions for policy-makers. Mentoring takes an important place in terms of what mentors bring to the induction process, their identity formation during the process, training of mentor teachers, how they contribute or not to identity formation of beginning teachers, problems associated with the mentoring process, what are best practices, and the use of tools such as electronic journals (Devos, 2010; Harrison, Dymoke, & Pell, 2006; Hennissen, Crasborn, Brouwer, Korthagen, & Bergen, 2010; Killeavy & Moloney, 2010; Kwan & López-Real, 2010; Sundli, 2007). Conditions associated with the support and mentoring needed to retain beginning teachers in the profession and assist them with their teaching difficulties were studied by Fantilli and McDougall (2009), Mitchell and Logue (2009), and Oberski and McNally (2007). Professional judgment and concerns, including those related to school socialisation of beginning teachers, are studied both longitudinally and with mixed methods (Johnson, Reiman, & Richard, 2007; Kelchtermans & Ballet, 2002; Watzke, 2006).

Mediations Through Facilitation and Collaboration

I understand mediations to be structured or semi-structured processes (such as partnerships, collaborative networks) or informal contexts (such as the workplace interactions) that facilitate learning and stimulate teachers to alter or reinforce teaching and educational practices. In most, but not all of these instances, people such as external researchers or peers play key roles. I have grouped the contributions in this area in three main parts: school–university partnerships, teacher co-learning and workplace learning.

School–University Partnerships
These articles examine how school–university (or teacher–researcher) partnerships bridge the gap between their different perspectives of professional development or highlight the importance of such a space as an area for joint work or joint contributions (Bartholomew & Sandholtz, 2009; Gravani, 2008). The articles report long-standing mixed methods studies on multi-site school partnerships assisted by university professors and improvement in science teaching through links between a university science centre and schools, and discuss both the valuable opportunities as well as complexities in these links (Buczynski & Hansen, 2010; Butler, Lauscher, Jarvis-Selinger, & Beckingham, 2004; Erickson, MinnesBrandes, Mitchell, & Mitchell, 2005; Hudson-Ross, 2001; Jewett & Goldstein, 2008; LePage, Boudreau, Maier, Robinson, & Cox, 2001; McCotter, 2001; Sandholtz, 2002; Sztajn, Hackenberg, White, & Allexsaht-Snider, 2007).

Teacher Co-learning
The importance of understanding how teachers work together and share practices with learning purposes is reflected in articles that look at teacher networks and teams, communities of practice and communities of learning, as well as peer coaching. Two studies illustrate the use of different research procedures such as surveys and ethnography to study conditions for the success of networks as well as effects of networks on teacher meanings, identity and agency (Hofman & Dijkstra, 2010; Niesz, 2010). Lesson study, the Japanese experience of teacher co-learning through mutual collaboration and feedback, is examined in three studies that link its effects to improvement of instruction, efficacy and collaboration and that review conditions that impact on its effectiveness (Fernández, Cannon, & Choksi, 2003; Lee, 2008; Puchner & Taylor, 2006). The productivity of teamwork focused on data collection and problem solving, case studies on communities of practice, peer-coaching trajectory and co-construction of situated assessments are the subject of another group of articles (Baildon & Damico, 2008; Gregory, 2010; Huffman & Kalnin, 2003; Schnellert, Butler, & Higginson, 2008; Zwart, Wubbels, Bolhuis, & Bergen, 2008). Finally three studies (Clausen, Aquino, & Wideman, 2009; Crockett, 2002;

Rueda & Monz, 2002) consider the effects of teacher enquiry groups on changes in beliefs and practices, collaboration in mixed-culture situations of teachers and assistant teachers as well as the early development of a learning community.

Workplace Learning
To some extent this is an 'umbrella' term for professional development that takes place formally or informally in schools and that is not assisted by outside facilitators. Some articles that look at teachers learning in school contexts draw on situated learning theory and consider this learning to be both individual and collaborative as well as facilitated or not by a range of factors including, as we shall see below, different school cultures and traditions (Kwakman, 2003; Mawhinney, 2010; Sato & Kleinsasser, 2004).

Conditions and Factors Influencing Professional Development (Learning and Change)

While several of the articles reviewed deal with factors that affect the quality, possibilities and success of teacher professional learning, there are some that focus more closely on macro societal conditions and the micro-contexts provided by school cultures.

Macro Conditions
Included under this concept are the nature and operation of educational systems, policy environments and reforms, teacher working conditions as well as historic factors that determine what is accepted or not as suitable forms for professional development. For example, a historical approach and a particular theoretical model for analysing policy implementation (McIntyre & Kyle, 2006) are used to explain why an attempt to establish an ungraded primary school system in a particular U.S. state education system was not sustainable over time and the effect on this failure of pressures from the community, politics and the media. With the exception of those who had better professional development, school support and whose beliefs were aligned with those of the reform, teachers reverted to old practices. An opposite example is provided in an ethnographic case-book study about seven South African unqualified teachers (Henning, 2000) who in the last years of Apartheid struggled against the odds to form a teachers' community. In 1991 they sought assistance to develop professionally from an all-white university. The willingness and commitment of partners on both

sides allowed for the successful development of a programme that combined contact education, distance education, school-based training and the systematic assessment of prior learning. All of which made the teachers' journey to greater professionalism a successful one. While policy reform environments may be supportive of teacher development as narrated in another case (Borko, Elliot, & Uchiyama, 2002), and as evidenced in the learning interaction of teachers participating in the National Board Certification in the United States (Coskie & Place, 2008; Park, Steve Oliver, Setar Johnson, Graham, & Oppong, 2007), a more critical stance is taken about the effects on teacher development of standards-based reforms and accountability environments, high-stakes assessment, the narrowing of professional development 'outcomes' to teacher test scores and the increased control and regulation over how professional development operates (Boardman & Woodruff, 2004; Cochran-Smith, 2001; Delandshere & Arens, 2001; Sandholtz & Scribner, 2006; Skerrett, 2010).

School Cultures

Different studies refer to school culture as an indicator of the school's ethos and social environment (traditions, beliefs). The concept covers the operation of the administrative and organisational structures, and how these interact to facilitate or constrict teacher workplace learning. Comparative studies of schools in different geographical locations and their opportunities for teacher learning serve to illustrate how beliefs, traditions, types of institutional arrangements affect the extent of teachers' informal engagement in pedagogic exchanges (Jurasaite-Harbison & Rex, 2010; Melville & Wallace, 2007; Muijs & Harris, 2006; Sato & Kleinsasser, 2004; Snow-Gerono, 2005). Professional development that incorporates all-school enquiry can either be hindered by the school's organisational context or on the contrary, under certain conditions, can contribute towards commitment to learning goals and collaboration in school (King, 2002). Subject departments as forms of school organisation have positive effects on teachers' professional growth and active pedagogic leadership provided they operate as communities that seek to have influence on the whole school environment (Knight, 2002; Melville & Wallace, 2007).

Effectiveness of Professional Development

While most of the studies reviewed consider some form of impact of professional development on teachers' knowledge and practice, including effects on pupils, some set out explicitly to explore the effectiveness of programmes on personal changes of teachers cognitions, beliefs and practice as well as pupil change and teacher satisfaction.

Teacher Changes in Cognition, Beliefs and Practice

Changes in cognition took several forms in the studies reviewed. Different modalities of professional development improved curricular knowledge and understanding in areas as diverse as reading comprehension and science, as well as fostering of student motivation (Cherubini, Zambelli, & Boscolo, 2002; Ermeling, 2010; Frey & Fisher, 2009; Levine & Marcus, 2010; Morais, Neves, & Alfonso, 2005; Seymour & Osana, 2003). Improvement in teacher knowledge was partially detected in a study of the effect of action research on three areas of teacher cognition: ideological (norms, values), empirical (connection between phenomena) and technical (methods). Only technical knowledge was improved (Ponte, Ax, Beijaard, & Wubbels, 2004). Partial results were also produced on teachers' conceptions and practices regarding student self-regulated learning (Hoekstra, Brekelmans, Beijaard, & Korthagen, 2009). Changes in teacher beliefs or expectations of student achievement in low-income communities were an outcome sustained over two years of professional development (Timperley & Phillips, 2003). The effects of a year long experience in developing literacy instruction skills resulted in high and low implementers. Differences between them were explained in terms of their levels of general, personal and collective efficacy (Cantrell & Callaway, 2008).

Student Learning

The effectiveness of communities of learning on the improvement of teaching practice and student achievement was supported by a review of 11 studies dealing with the subject (Vescio, Ross, & Adams, 2008). Three articles (Fishman, Marx, Best, & Tal, 2003; Lovett et al., 2008; Vogt & Rogalla, 2009) report on the effects of professional development on student reading outcomes in the first case, on science learning in the second, and on generally improved student outcomes as teachers learned to adapt teaching to individual student needs in the third. Comparison of two types of professional development related to reading comprehension instruction (a year-round intensive coaching and a short 13 hour course) had similar positive effects on student learning and self-efficacy perceptions, but with increased workload for teachers in the restricted course (Van Keer & Verhaeghe, 2005).

Teacher satisfaction increased in relation to professional development activities considered to be 'close to home' and to their needs and expectations, and when they contributed to the improvement of curricular understanding and increased self-efficacy (Lovett et al., 2008; Nielsen, Barry, & Staab, 2008; Nir & Bogler, 2008).

Specific Areas and Issues

A couple of articles consider both conceptually and empirically how teachers deal with aggressive behaviour or abused children and the degree to which they have been prepared appropriately (Alvarez, 2007; Walsh & Farrell, 2008). A few articles look at diverse forms of professional development activities with an eye on dilemmas, conflicts and limiting circumstances that for different reasons affect their effectiveness (Glazier, 2009; Hibbert, Heydon, & Rich, 2008; O'Sullivan, 2002; Tillema & Kremer-Hayon, 2002; Yamagata-Lynch, 2003; Yamagata-Lynch & Haudenschild, 2009). These articles highlight, for example, the dilemmas that facilitators and teacher participants have promoting self-regulated learning, the equivocal goal of preparing 'expert teachers' to become trainers of others, teacher tensions during activities due to competing responsibilities and pressures on their work lives arising from external expectations, the disturbing role of a 'cultural expert' within a professional development group, and possible misalignment between motives or background of teacher participants in professional development and those of the responsible entities. Professional development geared to new curriculum implementation assists the sharing of new knowledge with other teachers, but is also limited in terms of new pressures on their work lives by expectations of the programme and the school district.

TEACHER PROFESSIONAL DEVELOPMENT IN SELECTED ARTICLES

In this section, I discuss a group of nine articles published over the 10 year period that cover a number of the themes outlined in the first section. I have selected these particular papers not only because of their thematic approach but also because they study teachers in different geographical and cultural contexts, thus honouring the international character of teaching and teacher education. These papers represent ways of approaching teacher professional development along the following main thematic areas:

1. The learning of practicing teachers: how they learn, what they bring to their learning efforts and how these efforts are reflected in changes in cognition, beliefs and practices.
2. The embedded or situated nature of teacher professional learning and development: within the school environment and its culture, and in relation to how educational systems and policies affect their work lives.
3. The role of mediations in the quality of their learning: external facilitation of learning processes provided for example by school–university/researchers collaboration or by other teachers as collaborators, informal and teacher formal networking, and the use of specific teaching tools as sources for self-analysis and change.

The main characteristics of the selected papers are presented in Table 2.

How Teachers Learn to Learn? The Possibilities and Limitations
of Teacher Professional Development

The reason why I selected O'Sullivan's (2002) article to illustrate how teachers learn to learn is because of the extreme care with which the author unveils an experience with unqualified and under-qualified teachers. The participants were teaching English in 31 primary schools at lower and upper primary level. The setting was Namibia in the early years after its independence and at the end of the Apartheid regime. Only 24% of the 99 teachers had some form of qualification. The originality of the experience was that not only did the author design and implement the professional development activity but also researched its process. Appropriately, she chose an action research model based on Elliot's (1991) cycles of hypothesis, planning, action, monitoring and reflection, and the article centres on how these cycles were carried out during four circuits of workshops and follow-up activities in classrooms (June 1995–June 1997). The article also centres on the effort to develop reflective skills in the participants.

What we get is a detailed account of the teachers' interaction with the process and of how the author, slowly and painfully, interprets and reacts to what initially are hardly discernible signs of interest and involvement, by creatively applying the action research steps: retracing steps, redirecting and refocusing during workshops and in follow-up stages of the training circuits.

Table 2. Main Features of Selected Articles.

Authors	Topic	Type of Article	Subjects Studied	Location
James and McCormick (2009)	Teachers learning how to learn	Research based (quantitative and qualitative)	Teachers in secondary, primary and infant schools	England
Jenlink & Kinmuncan-Welsch (2001)	Teacher development facilitators' learning	Research based (qualitative, case stories)	Design team, facilitators and teachers in study groups	USA
Jurasaite-Harbison and Rex (2010)	School cultures and teacher learning	Research based (ethnographic study)	Teachers	Lithuania and USA
Sato and Kleinsasser (2004)	School cultures and teacher beliefs, practices and interactions	Research based (interviews, observations, documents)	Teachers	Japan
LePage et al. (2001)	Professor–teacher relationships in graduate programme	Research based (dialogic enquiry, interviews and short-answer surveys)	Teachers and university faculty	USA
O'Sullivan (2002)	Teacher learning in action research cycles	Research based (action research cycles, observation)	Unqualified and under-qualified practicing teachers	Namibia
Ross and Bruce (2007)	Teacher self-assessment as a source of change	Research based (qualitative case study)	Teachers	Canada
Schnellert et al. (2008)	Collaborative learning from use of situated assessment tools	Research based (qualitative data in cycles of collaboration)	Teachers and researchers	Canada
Vescio et al. (2008)	Impact of teacher learning communities	Research review	Research reports	USA and England

Source: http://www.scopus.com.scopeesprx.elsevier.com/home.url

As products of Apartheid education the participant teachers had been exposed for the most part of their education to structured directive teaching and rote learning. They had no prior experience of brainstorming, of volunteering ideas, and of sharing of views. Thus, the 'reflection' step in the first action research cycle proved difficult and ineffective. Rather than giving up and considering the method to be a failure, the author as facilitator resorted to refocusing the next three circuits of the process. This was done through posing and seeking to respond to three questions: (a) to what extent can reflective skills be developed, (b) how can they be developed and (c) how appropriate is the 'Western' model of reflective training to the Namibian context. The core of the remaining action research cycles consisted in examining what reflective skills were possible and how they could be developed. By being attentive to signs of change the author observed that through practice and reinforcement in question-asking as well as through group and pair discussions the teachers increased their confidence and participation. She also noticed that teacher reactions to unstructured lesson observations and videos were passive and so decided to provide them with a semi-structured observation form containing factual and reflective questions. This approach was successful in increasing teacher reflective analysis and involvement. Leading teachers critically to examine their own practice was more complicated, but again it was aided by prompts based on presenting examples of carelessly prepared materials so that teachers, in their student role, could notice the problem. In other words, she concluded, reflective learning as conceptualised in Western literature required adaptation if it was to be effective in the kind of situations described. She defined the adaptation as 'structured reflection'. This made it possible for her to respond affirmatively to the question about teachers being able to move along the reflective path. They could do so. But the pace was slower. In the time frame of the experience these teachers had reached a 'basic' stage of reflection, which was below Zeichner's (cited O'Sullivan, 2002) first stage of 'technical rationality'. They could see problems in their practice but not yet devise solutions for them. Had the programme been extended, these teachers would probably have reached the stage of 'technical rationality'. Kenneth Zeichner (Zeichner & Dahlström, 1999) who also contributed to teacher education in Namibia through a Bachelor of Education Initial Teacher Preparation Programme based on reflective learning might have a different opinion regarding O'Sullivan's conclusions. Nevertheless, the authors' experience and approach as narrated in this chapter provides substance to well-developed theories and approaches to teacher development that alert us to the importance and strength of prior beliefs and cultural values as factors that may affect its results and impact. The honest account of the author also highlights the importance of monitoring progress in learning and refocusing teaching when necessary as a key condition in any learning process. These procedures did allow for observed improvements of teaching in the participants classrooms.

The second article (Ross & Bruce, 2007) included in this section is also about the subjective reflective elements in teacher learning as facilitated through a structured process of self-assessment and includes research carried out in Ontario, Canada. It starts by proposing a model of teacher change centred on teacher self-assessment, which is embedded within the framework of social cognition theory. Self-assessment is seen as integrating three processes: (a) self-observation of aspects of instruction considered relevant to success, (b) self-judgments about meeting or not proposed goals and (c) self-reactions or interpretations of the extent to which goals have been attained and degree of satisfaction about the process. Self-assessment influences self-efficacy beliefs and in turn affects future decisions about teaching. The model also includes the influence of peers who may assist in drawing attention to specific elements of practice (in cases of co-observation), and provide feedback that supports or competes with the teacher's self-assessment, depending on how credible the peer teacher is considered to be. Finally, the model includes the participation of external agents in the process of teacher change. With all these elements at hand, the article narrates the results of work with seven teachers involved in an in-service programme designed to implement standards-based teaching in mathematics. Standards-based teaching in mathematics is described as being at the opposite end of 'traditional' mathematics teaching based on rules and procedures. The key feature of the study was a self-assessment tool constructed by the authors, which included 10 characteristics of standards-based mathematics teaching and a rubric with four levels of implementation based on fidelity to the standards.

Based on the model, the intervention consisted of a cycle beginning with the use of the self-assessment tool and rubrics by the teachers, followed by exposure to peer observation skills and information about teaching mathematics using the standards, peer observation of teaching and joint setting of teaching goals, analysis of the observation data and further input on standards' teaching skills, classroom experimentation during four weeks, peer observation, and further work on teaching skills. The article discusses results of the whole process on the basis of the example of one teacher and the usefulness of the self-assessment tool. It concludes that the tool reinforced the value of existing practices and strengthened beliefs about competence, but also provided information for improvement. It provided a common language for observation and discussion with peers and researchers. However, there were also problems with the assessment tool as noted by the case teacher: rigid in some parts, the actual teacher practices overlapped the categories, and changes suggested in the rubrics were too big to be accomplished in the period of time available (four weeks). The initial change model was modified as a result of the experiment to include effects on student achievement and the contribution of peers and researchers to the development of innovative instruction.

Awareness of shortfalls was provided by what the authors call 'negative data', or data that worked in the opposite direction of what was expected, indicating, for example, that teaching had become more and not less directive. And, in a similar way to what happened in the Namibian case, these shortfalls were explained on the basis of existing beliefs and the extent to which teachers recognised or not the need for change and therefore attempted to change their teaching practice. If there is a gap between beliefs and suggested practices, change will only occur if the gap is recognised: 'teachers who underrate their performance or have low self-efficacy are less likely to implement data' (Ross & Bruce, 2007, p. 155). The article also refers to other contextual elements that support change in the expected direction such as a history of successful mathematics teaching and support from school administrators.

The Situated Nature of Teacher Learning

The articles selected to represent this well-recognised condition of teacher professional development consider primarily what is known as workplace learning or the formal and informal processes that take place and are facilitated by schools. Traditions, administrative arrangements and strength of purpose or mission of a school affect how teachers perceive their work and how they interact professionally among themselves. The term 'school culture' has been widely used to express these aspects of school life and is used in the articles reviewed in this section.

Set in Lithuania and the United States, the article by Jurasaite-Harbison and Rex (2010) narrates a two-year ethnographic study that looks at how teachers in three different types of schools perceive themselves as learners and how their school cultures create opportunities for teachers' professional development. The authors define culture, following Anderson-Levitt (cited in Jurasaite-Harbison & Rex, p. 268) as 'an interactive web of meaning, whose parts are in continuous interaction with each other'. Two of the schools studied were secondary schools in Lithuania but one was a former Russian school that continued to provide for the Russian population, while the other was a newer school for Lithuanians. The third one was a mid-western United States elementary school. The article addresses the culture of these schools, how teachers viewed them as contexts for professional growth and the manner in which teachers engaged in professional interactions among themselves. Data was provided by observations of the schools and interviews with 11 teachers, as well as by videos, photographs and diverse documentation. To assess the extent to which the schools reflected external policies and structures, the authors also collected national educational documents. The article describes the methods of analysis and triangulation used to reach their descriptions, interpretations and conclusions.

Each one of the schools comprised a different microcosm. The Russian school had in the past a position of prestige and a tradition of excellence, but in its current condition as a school for Russian minorities, it was struggling for survival and for a valid place within the Lithuanian educational community. The Lithuanian school in a way represented the new world after independence, and tied its academic and social goals to this world. It was described as an elite school that used novel approaches to teaching, and that had well-trained teachers and democratic relations with the community. The American school was new in a community where parents wanted their children to prepare for university entrance. It was also a school that accepted and promoted the goals of the U.S. educational policy expressed in the No Child Left Behind (NCLB) document. The school is described as not having the need for a proper mission statement apart from the one embedded in the test-driven policies of NCLB. All three schools also differed in their approach to traditions. While the American school did not have any traditions to uphold, the Russian school sought to revitalise their old traditional events, an effort that was valued by the teachers but that involved hard work and stress on their part. The Lithuanian school banked on traditional events and social customs (i.e. meeting for tea) as opportunities for informal exchange and learning. Physical spaces were appropriate for interchange of teachers and visits to each other's classrooms in the Lithuanian and Russian schools, while this was not the case in the two-story building of the American school. The administrative arrangements for professional development also varied in each school. In the American school it was the central administration that provided a time and place for teachers of the same level to plan and to learn (generally on topics related to NCLB). The principal also provided support for teachers to attend conferences and workshops. But there were no in-school formal professional development activities. This was not the case in both Lithuanian schools where the vice-principals organised and led professional development activities for teachers. As far as informal learning among teachers, this was not supported in the Russian school where the emphasis was on top-down monitoring of quality, while the situation was reversed in the Lithuanian school.

As a result of the different contextual elements described above teachers related very differently to each other depending on the school to which they belonged. Using the concepts coined by Hargreaves (cited in Jurasaite-Harbison & Rex, 2010) of types of professional interchanges: 'tinkering, transferring knowledge, researching practice', the authors describe how these processes operated in each one of the schools. In the American school they were very much absent, being practically reduced to 'simple exchange or borrowing of materials and ideas'. There were, however, examples of 'collective tinkering' expressed as bouncing ideas off with others. Despite the introduction of peer coaching in the school, there was not much evidence of its practice. In the Russian school, some individual tinkering with ideas and trial and error occurred despite the lack of support for informal learning among teachers. Interaction depended on their being someone willing to do so. The Lithuanian school, on the contrary, exemplified a wide range of informal learning and interchange among teachers: experimenting of new ideas, classroom observation of colleagues, interchanges with student teachers. This was assisted by the fact that middle managers organised professional development activities, provided information on external ones as well as opportunity for informal learning. However, teachers in this school formed a closed community that made it difficult for a new teacher, who did not abide by the established mores, to remain in the school.

On the basis of their findings, the authors conclude that the most productive conditions for informal workplace learning is a teacher culture that encourages and values collaborative learning.

Moving to a different context, the next selected article examines teachers and teaching in an English high school department in Japan (Sato & Kleinsasser, 2004). The concept of 'technical school culture' is taken from Lortie (cited in Sato & Kleinsasser, 2004) and serves to define the culture of the school in terms of beliefs, practices and interactions. Through a yearlong study the authors responded to three main questions centred on (a) the beliefs, practices and interactions of 19 teachers studied (15 native Japanese), (b) how these beliefs, practices and interactions related to each other and (c) how the whole technical culture influenced individual teachers' beliefs, practices and interactions.

The examination of the general features of the school culture leads the authors to describe it as focused on management and on tasks that were not primarily related to teaching, communication and collaboration. Teaching English was observed to be extremely examination oriented, with teachers sharing the belief that it was important to teach in line with examination demands and to manage the classroom appropriately. Teaching as observed was in fact similar in its patterns. Teacher interactions included collaboration to sustain the established norms and values of their workplace, but not to sound out new ideas or discuss how their teaching was progressing. They described their teaching beliefs and interactions in a similar way to what the researchers had observed in the school and classrooms, supporting the notion that effectively there was a technical culture with the aforesaid characteristics. The prevalence of this general culture led individuals with different personal stands on teaching practices to subsume their beliefs under the general cover of three basic norms or values: examinations-oriented English, keeping pace and managing school tasks and students. Teachers had developed their concept and patterns of teaching by watching their colleagues at school. The effect was to produce a uniform style of teaching. There were no observed differences due to experience. The tendency of the older teachers was to teach English the same way as they always had, using a particular method based on grammar translation. Professional learning seemed to entail the improvement of teacher fidelity to the established technical culture. To progress in teaching meant to teach according to the textbook and to share handouts. Teachers did not have time to discuss in depth any substantive teaching issue and most did not attend professional development activities. If an individual teacher developed an innovative practice this was not shared with other teachers. In other words, the school did have a shared culture in which teachers reflected, interpreted and socially constructed English language teaching although 'not in the way some scholars want them to do or think they should' (Sato & Kleinsasser, 2004, p. 814).

Beliefs and practices were also the subject of a large study in 40 English primary and secondary schools (James & McCormick, 2009) in the context of a project directed to assisting students in 'learning how to learn' (LHTL). The relevant part of the article deals with those teaching practices that the research team generally stimulated and that promoted Assessment for Learning as a tool for teaching how to learn. Using a large data set involving surveys, interviews and observational records, the researchers examined how teachers in the participant schools behaved in their efforts to promote LHTL through work with assessments. They were able to distil three elements in the teaching practices that appeared conducive to learning how to learn: 'making learning explicit, promoting learning autonomy and pursuing a performance orientation in lieu of a learning or mastery orientation'. Teachers differed in the way they worked in relation to these principles, depending on their prior values and beliefs, and on the degree to which they were able to adhere, for example, to the importance of learning autonomy. The study considered the embedded nature of the teachers' learning processes by paying attention to the educational policy environment in which they taught and to the importance of collaboration and networking among the participating teachers. Thus, teachers who found it difficult to close the gap between believing in teaching to learn through the use of assessment and their own practice were those that felt constrained by a 'policy culture that encouraged rushed curriculum coverage, teaching to the test and a tick-box culture' (James & McCormick, 2009, p. 982). Also, while collaboration and networking proved to be a key element in teacher learning, its possibilities depended on the degree to which the schools' organisational structures and leadership were supportive and enabling. The study thus provided further support for the differing effects on professional development of school and policy environments.

Mediations

Mediations, in most education processes, are like springboards that provide the impetus for moving from one point to another. An important part of teacher learning is mediated through dialogues, conversations and interactions centred on materials and situations. Teacher professional development often involves horizontal sharing of ideas and experiences, active participation in projects or becoming aware of problems that need solutions. How others mediate teacher learning through these actions and the nature of such interactions is the subject of the next group of articles selected for this review.

The nature of university–school partnerships is discussed theoretically in an article by LePage et al. (2001) and studied empirically during one year through the experience of one professor and five teachers who were part of a 'non-traditional' master's programme offered at a U.S. university. The purpose of the programme was to enter into partnerships with schools and teachers through enrolling teams of teachers from individual schools. It is described as having a strong philosophical and moral component in the curriculum and an emphasis on confronting issues through analysis and research. In the second year of study, teachers worked as teams with a professor in the development of a research project. The article narrates the work of one such team. The purpose of their study was to explore the complexities of relationships between professors and teachers in a context where reciprocity was valued and teachers' struggle against confinement to a technician role was underscored and respected by the programme. This was done through several procedures: dialogic enquiry pursued by the team through monthly meetings of which each participant kept a journal, in-depth interviews of 10 alumni on the nature of professor–teacher relationships and short-answer surveys that were administered to 80 master's students at the beginning and end of their studies on the relationship to their professors. The researchers used all the data sources to study the nature of their mediations and deal specifically with issues of authority and hierarchy, role definitions, and contradictions in their different role relations. The process produced changes in hierarchical relations, from greater to lesser feelings of intimidation among the teachers, although a sense of distance still remained due to the professors' responsibility for assessment. Role definitions were marked by ambiguity. In part teachers equated their role as teachers of children with the professors' role, but more importantly their roles appeared confused due to what the authors described as the growing 'isomorphism' in teacher and professor definitions within the broader community. For example, teachers increasingly are urged to take on tasks such as research in classrooms that traditionally formed part of academia, while teacher educators are requested to develop skills normally defined as belonging to excellent classroom teachers. This convergence of roles causes difficulties in role definition, especially as the institutions themselves do not change as rapidly in the same direction. On the basis of their findings, the authors suggest changes in how teacher educators see their role and how they value teachers as partners, but also they propose that both sides collaborate in defining roles that do not blur distinctions or maintain traditional boundaries.

While the LePage study addressed role relationships between university professors and teachers, Jenlink and Kinnuncan-Welsch (2001) examined the role of facilitators in teacher development activities, seen from the side of facilitators. The article centres on case stories written by the facilitators of nine study groups of teachers who were part of a professional development activity in the United States. These stories resulted from a project in which three types of teams interacted: a design team of 3 university academics, a team composed of 12 teacher facilitators plus the design team, and 9 study groups of 5–14 teachers. The article centres on narratives written by three of the facilitators on their lived experiences after five months of work with the study groups. The sources from which these narratives were crafted include fieldnotes from participant observation, videotapes, reflective journals, critical moment stories and individual, peer and focus group interviews. The article presents three case stories, as seen in each case through the lenses of a different facilitator: how to get a group started and set the ground rules in one case, or how to handle domineering participants and maintain trust and motivation in another. The third case story, written after the end of the groupwork, was the joint facilitators' reflection of what the experience had meant for them: 'it has given me the skills and ability to not necessarily delegate more, but let other people take over the role and lead the conversation. It has given me the opportunity to participate versus always being in the leadership role' (Jenlink & Kinnuncan-Welsch, 2001, p. 717). The article ends by highlighting key elements involved in the process of facilitation, issues and outcomes of the process, and its effects on the facilitators' personal professional development: increased confidence, high degree of commitment, heightened responsibility of the self as learner and impact on their personal lives.

Finally, two other studies bring out the importance of teacher co-learning as being itself a mediating factor in the change of practices as well as in the improvement of student learning. One is a review of research on the impact of professional learning communities (Vescio et al., 2008) and the other an account of the effect on reflection and practice of teachers who engage collaboratively in the construction, scoring and interpretation of assessment data (Schnellert et al., 2008). Vescio et al.'s (2008) review covers 11 studies all centred on the impact of professional learning communities. These are described as teachers in schools, with shared values and norms, who work together collaboratively and reflectively on their improvement with a specific focus on student learning. Not all studies reviewed reported important changes in practice, but they did report changes in the school cultures due to four main characteristics: collaboration, a focus on student learning, teacher authority described as the ability of teachers to make decisions within their communities and in school governance, and finally recognition of the importance of teacher continuous learning. As far as improvement of student learning was concerned not all studies examined this outcome, but the eight that did reported improved student learning and the key contributing factor to this was the learning community's commitment to meeting student learning needs. The article by Schnellert et al. (2008) takes us closer into the learning experience of six teachers in one Canadian school. These teachers worked together with university researchers in the use of two learning tools designed to help develop and measure progress in literacy skills among students, part of a policy target known as Learning through Reading. The relevant part of the broader study was the collaboration of teachers in the use of these instruments, the interpretation of the data they produced, reflection on the meaning of the results and setting of goals, as well as the planning, enacting and reflection on their instructional strategies and the refinement of their teaching over time. All this occurred during what the authors call 'data-driven cycles of collaboration'. Analysis of the information provided by teacher interviews, field notes from planning meetings and classroom observations as well as classroom artefacts such as lesson plans and graphic organisers allowed the researchers to conclude that the collaborative reviewing of formative assessment data influenced all teachers' changes in teaching, although to varying degrees. They were also able to conclude that this was not related to years of experience but to the extent to which they had engaged in stages of collaborative and reflective enquiry.

CONCLUDING REFLECTIONS

At the end of this journey through so much that has been studied and written on teacher professional development over a decade, what perhaps more vividly stands out is the extent to which, at least in these publications, we have moved away from the traditional in-service teacher training model. What underlies the thematic emphasis of the studies reviewed, their assumptions and enquiry methods is a recognition that teacher learning and development is a complex process that brings together a host of different elements and is marked by an equally important set of factors. But also that at the centre of the process, teachers continue to be both the subjects and objects of learning and development.

The particular way in which background contextual factors interact with learning needs varies depending on the traditions, culture mores, policy environments and school conditions of a particular country. The starting point of teachers engaging in professional development in the Namibian study may not be relevant to teachers in Canada or The Netherlands. On the other hand, there is a similitude in the processes whereby teachers move from one stage to the next in different contexts, which appears to be supported in the research reviewed, although with different manifestations.

The effort to construct models of teacher development is also a way of searching for unifying threads in the midst of diversity. Cognitive theory and research have helped unveil some of the constant factors such as the role of prior beliefs and perceptions of self-efficacy as individual factors supporting or hindering change, while socio-cultural theory has directed the attention to the external situations that likewise affect change. The good news resulting from the research reviewed is that diverse formats of professional development have effects of some kind or degree. The not-so-good news is that we know little about how pervasive these changes are and to what degree they sustain continuous efforts to move ahead. It was clear from the successful experiences narrated that prolonged interventions are more effective than shorter ones, and that combinations of tools for learning and reflective experiences serve the purpose in a better way.

The power of teacher co-learning emerges very strongly from the studies reviewed. The road starts with informal exchanges in school cultures that facilitate the process, continues in networking and interchanges among schools and situations and is strengthened in formalised experiences such as courses and workshops that introduce peer coaching or support collaboration and joint projects. In whatever way, the lesson learned is that teachers naturally talk to each other, and that such a talk can take on an educational purpose. It also is true that in many places classroom teaching continues to be a solitary activity. Therefore to move from co-learning through talk to co-learning through observation and feedback is necessary as well as effective, as illustrated in experiences such as lesson study.

The traditional 'master' role of teacher educators and researchers is revised in a number of the studies reviewed. We read about partnership experiences between university professors and teachers in formal courses where roles and role-playing were investigated in order to further more productive engagements in learning and change. Other partnerships such as those generated by external researchers working with teachers as co-researchers contributed to modify the traditional separation between academia and the professions.

Finally, although the topic was not included in the selected articles, the wider list included a set of articles that highlighted the effects of policy environments centred on standardised examination results and restricted notions of teacher accountability. This is not a minor issue, as these policies have travelled the world and penetrated more strongly in precisely those contexts where teachers, working under difficult conditions, have limited opportunity to renew imaginatively their teaching through collaborative work among themselves. In the quest for higher examination scores, they are provided with 'outside experts' to teach them how to produce results in the short periods of time demanded by their education systems. The experiences in the articles reviewed run counter to such a model.

REFERENCES

Alvarez, H. E. (2007). The impact of teacher preparation on responses to student aggression in the classroom. *Teaching and Teacher Education, 23*(7), 1113–1126.

Baildon, M., & Damico, J. (2008). Negotiating epistemological challenges in thinking and practice: A case study of a literacy and inquiry tool as a mediator of professional conversation. *Teaching and Teacher Education, 24*(6), 1645–1657.

Bartholomew, S. S., & Sandholtz, J. H. (2009). Competing views of teaching in a school–university partnership. *Teaching and Teacher Education, 25*(2), 155–165.

Boardman, A. G., & Woodruff, A. L. (2004). Teacher change and "high-stakes" assessment: What happens to professional development? *Teaching and Teacher Education, 20*(6), 545–557.

Borko, H., Elliot, R., & Uchiyama, K. (2002). Professional development: A key to Kentucky's educational reform effort. *Teaching and Teacher Education, 18*(8), 969–987.

Borko, H., Jacobs, J., Eiteljorg, E., & Pittman, M. E. (2008). Video as a tool for fostering productive discussions in mathematics professional development. *Teaching and Teacher Education, 24*(2), 417–436.

Breault, R. A. (2010). Distilling wisdom from practice: Finding meaning in PDS stories. *Teaching and Teacher Education, 26*(3), 399–407.

Buczynski, S., & Hansen, C. B. (2010). Impact of professional development on teacher practice: Uncovering connections. *Teaching and Teacher Education, 26*(3), 599–607.

Burbank, M. D., & Kauchak, D. (2003). An alternative model for professional development: Investigations into effective collaboration. *Teaching and Teacher Education, 19*(5), 499–514.

Butler, D. L., Lauscher, H. N., Jarvis-Selinger, E., & Beckingham, B. (2004). Collaboration and self-regulation in teachers' professional development. *Teaching and Teacher Education, 20*(5), 435–455.

Cantrell, S. C., & Callaway, P. (2008). High and low implementers of content literacy: Portraits of teacher efficacy. *Teaching and Teacher Education, 24*(7), 1739–1750.

Castle, K. (2006). Autonomy through pedagogical research. *Teaching and Teacher Education, 22*(8), 1094–1103.

Cherubini, G., Zambelli, F., & Boscolo, P. (2002). Student motivation: An experience of inservice education as a context for professional development of teachers. *Teaching and Teacher Education, 18*(3), 273–288.

Clarke, D., & Hollingsworth, H. (2002). Elaborating a model of teacher professional growth. *Teaching and Teacher Education, 18*(8), 947–967.

Clausen, K. W., Aquino, A. M., & Wideman, R. (2009). Bridging the real and the ideal: A comparison between learning community characteristics and a school-based case study. *Teaching and Teacher Education, 25*(3), 444–452.

Cochran-Smith, M. (2001). The outcomes question in teacher education. *Teaching and Teacher Education, 17*(5), 527–546.

Coskie, T. L., & Place, N. A. (2008). The National Board Certification process as professional development: The potential for changed literacy practice. *Teaching and Teacher Education, 24*(7), 1893–1906.

Craig, C. J. (2003). What teachers come to know through school portfolio development. *Teaching and Teacher Education, 19*(8), 815–827.

Crockett, M. D. (2002). Inquiry as professional development: Creating dilemmas through teachers' work. *Teaching and Teacher Education, 18*(5), 609–624.

Day, C., & Leitch, R. (2001). Teachers and teacher education lives: The role of emotion. *Teaching and Teacher Education, 17*(4), 403–415.

De la Torre Cruz, M. J., & Casanova Arias, P. F. (2007). Comparative analysis of experiences of efficacy in in-service and prospective teachers. *Teaching and Teacher Education, 23*(5), 641–652.

Delandshere, G., & Arens, S. A. (2001). Representations of teaching and standards based reform: Are we closing the debate about teacher education. *Teaching and Teacher Education, 17*(5), 547–566.

Devos, A. (2010). New teachers, mentoring and the discursive formation of professional identity. *Teaching and Teacher Education, 26*(5), 1219–1223.

Doecke, B., Brown, J., & Loughran, J. (2000). Teacher talk: The role of story and anecdote in constructing professional knowledge for beginning teachers. *Teaching and Teacher Education, 16*(3), 335–348.

Elliot, J. (1991). *Action research for educational change.* Milton Keynes, UK: Open University Press.

Erickson, G., MinnesBrandes, G., Mitchell, I., & Mitchell, J. (2005). Collaborative teacher learning: Findings from two professional development projects. *Teaching and Teacher Education, 21*(7), 787–798.

Ermeling, B. A. (2010). Tracing the effects of teacher inquiry on classroom practice. *Teaching and Teacher Education, 26*(3), 377–388.

Fantilli, R. D., & McDougall, D. E. (2009). A study of novice teachers: Challenges and supports in the first years. *Teaching and Teacher Education, 25*(6), 814–825.

Fernández, C., Cannon, J., & Choksi, S. (2003). A US–Japan lesson study collaboration reveals critical lenses for examining practice. *Teaching and Teacher Education, 19*(2), 171–185.

Fishman, B. J., Marx, R. W., Best, S., & Tal, R. T. (2003). Linking teacher and student learning to improve professional development in systemic reform. *Teaching and Teacher Education, 19*(6), 643–658.

Frey, N., & Fisher, D. (2009). Using common formative assessments as a source of professional development in an urban American elementary school. *Teaching and Teacher Education, 25*(5), 674–680.

Glazier, J. A. (2009). The challenge of repositioning: Teacher learning in the company of others. *Teaching and Teacher Education, 25*(6), 826–834.

Gravani, M. N. (2008). Academics and practitioners: Partners in generating knowledge or citizens of two different worlds? *Teaching and Teacher Education, 24*(3), 649–659.

Gregory, A. (2010). Teacher learning on problem-solving teams. *Teaching and Teacher Education, 26*(3), 608–615.

Harrison, J., Dymoke, S., & Pell, T. (2006). Mentoring beginning teachers in secondary schools: An analysis of practice. *Teaching and Teacher Education, 22*(8), 1055–1067.

Henning, E. (2000). Walking with "barefoot" teachers: An ethnographically fashioned casebook. *Teaching and Teacher Education, 16*(1), 3–20.

Hennissen, P., Crasborn, F., Brouwer, N., Korthagen, F., & Bergen, T. (2010). Uncovering contents of mentor teachers' interactive cognitions during mentoring dialogue. *Teaching and Teacher Education, 26*(2), 207–214.

Hibbert, K. M., Heydon, R. M., & Rich, S. J. (2008). Beacons of light, rays, or suncatchers? A case study of the positioning of literacy teachers and their knowledge in neoliberal times. *Teaching and Teacher Education, 24*(2), 303–315.

Hobson, A. J., Ashby, P., Malderez, A., & Tomlinson, P. D. (2009). Mentoring beginning teachers: What we know and what we don't. *Teaching and Teacher Education, 25*(1), 207–216.

Hoekstra, A., Brekelmans, M., Beijaard, D., & Korthagen, F. (2009). Experienced teachers' informal learning: Learning activities and changes in behavior and cognition. *Teaching and Teacher Education, 25*(5), 663–673.

Hofman, R. H., & Dijkstra, B. J. (2010). Effective teacher professionalization in networks? *Teaching and Teacher Education, 26*(4), 1031–1040.

Hou, H.-t., Sung, Y.-T., & Chang, K.-E. (2009). Exploring the behavioural patterns of an online knowledge-sharing discussion activity among teachers with problem-solving strategy. *Teaching and Teacher Education, 25*(1), 101–108.

Hudson-Ross, S. (2001). Intertwining opportunities: Participants' perceptions of professional growth within a multiple-site teacher education network at the secondary level. *Teaching and Teacher Education, 17*(4), 433–454.

Huffman, D., & Kalnin, J. (2003). Collaborative inquiry to make data-based decisions in schools. *Teaching and Teacher Education, 19*(6), 569–580.

James, M., & McCormick, R. (2009). Teachers learning how to learn. *Teaching and Teacher Education, 25*(7), 973–982.

Jenlink, P. M., & Kinnuncan-Welsch, K. (2001). Case stories of facilitating professional development. *Teaching and Teacher Education, 17*(6), 705–724.

Jewett, P., & Goldstein, N. (2008). Catching sight of talk: Glimpses into discourse groups. *Teaching and Teacher Education, 24*(5), 1232–1243.

Johnson, L. E., Reiman, A. J., & Richard, W. (2007). Beginning teacher disposition: Examining the moral/ethical domain. *Teaching and Teacher Education, 23*(5), 676–687.

Jurasaite-Harbison, E., & Rex, L. A. (2010). School cultures as contexts for informal teacher learning. *Teaching and Teacher Education, 26*(2), 267–277.

Kelchtermans, G., & Ballet, K. (2002). The micropolitics of teacher induction. A narrative-biographical study on teacher socialisation. *Teaching and Teacher Education, 18*(1), 105–120.

Killeavy, M., & Moloney, A. (2010). Reflection in a social space: Can blogging support reflective practice for beginning teachers. *Teaching and Teacher Education, 26*(4), 1070–1076.

King, M. B. (2002). Professional development to promote schoolwide inquiry. *Teaching and Teacher Education, 18*(3), 243–257.

Knight, P. (2002). A systemic approach to professional development. *Teaching and Teacher Education, 18*(3), 229–241.

Koc, Y., Peker, D., & Osmanoglu, A. (2009). Supporting teacher professional development through online video case study discussions: An assemblage of preservice and inservice teachers and the case teacher. *Teaching and Teacher Education, 25*(8), 1158–1168.

Korthagen, F. A. J. (2004). In search of the essence of a good teacher: Towards a more holistic approach in teacher education. *Teaching and Teacher Education, 20*(1), 1–77.

Korthagen, F. A. J. (2010). Situated learning theory and the pedagogy of teacher education: Towards and integrative view of teacher behaviour and teacher learning. *Teaching and Teacher Education, 26*(1), 98–106.

Kucan, L., Palincsar, A. S., Khasnabis, D., & Chang, C.-I. (2009). The video viewing task: A source of information for assessing and addressing teacher understanding of text-based discussion. *Teaching and Teacher Education, 25*(3), 415–423.

Kwakman, K. (2003). Factors affecting teacher participation in professional learning activities. *Teaching and Teacher Education, 19*(2), 149–170.

Kwan, T., & López-Real, F. (2010). Identity formation of teacher-mentors: An analysis of contrasting experiences using a Wengerian matrix framework. *Teaching and Teacher Education, 26*(3), 722–731.

Lee, J. F. K. (2008). A Hong Kong case of lesson study – Benefits and concerns. *Teaching and Teacher Education, 24*(5), 1115–1124.

LePage, P., Boudreau, S., Maier, S., Robinson, J., & Cox, H. (2001). Exploring the complexities of the relationship between K–12 and college faculty in a nontraditional professional development program. *Teaching and Teacher Education, 17*(2), 195–211.

Levine, T. H., & Marcus, A. S. (2010). How the structure and focus of teachers' collaborative activities facilitate and constrain teacher learning. *Teaching and Teacher Education, 26*(3), 389–398.

Lovett, M. W., Lacerenza, L., de Palma, M., Benson, N. J., Steinbach, K. A., & Frijters, J. C. (2008). Preparing teachers to remediate reading disabilities in high school: What is needed for effective professional development? *Teaching and Teacher Education, 24*(4), 1083–1097.

Mawhinney, L. (2010). Let's lunch and learn: Professional knowledge sharing in teachers' lounges and other congregational spaces. *Teaching and Teacher Education, 26*(4), 972–978.

McCotter, S. S. (2001). Collaborative groups as professional development. *Teaching and Teacher Education, 17*(6), 685–704.

McIntyre, E., & Kyle, D. W. (2006). The success and failure of one mandated reform for young children. *Teaching and Teacher Education, 22*(8), 1130–1144.

Melville, W., & Wallace, J. (2007). Metaphorical duality: High school departments as both communities and organizations. *Teaching and Teacher Education, 23*(7), 1193–1205.

Mitchell, S. M., Reilly, R. C., & Logue, M. E. (2009). Benefits of collaborative action research for the beginning teacher. *Teaching and Teacher Education, 25*(2), 344–349.

Morais, A. M., Neves, I. F., & Alfonso, M. (2005). Teacher training processes and teachers' competence – A sociological study in the primary school. *Teaching and Teacher Education, 21*(4), 415–437.

Muijs, D., & Harris, A. (2006). Teacher led school improvement: Teacher leadership in the UK. *Teaching and Teacher Education, 22*(8), 961–972.

Mushayikwa, E., & Lubben, F. (2009). Self-directed professional development – Hope for teachers working in deprived environments. *Teaching and Teacher Education, 25*(3), 375–382.

Nielsen, D. C., Barry, A. L., & Staab, P. T. (2008). Teachers' reflections of professional change during a literacy-reform initiative. *Teaching and Teacher Education, 24*(5), 1288–1303.

Niesz, T. (2010). Chasms and bridges: Generativity is the space between educators' communities of practice. *Teaching and Teacher Education, 26*(1), 37–44.

Nir, A. E., & Bogler, R. (2008). The antecedents of teacher satisfaction with professional development programs. *Teaching and Teacher Education, 24*(2), 377–386.

Obserki, I., & McNally, J. (2007). Holism in teacher development: A Goethian perspective. *Teaching and Teacher Education, 23*(6), 935–945.

OECD. (2005). *Teachers matter. Attracting, developing and retaining effective teachers.* Paris: OECD.

Olson, M. R., & Craig, C. J. (2001). Opportunities and challenges in the development of teachers' knowledge: The development of narrative authority through knowledge communities. *Teaching and Teacher Education, 17*(6), 667–684.

O'Sullivan, M. C. (2002). Action research and the transfer of reflective approaches to in-service education and training (INSET) for unqualified and under-qualified primary teachers in Namibia. *Teaching and Teacher Education, 18*(5), 523–539.

Park, S., Steve Oliver, J., Setar Johnson, T., Graham, P., & Oppong, N. K. (2007). Colleagues' roles in the professional development of teachers: Results from a research study of National Board Certification. *Teaching and Teacher Education, 23*(4), 368–389.

Penlington, C. (2008). Dialogue as a catalyst for teacher change: A conceptual analysis. *Teaching and Teacher Education, 24*(5), 1304–1316.

Ponte, P., Ax, J., Beijaard, D., & Wubbels, T. (2004). Teachers' development of professional knowledge through action research and the facilitation of this by teacher educators. *Teaching and Teacher Education, 20*(6), 571–588.

Prestridge, S. (2010). ICT professional development for teachers in online forums: Analysing the role of discussion. *Teaching and Teacher Education, 26*(2), 252–258.

Puchner, L. D., & Taylor, A. R. (2006). Lesson study, collaboration and teacher efficacy: Stories from two school-based math lesson study groups. *Teaching and Teacher Education, 22*(7), 922–934.

Reis-Jorge, J. (2007). Teachers' conceptions of teacher-research and self-perceptions as enquiring practitioners – A longitudinal case study. *Teaching and Teacher Education, 23*(4), 402–417.

Romano, M. E. (2006). "Bumpy moments" in teaching: Reflections from practicing teachers. *Teaching and Teacher Education, 22*(8), 973–985.

Ross, J. A., & Bruce, C. D. (2007). Teacher self-assessment: A mechanism for facilitating professional growth. *Teaching and Teacher Education, 23*(2), 146–159.

Rueda, R., & Monz, L. D. (2002). Apprenticeship for teaching: Professional development issues surrounding the collaborative relationship between teachers and para-educators. *Teaching and Teacher Education, 18*(5), 503–521.

Runhaar, P., Sanders, K., & Yang, H. (2010). Stimulating teachers' reflection and feedback asking: An interplay of self-efficacy, learning goal orientation, and transformational leadership. *Teaching and Teacher Education, 26*(5), 1154–1161.

Sandholtz, J. H. (2002). Inservice training or professional development: Contrasting opportunities in a school/university partnership. *Teaching and Teacher Education, 18*(7), 815–830.

Sandholtz, J. H., & Scribner, S. B. (2006). The paradox of administrative control in fostering teacher professional development. *Teaching and Teacher Education, 22*(8), 1104–1117.

Sato, K., & Kleinsasser, R. C. (2004). Beliefs, practices and interactions in a Japanese high school English department. *Teaching and Teacher Education, 20*(8), 797–816.

Schnellert, L. M., Butler, D. L., & Higginson, S. K. (2008). Co-constructors of data, co-constructors of meaning: Teacher professional development in an age of accountability. *Teaching and Teacher Education, 24*(3), 725–750.

Schussler, D. L., Poole, I. R., Whitlock, T. W., & Evertson, C. M. (2007). Layers and links: Learning to juggle 'one more thing' in the classroom. *Teaching and Teacher Education*, *23*(5), 572–585.

Seymour, J. R., & Osana, H. P. (2003). Reciprocal teaching procedures and principles: Two teachers' developing understanding. *Teaching and Teacher Education*, *19*(3), 325–344.

Shank, M. J. (2006). Teacher storytelling: A means for creating and learning within a collaborative space. *Teaching and Teacher Education*, *22*(6), 711–721.

Sherin, M. G., & Han, S. Y. (2004). Teacher learning in the context of a video club. *Teaching and Teacher Education*, *20*(2), 163–183.

Skerrett, A. (2010). "There's going to be community. There's going to be knowledge": Design for learning in a standardised age. *Teaching and Teacher Education*, *26*(3), 648–655.

Snow-Gerono, J. L. (2005). Professional development in a culture of inquiry: PDS teachers identify the benefits of professional learning communities. *Teaching and Teacher Education*, *21*(3), 241–256.

Snow-Gerono, J. L. (2008). Locating supervision: A reflective framework for negotiating tensions within conceptual and procedural foci for teacher development. *Teaching and Teacher Education*, *24*(6), 1502–1515.

Sundli, L. (2007). Mentoring e a new mantra for education? *Teaching and Teacher Education*, *23*(2), 201–214.

Sztajn, P., Hackenberg, A. J., White, D. Y., & Allexsaht-Snider, M. (2007). Mathematics professional development for elementary teachers: Building trust within a school-based mathematics education community. *Teaching and Teacher Education*, *23*(6), 970–984.

Tillema, H. H., & Kremer-Hayon, L. (2002). "Practicing what we preach" – teacher educators' dilemmas in promoting self-regulated learning: A cross-case comparison. *Teaching and Teacher Education*, *18*(5), 593–607.

Timperley, H. S., & Phillips, G. (2003). Changing and sustaining teachers' expectations through professional development in literacy. *Teaching and Teacher Education*, *19*(6), 627–641.

Van Es, E. A., & Sherin, M. G. (2008). Mathematics teachers' "learning to notice" in the context of a video club. *Teaching and Teacher Education*, *24*(2), 244–276.

Van Keer, H., & Verhaeghe, J. P. (2005). Comparing the teacher development programs for innovating reading comprehension instruction with regard to teachers' experience and student outcomes. *Teaching and Teacher Education*, *21*(5), 543–562.

Vescio, V., Ross, D., & Adams, A. (2008). A review of research on the impact of professional learning communities on teaching practice and student learning. *Teaching and Teacher Education*, *24*(1), 80–91.

Vogt, F., & Rogalla, M. (2009). Developing adaptive teaching competency through coaching. *Teaching and Teacher Education*, *25*(8), 1051–1060.

Walsh, K., & Farrell, A. (2008). Identifying and evaluating teachers' knowledge in relation to child abuse and neglect: A qualitative study with Australian early childhood teachers. *Teaching and Teacher Education*, *24*(3), 585–600.

Warren Little, J. (2002). Locating learning in teachers' communities of practice: Opening up problems of analysis in records of everyday work. *Teaching and Teacher Education*, *18*(8), 917–946.

Watzke, J. L. (2006). Longitudinal research on beginning teacher development: Complexity as a challenge to concerns-based stage theory. *Teaching and Teacher Education*, *23*(1), 106–122.

Yamagata-Lynch, L. C. (2003). How a technology professional development program fits into teachers' work life. *Teaching and Teacher Education, 19*(6), 591–607.

Yamagata-Lynch, L. C., & Haudenschild, M. T. (2009). Using activity systems to identify inner contradictions in teacher professional development. *Teaching and Teacher Education, 25*(3), 507–517.

Zeichner, K., & Dahlström, L. (1999). *Democratic teacher education reform in Africa: The case of Namibia.* Boulder, CO: Westview Press.

Zwart, R. C., Wubbels, T., Bolhuis, S., & Bergen, T. C. M. (2008). Teacher learning through reciprocal peer coaching: An analysis of activity sequences. *Teaching and Teacher Education, 24*(4), 982–1002.

CHAPTER 10

THE EMERGENCE OF RESEARCH ON TEACHERS' PROFESSIONAL IDENTITY: A REVIEW OF LITERATURE FROM 1988 TO 2000 ☆

Douwe Beijaard, Paulien C. Meijer and Nico Verloop

ABSTRACT

The studies considered in this review of research on teachers' professional identity until 2004 can be divided into three categories: (a) studies in which the focus was on teachers' professional identity formation; (b) studies in which the focus was on the identification of characteristics of teachers' professional identity; and (c) studies in which professional identity was (re)presented by teachers' stories. Four essential features of teachers' professional identity could be derived from the studies. Many of the reviewed studies appeared to be studies on teachers' personal practical knowledge. However, in only a few studies was the relationship between this knowledge and professional identity made explicit. It is argued that, in future research on teachers' professional identity, more attention needs to be paid to the relationship between relevant concepts like "self" and

☆This chapter is a condensed version of Beijaard, D., Meijer, P.C., & Verloop, N. (2004). Reconsidering research on teachers' professional identity. *Teaching and Teacher Education, 20*(2), 107–128.

From Teacher Thinking to Teachers and Teaching: The Evolution of a Research Community
Advances in Research on Teaching, Volume 19, 205–222
ISSN: 1479-3687/doi:10.1108/S1479-3687(2013)0000019013

"identity," the role of the context in professional identity formation, what counts as "professional" in professional identity, and research perspectives other than the cognitive one that may also play a role in designing research on teachers' professional identity.

Keywords: Teacher professional identity; identity development; identity research

INTRODUCTION

In the last decades, teachers' professional identity has emerged as a separate research area (i.e., Bullough, 1997; Connelly & Clandinin, 1999; Knowles, 1992; Kompf, Bond, Dworet, & Boak, 1996). To explain what this concept means, several authors have drawn on the definition of identity used in the social sciences and philosophy. Of particular interest in this regard is the work of the symbolic interactionist Mead (1934) and the psychologist Erikson (1968). The latter focused on identity formation in social contexts and on the stages people pass through: owing to biological and psychological maturation, each stage has its own characteristics regarding the individual's interaction with his or her environment. Erikson outlined a chronological and changing concept of identity. Identity is not something one has, but something that develops during one's whole life. Mead used the concept of identity in relationship with the concept of self; he described in detail how the self is developed through transactions with the environment. According to Mead, self can arise only in a social setting where there is social communication; in communicating we learn to assume the roles of others and monitor our actions accordingly. Our concept of self can be defined as an organized representation of our theories, attitudes, and beliefs about ourselves (McCormick & Pressley, 1997). The world of the self may appear to the outsider to be subjective and hypothetical, but to the individual experiencing it, it has the feeling of absolute reality (Purkey, 1970). In general, the concept of identity has different meanings in the literature. What these various meanings have in common is the idea that identity is not a fixed attribute of a person, but a relational phenomenon. Identity development occurs in an intersubjective field and can be best characterized as an ongoing process, a process of interpreting oneself as a certain kind of person and being recognized as such in a given context (Gee, 2001). In this context, then, identity can also be seen as an answer to the recurrent question: "Who am I at this moment?"

The concept of identity is defined in various ways in the more general literature. It seems that the concept of professional identity is also used in different ways in the domain of teaching and teacher education. In some studies, the concept of professional identity was related to teachers' concepts or images of self (i.e., Knowles, 1992; Nias, 1989). It was argued that these concepts or images of self strongly determine the way teachers teach, the way they develop as teachers, and their attitudes toward educational changes. In other studies of professional identity, the emphasis was placed on teachers' roles (i.e., Goodson & Cole, 1994; Volkmann & Anderson, 1998), whether or not in relationship with other concepts, or on concepts like reflection or self-evaluation that are important for the development of professional identity (i.e., Cooper & Olson, 1996; Kerby, 1991). Furthermore, professional identity refers not only to the influence of the conceptions and expectations of other people, including broadly accepted images in society about what a teacher should know and do, but also to what teachers themselves find important in their professional work and lives based on both their experiences in practice and their personal backgrounds (Tickle, 2000). Both sides of professional identity seem strongly interwoven, but have been differently emphasized by researchers. Knowles (1992), therefore, characterized professional identity as an unclear concept in the sense of what, and to what extent, things are integrated in such an identity.

Thus, while it is clear that teachers' professional identity has emerged as a separate research area, it is, in our view, an area in which researchers conceptualize professional identity differently, investigate varying topics within the framework of teachers' professional identity, and pursue a diversity of goals. Against this background, we felt the need to gain greater insight into this research area and, through that contribute to a better understanding of what professional identity entails in teaching and teacher education, stimulate the discussion about this topic, and help in designing future research. In order to realize this, we attempted to answer the following questions:

1. What features are essential for research on teachers' professional identity?
2. How can current research on teachers' professional identity be characterized?
3. What problems need to be addressed in research on teachers' professional identity?

The answers to these questions are based on a review of the literature on teachers' professional identity in the period 1988–2000 in which we systematically analyzed how this concept was used in studies and ascertained what the results of these studies were.

Based on their focus of attention, the studies could be divided into three categories:

- studies in which the focus was on teachers' professional identity formation;
- studies in which the focus was on the identification of characteristics of teachers' professional identity as perceived by the teachers themselves or as identified by the researchers from the data they collected; and
- studies in which professional identity was (re)presented by teachers' stories told and written.

Below, we summarize the results of our analysis of these three categories of studies. For full details of this review we refer to Beijaard, Meijer, and Verloop (2004).

TEACHERS' PROFESSIONAL IDENTITY FORMATION

Research on teachers' professional identity formation is seen as relevant to teacher educators and mentors in schools in order to better understand and conceptualize the support student teachers need (i.e., Volkmann & Anderson, 1998). Particularly student teachers' biographies and the beliefs that are determined by these biographies are conceived of as important constituents of teachers' professional identity formation (Knowles, 1992; Sugrue, 1997; see also Kelchtermans, 1994). From this perspective, Bullough (1997) wrote:

> Teacher identity – what beginning teachers believe about teaching and learning as self-as-teacher – is of vital concern to teacher education; it is the basis for meaning making and decision making. [...] Teacher education must begin, then, by exploring the teaching self. (p. 21)

Research on teachers' professional identity formation also contributes to our understanding and acknowledgment of what it feels like to be a teacher in today's schools, where many things are changing rapidly, and how teachers cope with these changes. From this point of view, it is important to pay attention to the personal part of teachers' professional identity. What is found relevant to the profession, especially in light of the many educational changes currently taking place, may conflict with what teachers personally desire and experience as good. Such a conflict can lead to friction in teachers' professional identity in cases in which the "personal" and the "professional" are too far removed from each other (Korthagen, 2001).

From the review (for full details see Beijaard et al., 2004), the following major findings stood out. Student teachers can be equally successful in their professional identity formation although they follow different developmental paths (Antonek, McCormick, & Donato, 1997). This uniqueness of the process of identity formation is supported by the "theoretical" findings of Coldron and Smith (1999), who pointed to the need for teachers to be active in this process. Based on their theoretical analysis, they stated that teachers should participate in dialogue, be aware of the many approaches and ways of doing things, be engaged with a range of resources, and share ideas so that they can locate themselves. Striving for uniformity and conformity, then, would threaten the teacher's active location in the process of professional identity formation (Gee & Crawford, 1998). Dillabough (1999) concluded that the current conception of the teacher as a rational and instrumental actor ignores the notion of the authentic and discursive self.

Professional identity formation is a process involving many knowledge sources, such as knowledge of affect, teaching, human relations, and subject matter (Antonek et al., 1997). Student teachers' own lay theories should also be seen as such a source. Sugrue (1997) found that these lay theories begin with the student teachers' personalities, but that they are significantly shaped by (a) immediate family, (b) significant others or extended family, (c) apprenticeship of observation, (d) atypical teaching episodes, (e) policy context, teaching traditions, and cultural archetypes, and (f) tacitly acquired understandings. Lay theories are tacit or unarticulated and lead to forms of professional identity formation that differ from forms of professional identity formation derived from research-based theories of teaching. It is important to enhance student teachers' awareness of their own theories (Sugrue, 1997; see also Bullough, 1997). A (student) teacher's biography, then, is important in the process of identity formation. Knowles (1992) mentioned early childhood experiences, early teacher role models, previous teaching experiences, and significant or important people and significant prior experiences as relevant biographical categories.

Professional identity formation is often presented as a struggle because (student) teachers have to make sense of varying and sometimes competing perspectives, expectations, and roles that they have to confront and adapt to (Samuel & Stephens, 2000; Volkmann & Anderson, 1998; see also Bullough,

Knowles, & Crow, 1992; Mawhinney & Xu, 1997; Roberts, 2000). For example, Volkmann and Anderson (1998), who examined the professional identity formation of one beginning science teacher, found that this teacher's images of teaching conflicted with more general expectations of what makes a professional teacher. The three dilemmas this teacher struggled with were (a) feeling like a student while being expected to act like a teacher, (b) wanting to care for students while being expected to be tough, and (c) feeling incompetent in her knowledge of chemistry while being expected to behave like an expert. The results described by Goodson and Cole (1994) also follow this line. They found that teachers' sense of developing a (new) professional identity was contextually dependent on their developing notions of the professional community. Based on this, they concluded that

> In order for teachers to have opportunities to realize their individually-defined personal and professional potential, teaching and development need to be defined, interpreted, and facilitated within a broader institutional context. (p. 102)

CHARACTERISTICS OF TEACHERS' PROFESSIONAL IDENTITY

Some studies in this category drew attention to specific issues related to teachers' perceptions of professional identity, such as the teaching of low-status subjects in schools (Paechter & Head, 1996), increasing teachers' sense of professional identity to prevent burnout or attrition, e.g., by providing a sabbatical year (Gaziel, 1995; see also Moore & Hofman, 1988), and male teachers' reasons for entering primary education (DeCorse & Vogtle, 1997). Some other studies in this category indicated that it is important to benefit from teachers' perceptions of aspects of their professional identity, such as the subject they teach, their relationship with students, and interactions with colleagues. Knowledge of teachers' perceptions of aspects of their professional identity may, e.g., be useful in helping them to cope with educational changes (Beijaard, Verloop, & Vermunt, 2000), and serve as a basis for institutional and educational innovations (Nixon, 1996) or cooperation with colleagues (Mitchell, 1997). The last group of studies in this category attempted to make explicit what the occupational group shares or should share. Siraj-Blatchford (1993), for example, wanted to draw attention to what new teachers share and which is ignored by policy documents. Preuss and Hofsass (1991) argued that the implementation of a new role (teaching disabled students in "normal" classrooms owing to governmental policy) should have implications for teacher education.

The review (Beijaard et al., 2004) showed the following major findings regarding this issue. A shared sense or perception of professional identity is hard to identify in the studies on aspects of teachers' professional identity. The absence of a shared sense of professional identity in these studies is somewhat in contrast to the findings of Nixon (1996), who concluded that (university) teachers profess and practice values as an occupational group with a coherent professional perspective on teaching and learning.

The results of the studies related to specific issues are hard to compare. Taking again the study by DeCorse and Vogtle (1997) on men choosing to enter elementary education as an example, it was concluded that the most common reason for a male teacher to be or become an elementary teacher is the direct contact with and nurturing of children. In this, they do not differ from female teachers. Another finding concerning a specific issue was reported by Paechter and Head (1996) in their study on teachers' professional identity related to teaching low-status subjects. Teachers who teach such subjects tend to locate their professional identity in teaching in general rather than in their subject skills.

Experienced teachers seem to perceive relevant aspects of their profession (such as their interaction with students and their commitment to serving students) as positive (i.e., Beijaard, 1995). A teacher's positive self-perception of his or her professional identity appears to override his or her dissatisfaction with poor working conditions (Moore & Hofman, 1988). Measures taken to improve teachers' working conditions may influence teachers' perceptions of their professional identity positively (Gaziel, 1995). Moore and Hofman (1988), e.g., found that striving for quality by the school is consistent with a highly developed professional identity.

STORIES THAT (RE)PRESENT PROFESSIONAL IDENTITY

This category consists of only two publications that fit our selection criteria. Both emphasize, more than those about teachers' professional identity formation, the influence of teachers' professional landscape on their professional lives. Connelly and Clandinin (1999) see this landscape as a storied landscape. During the last two decades, the narrative research tradition gained much influence on research on teaching and teacher education. Generally speaking, from a narrative perspective, the practice of teaching is seen as constructed when teachers tell and live out particular stories (Elbaz-Luwisch, 2002).

The studies, particularly those of Connelly and Clandinin (1999), explicitly relate storytelling to teachers' (and researchers' as well as administrators') professional identity. In the studies on teachers' professional identity formation presented above this relationship remained much more implicit. In the review (Beijaard et al., 2004), the following major findings are reported. Brooke (1994) described her process of becoming a teacher in terms of a person "who teaches preschool" toward "being a preschool teacher." According to her, a professional has a certain body of assimilated knowledge in the field in which he or she works and the skill to use it effectively. Becoming a professional is for Brooke a process of interaction between what is found relevant by others in the vocation and what teachers value themselves. This implies a growth process characterized by learning from experiences and engaging in dialogue about these experiences with colleagues. Brooke pointed to issues of disagreement among colleagues which can lead to growth places. The stories in the work of Connelly and Clandinin (1999) give the reader a sense of what the narrators care about most, what motivates them, the conditions in which they carry out their work, and the dilemmas with which they live. These aspects of their professional lives usually remain hidden in a teaching life (Phelan, 2000). One such aspect is the relationship between identity and curriculum practice: when programs and curricula change, teachers lose a sense of themselves. School change, then, results in new stories to live by (Clandinin, 2003). However, teacher resistance against school change may also reflect an effort to maintain a story to live by. The tensions and dilemmas in the administrators' stories recounted by Connelly and Clandinin appear to be similar to those of teachers.

RECONSIDERING RESEARCH ON TEACHERS' PROFESSIONAL IDENTITY

In the introduction, we posed three questions. Based on the above review, we attempt to answer these questions in this section.

Features of Professional Identity

The concept of professional identity was defined differently or not defined at all in the studies we reviewed. The latter pertains particularly to the studies on teachers' characteristics of professional identity. These studies also showed much variety, ranging from the identification of characteristics that emerged from the data to teachers' perceptions of such characteristics that were already formulated by the researcher. On the basis of the studies on teachers' characteristics of professional identity, it is not possible to indicate which specific characteristics particularly shape teachers' professional identity. More indications of this can be derived from the studies on teachers' professional identity formation and the studies on stories that (re)present professional identity. Based on these studies, we identified the following features that, in our view, are essential for teachers' professional identity.

• Professional identity is an *ongoing process* of interpretation and reinterpretation of experiences (Kerby, 1991), a notion that corresponds with the idea that teacher development never stops and can be best seen as a process of lifelong learning (i.e., Day, 1999; Graham & Young, 1998). From a professional development perspective, therefore, professional identity formation is, in our view, not only an answer to the question "Who am I at this moment?", which we posed in the introduction to this chapter, but also an answer to the question "Who do I want to become?", which is in line with what Conway (2001) called the function of anticipatory reflection. Seeing professional identity as an ongoing process implies that it is dynamic, not stable or fixed.
• Professional identity implies both *person and context*. A teacher's professional identity is not entirely unique. Teachers are expected to think and behave professionally, but not simply by adopting professional characteristics, including knowledge and attitudes that are prescribed. Teachers differ in the way they deal with these characteristics depending on the value they personally attach to them. Feiman-Nemser and Floden (1986), e.g., wrote that there is no one teaching culture in a school and that every teacher, though limited by the context, may to some extent develop his or her own teaching culture.
• A teacher's professional identity consists of *sub-identities* that more or less harmonize. The notion of sub-identities relates to teachers' different contexts and relationships. Some of these sub-identities may be broadly linked and can be seen as the core of teachers' professional identity, while others may be more peripheral. It seems to be essential for a teacher that these sub-identities do not conflict, for example, that they are well balanced. During initial teacher training, student teachers often experience such conflict (i.e., Volkmann & Anderson, 1998). Experienced teachers

may experience such conflict in cases of educational change or change in their immediate working environment (i.e., Connelly & Clandinin, 1999). The more central a sub-identity is, the more costly it is to change or lose that identity.

- *Agency* is an important element of professional identity, meaning that teachers have to be active in the process of professional development (Coldron & Smith, 1999). This element of professional identity formation is in line with a constructivist view of learning, which means that learning – individually as well as in collaboration – takes place through the activity of the learner. There are various ways in which teachers can exercise agency, depending on the goals they pursue and the sources available for reaching their goals. In addition, it can be argued that professional identity is not something teachers have, but something they use in order to make sense of themselves as teachers. The way they explain and justify things in relation to other people and contexts expresses, as it were, their professional identity (Coldron & Smith, 1999).

Characterizing the Research

Researchers investigating the characteristics of teachers' professional identity must ask themselves to what extent their purposes fit in with how the concept of (professional) identity is generally defined. The above-mentioned features of professional identity (particularly its process and ever-changing nature) may imply that characteristics of professional identity can only be identified at a general and abstract level (Dillabough, 1999), or that it is probably better to place this research under another heading, for example, under the heading "professional characteristics" (Tickle, 2000).

The studies on teachers' professional identity formation and the stories that (re)present professional identity are small-scale and in-depth. They all more or less appeared to be studies on teachers' personal practical knowledge (i.e., Connelly & Clandinin, 1985, 1990; Clandinin & Connelly, 1996; Craig, 1998; Elbaz, 1983; Golombek, 1998). Clandinin (1992) defined this type of knowledge as "... carved out of, and shaped by, situations; knowledge that is constructed and reconstructed as we live out our stories and retell and relive them through processes of reflection" (p. 125). Most studies on teachers' professional identity formation demonstrated or reconstructed ways in which teachers build their personal practical knowledge from experiences in practice (Jeans, 1996; Taylor, 1989).

However, in most of these studies, the relationship between professional identity and personal practical knowledge was assumed but not explained. In the studies on stories that (re)present professional identity, particularly in that of Connelly and Clandinin (1999), this relationship was made explicit: the authors increasingly noticed that teachers' answers to their questions about knowledge seemed to be answers to questions about identity.

In the other, more general, literature (i.e., Bakhtin, 1981; Giddens, 1991), the emphasis is placed on the importance of narrative and dialogue in the construction of self. Though not made explicit in many of the studies reviewed above, this may also explain the relevance of stories or narratives in research on teachers' professional identity. This identity, then, is formed and re-formed by the stories we tell and which we draw upon in our communications with others. In other words, stories inadvertently shape teachers and teaching; they are not only chosen and managed by their tellers alone, but are also expressions of cultural values, norms, and structures passed on by the tellers (Rex, Murnen, Hobbs, & McEachen, 2002).

In some studies on teachers' professional identity formation, explicit attention was paid to the importance of teachers' contexts and to research-based knowledge of teaching, i.e., professional characteristics that are seen as relevant to teachers and that should have a role in identity formation as well (i.e., Sugrue, 1997). Doing justice to a teacher's context and the research-based knowledge of teaching that is available is in line with the notion that teachers' stories constitute their "core" identity, but, at the same time, that these stories are socially formed and informed (Gee, 2001). This notion about the influence of the context on teachers' professional identity is particularly reflected in the studies on stories that (re)present teachers' professional identity.

We argue, more than in most of the studies on professional identity formation and in line with the studies on stories that (re)present teachers' professional identity, that identity formation is a process of practical knowledge-building characterized by an ongoing integration of what is individually and collectively seen as relevant to teaching. Fig. 1, inspired by Jansz (1991), illustrates in more detail what we mean by this. In this figure, the unbroken arrows represent the process of professional identity formation that is often seen as "the" process by which teachers build their practical knowledge, beginning in Quadrant 1, passing through Quadrants 2, 3, and 4 and then again starting in Quadrant 1, etc. In reality, however, many other processes of identity formation also occur. These are represented by the broken arrows in Fig. 1. The studies on professional identity formation which we reviewed focused on the interaction between

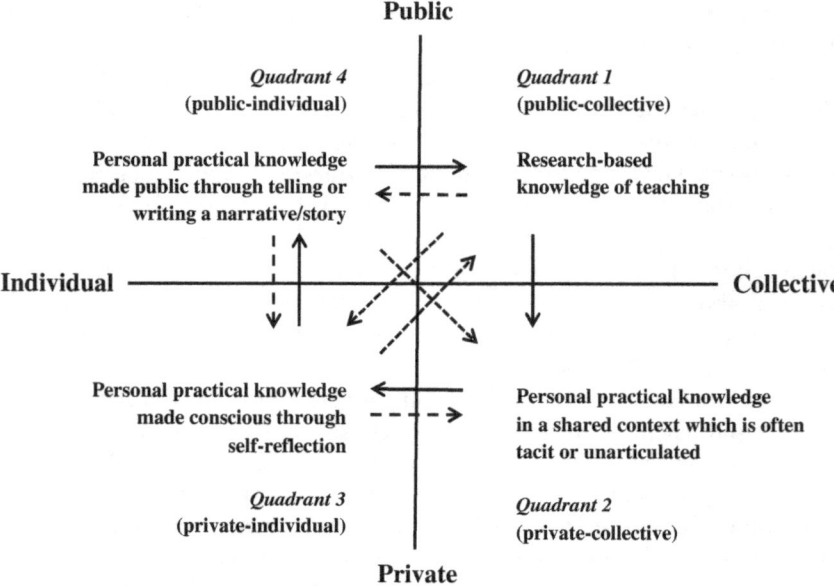

Fig. 1. Representation of Professional Identity Formation from a Teacher Knowledge Perspective.

Quadrants 2 and 3 and on the results of this interaction (Quadrant 4), i.e., public accounts of (student) teachers' personal practical knowledge. Fig. 1 indicates that research on teachers' professional identity formation should focus on more ways of identity formation and that this process can be very complex. In the next section, we pay more attention to this.

Problems that Need to be Addressed

Based on the studies reviewed, we would like to point to the following problems. First, it remains unclear how exactly the concepts of "identity" and "self" are related. Both concepts were often used to indicate the same thing, but seem to be different concepts. According to Nias (1989), "identity" forms part of "self." Through reflection, it can be argued, a person informs his or her identity, which may affect the self. This is in line with the work of Mead (1934) who made a distinction between "I" and "me" as two important components of "self." The "I" is, so to say, the active component of self: through reflection, the "I" articulates thoughts. "Me" is the identity that the self develops. The "me" owns those thoughts and recognizes, as it were, the voice of "I" as its own (Miller, 1973). From this point of view the "I" and "me" cannot exist without each other. However, this is only one point of view. In order to define professional identity, it is important to make explicit from what point of view we see a teacher's self, because this determines how we see his or her professional identity. For example, from a modernist point of view, "self" is strongly related to being authentic and fulfilling a pre-given individual autonomy, while from a post-modernist point of view, "self" is strongly related to how people organize their experiences in stories, which may differ in time and depend on context (i.e., Edwards, 1997). The studies we reviewed seem to represent a mixture of modern and post-modern ways of looking at "self."

Second, in most of the studies on professional identity formation, the emphasis was on the "personal side" (the left side of Fig. 1) and less on the context and how the "professional side" is seen in and by this context (the right side of Fig. 1). The need to pay explicit attention to the influence of the context (i.e., a teacher's landscape; Reynolds, 1996) on professional identity formation has been emphasized by Coldron and Smith (1999), Goodson and Cole (1994), and Connelly and Clandinin (1999). None of the studies, however, was explicit about the educational theories that are part of teachers' landscape as well and which also play a role in professional identity formation (see Fig. 1). Explicitly acknowledging this role of educational theories has implications for research. A structured, though open method of data collection seems desirable. By using a "structured" method, justice is done to what is contextually given and socially legitimated; by using an "open" method, justice is done to the personal norms and values teachers themselves find important. It seems to us that the studies we reviewed did not sufficiently or explicitly take into account such (and other) methodological implications of research on teachers' professional identity.

Third, we mentioned four features of teachers' professional identity, but it remains unclear what counts as "professional" in these features. These features may serve as a general framework on which to base professionality in teaching on and determine how a person can become a professional teacher. What counts as "professional," then, is related to ways in which teachers relate to other people (students, colleagues, parents; see also Richardson & Placier, 2001) and the responsibilities, attitudes, and behaviors they adopt as well as the knowledge they use which are, more or less, outside themselves. We argue that such aspects need to become common themes of research on teachers' professional identity. On the basis of the studies we reviewed, it is not yet possible to identify such common themes.

Fourth, and in addition to what was written above, a cognitive perspective underlies most studies on teachers' professional identity. From this perspective, the research results are based on written or verbal data collected from the teachers (i.e., portfolios and interviews). Understanding these data is only possible when data is also available about the teachers' contexts from a more sociological perspective, i.e., gained through (participant) observation and analysis of school documents and student materials. Furthermore, a teacher's biography is important for professional identity formation (i.e., Knowles, 1992; Sugrue, 1997). In the literature on teachers and teaching, "biography" seems to imply a perspective of its own, with the emphasis on life histories (Goodson, 1992; Kelchtermans, 1994). Life histories are not just "life stories," but stories that are embedded in a socio-historical context. The cognitive and the biographical perspectives on professional identity formation are both characterized by a narrative research approach. This cannot be said about the sociological perspective, though it is implied in the biographical perspective. In view of professional identity formation, we feel that more clarity is needed about these perspectives that can possibly be combined in research on teachers' professional identity.

CONCLUSION

In the introduction to this chapter, we identified teachers' professional identity as an emerging research area, particularly in the last decade. The number of studies available for the present review was limited, so that we consulted additional studies. The information we acquired from this additional group of studies was added to findings based on the studies we systematically analyzed. It can be concluded that, in most studies, the concept of professional identity was defined differently or not defined at all. The latter pertains particularly to the studies on characteristics of teachers' professional identity, a line of research we suggest should be placed under a heading other than that of "professional identity."

The concept of teachers' professional identity was defined most explicitly in studies on professional identity formation (i.e., Coldron & Smith, 1999; Goodson & Cole, 1994; Sugrue, 1997; Volkmann & Anderson, 1998) and in studies on stories that (re)present professional identity, e.g., the work of

Connelly and Clandinin (1999). Both categories of studies overlap in the sense that, in both, the emphasis was placed on personal practical knowledge. Differences between these categories of studies pertain to the influence of teachers' context ("landscape") on shaping professional identity and the relationship identified between teachers' personal practical knowledge, stories or narratives, and professional identity. This relationship between teachers' stories and their professional identity is in line with the other, more general, literature (i.e., Bakhtin, 1981; Gee, 2001; Giddens, 1991) and seems to be a sound theoretical basis for researching teachers' professional identity.

Based on the studies reviewed, we identified four features that, in our view, are essential for professional identity. They may function as a general framework for future research on teachers' professional identity. The current research on teachers' professional identity is not without problems. Different concepts were used to indicate the same thing, or it was not clarified how they are related; this pertains particularly to the concepts of "self" and "identity." We argued for better conceptual clarity of these concepts. We also argued that more attention should be paid to the role of context in professional identity formation and to what counts as professional in teachers' professional identity. In our opinion, the "professional landscape" metaphor (Connelly & Clandinin, 1999) may offer a perspective for this: teachers are part of this landscape, as are "relevant others" (researchers, policy makers, school administrators, teacher educators, etc.) who represent different aspects of the landscape. We believe that a permanent dialogue between these actors in the professional landscape may lead to a better insight into what counts as professional in teachers' professional identity.

REFERENCES

Antonek, J. L., McCormick, D. E., & Donato, R. (1997). The student teacher portfolio as autobiography: Developing a professional identity. *Modern Language Journal, 81*(1), 15–27.

Bakhtin, M. M. (1981). *The dialogic imagination: Four essays by M.M. Bakhtin.* Austin, TX: University of Texas Press.

Beijaard, D. (1995). Teachers' prior experiences and actual perceptions of professional identity. *Teachers and Teaching: Theory and Practice, 1*(2), 281–294.

Beijaard, D., Verloop, N., & Vermunt, J. D. (2000). Teachers' perceptions of professional identity: An exploratory study from a personal knowledge perspective. *Teaching and Teacher Education, 16,* 749–764.

Beijaard, D., Meijer, P. C., & Verloop, N. (2004). Reconsidering research on teachers' professional identity. *Teaching and Teacher Education, 20*(2), 107–128.

Brooke, G. E. (1994). My personal journey toward professionalism. *Young Children*, *49*(6), 69–71.

Bullough, R. V. (1997). Practicing theory and theorizing practice. In J. Loughran & T. Russell (Eds.), *Purpose, passion and pedagogy in teacher education* (pp. 13–31). London: The Falmer Press.

Bullough, R. V., Knowles, G., & Crow, N. A. (1992). *Emerging as a teacher*. London: Routledge.

Clandinin, D. J. (1992). Narrative and story in teacher education. In T. Russell & H. Munby (Eds.), *Teachers and teaching: From classroom to reflection* (pp. 124–137). Sussex: The Falmer Press.

Clandinin, D. J. (2003). Stories to live by on landscapes of diversity: Interweaving the personal and professional in teachers' lives. Key note paper presented at the 11th conference of the International Study Association on Teachers and Teaching (ISATT), Leiden, The Netherlands.

Clandinin, D. J., & Connelly, F. M. (1996). Teachers' professional knowledge landscapes: Teacher stories – stories of teacher – school stories – stories of schools. *Educational Researcher*, *25*(3), 24–30.

Coldron, J., & Smith, R. (1999). Active location in teachers' construction of their professional identities. *Journal of Curriculum Studies*, *31*(6), 711–726.

Connelly, F. M., & Clandinin, D. J. (1985). Personal practical knowledge and the modes of knowing. In E. Eisner (Ed.), *Learning and teaching the ways of knowing* (pp. 174–198). Chicago, IL: University of Chicago Press.

Connelly, F. M., & Clandinin, D. J. (1990). Stories of experience and narrative inquiry. *Educational Researcher*, *19*(5), 2–14.

Connelly, F. M., & Clandinin, D. J. (1999). *Shaping a professional identity: Stories of education practice*. London, Ontario: Althouse Press.

Conway, P. (2001). Anticipatory reflection while learning to teach: From a temporally truncated to a temporally distributed model of reflection in teacher education. *Teaching and Teacher Education*, *17*, 89–106.

Cooper, K., & Olson, M. R. (1996). The multiple 'I's' of teacher identity. In M. Kompf, W. R. Bond, D. Dworet & R. T Boak (Eds.), *Changing research and practice: Teachers' professionalism, identities and knowledge* (pp. 78–89). London: The Falmer Press.

Craig, C. J. (1998). The influence of context on one teacher's interpretive knowledge of team teaching. *Teaching and Teacher Education*, *14*, 371–383.

Day, C. (1999). *Developing teachers, the challenge of lifelong learning*. London: The Falmer Press.

DeCorse, C. J. B., & Vogtle, S. P. (1997). In a complex voice: The contradictions of male elementary teachers' career choice and professional identity. *Journal of Teacher Education*, *48*(1), 37–46.

Dillabough, J. A. (1999). Gender politics and conceptions of the modern teacher: Women, identity and professionalism. *British Journal of Sociology of Education*, *20*(3), 373–394.

Edwards, R. (1997). *Changing places? Flexibility, lifelong learning and a learning society*. London: Routledge.

Elbaz, F. (1983). *Teacher thinking: A study of practical knowledge*. London: Croom Helm.

Elbaz-Luwisch, F. (2002). Writing as inquiry: Storying the teaching self in writing workshops. *Curriculum Inquiry*, *32*, 403–428.

Erikson, E. H. (1968). *Identity, youth and crisis.* New York, NY: W.W. Norton.

Feiman-Nemser, S., & Floden, R. E. (1986). The cultures of teaching. In M. C. Wittrock (Ed.), *Handbook of research on teaching* (pp. 505–526). New York, NY: Macmillan.

Gaziel, H. H. (1995). Sabbatical leave, job burnout and turnover intentions among teachers. *International Journal of Lifelong Education, 14*(4), 331–338.

Gee, J., & Crawford, V. (1998). Two kinds of teenagers: Language, identity, and social class. In D. Alvermann, K. Hinchman, D. Moore, S. Phelps & D. Waff (Eds.), *Reconceptualizing the literacies in adolescents' lives* (pp. 225–245). Mahwah, NJ: Erlbaum.

Gee, J. P. (2001). Identity as an analytic lens for research in education. In W. G. Secada (Ed.), *Review of research in education* (Vol. 25, pp. 99–125). Washington, DC: American Educational Research Association.

Giddens, A. (1991). *Modernity and self-identity: Self and society in the late modern age.* Cambridge, UK: Polity Press.

Golombek, P. R. (1998). A study of language teachers' personal practical knowledge. *TESOL Quarterly, 32*(2), 447–464.

Goodson, I. (Ed.). (1992). *Studying teachers' lives.* London: Routledge.

Goodson, I. F., & Cole, A. L. (1994). Exploring the teacher's professional knowledge: Constructing identity and community. *Teacher Education Quarterly, 21*(1), 85–105.

Graham, R., & Young, J. (1998). Curriculum, identity, and experience in multicultural education. *The Alberta Journal of Educational Research, 44*(4), 397–407.

Jansz, J. (1991). *Person, self, and moral demands.* Leiden, the Netherlands: Leiden University DSWO Press.

Jeans, B. A. (1996). The construction of professional identity. *International Journal of Psychology, 31*(3/4), 201–224.

Kelchtermans, G. (1994). *De professionele ontwikkeling van leerkrachten basisonderwijs vanuit het biografisch perspectief [The professional development of elementary teachers from the biographical perspective].* Leuven: University Press.

Kerby, A. (1991). *Narrative and the self.* Bloomington, IN: Indiana University Press.

Knowles, G. J. (1992). Models for understanding pre-service and beginning teachers' biographies: Illustrations from case studies. In I. F. Goodson (Ed.), *Studying teachers' lives* (pp. 99–152). London: Routledge.

Kompf, M., Bond, W. R., Dworet, D., & Boak, R. T. (Eds.). (1996). *Changing research and practice: Teachers' professionalism, identities and knowledge.* London: The Falmer Press.

Korthagen, F. A. J. (2001). *Waar doen we het voor? Op zoek naar de essentie van goed leraarschap [What are we doing it for? Searching for the essence of good teaching].* Utrecht, the Netherlands: University of Utrecht IVLOS.

Mawhinney, H., & Xu, F. (1997). Restructuring the identity of foreign-trained teachers in Ontario schools. *TESOL Quarterly, 31*(3), 632–639.

McCormick, C. B., & Pressley, M. (1997). *Educational psychology: Learning, instruction, assessment.* New York, NY: Longman.

Mead, G. J. (1934). *Mind, self and society.* Chicago, IL: University of Chicago Press.

Miller, D. (1973). *George Herbert Mead: Self, language and the world.* Chicago, IL: University of Chicago Press.

Mitchell, A. (1997). Teacher identity: A key to increased collaboration. *Action in Teacher Education, 19*(3), 1–14.

Moore, M., & Hofman, J. E. (1988). Professional identity in institutions of higher learning in Israel. *Higher Education, 17*(1), 69–79.

Nias, J. (1989). Teaching and the self. In M. L. Holly & C. S. McLoughlin (Eds.), *Perspective on teacher professional development* (pp. 151–171). London: The Falmer Press.

Nixon, J. (1996). Professional identity and the restructuring of higher education. *Studies in Higher Education, 21*(1), 5–16.

Paechter, C., & Head, J. (1996). Gender, identity, status and the body: Life in a marginal subject. *Gender and Education, 8*(1), 21–29.

Phelan, A. M. (2000). A knot to unfurl (A book review of "Shaping a professional identity: Stories of education practice" by M. F. Connelly & D. J. Clandinin, 1999, London, ON: Althouse Press). *Alberta Journal of Educational Research*, 46, 288–290.

Preuss, E., & Hofsass, T. (1991). Integration in the Federal Republic of Germany: Experiences related to professional identity and strategies of teacher training in Berlin. *European Journal of Teacher Education, 14*(2), 131–137.

Purkey, W. W. (1970). *Self-concept and school achievement.* Englewood Cliffs, NJ: Prentice-Hall.

Rex, L. A., Murnen, T. J., Hobbs, J., & McEachen, D. (2002). Teachers' pedagogical stories and the shaping of classroom participation: "The Dancer" and "Graveyard Shift at the 7-11". *American Educational Research Journal, 39*, 765–796.

Reynolds, C. (1996). Cultural scripts for teachers: Identities and their relation to workplace landscapes. In M. Kompf, W. R. Bond, D. Dworet & R. T. Boak (Eds.), *Changing research and practice: Teachers' professionalism, identities and knowledge* (pp. 69–77). London: The Falmer Press.

Richardson, V., & Placier, P. (2001). Teacher change. In V. Richardson (Ed.), *Handbook of research on teaching* (pp. 905–947). Washington, DC: American Educational Research Association.

Roberts, L. (2000). Shifting identities: An investigation into student and novice teachers' evolving professional identity. *Journal of Education for Teaching, 26*(2), 185–186.

Samuel, M., & Stephens, D. (2000). Critical dialogues with self: Developing teacher identities and roles – A case study of South Africa. *International Journal of Educational Research, 33*(5), 475–491.

Siraj-Blatchford, I. (1993). Educational research and reform: Some implications for the professional identity of early years teachers. *British Journal of Educational Studies, 41*(4), 393–408.

Sugrue, C. (1997). Student teachers' lay theories and teaching identities: Their implications for professional development. *European Journal of Teacher Education, 20*(3), 213–225.

Taylor, C. (1989). *Sources of the self: The making of the modern identity.* Cambridge, MA: Harvard University Press.

Tickle, L. (2000). *Teacher induction: The way ahead.* Buckingham: Open University Press.

Volkmann, M. J., & Anderson, M. A. (1998). Creating professional identity: Dilemmas and metaphors of a first-year chemistry teacher. *Science Education, 82*(3), 293–310.

CHAPTER 11

THE MORAL MATTERS OF TEACHING: A FINNISH PERSPECTIVE

Kirsi Tirri, Auli Toom and Jukka Husu

ABSTRACT

This chapter provides a synthesis of the literature having to do with the moral matters of teaching. It is organized around three themes: (a) teacher's professional ethics and values, (b) teacher's moral sensitivity, action, and judgment, and (c) school ethos and community. Each theme is first dealt with separately. Then, the themes are related to one another to show the interconnectedness between and among them. Exemplars in this work are drawn from the authors' and others' substantial body of research conducted in Finland. The research findings, however, have an applicability that extends beyond national borders. The intent of this work is to stimulate discussion and to advance what is known about the moral nature of teaching through using a range of research methods and conducting studies in live school settings.

Keywords: Moral act of teaching; teaching dispositions; dilemmas of teaching

From Teacher Thinking to Teachers and Teaching: The Evolution of a Research Community
Advances in Research on Teaching, Volume 19, 223–239
ISSN: 1479-3687/doi:10.1108/S1479-3687(2013)0000019014

INTRODUCTION: WHAT IS MORAL IN TEACHING?

A number of years ago, Colnerud (2006) invited those interested in the moral dimensions of teaching profession to discuss and renew the field of teacher ethics. Her invitation did not mean that the research on ethical/ moral issues in teaching had been weak or futile. Rather her aim was to foster investigations into why is it so hard to be a (morally) good teacher. Systematic research on this crucial topic has been scattered (Sanger, 2008). So far, research has revealed that most teachers are not always aware of the impact of their actions and decisions (Husu, 2005a; Jackson, Boostrom, & Hansen, 1993; Tirri, 1999; Toom, 2006). Furthermore, teachers have reported that they are ill-prepared for dealing with ethical dilemmas that they encounter in their work (Husu & Tirri, 2001; Lyons, 1990; Tirri, 1999, 2009). Teachers are called upon to mediate many private and public interests pertaining to personal, professional, organizational, and societal values. Their work often presupposes mediation of conflicting values that relate to guarding and promoting "the best interests of students" (Husu & Tirri, 2003; Husu & Toom, 2008; Tirri & Husu, 2002). The challenge for teachers is to take a holistic approach to school pedagogy (Tirri, 2008, 2011) and to foster purpose and the well-being of their students (Bundick & Tirri, in press; Soini, Pietarinen, Pyhältö, & Tirri, in press; Tirri, 2012; Tirri & Ubani, 2013).

Van Manen and Li (2002) argue that the modern pedagogical task of teaching is ambiguous because contemporary policy perspectives and public discourses on education tend to focus on issues that are largely external to teachers' daily concerns: productivity, accountability measures, instructional technology, and so forth. The point is that these perspectives and orientations do not adequately reflect how teachers experience their duties of school life. Teachers are mostly concerned with the success of their students, their personal relationships with students and colleagues, and the interpersonal and emotional dimensions of their actions. In this sense, the focus of teachers tends to be on the complexity of daily interactions with their students and colleagues. Thus, teachers' work can be seen as a pedagogical challenge to knowing how to deal in appropriate ways with the contingencies of everyday events of school life (Husu, 2001; Kansanen et al., 1999; Tirri & Puolimatka, 2000).

From this perspective, pedagogy makes the practice of teaching possible in the first place. According to Simon (1992, p. 62), pedagogy itself is an ethical vision. Such a vision makes teaching a reflective practice, and accordingly, school teaching "an interpretative or deliberative science – a branch of moral or social philosophy" (Hamilton, 2001, p. 121). Naturally, we must keep in mind that the problems within this field cannot be solved. But when problems are made explicit and analyzed, we can understand them better, and thus we can formulate more nuanced opinions about them and responses to them. Exploring the conditions of pedagogical practices can make teachers' work more visible and give them more control over what they are doing (Husu & Toom, 2008; Sanger, 2008).

In this chapter we primarily present and discuss recent Finnish research on the moral core of teaching. Our review includes published research in English on teachers' ethics, morality, and the moral perspectives on teaching during the last decade and the prior work on this theme. We have grouped these studies around three main themes: (a) teacher's professional ethics and values, (b) teacher's moral sensitivity, action, and judgment, and (c) school ethos and community. We present each theme in detail in order to show their specific characteristics as well as their interconnectedness with one other. However, the purpose of our contribution is not to present the complete picture of the research within this area, but rather to show its temporary condition in the Finnish context. Our goal is to synthesize positions that often appear separate and disconnected or even in conflict. We hope this review will stimulate discussion and hopefully lead to new understandings of the topic.

TEACHER'S PROFESSIONAL ETHICS AND VALUES

Professional ethics concerns those norms, values, and principles that should govern the conduct of teachers. It emphasizes the inherent normative meanings that determine the appropriateness of teachers' professional practices. It is well known that the term ethics finds its roots in the Greek language (*ethikos, ethos*: character, standards, custom, convention), while the term *moral* comes from Latin (*mos, moris*: convention, custom, conduct). Both refer to human conduct and are expansive in their meanings (Husu & Toom, 2008). However, ethics has come "to denote the theory of morality and the considered principles of conduct while moral has come to cover everyday, not often reflected, conduct" (Colnerud, 2006, p. 367). The normative core of professional ethics, therefore, provides ways to appraise the merits and to judge the significance of educational practices taking place in schools. Within this kind of ethical rationality, the teacher approaches the problem of what to do in a given situation with actions based on reason that are mainly ethical by their nature. At this stage, "ethical" means conscious deliberation and sticking to ethical ideals and principles, regardless of the consequences. This is ethics at a descriptive level. Consequently, problem finding and problem understanding are activities needed at this phase (Husu & Toom, 2008). Within this topic, we define and present two specific areas of research: *ethical codes* and *standards of the teaching profession.*

Ethical Codes

In Finland, the professional ethical codes for teachers clarify the teachers' roles and relationships in their work (Trade Union of Education in Finland, 2010; Tirri, 2010). We know from the empirical research concerning Finnish teachers that they value professional commitment in terms of caring and cooperation in critical situations in their work (Hanhimäki & Tirri, 2008, 2009; Tirri, 1999, 2003). We have studies on the pedagogical values identified by teachers (Husu & Tirri, 2007; Tirri & Husu, 2006), the values underlying urban school principals' work (Hanhimäki & Tirri, 2008), and ethically sensitive responses of teachers in critical incidents at school (Hanhimäki & Tirri, 2009). We have also developed an instrument to measure teachers' and students' ethical sensitivity in the context of teaching (Tirri & Nokelainen, 2007, 2011).

Standards of the Teaching Profession

In addition to personal values, teachers need to consider the ethical standards of their profession. Professional ethics include reflection on the values and virtues of a teacher. According to empirical studies, teachers cannot separate their own moral character from their professional self. The stance of teachers' moral character functions as a moral approach in teachers' reasoning, guiding their ways of interacting with pupils and giving them hope for the future. The professional approach in teachers' reasoning includes rules and principles guiding their pedagogical practice and decision-making. These rules and principles build teachers' professional character in their practical knowing (Tirri, Husu, & Kansanen, 1999).

Within this research topic, Max Weber's (1978, pp. 212–215) notion of "ethics of intention" describes the scene. The ethics of intention is concerned with sticking to ethical principles and ideals and how these actually work and not mixing them with practice. If we want to characterize ethical activities at this stage, we are *trying* or *attempting* to bring something about, or we are *aiming* at something; the ethics of intention are the *point or purpose* of the action; they are part of our *plan* (Shaw, 2006, p. 188). However, ethics of intention is not what actually happens in the moral practice of teaching.

TEACHER'S MORAL ACTION AND JUDGMENT

The moral work of teaching (Sanger & Osguthorpe, 2013) implies that teachers have their own beliefs, that they actively play a role in constructing those beliefs, and that, at least to some extent, teachers are able to guide their teaching practices on the beliefs they hold. The question of how to translate ethical principles and codes into lived pedagogical practice arises as we enter into the practice of teaching. It is a well-known fact that single-minded pursuit of ideals and principles is not a good thing in a classroom and may lead to undesirable consequences. Situations should also be interpreted through a calculation of the probable positive and negative consequences (short and long term) of a particular educational decision and action. Once the likely outcomes are predicted, the alternatives that provide the greatest benefit and least harm may be chosen. The best interests of students are served if the negative consequences are minimized and positive benefits are maximized (Husu & Toom, 2008).

The problems teachers face in their work relate most closely to those questions referred to as "uncertain practical questions" (Gauthier, 1963; Reid, 1979). These are challenges that have to be resolved, even if the response is a decision to do nothing (Toom, 2006, 2012). The grounds on which decisions should be made are often uncertain. Nothing can tell teachers infallibly which method should be used, what evidence should be taken into account or rejected, what kinds of arguments should be given precedence, and so forth. In addition, teachers always have to take the existing state of affairs into account. Teachers are never free from past or present contexts and their arrangements. In this uncertain environment, teachers have to take stances (Husu, 2002b, 2003). What distinguishes pedagogical judgment from mere descriptive thinking and reflection is that judgment in moral practices involves some evaluation of a situation and of persons in question: it is a *discriminating* and *normative* form of thought and action (Hostetler, 1997, p. 8). Within this topic, we have defined and present three various areas of research: (1) professionalism and commitment, (2) moral sensitivity in teaching and phronesis, and (3) the combination of ethical competence with action competence.

Professionalism and Commitment

As stated, teacher's work requires professional behavior from the teacher. In many difficult situations, teachers are called to act according to their professional codes instead of allowing their personal preferences to dominate their decisions. Teachers' work includes conflicts with parents and colleagues (Tirri & Husu, 2002). Many times teachers cannot separate their professional selves from their personal moral character. However, teachers are mostly committed to their students and this emotional commitment helps them in difficult situations. Cooperation and caring can bring positive resolutions to difficult conflicts. Many cases may remain unresolved or take a long time to close and that makes teachers tired and worried. Professionalism and commitment are part of teachers' challenges in their everyday work in schools.

The centrality of professional commitment was also present in a study on teacher's practical action and knowledge (Gholami & Husu, 2010), where teachers warranted their practical knowledge claims with "moral ethos." The particular study also indicated that the concept of "care," including care about professional responsibilities generally and care about students specifically, was placed at the heart of the professional moral ethos. The teachers tried to warrant their practical knowledge in terms of their professional responsibilities and their desire to provide a good educational environment in which to nurture students. Care was characterized by the following three features: teachers tried to provide "equal educational opportunities" for their students, they tried to do their "best" in pedagogical encounters with their students, and they tried to hold back "rebuttal pedagogy" related to the main knowledge claim (Gholami & Husu, 2010).

Moral Sensitivity in Teaching

To respond to a situation in a moral way, a teacher should be able to perceive and interpret events in ways that lead to ethical action. The teacher must be sensitive to situational cues and must be able to visualize various alternative actions in response to that situation. A morally sensitive person draws on many skills, techniques, and components of interpersonal sensitivity. These include taking the perspective of others (role taking), cultivating empathy for a sense of connection to others, and interpreting a situation based on imagining what might happen and who might be affected. According to Muriel Bebeau and her colleagues, moral sensitivity is the awareness of how our actions affect other people. It involves being aware of the different possible lines of action and how each line of action could affect the parties involved (including oneself). Moral sensitivity involves imaginatively constructing possible scenarios (often from limited cues and partial information), knowing cause-consequent chains of events in the real world, and having empathy and role-taking skills. Moral sensitivity is necessary to become aware that a moral issue is involved in a situation. (Bebeau, Rest, & Narvaez, 1999, p. 22)

We have developed an instrument to study teachers' ethical sensitivity in the context of teaching (Tirri & Nokelainen, 2007, 2011). The instrument has been used in different cultural contexts with Finnish, Iranian, and Dutch teachers and students (Gholami & Tirri, 2012a; Kuusisto, Tirri, & Rissanen, 2012; Schutte, Tirri, & Wolfensberger, under review). Our results indicate that the instrument is reliable across different cultures and yields similar trends with different populations. Generally, teachers evaluate their ethical sensitivity quite high with an emphasis on caring ethics. Females and high-ability students tend to score higher in ethical sensitivity than males or average-ability students (Gholami & Tirri, 2012a, 2012b; Kuusisto, Tirri, & Rissanen, 2012; Schutte, Tirri, & Wolfersberger, under review; Tirri & Nokelainen, 2007).

Phronesis: Combining Ethical Competence with Action Competence

We adopt Aristotle's *phronesis* perspective to study teachers' moral reasoning in pedagogical situations (Husu, 2001, 2002a, 2003). *Phronesis* is not a cognitive capacity that a teacher has at her/his disposal. Rather, it is closely bound up in the kind of person that the teacher is. Thus, *phronesis* for a teacher has "its own personality which is rooted in a definite ethos with its own favored dispositions and habits" (Dunne, 1993, p. 273). The teacher's actions and her/his possibilities can only be found within particular situations, informed by particular histories and school institutions. Consequently, the teacher sees it not only as a way of behaving in particular contexts, but also as her/his "way of being" that arises in those situations. Three various codes – rational, situational, and moral character codes – can be used as interpretative lenses to study pedagogical cases. These three interpretations of *phronesis* cannot be separated from each other. Rather, each interpretation is linked to the others. The combination of the different interpretations comprises the concept of *phronesis* as a totality (Husu, 2005a). In this form, the nature of practical knowing contrasts with the certainty often attributed to the concepts of "formal" or "propositional" knowledge (Fenstermacher, 1994).

Within this research topic, according to Weber's (1978) distinction, it is important to notice that teachers are not choosing between ethics and practicalities; they operate between two sorts of ethics. Embedded in implicit, moral practices of school life, teachers should not do away with their ethical principles and ideals (ethics of intention). Instead, their purposes need to be completed by their concern for consequences (ethics of responsibility) (Husu, 2003). It is always about balancing and negotiating between pros and cons, and trying to find the reasonable course of action (Husu & Toom, 2008). This ethics of responsibility goes even beyond the classroom, and is concerned with the ethical commitments of an entire school. Foremost, ethical teaching is indirect and informal, sometimes even hidden. It is, as Bullough (2011) suggests, "a matter of living within a shared institutional context" (p. 26).

SCHOOL ETHOS AND COMMUNITY

In schools, ethical dilemmas are often interpreted through a calculation of the probable positive and negative consequences (short and long term) of a particular educational decision. Once the likely outcomes are predicted, the alternatives that provide the greatest benefit and least harm may be chosen. The best interests of students are served if the negative consequences are minimized and positive benefits are maximized (Walker, 1998, p. 300). In many cases, teachers' aims for any particular student are entangled with teachers' aims for each of the other youths in the class and in the school's professional community (Husu, 2003). It is clear that in practice teachers deal with most of the ethical dilemmas at school, which always happens in the context of the school and within its possibilities and restrictions. These separate events and decisions of individual teachers build up the practices and norms reflecting the pedagogical atmosphere and ethos of the school context. Together with educational leadership, the collective responsibility is positively supported and constructed at schools. Schools are places to educate youth to be active citizens in democratic societies (Toom & Husu, 2012), and thus they necessarily exist with moral spheres (i.e., Kane, 1996). Within this topic, we define and present three strands of research: (1) principals as supportive leaders of schools, (2) cooperation as an indispensable quality of school, and (3) collective values of school and caring school culture.

Principals as Supportive Leaders of Schools

The principals play a very central role in formulating the general pedagogical ethos of their school. In one of our studies on principals (Hanhimäki & Tirri, 2008), they reflected many of the typical qualities of moral exemplar identified by Colby and Damon (1992). These qualities include a generalized respect for humanity that was mentioned in many interviews; a tendency to be inspiring to others, a quality that was reflected in teachers', parents', and students' interviews; and a sense of realistic humility about one's importance relative to the world at large, implying a relative lack of concern for one's own ego. All the principals served a greater purpose in that they hoped to improve the lives of their students and the school community, not only to advance their own career (Hanhimäki & Tirri, 2008). The principals also shared the values of tolerance, care, and equality of people (Hanhimäki & Tirri, 2008). These values guided their work in the school-based projects and led to their cooperation with teachers, students, and families. All the principals had knowledge of different networks inside and outside of school that helped them to provide the best possible education for their students. The principals viewed the school as an important institution in a society, an institution where students can learn democracy and human rights (Hanhimäki & Tirri, 2008). The four principals in the Hanhimäki and Tirri study differed in their leadership roles. One elementary school principal was more present in his schools; the other delegated more leadership responsibilities to vice-principals and other personnel. One secondary school principal was very informal and motherly in her work; the other was more professionally oriented and business-like. All of the four principals had a unique moral profile that reflected their role and characteristics as an emotional and ethical leader of their schools (Hanhimäki & Tirri, 2008). Teachers, parents, and students also viewed the principals as moral exemplars. The principals' personal qualities, values, and social skills created an atmosphere in urban schools that made cooperation and respect possible. The principals of urban schools shared some common values and characteristics needed to educate diverse students. They had strong self-awareness and an ability to keep disruptive emotions and impulses under control. They were also able to adapt to new challenges and to see the upside in the events. Teachers reported that their principals had high personal standards that drove them to constantly seek improvements in their leadership practices (Hanhimäki & Tirri, 2008).

Teachers also reported situations in which the role of the principal and his/her characteristics or leadership qualities played a central part in coping with or resolving a critical incident in their school contexts. In these incidents, principals displayed their leadership qualities through exemplary behavior and their abilities to cooperate with different parties. This professional attitude also manifested itself in their commitment to educate themselves and to develop their school communities. Furthermore, they respected people from diverse religious and ethical backgrounds and cared for themselves, their teachers, and students from different families (Hanhimäki & Tirri, 2009).

The teachers of the urban schools ($N = 124$) evaluated their principals' emotional leadership (Nokelainen & Tirri, 2007) with an Emotional Leadership Questionnaire (ELQ) that operationalizes four domains of EI with 51 items (Goleman, Boyatzis, & McKee, 2002). The teachers' task was to assess their principals' EL characteristics on four dimensions of the ELQ: (1) self-awareness, (2) self-management, (3) social awareness, and (4) relationship management. Teachers viewed their principals very positively in the dimensions measuring principals' personal characteristics. According to the teachers' evaluations, the principals of urban schools in the study had quite strong self-awareness. Furthermore, the principals were able to keep disruptive emotions and impulses under control, adapt to new challenges, and see the upside in events. Teachers were also quite satisfied with their principals' high personal standards that drove them to constantly seek improvements in performance, to monitor parents' and students' satisfaction carefully to ensure they are getting what they need, and to resolve disagreements and to generate an atmosphere of friendly collegiality (Hanhimäki & Tirri, 2008; Nokelainen & Tirri, 2007).

Cooperation as an Indispensable Quality of School

The most constructive emotional component of a school community is cooperation. In school cultures serving multicultural families, respect opens many doors to cooperation. In earlier empirical studies on moral dilemmas with minority groups, compromise has been shown to be the best solution to intercultural misunderstandings (Tirri, 1999). Open discussion of rules and norms is needed to establish some guidelines for organizational morality. In this moral discourse, respect and cooperation are the ethical sensitivity skills needed to meet and understand diverse families. Common rules in schools also educate teachers, parents, and students to respect each other, care for each other, and attend to their ethical sensitivity. Good manners can promote an ambiance in the school community that can help to build a more positive and inclusive whole school culture.

Collective Values of School

In a collaborative action research project with 2 educational researchers and 24 elementary school teachers, we used the value clarification process to recognize, articulate, and express the beliefs and values of a particular school community (Husu & Tirri, 2007; Tirri & Husu, 2006). The researchers analyzed the nature of values expressed by the teachers and established a framework for school values. The school values reflected individual, social, and relational values. According to the teachers, all these meta-values are important in a pedagogical context. The most important values chosen by teachers came from three categories of values: social, relational, and individual. The statement, "Teachers emphasize the interests of their community more than individuality and selfishness," for example, reflected important social values of the school and was chosen because it represented the social ethos of the school. The statement, "Teachers educate to tolerate differences," for instance, reflected important relational values of the school and was chosen to convey the relational ethos of the school. Individual values were reflected in these third statements, "Teachers aim to complete their tasks" and "Teachers try to evaluate their work honestly." These choices allowed the teachers to actualize in their school ethos and embed it in their own behaviors. Our aim was to support this schools' desire to create a pedagogical environment that is sensitive to numerous individual backgrounds in such areas as justice, self-esteem, and consideration. The process of values clarification, we aver, should be anchored to real values expressed in real-world school situations (Husu & Tirri, 2001). If a teacher says she/he values honesty, we ask her/him to explain what that would mean to her/him in terms of real-world classroom or school behavior. Consequently, we, as researchers, encourage teachers to identify practical examples where there is a gap between values and behavior, either on an individual level or an organizational level. We aim to develop methods that bring behavior in line with our values. At best, value clarification provides an opportunity to take the first step on the road of getting to know our values – and finally, live them (Husu & Tirri, 2007).

Caring School Culture

Caring was the most evident emotional stance of both principals and teachers. They all agreed that successful and safe school culture is built on caring. They agreed with Noddings (1992) that caring should be about the others but also should include caring about places and ideas. Where family and diversity are concerned, a lack of caring often is identified as a source of difficulty. Sometimes students are not cared for enough at home and school needs to find those in need of care. In multicultural families experiencing difficulties, schools have arranged extra help and found advocates for the students. In urban schools, respect is often the way to demonstrate ethical sensitivity to families of diverse religious and ethical backgrounds (Hanhimäki & Tirri, 2009). Schools also cared for the children by supporting their whole family. The success of these schools was very much based on their flexible integration and curriculum planning. Students with special needs had individually tailored and personalized curricula to meet their needs. This approach has produced good learning results even with struggling students from socially disadvantaged backgrounds. Taken together, an atmosphere of caring, an effort to meet the needs of individual students from diverse backgrounds, and respect for different families have created conditions for success and emotional well-being of students within the context of schools (Hanhimäki & Tirri, 2009).

Within this research topic, it is reasonable to assume that all pedagogical situations are contingent, and thus the various opinions and needs of both students and teachers have to be taken into account in solving educational problems in practice at schools (i.e., Husu & Toom, 2008). It is important to compromise and be "open to change for the sake of preserving integrity in relationships with other people" (Hostetler, 1997, p. 70). Consequently, where students and parents (and other stakeholders) are concerned, there is a lesson to learn: teachers and schools cannot do it *for* you, but they can – or at least should try to – do it *with* you.

DISCUSSION: REFLECTING ON THE NEXT STEPS

In this chapter, we have reviewed the recent Finnish research on the moral core of teaching and summarized – through the use of examples – three main topic areas: (1) teacher's professional ethics and values, (2) teacher's moral sensitivity, action, and judgment, and (3) school ethos and community. Our survey of the literature shows that various theoretical and methodological approaches have been used, and these have opened up multiple under-standings of both broad structural aspects and more specific notions related to the moral work of teaching. We hope that this synthesis of the moral matters of teaching will help others to better understand the problems teachers face in their work, the dynamics of educational contexts, and the impact of different approaches on teachers and students. As a result, our ability to understand the moral work of teaching should reach a level of deeper understanding (Sanger & Osguthorpe, 2013). We also think that using more than one research approach increases the trustworthiness of findings, because each approach serves as a check on the other(s).

Based on our findings, we suggest that schools should be aware of the importance of values, bring them to the fore, and give students and teachers time to reflect on and discuss such issues (Husu & Tirri, 2007, p. 400). As for pre-service teachers, they encounter the moral nature of teaching by addressing these issues explicitly – not only implicitly – in teacher education courses. These aims would be successfully supported by systematic research on moral matters of teaching as well as by developing appropriate research methods to investigate them and tools to reflect on them (Hansen, 2001; Husu, 2005b; Husu, Patrikainen, & Toom, 2007; Husu, Toom, & Patrikainen, 2008).

Taken together, this work related to the moral nature of teaching contributes to the establishment and maintenance of a strong bond of trust between teacher and students (Hargreaves, 1998; Troman, 2000). Trust is of prime importance in teaching. Trust ensures that participating individuals at every level of the educational system can be allowed greater freedom and afforded greater autonomy (Cook-Sather, 2002, p. 4). Also, trust is a pre-condition for cooperation (Gambetta, 1988). In pedagogical encounters, high levels of trust among participants (teachers, students, parents) for prerequisite for the development of a "communitas" recognizable for its "strong feeling of camaraderie, sense of common destiny, [and] mutual support" (Woods, 1995, p. 93). These experiences of trust in the daily live of schools have deep and lasting impact on individuals and their communities (Toom & Husu, 2012).

REFERENCES

Bebeau, M., Rest, J., & Narvaez, D. (1999). Beyond the promise: A perspective on research in moral education. *Educational Researcher, 28*(4), 18–26.

Bullough, R. V., Jr. (2011). Ethical and moral matters in teaching and teacher education. *Teaching and Teacher Education, 27*, 21–28.

Bundick, M., & Tirri, K. (in press). Teacher support and competencies for fostering youth purpose and psychological well-being: Perspectives from two countries. *Applied Developmental Science.*

Colby, A., & Damon, W. (1992). *Some do care: Contemporary lives of moral commitment*. New York, NY: The Free Press.

Colnerud, G. (2006). Teacher ethics as a research problem: Syntheses achieved and new issues. *Teachers and Teaching: Theory and Practice, 12*(3), 365–385.

Cook-Sather, A. (2002). Authorizing students' perspectives: Toward trust, dialogue, and change in education. *Educational Researcher, 31*(4), 3–14.

Dunne, J. (1993). *Back to the rough ground: Practical judgement and the lure of technique*. Notre Dame, IN: University of Notre Dame Press.

Fenstermacher, G. D. (1994). The knower and the known: The nature of knowledge in research on teaching. *Review of Research in Education, 20*, 3–56.

Gambetta, D. (1988). Can we trust trust? In D. Gambetta (Ed.), *Trust: Making and breaking cooperative relations* (pp. 213–237). Oxford: Basil Blackwell.

Gauthier, D. P. (1963). *Practical reasoning: The structure and foundations of prudential and moral arguments and their exemplifications in discourse*. London: Oxford University Press.

Gholami, K., & Husu, J. (2010). How do teachers reason about their practice? Representing the epistemic nature of teachers' practical knowledge. *Teaching and Teacher Education, 28*(6), 1520–1529.

Gholami, K., & Tirri, K. (2012a). The cultural dependence of the ethical sensitivity scale questionnaire: The case of Iranian Kurdish teachers. *Education Research International*. doi:10.1155/2012/387027

Gholami, K., & Tirri, K. (2012b). The teachers' perceived dimensions of caring practice: A quantitative reflection on the moral aspect of teaching. *Education Research International*. doi:10.1155/2012/954274

Goleman, D., Boyatzis, R., & McKee, A. (2002). *Primal leadership: Realizing the power of emotional intelligence*. Boston, MA: Harvard Business School Press.

Hamilton, D. (2001). In Schwabian fields. A review essay of Teaching as reflective practice: The German didactic tradition. In I. Westbury, S. Hopmann, & K. Riquarts (Eds.), *Pedagogy, Culture and Society, 9*, 119–128.

Hanhimäki, E., & Tirri, K. (2008). The moral role and characteristics of Finnish urban school principals. *Journal of Research in Character Education, 6*(1), 53–65.

Hanhimäki, E., & Tirri, K. (2009). Education for ethically sensitive teaching in critical incidents at school. *Journal of Education for Teaching, 35*(2), 107–121.

Hansen, D. T. (2001). Teaching as a moral activity. In V. Richardson (Ed.), *Handbook of research on teaching* (4th ed., pp. 826–857). Washington, DC: American Educational Research Association.

Hargreaves, A. (1998). The emotional politics of teaching and teacher development: With implications for educational leadership. *International Journal of Leadership in Education, 1*(3), 315–336.

Hostetler, K. D. (1997). *Ethical judgement in teaching*. Boston, MA: Allyn & Bacon/Longman.

Husu, J. (2001). Teachers at cross-purposes: A case report of ethical dilemmas in teaching. *Journal of Curriculum & Supervision, 17*(1), 67–89.

Husu, J. (2002a). *Representing the practice of teachers' pedagogical knowing*. Research in Educational Sciences 9. Turku: Finnish Educational Research Association.

Husu, J. (2002b). Navigating through the pedagogical practice – Teachers' epistemological stance towards pupils. In C. Sugrue & C. Day (Eds.), *Developing teachers and teaching practice: International research perspectives* (pp. 58–72). London: Routledge.

Husu, J. (2003). Real world pedagogical ethics - Mission impossible? *Teacher Development*, 7(3), 311–326.
Husu, J. (2005a). Exploring the landscape of teachers' tacitly implied ethics: An Aristotelian uncovering. In M. Kompf (Ed.), *Connecting policy and practice: Challenges for teaching and learning in schools and universities* (pp. 83–91). London: Routledge.
Husu, J. (2005b). Analyzing teacher knowledge in its interactional positioning. In D. Beijard, P. C. Meijer, G. Morine-Dershimer & H. Tillema (Eds.), *Teachers professional development in changing conditions* (pp. 117–131). New York, NY: Springer.
Husu, J., Patrikainen, S., & Toom, A. (2007). Developing teachers' competencies in reflecting on teaching. In J. Butcher & L. McDonald (Eds.), *Making a difference: Challenges for teachers, teaching and teacher education* (pp. 127–140). Amsterdam: Sense Publishers.
Husu, J., & Tirri, K. (2001). Teachers' ethical choices in sociomoral settings. *Journal of Moral Education*, 30(4), 361–375.
Husu, J., & Tirri, K. (2003). A case study approach to study one teacher's moral reflection. *Teaching and Teacher Education*, 19(3), 345–357.
Husu, J., & Tirri, K. (2007). Developing whole school pedagogical values – A case of going through the ethos of "good schooling." *Teaching and Teacher Education*, 23(4), 390–401.
Husu, J., & Toom, A. (2008). Ethics, moral, politics – The (un)broken circle of good and caring pedagogical practice. In A. Kallioniemi, A. Toom, M. Urbani, H. Linnansaari & K. Kumpulainen (Eds.), *Ihmistä kasvattamassa: koulutus – arvot – uudet avaukset [Cultivating humanity: Education – values – new discoveries]* (pp. 215–230). Turku: Finnish Educational Research Association.
Husu, J., Toom, A., & Patrikainen, S. (2008). Guided reflection as a means to demonstrate and develop student teachers' reflective competencies. *Reflective Practice*, 9(1), 37–51.
Jackson, P. W., Boostrom, R., & Hansen, D. T. (1993). *The moral life of schools*. San Francisco, CA: Jossey-Bass.
Kane, R. (1996). . *Through the moral maze: Searching for absolute values in a pluralistic world.* New York, NY: Paragon House.
Kansanen, P., Tirri, K., Meri, M., Krokfors, L., Husu, J., & Jyrhämä, R. (1999). Moral perspectives in teachers' thinking. In M. Lang, J. Olson, H. Hansen & W. Bünder (Eds.), *Changing schools/changing practices: Perspectives on educational reform and teacher professionalism* (pp. 109–116). Louvain: Garant.
Kuusisto, E., Tirri, K., & Rissanen, I. (2012). Finnish teachers' ethical sensitivity. *Education Research International.* doi:10.1155/2012/351879
Lyons, N. (1990). Dilemmas of knowing: Ethical and epistemological dimensions of teacher's work and development. *Harvard Educational Review*, 60, 159–181.
Noddings, N. (1992). *The challenge to care in schools: An alternative approach to education.* New York, NY: Teachers College Press.
Nokelainen, P., & Tirri, K. (2007). Empirical investigation of Finnish school principals' emotional leadership competencies. In S. Saari & T. Varis (Eds.), *Ammatillinen kasvu. Professional growth. Festschrift for Pekka Ruohotie* (pp. 424–438). Helsinki: OKKA.
Reid, W. (1979). Practical reasoning and curriculum theory: In search of a new paradigm. *Curriculum Inquiry*, 9, 187–207.
Sanger, M. N. (2008). What we need to prepare teachers for the moral nature of their work. *Journal of Curriculum Studies*, 40(2), 169–185.

Sanger, M. N., & Osguthorpe, R. D. (2013). Modeling as moral education: Documenting, analyzing, and addressing a central belief of preservice teachers. *Teaching and Teacher Education, 29*(1), 167–176.

Schutte, I., Tirri, K., & Wolfersberger, M. (under review). The relationship between ethical sensitivity, high ability and gender in higher education students.

Shaw, J. (2006). Intention in ethics. *Canadian Journal of Philosophy, 36*(2), 187–224.

Simon, R. I. (1992). *Teaching against the grain: Texts for a pedagogy of possibility.* Toronto: OISE Press.

Soini, T., Pietarinen, J., Pyhältö, K., & Tirri, K. (in press). Strategies for well-being and ethically sustainable problem-solving in teacher–student interaction. In D. Jindal-Snape & E. Hannah (Eds.), *Interprofessional ethics.* Bristol: Policy Press.

Tirri, K. (1999). Teachers' perceptions of moral dilemmas at school. *Journal of Moral Education, 28*(1), 31–47.

Tirri, K. (2003). The teacher's integrity. In F. Oser & W. Veugelers (Eds.), *Teaching in moral and democratic education.* Bern: Peter Lang.

Tirri, K. (Ed.). (2008). *Educating moral sensibilities in urban schools.* Rotterdam: Sense Publishers.

Tirri, K. (2009). Ethical dilemmas in confirmation school experienced by Finnish confirmation school teachers. In G. Skeie (Ed.), *Religious diversity and education in Europe* (Vol. 11, pp. 223–233). Munster: Waxmann.

Tirri, K. (2010). Teachers' values underlying their professional ethics. In T. Lovat, N. Clement & R. Toomey (Eds.), *International handbook on values education and student well-being* (pp. 153–163). New York, NY: Springer.

Tirri, K. (2011). Holistic school pedagogy and values: Finnish teachers' and students' perspectives. *International Journal of Educational Research, 50*(3), 159–165.

Tirri, K. (2012). The core of school pedagogy: Finnish teachers' views on the educational purposefulness of their teaching. In H. Niemi, A. Toom & A. Kallioniemi (Eds.), *Miracle of education: The principles and practices of teaching and learning in Finnish schools* (pp. 55–66). Rotterdam: Sense Publishers.

Tirri, K., & Husu, J. (2002). Care and responsibility in "the best interest of the child": Relational voices of ethical dilemmas in teaching. *Teachers and Teaching: Theory and Practice, 8*(1), 65–80.

Tirri, K., & Husu, J. (2006). Pedagogical values behind teachers' reflection of school ethos. In M. B. Klein (Ed.), *New teaching and teacher issues* (pp. 163–182). New York, NY: Nova Science.

Tirri, K., Husu, J., & Kansanen, P. (1999). The epistemological stance between the knower and the known. *Teaching and Teacher Education, 15*, 911–922.

Tirri, K., & Nokelainen, P. (2007). Comparison of academically average and gifted students' self-rated ethical sensitivity. *Educational Research and Evaluation, 13*(6), 587–601.

Tirri, K., & Nokelainen, P. (2011). *Measuring multiple intelligences and moral sensitivities in education.* Rotterdam: Sense Publishers.

Tirri, K., & Puolimatka, T. (2000). Teacher authority in schools: A case study from Finland. *Journal of Education for Teaching: International Research and Pedagogy, 26*(2), 157–165.

Tirri, K., & Ubani, M. (2013). Education of Finnish student teachers for purposeful teaching. *The Journal for the Education of Teaching, 39*(1), 21–29.

Toom, A. (2006). *Tacit pedagogical knowing: At the core of teacher's professionality.* Research Report 276, Department of Applied Sciences of Education, University of Helsinki, Helsinki.

Toom, A. (2012). Considering the artistry and epistemology of tacit knowledge and knowing. *Educational Theory*, *62*(6), 621–640.

Toom, A., & Husu, J. (2012). Finnish teachers as "makers of the many": Balancing between broad pedagogical freedom and responsibility. In H. Niemi, A. Toom & A. Kallioniemi (Eds.), *Miracle of education: The principles and practices of teaching and learning in Finnish schools* (pp. 39–54). Rotterdam: Sense Publishers.

Trade Union of Education in Finland. (2010). *Code of ethics for Finnish teachers*. Helsinki: Trade Union of Education in Finland.

Troman, G. (2000). Teacher stress in the low-trust society. *British Journal of Sociology of Education*, *21*(3), 331–353.

Van Manen, M., & Li, S. (2002). The pathic principle of pedagogical language. *Teaching and Teacher Education*, *18*(2), 215–224.

Walker, K. (1998). Jurisprudential and ethical perspectives on "the best interests of children." *Interchange*, *29*, 287–308.

Weber, M. (1978). Politics as a vocation. In W. G. Runciman (Ed.), *M. Weber selections in translation* (pp. 212–225). Cambridge, MA: Cambridge University Press.

Woods, P. (1995). *Creative teachers in primary schools*. Buckingham: Open University Press.

CHAPTER 12

IN SEARCH OF THE ESSENCE OF A GOOD TEACHER: TOWARD A MORE HOLISTIC APPROACH IN TEACHER EDUCATION☆

Fred A. J. Korthagen

ABSTRACT

There are two central questions determining the pedagogy of teacher education: (a) What are the essential qualities of a good teacher; and (b) How can we help people to become good teachers? Our objective is not to present a definitive answer to these questions, but to discuss an umbrella model of levels of change that could serve as a framework for reflection and development. The model highlights relatively new areas of research, viz., teachers' professional identity and mission. Appropriate teacher education interventions at the different levels of change are discussed, as well as implications for new directions in teacher education.

Keywords: Teacher characteristics; teacher competences; teacher education; pedagogical task; teacher identity; mission

---

☆This chapter is a slightly adapted version of Korthagen, F. A. J. (2004). In search of the essence of a good teacher: Towards a more holistic approach in teacher education. *Teaching and Teacher Education, 20*(1), 77–97. Reprinted with permission of Elsevier.

From Teacher Thinking to Teachers and Teaching: The Evolution of a Research Community
Advances in Research on Teaching, Volume 19, 241–273
Copyright © 2013 Elsevier
All rights of reproduction in any form reserved
ISSN: 1479-3687/doi:10.1108/S1479-3687(2013)0000019015

Consciously, we teach what we know; unconsciously, we teach who we are.
                                                        –Hamachek (1999, p. 209)

INTRODUCTION

> *A practical example:* A teacher educator is having a supervisory session with Judith, a student teacher in mathematics. Judith is annoyed with a student named Peter. She has a feeling that Peter is trying to get away with as little work as possible. Today was a good example. In the previous lesson, she had given the class an assignment for the next three lessons in which they were to work in pairs. The assignment would be wrapped up in the third lesson with a report. Today was the second day. Judith expected all the students to be hard at work, and during this lesson, she was to answer questions from students experiencing problems. Then she noticed that Peter was working on a completely different subject. Seeing this, her response was "Oh, so you're working on something else … looks like you're going to fail this assignment, too!" In retrospect, she is dissatisfied with her reaction, which she realizes was not effective.

In this example it was clear to the supervisor and to Judith herself that in the specific confrontation with Peter, Judith was not really being a "good teacher." But what was the underlying cause of it in Judith? Lack of competencies? Or was it that she does have the right competencies, but just did not use them? Or is she perhaps allergic to Peter? Or does she have an ineffective view of the role of a teacher?

And, even if the teacher educator or Judith would know this underlying cause or if they would unravel it in the course of the supervisory meeting, would it be clear how to help Judith in dealing with such situations? How could she become a "good teacher?" Would that require modeling, instruction, training, or reflection?

These are questions simple to ask, but not so simple to answer. At the same time, the situation and the questions that surface are characteristic of many others occurring each day in teacher education. They bring us to the heart of the pedagogy of teacher education.

This is why this chapter discusses two central questions determining the design of teacher education programs and the work of teacher educators:

1. *What are the essential qualities of a good teacher?*
2. *How can we help people to become good teachers?*

However, the objective of this chapter is not to present definitive answers to these questions, which according to Hamachek (1999) are still unresolved. We believe the answers may be different depending on the context, and perhaps it is even impossible or pedagogically undesirable to formulate a definitive description of "the good teacher." So, we believe it would be too ambitious to try to introduce any norm describing what a good teacher should look like. However, we do intend to offer a framework for any serious discussion of such a norm. What we wish to point out is that any attempt to describe the essential qualities of a good teacher should take into account that various levels are involved that fundamentally differ from each other. The level of teacher competencies is just one of these. We will introduce a model clarifying this point, and offering a framework for thinking about the two questions.

There are various reasons why such a framework may be important, especially at the present time. The first reason has to do with the changes in the aims and methods of teacher education taking place worldwide, due in part to the serious shortages of teachers. In many places, short-track teacher education programs have been introduced, and more and more of the actual education of teachers is taking place inside the schools. This raises a number of questions about the quality of these programs, questions that can only be answered when we have some kind of answer to the question "what is a good teacher?" Sometimes, the complexity of this question seems to be overlooked by policy-makers.

The second reason why the two questions may be important is that in teacher education there is considerable emphasis on promoting reflection in teachers, but at the same time, it is not always clear exactly *what* teachers are supposed to reflect *on* when wishing to become better teachers. What are important contents of reflection?

Finally, the pedagogy of teacher education strongly builds on insights from other disciplines, especially psychology. In that respect, it is important to note that new developments have taken place within psychology and psychotherapy, developments that have not yet much influenced main-stream thinking about teacher education. Hence, one of the objectives of this chapter is to discuss these developments, such as transpersonal psychology, positive psychology, the status-dynamic approach in psychotherapy, and to consider their implications for the work of teacher educators.

A THEORETICAL MODEL FOR FRAMING THE QUESTION "WHAT IS A GOOD TEACHER?"

Trying to put the essential qualities of a good teacher into words is a difficult undertaking. At present, all over the world, many attempts are being made to describe these qualities by means of lists of competencies, something that seems to be strongly supported by policy-makers (Becker, Kennedy, & Hundersmarck, 2003). However, doubts have been raised about the validity, reliability, and practicality of such lists, and many researchers question whether it is actually possible to describe the qualities of good teachers in terms of competencies (i.e., Barnett, 1994; Hyland, 1994).

It is remarkable that in this respect, history is repeating itself. Around the middle of the twentieth century, the "performance-based" or "competency-based" model in teacher education started to gain ground. The idea was that concrete, observable behavioral criteria could serve as a basis for the training of novices. For a number of years, so-called process-product studies were carried out in an effort to identify the teaching behaviors that displayed the highest correlation with the learning results of children. This was then translated into the concrete *competencies* that should be acquired by teachers.

This development, however, led to serious problems. In order to ensure sufficient validity and reliability in the assessment of teachers, long detailed lists of skills were formulated, which gradually resulted in a kind of fragmentation of the teacher's role. In practice, these long lists proved highly unwieldy. Moreover, it was becoming increasingly apparent that this view of teaching took insufficient account of the fact that a good teacher cannot simply be described in terms of certain isolated competencies, which can be learned in a number of training sessions: "In the first place, it is a fallacy to assume that the methods of the experts either can or should be taught directly to beginners" (Combs, Blume, Newman, & Wass, 1974, p. 4).

Moreover, Lowyck (1978, p. 215) stressed that teaching behavior can only be understood when the original context of the specific teaching behavior is included in the interpretation. Others criticize the competency-based model because it is rigid and pedagogically wrong (i.e., Hyland, 1994). In this light, it is noteworthy that in many places in the world we are still seeing the revival of a view of teaching and teacher education focusing on competencies.

Around 1970, a contrasting view of the way teachers should be educated emerged, known as Humanistic-Based Teacher Education (HBTE), in which more attention was directed toward the person of the teacher. HBTE originated in humanistic psychology, a movement whose well-known representatives were Rogers and Maslow. It was promoted, among others, by Combs et al. (1974) at the University of Florida in Gainesville, and by the University of California School of Education at Santa Barbara, where George Brown and his colleagues pursued the notion of "confluent education" in which thinking and feeling "flow" together in the learning process (i.e., Shapiro, 1998). Joyce (1975, p. 130) notes that HBTE stresses above all the *unicity and dignity of the individual*. In this view of education, a central role is reserved for personal growth (Maslow, 1968, uses the term self-actualization). As Joyce (1975, p. 132) maintains, the viewpoint of HBTE cannot be reconciled with the laying down of standardized teaching competencies.

HBTE failed to obtain broad support. However, the fact that this movement focused attention on the *person of the teacher* was of importance to the further development of teacher education. For example, Combs et al. (1974) devote an entire chapter to "the self" of the effective teacher.

This classical controversy between a competency-based view of teachers and an emphasis on the teacher's self can still be found in present discussions on teaching and teacher education. Where policy-makers generally focus on the importance of outcomes in terms of competencies, many researchers emphasize the more personal characteristics of teachers (i.e., Tickle, 1999), such as enthusiasm, flexibility, or love of children. However, we may have to guard ourselves against narrowing down the discussion to this classical dichotomy. More factors seem to be involved. In order to broaden the discussion, the model visualized in Fig. 1 may be helpful. This so-called "onion model" is an adaptation of what is known in the literature as Bateson's model (i.e., Dilts, 1990).[1] It shows that there are various levels in people that can be influenced. Only the outer levels (environment and behavior) can be directly observed by others. In the remainder of the present section, we will discuss each of the levels, which can be seen as different perspectives from which we can look at how teachers function. From each perspective, there will be a different answer to the question of the essential qualities of a good teacher, while it is also possible to employ various perspectives parallel to one another.

The outermost levels are those of the *environment* (the class, the students, the school) and *behavior*. These are the levels that seem to attract the most attention from student teachers: they often focus on problems in their classes, and the question how to deal with these problems.

Very influential to the level of behavior is the next level, the level of *competencies* (the latter including knowledge, i.e., subject matter knowledge). We have already discussed this level.

The onion model

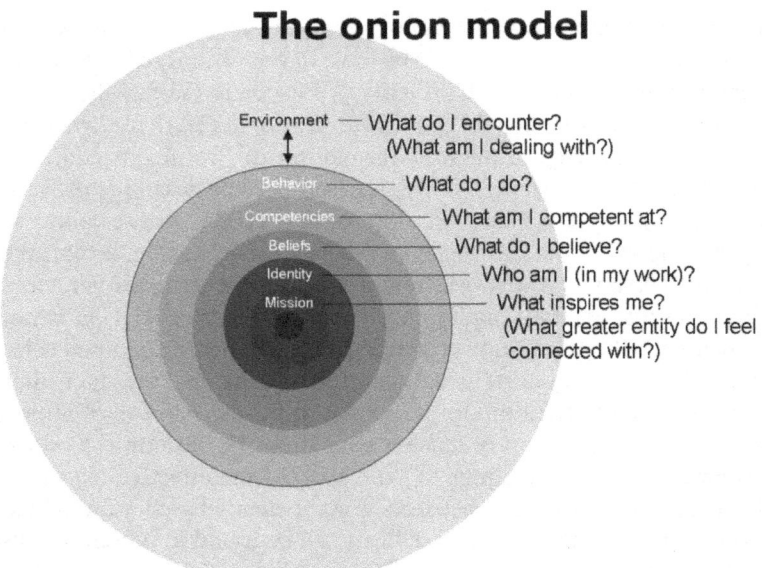

Fig. 1. The Onion: A Model of Levels of Change.

In order to make a clear distinction between the levels of behavior and of competencies, it is important to stress that competencies are generally conceived of as *an integrated body of knowledge, skills, and attitudes* (Stoof, Martens, & Van Merriënboer, 2000). As such, they represent a potential for behavior, and not the behavior itself. It depends on the circumstances whether the competencies are really put into practice, that is, expressed in behavior (Caprara & Cervone, 2003).

Before discussing the other three levels, we can at this point already note an important assumption behind the model, namely that the outer levels can influence the inner levels: the environment can influence a teacher's behavior (a difficult class may trigger other reactions from the teacher than a friendly one), and through behavior that is repeated often enough, one develops the competency to also use it in other circumstances. A reverse influence, however, also exists, that is, from the inside to the outside. For example, one's behavior can have an impact on the environment (a teacher who praises a child may influence this child), and one's competencies determine the behavior one is able to show.

We will now discuss the next three levels in more detail. First, we realize that a teacher's competencies are determined by his or her *beliefs*. For example, if a teacher believes that attention to pupils' feelings is just "soft" and unnecessary, he or she will probably not develop the competency to show empathic understanding. The level of beliefs has begun to draw international attention since about 1980 under the influence of the so-called cognitive shift in psychology. Researchers studying the behavior of teachers and how they were trained stressed that it is important to know what teachers think, and what their beliefs are (i.e., Clark, 1986; Pajares, 1992). The beliefs teachers hold with regard to learning and teaching determine their actions, a point often overlooked in the more behaviorist approach. Various authors (i.e., Feiman-Nemser, 1983) state that teachers have themselves spent many years as students in schools, during which time they have developed their own beliefs about teaching, many of which are diametrically opposed to those presented to them during their teacher education. For example, they may have developed the belief that teaching is transmission of knowledge, and most teacher educators find this belief not very beneficial to becoming a good teacher (Richardson, 1997). However, in most cases, it is these old beliefs that prevail (Wubbels, 1992).

This has led to a development in teacher education in which the emphasis is less on the transfer of scientific knowledge (or "formal knowledge," as Fenstermacher, 1994, calls it), and more on becoming conscious of one's own "personal practical knowledge" (Clandinin, 1986). This practical knowledge usually takes the form of *images*. An example is the image of a teacher that many teachers have retained from their own school days: someone standing at the front of the classroom and explaining things. Korthagen and Lagerwerf (1996) emphasize that not only visual images or purely cognitive aspects are involved here, but also emotional (compare Hargreaves, 1998), volitional, and behavioral aspects. They use the term "Gestalts" to refer to cohesive wholes of earlier experiences, role models, needs, values, feelings, images, and routines, which are – often unconsciously – evoked by concrete situations (see for an elaboration of the concept of Gestalt, Korthagen & Lagerwerf, 1996; Korthagen, Kessels, Koster, Lagerwerf, & Wubbels, 2001). To take an example: a student teacher is faced with a student he sees as unmotivated. This student immediately triggers old images and feelings, along with the desire to change something in that student and its accompanying behavioral inclination. It is not inconceivable that, at a stroke, all the knowledge provided during his professional preparation will be nullified, and replaced by that Gestalt. The student teacher may for example seek a confrontation with the student, even though the theory on interpersonal classroom behavior (Wubbels & Levy, 1993) says that in such a situation the teacher would do better to opt for cooperative rather than oppositional behavior.

More recently, many researchers have turned to the stories of teachers. This so-called "narrative approach" is based on the premise that the ways in which teachers think about education is embedded in the stories they tell each other and themselves (Carter, 1993). Moreover, a shift of accent within this narrative approach gradually became apparent. Initially, it was considered important to find out how teachers thought about education. Today, more and more attention is being paid to the *beliefs people have about themselves*. This is the fifth level in the onion model, the level referring to how one defines oneself, in other words, to how a person sees his or her *(professional) identity*. This brings us to the fifth level in Fig. 1, which we will now describe in more detail, as there are some interesting developments in this area.

TEACHERS' PROFESSIONAL IDENTITY AND ITS DEVELOPMENT

The Concept of Professional Identity

Interest in the theme of professional identity may seem to be of fairly recent date, although in this respect the humanistic-based approach (HBTE) was ahead of its time. From quite early on, it was customary within this movement for teachers to reflect on such questions as "who am I?", "what kind of teacher do I want to be?", and "how do I see my role as a teacher?", all of which are essential questions when it comes to developing a professional identity.

It is not surprising that at present the theme of professional identity receives renewed attention: in the recent past there have been a great many significant developments in the ways in which we look at learning and teaching, and views of the role of the teacher have rapidly shifted from someone transferring knowledge to someone guiding students. This means that teachers are expected to adopt a different view of their role, and a different answer to the question "who am I as a teacher?" McLean (1999, p. 55) concludes that after decades in which "the person" was largely absent from the theory on how best to educate teachers, we are now witnessing a surge of interest in the question of how beginning teachers think about themselves and how they undergo the substantial personal transformations they pass through as they become teachers.

A good example of that shift in accent is to be found in the work of Kelchtermans and Vandenberghe (1994), who studied the influence on the professional development of teachers of so-called critical life events, phases, and significant others (see also Tripp, 1994). Due to the biographical perspective chosen by Kelchtermans, it became clear that the way teachers saw their role was to a large extent colored by the events and individuals in their lives. This had previously been emphasized by Crow (1987), who used the term "teacher role identity," and by Knowles (1988), who introduced a Biographical Transformation Model to explain the relationships between early childhood experiences with significant others, teacher role identity, and classroom actions. Interesting examples are presented by Mayes (2001), who shows how his student teachers' beliefs about the world and about themselves are shaped and inhibited by their upbringing. A student who has grown up in a closed religious environment can have a hard time when confronted with completely different views of the world, and this may start to undermine his or her self-concept.

A study carried out by Koster, Korthagen, and Schrijnemakers (1995) into the influence of positive and negative role models brought to light clear examples of the extent to which student teachers were influenced by certain teachers in their own past. Those examples illustrate how past role models shape the professional self-image of teachers. This point may be considered of enormous importance to teacher education. As Tusin (1999, p. 27) states, "behavior is a function of self-concept, which makes self-concept an essential aspect of teaching and learning to teach." Hamachek (1999, p. 209) says that "the more that teachers know about themselves – the private curriculum within – the more their personal decisions are apt to be about how to pave the way for better teaching."

During the twentieth century, an enormous amount of research has been carried out in psychology and philosophy on issues such as "identity" and the "self." However, as the theme of teacher identity has only recently begun to attract the widespread attention of researchers in the area of teaching and teacher education, Beijaard, Verloop, and Vermunt (2000) note that a largely unexplored territory lies ahead of us. How can we translate the wealth of psychological and philosophical literature to teaching and teachers? In the few publications devoted to this subject, we find no clear definition of the concept of teachers' professional identity. In this chapter, we endorse the definition put forward by Beijaard (1995): "Who or what someone is, the various meanings people can attach to themselves, or the meanings attributed by others." This is related to Gecas's (1985, p. 739) statement that identity "gives structure and content to the self-concept, and anchors the self to social systems." Both authors attribute great importance to the notion of "self-concept." On the basis of the interviews Nias (1989) conducted with teachers, she concludes that the concept of self is indeed crucial to a proper understanding of how teachers function. However, one problem presenting itself is the fact that if we look at the literature devoted to developmental psychology in order to clarify the notion of self-concept, we find an overwhelming number of concepts centered around the term "self." These include such terms as the actual self, the true self, the essential self, the ideal self, the possible self, as well as the social self, the emotional self, and the learning self. Moreover, there is considerable confusion about the difference between terms such as self-image, self-concept, self-conception, self-experience, and self-appreciation. There are also the more process-centered notions, including self-development, self-actualization, and self-realization. And this is just a random selection drawn from the extensive body of literature devoted to the "self," which also encompasses the debate concerning the differences between self and ego, and between self and personality. This body of literature becomes even more overwhelming and confusing if we also take the literature on identity formation that is more philosophical into account.

No doubt, many readers will see the above as evidence of a certain scientific vagueness surrounding the level of identity, promoting the idea that we would do better to forget about the whole notion of professional identity. However, a similar confusion of tongues occurs in the case of concepts much better known within the world of teaching and teacher education, including competencies (i.e., Eraut, 1994) and beliefs (i.e., Pajares, 1992). It is a challenge to further clarify such concepts in order to make them manageable for educational purposes. Indeed, this represents a major field of research as far as the theme of teachers' professional identity is involved. In the next section, we will try to take some further steps in developing a frame of reference for such research.

It is true to say that within the literature, a reasonable consensus is to be found with respect to the core idea of "self-concept." A common definition of the term is "an organized summary of information, rooted in observable facts concerning oneself, which includes such aspects as traits of character, values, social roles, interests, physical characteristics and personal history" (Bergner & Holmes, 2000; Kihlstrom & Klein, 1994).[2] On the basis of that definition, it is not so difficult to distinguish between a "personal self" and a "professional self," by focusing on the difference between a summary dealing with the entire body of information on one's personal functioning, and a summary of the information dealing with one's professional functioning.

With respect to teacher education, it is interesting to speculate on how far apart the two could lie. Although there are some who prefer to make a clear distinction between these two identities, most researchers in this area agree that excessive inconsistencies between one's personal and professional identities would in the long run give rise to friction within the individual teacher (i.e., Nias, 1989, p. 42). It is precisely because such friction must be prevented so that the professional identity of the teacher merits the attention of educators, even more than in professions where it is easier to separate the individual from his professional performance (McLean, 1999).

The Development of Teachers' Professional Identity in Teacher Education

We may ask ourselves whether teacher education can also contribute to the development of the professional identity of teachers. This is of no doubt to Bullough (1997), who states, "Teacher identity – what beginning teachers believe about teaching and learning and self-as-a-teacher – is of vital concern to teacher education; it is the basis for meaning making and decision making. [...] Teacher education must begin, then, by exploring the teaching self" (p. 21).

A major problem here is the fact that self-concepts are extremely resistant to change, even in the light of facts that clearly contradict them (Swann, 1992). Indeed, all experienced teacher educators know that when student teachers have a negative self-concept, it is extremely difficult to bring them round to a different way of thinking about themselves, even when they are confronted with examples of situations in which they performed in an outstanding manner. The reverse situation is at least as problematic, that is, trying to convince students with an unrealistically positive self-concept that their professional performance leaves something to be desired. The classic, psychoanalytical explanation for this phenomenon is that it involves a mechanism designed to protect the ego (Freud, 1986[1936]). This particular problem has taken on a different perspective as a result of an interesting shift in the theory surrounding the self-concept. Bergner and Holmes, representatives of the *status-dynamic approach* within psychotherapy, proposed to define the self-concept as a concise formulation of one's own status (Bergner & Holmes, 2000, p. 36). The notion of "status" refers to the overall conception of one's own place or position in relation to all the elements in one's world, including oneself. In this view, the self-concept is a relational concept: our self-concept is largely determined by how we see our relationships with significant others. This concurs with the view expressed by Sleegers and Kelchtermans (1999, p. 369). They consider the professional identity of teachers the result of temporary meanings related to themselves and their profession, which teachers construct by interacting with their environment. This is also in line with the systems approach chosen by Watzlawick, Beavin, and Jackson (1968), who see interpersonal relations as part of a system formed by those participating in the relationship. As a result of the imperative nature of the system, the participants' perceptions of the relation are difficult to alter once it has taken shape. This explanation for the fact that self-concepts are difficult to alter deviates from the classic one, which makes use of the notion of "ego-protective mechanisms," for which, in the view of Bergner and Holmes (2000), there is insufficient empirical support.

The status-dynamic approach may have very practical consequences for the supervision of teachers: Bergner and Holmes (2000) state that it is not effective to try to change the unrealistic self-concepts of people by confronting them with conflicting information. Even promoting reflection on one's own self-concept probably has only a conservative effect. What does help is putting people into a situation that creates a different status, a different definition of the relationship. A well-known example from teacher education consists in placing a student with a highly negative self-concept in an easy, friendly class. Another example is the deliberate use of the supervisory relationship: in this relationship, the experience of a certain status can be evoked in the student. One need only think of the status of unconditionally acceptable person which Carl Rogers (1969) emphasized, and which Borich (1999, p. 112, 113) translates into the relationship between the teacher educator and the student teacher. Bergner and Holmes (2000) believe that in the same way other status types can be created, for example, by approaching the person as being someone important who has within him a great potential for change, who has the capacity to be a change agent, etc. They describe this approach as "This is who you are, and I will treat you as such." There are many educators who have been doing this for years (i.e., Korthagen et al., 2001, p. 125), but recent developments in the field of psychotherapy have now provided a theoretical basis for their practice.

Reflection on professional identity is emphasized in many current teacher education programs. In our own, for example, students are asked to reflect on positive and negative role models from the time when they themselves were students in primary or secondary school. This appears to help them in making implicit influences explicit, and to consciously choose what kind of teacher they want to be. Tripp (1994, p. 74) says this kind of reflection is essential for teachers. In our own program, we also make use of exercises such as the "life path" in which students draw a time line indicating important events and persons that were – or still are – influential in their development as teachers. A variation on this has been developed by Pope and Denicolo (2001), and is called the "river of experience" in which a meandering river is used as a metaphor for teachers' personal biographies. Through such techniques, teachers may chart what Pinar (1986) calls their "Architecture of Self." A well-known other method in teacher education aimed at making teachers aware of their professional identities is the exchange of stories (Clandinin, 1992; McLean, 1999). Related approaches are described by Bullough (1997). Currently, many teacher educators use portfolios as a means to promote student teachers' reflections on their professional identities (see Bullough, 1993, for an exploration of the potential of portfolios for deepening reflection).

Activities such as these are examples of "constructing life through language" (Van Huizen, 2000, p. 41), and the co-construction of professional identity that takes place within interpersonal communication (Van Huizen, 2000, pp. 62, 65). It is important to point out that in the absence of such activities, teachers are usually not very interested in their professional identity, especially not during periods of actual teaching (Korthagen & Lagerwerf, 1996). Professional identity, then, often takes on the form of a Gestalt: an unconscious body of needs, images, feelings, values, role models, previous experiences, and behavioral tendencies, which together create a sense of identity. This Gestalt influences the outer levels of beliefs, competencies, and behavior. The methods described (such as the "life path" and story-telling) help students to become aware of that Gestalt. This in turn leads to what Kelchtermans and Vandenberghe (1994) refer to as "self-understanding." On the basis of such self-understanding, teachers are able to make choices that are more conscious when compared to their previous, more unconscious teaching behavior, and that are related to their own further professional development. Here, we see how the biographical perspective in research can be translated into teacher education practices.

However, as Bullough and Baughman (1997) show, fundamental changes in teacher identity do not take place easily: identity change is a difficult and sometimes painful process, and often there seems to be little change at all in how teachers view themselves.

THE LEVEL OF MISSION

In the form in which the model of Fig. 1 appears in the literature, a sixth level is also relevant to the present discussion. Dilts (1990) calls it the "spirituality level." We will refer to it as the "level of mission" in that, according to various authors, this level is concerned with such highly personal questions as to what end the teacher wants to do his or her work, or even what he or she sees as his or her personal calling in the world. In short, the question of what it is deep inside us that moves us to do what we do. This level has been called a "transpersonal level" in so-called transpersonal psychology (i.e., Scotton, Chinen, & Battista, 1996), because it is about becoming aware of the meaning of one's own existence within a larger whole, and the role we see for ourselves in relation to our fellow man. Where the identity level is concerned with the personal singularity of the individual, the spirituality level is about "the experience of being part of meaningful wholes and in harmony with superindividual units such as family, social group, culture and cosmic order" (Boucouvalas, 1988). In short, it is about giving meaning to one's own existence. The central question at this level is "why do I exist?", in other words, what is at the root of my personal inspiration? The word "inspiration" comes from the same Latin word as "spiritual." However, the term "spirituality level" occasionally evokes undesirable associations with the New Age movement.[3] This has prompted us to use the term "level of mission." In this context, it is also interesting to mention a suggestion put forward by Mike Bourcier (personal communication). He refers to this level as "the level of interconnectedness." The central question at this level can then be reformulated as "with which larger entity do I feel connected?" As will also be clear from the above quote from Boucouvalas (one of the authors writing about transpersonal psychology; see also Boucouvalas, 1980), the answer could be of a religious nature, or it could focus on the commitment to one's fellow man, to the environment, to an ideal such as World Peace, etc. For teachers, we can think of ideals such as creating more acceptance of differences between people, creating feelings of self-worth in children, and so forth. In any case, we are talking about deeply felt, personal values that the person regards as inextricably bound up with his or her existence. People are not always equally aware of this level in themselves. Occasionally, however, it can suddenly demand attention, as when through certain circumstances everything in your life grinds to a halt, for example, when faced with the loss of a loved one.

As we intend to demonstrate in the next section, the level of mission can be of direct relevance to teachers, and it may acquire a very concrete significance in their professional development. This has previously been emphasized by Mayes (2001).

CORE QUALITIES AND POSITIVE PSYCHOLOGY

One more issue is important to the understanding of the model of levels of change. Related to the deeper levels are people's *personal qualities*, for example, creativity, trust, care, courage, sensitivity, decisiveness, spontaneity, commitment, and flexibility (Tickle, 1999). Attention for such personal qualities is strongly influenced by the work of the past president of the American Psychological Association (APA), Seligman, and his colleague Csikszentmihalyi, well known for his publications on "flow." Seligman and Csikszentmihalyi (2000, p. 7) state that for too long psychology has focused on pathology, weakness, and damage done to people, and hence on "treatments." They say that, although this focus has been successful in some limited areas, "treatment is not just fixing what is broken; it is nurturing what is best." One can easily relate this to certain approaches toward the improvement of education, including some competency-based approaches, which often start from a deficiency model.

Partly returning to the roots of humanistic psychology, but also critical of its lack of empirical research, Seligman and Csikszentmihalyi (and many other psychologists at present working within *positive psychology*; see Aspinwall & Staudinger, 2003) emphasize the importance of positive traits in individuals, which they call "character strengths." For the scientific identification of these strengths, they also make use of philosophical literature on *virtues*, as "character strengths are the psychological ingredients – processes or mechanisms – that define the virtues." Examples of such strengths are creativity, courage, kindness, and fairness, but also spirituality, and transcendence ("strengths that connect us to the larger universe," Peterson & Seligman, 2000). The latter examples illustrate the connections made within positive psychology to transpersonal psychology.

Strengths are fundamental to what Diener (2000) calls subjective well-being. A central issue in positive psychology is how a person's values and goals (ideals) mediate between external events and the quality of experience, something that is directly relevant to teacher education. Peterson and Seligman (2000), using their terminology of strengths, emphasize that although these strengths can and do produce desirable outcomes, they are morally valued in their own right, even in the absence of obvious beneficial outcomes: "Although strengths and virtues no doubt determine how an individual copes with adversity, our focus is on how they fulfill an individual." This illustrates that these personal strengths are not only related to the level of identity, but also to the level of mission. Peterson and

Seligman add that when people are referring to their strengths, this correlates with a feeling of "this is the real me," that they show "a feeling of excitement when displaying a strength," and – very important to our discussion – "a rapid learning curve as themes are attached to the strength and practiced."

The way Seligman and other psychologists within this new field write about strengths clarifies that they are synonymous to what Ofman (1992, p. 33) calls "core qualities." He states that such core qualities are always potentially present. He maintains that the distinction between qualities and competencies lies primarily in the fact that qualities come from the inside, while competencies are acquired from the outside. This is in accordance with the model of levels of change: competencies such as the ability to take into account different learning styles or to reflect systematically are located at the level of competencies, while core qualities are found at the deeper levels of change. Almaas (1987, p. 175) talks about *essential aspects*, which he considers absolute in the sense that they cannot be further reduced, or dissected into simpler component parts. We prefer the term "core quality," as it stresses the difference with the concept of "core competence" (often used in the literature on competency management, for example, by Prahalad & Hamel, 1990).

It should be stressed that when someone is brought into touch with a core quality, it may be important to support him or her in taking the step toward actualization of that quality. This means that an important aim of supervision may be to facilitate the process whereby the inner levels of change influence the outer levels. Thus, we concur wholeheartedly with Lipka and Brinthaupt (1999, p. 228), who maintain that "an excessive focus on 'self' at the expense of 'other' will be counterproductive." What matters is developing effective personal behavior. To that end, it is vital that teachers are not only cognitively aware of their core qualities, but also emotionally in touch with those qualities, that they take the step leading to conscious decisions to make use of those core qualities and then carry out those decisions. Often, this may initially require help from a teacher educator.

WHAT IS A GOOD TEACHER?

On the basis of the previous analysis, we conclude that the first question from which we started, namely "what are the essential qualities of a good teacher?", cannot be answered in a simple way, and that a list of competencies is in any case inadequate to answer it. On the other hand, the model of levels of change may offer a helpful framework for thinking about this question, as it clarifies the variety of relevant aspects that should be taken in to account. We should not forget, however, that a "good teacher" will not always show "good teaching": although someone may have excellent competencies, the right beliefs, and an inspirational self and mission, the level of the environment may put serious limits on the teacher's behavior (i.e., Zeichner & Gore, 1990). This is another indication that awareness of the levels may help to understand such limitations: often there are discrepancies between the six levels. Such discrepancies often lead to problems for the teacher (in the form of inner tensions), for others in his or her environment (if the teacher does not show adequate behavior), or both. Stated more positively, with more balance between the various levels, the teacher will experience less inner and outer frictions. Ideally, there is a complete "alignment" of the levels, which means that the teacher's behavior, competencies, beliefs, identity, and mission together form one coherent whole matching the environment. This seems an ideal that can take a lifetime to attain, if attained at all. As Shaw (1975, p. 445) states in a wonderful chapter on this issue (entitled "Congruence"), "Such authenticity has no equivalent; it is the development and expression of one's Self through direct, personal experience and creation of one's language and meanings over time."

HOW CAN WE HELP STUDENTS TO BECOME GOOD TEACHERS?

This brings us to the second central question set out in the introduction of this chapter, namely: How can we help people to become good teachers? The onion model can make a contribution to finding an answer to that question. For example, it provides support in supervising the reflection processes of teachers, because it focuses attention on the possible contents of that reflection. Many models for reflection are in fact phase models (Pope & Denicolo, 2001, p. 63), describing the reflection *process*, and make no pronouncements on the question of what teachers can reflect *on*. In this sense, the model of levels of change (the "onion") supplements such process models of reflection, in that it helps educators to determine on which levels the teacher is having problems, as well as on which levels the supplement might lie that should take shape.

Let us look at the practical example of Judith, with which we started this chapter. In this example, the different levels in Fig. 1 can be concretized as follows:

1. *The environment*: what Judith encounters, that is, everything outside herself. In the present example, this is Peter and the way he is behaving.
2. *Behavior*: both Judith's less effective behaviors, such as an irritated response, and other – possibly more effective – behaviors.
3. *Competencies*: for example, the competency to respond in a constructive manner.
4. *Beliefs*: perhaps Judith's beliefs that Peter is not motivated or even that he is trying to cause trouble.
5. *Professional identity*: how does Judith view her own professional role here? For example, does she see a social-pedagogical role for herself in relation to Peter?
6. *Mission*: what is the calling that has led Judith to become a teacher? It is not uncommon for our own mathematics student teachers to be enthusiastic about their subject; in fact they often find their main inspiration in mathematics, and – at least at the beginning of their professional preparation – much less in their relationship with students at school.

For the teacher educator, an important question should be: What is it that is bothering Judith in this situation? In terms of the model in Fig. 1, the question is on which level lies her *concern*. In the so-called "realistic" view of teacher education formulated by Korthagen et al. (2001), concerns are seen as the driving force of learning. Perhaps, Judith is beginning to wonder whether different behavior would be better (the level of behavior), or she may be questioning her role as a teacher (identity level). The educator may have to help Judith in becoming aware of her concern and the level on which it is located, but must also keep in mind whether – and how – the other levels are involved. For example, if Judith intends to change her behavior, an important question is whether she has the competency to do so. And in order to develop this competency, the level of beliefs may well deserve attention.

The type of intervention required to change behavior may not be the same as that needed to promote awareness of one's professional identity or mission. Table 1 on next page indicates how, on the basis of the existing literature on the education of teachers, we can relate the various levels to appropriate interventions in teacher education. The right-hand column in this table was strongly influenced by a theory put forward by Gallimore and

Table 1. Relation Between the Levels of Change and Interventions in Teacher Education.

Levels	Appropriate Interventions
1. Environment	Creating a suitable learning environment
2. Behavior	Modeling and contingency management
3. Competencies	Instruction, training, and coaching
4. Beliefs	Conceptual-change approaches
5. Professional identity	?
6. Mission	?

Tharp (1992) on "assisted performance." They based many of their ideas on neo-Vygotskian concepts, and distinguished six types of intervention: modeling, contingency management, giving feedback, instructing, questioning, and cognitive structuring.

We will now look briefly at the right-hand column of Table 1:

1. In order to help student teachers become acquainted with the "environment" relevant to the professional development of a teacher, it is important to offer them a suitable learning environment. For example, a school where the teaching is highly traditional would be less appropriate for acquainting oneself with new teaching practices. Many institutions of teacher education try to create a fruitful teaching environment through collaboration with professional development schools (Darling-Hammond, 1994).

2. Modeling consists of showing students what is suitable behavior, so that they can imitate it. This requires that teacher educators "teach what they preach" (Lunenberg & Korthagen, 2003). When students are experimenting with new behavior, it is important to refine that behavior by both correcting and rewarding them. Gallimore and Tharp (1992) call this contingency management.

3. Instruction, training, and coaching are major components of the direct instructional model, which has been dealt with in detail by, among others, Rosenshine and Stevens (1986). As this model is widely known, it will not be further discussed here.

4. The essence of conceptual change is altering students' existing views. A well-known example is the common conception among students that teaching consists of "transferring" knowledge, while today's educators strive to help their students develop views that are more appropriate to a constructivist view of teaching. Conceptual-change strategies often consist

of the following steps (see also Korthagen, 1992; Wubbels, Korthagen, & Dolk, 1992):

a. First, the student is encouraged to reflect on a concrete experience during teaching practice.
b. Next, the student is helped to become aware of the often-implicit beliefs playing a role in his or her perception of – and behavior in – this and other, similar situations.
c. Then, through examining the disadvantages of that belief together with the student, dissatisfaction with the existing belief is created.
d. The student is then offered an alternative – scientifically sound – theory.
e. Finally, alternative behavior based on that theory is practiced.

Posner, Strike, Hewson, and Gertzog (1982) stress that the alternative theory must be intelligible, plausible, and fruitful in the eyes of the student in order to lend it a higher "status" than the existing belief.[4]

5 and 6. In the literature on the pedagogy of teacher education, relatively little attention has been devoted to interventions aimed at the levels of professional identity and mission. A relatively recent exception is Mayes (2001) who shows how a transpersonal perspective can lead to a broadening of the concept of reflection in teacher education. Another noteworthy exception is Palmer (1998), who focuses on teaching "from within" and stresses the importance of the call to, the pain, and the joy of teaching. His in-service work with teachers is based on his belief that "good teaching cannot be reduced to technique; good teaching comes from the identity and integrity of the teacher" (p. 10). Palmer's work shows similarities with Hansen (1995), who focuses on *the call to teach*. Newman (2000) studied the ideals and dreams of teachers and how these could be used in teacher education. Other exceptions are Allender (2001), who describes how he works with student teachers on the relation between self, others, and pedagogy, and Ayers (2001), who – while talking about educators – states that "our calling after all, is to shepherd and enable the callings of others."

When thinking about interventions on the fifth and sixth levels, one might expect the conceptual-change approaches to be useful here as well. On the other hand, these levels are concerned with self-concepts, which, as we have seen, are not easily influenced. In various therapeutic approaches, specific techniques are used to influence self-concepts and awareness at the level of mission. We have already looked at Rogerian interventions, which are designed to influence self-concepts. Psychosynthesis (a branch of transpersonal psychology founded by Assagioli) deals specifically with the level of mission, making use of such techniques as guided fantasies, drawing, and meditation (Assagioli, 1965; Parfitt, 1990; Whitmore, 1986). The use of the latter interventions within teacher education is still in its early stages, and sometimes evokes resistance (see Mayes, 2001). In the next section, a number of interventions will be described that seem promising, so that it may be possible to replace the question marks in Table 1 with concrete interventions suitable for teacher education.

To our discussion of Table 1, a comment must be added. Because the various levels influence one another, it is quite possible that a particular intervention can be employed on another level as well. For example, Wubbels (1992) emphasizes that it is possible to influence beliefs through interventions making much less use of reflection than the conceptual-change approach described above. For example, the views of a student teacher may change when starting teaching at a different school (influence via the level of the environment), or when he is helped to develop new behavior by means of modeling (level of behavior).

We are now gradually approaching a general answer to the second question with which we started this chapter, namely, how can we help someone to become a good teacher? The essence of this answer is: it may be important to focus on the level at which the person has a concern, but it is also helpful to extend the attention to include other levels, while keeping different types of intervention in mind. In short, the model of levels of change can help educators to provide tailor-made support to their students.

It would be interesting to systematically study the effects of integrated efforts at various levels. The hypothesis could then be tested that maintains that the process of professional development among teachers stagnates when problems on a specific level are not tackled by descending to a deeper level. Such research will demand a clearly defined theoretical foundation with respect to the various levels. For the outer levels of the model in Table 1, considerable theoretical material is available. However, when it comes to the theory surrounding the level of mission, very little research has been done. This is unfortunate for the field of teaching and teacher education since there are still many people who choose to become teachers, because they feel that they have a "calling" (i.e., Hansen, 1995). This is an aspect seldom mentioned in professional profiles and lists of teaching competencies. Almost nowhere do we find any mention of how important it is to be a teacher with all your heart and soul, and this is one reason why so little attention is devoted to the question of suitable interventions at the level of mission.

CONCRETE APPLICATIONS: THREE PROJECTS

Precisely because the inner levels of the model receive relatively little interest, we have started a number of projects aiming at the levels of professional identity and mission. They focus on student teachers, experienced teachers, and teacher educators, respectively. Through these projects, we are gradually gaining more insight into the interventions that may be suitable to replace the question marks in Table 1. As most reports on these projects have only been published in Dutch, they are briefly summarized in the next three sub sections.

A Workshop for Student Teachers[5]

We developed and researched a workshop (of four mornings/afternoons) for student teachers entitled "Did you encounter your students or yourself?" The workshop, which was held toward the end of the one-year postgraduate program, attracted students who during their teaching practice had been forced to face up to certain truths about themselves. Many of them were suffering from feelings of insecurity, and almost all were grappling with questions at the level of identity or mission, such as "Am I willing – and able – to adopt the kind of behavior that is apparently necessary to maintain classroom discipline? Does this behavior suit me? Do I still want to become a teacher? Is there actually room for what inspired me to become a teacher in the first place? In the workshop, we used a number of techniques designed to promote reflection in order to help the students to acquire a greater awareness on the levels of identity and mission. Elsewhere, we describe the workshop in more detail, its background and the interventions employed, together with an evaluation of the processes involved and their effects (Korthagen et al., 2001, pp. 266–269; Korthagen & Verkuyl, 2007).

After the workshop, in which we used many structures aiming at an awareness of the deeper levels, the students reported that reflection on these levels (which we call "core reflection"; Korthagen, Kim, & Greene, 2013) had not often taken place during the teacher education program (which focuses on the promotion of reflection!), and that they considered it a valuable addition. In the workshop, it appeared to serve as a springboard for a fresh examination of both their career choice and their concrete teaching behavior. In the latter case, this involved the important shift from the inner levels of the model to the outer levels, for example, by reflection on the question how to translate one's core qualities into concrete behavior in a specific situation.

In all, the workshop succeeded in focusing serious attention on professional identity and personal inspiration (mission). We believe that by stressing core reflection, we can counter the unconscious socialization and adaptation to a traditional school culture (i.e., Zeichner & Gore, 1990). Core reflection helps students to consciously direct their own development, in accordance with their personal identity, and their inspiration and enthusiasm for their profession (Korthagen et al., 2013).

A Project with Experienced Teachers

Core reflection was also a part of a project involving experienced teachers in primary and secondary education. In this group, a variety of structures were used focusing on raising (renewed) awareness of one's own professional identity, and one's "pedagogical mission" in relation to the moral and social development of children. These included a "contrast analysis" (in which reflection on the contrast between a positive and negative teaching experience leads to more awareness of the level of mission; see www.korthagen.nl), and the "wall," an exercise in making one's own pedagogical views explicit by means of paper bricks bearing statements (Korthagen et al., 2001, pp. 162–163). Within the framework of this project, the participants also selected a concrete case they were struggling with. Then, on the basis of this case, they worked together in small groups, supporting one another as they tried to identify their individual pedagogical ideals and ways to put them into practice. At the end of the project, these teachers reported that it had become clear to them how little their school cultures were directed toward reflection and collaboration with colleagues on matters related to the personal develop- ment of children. (This observation concurs with Klaassen [2002, p. 151], who states that "an erosion of teachers' pedagogical sensibilities is occurring.") The ground we had traveled with our teachers had inspired them, and they said they hoped their colleagues would also have an opportunity to take part in a project like this. Especially mentioned was the importance of the interaction with colleagues. In a reflection on the project, one participant wrote:

> Of course, after a discussion like that, you keep thinking about yourself, the way you function as a teacher. It gives you new insights into yourself, makes you face up to a side of yourself you didn't know of, and maybe would prefer not to know. You can't close your eyes to truths like this, and they keep revolving inside your head. During the lessons that follow, you find yourself stopping in order to think about interventions, decisions,

remarks and feelings. What am I like, how do I think and act as a teacher? What do I
consider really important?[6]

It will be clear from this quote that the levels of identity and mission had
come to occupy an important place in the thinking of this teacher. There
appeared to be many participants in this project whose pedagogical ideals
had received a shot in the arm, against the background of their colleagues in
their schools. In the midst of the rough and tumble of everyday life, we
believe there are a frightening number of teachers striving on their own to
give shape to the ideals they have – or had when they chose to take up a
teaching career. As one of the teachers in this project said, "Everyone who
decides to work with people must have ideals. Everyone has that 'level'
inside, but at a certain moment you can decide to close the hatch."

Teacher shortages have received a great deal of attention, and in many
countries teacher educators are doing their best to attract people to the
profession. However, in view of the prevalence of burnout among
experienced teachers, it is perhaps no less important to retain those already
teaching. Research has shown that the loss of ideals, and what people
experience as a lack of support when it comes to the realization of those
ideals, plays an important part in cases of burnout and, in some cases, the
decision to resign from present position (Freudenberger & Richelson, 1980).
Edelwich and Brodsky (1980, p. 14) even define burnout in terms of the loss
of ideals and meaningfulness, characterizing it as a "progressive loss of
idealism, energy, purpose, and concern as a result of conditions of work."
We conclude that an important working condition for teachers is sufficient
attention to their personal ideals, and collegial support in realizing those
ideals. In short, for many teachers finding answers to the question "What's
the sense of it all?" is not a luxury, but a necessity if they are to continue to
put their hearts and souls into their work (Palmer, 1998).

A Professional Development Course for Educators

The principle of congruence (Korthagen et al., 2001, p. 48) implies that
educators wanting to promote core reflection in student teachers will
themselves have to be actively involved in such reflection. Moreover, it is of
crucial importance that they acquire the specific competencies necessary to
stimulate core reflection. As McLean (1999, p. 74) observes, teacher
educators often find it difficult to support reflection processes focusing on
the person of the (student) teacher. It is for these reasons that we have

turned our attention to the teacher educators themselves. We have now organized a number of courses in which educators learn how to include the levels of professional identity and mission in their work with student teachers. In these courses, teacher educators are helped to focus more on the ideals of the people they work with, on their calling to the profession, and on their core qualities, but also on the limitations teachers themselves create, for example, by negative thinking. The courses also aim at promoting the translation of people's core qualities into competencies and actual behavior, and on overcoming their self-created inhibitions.

In these courses, "homework assignments" focus on the actual implementation of core reflection in everyday practices in teacher education. In most cases, the participants discover that a mere awareness of the tension between an ideal and inhibiting beliefs, feelings, and images serves to clarify the problem that lies at the root of many other problems the teacher is facing. To take an example: during the teacher education program, a student teacher becomes aware of an area of tension between his ideal "to be myself in my work" and his inhibiting belief that this is something that only experienced teachers can achieve. By means of this process of awareness-raising, he gradually realizes that his nervousness in the classroom, the minor conflict that he had the other day, as well as the uninspiring assignments he devises for his students, all have to do with that underlying area of tension. On the one hand, he wants to feel confident and relaxed, while in fact he is restrained by the belief that this is something reserved for "later." In this way, his stronger side (his core qualities) cannot be fully realized. By means of such core reflection, that is, reflection that takes the levels of identity and mission into account, a solution becomes possible more fundamental than would have been possible if his reflection had been restricted to the level of behavior, skills, or beliefs.

According to the evaluations of the participants, our professional development courses for educators appear to fill a gap in their professional development. For one thing, the participants appreciate the fact that core reflection – unlike other, more therapeutic, approaches – does not require them to delve into the past and the accompanying, often painful, memories, even though it is in itself a very deep and probing process. In core reflection, the depth is reflected above all in the process of tapping into one's inner potential for the benefit of professional development, which concurs with the perspective of positive psychology on personal growth. This is a considerable advantage for supervisors, who – quite rightly – take pains to respect the private lives of their students and to avoid a therapeutic role.[7]

CONCLUSIONS AND IMPLICATIONS

In this chapter, two questions were raised that are of importance in any form of teaching: (a) What are the essential qualities of a good teacher; and (b) How can we help people to become good teachers? Various possible answers were summarized in the model of levels of change. In answering the second question, the different levels were linked to possible interventions.

Special attention was focused on professional identity and mission, because until now not much theoretical research has been devoted to these levels.

Our discussion of core qualities has brought us to an area that, until now, has received surprisingly little attention from educators and researchers. In the view of Tickle (1999, p. 123): "In policy and practice the identification and development of personal qualities, at the interface between aspects of one's personal virtues and one's professional life, between personhood and teacherhood, if you will, has had scant attention." Tickle mentions such qualities as empathy, compassion, understanding, and tolerance, love, and flexibility. However, as noted previously, they are rarely included in official lists of teacher competencies and assessment procedures. Tickle is possibly correct when he emphasizes that these are essential qualities for teachers. He even maintains, "the teacher as a person is the core by which education itself takes place" (p. 136). This opinion is concurrent with our thinking in terms of core reflection.

In order to explore interventions on the levels of identity and mission, we briefly described three projects, which are largely terra incognita in the field of teacher education. This is remarkable in the light of Nias's (1989) conclusion that self-concepts and core values are sources of stability for teachers, through which they maintain a sense of purpose in their work (see also Tickle, 2000, p. 91).

Focusing on core reflection during initial and in-service teacher education can also make teachers more aware of the core qualities of students at school, so that they are better able to direct them in making use of their own core qualities, at school and throughout the rest of their lives. This is what Stoddard (1991, p. 221) calls "education for greatness," that is; education aiming at the development of great human beings, who are valuable contributors to society. On the basis of research into the lives of outstanding people, Stoddard and her colleagues found three "qualities that stand out in those who made significant contributions: a strong sense of self-worth, deep feelings of love and respect for all people, and an insatiable hunger for truth and knowledge."

She states that being aware of the importance of developing such qualities in people helps us "to concentrate on human development – maximum individual achievement – instead of curriculum development with its twin brothers: minimum competence and standardized achievement" (p. 222). In short, the topic that we touch on here is one of the pedagogical goals of identity development in children (Korthagen et al., 2001, pp. 263–267). It will be evident that this makes it even more important that teachers examine the "core levels" – in themselves and in children – and the ways these affect the other levels. In our view, it may ultimately be a question of raising awareness, among both teachers and teacher educators, of the interaction between all levels of change – whether in the student, the teacher, or the educator.

In particular, we feel it is important for teachers to learn how they can get (back) in touch with their core qualities, and how they can stimulate these qualities in their students. This will lead to a deeper involvement in the learning process among teachers as well as students. It is precisely this involvement that is in danger of being lost when a technical, instrumental approach to competence is employed.

This discussion may give the impression that we consider the inner levels more important than the outer. That is not so. In this chapter, we have focused more on the inner levels, because they have received far less attention in the literature on teaching and teacher education than the outer levels. However, all the levels are of fundamental importance to the professional development of teachers, and educators must be capable of intervening on all levels. It should be noted that in many cases it is sufficient to confine interventions to the outer levels. In fact, in a case where a student teacher is having serious discipline problems with a certain class, and will have to teach that same class tomorrow, it would probably be most effective to focus exclusively on the outer levels, namely on those of the environment (the class) and his own interpersonal behavior. However, if after the teaching practice period this student teacher has doubts about his or her own reasons for becoming a teacher, the inner levels come into play. The issues of mission and core qualities may then become relevant.

Looking at teachers from the perspective of the different levels may add validity to scientific analyses of how teachers function, and may broaden our view of what makes a good teacher. It counterbalances the somewhat frightening emphasis on specific aspects, such as competencies. From a more integrative perspective, a good teacher may be characterized by a state of harmony between the various levels. This means that a teacher educator will ideally devote attention to all the levels – preferably in relation to one another – depending on the phase in the teacher education program, the developmental process of the individual student teacher, and the specific problem at hand. In other words, in line with Harris, Guthrie, Hobart, and Lundberg (1995), we propose a more holistic approach toward teacher development in which competence is not equated with competencies, and which tries to find a realistic middle ground between views based on different paradigms, for example, between humanistic and behaviorist perspectives. Moreover, we believe it may be important that teacher education incorporates insights from transpersonal and positive psychology, as explained above. This implies demands on the professionalism of the educator, demands not limited to the level of competencies. For example, taking the model of levels of change seriously requires that teacher educators stay in touch with their own core qualities as a prerequisite for promoting the development of core qualities in prospective teachers. For, as Marianne Williamson (1992) reminded us in her book *Return to love*, "If we let our own light shine, we unconsciously give other people permission to do the same" (pp. 190–191).

NOTES

1. In the literature, one often finds references to "the Bateson model" in which the levels are visualized as stacked (i.e., Dilts, 1990). However, Gregory Bateson (1904–1980) never described such a model, not even in the publications to which many authors refer. Thus, the form of the model that appears in Fig. 1 cannot in fact be described as "the Bateson model" either. In the present chapter, we refer to "a model of levels of change," or briefly "the onion."

2. This modern formulation is remarkably similar to the description that James put forward over a hundred years ago, when he defined the self of a person as "the sum total of all that he can call his" (James, 1890).

3. This is even more striking in view of the fact that the original meaning of the word "psyche" is spirit or soul. Various authors point out that in this sense psychology appears to have distanced itself from its roots. For example, Graham (1986, p. 21) is critical of this development: "Bereft of its soul or psyche, psychology became an empty or hollow discipline; study for its own sake." Graham points to transpersonal psychology as a branch of psychology striving to re-establish the link with the concept of "soul."

4. However, this does not necessarily mean that the student will then actually act differently (Korthagen & Lagerwerf, 1996).

5. This workshop was devised and carried out by Hildelien Verkuyl and the author of this chapter.

6. Thanks go to Kristel Peters for this quote.

7. After the original publication of this chapter in 2004, the theory and practice of core reflection have been further elaborated. See for an overview: Korthagen et al. (2013) and www.korthagen.nl.

ACKNOWLEDGMENTS

The ideas developed in my work on core reflection build on my cooperation with Angelo Vasalos. I would also like to thank three anonymous reviewers for their stimulating comments.

REFERENCES

Allender, J. S. (2001). *Teacher self: The practice of humanistic education.* Lanham: Rowman & Littlefield.

Almaas, A. H. (1987). *Diamond heart, book 1.* Berkeley, CA: Diamond Books.

Aspinwall, L. G., & Staudinger, U. M. (Eds.). (2003). *A psychology of human strengths: Fundamental questions and future directions for a positive psychology.* Washington, DC: American Psychological Association.

Assagioli, R. (1965). *Psychosynthesis: A manual of principles and techniques.* New York, NY: Penguin.

Ayers, W. (2001). *To teach: The journey of a teacher* (2nd ed.). New York, NY: Teachers College Press.

Barnett, R. (1994). *The limits of competence: Knowledge, higher education and society.* Buckingham: Open University Press.

Becker, B. J., Kennedy, M. M., & Hundersmarck, S. (2003). *Hypothesis about "quality:" A decade of debates.* Paper presented at the Annual Meeting of the American Educational Research Association.

Beijaard, D. (1995). Teachers' prior experiences and actual perceptions of professional identity. *Teachers and Teaching: Theory and Practice, 1*(2), 281–294.

Beijaard, D., Verloop, N., & Vermunt, J. D. (2000). Teachers' perceptions of professional identity: An exploratory study from a personal knowledge perspective. *Teaching and Teacher Education, 16,* 749–764.

Bergner, R. M., & Holmes, J. R. (2000). Self-concepts and self-concept change: A status dynamic approach. *Psychotherapy, 37*(1), 36–44.

Borich, G. D. (1999). Dimensions of self that influence effective teaching. In R. P. Lipka & T. M. Brinthaupt (Eds.), *The role of self in teacher development* (pp. 92–117). Albany, NY: State University of New York Press.

Boucouvalas, M. (1980). Transpersonal psychology: A working outline of the field. *Journal of Transpersonal Psychology, 12*(1), 37–46.

Boucouvalas, M. (1988). An analysis and critique of the concept "self" in self-directed learning: Toward a more robust construct for research and practice. In M. Zukas (Ed.), *Proceedings of the Trans-Atlantic dialogue conference* (pp. 56–61). Leeds, England: University of Leeds.

Bullough, R. V. (1997). Practicing theory and theorizing practice in teacher education. In J. Loughran & T. Russell (Eds.), *Purpose, passion and pedagogy in teacher education* (pp. 13–31). London: The Falmer Press.

Bullough, R. V. (1993). Case records as personal teaching texts for study in preservice teacher education. *Teaching and Teacher Education, 9*(4), 385–396.

Bullough, R. V., & Baughman, K. (1997). *First year teacher eight years later: An inquiry into teacher development.* New York, NY: Teachers College Press.

Caprara, G. V., & Cervone, D. (2003). A conception of personality for a psychology of human strengths: Personality as an agentic, self-regulating system. In L. G. Aspinwall & U. M. Staudinger (Eds.), *A psychology of human strengths* (pp. 61–74). Washington, DC: American Psychological Association.

Carter, K. (1993). The place of story in the study of teaching and teacher education. *Educational Researcher, 22*(1), 5–12.

Clandinin, D. J. (1986). *Classroom practice: Teacher images in action.* London: The Falmer Press.

Clandinin, D. J. (1992). Narrative and story in teacher education. In T. Russell & H. Munby (Eds.), *Teachers and teaching: From classroom to reflection* (pp. 124–137). London: The Falmer Press.

Clark, C. M. (1986). Ten years of conceptual development in research on teacher thinking. In M. Ben-Peretz, R. Bromme & R. Halkes (Eds.), *Advances of research on teacher thinking* (pp. 7–20). Lisse: Swets & Zeitlinger.

Combs, A. W., Blume, R. A., Newman, A. J., & Wass, H. L. (1974). *The professional education of teachers: A humanistic approach to teacher preparation.* Boston, MA: Allyn & Bacon.

Crow, N. A. (1987). *Socialization within a teacher education program.* Unpublished doctoral dissertation. University of Utah.

Darling-Hammond, L. (1994). *Professional development schools: Schools for developing a profession.* New York, NY: Teachers College Press.

Diener, E. (2000). Subjective well-being: The science of happiness and a proposal for a national index. *American Psychologist, 55*(1), 15–23.

Dilts, R. (1990). *Changing belief systems with NLP.* Cupertino: Meta Publications.

Edelwich, J., & Brodsky, A. (1980). *Burn-out.* New York, NY: Human Sciences Press.

Eraut, M. (1994). *Developing professional knowledge and competence.* Londen: The Falmer Press.

Feiman-Nemser, S. (1983). Learning to teach. In L. Shulman & G. Sykes (Eds.), *Handbook of teaching and policy* (pp. 150–170). New York, NY: Longman.

Fenstermacher, G. D. (1994). The knower and the known: The nature of knowledge in research on teaching. *Review of Research in Education, 20,* 3–56.

Freud, A. (1986[1936]). *The ego and the mechanisms of defence* (rev. ed.). London: The Hogarth Press.

Freudenberger, H. J., & Richelson, G. (1980). *Burn-out.* Garden City: Archor Press.

Gallimore, R., & Tharp, R. (1992). Teaching mind in society: Teaching, schooling, and literate discourse. In L. C. Mol (Ed.), *Vygotsky and education: Instructional implications and applications of sociohistorical psychology* (pp. 175–205). Cambridge: Cambridge University Press.

Gecas, V. (1985). Self-concept. In A. Kuper & J. Kuper (Eds.), *The social science encyclopedia* (pp. 739–741). London: Routledge.

Graham, H. (1986). *The human face of psychology.* Philadelphia, PA: Open University Press.

Hamachek, D. (1999). Effective teachers: What they do, how they do it, and the importance of self-knowledge. In R. P. Lipka & T. M. Brinthaupt (Eds.), *The role of self in teacher development* (pp. 189–224). Albany, NY: State University of New York Press.

Hansen, D. T. (1995). *The call to teach.* New York, NY: Teachers College Press.

Hargreaves, A. (1998). The emotional practice of teaching. *Teaching and Teacher Education, 14*(8), 835–854.

Harris, R., Guthrie, H., Hobart, B., & Lundberg, D. (1995). *Competency-based education and training: Between a rock and a whirlpool.* South Melbourne: Macmillan Education Australia.

Hyland, T. (1994). *Competence, education and NVQs: Dissenting perspectives.* London: Cassell.

James, W. (1890). *The principles of psychology.* New York, NY: Holt.

Joyce, B. R. (1975). Conceptions of man and their implications for teacher education. In K. Ryan (Ed.), *Teacher Education, 74th yearbook of the National Society for the Study of Education* (pp. 111–145). Chicago, IL: University of Chicago Press.

Kelchtermans, G., & Vandenberghe, R. (1994). Teachers' professional development: A biographical perspective. *Journal of Curriculum Studies, 26,* 45–62.

Kihlstrom, J., & Klein, S. (1994). The self as a knowledge structure. In R. Wyer & T. Srull (Eds.), *Handbook of social cognition* (2nd ed., pp. 152–208). Hillsdale, NJ: Erlbaum.

Klaassen, C. A. (2002). Teacher pedagogical competence and sensibility. *Teaching and Teacher Education, 18*(2), 151–158.

Knowles, J. G. (1988). *Models for understanding preservice and beginning teachers' biographies:* Illustrations from case studies. Paper presented at the annual meeting of the American Educational Research Association, New Orleans.

Korthagen, F. A. J. (1992). Techniques for stimulating reflection in teacher education seminars. *Teaching and Teacher Education, 8*(3), 265–274.

Korthagen, F. A. J., Kessels, J., Koster, B., Lagerwerf, B., & Wubbels, T. (2001). *Linking practice and theory: The pedagogy of realistic teacher education.* Mahwah, NJ: Lawrence Erlbaum.

Korthagen, F. A. J., Kim, Y. M., & Greene, W. L. (Eds.). (2013). *Teaching and learning from within: A core reflection approach to quality and inspiration in education.* New York, NY: Routledge.

Korthagen, F. A. J., & Lagerwerf, A. (1996). Reframing the relationship between teacher thinking and teacher behaviour: Levels in learning about teaching. *Teachers & Teaching: Theory and Practice, 2*(2), 161–190.

Korthagen, F. A. J., & Verkuyl, H. (2007). Do you encounter your students or yourself? The search for inspiration as an essential component of teacher education. In T. Russell & J. Loughran (Eds.), *Enacting a pedagogy of teacher education: Values, relationships and practices* (pp. 106–123). London: Routledge.

Koster, B., Korthagen, F. A. J., & Schrijnemakers, H. G. M. (1995). Between entry and exit: How student teachers change their educational values under the influence of teacher education. In F. Buffet & J. A. Tschoumy (Eds.), *Choc démocratique et formation des enseignants en Europe* (pp. 156–168). Lyon: Presses Universitaires de Lyon.

Lipka, R. P., & Brinthaupt, T. M. (1999). How can the balance between the personal and the professional be achieved? In R. P. Lipka & T. M. Brinthaupt (Eds.), *The role of self in teacher development* (pp. 225–228). Albany, NY: State University of New York Press.

Lowyck, J. (1978). *Procesanalyse van het onderwijsgedrag [Process analysis of teaching behavior].* Leuven: Universiteit Leuven.

Lunenberg, M., & Korthagen, F. A. J. (2003). Teacher educators and student-directed learning. *Teaching and Teacher Education, 19*(1), 29–44.

Maslow, A. H. (1968). *Toward a psychology of being* (2nd ed.). Princeton, NJ: Van Nostrand.

Mayes, C. (2001). A transpersonal model for teacher reflectivity. *Journal of Curriculum Studies, 33*(4), 477–493.

McLean, S. V. (1999). Becoming a teacher: The person in the process. In R. P. Lipka & T. M. Brinthaupt (Eds.), *The role of self in teacher development* (pp. 55–91). Albany, NY: State University of New York Press.

Newman, C. S. (2000). Seeds of professional development in pre-service teachers: A study of their dreams and goals. *International Journal of Educational Research, 33*(2), 125–217.

Nias, J. (1989). *Primary teachers talking: A study of teaching as work.* London: Routledge.

Ofman, D. D. (1992). *Bezieling en kwaliteit in organisaties* [Soul and quality in organizations]. Cothen: Servire.

Pajares, M. F. (1992). Teachers' beliefs and educational research: Cleaning up a messy construct. *Review of Educational Research, 62*(3), 307–332.

Palmer, P. J. (1998). *The courage to teach.* San Francisco, CA: Jossey-Bass.

Parfitt, W. (1990). *The elements of psychosynthesis.* Dorset: Element Books.

Peterson, C., & Seligman M. E. P. (2000). *Values in action (VIA): Classification of strengths.* Philadelphia, PA: Values In Action Institute. http://www.positivepsychology.org/taxonomy.htm

Pinar, W. (1986). *Autobiography and the architecture of self.* Paper presented at the annual meeting of the American Educational Research Association, Washington, DC.

Pope, M., & Denicolo, P. (2001). *Transformative education.* London: Whurr.

Posner, G. J., Strike, K. A., Hewson, P. W., & Gertzog, W. A. (1982). Accommodation of a scientific conception: Towards a theory of conceptual change. *Science Education, 66,* 211–227.

Prahalad, C. K., & Hamel, G. (1990). The core competence of the corporation. *Harvard Business Review,* May–June, 79–91.

Richardson, V. (Ed.). (1997). *Constructivist teacher education.* London: The Falmer Press.

Rogers, C. R. (1969). *Freedom to learn.* Columbus, OH: Merrill.

Rosenshine, B., & Stevens, R. (1986). Teaching functions. In M. Wittrock (Ed.), *Handbook of research on teaching* (3rd ed., pp. 376–391). New York, NY: Macmillan.

Scotton, B. W., Chinen, A. B., & Battista, J. R. (1996). *Textbook of transpersonal psychiatry and psychology.* New York, NY: Basic Books.

Seligman, M. E. P., & Csikszentmihalyi, M. (2000). Positive psychology: An introduction. *American Psychologist, 55*(1), 5–14.

Shapiro, S. B. (1998). *The place of confluent education in the humanistic potential movement.* Lanham, MD: University Press of America.

Shaw, F. S. (1975). Congruence. In W. Pinar (Ed.), *Curriculum theorizing* (pp. 445–452). Berkeley, CA: McCutchan.

Sleegers, P., & Kelchtermans, G. (1999). Inleiding op het themanummer: Professionele identiteit van leraren [Introduction to the theme issue: Teachers' professional identity]. *Pedagogisch Tijdschrift, 24*(4), 369–373.

Stoddard, L. (1991). The three dimensions of human greatness: A framework for redesigning education. In R. Miller (Ed.), *New directions in education* (pp. 219–232). Brandon, VT: Holistic Education Press.

Stoof, A., Martens, R. L., & Van Merriënboer, J. J. G. (2000). *What is competence? A constructivist approach as a way out of confusion.* Paper presented at the Onder wijsresearchdagen [The conference of the Dutch Educational Research Association], Leiden.

Swann, W. (1992). Seeking "truth," finding despair: Some unhappy consequences of a negative self-concept. *Current Directions in Psychological Science, 1,* 15–18.

Tickle, L. (1999). Teacher self-appraisal and appraisal of self. In R. P. Lipka & T. M. Brinthaupt (Eds.), *The role of self in teacher development* (pp. 121–141). Albany, NY: State University of New York Press.

Tickle, L. (2000). *Teacher induction: The way ahead.* Buckingham: Open University Press.

Tripp, D. (1994). Teachers' lives, critical incidents, and professional practice. *Qualitative Studies in Education, 7,* 65–76.

Tusin, L. F. (1999). Deciding to teach. In R. P. Lipka & T. M. Brinthaupt (Eds.), *The role of self in teacher development* (pp. 11–35). Albany, NY: State University of New York Press.

Van Huizen (2000). *Becoming a teacher: Development of a professional identity by prospective teachers in the context of university-based teacher education.* Doctoral dissertation. Utrecht University, Utrecht.

Watzlawick, P., Beavin, J. H., & Jackson, D. D. (1967). *Pragmatics of human communication.* New York, NY: W.W. Norton.

Williamson, M. (1992). *A return to love: Reflections on the principles of a course in miracles.* New York, NY: Harper Collins.

Whitmore, D. (1986). *Psychosynthesis in education: A guide to the joy of learning.* Rochester, VT: Destiny Books.

Wubbels, T. (1992). Taking account of student teachers' preconceptions. *Teaching and Teacher Education, 8*(2), 137–149.

Wubbels, T., Korthagen, F., & Dolk, M. (1992). *Conceptual change approaches in teacher education: Cognition and action.* Paper presented at the annual meeting of the American Educational Research Association, San Francisco, CA.

Wubbels, T., & Levy, J. (1993). *Do you know what you look like?* London: The Falmer Press.

Zeichner, K. M., & Gore, J. M. (1990). Teacher socialization. In W. R. Houston (Ed.), *Handbook of research on teacher education* (pp. 329–348). New York, NY: Macmillan.

CHAPTER 13

REFLECTIVE CLASSROOM PRACTICE: CASE STUDIES OF HONG KONG STUDENT TEACHERS AT WORK ☆

Ora W. Y. Kwo

ABSTRACT

This chapter addresses the nature of reflective classroom practice in a Hong Kong setting where action research has been undertaken by both the student teachers and the teaching practice supervisor. It is based on a cross-case study of the processes through which student teachers learn to teach. Specifically, the analysis focuses on how student teachers reflect on their experiences in learning to teach. The data are based on student teachers' reported thoughts about their learning over a period of 1 year. The results contribute to the understanding of reflective classroom practice by highlighting first, student teachers' perceptions about learning to teach and second, their reviews on classroom practice. The discussion also adds to the literature on teacher development taken from

☆This chapter was first published in 1996, in the journal *Teachers and Teaching: Theory and Practice, 2*(2), 273–298. Reprinted with permission from the publisher, Taylor & Francis Ltd, www.tandfonline.com.

From Teacher Thinking to Teachers and Teaching: The Evolution of a Research Community
Advances in Research on Teaching, Volume 19, 275–303
ISSN: 1479-3687/doi:10.1108/S1479-3687(2013)0000019016

the novice-expert research tradition. Accordingly, implications for
curriculum development in teacher education are drawn.

Keywords: Reflective practices; teacher induction programs; student teachers

CRITICAL ISSUES IN LEARNING TO TEACH

Meaning of Teaching Experience

A prominent theme in research on teacher development concerns expert and novice teaching. The terms 'experienced', 'effective' and 'expert' have been used widely, in parallel to 'probationer', 'beginner' and 'novice' in many studies. Emerging from the findings are the schema differences between expert and novice teachers: their prior knowledge (Calderhead, 1983; Housner & Griffey, 1985), their awareness of classroom events (Carter, Sabers, Cushing, Pinnegar, & Berliner 1987; Housner & Griffey, 1985; Peterson & Comeaux, 1987), their prediction of learning misconceptions (Borko & Livingston, 1989) and their concepts of routines (Berliner, 1993; Doyle, 1979; Parker & Gehrke, 1986). While it is reasonable to see teachers' schemata as developing with experience, experience should not be equated with expertise. Amongst the important questions is how novices develop their schemata during initial teacher education.

Within most teacher education programmes, teaching practice is an important component (Stones, 1987). In the teaching practice component of most courses, student teachers spend several weeks in schools where they are guided by tutors from the training institutions and commonly by on-site co-operating teachers. The guidance mostly consists of occasional observations by tutors or co-operating teachers, and their post-lesson comments. Much of the student teachers' time on extended practice is spent without guidance. Calderhead (1987) found that as most students were driven by concerns with assessment, they rarely experimented for effective instruction. They were also resistant to much of the specific feedback from college tutors. Calderhead showed that only towards the end of the field experience, when most student teachers knew that they could maintain control, did they become more willing to experiment. However, experimental lessons were rarely supervised.

The limited effects of the conventional practicum call for reconceptualization and reforms. Schön's (1983, 1987, 1991) perspectives on the nature of professional knowledge raises many questions about the meaning of classroom practice in teacher education. As emphasised by Calderhead (1991), learning to teach is different from other forms of learning in academic life: changing teachers' knowledge does not necessarily result in changes in their practice. Student teachers need to be assisted to reflect on their new roles as teachers. Research on reflective teaching should explore how student teachers develop new frames on which new understandings can be built. Furthermore, recent reform efforts are highlighted by partnership and school-based models (i.e., Booth, Furlong, & Wilkin, 1990; McIntyre, Hagger, & Wilkin, 1993). To enhance the knowledge base for supervision, the meaning of practicum should be investigated from student teachers' perspectives.

Parallel to this concern, it is important to consider the mixed backgrounds of student teachers on entry to teacher education programmes. Research can generate new insights by exploring whether and to what extent former teaching experiences facilitate their acquisition of the meaning of practice.

The Nature of Reflections in the Practicum

Extended from Stones' (1987) concern for the lack of guidance in the conventional practicum are criticisms on the quality of guidance during the practicum. Alongside the recent trend in practicum which emphasises theory–practice integration through reflection, many studies document the restricting impact of supervisory guidance on learning to teach (i.e., Ben-Peretz & Rumney, 1991; Korthagen, 1988; Livingston, 1990). Despite the important arguments for reflections in learning to teach, student teachers do not appear to be readily engaged in significant reflections. Emphasis on reflective teaching by itself is no simple solution to problems in learning to teach. Innovations from an established institutionalised structure naturally create tensions which render the goals difficult to attain. For instance, as pointed out by Livingston (1990), student teachers need integrated support from co-operating teachers and supervisors to engage in reflective practice. Student teaching as currently structured provides little time or encouragement for reflection. Alternatively, student teachers' stage of development should be considered. Berliner (1988) argued that novice teachers may have too little experience to reflect on until extensive classroom experience has been acquired. Mcnally, Cope, Ingus, and Stronach (1994, p. 229) further queried whether it is actually *in service* that teachers may have a greater need for the input from higher education in promoting reflection, and in revisiting early experiential learning. In a recent study the author has noted that, at least in her sample, student teachers develop over time by engaging in more active reasoning and evaluation (Kwo, 1994a). However, despite the increased awareness of problems, generally no major decisions were reached to tackle the problems and alter directions of the lessons. Without suggesting that self-reflection is inappropriate for novice teachers, it is important to be cautious about the ambitious expectations of initial teacher education. There is a need to reach realistic expectations of student teachers from an understanding of the complicated demands on them.

Learning to teach requires the ability to face multi-faceted demands other than those in the cognitive domain. For readiness in learning to teach, student teachers have to move beyond initial concerns, such as socialisation into traditional roles (Calderhead & Robson, 1991; McCullough & Mintz, 1992). Teachers should be helped to formulate their individual selves and personal agendas. There are affective issues concerning their coping with their own emotions, such as described in the studies of Szpiczka (1990), Woods (1991) and Cole and Knowles (1993).

There are also social dimensions concerning their communication with co-operating teachers (i.e., Clift, Meng, & Eggerding, 1994) and inter-personal relationships with their pupils (i.e., Kagan & Tippins, 1991). Regarding these competing demands on the student teachers, teacher educators should be sensitive to the developmental stage of student teachers. Critically reporting the alarming effects of an innovative programme which incorporate the latest ideas about reflective pedagogy, Eisenhart, Behm, and Romagnano (1991) concluded that students might have been forced to need certain strategies the relevance of which they could not see, and therefore, teacher education should be more sensitive to the needs of novices in order to help them leave the programme with more confidence in the skills they have acquired and a clearer view of the identities they are striving for. The research literature has converged in a general concern to pursue under-standing of how student teachers learn to teach.

THE FRAME OF THE STUDY

The study reported here arises from a concern to narrow the gap between those who primarily do research and those who primarily deliver teacher education. Teacher education is viewed by the author as both a situation for studying learning patterns of student teachers and a factor influencing those learning patterns. It is important to acknowledge the potential for constructive innovations through teacher educators' own integration of research and practice. The context of this study is a teacher education programme which basically follows the academic tradition, with theoretical foundations of professional education, some academic preparation in the subjects that the students are to teach, and the student practicum. The researcher was the supervisor of the student teachers under investigation. Acquiring the spirit of the reflective practitioner in pursuing personal knowledge for her professional role, she attempted to integrate her action research with reforms in curriculum design (Kwo, 1994b).

By considering the critical issues in learning to teach, this study focuses on the understanding of student teachers' reflective classroom practices. It aimed to investigate the patterns of learning to teach by adopting a 'second-order' research perspective (Marton, 1981). Specifically, it addresses the question of how student teachers reflect on their experiences in learning to teach. By comparing the reviews of three student teachers with former teaching experience and three student teachers with absolutely no teaching experience at all, the study is able to explore the significance of former teaching experience on readiness for reflection. The analysis focuses on the student teachers' perceptions about learning to teach and their reviews on classroom practice.

Design and Methodology

Setting and Sample

It is often assumed that student teachers in pre-service teacher education programmes have little or no teaching experience. However, this assumption is not always valid. In Hong Kong, graduates are permitted to teach without professional qualifications in teaching. The initial start and ceiling points of their salary are lower than those of professionally qualified teachers, and many such graduates choose to gain training after entering the profession. This can be done either part-time or full-time. The dichotomy between in-service and pre-service training is therefore blurred; while many participants in the full-time programmes have no teaching experience, others have substantial experience.

The researcher collected a full set of data from 15 student teachers on the 1-year full-time Postgraduate Certificate of Education Programme at the University of Hong Kong, who are majoring in English language teaching.

Table 1. Personal Data of Student Teachers.

Student Teacher	Gender	Native Language	Origin	Age	Years of Teaching Experience
1	F	English	England	28	3 + PT
2 Sophie	F	Chinese	Hong Kong	22	0
3	F	Chinese	Hong Kong	34	1
4	F	English	Pakistan	42	2 + PT
5 Susan	F	Tagalog	Philippines	26	4
6	M	English	Scotland	24	2 + PT
7	F	Japanese	Japan	37	PT
8	M	Chinese	Hong Kong	22	PT
9	F	Chinese	Hong Kong	40	PT
10	M	Chinese	Hong Kong	27	2
11 Juliet	F	Chinese	Hong Kong	42	5
12 Joy	F	Chinese	Taiwan	25	0
13	F	Chinese	Hong Kong	41	2
14 Heidi	F	Chinese	Vietnam	30	5
15 Rita	F	Chinese	Hong Kong	22	PT

Note: PT, part-time.

As shown in Table 1, the majority of students were female, and two-thirds of them were native speakers of Chinese. Despite these dominant features, however, the group was heterogeneous in terms of geographic origin, age and teaching experience.

In order to explore the significance of former teaching experience on their reflections, six students were selected for data analysis. These were the three with most and the three with least teaching experience. For reporting here, the students in the first group are called Susan, Juliet and Heidi, while those in the second group are called Sophie, Joy and Rita. It just happened that all the selected subjects were female.

Structure of the Curriculum

The year's course was divided into three terms. The pattern in each term was as follows.

Term 1. In Term 1 three weeks of School Experience were scheduled between two periods of course work on campus. The topics presented before the School Experience gave student teachers some basic background for practical teaching.

Pedagogical knowledge in the teaching of language skills was introduced with attention to planning, teaching and evaluation.

Through the School Experience, the student teachers gained acquaintance with a classroom reality in which they could expand learner knowledge and apply the pedagogical knowledge and skills to which they had been initially exposed in the course. In this way, they were prepared to pursue knowledge about teaching from practical experience.

After the School Experience, the pedagogical knowledge in the teaching of language skills was reviewed in relation to content knowledge in various aspects of applied linguistics. Building on the skills in planning, teaching and evaluation was a perspective beyond lessons: curriculum design was considered with emphasis on critical use of textbooks and material development.

Term 2. Course work in Term 2 mainly focused on preparation for a 7-week period of main teaching practice. The student teachers were prepared with skills in observation, analysis and evaluation of video-recorded lessons. These skills were essential prerequisites for peer coaching during the main teaching practice, which demanded capability in problem-solving and communication. The course work before the Main Teaching Practice concluded with an examination in which individuals had to analyse independently a video-recorded lesson after viewing it together in class.

During the main teaching practice, alongside the further acquisition of learner knowledge and application of pedagogical knowledge and skills, each student teacher was engaged in the expansion of teaching repertoires and meta-cognition through conducting a classroom action-research project as the final assignment. The supervisory school visits provided support on both action research and classroom teaching.

Term 3. Term 3 covered areas in relation to the general progress of student teachers. Forums encouraged reflection on the main teaching practice. The schedule also included student teachers' presentations of classroom action research and teachers' global responsibilities and professional development.

Datasets

Data were collected throughout the year, both during course work on university campus and when the student teachers were working in schools for teaching practice. Three major sets of data were generated from the student teachers: their written reviews of their learning experiences during the course; their action research assignments; and videotapes of lessons recorded at the beginning and the end of teaching practice. From the three sets of data, patterns in learning to teach could be studied to illustrate three dimensions: student teachers' reflections on learning experiences, their development of personal knowledge about teaching and their actual development in classroom practice.

The study will eventually aim to reach a triangulation of three sources of data. However, this chapter focuses on student teachers' reflections on learning experiences by analysing the first dataset. In particular, the analyses focus on their perceptions about learning to teach and their reviews on classroom practice.

Student teachers' written reviews of their learning experiences were collected over six points of the course: on entry, before and after two blocks of teaching practice, and at the end of the course. The specific questions to which they responded are as follows:

1. On entry to the course:
    What do you see as essential qualities of a teacher which you are striving to develop?
2. Before the School Experience:
    From the course, what do you see as new learning experience to you? What are your major concerns/worries about the forthcoming teaching practice?
3. After the School Experience:
    What insights about teaching have you gained from the teaching practice, and in what ways have you developed as a teacher?
    What are the major problems you have encountered, and what are the strategies you have adopted to cope with these problems?
4. Before the Main Teaching Practice (same questions as 'before the School Experience')
5. After the Main Teaching Practice (same question as 'after the School Experience')
6. At the end of the course:
    From your perspective, how far have you developed yourself over the course in the essential qualities of a teacher which you have been striving to develop? If necessary, elaborate or modify your views about the essential qualities of a teacher.

Data Analysis
The data were analysed in an interactive process of data reduction and verification (Miles & Huberman, 1984, pp. 21–23). Following that, the phenomenographic method (Marton & Saljö, 1984) was used. The analysis emphasised an objective review of the data without any imposition of

theories. The theoretical perspectives were considered only after an intrinsic understanding of the original data was established. Case descriptions were examined repeatedly until some apparent categories emerged from the data. These categories were set up tentatively as hypotheses to check all the scripts again and again. The categories were revised, when they were found to be unable to account for some data. The whole process of data analysis was iterative and interpretative. Finally, general patterns were drawn about over-time changes and variations between the experienced and the inexperienced student teachers. Although there was some overlapping of common categories shared by the two groups of student teachers, collectively the data displayed some specific trends of the changes that took place in learning to teach. The report of findings which follows begins with a summary of the data, and then turns to discussion, which is illustrated with quotations from student teachers' reported thoughts.

FINDINGS

Perceptions about Learning to Teach

Student teachers' perceptions about learning to teach are summarised in Tables 2 and 3, respectively.

Changing Conceptions of Teaching

With some overlap between experienced and inexperienced student teachers, it is possible to trace similarities and differences in their conceptions of the essential qualities of a teacher. There seems to be a continuum from what a student might look for to a broader awareness of a teacher's professional competence and commitments to a societal role. Initially, it is natural that student teachers with no teaching experience tend to view teacher qualities from the learners' angle, as they have come from many years of classroom experience as students. For instance, words like 'fair', 'friendly', 'care without prejudices' were used. In contrast, student teachers with teaching experience apparently began the course with a more sophisticated view about essential teacher qualities which were beyond abilities in classroom instruction, to the extent they were concerned with their personal qualities, and the facilitation of pupils' character development.

A major change over time concerned the meaning of teaching in relation to learning. Teaching has been traditionally taken as a transmission of

Table 2. Experienced student-teachers' perceptions about learning to teach.

Susan	Heidi	Juliet
On Entry: perception of essential teacher qualities		
• Able to develop student-centred teaching • Character moulder	• Help academic and spiritual development • Humble, honest, consistent dedicated	• Keep to learn • Positive towards students • Honest, enthusiastic
Before School Experience: perceived new learning		
• Keen to try out some strategies and check their effectiveness	• Realised my problem in the past: too much teacher talk • Fascinated by the student-centred method from pupils	• Aware of previous mistakes: too much teacher talk, spent too much time marking, demanded total silence
After School Experience: insights and development		
• Learned to manage mixed-ability students • Learned to motivate students by positive feedback • Saw the need to develop a flexible teacher personality	• Realised there is a long way to go to get rid of the old habit of talking too much • Tried out various strategies related to student-centred teaching	• Realised some principles of teaching generalisable for different student levels • Tried out various strategies related to students-centred teaching
Before Main Teaching Practice: perceived new learning		
• Realised the shortcomings in previous teaching and wanted to make up for them • Hoped to make a quality leap in teaching methods	• Concentrated on reducing teacher talk • Continued using various strategies related to student-centred teaching	• More confident • Keen to replace rooted thinking from the past with current thinking • Saw the connections between different courses • Improved learning ability

After Main Teaching Practice: insights and development

• Enjoyed developing strategies in teaching	• Able to plan for teaching	• Increased feelings of inadequacy
• Able to introduce preliminary activities to motivate students successfully	• Able to foster a secure climate for learning	• Able to apply into practice what has been learned from the course without disciplinary problems
• Used a lot of evaluation techniques to measure learning	• Realised that learners are what the teacher expects them to be	• Convinced of value of student-centred teaching

At the end: evaluation of self-development

• Confirmed the belief in student-centred teaching	• Learned to be a facilitator	• Painful process in getting rid of the old ideas and traditional style of teaching
• Prepared to be a student-centred teacher	• Confirmed the belief that students could learn even without non-stop teacher talk	• Expanded my teaching strategies and knowledge of subject matter
	• Confirmed the belief that students could learn in many ways and modes	• Grown into a better person

Table 3. Inexperienced student-teachers' perceptions about learning to teach.

Sophie	Joy	Rita
On Entry: perception of essential teacher qualities		
• Not a commander but friendly and helpful • Knowledgeable • Teach systematically and efficiently • Fair grading system	• Patient and loving to students • Fluent spoken English • Good communication skills • Good explanation ability	• Enthusiastic in teaching • Care for students without prejudice • Prepare before lessons • Able to learn continually
Before School Experience: perceived new learning		
• Realised that the four skills could be taught in terms of a series of stage • Realised that English can be taught in a lively way by using different teaching aids	• Realised teaching is a job of a lot of preparation and making assumptions about the learning process	• Changed my conceptions about teaching: not that easy • Realised the use of various techniques was essential for effective teaching • Teaching does not mean testing
After School Experience: insights and development		
• Treated students as friends, sisters; helped them but not punished them • Realised that students wanted more participation	• Important to be patient • Able to set up a reasonably good relationship with students	• Strengthened the belief that teachers played a vital role in students' growth • Realised that good relationship with students is important • Be flexible in teaching
Before Main Teaching Practice: perceived new learning		
• Learned to produce materials • Acquired techniques in observation • Learned to integrate the four language skills	• Teachers should help each other to improve teaching • More confident to give help to the partners • Not satisfied with the school reality: teachers unwilling to observe each other teaching	• Realised the importance of integrated learning • Teachers must work very hard to make a lesson interesting

After Main Teaching Practice: insights and development

- Important to be strict with students
- Important to be patient
- Should teach students how to behave

- Tried to make every lesson student-centred
- Had some good interaction with learners
- Observed and learned from peer teachers

- Had good rapport with students
- Tried many activities
- Got more organised
- Learned to adjust teacher talk to students' levels
- Learned from peers

At the end: evaluation of self-development

- Realised that diligence is an essential quality of a teacher
- Learned to be patient
- Avoid prejudice
- Friendly with students

- Critical of myself
- Uprooted my previous understanding about teaching
- Found many interesting methods to motivate students
- Learned to innovate ideas and modify them for teaching different groups of students

- Renew enthusiasm in teaching
- Able to set up a good rapport with students

knowledge, which may be what most student teachers experienced in their classrooms in the past as learners. According to this conception, fluent teacher talk and good communication skills were important qualities, and these were especially apparent in initial reports by inexperienced student teachers. The course highlighted an alternative conception of teaching which emphasised the facilitation of learning, and most participants were challenged to re-consider the former conception of teaching. Susan was an exceptional case because of her previous educational and teaching experience, as she had been exposed to ideas about student-centred teaching in a short course prior to the PCEd programme. She set off with a specific regard for student-centred teaching and concluded the course with confirmation of the value of this approach.

In cases of experienced student teachers like Heidi and Juliet, after only 4 weeks of course work, they reported having identified problems in their former teaching for being teacher-centred. Subsequently they repeated their concerns about having to get rid of the old thinking and habits to make way for teaching for facilitation of learning. Their established concept of teaching was dismantled, while they were open to re-construction of a new one. Along a similar move towards more student-centred teaching, the conception of teaching amongst inexperienced teachers like Sophie, Joy and Rita apparently became more complicated over time. They realised that teaching is demanding, if it is to facilitate learning rather than testing learners' abilities. They also reported an expansion of their teaching repertoire to consider a range of methods.

Some illustrations may help to show the change in conception of these teachers. Before the School Experience, Sophie remarked that she 'never thought that English composition can be taught in class'. While her previous English teachers might never have taught her explicitly how to approach composing English writing, it was possible that she was never aware of the procedures as a student. Either possibility could change her conception of teaching from a simple to a more complicated one. Similarly, Rita's previous image of an English teacher was simply one busy with marking, and her report was most illustrative: 'Drawing on my former experience as a student, I supposed teaching English not to be that difficult except the workload of marking. Teachers only need to go through the textbooks ... the course makes me realise that the job of teaching English is not that easy.'

Joy also reported seeing teaching as 'a job of a lot of preparation and making assumptions about learning'. Like experienced teachers, the inexperienced student teachers also displayed conceptual changes. Their original conception of teaching might have been associated with their observation of their former teachers. As critically reviewed by Joy,

> I have uprooted my understanding of teaching, which was planted in me a long time ago as I was a secondary school student ... many of the ways my teachers used to teach me were rubbish ... I am glad to have begun to find many interesting methods to motivate and help students to learn.

With a different focus, Rita also mentioned her schema change:

> My enthusiasm before joining the course was strong, but it has become more concrete now, as supported by a teaching schema in my mind.

On entry to the course, all the experienced student teachers except Susan saw teaching as transmitting knowledge, whereas the inexperienced student teachers held a rather simplistic view about teaching. At the end of the course, having gone through their personal processes of learning to teach, both groups seemed to have adopted a more student-centred conception of teaching. They also generally reported an awareness of using different methods to facilitate learning.

Learning Processes over the Course
There were apparent differences between the experienced and inexperienced student teachers in their reviews of learning over the year. The experienced student teachers were able to identify their problems, and hence the focus of learning more specifically. With some developed schemata about teaching, they selected what they needed, and in different ways reached a higher level of conceptualization and practice about how to facilitate learning. In pursuing student-centred teaching, Susan reported her new understanding:

> I realized the futility of preparing too many tasks if they do not help learners to understand what is supposed to be learned. Instead, I saw how important it is to be equipped with a direct but well-structured lesson plan designed to meet the cognitive styles and needs of the learners.

Heidi and Juliet were critical of their previous teaching styles, and hence, open to new alternatives. Having identified her problems in teacher talk, Heidi concluded that

> students can learn without my non-stop teacher talk – individually, in pairs as well as in groups. They need not be spoon-fed all the time ... An effective teacher need not be a walking encyclopedia, but should be one who can facilitate and motivate the learners to learn by themselves.

Along a similar vein in challenging the self to pursue changes, Juliet's reflections were most vivid:

> After 5 years of teaching, I have genuinely built myself up with a certain amount of confidence as well as a certain amount of prejudice. It took me almost a year to humble myself, to renew my mind and to refill my teaching life with some fresh ingredients.

Seeing alternatives through their reflective practice, both Heidi and Juliet made fundamental changes in their conception of teaching. While that might have been a slow and painful process, it was most encouraging to see the possibility that the established schemata of experienced teachers can be changed.

For the inexperienced student teachers, the initial teaching practice made them aware of the complicated demands in teaching, not something they could understand when they were students. In contrast to experienced teachers, Sophie, Joy and Rita shared a more prominent concern for survival in teaching practice. Rather than applying the ideas they came across in the course, they tended to focus more on relationships with students. Compared to experienced teachers, their practice of student-centred teaching was rather limited and *ad hoc*. Their shared concern for good rapport with their pupils was less specific on pedagogical considerations. For instance, after the School Experience, Sophie described her insights in seeing the importance of friendly relationships with students and student participation, and then concluded her learning before the Main Teaching Practice in an itemised list. However, there was no elaboration on the meaning of the items. It was likely that her attention was diverted to the mechanics of teaching procedures, as taken from the notes of the course. She was not yet ready to be engaged in extensive reflections for sorting learning priorities like her experienced counterparts. It seems that given the two blocks of teaching practice which had exposed the inexperienced student teachers to the complicated reality of the classroom, the contents to be learned were too plentiful for them to select their priorities consciously. With Sophie's emphasis on diligence, Joy's embrace of new methods and self-criticism and Rita's renewed enthusiasm about teaching, they all made some progress. Yet, they all seemed to realise that there was a long way for them to go in achieving their goals of learning.

Reviews of Classroom Practice

The student teachers' reviews of classroom practice are summarised in Tables 4 and 5. Given the shared direction in conceptual change towards

Table 4. Reviews of classroom practice by experienced teachers.

Susan	Heidi	Juliet
Concerns before School Experience	Concerns before School Experience	
• Afraid there is not a wide range of audio-visual resources	• Whether I meet students' expectations • Discipline problems • Establish 'good relation' with colleagues • Afraid to work with a difficult teacher-tutor	• No knowledge of students' background and school rules • Does the teacher-tutor have the same philosophy of teaching as mine? • How much can I apply what I have learned to real situations?
Problems and strategies in School Experience		
• Assessment of teaching practice	• Afraid to teach a large class • Afraid that students are not co-operative and therefore I can't apply theory to practice	• Do not have the same worries as those before School Experience • How to make the Main Teaching Practice meaningful to me and students • Wish MTP can reinforce my commitment to teaching career
Concerns before Main Teaching practice		
• Traffic noise outside classroom – Used a microphone – Repeated the important answers – Used more eye-contact – Used more individual, pair, group work to reduce teacher talk	• Teacher-tutor not friendly – Listened to her negative comments without defence • Class teacher: negative about the students – Ignored negative opinions – Took a positive attitude – Set to motivate students	• Took too much time to plan – Focused on 2-3 objectives • Not enough time to cover what was planned – Minimised teacher-talk – Avoided repeating students' answers – Lower achievers were passive • Not know how to assess their understanding of my teaching – Talked to them during the lunch time – Got feedback from their facial expressions – Male instructions clear and simple

Table 4. (*Continued*)

Susan	Heidi	Juliet
Problems and strategies in Main Teaching Practice		
• Coped with differences between Form Three and Form Six students	• The teacher-tutor was too busy	• Students good at mathematics not motivated to learn English
– Adjust teaching methods to students' differences in personality	• Benefited from the peer-coaching	• Students had their own culture: make jokes all the time
		• Some students never handed in their homework
		– Talked to them after class
		– Established good relationship with them

Table 5. Reviews of classroom practice by inexperienced teachers.

Sophie	Joy	Rita
Concerns before School Experience	• How to keep smiling even if students don't respond	• Nervous when facing unfamiliar faces
• How to break silence	• How to assess students' understanding	• My oral English may not be fluent
• How to deal with naughty students	• How to cope with students' different levels and students who might challenge me on purpose	
• How to build up friendly relations with students and teachers		
Problems and Strategies in School Experience	• Too much work	• Not enough time to prepare the lessons
• School was far away	• How to treat adolescents properly without hurting them	• Appreciate peer-coaching and how to get more help from the partner
• Students' English was poor	• How to learn more from peer partners without taking too much of their time	
• School environment was noisy		
• How to arouse students' interest in learning English		
• How to deal with students who finish work faster and keep on talking		
• How to apply good teaching ideas to the students with low standard		
Concerns before Main Teaching Practice	• Hard to meet the teacher-tutor's demand: teach in her ways	• Put too much into one lesson and the plan left unfinished
• One girl hurt herself and two girls felt sick but refused to go to the sick room	– Insisted on practising what I have learned from the course	• How to deal with passive and inattentive students
– Stayed calm and tried to behave like a sister	• Hard to finish a lesson as planned	• Students spoke too softly to be heard
• Students spoke too softly to be heard	• Hard to assess students' understanding	– Repeated or rephrased their answers
– Encouraged them to speak louder	• Hard to explain everything in perfect English	– More pair or group work
• Very upset about students' mistakes in their exercises: wondering if I am a good teacher	– More preparation	
	• Felt uncertain if I should show anger about students, lateness	

Table 5. (*Continued*)

Sophie	Joy	Rita
	• How to organise the blackboard • Hard to tackle with different levels	• Not experienced and inadequate knowledge – Anticipate to learn more from the course

Problems and strategies in Main Teaching Practice

Sophie	Joy	Rita

• Students' English was poor
  – Gave them simple questions to answer
• Traffic noise outside classroom
  – Used a microphone
  – Gave them written work
• Boys and girls unwilling to work together
  – Set games for them which required competition
• Two boys daydreaming
  – Got them to answer my questions
	• How to develop dynamic interaction with students
	  – Memorised their names
	  – Treated different classes differently
	  – Established direct and active communication
	• Hard to give precise instructions
	  – Used cue cards with questions
	  – Refrained from speaking too fast and thought before responding to questions raised on the spot
	• Not enough time for marking
	  – Used weekends
	  – Introduced peer-checking
		• Hard to recognise the students of three classes within seven weeks
		  – Got the seating plans of each class
		• Sometimes unable to spot the mistakes in students' oral English
		  – Improved my English: both listening and speaking
		• Time constraints: too much work pressure

student-centred teaching (as analysed previously), the study also traces how the student teachers viewed their own practice. The analysis turns to the changes in their focus of attention and identification of problems and strategies. Judging from individual cases, it was difficult to identify common patterns. However, patterns are shown over comprehensive and repeated reviews of the data.

Focus of Attention

Emerging from the data on concerns and worries about teaching practice is a developmental trend over the course of learning to teach. This trend can be used to map the possible stages of learning. The inexperienced students may cover the first part of the journey, whereas the experienced ones may cover the latter part.

Classroom Management.   Setting up the basic routines in teaching seemed to worry the new teachers most. The main concerns of Sophie, Joy and Rita before the School Experience were not pedagogically related so much as how to deal with naughty students, how to cope with students who might challenge the new teacher on purpose and even simply how to face unfamiliar faces. Interestingly, the experienced group did not focus so much on classroom management, though Heidi did express concerns for discipline problems.

Self-Image and Relationship with Colleagues.   Again, the concern for self-image and social relationship was not related so much to subject matter or pedagogy as to another aspect of basic survival. Worries about self-image were explicitly mentioned by Sophie:

> I may be too young to be a teacher. I laugh easily, and behave like a girl.

> I am nervous about speaking in front of a class.

Similarly, Joy was concerned about her image, and wondered how she could keep smiling even at a lack of student response. On the other hand, experienced student teachers did not mention their self-image. Instead, both Heidi and Rita expressed their concerns for relationships with their colleagues, especially their teacher-tutors. Susan showed no concern for this aspect.

Pedagogy.   The focus on pedagogy shows a concern for the applicability of teaching methods, use of materials and audio-visual resources. To experienced student teachers, this is a central concern. Even before the School Experience, Susan expressed her worry about the possible lack of audio-visual resources. By the time of the Main Teaching Practice, her concern had extended to assessment. The concern about 'applying theory to practice' was mentioned by both Heidi and Juliet. Juliet's concern was particularly ambitious: she wanted to make her Main Teaching Practice so meaningful that it would reinforce her commitment to the teaching career. By contrary, the inexperienced student teachers' expressions of this concern were more rather vague. As reviewed by Sophie after the School Experience,

> What we have learnt is useful, but it may not be applicable to students of lower ability – they hate speaking in English. If we don't correct them, they will never know that they are wrong.

While her view may be considered simplistic, her focus was by then apparently beyond basic survival and had moved to the complexities of applying teaching methods.

Learners and Learning. The concerns for learners and learning are also shared by both groups, though the responses to this concern were quite different. An instance can be drawn from their thoughts about learners' low standard. By the Main Teaching Practice, Sophie was concerned about learning, but felt rather helpless about the learners described by her teacher-tutor:

> She told me that I have to teach a remedial class, and the students are very passive and most of them fail in a test ... I fear that I would be disappointed. I recall how upset I was in the School Experience, when my students made lots of mistakes in their exercises.

It seemed that her limited practice did not lead her to a state of confidence in coping with this concern. In contrast, the response by an experienced student teacher, Heidi, to the similar encounter was very different. As reported by Heidi,

> Without defence, I listened to my teacher-tutor's negative comments about the class. But then I ignored these comments, and took a positive attitude to motivate the students.

In her latter experience, she concluded that 'learners are what the teacher expects them to be', and she was pleased that the class considered to be the second worst actually improved a lot in response to her effort.

The Self in Relation to Problems
Focusing on the data on student teachers' identification of problems and coping strategies, it is possible to trace a pattern in their learning process: from passively tolerating environmental constraints to actively initiating

changes. Again, with some overlap between the two groups, differences also arise out of this trend. The inexperienced student teachers tended to identify problems as arising from the environment rather than from their personal abilities. Furthermore, the inexperienced student teachers reacted rather passively to environmental constraints, with little mention of the power from within their selves. In contrast, the experienced ones were more ready to be critical of themselves with identification of personal weaknesses. They were also able to search within themselves for resources to initiate changes in the environment. The learning process seems to be characterised by the changing self in relationship to problems. Apparently, personal maturity has a part to play, as the process of learning to teach requires the student teacher to move from a learner role to a teacher role.

During the School Experience, Sophie seemed to be daunted by numerous environmental problems concerning which she made little mention of coping strategies. Her overall query as to whether she was a good teacher probably added to her sense of inadequacy. By the Main Teaching Practice, she was still bothered by non-pedagogical issues, such as the distance to the school and the low English standard of students. Nevertheless, she began to identify some pedagogical problems, and mentioned what she could do about them. This shift in the perception of the self in relation to problems showed her significant progress in learning to teach. Both Joy and Rita also shared this pattern in the move towards the search for strategies from within the self. In particular, Joy seemed to have made considerable progress. During the School Experience, she identified many problems, but had few strategies to cope. In contrast, her Main Teaching Practice was completed with a rich exploration of strategies which focused on improvement of her interaction with students. Amongst the experienced student teachers' more active response to problems, Susan came up with multiple alternatives to tackle the noise outside the classroom, and Juliet reached for some depth in her rapport with students by trying to understand and accept the students' culture. The data demonstrated that by the end of the two blocks of teaching practice, the student teachers made some clear changes in the ways they identified and responded to problems. While the progress was considerable for many, the teaching practice can only provide a start for them to see the growing strength in the self in dealing with problems. There is a longer way beyond the course for further maturation, both personally and as a teacher.

Flexibility and Adaptability
Emerging from the data on student teachers' identification of problems and coping strategies was another feature of their learning: progress towards

greater flexibility and adaptability. Flexibility refers to their responses to problems, whereas adaptability refers to their interaction with students. Some overall differences between the two groups can be identified: the experienced student teachers tended to be more flexible and more adaptable than the inexperienced student teachers. From different starting points, they showed a common direction in their progress.

In tackling the noise problem outside the classroom, Susan's considerations were multi-faceted, ranging from using more eye-contact to balancing teacher talk with other learning activities. While using the microphone, she was also trying to deal with its constraint to her mobility within the classroom by reducing the reliance on teacher talk and involving students in independent work in pairs or groups. Her flexibility was shown in the ways she searched for different strategies, while being aware of the conflicting nature of the chosen strategies. Although a microphone can be used to tackle the noise problem, it presents another problem in restricting interaction with students. Facing a similar problem, Sophie had a less elaborated response: apart from the use of the microphone, she resolved the noise problem only by giving students written work. Another example in comparing flexibility can be located in their relationships with teacher-tutors. During the School Experience, Joy handled her disagreement with her teacher-tutor with a direct confrontation, which led to an unhappy relationship between them. Compared to Heidi's quiet work on alternatives (as discussed previously), Joy was not tactful, and lacked flexibility in reaching a compromise. This incident illustrated a new teacher's dilemma in dealing with competing demands. Often a painful choice has to be made when there is a lack of flexibility to cope with both. On pedagogical strategies, however, Joy made considerable progress in becoming more flexible. In order to improve her teacher talk, she came up with different strategies, ranging from the use of cue cards to a conscious effort to refrain from speaking too fast, allowing herself time to organise her response to impromptu questions.

Adaptability was more apparent in experienced student teachers who were rather observant of the differences amongst students. Susan gave a detailed description of her students:

> I found Form Three students quite playful and talkative, while the Form Six students were very serious and quiet. They wanted to learn more about life. I included more games and discussions about teenagers in my Form Three class, but focused more on serious topics (e.g. friendship, communism, etc.) in my Form Six class. I also had to change my personality, when going into a different class. I was very serious to my Form Six class, but more ready to crack jokes with my Form Three class.

In her development of a warm rapport with students, Juliet faced an unexpected dilemma that the students were too casual with her and she felt threatened. However, she decided that she had to 'develop a stronger sense of humour and become more adaptable to their culture in order to minimise the generation gap'. That provided another illustration of the adaptability of an experienced student teacher. In less depth, inexperienced student teachers also considered students' characteristics in the Main Teaching Practice. Rita was conscious of the importance of recognizing students personally, even though she had to take up three classes with little contact time with each class. Joy mentioned 'designing tasks to channel the students' energy and modifying activities according to the levels of students'. At different points in their process of learning to teach, both groups of student teachers seemed to demonstrate more adaptability over-time.

FORMER TEACHING EXPERIENCE AND READINESS FOR REFLECTIONS

The findings of this study add to the literature on student teachers' professional learning. The meaning of learning from course work and practicum was drawn from student teachers' perspectives. In particular, by analysing the differences between experienced and inexperienced student teachers, the chapter highlights the significance of earlier teaching experience for various aspects of student teachers' reflective classroom practice. Although the student teachers with no previous teaching experience did not enter the learning process with such developed teaching schemata as their experienced counterparts, they did have some entry perspectives about teaching which were challenged during the course. Equally, rather than simply expanding the existing schemata, the experienced student teachers had to get rid of some old ideas in order to make space for changes. The course on which this study was based was designed to address the critical issues about training effects. Through engagement in various forms of reflection, such as classroom action research and regular reviews of their learning experiences, student teachers were required to play an active and constructive role in their own learning. Consequently they all underwent critical re-consideration of their former conceptions of teaching, as inherited unconsciously during years of socializing experiences in classrooms as learners. To a certain extent, in having re-lived the socialised experiences as teachers, those with teaching experience prior to initial training had to carry more weight when going through the critical reviews. On the other hand, once they realised their weaknesses, they tended to approach their learning processes with better focus, whereas the inexperienced student teachers faced initial difficulties in prioritizing their learning focus.

While previous teaching experiences certainly played a part in reflective classroom practice, the findings of this study do not agree with Berliner's (1988) assertion that novice teachers may have too little experience to reflect on until extensive classroom experience has been acquired. Despite the limitation of time, the inexperienced student teachers were able to get into elaborated reflections of their practice. They tended to come up with more problems than coping strategies. From a comparison of the detailed accounts of concerns, perceptions of problems and new insights of the two groups of student teachers, some essential features of various patterns of reflections were captured. The question is not so much whether student teachers are ready to reflect, but rather the support or guidance needed in the course of learning to teach. A further question concerns the extent to which they can be expected to benefit from their reflections. The necessary support went beyond what the supervisor's classroom visits could offer. As mentioned in the reviews, peer coaching was a valuable source of support. Concerning the question of whether the student teachers might have benefited from reflection, it is necessary to consider the data from video-lessons. Meanwhile, it is worth acknowledging the power of video-recording as a powerful source of stimulus which assisted recall of what happened. By reviewing the lessons, the student teachers were sensitised to critical details which would not otherwise have come to their notice. It is probable that the multiple resources in the course had made it easier for the student teachers to be engaged in reflections. Former teaching experience is therefore not necessarily a prerequisite for readiness to reflect.

IMPLICATIONS FOR CURRICULUM DEVELOPMENT IN TEACHER EDUCATION

As the major objectives of the course included facilitating the ability of student teachers to explore and experiment with a broad range of approaches in teaching, and to pursue a wide repertoire of problem-solving strategies (Kwo, 1994b), the findings indicate the ways student teachers responded to their course experiences. The extent to which the objectives were achieved was partly revealed in student teachers' own words: their own assessment of their learning experiences, and how they concluded their own understanding of the nature of teaching. If teacher education has to target the nature of student teachers' conceptions and competence levels on entry to the course, it is important to refrain from unrealistic assumptions. This study describes some differences between groups of experienced and inexperienced student teachers. The schemata differences and the range of teaching competence amongst student teachers were apparent. Rather than taking the differences as constraints, the course accommodated the differences by nurturing individual development through promoting reflective teaching. Individuals started from where they were, progressed over the year in a similar direction towards student-centred teaching and reached different points in their development at the end of the course. Progress in this shared direction was essentially based on a culture of inquiry ingrained in the practice of reflective teaching. Throughout the analyses, the supervisor-researcher was constantly reminded by the data of the importance of acknowledging and accepting the individuality of student teachers, in order to facilitate them in their 'pursuit of personal excellence' (as explicitly set out in the objectives). Parallel to the student teachers' progress from a transmission mode to a student-centred mode of teaching, the study also enabled the supervisor-researcher to undergo a reinforcement of training practice in the spirit of the course objectives. Learning together with student teachers was crucial in empowering the supervisor-researcher to help sustain the harmonious culture of inquiry amidst the tension each individual experienced in facing the problems.

The open curriculum of the course provided the framework to build a context of reflective teaching. Rather than being simply a matter of rational planning, the curriculum requires contributions from the participating student teachers and the supervisor. This study shows positive signs concerning the collegiality amongst student teachers, and the benefits in learning they gained from one another. The personality differences amongst the student teachers may be exciting for peer coaching, but they may also cause difficulty when there are clashes, which could be a subject for future research. Parallel to the school context, teaching at the university requires the supervisor to be actively involved in reflection on the teaching-learning processes that the student teachers experienced. The self-education of the supervisor-researcher was an implied but essential part of the curriculum for building up the desirable context in training for reflective teaching. Indeed there is an intimate connection between teaching and learning. Learning to teach and teaching to learn are simultaneous activities for student teachers as well as for reflective practitioners who seek to improve themselves.

Conditions for reflective teaching include the entire environment and the persons associated with it.

ACKNOWLEDGEMENTS

The author acknowledges the receipt of financial support for this work from the Committee on Research and Conference Grant of the University of Hong Kong. She also acknowledges the help of Dr Wen Qiu-fang of Nanjing University of the People's Republic of China.

REFERENCES

Ben-Peretz, M., & Rumney, S. (1991). Professional thinking in guided practice. *Teaching and Teacher Education, 7*, 517–530.

Berliner, D. C. (1988). Implications of studies on expertise in pedagogy for teacher education and evaluation. In *New directions for teacher assessment* (proceedings of the 1988 ETS invitational conference), Educational Testing Service, Princeton, NJ (pp. 39–68).

Berliner, D. C. (1993). Some characteristics of experts in the pedagogical domain. In F. K. Oser, A. Dick & J.-L. Patry (Eds.), *Effective and responsible teaching: The new synthesis.* San Francisco, CA: Jossey-Bass.

Booth, M., Furlong, J., & Wilkin, M. (Eds.). (1990). *Partnership in initial teacher training.* London: Cassell Educational.

Borko, H., & Livingston, C. (1989). Cognition and improvisation: Differences in mathematics instruction by expert and novice teachers. *American Educational Research Journal, 25*, 473–498.

Calderhead, J. (1983). *Research into teachers' and student teachers' cognitions: Exploring the nature of classroom practice.* Paper presented at the annual meeting of the American Educational Research Association, Montreal, Canada.

Calderhead, J. (1987). The quality of reflection in student teachers' professional learning. *European Journal of Teacher Education, 10*, 269–278.

Calderhead, J. (1991). The nature and growth of knowledge in student teaching. *Teaching and Teacher Education, 7*, 531–535.

Calderhead, J., & Robson, M. (1991). Images of teaching: Student teachers' early conceptions of classroom practice. *Teaching and Teacher Education, 7*, 1–8.

Carter, K., Sabers, D., Cushing, K., Pinnegar, S., & Berliner, D. C. (1987). Processing and using information about students: A study of expert, novice, and postulant teachers. *Teaching and Teacher Education, 3*, 147–157.

Clift, R. T., Meng, L., & Eggerding, S. (1994). Mixed messages in learning to teach English. *Teaching and Teacher Education, 10*, 265–279.

Cole, A. L., & Knowles, J. G. (1993). Shattered images: Understanding expectations and realities of field experiences. *Teaching and Teacher Education, 9*, 457–471.

Doyle, W. (1979). Making managerial decisions in classrooms. In D. L. Duke (Ed.), *Classroom management (Yearbook of the National Society for the Study of Education).* Chicago, IL: University of Chicago Press.

Eisenhart, M., Behm, L., & Romagnano, L. (1991). Learning to teach: Developing expertise or rite of passage? *Journal of Education for Teaching, 17,* 51–71.

Housner, L. D., & Griffey, D. C. (1985). Teacher cognition: Differences in planning and interactive decision making between experienced and inexperienced teachers. *Research Quarterly for Exercise and Sport, 56,* 45–53.

Kagan, D. M., & Tippins, D. J. (1991). How teachers' classroom cases express their pedagogical Beliefs. *Journal of Teacher Education, 42,* 281–291.

Korthagen, F. A. J. (1988). The influence of learning orientations on the development of reflective teaching. In J. Calderhead (Ed.), *Teachers' professional learning* (pp. 35–50). London: Falmer.

Kwo, O. (1994a). Learning to teach: Some theoretical propositions. In I. Carlgren, G. Handal & S. Vaage (Eds.), *Teachers' minds and actions: Research on teachers' thinking and practice* (pp. 215–231). London: Falmer.

Kwo, O. (1994b). Towards reflective teaching: curriculum development and action research. In D. Li, D. Mahoney & J. Richards (Eds.), *Exploring second language teacher education* (pp. 113–130). Hong Kong: City Polytechnic of Hong Kong.

Livingston, C. C. (1990). *Student teacher thinking and the student teaching curriculum.* Unpublished doctoral dissertation, University of Maryland, College Park, MD.

Marton, F. (1981). Phenomenography: Describing conceptions of the world around us. *Instructional Science, 10,* 177–200.

Marton, F., & Saljö, R. (1984). Approaches to learning. In F. Marton, D. Hounsell & N. J. Entwistle (Eds.), *The experience of learning* (pp. 39–58). Edinburgh: Scottish Academic Press.

McCullough, L. L., & Mintz, S. L. (1992). Concerns of pre-service students in the USA about the practice of teaching. *Journal of Education for Teaching, 18,* 59–67.

McIntyre, D., Hagger, H., & Wilkin, M. (Eds.). (1993). *Mentoring: Perspectives on school-based teacher education.* London: Kogan Page.

McNally, J., Cope, P., Ingus, B., & Stronach, I. (1994). Current realities in the student teaching experience: A preliminary inquiry. *Teaching and Teacher Education, 10,* 219–230.

Miles, M. B., & Huberman, A. M. (1984). *Qualitative data analysis: A sourcebook of new methods.* Newbury Park, CA: Sage.

Parker, W. C., & Gehrke, N. J. (1986). Learning activities and teachers' decisionmaking: Some grounded hypotheses. *American-Educational Research Journal, 23,* 227–242.

Peterson, P. L., & Comeaux, M. A. (1987). Teachers' schemata for classroom events: The mental scaffolding of teachers' thinking during classroom instruction. *Teaching and Teacher Education, 3,* 319–331.

Schön, D. A. (1983). *The reflective practitioner.* London: Temple Smith.

Schön, D. A. (1987). *Educating the reflective practitioner.* San Francisco, CA: Jossey-Bass.

Schön, D. A. (Ed.). (1991). *77K reflective turn.* New York, NY: Teachers College Press.

Stones, E. (1987). Student (practice) teaching. In M. J. Dunkin (Ed.), *The international encyclopedia of teaching and teacher education* (pp. 681–685). Oxford: Pergamon.

Szpiczka, N. A. (1990). *Preservice teachers' perspectives on student teaching.* Unpublished doctoral dissertation, Syracuse University, Syracuse, NY.

Woods, H. E. (1991). *The student teaching experience: A qualitative examination.* Unpublished doctoral dissertation, Oregon State University, Corvallis, OR.

CHAPTER 14

TEACHER EDUCATION IN BRAZIL ☆, ☆☆

Maria Inês Marcondes

ABSTRACT

Teacher education for the elementary level in Brazil is examined and the main problems school teachers and teacher educators face are discussed. Some current educational policies in Brazilian education are described and analysed.

Keywords: Teacher education; education in Brazil; teacher preparation programs; teacher induction programmes

☆This is a revised version of a paper presented at the symposium 'Relating Research and Practice in Teacher Education: International Perspectives', chaired by Professor Kenneth Zeichner, in the American Educational Research Association Annual Meeting 1997, 24–28 March, Chicago, IL, USA.
☆☆This article was first published in 1999, *Journal of Education on Teaching: International research and pedagogy*, 25(3), 203–213. Reprinted with permission from the publisher, Taylor & Francis Ltd, www.tandfonline.com.

From Teacher Thinking to Teachers and Teaching: The Evolution of a Research Community
Advances in Research on Teaching, Volume 19, 305–319
ISSN: 1479-3687/doi:10.1108/S1479-3687(2013)0000019017

INTRODUCTION

In this chapter I hope to contribute to the debate on Brazilian education and to make some important issues known to a wider readership. My comments reflect my experience as a teacher in elementary school, as a teacher educator and also as a university researcher for the last 15 years. For the past five years I have also been working at the university in a special teacher education programme for in-service teachers. I begin by providing a brief contextualisation of elementary education in Brazil (see also Feldens, 1986a, 1986b; Feldens & Duncan, 1988; Moraes, 1989).

PROBLEMS FACING BRAZILIAN SCHOOL TEACHERS

Brazil is made up of 27 states and more than 4,500 municipalities with the responsibility of providing primary education, while the states and federal government provide secondary education.

It is not necessary to have a university degree to become an elementary school teacher in Brazil. Instead there is a special course for elementary school teachers, corresponding to high school level. The official course required for teaching at elementary level in Brazil is called 'Magistério'. The great majority of the students taking this degree are female students, and nowadays these future elementary school teachers come from low middle class families with little education and their choice of profession represents upward social mobility.

Those teachers who have taken a complete degree, and who have attended better schools and are better educated, are mainly concentrated in urban areas in the South and Southeast regions of the country. Elementary school teachers with the lowest levels of education are found mainly in rural areas in the Northeast and Middle-West regions of the country, although in all regions, especially in rural areas, there is a high percentage of elementary school teachers who have not graduated and in some cases have not even finished their elementary education themselves. So these teachers have limited schooling, sometimes no more than three years of elementary school. They are known as 'lay teachers' (IBGE-PNAD, 1995).[1]

This does not imply that the low educational level of these teachers makes them in any sense directly responsible for the poor results of our elementary education. Even those who are considered to be good teachers do not feel stimulated to do a good job. Besides facing problems such as schools with few material conditions and resources, Brazilian teachers feel their careers have been undervalued. Salaries in Brazil are very low (varying from the equivalent of US \$25–200 monthly) and their profession has a low status in society.

Because of these bad conditions and poor pay few people want to be teachers and many teachers have other jobs to complement their salaries. Also many leave their present jobs as teachers to get other jobs with better salaries. Paiva, Junqueira, and Muls (1997) carried out a study of the salaries of teachers working in the municipal schools of the city of Rio de Janeiro during the period from May 1979 to May 1996, and the interviews with teachers, students and parents in that city's public schools demonstrated the contradictions between the rhetoric in favour of education, with emphasis on basic education and the impoverishment of elementary school teachers.

According to the Educational Census of 1994, there were approximately 1,375,000 elementary school teachers in Brazil in 1994; among these, 1,186,000 taught at public schools and 189,000 taught in private schools. Approximately 280,820 of the total taught in rural areas and most of the time at schools where there was only one classroom. In such schools the teacher has to teach several different levels at the same time in the same classroom, the so-called 'multi-grade class'. This happens because there are not enough teachers for all grades, especially in rural areas.

One of the main problems school teachers face in the school system in Brazil is school failure and grade repetition. Some of the determinants of school failure and grade repetition such as, for instance, malnutrition, clearly cannot be related to the school system and have to do with social and economic status. Many poor families have such low incomes that they have difficulty in keeping their children in school and out of the workforce. In many cases, children start working at a very early age in order to help their parents to earn money to make a living.

However, explanations for school failure and grade repetition can also be related to the general low quality of some schools. There are unprepared teachers with low levels of education, low salaries and few material resources such as textbooks and audio-visual equipment. The working conditions in classrooms are also poor. Altogether, these factors contribute strongly to the teachers' and students' lack of motivation.

An important study conducted by Gatti et al. (1981) intended to analyse different factors that might explain school failure in the first grade. Two public schools were selected. One of them lacked resources and served a low socio-economic status population. The other had better resources and a higher socio-economic status population. Data were collected on students (through medical examinations and psychological testing) and their families, teachers, supervisors and principals (through interviews and observation). The main conclusion was that school failure cannot be attributed to any one isolated factor. It seems that the public school was not prepared to work with low socio-economic status students and had no intention of doing so. What the school had been doing was to structure itself to teach an ideal child who was rarely, if ever, to be found in its classrooms (Gatti et al., 1981).

The great majority of students in the public elementary school system come from the poor population (IBGE/PNAD, 1988). These data show that 54% of Brazilian children from 0 to 14 years old come from families of very low income, less than $250 per year, and are concentrated in slums at the periphery of big cities. Educational data reveal that 90% of children in urban areas study at public schools. These children come from the poorest families and generally fail school examinations.

Teachers feel that they are not prepared to teach poor children, with economic, social and cultural background different from their own and most of the time they do not know how to teach poor children. Teacher education programmes take as reference the white, middle class student. When teachers face a different reality they think it is difficult and sometimes impossible to teach poor students because they imagine these students are incapable of learning and will fail anyway.

SPECIFIC PROBLEMS

Teacher educators in Brazil thus face many important and difficult problems. I will now discuss some of them.

Lack of Direct Connection between Theoretical Studies and
the Practical World

Teacher education is not an easy task. Teacher education programmes frequently fail to establish relations between theory and practice. Consequently, it is very difficult to establish the connections between the theory that has been learned in courses they take in training institutions and the practice in schools. It seems they are completely different worlds and teachers feel unable to make connections just by themselves.

Liston and Zeichner (1991), using Confrey's approach, remind us that teachers and researchers engage in knowledge production and use it in different ways. School teachers are more concerned with solving practical problems, while researchers tend to be influenced by the discipline-oriented inquiries and practices of fellow researchers. In other words, school teachers and researchers engage in 'knowledge production and use', having different purposes in mind and within different social and institutional contexts.

> In effect, we sense that although both teachers and researchers engage in knowledge production and use, they do so with different purposes in mind and within different social and institutional contexts. (Liston & Zeichner, 1991, p. 126)

It is important to ask what kind of knowledge is seen as essential for teachers. What kind of theoretical and practical knowledge is important to be included in a teacher education programme? Who produces valid, reliable knowledge about teaching? What strategies and contents would be more useful in teacher education programmes? How can we join academic and practical interests in a curricular proposal for a teacher educational programme? What kind of theory or theoretical approaches is important for daily practices in schools?

Quite often research findings do not reach school teachers. The communication and discussion of these research findings are restricted to meetings in which school teachers do not participate. So, as the participation of school teachers in research meetings is restricted, the communication of research findings remains restricted to the academy. Most of the time, research on teachers is not conducted by teachers but is formulated by teacher educators or research experts on teachers, often ignoring the concrete reality of teachers and the ways they deal with the problems they have to face daily in the classrooms. In most of the cases the teacher participates in the research only when it involves applying a new method or a new approach to the curriculum, as part of the experiment. This is a very restricted view of the role of teachers in educational research.

It is also important to keep in mind that research on teacher education is mostly conducted by university professors or by students belonging to a Master or a Doctorate programme, and most of the time they result in a dissertation or a thesis. School teachers are not the main researchers on their own practice.

Lack of Inclusion of Practical Knowledge and Expertise Developed by Successful Teachers

Another problem is that teacher education programmes often ignore the kind of practical knowledge and expertise that some of the successful teachers have developed through their experience as teachers. Even programmes for in-service teachers tend to ignore the kind of knowledge that is produced by teachers in everyday practice and in their experience in the classroom.

These programmes do not take into consideration the experience of teachers themselves and do not consider very often their previous experience as students. Instead of seeing teachers as potential producers of knowledge, they often see them just as a passive audience. Only rarely is this practical knowledge of elementary school teachers taken as a starting point for the development of their own education. Teacher educators often forget that the teachers have their own ideas about how to act in the classroom and that these ideas are the product of their reflections upon situations they have to face. They frequently want to share their difficulties and talk about their students with other teachers. However, teacher education programmes often see these teachers disconnected from their concrete reality, their practice and their own story. Again, most of the time theoretical issues are discussed from the point of view of an idealised school, with idealised students corresponding to white, middle class students, whom the teachers expect to be well behaved during classroom activities. When teachers get their first job they discover that this is not the reality of most of our students in the public system. After this initial shock they either accommodate to doing their job mechanically and often giving it up, or they develop their own way of dealing with the situation they are faced with.

Research on teachers' frequent blames the way they act in the classroom for the bad results of education. It is said that things go wrong because of the teachers' behavior and they are often reported in the academic research in a negative way. In consequence, teachers feel used by academic researchers as they allow them to be close to their work and at the time the research report is written they feel academic researchers are 'largely insensitive to the complex circumstances with which they are faced in their work and [they] frequently feel exploited by university researchers' (Zeichner, 1995, p. 155).

BRAZILIAN TEACHER EDUCATION TODAY

Currently Brazilian education faces the challenges of globalisation. The dominant view is that globalisation reflects a global economic pressure, seen as inexorably determining educational policy in countries like Brazil. To cope with globalisation the country has to modernise education and teacher education. Educational reforms have been proposed to facilitate adaptation to new needs of the work market. The official rhetoric has as its priority to improve quality in education to cope with globalisation. Quality will be attained in relation to the implementation of a national system of evaluation and the establishment of a national curriculum. Both are essential elements, according to the neo-liberal ideology, to attain quality in education.

Two elements of recent Brazilian educational policy of the 1990s are seen as important elements to modernise education to meet new needs of globalisation: the implementation of a national system of evaluation and the establishment of national parameters of curriculum (a national curriculum). I discuss in the following sections some issues related to a recent document of the Ministry of Education, in its preliminary version, establishing new guidelines for teacher education to prepare Brazilian teachers for the needs of globalisation.

THE IMPLEMENTATION OF A NATIONAL SYSTEM OF EVALUATION: EDUCATIONAL QUALITY IN QUESTION

The *Sistema de Avaliação do Ensino Básico* (National System of Evaluation of Elementary School) has as its main purpose to improve quality in education. The first national evaluation took place in 1990, the second in 1993 and the third in 1995. I will refer to these three phases using the critical analysis developed by Maluf as main reference (1996).

The systematisation of the information for planning and decision-making can be seen as an important positive aspect of the system. Some questions the programme is seeking to answer are:

• How are the policies adopted making possible school access and the improvement of quality in teaching?
• What are the changes in working conditions and in the pedagogical competence of teachers?
• How are the school managements to become more efficient and democratic?

The main instrument is the students' performance test in different subjects (Portuguese language, mathematics and science) that are considered the basic curriculum. It is not unusual when the system is based on tests to measure students' performance, for teachers to become more interested in preparing students for those tests. Teachers start to teach their subjects according to public examination requirements.

However, according to Maluf (1996), the evaluation system has presented many problems since its conceptualisation, its 'design', process of implementation and the dissemination of its findings.

In relation to its conceptualisation, it would be essential first of all to discuss what 'quality' means. This meaning needs to be agreed before designing the programme. It is also necessary at this stage to decide how it could be applied in concrete terms. It would be necessary to have a national definition about the standards of quality that could be translated into contents and skills to be developed before defining the conception and the implementation of the evaluation system. We have to stimulate the debate about what kind of quality in education we are searching for. What does quality means? What are the best indicators to measure quality? How can quality be measured in practical terms? These are important questions to be answered.

The lack of participation of states and municipalities in the earlier definition of the basic guidelines of the evaluation programme was deleterious to the development of evaluation procedures and their regional application. According to Maluf (1996), a condition of fundamental importance is to rethink the national system of evaluation on a new basis. Such a change could transform the current design of the programme. Participants – states and municipalities – could then be directly involved in decision-making instead of acting merely as executors of an external action that is exclusively oriented to the results of learning. This way, it would be possible to establish some objectives that can be shared by all participants and will satisfy the needs of different regions of the country.

In considering the results of the examinations, a tendency to reward or to punish teachers and schools was detected. A more desirable outcome will be when the main objective becomes the reorientation of teaching and learning processes and not the control over schools. This control is associated, according to Young (1998), with the neo-liberal economic policies that will 'lead to attempts to cut public expenditure, and to maximize the economic benefits of educational spending by increasing its efficiency and directing its goals to economic rather than social or cultural ends'.

I suggest that it is really important that research findings have to be offered to teachers and school staff, with general or specific orientations that can allow them to study and use these findings to improve their own practice. To reach the main objective of the national system of evaluation, to improve quality of the teaching and learning process, it is necessary to transform results into alternatives to intervention, improving our research knowledge about the process that can lead to different results.

We may conclude that the adoption of a national system of evaluation can be seen as part of a centralisation strategy of the Ministry of Education, and putting this system of evaluation into practice could lead to the need for a national curriculum.

The Establishment of National Curriculum Parameters: in Search of Quality ...

In a recent analysis by Marcondes, Tura, and Macedo (1998) the definition of a national curriculum in Brazil is seen as the national system of evaluation, in the context of the prevalence of neo-liberal policies in Latin America and the globalisation of the economy. From the authors point of view, however, in Brazil, a country with continental dimensions, with enormous ethnic, regional, social and economic diversities, such a generic definition may lead to a dissociation from the concrete reality of the country.

The establishment of national curriculum parameters emerged according to the experts of the Ministry of Education as a necessity for putting the system of evaluation into practice. This analysis refers only to the introductory document of national curriculum parameters for elementary schools (Ministério da Educação, Secretaria do Ensino Fundamental, Brasília, Brazil, 1997). The document's theoretical basis is 'curriculum development' (Pinar, Reynolds, Stattery & Taubman 1995), meaning that curriculum is viewed from a technical point of view as giving particular relevance to curriculum design. Throughout the document, there is a belief that education can be changed through changes in the curriculum. Factors such as the improvement of teachers' practice, better working conditions and wages are isolated from the analysis of historical conditions.

According to the curriculum development approach, selecting contents is considered a fundamental task. There is no questioning of the nature of knowledge or of its political nature. Contents are seen as if they were neutral, promoting social equity by themselves and having their own value. The document presents recurrent failures, students' insufficient apprenticeship, lack of interest in school tasks and irrelevant contents as the main unrelated problems of education and a curriculum revision is proposed as a solution to all these problems. As a matter of fact, throughout the document, the concept of quality is related to the teaching and learning processes.

The concern with quality interferes in the document's general argument. Brazilian education needs to be reorganised in order to prepare citizens for the global market. The insertion of the country in the context of globalisation, in the scientific and technological changes and in the ethical reorientation of society, brings immense tasks to schools.

Quality is understood as teaching/learning quality. The emphasis is on what is more evident, while a more critical analysis is left undone. Quality is related to micro-sociological dimensions. In spite of presenting the need for an educational practice adapted to all students' needs, quality is understood as a demand for the existence of a national curriculum proposal.

According to Cunha (1996, p. 22), the document viewed school as 'omnipotent' to face school failure. School failure is considered as if it were a problem with internal causes; thus, a good school would be capable of fighting and eliminating school failure. Arguing against this 'omnipotent' view, Cunha (1996, p. 22) mentioned among out-of-school causes of bad results in Brazilian schools the maldistribution of income and poverty of a great part of the population. However, it is doubtful that it is possible to change this situation by selecting curricular contents.

Related to the educational system, wage policies and bad conditions of work are responsible for attracting people not well qualified and not motivated. Many teachers give up their jobs during the first five years of profession. Teachers' lack of motivation due to their career being under-valued leads to a routine in their daily practices and they end up doing their work mechanically.

Cunha (1996) referred to the management patterns of the public system as 'zigzag' administration. Teachers tend not to believe in the orientation proposed by the Secretary of Education due to constant changes since each administrative proposes a different approach.

The way to reach quality is through the national curriculum parameters, although the relation between 'national evaluation' and 'national curriculum' is not clear. No data indicate how the change from 'evaluation' to 'intervention' in quality will take place.

According to Marcondes et al. (1998) in a country as big as Brazil, to which regional (social and economic) differences are added, along with a variety of tendencies in pedagogy, it becomes hard to accomplish this homogeneity of contents, and it is naïve to believe that this will reduce the inequality of opportunities in education. It is easier to assume that the interest in curriculum change focuses mostly on a need for the legitimization of changes which the current government intends to achieve, as a way of opening the economy to the world' s market globalisation

(Popkewitz, 1991). The idea of a national curriculum is thus associated with the neo-liberal policy in order to train workers according to standards required by the market. Furthermore, it serves as a guide for government funding, providing subsidies for redistributing political funds which are reduced day by day (Anderson, 1995).

The existence of national curriculum parameters does not necessarily ensure learning/teaching quality as is suggested, if we remember that it is related not only to internal but also to external conditions. As a consequence of the establishment of a national system of evaluation and of a national curriculum, the Ministry of Education believes teacher education must be revised.

Curriculum and Main Pedagogical Guidelines

A recent document of the Ministry of Education proposes a teacher education programme of quality considering the current necessities of Brazilian society, *Referencial Pedagógico – Curricular para a Formação de Professores da Educação Infantil e Séries Iniciais do Ensino Fundamental (Pedagogical – Curricular Orientations for Teacher Education to Pre-school and Initial Grades of Fundamental Level)*. In this section I refer to a document still in its preliminary version, having as its main objective to give support for teacher education in educational systems and in graduation institutions indicating main guidelines that can be adapted to local necessities.

While I believe it is important to rethink teacher education, I believe this document can be seen only as part of an effort to overcome the main problems of teacher education. It is known that discourse alone cannot transform practice. So, many practical actions besides changing curriculum and main pedagogical guidelines would be necessary to transform the teaching profession as a whole, such as improving wages and giving better working conditions for teachers, especially for those who work in elementary education. I do not deny the importance of rethinking teacher education emphasised throughout the document of the Ministry of Education, but it is not enough to propose this; surely we cannot rethink teacher education without taking into consideration the socio-political context.

According to the Ministry of Education's proposal, teachers' professional knowledge must be improved because of (a) the rapid growth and change in scientific knowledge; (b) changes in students' way of thinking due to the quick evolution of society, models of production and income distribution; (c) the progress of investigations in the professional knowledge of the teachers; and (d) teachers' personal development, which includes their own lives and, consequently, their careers.

The first part of the document aims to give a brief overview of the conditions in which teacher education takes place. This overview extensively uses quantitative data and tables. We cannot deny the importance of this kind of information, although it is shown in a purely descriptive way, without a more critical analysis.

In the second part of the document, some important concepts are presented based on theoretical studies and educational research in Brazil and abroad, strongly influenced by North American authors, some of them translated into Portuguese and published in Portugal. Many concepts derived from North American, Canadian and English authors are mentioned in the text, although the authors themselves are not cited, and only listed at the end of the document as references.

The themes are basically related to the nature of the teaching profession: continuing professional development of teachers, evaluation of teacher education, initial teacher education, in-service teacher education, distance education, and so on. Concepts such as 'teacher as a reflexive practitioner' are extensively used. However, although we cannot deny the great importance of these ideas, we think that it is important to adapt them to the Brazilian context.

The third part of the document comprises the main guidelines proposed by the Ministry of Education for teacher education programmes for elementary schools throughout the country. Curriculum is viewed as a plan of studies in a more specific way. Some objectives for initial training are focused. The importance of theoretical studies linked to such disciplines as psychology, sociology, anthropology and philosophy (in this order of importance) is reaffirmed. There is an explicit reaffirmation of the importance of psychological knowledge for teachers in order to deal successfully with the national curriculum parameters. According to the document, learning is a psychological act, so psychology is a necessary resource for the development of the teaching practice. Teachers have to be aware of 'different learning theories', 'motivation', 'student interaction' and 'the importance of self-esteem' among other concepts. All these concepts are viewed as important tools for planning learning activities according to a Tylerian view (one of the basic references of the national curriculum parameters).

In relation to the teacher practicum the document uses as main concepts 'critical reflection' as 'reflection-in-action, reflection-on-action ...' based on Donald Schön's (1983) approach, although Schön is not explicitly mentioned in the text. So, teachers will not be able to understand this meaning in any fundamental way in the Brazilian context. The 'practicum' placement is the school and school teachers will work, in collaboration acting as supervisors, with student teachers. It is important to put into question what the real working conditions of school teachers are, so that they have, in addition to all their duties, the responsibility to act as a 'model' for student teachers. The document did not mention if they will be paid for this function and this is an important consideration in our context because elementary school teachers live today 'in a process of professional distress and impoverishment' (Paiva et al., 1997). It would be urgent and necessary to rethink and establish a new policy for teachers who will be in contact with student teachers in everyday practice.

As an overall comment on the document I suggest that it is important to include the voices of elementary school teachers in the process of establishing new guidelines for teacher education. Top-down educational reforms that are conceptualised without the active involvement of teachers may not be successful. I realise the importance of a document like that which can incorporate important guidelines and stimulate consensus on certain basic ideas about what is evidently of great importance for the educational field as a whole as well as for teacher education. But once again we cannot be naïve to the point of believing that a written document will be strong enough to change educational practice.

CONCLUSION

In a very thoughtful paper, Young (1998) pointed out that 'Becoming competitive is not just providing existing education at a lower cost; it requires a fundamentally new approach to the relationship between education and economy' (p. 52). And in our analysis we can say that the dominant economic view in Brazil (although not exclusive) has a limited view of educational problems. For instance, in order to improve quality in Brazilian education, economists must not ignore wages and conditions of work of teachers in their analysis, especially of those who work in elementary schools, all central factors in this process.

The national evaluation system was conceptualised and implemented before the conceptualisation and implementation of the national curriculum. So the process was inverted, the criteria of evaluation being established before the national curriculum parameters were defined. The Ministry put in practice an evaluation based on tests of students' performance in public schools in practice without having established previously a national curriculum for the educational systems of the states without a consensus about what was going to be evaluated. It is important to ask: is evaluation a part of the curriculum design? Or, will evaluation be the determinant of the curriculum?

Improving the quality of pedagogical practice is seen as the capacity of the school system to plan, apply and evaluate a curriculum adjusted to the diversity of skills, interests and motivations of all students. In this way we end up placing the emphasis on the 'how to do' and overlook the political character of the discussion about teaching quality, and important questions, such as 'who is really benefiting from this quality teaching?' 'What kind of idea of world and society can it develop?' These questions are left out of the debate.

We are conscious that we surely need a quality educational programme, but we certainly need much more than that. It is necessary to improve the social conditions of the population in general as quality housing, health care and more decent wages. The implementation of a quality educational programme without a social programme will be almost worthless. It is important here to quote Zeichner who, although speaking from a different reality, reminds us that schools are part of society:

> Although we must do the best in our schools and in our universities, we must also link up with those who are struggling in various others sectors in our society for the achievement of the social and economic pre conditions that will enable our educational efforts to be more successful. (Zeichner, 1993)

Although our reality is a special one, many of the questions presented in this chapter are probably similar to the questions raised by teacher educators and researchers from other countries.

NOTE

1. IBGE-Brazilian Institute of Geography and Statistics/PNAD is the Brazilian Annual Labour Force Survey.

REFERENCES

Anderson, P. (1995). Balanço do neoliberalismo. In E. Sader & P. Gentili (Eds.), *Pós-liberalismo: as políticas sociais e o estado democraâtico* (pp. 9–23). São Paulo: Paz e Terra.

Cunha, L. A. (1996). Os parâmetros curriculares nacionais para o ensino fundamental: convívio social e ética. *Cadernos de Pesquisa, 99*, pp. 60–72.

Feldens, M. G. (1986a). Perceived problems of teachers: The Brazilian case. *Journal of Education for Teaching, 12*(3), 233–243.

Feldens, M. G. (1986b). The state of art in teacher education in Brazil. *Journal of Education for Teaching, 12*(1), 85–96.

Feldens, M. G., & Duncan, J. K. (1988). Brazilians speak about their schools: Implications for teacher education. *Journal of Education for Teaching, 14*(2), 105–123.

Gatti, B. A., Patto, M. H., da Costa, M. L., Kopit, M., & Almeida, R. M. (1981). A reprovação na primeira série do primeiro grau: um estudo de caso. *Cadernos de Pesquisa, 38*, 3–13.

IBGE-PNAD. (1988). *Pesquisa Nacional por Amostra de Domicílios/PNAD*, IBGE (Brasil).

IBGE-PNAD. (1995). *Pesquisa Nacional por Amostra de Domicílios/PNAD*, IBGE (Brasil).

Liston, D. P., & Zeichner, K. M. (1991). *Teacher education and the social conditions of schooling.* New York, NY: Routledge.

Maluf, M. M. B. (1996). Sistema nacional de avaliação da educação básica: análise e proposições. *Estudos em Avaliação Educacional, 14*, 5–38.

Marcondes, M. I., Tura, M. L., & Macedo, E. (1998). *Analyzing citizenship, quality and cultural diversity concepts.* Paper presented at American Educational Research Association, San Diego, CA.

MEC. (1997). *Parâmetros Curriculares Nacionais.* Brasília, Secretaria do Ensino, Fundamental.

Moraes, V. R. P. (1989). Students' views of schooling and teaching and their implications for teacher education: A Brazilian study. *Journal of Education for Teaching, 15*(3), 261–269.

Paiva, V., Junqueira, C., & Muls, L. (1997). Prioridade ao Ensino Básico e Pauperização Docente. *Cadernos de Pesquisa, 100*, 109–119.

Pinar, W., Reynolds, W. M., Stattery, P., & Taubman, P. M. (1995). *Understanding curriculum.* New York, NY: Lang.

Popkewitz, T. (1991). *A political sociology of school reform: Power knowledge in teaching. Teacher education and research.* New York, NY: Teachers College.

Schön, N. D. (1983). *The reflective practitioner: How professionals think in action.* New York, NY: Basic Books.

Young, M. (1998). Rethinking teacher education for a global future: Lessons from the English. *Journal of Education for Teaching, 24*(1), 51–62.

Zeichner, K. M. (1993). Connecting genuine teacher development to the struggle for social justice. *Journal of Education for Teaching, 19*(1), 5–20.

Zeichner, K. M. (1995). Beyond the divide of teacher research and academic research. *Teachers and Teaching: Theory and Practice, 1*(2), 153–172.

CHAPTER 15

REFLECTIVE PRACTICE IN THE TEACHING PROFESSION: THE CASE OF TRAINING AND RESEARCH PRACTICES IN THE FRENCH COMMUNITY IN BELGIUM

Sephora Boucenna and Evelyne Charlier

ABSTRACT

The idea of reflective practice, a concept that is currently in vogue in educational circles, is taken up in this chapter. Having to do with training and research practices in the French community in Belgium, this chapter revolves around two major themes: an overview of training as approached in French-speaking Belgium and a summary of teaching and research issues addressed by researchers in this particular part of Europe. In the final analysis, important matters having to do with socialization and intelligibility and their relationship to reflective practice are probed. These considerations are of major significance to educators worldwide.

Keywords: Reflection; reflective practice; reflective processes; Belgium

From Teacher Thinking to Teachers and Teaching: The Evolution of a Research Community
Advances in Research on Teaching, Volume 19, 321–338
Copyright © 2013 by Emerald Group Publishing Limited
All rights of reproduction in any form reserved
ISSN: 1479-3687/doi:10.1108/S1479-3687(2013)0000019018

Are reflective practices, which are currently highly regarded currently, a new avenue to overcome the "uneasiness" in education identified by teachers and researchers in the field? This "malaise" has been the subject of considerable research investigation. Some scholars question the factors involved in the dropout rate of novice teachers: one in three teachers leave the profession within the first 5 years of working in the field.[1] Other studies attribute the suffering of teachers to the shift in relationship between them and their students (Dubet, 1998).

Some consider the in depth use of reflective practices of those working in the field of education as a potential means to meet the needs of teachers in their professional context. This hypothesis is now widely acclaimed by teachers and researchers. Paquay and Sirota (2001) write that if the implementation of reflective practice has not been the subject of research as such, it

> is part of a general occupational analysis, that sets aside the analysis of external factors and approaches working conditions and workplace situations, especially for those professions dealing with other humans confronted with misery, in frameworks where legitimization is wavering and uncertain. Prior definition of the task and the role is no longer sufficient, as teachers are constantly required to reinvent ways of working in their daily activity, from the classroom to discussions in the staff common room. (p. 8)

In the same essay, the researchers state that, in the face of publicly displayed social unrest, the professionalization of teachers (of which the development of reflective practices is an essential part) has become a reiterated demand of a profession in trouble.

We deliberately quote this passage because, although it is excerpted from an editorial introducing international research, the first author is from the French community of Belgium, and he knows the context well. That the loss of legitimacy of which the authors speak comes from public authorities (through successive decrees aimed at normalizing practice) or students (whose behavior is seen as a source of anxiety by some teachers) seem to be a source of educators' discomfort.

In this chapter, we present a nonexhaustive inventory of training practices and research in education and teacher training in French-speaking Belgium. We subsequently analyze these practices by questioning the tensions that penetrate them with a view to developing a model of these practices that sets these tensions in perspective with respect to the discomfort felt by teachers.

To analyze educational systems, we focus on those topics that are the subject of reflective practice, which can be accessed through oral evidence and found in the literature. We have tried to determine whether the analysis focused on the activity of the participants engaged in reflection and the processes present in the activity, on the contents of those situations analyzed, on values, or on the professional behaviors of teachers. We also tried to identify the objectives of the reflective methods that were a part of the training. Finally, before identifying the approaches used to engage audience in reflective exercises, we wanted to identify the material used to support those exercises. Were they written or oral histories, classroom activities, or professional writing? Hence, our analysis concerns three issues: the topics of the research studies, their stated purposes, and the methodologies used to the collect and process the reflective material.

This chapter is divided into two main parts. The first part provides an overview of ways of training in French-speaking Belgium that enabled us to develop a classification of the systems present based on their logic and the aims that underpinned them. The second part offers an overview of themes and research issues currently being addressed by researchers in this part of Europe. We contacted a total of 21 colleagues: nine people from five universities in French-speaking Belgium (assistants and academics), and 12 higher education teachers in 3-year post-secondary training programs. We received many responses. We have chosen not to mention our colleagues who were contacted, partly because practices are constantly evolving and we do not wish to reduce the richness of our colleagues' practices by attributing labels to their work. In addition, our study was not intended to be exhaustive.

TRAINING PRACTICES

The Context: French-Speaking Belgium

Initial teacher training in French-speaking Belgium is organized according to three possible curricula, each involving courses at higher education institutes or universities and practicum in schools. A 3-year curriculum, starting at the end of secondary education (18 year of age), trains infant and primary school teachers who will teach students from 2.5 to 12 years old. Training takes place in nonuniversity higher education institutions. A second curriculum, taking place in the same institution, which also lasts 3 years, trains teachers for lower secondary school (12–15-year olds). These are so-called "aggregated" graduates of lower secondary education (AESI). The third curriculum prepares upper secondary teachers who have the title of Associate of upper secondary education (AESS). This course is taught in universities in two ways. The first involves 5 years of university study with a bachelor in a given subject (180 credits or ECTS), followed by a master (120 credits) in any discipline. In addition, there is "the aggregation for upper secondary education," which corresponds to a training program (practicum) of 30 credits during the 6th year. The second formula also includes a bachelor of 180 credits in a given discipline, but it is followed by a master's degree in didactics, corresponding to 2 years of study and 120 credits, 30 of which are dedicated to teacher training. Finally, there is the "Certificate of Pedagogical Aptitude Suitable for Higher Education" (CAPAES), the teaching qualification required to teach in higher education. This is only available to those already teaching in higher education and can be acquired during the first 6 years of higher education teaching.

According to our interview data, many teachers in further education and university perceive initial teacher training as being split between "theory and practice," where theoretical courses take place in further education at university and practice takes place in periods of teaching practice in schools. It is this perception that leads prospective and practicing teachers to consider initial training "fragmented."

The emergence and proliferation of training approaches using reflective methods are therefore perceived as "resources to promote the integration of different forms of learning." In February 2001, the decree defining the initial training for "aggregated" upper secondary education (AESS) was revised. In the thirteenth and final item of a list of skills, it was declared that the future "aggregated" teacher must be able to "take a reflective stance on his or her practice and organize his or her ongoing training."[2] A year earlier, a decree was published defining the initial training of teachers and "aggregated" lower secondary education (AESI) in which this 13th competence was also to be found. The notion of reflectiveness became publicly acknowledged. More than that, it became an educational imperative and would gradually modify training practices with the introduction of a reflective dimension and reflective terminology into curricula. But what does "taking a reflective stance" mean? The decree did not specify. Could this lack of information be due to the nature of reflectiveness? One thing is clear; the term covers a wide range of practices and takes on numerous forms.

A similar trend can be observed in other countries. As emphasized by Tardif, Borges, and Malo in their introduction to the collective work entitled "The Reflective Shift in Education," reflective design has prevailed (...) in various countries amongst those political, academic and educational authorities that shape the teaching profession and teacher training. In the 1990s, the majority of teacher training in Europe, North America and Latin America had made the move to reflectiveness. Reflection (or reflectiveness) is now considered a core competence of the teacher. (Tardif, Borges, & Malo, 2012, p. 11)

But which groups are affected? Are only initial teacher education programs affected?

Relevant Audiences (Trainers and Trainees)

We would like to point out that the information in this chapter represents the point of view of those who were willing to testify about their practices. It is not for us to decide, on the basis of the data collected, that a particular practice stems from reflectiveness or an analysis of practices. It is the people who were interviewed that decide. As a result, we will inventory a wide variety of options.

We would, however, like to begin by specifying what we mean by reflectiveness and the analysis of professional practices. By "reflectiveness," we mean those analytical activities that produce "statements about relationships between what exists" (Barbier, 2011, p. 30) and that take the form of knowledge developed by the subject about himself as he interacts with the environment. Various aspects of the subject (cognitive, emotional, affective, conative, interpersonal, behavioral, postural) may be involved in the analysis, the results of which are formalized through communication in a shared language. By "analysis of practices" we mean those analytical activities that focus exclusively on professional practices in the form of "statements of a subject about his own activities" (Barbier, 2011, p. 103) on the one hand and the professional activities themselves or traces of them on the other hand. The practices and professional activities are not necessarily those of the subject doing the analysis. Training methods that employ reflectiveness are used not only in initial training but also in ongoing training.

Those systems that aim to develop reflective practice in initial teacher training affect all future teachers. However, depending on the levels for which they are destined, teachers are not trained in the same processes and there are differences between practices in further education (teacher training) institutions and in universities, both of which are sites of teacher education in Belgium. University-educated teachers from 5-year programs, a large part of whose training is subject matter based, seem less concerned by such systems than those prepared in 3-year teacher training institutions.

There are, however, some exceptions. Students in physical education, educational sciences, health care, and psychology have been introduced to this approach over the past 15 years. Psychology professors have adopted the concept faster than their colleagues in didactics. Among their missions, they clearly identify the development of reflective skills in their students. As a result, in the "aggregation" curriculum several courses revolve around reflective practices. Introductory seminars and those seminars designed to accompany or follow up on practicum in schools have become privileged spaces for the development of reflective practice in both further education institutions and universities. Also concerned by these approaches are the CAPAES students, whose training is at the intersection between initial and further training.

Contrary to initial training, in-service teacher professional development does not decree driving the adoption of reflective practices. Its use depends on the convictions of a number of trainers. It is probably for this reason that reflective practices are less visible in in-service training, but that does not imply that such initiatives are rare. In fact, there are many others who are responsible for organizing and delivering such training. Not only are teachers in higher education institutions and universities responsible for a number of initiatives, but certain training organizations also take responsibility for the task. These courses target all teachers, although participation is generally on a voluntary basis. Note that these courses concern not only teachers, but also those who supervise teachers and other related professionals such as those who accompany preservice teachers to their practicum sessions in schools, educational advisers, inspectors, school principals, branch coordinators, and teacher trainers themselves.

Preferred Approaches

The decrees of 2000 and 2001 did not specify the framework needed to implement practices that support the development of reflectivity in future teachers. As a result, systems abound and are varied in nature. The following passages present approaches by various university and higher education colleagues that were selected from their written testimonies that suggest a formalization of their practices:

- Such practices can take the form of an exchange of experience at the end of a practicum. Students are invited to present both positive and negative situations they have experienced and to draw guidelines for the future.

- They can also take the form of a comparison of experience in which experienced teachers attend student presentations and then present those of their own practices that took place in situations similar to those experienced by the student teachers.
- Another possibility is a review following a visit during the student's practicum. The student is invited to describe how he experienced the teaching sequence he has just used and to explain his actions. The interview may be based, where appropriate, on a written report of such a course, a portfolio or a logbook.
- Portfolios, diaries, and other reflective writings subsequent to a practicum (reports, for example) invite authors to produce written descriptions (testimonies of experience, descriptions of professional situations, notes on emotions, ...), written assessments (level of satisfaction, changes in practices or developments in perspectives, ...), written analysis (identification of the nature of learning achieved, case analysis showing the appropriation of concepts proposed in courses, questions about practices, ...), and prescriptive writing (drawing up rules, ...). Depending on the context, these writings are communicated on paper or via digital media.
- Workshops about incidents (inspired by data collection methods from anthropology then adopted by businesses to produce qualitative assessments) enable the critical analysis of problem situations.
- Professional co-development in peer groups (often referred to as intervision–supervision between colleagues), an approach close to problem solving techniques, offers an opening to problematization.

In the same vein, several analytical approaches to practices invite participants to describe their practices from real or virtual situations, to problematize and to analyze them and then to generate theories to guide future actions (Charlier, Beckers, & Boucenna, in press). Among these approaches we would like to mention: the educational lookalike (Clot, 1999), simple self-confrontation (Theureau, 1992), the "explicitation" interview (Vermersch, 1994), the training group in the analysis of educational situations (Fumat, Vincens, & Richard, 2003), and more recently the exchange group for reflective analysis of professional practices (Vacher, 2010). Other approaches introduce transitional stages to support changes in stance that can occur between an evaluation exercise and exercise analysis. These approaches are based on the assumption that the natural reaction of a teacher will be to evaluate practice (either his own or that of others). Thus, through them, the participants are invited to follow their natural reactions and then explore models of intelligibility that enable them to analyze not only their practices but also their initial judgments of them. All of these approaches use a variety of media including writing, oral narrative, a filmed story or a filmed professional situation.

Our survey indicates that the individual who serves as the catalyst of reflective approaches or the analysis of practices can serve different functions depending on the approach. She/he could be a subject-based expert, in which case, she/he intervenes on the content with a view to equipping participants pedagogically. This approach to developing reflective capacities can sometimes lead the trainer to assume a role as evaluator of practices. In other approaches, the catalyst limits her/his intervention to questions of method, overseeing the work of participants and orienting types of exchange between participants by intervening in the process of analysis. She/he does not intervene in questions directly concerning the content, which is the subject of the analysis.

In both cases, the catalyst/trainer uses the time of the analysis of practices to encourage teachers to use concepts and theories produced by the profession, by research in education, psychology, ergonomics, or other disciplines as tools to analyze the professional situations explored. In other cases, he invites participants to enrich their analysis with personal theories.

Aims: Socialization or Intelligibility?

Our interviews with educators from initial and in-service training as well as the analysis of reflective processes and systems (or those aimed at the development of reflectivity) led us to identify two distinct objectives: one having to do with socialization and the other concerning intelligibility.

The first leads trainers to seek to develop professional practices that participating teachers do not use in their current practices. For students in initial training, the aim is to familiarize them with processes expected of professionals by using reflective approaches. These processes are promoted by educators who do not necessarily have the same teaching (pre)occupations (university teachers have not necessarily taught teenagers and teachers in further education institutions do not teach 2-to-12-year olds). As a result, the processes are perceived by students as "academic knowledge." Hence the apparent, albeit long-standing, conflict between theory and practice emerges. Everything that is proposed in a school setting (during further education and university courses) is seen both by teachers and by students as theoretical, even if when time is devoted to practice. These courses are inspired by academic research and are built on pedagogical models developed by educators who have formalized their practices and political and ideological options. Students acknowledge neither the professional legitimacy of the search results nor the contributions of educators they consider out of touch with the reality of down-to-earth teaching. This may explain why steps aimed at the development of reflective skills, devised by trainers to create bridges between the practicum experience and the content of courses, are seen as "theoretical" by students. This vision contrasts with that of the trainers for whom developing reflective practices in future teachers aims to equip them pragmatically for pertinent work in the field. By way of conclusion, the aim of this first category of approaches is the integration of new elements in the practices of the actors involved. Our analysis points to the emergence of a "socializing function" underpinned by certain approaches aimed at reflectivity. By socializing function we mean a will to socialize in the sense defined by Lahire (2013) where individuals are shaped by society.

The second aim is found in approaches where the center of focus is the development of "analyzed knowledge" on the part of participants. The aim is not only to get people to see themselves as "active agents," bearers of "values in action," and "reference systems," but also to invite them to examine the systems and environments in which they operate in order to identify the underlying logic. These approaches are designed to develop a critical perspective on the part of teachers with respect to political, scientific, and educational institutions. Intelligibility is the prime aim. The teacher learns to analyze his/her professional activity by considering it as an interaction or a constellation of interactions within a given environment. This understanding of the milieu may diminish feelings of guilt and thereby reduce the possible discomfort often encountered in the teaching world. The resulting adjustments are not limited to actions and professional attitudes. They may also affect the professional stance and how teachers position themselves in relation to a given environment. We can conclude that the characteristic aim of such approaches is the development of self-understanding in interaction with the environment on the part of the educators involved. As a result, our analysis points to a second function that we will call the "intelligibility function" underpinning certain approaches that generate reflectivity.

Analysis: Professional Logic or Scholastic Logic?

Equipping teachers (or future teachers) so that they become "reflective practitioners, that is to say, practitioners who can think about their own practices, objectifying, sharing and improving them, introducing innovations to improve their efficiency" (Paquay & Sirota, 2001, p. 5) aims to intervene in the teaching performance of these teachers. The objective is to improve performance. These processes may concern current employability or extend to the teaching practice throughout the life of their career. In these approaches, the "analysis," whether it be prior to, during, or after the practicum, aims to encourage the assimilation of concepts and theories developed in the courses in further education institutions or universities. This assimilation or transfer within practices is based on the conviction of the promoters of these programs and approaches that it will serve to improve the performance of teachers.

The educational world is also subject to the criteria that drive the world of work as a producer of goods and merchant services: productivity and efficiency. These criteria have extended their hold to areas that 60 years ago were not concerned with them. This is the case of education and health, but also of former public services like transportation and communications. The worker's skills have become the unit of measure of his/her performance and the reference for any future acquisition of competencies. We refer to this approach as "professional logic" that is characterized by its dominant intention to produce skills. Insofar as certain approaches that are designated as reflexive and seek to increase the performance of teachers as professionals, we can hypothesize that they subscribe partly or wholly to this logic.

From a completely different perspective, equipping teachers to develop knowledge about their practices and their environment is based on an ideological conception according to which she/he who studies and produces knowledge forges his/her personal happiness. As such, exercises become reflective moments dedicated to study of oneself, of others, and of interactions. The main intention in this kind of logic, which we call "scholastic logic," is purely the production of knowledge. We chose the term "scholastic" in its etymological sense, namely, that time is not dedicated to productive work, but to leisure devoted to study. Study is therefore part of leisure and as such it is not an activity dedicated to economic production.

If "professional logic" and "scholastic logic" are present in the same field of activity, that may create tension as they represent opposing intentions. These differing logics are not necessarily due to different individuals. In an organization or an institution, it is possible that people become points of tension produced by the coexistence of the two logics within the same field of activity, because, whether consciously or not, they are moved by both.

Similarly, the socializing function may be at odds with the function of intelligibility. Pursuing the development of specific professional acts is part of a project to transform the world in a way that it corresponds to an ideal. The expected product, the contours of which we delimit and the features of which we define, colors the impact on others. The aim is, in fact, to train teachers who have a given set of characteristics. The intelligibility function also corresponds to a project to change the world. However, the project is not so much focused on the product as on the process. The objective is to get the teacher to act in a particular way without necessarily saying what the characteristics of the teacher will finally be. As a result, the work of teacher trainer is not structured around a defined "profile of the teacher," but is rather the teacher's action. The reflectivity of the teacher is not thought of as a means to acquire skills, but as a way of understanding oneself and the environment. Understanding provides no map of how it will guide the actions of the teacher in the future. Consequently, training that develops reflective practices or approaches that use analytical practices can be made sense of on a twofold axis (see Fig. 1). The first axis depicts the tension between professional logic and scholastic logic. The second axis shows the tension between the socializing function and the function of intelligibility. Such an interpretative framework is not designed to classify an approach or a course of action in terms of a particular logic or function. That would be counterproductive. Instead, it enables us to identify the extent to which approaches are not necessarily due to a particular logic or a single function. If it is possible to identify the dominant function and intention, it is equally possible to identify potential tensions insofar as the dominant trend can be counteracted by the minor trend. Thus for a reflective approach, we can identify that the dominant intention is to produce skills, but its function is more intelligibility than socializing. This

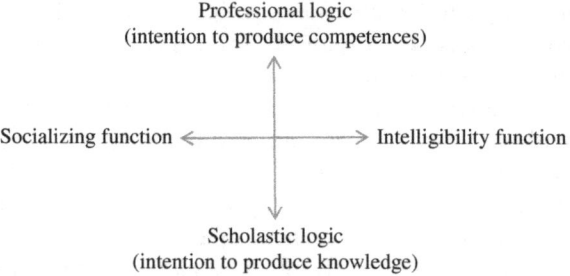

Fig. 1. Tensions in Reflective Practice.

is the case of those approaches that seek to professionalize teachers and thus support the process of improving their mastery of school milieus while offering to build ways of understanding those environments. But if, in the example given, it is a process of intelligibility for teachers, it is possible to identify a minor socializing function. Indeed, it comes down to analyzing the practices of teachers in a particular mode so as to produce an interpretative framework, which then allows for the identification of levers for action.

This tool (Fig. 1) provides an interpretative framework that enables a nuanced understanding of approaches and reflective systems. However, it would appear that in a clear majority of the courses about which we obtained information, the dominant intention was to produce skills with socialization as the main function. It is therefore legitimate to raise questions about the context of this result. Is it specific to our collection of data? Is it specific to the context of the Belgian French-speaking community? Or does this trend also exist in other European contexts, or even further afield in the ISATT (International Study Association on Teachers and Teaching) community at large?

An Interpretative Framework for Discomfort Perceived at School

Finally, in the analysis of practices we find the same tensions that are found in schools. Bourgeois and Durand, in their introduction to the book *Learning at Work* question the fascination for support systems of all kinds. As a hypothetical response they offer the discovery of the self-evidence: *"Like Mr. Jordan, do we not discover the obvious: that people have been learning in the work context ... since the dawn of time"* (Bourgeois & Durand, 2012, p. 9, italics in original). They put forward two hypotheses about the pendulum swing in which the model of training is replaced by the acquisition of "skills on the job" (*ibid.*, p. 10). Training alone is not enough to prepare professionals. The organization of this training represents a cost and is therefore a luxury that our employers, given the "financial crisis," can no longer afford the same way they could decades earlier. If we adhere to the idea of the pendulum swing, where professional learning takes place first in the workplace, then in a setting outside work only to return to the workplace, our hypothesis is necessarily different. Professional and scholastic logics alternately occupy the field of training. Today it would seem that scholastic logic is progressively being excluded from the world of school only to be replaced exclusively by professional logic. The negotiated divisions between areas dominated by one or another are being questioned; scholastic logic is gradually disappearing from schools. These systems, whether in initial or in-service training, in the pursuit of socialization or intelligibility, have given rise to abundant literature that formalizes training and support practices. These writings are often considered scientific as their authors are from universities or higher education institutions specializing in 3-year post-secondary teacher training and their formalization or models are sometimes accompanied by research questions. But what about research practices? How do they relate to these different functions and intentions?

RESEARCH PRACTICES

Research that focuses on the concept of reflectiveness, reflective practices, and approaches to the analysis of professional practices is still in an embryonic stage in French-speaking Belgium. In this second section, we present what attracts the attention of researchers, the fields they explore, the nature of the material collected, and the methods of collecting and processing the data used. This collection is far from complete, but it reflects current trends in this field of research.

The Research Study

Regarding research studies, given that reflective practices are also decreed to be professional competencies, many educators are interested in identifying factors conducive to the development of such practices. Conditions required by such practices and environments in which they can be developed constitute a challenge to teacher trainers. In Table 1, readers will find some examples of research questions that fall into this category.

A great deal of the research we have encountered addresses the field of initial training of teachers. It is not surprising then that teacher trainers seek to evaluate mandatory competencies. The evaluation may involve indicators of reflective practices in future teachers. It may also involve indicators of practices of those teacher trainers who organize activities meant to develop reflectivity. To evaluate emerging or existing reflective practice, indicators are needed. In its own way, this research questions the notion of reflectiveness. Either the questions rely on existing definitions of reflectiveness proposed by that field of research or, based on the variety of practices expressed, they redefine the notion by expanding on it (see Table 2). We ask: What is the value of a scientific definition, if it does not deal in one way or another with reality?

In an attempt to map the contours of reflective practice, some research studies the various forms the practice takes. They do so by questioning the appropriation of reflective approaches or the nature of the media used to engage in a reflexive exercise or they compare the effects of the varied approaches present (see Table 3).

In addition to research that seeks to identify factors optimizing approaches or the favorable characteristics of certain circumstances with a view to boosting performance, there is also research aimed at intelligibility. Some research attempts to understand the mental or identity-related mechanisms that correspond to reflectivity, while other research questions the social relations identified in this type of activity.

Table 1.   Examples of Research Questions That Address Factors Favorable to the Development of Reflective Practice.

- What training and mentoring practices of future students are favorable to the development of reflective practice?
- What are the characteristics of the work environment that can support teachers at the start of their career in the pursuit of reflective practices learnt in initial training?
- How do you evaluate systems designed by researchers and teachers at university or further education institutions, but also media meant to develop reflectiveness in students, with a view to developing reflective practice in the long term?
- How do trainee teachers react to practices designed to develop reflectiveness?
- What are the professional actions of trainers who advocate reflective approaches?

Table 2.   Examples of Research Questions That Develop Tools to Assess the Presence/Absence of Reflective Practice.

- What are the indicators of the presence or absence of reflective practice? When can one assert that there is reflective practice in student teachers?
- What indicators of reflectiveness reveal linguistic practices that are potentially differentiated and differentiating?
- Can we identify levels of reflectiveness in future teachers?
- What are the differences between practices declared by trainers to develop reflectiveness in their trainee teachers and practices observed by the researcher?

Table 3. Examples of Research Questions Aimed at Identifying
Different Forms of Reflective Practices or Practices Designed to Develop
Reflectiveness and Their Effects.

- Based on common benchmarks that delimit reflective practice, how and on what do teacher trainers develop different practices?
- What are the characteristics of oral reflectiveness compared to written reflectiveness?
- What are the effects of mentoring and coaching when they use reflective approaches?

The Target Groups Studied

Two target groups were studied in connection with the research studies mentioned earlier. The first were the beneficiaries, that is, students who intend to teach, young teachers, those who are entering the profession and even experienced teachers. The second were teacher trainers (whether in initial training or in-service training) who employed approaches that analyze practices or incorporate reflective dimensions.

The Material

The material collected was essentially discursive. It was the discourse that is studied, whether written or oral. When data collection focuses on evidence of teaching activities as is the case in classroom situations that are video-recorded, participants engage in conversations about that evidence. The conversation constitutes the research material. Teachers' log books are also used as data collection tools. Sometimes, the researcher uses his/her own observations as evidence. In this case, there are no other tools used. But it remains discursive. No multimodal treatment (treatment that does not favor speech as the unique access to the subject's activity but rather focuses on the body, voice, postures, intonations, etc.) was significant in the research study.

Situations in which reflective material is collected can be deliberately set up (structured or semi-directive interviews, questionnaires, ...) or they can be anchored in practices taking place in the authentic situations of the actors being studied. For the majority of the reflective material read, the research focused on representations. Some research on teaching practices and their effectiveness does not analyze practices or procedures likely to develop reflectiveness, but instead uses the reflective approach as a method of data collection. What was once the object of study becomes the research methodology capable of producing a collection of reflective material. What we found in French Belgium was that there was little discussion of methodologies to treat and analyze reflective material or, when there was, it remained rather vague on the issue, except in the case of Ph.D. thesis for which there was an obligation to describe clearly the methodology.

PROFESSIONAL LOGIC: THE DOMINANT INTENT OF RESEARCH IN THE FIELD OF REFLECTIVE PRACTICE?

The vast majority of work encountered refers to authors of reference in efforts to define reflectiveness; Schon's work is widely cited. Very few studies attempt to develop the notion of reflectiveness both conceptually and theoretically. However, there is a broader movement to operationalize the concept so as to develop criteria that serve as indicators to detect and assess reflective practice. If we summarize the research studies to which we had access, research is mainly driven by the issue of performance. Concern is currently focused on factors involved in reflectiveness or the development of reflective practice and whether they support the process or slow it down. Organizational environments are surveyed; the nature of interactions between various players (teachers, students, principals) involved is discussed as well as factors influencing commitment, not to mention the significant interest paid to the effects of participation in such efforts.

Given these topics, we can hypothesize that the research is influenced by the professional logic that drives much of the analysis of practices in French-speaking Belgium. Most energy is concentrated on the ability to optimize the skills of teachers. This optimization also involves the development of reflective skills. Little research focuses on conceptualization. Indeed, research targeting the identification of indicators does not involve procedural and conceptual exploration of reflectiveness. It sets out to generate behaviors in which it is possible to operationalize a concept that seems stabilized by previous productions.

This chapter did not set out to compare and contrast results from French-speaking Belgium with those of other countries to which ISATT members belong, for example. Rather, the approach has been to explore practices that have not necessarily been discussed in other publications. It was an inquiry into what is done, but which is not well known elsewhere. We were impressed by the quantity of approaches (there are many versions of the same approaches, but we had access to more than 25 methods) that claim to support, develop, or continue a reflective process. Such an exercise cannot be achieved by a review of the literature needed to enable an effective comparison. But significant questions worthy of future inquiry remain: What is the dominant logic that drives training practices in the field of reflective practice? Are they specific to particular organizational environments that characterize certain countries or are they more broadly common to various contexts?

CONCLUSIONS

This chapter is the result of an encounter between, on the one hand, a team of researchers/teacher trainers and, on the other hand, colleagues who work in the field of training practices and research aimed at reflective practices and approaches to the analysis of professional practices. On the basis of a concept and convictions but also training experience and "scientific" work, we have shifted our attention to concentrate on practices closer to home, that is, French Belgium. For us, this chapter is a reflexive exercise, because we have formalized our practices and those of colleagues to produce an interpretative framework that takes into account those practices. We have been able to identify intentions embodied in two underlying logical systems that drive reflective approaches and training to develop reflectiveness. On one side, there is professional logic that is characterized by the dominant intention to produce skills, and on the other hand, there is scholastic logic that is characterized by its dominant intention to build knowledge. We have also identified two functions that can characterize these reflective approaches: the "socializing function" whose main objective is the integration of new elements in the practices of the actors involved and the "function of intelligibility" whose main objective is the understanding of self, the environment, and interaction with that environment.

The analysis of the training taking place in the French Community of Belgium highlighted that the dominant intention of a sizeable majority of training concerns the production of skills for which the main function is socialization. In addition, the research material studied, on the basis of the topics with which it deals, leads us to suggest that research takes into account the issues conveyed by the professional logic that drives a large part of the analysis of practices in the French-speaking Belgian landscape, namely the optimization of the skills of teachers. We note that little research focuses on the elaboration of a conceptual or theoretical framework of reflectivity. Does such a conclusion correspond to specific characteristics of the French community of Belgium or is it a phenomenon that transcends those boundaries? This is a question we leave with members of the ISATT community and other international scholars who will read our work.

NOTES

1. CEF, Avis 111, www.eunec.eu/sites/www.eunec.eu/files/.../cef_avis_111_1.pdf
2. Information was provided by José Wolf, professor in Educational Sciences, at ULB.

ACKNOWLEDGMENTS

Appreciation is extended to Bernadette Charlier, a section editor of this volume and member of the ISATT Executive Committee, who aided in its inclusion and in its translation.

REFERENCES

Barbier, J.-M. (2011). *Vocabulaire d'analyse des activités*. Paris: PUF.
Bourgeois, E., & Durand, M. (2012). L'apprentissage au travail en question. Dans Bourgeois E., Durand M., *Apprendre au travail* (pp. 9–15). Paris: PUF.
Charlier, E., Beckers, J., & Boucenna, S. (in press). *Démarches et outils pour soutenir l'activité réflexive*. Bruxelles: De Boeck.
Clot, Y. (1999). *La fonction psychologique du travail*. Paris: Presses Universitaires de France.
Dubet, F. (1998). Les figures de la violence à l'école. *Revue Française de pédagogie, 123*, 35–46.
Fumat, Y., Vincens, C., & Étienne, R. (2003). *Analyser les situations éducatives*. Paris: ESF.
Lahire, B. (2013). *La socialisation*. Paris: Encyclopædia Universalis, France.
Paquay, L., & Sirota, R. (2001). La construction d'un espace discursif en éducation. Mise en œuvre et diffusion d'un modèle de formation des enseignants: le praticien réflexif. *Recherche et Formation, 36*, 5–16.
Tardif, M., Borges, C., & Malo, A. (2012). *Le virage réflexif en éducation*. Bruxelles: De Boeck.
Theureau, J. (1992). *Le cours d'action: Analyse sémiologique. Essai d'une anthropologie cognitive située*. Berne: Peter Lang.
Vacher, Y. (2010). *Pratique réflexive et professionnalisation au cœur de la formation des enseignants stagiaires: Quelle opérationnalisation pour réduire les tensions? Un exemple à l'IUFM de Corse*. Doctoral Thesis, Université de Genève, Geneva, Switzerland.
Vermersch, P. (1994). *L'entretien d'explicitation*. Paris: ESF.

CHAPTER 16

BEYOND THE REACH OF LEADING: EXPLORING THE REALM OF LEADERSHIP AND LEARNING

Michael Schratz

ABSTRACT

Over time, the orientation of educational leadership has changed as new paradigms have been introduced. These new paradigms have afforded increased insights into school milieus and actions and nonactions of teachers. The view of leadership that is currently in vogue connects acts of leading with acts of learning. According to this worldview, transformation occurs when students, teachers, and systems of education learn from experience in mutually beneficial ways. Strictly speaking, teachers are the true leaders of learning. As for school leaders, they facilitate student and teacher growth and take a reflective stance to issues at hand. In this scenario, school leaders as agents of change extend the reach of leading into the realm of leadership and learning.

Keywords: Leadership; learning; teaching; experience; reflective stance; change

From Teacher Thinking to Teachers and Teaching: The Evolution of a Research Community
Advances in Research on Teaching, Volume 19, 339–356
Copyright © 2013 by Emerald Group Publishing Limited
All rights of reproduction in any form reserved
ISSN: 1479-3687/doi:10.1108/S1479-3687(2013)0000019019

In almost all countries around the world the education systems are presently under significant pressure. Discussions on the implementation of standards (for teaching, school quality, the profession, etc.) suggest that professionals in education will undergo stricter external control in their work than ever before. Rhetoric on *quality improvement* dominates educational policy discourse in many areas, and policy borrowing and lending dominates national and international policy arenas. The side effects of these debates on reform and renewal appear at all levels of the system, where they have a formative effect on the professional work and professionalism of educators. On the micro-level, the arena where the actors have to put national/global policy aspirations into practice, school leadership has become the buzz word which seems to carry all the hopes and expectations for the transformation of school systems. Hargreaves and Shirley (2009) have pointed out three distinct ways of change and set out their Fourth Way pointing to an "inspiring future for educational change."

On the publication front, however, leadership has experienced several turns which signal a number of paradigms, particular modes (sometimes even fashions) of certain times and sometimes also reflecting certain values. These leadership trends and orientations are apparent in the following titles: Why leaders can't lead (Bennis, 1989), leadership as an art (Pree, 1989), transformational leadership (Tichy & Devanna, 1990), visionary leadership (Nanus, 1992), principle-centered leadership (Covey, 1992), moral leadership (Sergiovanni, 1992), authentic leadership (Terry, 1993), the leadership paradox (Deal & Peterson, 1994), the leadership trapeze (Wilson, George, & Wellins, 1994), enlightened leadership (Oakley & Krug, 1994), leadership from within (Bender & Hellman, 1997), alpha leadership (Deering, Dilts, & Russell, 2002), ethical leadership (Strike, 2007), distributed school leadership (Harris, 2008), motion leadership (Fullan, 2010), blundering leadership (Arnott & Holmgren-Hoeller, 2010) dealing with missteps by school administrators, radical leadership (Sprenger, 2012), and self-leadership (Furtner & Baldegger, 2013).

The different interpretative turns have rendered the term "leadership" multifaceted, which – in its over-use – could devaluate it to a so-called "plastic word" (Pörksen, 1995) losing its inherent potential. The present debates linking leadership with learning opens new possibilities, which is the theme of this chapter.

SHIFTING THE RESEARCH FOCUS ON EDUCATIONAL LEADERSHIP

In England, and similarly in other countries, for a long time a "headmaster tradition" dominated as a model of moral leadership, which was closely related to the moral order and the social order of the wider society. This tradition placed a premium upon leaders with a strong and assertive personality. During the late 1980s and 1990s neoliberal market policies reformed schooling and introduced concepts of a national curriculum, local management of schools, and stronger accountability of state schooling to parents who may choose where to place their children. Through the process of decentralization, school heads have become more managerially autonomous, but they have become less educationally autonomous compared to the 1970s (Møller & Schratz, 2008) because of the different forms of accountability enforced through national standards and mandatory school inspections. This movement has been globalized through transnational assessment regimes like Programme for International Student Assessment (PISA), which have put pressure on countries to compare results of the outcome of schooling.

Decentralization and higher degrees of autonomy of schools and the transfer of budgets from the authorities to the individual schools as such, however, do not guarantee quality improvement. School reforms only seem to prove successful when they have an effect on the pedagogical processes in the classroom and on students' achievement. The advocates for the success of schools are, on the one hand, the school leaders, who are in authority and accountable for the quality of the school, and the teachers who, on the other hand, are responsible for the quality of their teaching in the classrooms and their students' achievement (Firestone & Riehl, 2005; Hall & Hord, 1987). However, there is little that is known about the inner workings of this codependency.

School leaders can only indirectly influence the learning processes of the students (Hallinger & Heck, 1998), since they spend most of the time outside the classroom. Their influence only materializes through other people, measures, and organizational factors like school climate. School heads have become important advocates for creating favorable conditions for teaching and learning and for setting and reaching ambitious goals. They spur the performance of others by influencing motivation, commitment, and working conditions of the teachers who work face-to-face with students in classrooms. Blase and Blase (1994) and Blase (1995) tried to instantiate what effective, facilitative, empowering leadership looks like and what approaches to leadership produce the remarkable benefits that are the trademark of empowered teachers. They concluded that strategies, structures, and activities differ considerably from one school leader to another and from one school to another.

Pont, Nusche, and Moorman (2008) direct attention to the decisive role of school leadership for school reform. They assert that "It bridges educational policy and practice" (p. 19). To fulfill this visionary goal researchers have shifted their efforts by bringing school leadership in closer contact with student learning (i.e., MacBeath, Frost, Swaffield, & Waterhouse, 2006; MacBeath & Moos, 2004; MacBeath & Townsend, 2010; Schratz, 2007). The term *Leadership for Learning* was introduced to bridge the gap between the two paradigms. At its heart are the following key questions, which are of far-reaching significance:

- What is understood by the term "leadership?"
- What is the role of learning in schools?
- What connection exists between leadership and learning?

The answer to these important queries may help reveal the complexity of *leadership, learning,* and *leadership for learning* in individual schools and in school systems as a whole. Each of these central concepts – that is, leadership, learning, and leadership for learning – will now be briefly described.

Focus on Leadership

In several countries the ascendancy of school leadership is linked to government's goals of raising educational standards and modernizing the education system and therefore "the primacy of leadership is part of a wider agenda of transformation across public services where leaders are the vehicle by which policy reforms can be implemented and change realized" (Forrester & Gunter, 2009, p. 67). This kind of "functional organizational leadership" is a managerial approach of neoliberal policy-making rather than leadership which is associated with being visionary, motivational, inspirational, and innovative. Due to the discrepancies between reality and the ideal, conceptions of leadership in recent years have been increasingly characterized by notions of personal leadership. As a result, there is a delineation of characteristics which apply to individual leaders and strategies for influencing the behavior of their associates. According to Stähle, "A concept of leadership represents a (normative) system of recommendations for action on the manager's part, both in reference to personal responsibility and their personal leadership tasks. Leadership concepts are based explicitly or implicitly upon one or more leadership theories" (Stähle, 1999, p. 839).

In order to characterize the qualities of both management and leadership, Hinterhuber's theoretical model (2003) can be helpful, in that it attributes differentiating attitudes, mindsets, and actions to *Management* and *Leadership*, modeling them along the Eastern conception of Yin-Yang (see Fig. 1).

According to the Yin-Yang metaphor, there is no clear-cut division between management and leadership, and yet their features are distinct. There is no "either – or" but an "as well as." Management carries elements of leadership and vice versa. They can be differentiated in theory, but, in practice, they are interwoven. Management is more a state of behavior referring to norms; leadership is more a (moral) attitude of influence. Behaving (managing) without a moral attitude is just as problematic as leading without acting according to (given) norms. Competency in management is easier to acquire than the capacity to lead, not the least because leadership is never a solo act. This is because leadership is a social activity, which enables others to rise to their individual challenges and meet them with the necessary measures. It is the school leaders who are in contact with many different stakeholders (not just within the school but in society at large: the community, politicians, the public, etc.) and they are also the ones to register and respond to differing (and at times conflicting) interests. Leadership can only be effective in so far as leaders are willing to accept and work to their own moral (and policy) agendas, but these need to be

Fig. 1. Interrelation between Management and Leadership (Hinterhuber, 2003).

grounded within the political framework in which their education systems operate, since the weight of normative pressures bears differently upon varying educational contexts (i.e., Portin et al., 2005).

The culturally embedded trends, according to Senge, "are based not on the laws of physics but on human habits, albeit habits on a large scale. These habitual ways of thinking and acting become embedded over time in social structures we enact, but alternative social structures can also be created" (Senge, 1990, p. xiii). In his structuration theory, Anthony Giddens (1984)

> talks of the duality of structure in which social structures are not fixed sets of rules and resources but are features of social systems that have to be recreated in the specific moment of action. Such recreation can only take place when human agents act in this way or that and a powerful influence at that point is the reflexivity and knowledgeability. (Frost, 2006, p. 23)

Therefore the implication of Giddens' theory of action is that social (or organizational) structures can be modified by the agency of individuals.

In the context of daily work, management and leadership are social activities which cannot be separated from each other: They are relational concepts and not individual activities. Therefore, they can only be dealt with separately for analytical purposes. In this respect, leadership is a social activity setting a direction and developing a vision. It is about aligning people and inspiring them, which should enable others to rise to their individual challenges and meet them with the necessary measures. Leadership is also about agency: "We make choices which have moral dimensions ... agency as a capacity to act and reflect on the consequences" (*ibid.*). Management is more a state of behavior referring to norms; leadership is more a (moral) attitude of influence. This is important because it views agency as a driving force for leadership for learning.

Focus on Learning

In the context of "Leadership for Learning" *learning* does not only refer to students' experiences in the classroom but also to professional learning experiences of the professionals involved in the arena of schooling. Since learning is not a visible process, it cannot be observed or measured. In this sense, learning is always about something we do not know (yet). Tests both on the micro level (classroom) and macro level (system, i.e., PISA) do not assess learning as such, but only its results. Therefore, student achievement results only show how students respond to certain test items and do not mirror a student's capacity for learning. Learning is characterized by a high interconnectedness between cognitive, emotional, and actional processes (Roth, 2001) and, as such, is a total human experience – "Learning is the most personal thing in the world. It is as personal as one's own face or a fingerprint. Even more individual than one's love-life"[1] (as cited in Kahl, 1999, p. 109).

Rather than focusing on the results of learning further research in the context of leadership for learning calls for a reappraisal of the relationship between teaching and learning. Only if teaching is regarded as a responsive, interdependent, and relational encounter (Tomlinson, 2008) it can be mindful of learning (Schratz, 2009) and is constituted by the experiences both teachers and students make. Understanding learning *as* experience (Meyer-Drawe, 2008) rather than learning as a product *out of* experience, it becomes evident that learning and teaching processes are irrevocably intertwined and codetermining. In a phenomenological approach Schratz, Schwarz, and Westfall-Greiter (2012) used vignettes as a means of capturing in words the researchers' experiences of the experience of others. The findings do not only render deep insights into phenomena of learning but also offer a fresh look at the relationship between teaching and learning on the one hand and leading on the other.

A distinguishing feature of learning is that it possesses the potential for development. How ready, however, are all actors involved to express this potential? It depends on whether they move from unconscious incompetence to conscious incompetence and from conscious competence to unconscious competence (cf. Howell & Fleishman, 1982; see Fig. 2).

What we require in order to develop is not immediately evident to us. When learning something new, we perceive it as a time of emotional incompetence and loss of security. The old competence does not work any more; the new one has not yet been experienced. Each step away from a hitherto existing state of competence ushers in uncertainty – but it also opens the way toward the possibility of embracing something new. Experience proves, however, that new knowledge, skills, and attitudes needed to face impending challenges, must first be acquired. In a school setting it is very important that teachers create confidence and belief into the students' capacity as learners. To gain competence students have to be confident that they will succeed. Believing in our own capacities plays a significant role here, as does the appreciation expressed by others, who value the mistakes we might make along the way from conscious incompetence to conscious competence as necessary steps in our learning process. Schein (2003) pointed out

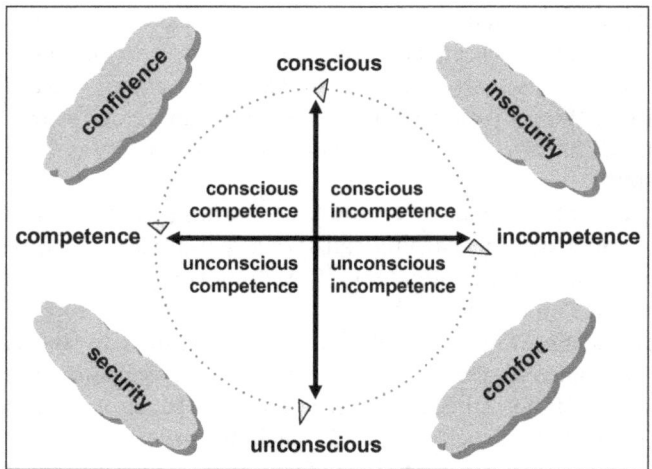

Fig. 2.   From Unconscious Incompetence to Unconscious Competence.

> In order for creative learning to start, *our urge to survive must be greater than our fear of learning.* Somehow we must reach the psychological condition where our fear or sense of guilt in not learning is greater than our dread of moving into something new, something unpredictable – into the state of temporary incompetence. (p. 5)

When newly gained knowledge, skills, and attitudes are mastered to the point of becoming unconscious, they can be perfected and integrated into our repertoire, so that it is no longer necessary for us to consider each step to take. Only then do we reach a certain self-assurance and independence in dealing with such knowledge or skills even in unusual, unforeseen circumstances. Students learning, however, never takes place in a vacuum, but is intertwined and codetermined by the actions taken by the teachers (directly) and the school leader (indirectly).

Focus on Leadership for Learning

After examining the notions of management and leadership and after considering learning as an experience between (un)consciousness and (in)competence we still have yet to find the answer to the question how leadership and learning relate to each other. The terms "leading" and "learning" belong to different domains of the pedagogical discourse, and they are associated with different actors in the educational arena.

Leadership is characterized by the fact that people are "led" to interact in certain settings so as to perform according to the desired aims or to undertake certain tasks. Learning, on the other hand, is a process which should lead to the acquisition of new knowledge or skills. Leaders, teachers, and learners are the protagonists who have to interact in a meaningful way to achieve the desired results. This leads to the following questions: How does leadership interact with teaching and learning? How do school leaders, teachers, and learners interact? In practice, these questions cannot be answered separately since leadership resides "in a collective relationship where participants are both 'shapers of' and 'shaped by' one another" (Donaldson, 2001, p. 41).

Research findings from a multilateral project (MacBeath et al., 2006) show that the following three learning spheres have to complement each other: the learning of the students, of the professionals, and of the system (see Fig. 3).

The model in Fig. 3 points to the ideal situation of matching learning experiences on all three levels: The more coherence there is between school (system) policies and practice, the more successfully leadership will be connected with practice. If all members in school see themselves as learners then the chances are high that the school is a learning school (Schratz & Steiner-Löffler, 1998) and as such a successful school, which makes

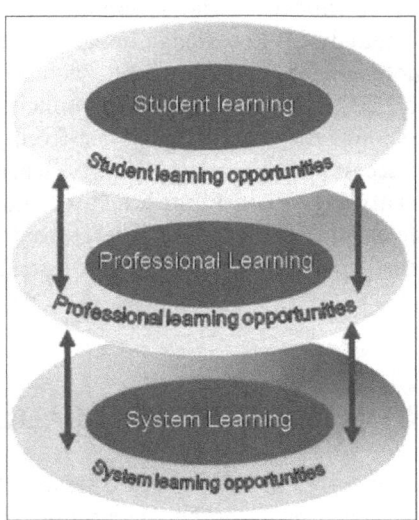

Fig. 3. Connecting Leadership with Learning.

connections between leading, learning and teaching, leading change, leading the organization, leading self and others. In Kruse and Seashore Louis's words, "More leadership from more people is not a goal in itself, but is one of the means of enriching your opportunities and potential for improving learning processes and outcomes ... The foundation of intensified leadership is rooted in the interactions between school organisation members" (Kruse & Seashore Louis, 2009, p. 79). It is the teachers who are leaders of learning – as individuals, as teams, and as a profession. Therefore, Hargreaves and Fullan (2012) argue that

> sustainable improvement can ... never be done to or even for teachers. It can only ever be achieved by and with them ... If we want to improve teaching and teachers, we must therefore improve the conditions of teaching that shape them, as well as the cultures and communities of which they are a part. We must invest in developing teachers' capabilities and give them time to sharpen these capabilities to a high standard. (p. 45)

The stronger learning cultures in individual schools are in an education system, the more successful countries are. A good example of such a cohesive system is Finland, which has often been portrayed as the "miracle of education," but whose success is only seen as a "side product" in the development of the country's educational system by the Finns themselves (Niemi, Toom, & Kallioniemi, 2012, p. 20). Policies build on the expertise of teachers, who are many-sided experts in their fields. "They must have a wide view of every aspect of education and schooling. Teachers need content knowledge and the pedagogical knowledge integrated with it ... An understanding of the wholeness of education and schooling is important for developing curricula" (*ibid.*, p. ix). Purposeful policies build on the high standards of teachers and form a learning system from preschool education to the end of upper secondary education. Equity, learning, and education have long been the central factor in Finnish history and teachers used to be called "candles of the nation" (*ibid.*, p. 21). Therefore, teachers have become key actors in the transformation of teaching and learning in particular and schooling at large.

BEYOND THE REACH OF LEADERSHIP

As teachers are the key actors in the process of leadership for learning, we have to look closer at the connection between school leaders and teachers. As was depicted in Fig. 3, successful schools can be found where there is coherence between (school) policy and practice. Hargreaves and Shirley (2009) suggested

> The challenge of coherence is not to clone or align everything so it looks the same in all schools ... The challenge, rather, is how to bring diverse people together to work skillfully and effectively for a common cause that lifts them up and has them moving in the same direction with an impact on learning, achievement, and results. (pp. 94–95)

The leadership challenge how to get diverse people moving into the same direction lies beyond the reach of an individual (school) leader. The book titles on leadership mentioned in the introduction (*Setting the leadership sense*) give a vivid impression of the different leadership voices in taking up the challenge.

In order to reduce the complexity of leadership among the actors involved in school we can use Giddens' (1984) differentiation between structure (vertical–lateral) and agency (transactional–transformational) (see Fig. 4).

Leadership activities in schools can neither be separated from the organizational (power) *structure* in which they are set and from the *agency* of the people involved (as so-called "leaders" or "followers"). For Giddens (1984), self, body, and memory are intimately related when leaders act, at the same time there are institutional aspects which influence leadership activities like deep structures which leaders are only partially conscious of (Tye, 2000). In Fig. 4 the first axis refers to the (power) structure between *vertical* and *horizontal* leadership. The second axis refers to the aspect of (human) agency, which moves between two leadership modes: *transactional* and *transformational*. Whereas transactional leadership works at the level of need satisfaction (award systems) aiming at stability, transformational leadership builds on consciousness rising toward significant change in the life of people and organizations (Burns, 1978). According to the two axes in

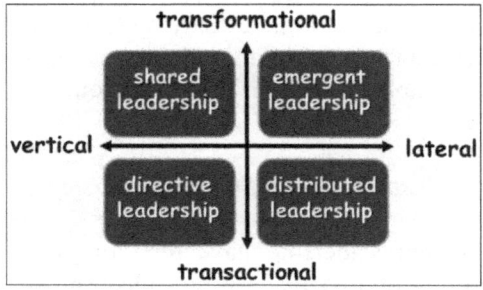

Fig. 4. Modes of Leadership: Structure and Agency.

Fig. 4 on the previous page, we can form four quadrants which highlight four orientations of leadership with a view to the relationship between school heads and teachers, which will be covered in the following sections.

Directive Leadership

If school leaders' beliefs and actions originate in a vertical and transactional understanding their behavior and actions can be characterized as directive leadership. It can be described as "leadership that primarily relies on position power, which at times has been referred to as legitimate power ..., emphasizes the need to provide direction to subordinates" (Pearce & Sims, 2002, pp. 173–174) and "involves planning subordinates' roles and responsibilities ... Representative behaviours of the directive leadership type include (a) issuing instructions and commands and (b) assigning goals" (*ibid.*, p. 174).

School leaders exercising directive leadership take over responsibility and tend to eliminate personal responsibility on the part of the teachers. "Motivation is doomed to fail," Sprenger (1991, p. 154) argues. He considers that achievement is an interplay of the three dimensions "willingness," "ability," and "possibility" and believes that willingness is a matter of the individual and not of the person in the leading position (Sprenger, 1991). Turnbull's (2005) study reveals that new teachers want to take over responsibility from the very beginning of their career by being involved in school-level decision-making. They report that teachers are often surprised and disillusioned that they seem to have considerably less involvement and influence than expected. These findings point to needs and expectations in two directions: (a) to include novice teachers earlier in decision-making processes when they start their careers; and (b) to incorporate education in school-based management as a means to better prepare new teachers for the political realities of the profession. A study by Clayton and Schoonmaker (2007) demonstrates that engaging in leadership is an important aspect in holding academically able teachers in the profession.

Distributed and Shared Leadership

Distributed and shared leadership have their origin in the theory that complex organizations, and particularly so-called knowledge organizations like schools, cannot be led through command and control by exceptional leaders but need to build on the distributed knowledge available. Its focus is on "how school leaders promote and sustain conditions for successful schooling in interaction with others, rather than on what structures and programmes are necessary for success" (Timperley, 2005, p. 395). According to Harris (2008) the terms distributed and shared leadership have been competing and sometimes conflicting and it is clear for her "that the idea of distributed leadership overlaps substantially with shared" (p. 33). In Fig. 4 the distinction is made by the vertical and horizontal axis.

If leadership is mainly distributed in a transactional mode (i.e., using reward systems to achieve maximal motivation) or hierarchically motivated (i.e., delegation principle, middle management) it fits into the bottom right quadrant (*distributed leadership*). In larger schools subject leaders form part of the distribution of leadership and are supposed to carry out their curricular tasks in accordance with the national requirements (i.e., educational standards) and the school's vision. In her research, Friedman (2011) shows the importance for school heads to realize and recognize the important position of subject leaders. If school heads narrow the subject leaders' role to mainly managerial aspects of their result-based departments, they feel not trusted and limited in their distributed leadership. In another study, Timperley (2005) found that teacher leaders with high acceptability among their colleagues were not necessarily those with expertise, and conversely, "the micro-politics within a school can reduce the acceptability of those with expertise" (p. 418).

Hargreaves (2002) reports that most research does not mention trust as a source of positive emotions, which seems a prerequisite for collaboration in school. One of the strongest sources of negative emotions in distributed leadership seems to be betrayal, which he finds in three forms: competence, contract, and communication betrayal. Kelchtermans (2011) argues for an encompassing conceptual framework on leadership in schools that allows to acknowledge and integrate both the concentrated and distributed approaches to leadership, as well as both the task dimension and the emotional dimension of school leadership. If leadership is shared through mutual understanding and trust, responsibility will be a collegial effort. Then we refer to the top left quadrant in Fig. 4 (*shared leadership*), which Senge et al. (1999) referred to through the metaphor, the "dance of change," with a view to mutual responsibilities. Good schools cope with the growing responsibilities for the development of young people not only segmentary, but look at it in its entity and are answerable to the parties involved and the public through shared leadership (Fauser, Prenzel, & Schratz, 2008).

Emergent Leadership

The school head–teacher relationship must be understood from their respective professional biographies and the particular context of the school and is highly sensitive to values and purposes which are at stake (Blase & Blase, 1994). Harris, Day, and Hadfield (2010) take up the issue of school leadership from the perspective of the teachers and point out that teachers appear to have fairly clear and consistent positions about what is required for good leadership. Therefore, creating a mindset of change cannot be imposed or enacted on a person; it is a human being's innate capacity to create new knowledge. Emergent leadership builds on the concept of "presencing," leading from the future as it emerges (Scharmer, 2007). For him the essence of leadership builds on everybody's capacity to feel in the here and now which future possibilities urge for evolvement without "downloading the patterns of the past." To activate this vital potential as a leader, for him three preconditions are necessary: an *open mind*, an *open heart*, and an *open will*. Opening the mind is based on our intellectual capacity which allows us to see things "with fresh eyes," which asks for a new perspective on leadership practice. Opening the heart relates to our ability to access our emotional intelligence, which asks for empathy to feel the sensibility of the field. Opening the will "relates to our ability to access our authentic purpose and self ... It deals with the fundamental happening of the letting go and letting come" (*ibid.*, p. 41).

This emergent leadership perspective puts empowerment at the center. In this view, power is not only a gift, but a right: "power is exercised with others in collaborative efforts that include students and have the students' welfare at their center" (Blase, 1995, p. 149). In this way leadership becomes a collaborative endeavor involving all teachers (Lambert, 1998) creating a strong leadership culture. Changing the culture of a school is not easy to achieve. Emergent leadership uses energy as a lever for promoting change, because it is easier to influence the energy of a system than to change the culture. Loehr and Schwartz (2003) argue that "positive energy rituals ... are key to full engagement and sustained high performance" (p. 16) and not the time invested. The intensity of organizational energy is an indicator of how much emotional, mental, and behavioral potential can be mobilized to reach the goals. It is an indication of the vitality, intensity, and velocity of innovation processes (Bruch & Vogel, 2005).

OUTLOOK: A SYSTEMS PERSPECTIVE

Implementing leadership concepts for innovation and change is often seen as merely organizational or technological question, turning complexity into a series of (trans)actions from policy to practice. However, dealing with complexity does not mean creating more complex structures of planning, acting, controlling, and developing systems. The shift to an organic understanding of growth is related to openness and trust, which best help in reducing complexity of systems: Speaking openly opens others. In our leadership work through the Leadership Academy (Schley & Schratz, 2010), we have been actors and observers of a shift in mindset and culture, overcoming the traditional abyss between policy and practice. The field work with many stakeholders on all levels of the system has taught us the wisdom of many in the collective intelligence of practice and opened up new dimensions of dealing with system-wide development.

The performance of the school system is based on an understanding of the different situations, contexts, demands, and challenges within each organizational unit. Consequently, developing performance is not simply achieved by sending individuals on a training course but a journey through the "field structure of attention" (Scharmer), which builds on different modes of (self-)awareness. Self-awareness, in Owen's view, "is knowing how your actions affect other people" (2009, p. 287). We are becoming aware of an emergent leadership culture which can be characterized by a spirit of innovation, commitment, and new attitudes for dealing with complexity, facing dynamics, taking risks, and learning from mistakes. After all, for Stenhouse et al. "[i]t is teachers who in the end will change the world of the school by understanding it" (Stenhouse, Rudduck, & Hopkins, 1985).

NOTE

1. Translations from original German texts into English are my own.

REFERENCES

Arnott, T., & Holmgren-Hoeller, G. (2010). *Blundering leadership: Missteps by school administrators.* Lanham, MD: Rowman & Littlefield Education.
Bender, P. U., & Hellman, E. (1997). *Leadership from within.* Toronto: Stoddart.
Bennis, W. G. (1989). *Why leaders can't lead: The unconscious conspiracy continues* (1st ed.). San Francisco, CA: Jossey-Bass Publishers.

Blase, J. (1995). *Democratic principals in action: Eight pioneers.* Thousand Oaks, CA: Corwin Press.

Blase, J., & Blase, J. R. (1994). *Empowering teachers: What successful principals do.* Thousand Oaks, CA: Corwin Press.

Bruch, H., & Vogel, B. (2005). *Organisationale energie.* Wiesbaden: Gabler.

Burns, J. M. (1978). *Leadership.* New York, NY: Harper & Row.

Clayton, C., & Schoonmaker, F. (2007). What holds academically able teachers in the profession? A study of three teachers. *Teachers and Teaching: Theory and Practice, 13*(3), 247–267.

Covey, S. R. (1992). *Principle-centered leadership.* New York, NY: Simon & Schuster.

Deal, T. E., & Peterson, K. D. (1994). *The leadership paradox: Balancing logic and artistry in schools* (1st ed.). San Francisco, CA: Jossey-Bass Publishers.

Deering, A., Dilts, R., & Russell, J. (2002). *Alpha leadership: Tools for business leaders who want more from life.* New York, NY: Wiley.

de Pree, M. (1989). *Leadership is an art.* New York, NY: Dell.

Donaldson, G. A. (2001). *Cultivating leadership in schools: Connecting people, purpose and practice.* New York, NY: Teachers College Press.

Fauser, P., Prenzel, M., & Schratz, M. (Eds.). (2008). *Was für Schulen! Profile, Konzepte und Dynamik guter Schulen in Deutschland: Der Deutsche Schulpreis 2007.* Seelze: Klett/ Kallmeyer.

Firestone, W. A., & Riehl, C. (Eds.). (2005). *Critical issues in educational leadership series. A new agenda for research in educational leadership.* New York, NY: Teachers College Press.

Forrester, G., & Gunter, H. M. (2009). School leaders: Meeting the challenge of change. In C. Chapman & H. Gunter (Eds.), *Radical reforms. Perspectives on an era of educational change* (pp. 67–79). New York, NY: Routledge.

Friedman, H. (2011). The myth behind the subject leader as a school key player. *Teachers and Teaching: Theory and Practice, 17*(3), 289–302.

Frost, D. (2006). The concept of "agency" in leadership for learning. *Leading & Managing, 12*(2), 19–28.

Fullan, M. (2010). *Motion leadership: The skinny on becoming change savvy.* Thousand Oaks, CA: Corwin; Ontario Principals' Council; School Improvement Network; NSDC; American Association of School Administrators.

Furtner, M., & Baldegger, U. (2013). *Self-leadership und führung: Theorien, modelle und praktische Umsetzung.* Wiesbaden: Springer.

Giddens, A. (1984). *The constitution of society: Outline of the theory of structuration.* Cambridge: Polity Press.

Hall, G. E., & Hord, S. M. (Eds.). (1987). *Change in schools: Facilitating the process.* Albany, NY: State University of New York.

Hallinger, P., & Heck, R. H. (1998). Exploring the principal's contribution to school effectiveness. *School Effectiveness and School Improvement, 9*(2), 157–191.

Hargreaves, A. (2002). Teaching and betrayal. *Teachers and Teaching: Theory and Practice, 8*(3), 393–407.

Hargreaves, A., & Fullan, M. (2012). *Professional capital: Transforming teaching in every school.* London: Routledge.

Hargreaves, A., & Shirley, D. (2009). *The Fourth Way: The inspiring future for educational change.* Thousand Oaks, CA: Corwin Press.

Harris, A. (2008). *Distributed school leadership: Developing tomorrow's leaders.* London: Routledge.

Harris, A., Day, C., & Hadfield, M. (2010). Teachers' perspective on effective school leadership. *Teachers and Teaching: Theory and Practice, 9*(1), 67–77.

Hinterhuber, H. H. (2003). *Leadership: Strategisches Denken systematisch schulen von Sokrates bis Jack Welch.* Frankfurt am Main: Frankfurter Allgemeine Zeitung.

Howell, W. C., & Fleishman, E. A. (1982). *Information processing and decision making. Human performance and productivity: Vol. 2.* Hillsdale, NJ: L. Erlbaum.

Kahl, R. (1999). Der Neugierologe. *GEO-WISSEN, 1,* 106–109.

Kelchtermans, G. (2011, July). Living the Janus-head: Leaders and leadership in schools. Paper presented at the 15th biennial conference of the International Study Association on Teachers and Teaching (ISATT), Braga, Portugal.

Kruse, S. D., & Seashore Louis, K. (2009). *Building strong school cultures: A guide to leading change. Leadership for learning series.* Thousand Oaks, CA: Corwin.

Lambert, A. (1998). How to build leadership capacity. *Educational Leadership, 55*(7), 17–19.

Loehr, J. E., & Schwartz, T. (2003). *The power of full engagement: Managing energy, not time, is the key to high performance and personal renewal.* New York, NY: Free Press.

MacBeath, J., & Moos, L. (2004). *Democratic learning: The challenge to school effectiveness.* London: Routledge.

MacBeath, J., & Townsend, T. (Eds.). (2010). *International handbook on leadership for learning.* New York, NY: Springer.

MacBeath, J., Frost, D., Swaffield, S., & Waterhouse, J. (2006). *Making the connections: The story of a seven country odyssey in search of a practical theory.* Cambridge: Cambridge University.

Meyer-Drawe, K. (2008). *Diskurse des Lernens.* München: Fink.

Møller, J., & Schratz, M. (2008). Leadership development in Europe. In J. Lumby, G. Crow & P. Pashiardis (Eds.), *International handbook on the preparation and development of school leaders* (pp. 341–366). New York, NY: Routledge.

Nanus, B. (1992). *Visionary leadership: Creating a compelling sense of direction for your organization.* San Francisco, CA: Jossey-Bass.

Niemi, H., Toom, A., & Kallioniemi, A. (Eds.). (2012). *Miracle of education: The principles and practices of teaching and learning in Finnish schools.* Boston, MA: Sense Publishers.

Oakley, E., & Krug, D. (1994). *Enlightened leadership: Getting to the heart of change.* New York, NY: Simon & Schuster.

Owen, J. (2009). *How to lead: What you actually need to do to manage, lead and succeed.* New York, NY: Pearson Prentice Hall.

Pearce, C. L., & Sims Jr., H. P. (2002). Vertical versus shared leadership as predictors of the effectiveness of change management teams: An examination of aversive, directive, transactional, transformational, and empowering leader behaviors. *Group Dynamics: Theory, Research, and Practice, 6*(2), 172–197.

Pont, B., Nusche, D., & Moorman, H. (2008). *School leadership development: Policy and practice. Improving school leadership: Vol. 1.* Paris: OECD.

Pörksen, U. (1995). *Plastic words: The tyranny of a modular language.* University Park, PA: Pennsylvania State University Press.

Portin, B., Bagakis, G., Frost, D., MacBeath, J., Møller, J., Moos, L., Skedsmo, G., & Swaffield, S. (2005, April). International politics and local school development: Emerging themes from a seven-nation study. Paper presented at the annual meeting of the American Educational Research Association, Montreal.

Roth, G. (2001). *Fühlen, Denken, Handeln: Wie das Gehirn unser Verhalten steuert.* Frankfurt am Main: Suhrkamp.

Scharmer, C. O. (2007). *Theory U: Leading from the future as it emerges: The social technology of presencing.* Cambridge, MA: Society for Organizational Learning.

Schein, E. H. (2003). Angst und Sicherheit. Die Rolle der Führung im Management des kulturellen Wandelns und Lernens. *Organisationsentwicklung, 3,* 4–13.

Schley, W., & Schratz, M. (2010). Developing leaders, building networks, changing schools through system leadership. In J. MacBeath & T. Townsend (Eds.), *International handbook on leadership for learning* (pp. 267–296). New York, NY: Springer.

Schratz, M. (2007). Leading and learning: "Odd couple" or powerful match? *Leading & Managing, 12*(2), 40–53.

Schratz, M. (2009). "Lernseits" von Unterricht. Alte Muster, neue Lebenswelten – was für Schulen? *Lernende Schule, 12*(46-47), 16–21.

Schratz, M., Schwarz, J. F., & Westfall-Greiter, T. (2012). *Lernen als bildende Erfahrung: Vignetten in der Praxisforschung.* Innsbruck: Studien Verlag.

Schratz, M., & Steiner-Löffler, U. (1998). *Die lernende Schule: Arbeitsbuch pädagogische Schulentwicklung.* Weinheim: Beltz.

Senge, P. M. (1990). *The fifth discipline: Mastering the five practices of the learning organization* (1st ed.). New York, NY: Doubleday/currency.

Senge, P. M., Kleiner, A., Roberts, C., Ross, R., Roth, G., & Smith, B. (1999). *The dance of change: The challenges of sustaining momentum in learning organizations* (1st ed.). New York, NY: Currency/Doubleday.

Sergiovanni, T. J. (1992). *Moral leadership: Getting to the heart of school improvement.* San Francisco, CA: Jossey-Bass Publishers.

Sprenger, R. K. (1991). *Mythos Motivation: Wege aus einer Sackgasse.* Frankfurt am Main: Campus.

Sprenger, R. K. (2012). *Radikal führen.* Frankfurt am Main: Campus.

Stähle, W. H. (1999). *Management: Eine verhaltenswissenschaftliche Perspektive.* München: Vahlen Franz.

Stenhouse, L., Rudduck, J., & Hopkins, D. (1985). *Research as a basis for teaching. Readings from the work of Lawrence Stenhouse.* Portsmouth NH: Heinemann Educational Books.

Strike, K. A. (2007). *Ethical leadership in schools: Creating community in an environment of accountability.* Thousand Oaks, CA: Corwin Press.

Terry, R. W. (1993). *Authentic leadership: Courage in action* (1st ed.). San Francisco, CA: Jossey-Bass Publishers.

Tichy, N. M., & Devanna, M. A. (1990). *The transformational leader: The key to global competitiveness* (2nd ed.). New York, NY: Wiley.

Timperley, H. (2005). Distributed Leadership: Developing theory from practice. *Journal of Curriculum Studies, 37*(4), 395–420.

Tomlinson, C. A. (2008). *The differentiated school: Making revolutionary changes in teaching and learning.* Alexandria, VA: Association for Supervision and Curriculum Development.

Turnbull, B. (2005). Facilitating early career leadership through pre-service training. *Teachers and Teaching: Theory and Practice, 11*(5), 457–464.

Tye, B. B. (2000). *Hard truths: Uncovering the deep structure of schooling.* New York, NY: Teachers College Press.

Wilson, J. M., George, J., & Wellins, R. S. (1994). *Leadership trapeze: Strategies for leadership in team-based organizations.* San Francisco, CA: Jossey-Bass.

CHAPTER 17

THE NEW LIVES OF TEACHERS [☆]

Christopher Day

ABSTRACT

In this chapter, the author, drawing on his extensive career as a researcher and teacher educator, examines variations in the work and lives of teachers and the educational backdrops with which they interact – what Ivor Goodson called the 'genealogies of context'. His work develops Michael Huberman's seminal research on the lives of secondary teachers and, in doing so, provides empirical evidence which challenges linear views of the development of teacher expertise and highlights the key roles of professional identity, commitment and school culture in career long effective and successful teaching.

Keywords: Teachers lives; identity; commitment; teacher educators

Depending on our own ontological and epistemological positioning we may believe that it is (a) the meganarratives or grand stories (Cohen & Garet, 1975) of broader performativity, results driven, contexts which determine the changes in nature, shape and direction of the new work and lives of teachers; or (b) the accumulation and persistence of what are sometimes called 'small stories' (Georgakopoulou, 2004) show that these only influence

---

[☆]The reprinting of this article from *Teacher Education Quarterly* has been authorized by the journal and the author.

From Teacher Thinking to Teachers and Teaching: The Evolution of a Research Community
Advances in Research on Teaching, Volume 19, 357–377
ISSN: 1479-3687/doi:10.1108/S1479-3687(2013)0000019020

and thus may be mediated by individual and collective agency aided by a strength of vocation, the passion of moral purpose. Some researchers position themselves in a critical sociological perspective, often using Bourdieu (1970) or Foucault (1976) as their theoretical mentors. These researchers tend to write about teachers and schools as victims of policy-driven imperatives as bureaucratic surveillance and new pervasive forms of contractual accountability which (wrongly) assume a direct causal link between good teaching, good learning and measurable student attainments persist and increase. I see research evidence of this but research evidence, also, of teachers who remain skilful, knowledgeable, committed and resilient regardless of circumstance

I subscribe to what Judyth Sachs identifies as the 'activist professional' (Sachs, 2003). By a predisposition to hope, persistence in believing that I can make a difference to the lives of those who I teach, knowledge of a range of research and by conducting research which keeps me close to teachers, for example, through a networked learning community of schools in one city in England, now about to celebrate a decade of teacher inquiry endeavours, I am persuaded that, like me, many teachers, despite some 'bumpy moments', also maintain their commitment to teach to their best across a career and in changing, sometimes challenging, circumstances. We see this in the in-depth work of Susan Moore Johnson and her colleagues (2004) with new teachers, in Nieto (2003) and Hansen's (2001) writings, in the professional learning communities reported by Ann Lieberman and Bob Bullough's recent writings of happiness, hope and hopefulness.

NEW LIVES, OLD TRUTHS

The work and lives of teachers have always been subject to external influence as those who are nearing the end of their careers will attest, but it is arguable that what is new over the last two decades is the pace, complexity and intensity of change as governments have responded to the shrinking world of economic competitiveness and social migration by measuring progress against their position in international league tables. This is in part the reason I have called this address the 'New Lives of Teachers'. Parallel to these are the growing concerns with the new generation of 'screen culture' children who, suggests one author (Greenfield, 2008), spend more time interacting with technology than with family or at school and whose attention span and sense of empathy are diminishing alongside real and potential conflicts in increasingly heterogeneous societies.

As a result, there are regularly repeated claims that teacher educators are failing to prepare their students well enough and so, as in my own country, governments promote apprenticeship models of training (not education) (Donaldson, 2011; Hobson et al., 2009; Holmes Report, 1986). 'Teach for America' is one of the models borrowed by my own current government. Schools are encouraged to become 'Teaching Schools' which buy in teacher educators, who themselves are subject to new functionalist performativity demands. In these forms of teacher education students spend most of their time in schools learning the craft of teaching but not necessarily developing their thinking, capacities for reflection and their emotional understandings; for teaching at its best is an intellectual and emotional endeavour.

In the new lives of teachers, schools and classrooms have become, for many, sites of struggle as financial self-reliance and pressure for ideological compliance have emerged as the twin realities. Externally imposed curricula, management innovations and monitoring and performance assessment systems have been introduced but have often been poorly implemented, and resulted in periods of destabilisation, increased workload, intensification of work and a crisis of professional identify for many teachers who perceive a loss of public confidence in their ability to provide a good service.

Governments seem not quite to realise the results of a range of robust, well documented research that tell us: (a) teachers' commitment to their work will increase student commitment (Bryk & Driscoll, 1988; Louis, 1998; Rosenholtz, 1989); and (b) enthusiastic teachers (who are knowledgeable and skilled) who have a sense of vocation and organisational belonging work harder to make learning more meaningful for students, even those who may be difficult or unmotivated (Day & Leithwood, 2007; Guskey & Passaro, 1994). While governments in different countries of the world have introduced reforms in different ways at different paces, change is nevertheless not optional but, it is said, is a part of the 'post-modern' condition, which requires political, organisational, economic, social and personal flexibility and responsiveness (Hargreaves, 1994). Little wonder that the post-modern condition for many teachers represents more of a threat than a challenge, or that many are confused by the paradox of decentralised systems (i.e. local decision-making responsibilities), alongside increased public scrutiny and external accountability, and the associated bureaucratic burdens.

There are many other examples worldwide and educational researchers continue to critique policy and its consequences for recruitment, quality and retention. However, it is important, having set the scene, to look more closely at what a range of research tells us about the new lives of teachers in terms of their continuing capacity to teach to their best.

Lessons from Michael Huberman's Research

More than 30 years ago, Huberman conducted a preliminary study (1978–1979) with 30 teachers followed by an extended study (1982–1985) with 160 secondary-level teachers of all subjects in Geneva and Vaud two cantons (districts) of Switzerland. Roughly two-thirds taught at lower secondary and the rest at upper secondary. There were slightly more women than men. Four 'experience groups' were chosen: 5–10 years of experience, 11–19 years of experience, 20–29 years of experience and 30–39 years of experience. During a series of 5-hour interviews, informants were asked to review their career trajectory and to see whether they could carve it up into phases or stages, each with a theme and identifiable features.

The career development 'process' that Huberman's (1995) research revealed, filled as it is with 'plateaux, discontinuities, regressions, spurts and dead ends' (p. 196), has become the touchstone for researchers in this field worldwide.

Writing in 1995 about professional careers and professional development, Huberman (1995) stated:

> The hypothesis is fairly obvious: Teachers have different aims and different dilemmas at various moments in their professional cycle, and their desires to reach out for more information, knowledge, expertise and technical competence will vary accordingly ... A core assumption here is that there will be commonalities among teachers in the sequencing of their professional lives and that one particular form of professional development may be appropriate to these shared sequences ... (p. 193)

He suggested that we:

> can begin to identify modal profiles of the teaching career and, from these, see what determines more and less 'successful' or 'satisfactory' careers ... identify the conditions under which a particular phase in the career cycle is lived out happily or miserably and, from these, put together an appropriate support structure. (Huberman, 1995, p. 194)

However, in a typical self-critical note – a characteristic worthy of the best researchers – he warned of the ways in which ontogenetic, psychological research underestimates, as he had the organisational effects and the importance (and influence) of social and historical factors. In addition, there continues to be a need to conduct empirical research on teachers' professional life trajectories in all countries, for, as he acknowledged, his own work was limited by the cultural effect of a homogeneous teaching population and did not take place in times of turbulence in teaching.

Huberman was not afraid to speak to policy-makers directly with the power of his findings:

> Minimally, sustaining professional growth seems to require manageable working conditions, opportunities – and sometimes demands – to experiment modestly without sanctions if things go awry, periodic shifts in role assignments without a corresponding loss of prerequisites, regular access to collegial expertise and external stimulation, and a reasonable chance to achieve significant outcomes in the classroom. These are not utopian conditions. It may just be the case, in fact, that they have not been met more universally because policy and administrative personnel have not deliberately attended to them. (1995b, p. 206)

Michael Huberman's research provided a springboard for much of my own and others. Until recently, however, there have been few large-scale longitudinal studies of teachers' lives and work and even those have tended to focus upon the first 0–5 year period of teaching, perhaps since this is where traditionally there has been considerable attrition (Moore Johnson, 2004). The 'VITAE' project was a four-year national mixed methods study of 300 primary and secondary teachers in 100 schools in seven regions of England who were in different phases of their professional lives (Day, Sammons, Stobart, Kington, & Gu, 2007). That study, which I was privileged to lead, was designed to investigate variations in teachers' effectiveness over their careers. Effectiveness was defined as that which was both perceived by teachers themselves and by student progress and attainment which was measured in terms of attainment results over a three-year consecutive period. It is complemented by the work of my colleagues in the International Successful School Principals Project (ISSPP), a 14 country, highly collaborative research network of researchers which now has the largest international collection of now more than 100 case studies of principals who have built and sustained success in different contexts and sectors (Day & Leithwood, 2007; Moos, Day, & Johansson, 2011); and by the findings of a national, three-year mixed methods project in England which focussed upon associations between effective school principals and pupil outcomes (Day et al., 2011). The findings of these and other recent research in this area (i.e., Robinson, Hohepa, & Lloyd, 2009) are profoundly important for their contributions to knowledge of conditions which contribute to teacher quality, retention and achievement (e.g. values, democratic leadership, collegiality, professional learning, learning communities, and forms of distributed leadership and trust) in ways which go far beyond those available to Michael Huberman.

The leadership literature tells us much about school environments in which teachers flourish and in which they are likely to sustain commitment as well as competence, a sense of well-being and positive professional identity; and teachers over the years are consistent in telling us that where they experience sustained support, both personally outside and professionally inside their workplace, they are able not only to cope with but also positively manage adverse circumstances – in other words, to be resilient.

It is this close connection between teachers' lives, their work, its contexts and its effectiveness for students and school leadership which marks the focus of my own work over the last decade in particular. 'New Lives, Old Truths', in fact, is the title of the final chapter of the second book which arose from the VITAE project. Whereas the first, 'Teachers Matter: Connecting Work, Lives and Effectiveness' (Day et al., 2007), reported on and discussed the mixed methods project design and findings about variations in teachers' perceived and measured effectiveness and the reasons for this, the second, 'The New Lives of Teachers' (Day & Gu, 2010) draws primarily upon new qualitative data drawn from the project in order to tell the stories of teachers in what my co-author, Qing Gu, and I identified as teachers' 'professional life phases' (PLPs) in order to distinguish these from career phases, a term usually associated more with role changes.

What we learnt about teachers who experience these PLPs enabled us to identify generic similarities and differences within each phase. It also allowed the identification of critical incidents or phases and, through these, provided new insights into positive and negative variations in personal, workplace and socio-cultural and policy conditions which teachers experience across a career and the consequences for teacher and students if support is not available. We found that teachers' ongoing capacities, commitment and passion to teach to their best for the benefit of their students relate to:

- professional life phase;
- the relative instability and stability of their sense of identity – so important to their sense of self-efficacy and agency; and
- a passion for teaching: commitment, well-being and effectiveness.

Professional Life Phases

We identified six professional life phases. We found that teachers' commitment, well-being, identity and effectiveness varied within and between these

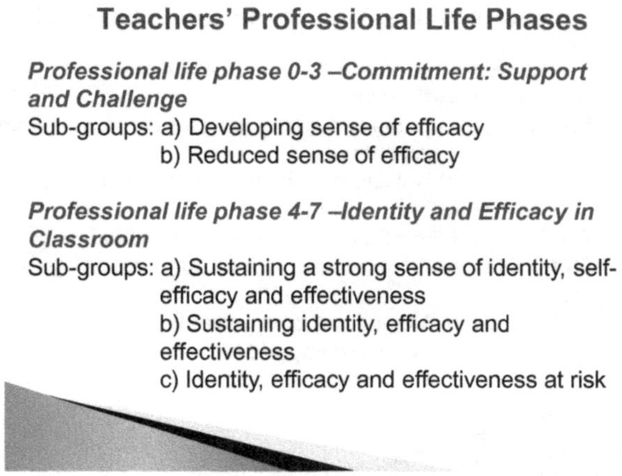

Teachers' Professional Life Phases

Professional life phase 0-3 –Commitment: Support and Challenge
Sub-groups: a) Developing sense of efficacy
b) Reduced sense of efficacy

Professional life phase 4-7 –Identity and Efficacy in Classroom
Sub-groups: a) Sustaining a strong sense of identity, self-efficacy and effectiveness
b) Sustaining identity, efficacy and effectiveness
c) Identity, efficacy and effectiveness at risk

Fig. 1. Teachers' Professional Life Phases 1–7.

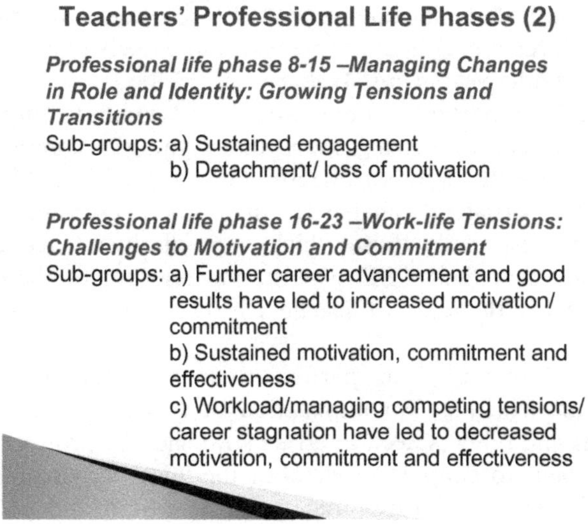

Teachers' Professional Life Phases (2)

Professional life phase 8-15 –Managing Changes in Role and Identity: Growing Tensions and Transitions
Sub-groups: a) Sustained engagement
b) Detachment/ loss of motivation

Professional life phase 16-23 –Work-life Tensions: Challenges to Motivation and Commitment
Sub-groups: a) Further career advancement and good results have led to increased motivation/commitment
b) Sustained motivation, commitment and effectiveness
c) Workload/managing competing tensions/career stagnation have led to decreased motivation, commitment and effectiveness

Fig. 2. Teachers' Professional Life Phases 8–23.

and that, within each phase, there were those whose commitment was rising, being sustained despite challenging circumstances, or declining (Figs. 1–3).

The majority of teachers in the VITAE research maintained their effectiveness but did not necessarily become more effective over time.

Teachers' Professional Life Phases (3)

Professional life phase 24-30 – Challenges to
Sustaining Motivation
Sub-groups: a) Sustained a strong sense of motivation and
                    commitment
              b) Holding on but losing motivation

Professional life phase 31+ – Sustaining/Declining
Motivation, Ability to Cope with Change, Looking to
Retire
Sub-groups: a) Maintaining commitment
              b) Tired and trapped

Fig. 3.   Teachers' Professional Life Phases 24–31+.

Indeed, we found that the commitment of teachers in late professional life phases, though remaining high for many, is more likely to decline than those in early and middle years (Fig. 4).

It is especially important to note also that the commitment and resilience of teachers in schools serving more disadvantaged communities where relational ties are the 'sources of reservoirs of resilience' (Tonnies, 2001, p. 27) are more persistently challenged than others. One implication of this is that schools, especially those which serve disadvantaged communities, need to ensure that their CPD provision is relevant to the commitment, resilience and health needs of teachers in each of their professional life phases.

Given the nature of teaching, particularly in inimical reform contexts, this is, perhaps unsurprising. An implication of this finding is that national organisations and schools need to target strategies for professional learning and development to support teachers in the later phases of their careers. Teachers will move backwards and forwards within and between phases during their working lives for all kinds of reasons concerning personal history, psychological, social and systemic change factors. Taking on a new role, changing schools, teaching a new age group or new syllabus or learning to work in new ways in the classroom will almost inevitably result in development disruption, at least temporarily. It is clear from this that there are problems, in a changing world, with assuming that the acquisition of expertise through experience marks the end of the learning journey.

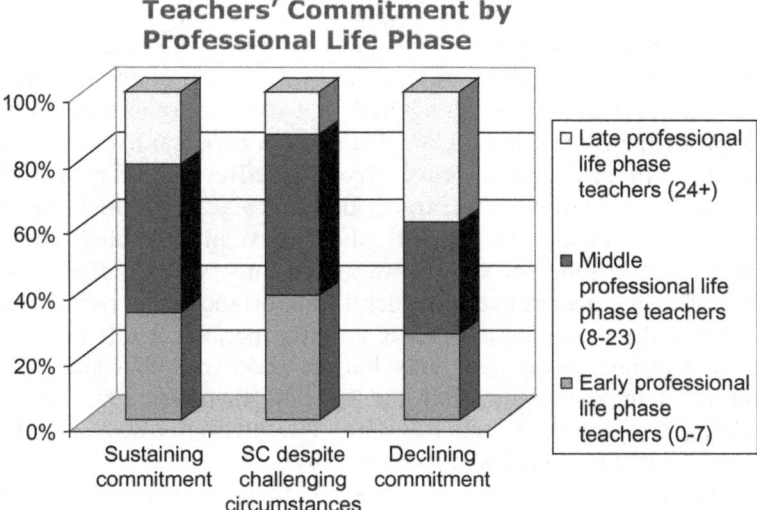

Fig. 4. Teachers' Commitment by Professional Life Phase (Day et al., 2007).

Huberman's work also provides an important in principle critique of linear, 'stage' models of professional development which ignore the complexity and dynamic of classroom life, the discontinuities of learning; and points to the importance of continuing regular and differentiated opportunities for deliberative, systematic reflection 'on' and 'about' experience as a way of locating and extending understandings of the broad and narrow contexts of teaching and learning, and reviewing and renewing commitment and capacities for effectiveness.

Becoming an expert does not mean that learning ends – hence the importance of maintaining the ability to be a lifelong inquirer. Experienced teachers who are successful, far from being at the end of their learning journeys, are those who retain their ability to be self-conscious about their teaching and are constantly aware of and responsive to the learning possibilities inherent in each teaching episode and individual interaction.

Teacher Identity: The Person in the Professional

'Being a teacher seems to involve a special relationship with other people that you don't find in most professions ...' (Trier, 2001, p. 35). Much research literature demonstrates that events and experiences in the personal lives of teachers are intimately linked to the performance of their professional roles (Ball & Goodson, 1985; Goodson & Hargreaves, 1996). In her research on the realities of teachers' work, Acker (1999) describes the considerable pressures on teaching staff, not just arising in their work but also from their personal lives. Complications in personal lives can become bound up with problems at work. Woods, Jeffrey, and Troman (1997, p. 152) and David Hansen (2011) argue, also, that teaching is fundamentally a matter of values. People teach because they believe in something. They have an image of the 'good society'. If we are to understand the new lives of teachers, then, it is necessary to consider the importance of the part the person plays within the professional. This is essential because a raft of literature points to teaching as an essentially human endeavour in which who the teacher is as important as what she teaches (Beijaard, 1995; Bullough, Knowles, & Crow, 1991; Hamachek, 1999; Kelchtermans, 2009; Korthagen, 2004; Nias, 1989; Palmer, 2007; Russell, 2007).

'(P)aying attention to the connection of the personal and the professional in teaching … may contribute to educational goals that go far beyond the development of the individual teacher' (Meijer, Korthagen, & Vasalos, 2009, p. 308). Several researchers (Hargreaves, 1994; Nias, 1989, 1996; Nias, Southworth, & Campbell, 1992; Sumsion, 2002) have also noted that teacher identities are not only constructed from the more technical aspects of teaching (i.e. classroom management, subject knowledge and pupil test results) but, as Van Den Berg (2002) explains, 'can be conceptualised as the result of an interaction between the personal experiences of teachers and the social, cultural and institutional environment in which they function on a daily basis' (p. 579).

It matters enormously what kind of person the teacher is because 'those of us who are teachers cannot stand before a class without standing for something … teaching is testimony' (Paterson, 1991, p. 16). There is, then, an unavoidable interrelationship between the personal and the professional if only because the overwhelming evidence is that teaching demands significant personal investment. So when we think of the importance to good teaching of a positive, stable identity, it is necessary to construe such identity as being made up of these elements.

Dimensions of Identity: Professional identity is influenced by biography and experience, life outside the school and reflects social and policy expectations of what a good teacher is, workplace conditions and relationships and the educational ideals of the teacher. The VITAE project found that professional identity was, for the 300 participating teachers, a composite of the interaction in different work scenarios between socio-cultural/policy, workplace and personal dimensions and that it was not always stable or positive (Day & Kington, 2008; Day et al., 2011).

Interviews with these teachers over a three-year period revealed four scenarios or sites of struggle which reflected different relationships between the three dimensions of identity:

- The first was holding the three in balance. The dominant characteristics of this group of teachers included being highly motivated, committed and self-efficacious.
- In the second scenario, one dimension was dominant, for example, immediate school demands dominating and impacting on the other two.
- In the third scenario two dimensions dominated and impacted on the third.
- The fourth scenario represented a state of extreme fluctuation within and between each dimension.

Teachers from across the professional life phases who expressed a positive sense of agency, resilience and commitment in all scenarios spoke of the influence of in-school leadership, colleague and personal support. The supporting factors mentioned most frequently by teachers who expressed a positive, stable sense of identity (67%) were:

- *Leadership* (76%). It is good to know that we have strong leadership who has a clear vision for the school (Larissa, year 6).
- *Colleagues* (63%). We have such supportive team here. Everyone works together and we have a common goal to work towards (Hermione, year 2). We all socialize together and have become friends over time. I do not know what we'd do if someone left (Leon, year 9).
- *Personal* (95%). It helps having a supportive family who do not get frustrated when I'm sat working on a Sunday afternoon and they want to go to the park (Shaun, year 9).

Teachers who judged their effectiveness to be at risk or declining (33%) spoke of negative pressures. Those mentioned most frequently were:

- *Workload* (68%). It never stops, there is always something more to do and it eats away at your life until you have no social life and no time for anything but work (Jarvis, year 6). Your life has to go on hold – there is not enough time in the school day to do everything (Hermione, year 2).
- *Student behaviour* (64%). Over the years, pupils have got worse. They have no respect for themselves or the teachers (Jenny, year 6). Pupil

behaviour is one of the biggest problems in schools today. They know their rights and there is nothing you can do (Kathryn, year 9).
- *Leadership* (58%). Unless the leadership supports the staff, you are on your own. They need to be visible and need to appreciate what teachers are doing (Carmelle, year 2). I feel as if I'm constantly being picked on and told I'm doing something wrong (Jude, year 9).

An implication of this finding is that strategies for sustaining commitment in initial and continuing professional development programs should differentiate between the needs of teachers in different phases of their professional lives and experiencing different sites of struggle which may threaten their sense of positive stable identity and sense of well-being.

A Passion for Teaching: Commitment,
Well-being and Effectiveness

A lesson from the VITAE project and a range of research internationally (Day, 2004) is that passion for teaching, a commitment to understand and educate every learner, is necessary if teachers are to teach to their best, but that this may grow or die according to changes in personal and work circumstances. Being passionate about others' learning and achievement creates energy and fuels determination, conviction and commitment. Yet passion should not be regarded only as a disposition – people are not born, nor do they die, passionate. Whilst many teachers enter the profession with a sense of vocation and with a passion to give their best to the learning and growth of their pupils, for some, these become diminished with the passage of time, changing external and internal working conditions and contexts and unanticipated personal events. They lose their sense of purpose and well-being which are so intimately connected with their positive sense of professional identity and which enable them to draw upon, deploy and manage the inherently dynamic emotionally vulnerable contexts of teaching in which they teach and in which their pupils learn.

Without organisational support, bringing a passionate and resilient self to teaching effectively every day of every week of every school term and year can be stressful not only to the body but also to the heart and soul, for the processes of teaching and learning are rarely smooth, and the results are not always predictable. Thus, the commitment, hope and optimism with which many teachers still enter the profession, unless supported within the school, may be eroded over time as managing combinations of low level disruption from those who don't wish to learn or cannot, or interfere with others' opportunities to learn, increasing media criticisms and lack of work–life balance take their toll on professional well-being.

Teacher well-being is both a psychological and social construct, '… a dynamic state, in which the individual is able to develop their potential, work productively and creatively, build strong and positive relationships with others, and contribute to their community' (Foresight Mental Capital and Wellbeing Project, 2008, p. 10). To achieve and sustain a healthy state of well-being, teachers need to manage successfully a range of cognitive and emotional challenges in different, sometimes difficult sites of struggle which vary according to life experiences and events, the strength of relationships with pupils and parents, the conviction of educational ideals, sense of efficacy and agency and the support of colleagues and school leadership. As Moore Johnson (2004) reminds us, '… anyone familiar with schools knows that stories about the easy job of teaching are sheer fiction. Good teaching is demanding and exhausting work, even in the best of work places …' (2004, p. 10).

Experience and research, then, suggest that, in terms of nurturing well-being, a dichotomy between promoting technical competence and personal growth among teachers is a false economy. Rather, teachers at their best combine their professional craft expertise with their personal commitment, experience and values in their work in the knowledge that teaching cannot be devoid from an interest in and engagement with the learner. In other words, it is the extent to which both learner, teacher and teaching content are all fully 'present' which will influence, in interaction with the internal and external environments, the quality of the process and its results. This journey of the personal and the professional in the here and now of teaching is what Csikszentmihalyi (1990) calls 'flow' and Rodgers and Raider-Roth (2006) term, 'presence', '(p)resence from the teacher's point of view is the experience of bringing one's whole self to full attention so as to perceive what is happening the moment' (Rodgers & Raider-Roth, 2006, p. 267).

Many writers on teacher education focus on the role and presence of the teacher in the classroom (Meijer et al., 2009), emphasising the need for personal strengths or core qualities such as care, courage, fairness, kindness, honesty, perseverance (Fredrickson, 2002; Noddings, 2003; Palmer, 2004; Seligman, 2002; Sockett, 1993). Others have combined this with research on the nature, purposes and forms of reflection in, on and about education (Schön, 1983), and developed humanistic pedagogies of teacher education which emphasise the importance to good teaching practice of understanding and interrogating teachers' own belief systems (Loughran, 2004) and the interchange between these teaching contexts and purposes (Korthagen & Vasalos, 2005).

Teacher presence, whilst a necessary condition for successful teaching, is, however, not sufficient to achieve optimal learning. Students themselves must also be willing and able to be present. At this point, it is worth once again bringing to the attention of policy-makers the observation that there is no necessary direct cause and effect relationship between high quality teaching and student learning (Fenstermacher & Richardson, 2005).

Five key observations about the qualities evident in good teaching and teachers have been made by researchers across the world:

- Good teaching is recognised by its combination of technical and personal competencies, deep subject knowledge and empathy with the learners (Hargreaves 1998; Palmer, 1998). Teachers as people (the person in the professional, the being within the action) cannot be separated from teachers as professionals (Nias, 1989). Teachers invest themselves in their work. Teaching at its best, in other words, is a passionate affair (Day, 2004).
- Good teachers are universally identified by students as those who care. They care for them as part of their exercise of their professional duty and their care about them is shown in the connectiveness of their everyday classroom interactions as well as their concern for their general well-being and achievement (Ashley & Lee, 2003; Fletcher-Campbell, 1995; Noddings, 1992).
- Teachers' sense of identity and agency (the means by which they respond, reflect upon and manage the interface between their educational ideals, beliefs, work environments and broader social and policy contexts) are crucial to their own motivation, commitment, well-being and capacity to teach to their best. It is how they define themselves as 'teacher' (Day & Lee, 2011; Schutz & Zembylas, 2009).
- The extent to which teachers are able to understand emotions within themselves and others is related to their ability to lead and manage teaching and learning. Good teaching, 'requires the connection of emotion with self-knowledge' (Denzin, 1984; Harris, 2007; Zembylas, 2003, p. 213).
- To be a good and effective teacher over time requires hopefulness and resilience, the ability to manage and lead in challenging circumstances and changing contexts (Bullough, 2011; Day & Gu, 2010; Gu & Day, 2007).

THE ROLE OF TEACHER EDUCATOR RESEARCHERS

Finally, I want to grasp a difficult nettle which continues to be a source of discussion in universities and colleges. It concerns the role, influence and impact of teacher educators who are also researchers as part of their commitment to learning. In his paper in *Teacher Education Quarterly* Bob Bullough (2008) wrote that in the current political context, researchers have, as Goodson (1992) earlier argued, a special obligation: 'to assure that the teacher's voice is heard, heard loudly, heard articulately' (p. 112). It would be difficult not to agree with Bob Bullough that, '... At this moment in time, as we research teachers' lives there may be no more important task before us than championing the cause of teachers and making clear the ineluctable connection between their well-being and the well-being of children' (Bullough, 2008, p. 23).

However, in involving ourselves in research with teachers and schools, as university researcher educators and researchers we also need appropriate competencies:

> ... the competence to cross borders, cultures and dialects, the learning and translating of multiple languages (the political, the everyday, the academic) and the courage to transgress when faced with social injustices ... How we practice our authority is then the issue, not what we claim or profess: if we believe in something then we have to practice it. (Walker, 1996, pp. 407–425)

Finley's (2005) metaphor of 'border crossings', together with Tony Becher's (1989) metaphor of 'tribes and territories' provide vivid illustrations of the persisting separation cultures both between university researchers and between researchers and teachers. In addition, the environments in which teachers teach and in which our research is conducted have become more problematic. So-called neo liberal, 'performativity', results driven agendas have invaded and changed our worlds of work, threatening hard won and treasured practices and professional identities. In academia, we see this especially through the creeping erosion of time to conduct research, as bureaucratic procedures continue to increase; through the rise of research funding which is tied to short-term government agendas in some countries; and, in others, the imposition of national research assessment exercises associated with league tables and increases or decreases in finance, social citation indexes and judgements of research worthiness based upon evidence of impact on the user communities.

The implications of drawing lines of separation between policy-makers, professional researchers (from the academy) and 'other' researchers (in schools) without considering their complementarity and respective development need to be carefully considered, lest continuing separation does a disservice to all. The evidence still points to a lack of use by teachers of much research where they themselves have not been involved in the research process. We know well that, 'the gap between educational research and practice is a more complex and differentiated phenomenon than commonly assumed in the international literature' (Vanderlinde & van Broak, 2010, pp. 311–312).

The separation between the school teaching, policy-making and academic communities which exists partly because of history, partly because of function and partly because of collusion *need not continue*. Worlds which emphasise the systematic gathering of knowledge, the questioning and challenge of ideology, formal examination of experience, professional criticism and seemingly endless discussion of possibilities rather than solutions, need not necessarily conflict with those dominated by unexamined ideology, action, concrete knowledge and busyness. Although it is interesting to observe that as researchers from universities and other agencies seek to work more closely with teachers and schools, policy formulation becomes more distant, there are examples of growing understandings of the possibilities for their complementarity. Research needs to be more open, more amenable to those interest groups which seek to influence policy. Part of higher education's responsibility is to use our 'room to manoeuvre', to critique policy where it flies in the face of research, to be rigorous in our own research, whether separate from or in collaboration with teachers; and to communicate with rather than colonise the voices of practitioners. In order to do this we need to maintain and develop critical engagement with policy-makers, interest groups and practitioners.

Ball and Forzani (2007) claim that:

> At the center of every school of education must be scholars with the expertise and commitment necessary to study educational transactions ... (and that) ... if they do not work actively to disseminate that knowledge among policy makers and members of the public, then educational problem solving will be left to researchers and professionals without the requisite expertise ... Educational researchers must also arm themselves with the special analytical skills that will allow them to usefully bridge the alleged divide between theory and practice. It is along this divide that educational researchers have special expertise. (p. 537)

Essentially, Ball and Forzani are identifying what we call in England, 'the elephant in the room', something so obvious that we often overlook its huge importance. In this case, there are two elephants: researcher independence and moral purpose. Whilst all of us would support Ivor Goodson's articulation of the researcher as independent, 'a public intellectual, not a servant of the state' (Goodson, 1999), I would argue that alongside independence is moral purpose, a sense of deep responsibility of contributing to the 'betterment' of society though our work on, about, with and for teachers. As researchers, we do need to acknowledge what research tells us about ourselves, our endeavours and our influence (or lack of it). There are sceptics among teachers and policy-makers – and even researchers of different ontological and epistemological dispositions – about the intrinsic value of research and about its relevance, language and applicability. However, there are also examples of research which do lead to greater educational understandings, influence policy and practice, and ultimately, make a difference to the contexts and quality of teachers' and childrens' experiences in schools and classrooms.

No single model of research will necessarily be best fitted to bridge the gap. However, whether research is constructed and conducted primarily for the purpose of furthering understanding or for more direct influence on policy-makers and practitioners, whether it is on, about or for education, the obligation of all researchers is to reflect upon our broader moral purposes and measure the worth of our work against their judgement of the extent to which we are able to realise this as we continue to develop our work.

THE CHALLENGE TO BE THE BEST

The challenge for university faculties, schools and departments of education, then, is to engage in strategic planning in which our capacity to respond to schools' agendas as well as to take forward those of the academy can be heightened. In developing new kinds of relationships with schools and teachers, we will be demonstrating a service-wide commitment in which traditional expertise (e.g. in research and knowledge production) is combined with new expertise in cooperative and collaborative knowledge creation, development and consultancy that are part of a more diverse portfolio that connects more closely with the needs of the school community at large. Such a portfolio would demonstrate the commitment of university educators to improving teaching and learning in collaboration with schools and teachers through capacity-building partnerships through, for example, participatory forms of research, in addition to an ongoing commitment to producing knowledge about education and generating knowledge for education (Carr & Kemmis, 1986), through more traditional forms of outsider research which could be utilised and tested by the system for which it has been produced, both directly and indirectly. Currently perceived problems of credibility, relevance of research and fitness for purpose of programmes of study would thus be minimised.

The challenge to be the best, then, not only applies to teachers, but also to us as researchers whose work aims to further understandings of their work and lives in their personal, work place and policy-related contexts and, in some cases, to influence them. To be the best ourselves requires us to be partisan (we are for teachers) but dispassionate, to be both close up and distant to our work and, like teachers at their best, to monitor and reflect on the efficacy, processes and impact of our work upon the policy and practice communities we seek to influence. Like Michael Huberman, to whom the work of all who are engaged in research on the work and lives of teachers owes a lasting debt, I urge us all to be active always in checking out and giving voice to the connections, at all levels, between policy, research and practice, and most of all to become and remain, with integrity and passion, as he was and I remain, 'recklessly curious'.

REFERENCES

Acker, S. (1999). *The realities of teachers' work: Never a dull moment*. London: Cassell.
Ashley, M., & Lee, J. (2003). *Women teaching boys: Caring and working in the primary school*. Stoke on Trent: Trenthan Books.
Ball, D. L., & Forzani, F. M. (2007). What makes education research "educational?" *Educational Researcher*, 36(9), 529–540.
Ball, S. J., & Goodson, I. (1985). *Teachers' lives and careers*. Lewes: Falmer Press.
Becher, T. (1989). *Academic tribes and territories. Intellectual enquiry and the cultures of disciplines*. Milton Keynes: The Society for Research into Higher Education and Open University Press.
Beijaard, D. (1995). Teachers' prior experiences and actual perceptions of professional identity. *Teachers and Teaching: Theory and Practice*, 1, 281–294.
Bourdieu, P. (1970). *La Reproduction. Elements pour une th~orie du syst~me d'enseignement* (Paris, Editions de iinuit) (with J. C. Passeron). *Reproduction in education, society, and culture* (1977, R. Nice, Trans.) (2nd ed., 1990, with a new preface by Bourdieu). London: Sage.
Bryk, A., & Driscoll, M. (1988). *The high school as community: Contextual influences and consequences for students and teachers*. Madison, WI: University of Wisconsin, National Center on Effective Secondary Schools.
Bullough, R. V. (2008). The writing of teachers' lives – Where personal troubles and social issues meet. *Teacher Education Quarterly*, 35(4), 7–26.
Bullough, R. V. (2011). Hope, happiness, teaching and learning. In C. Day & J. C. K. Lee (Eds.), *New understandings of teacher's work: Emotions and educational change* (pp. 17–32). New York, NY: Springer.

Bullough, R. V., Jr., Knowles, J. G., & Crow, N. A. (1991). *Emerging as a teacher*. London: Routledge.

Carr, W., & Kemmis, S. (1986). *Becoming critical. Education, knowledge and action research*. Lewes: Falmer Press.

Cohen, D. K., & Garet, M. S. (1975). Reforming educational policy with applied social research. *Harvard Educational Review, 45*(1), 17–43.

Csikszentmihalyi, M. (1990). *Flow: The psychology of optimal experience*. New York, NY: Harper & Row.

Day, C. (2004). *A passion for teaching*. London: Routledge Falmer.

Day, C., & Gu, Q. (2010). *The new lives of teachers*. London: Routledge.

Day, C., & Lee, J. C. K. (Eds.). (2011). *New understandings of teacher's work: Emotions and educational change*. London: Springer.

Day, C., & Leithwood, K. (Eds.). (2007). *Successful principal leadership in times of change: International perspectives*. Dordrecht: Springer.

Day, C., & Kington, A. (2008). Identity, well-being and effectiveness: The emotional contexts of teaching. *Pedagogy, Culture & Society, 16*(1), 7–23.

Day, C., Sammons, P., Leithwood, K., Hopkins, D., Gu, Q., Brown, E., & Ahtaridou, E. (2011). *School leadership and student outcomes: Building and sustaining success*. Maidenhead: Open University Press.

Day, C., Sammons, P., Stobart, G., Kington, A., & Gu, Q. (2007). *Teachers matter: Connecting lives, work and effectiveness*. New York, NY: McGraw Hill.

Denzin, N. (1984). *On understanding emotion*. San Francisco, CA: Jossey-Bass.

Donaldson, G. (2011). *Teaching Scotland's future: Report of a review of teacher education in Scotland*. Edinburgh: The Scottish Government.

Fenstermacher, G. D., & Richardson, V. (2005). On making determinations of quality in teaching. *Teachers College Record, 107*(1), 186–213.

Finley, A. (2005). Arts-based inquiry: Performing revolutionary pedagogy. In N. K. Denzin & Y. S. Lincoln (Eds.), *Handbook of qualitative inquiry* (3rd ed., pp. 681–694). Thousand Oaks, CA: Sage.

Fletcher-Campbell, F. (1995). Caring about caring? *Pastoral Care*, September, pp. 26–28.

Foresight Mental Capital and Wellbeing Project. (2008). *Final project report*. London: The Government Office for Science.

Foucault, M. (1976). *The history of sexuality: The will to knowledge* (Vol. 1). London: Penguin Books.

Fredrickson, B. L. (2002). Positive emotions. In C. R. Snyder & S. J. Lopez (Eds.), *Handbook of positive psychology* (pp. 120–134). Oxford: Oxford University Press.

Georgakopoulou, A. (2004, May). *Narrative analysis workshop: How to work with narrative data*. Paper presented at Narrative Matters 2004: An interdisciplinary conference on narrative perspectives, approach, and issues across the humanities and social sciences, Fredericton, New Brunswick, Canada.

Goodson, I. F. (1992). Life histories and the study of schooling. *Interchange, 11*(4), 62–76.

Goodson, I. (1999). The educational researcher as a public intellectual. *British Educational Research Journal, 25*(3), 277–297.

Goodson, I., & Hargreaves, A. (Eds.). (1996). *Teachers' professional lives*. London: Falmer Press.

Greenfield, S. (2008). *Autonomy, creativity and social relationships in early learning*, Researcher-Practitioner Seminar, Oxford Brookes University.

Gu, Q., & Day, C. (2007). Teachers' resilience: A necessary condition for effectiveness. *Teaching and Teacher Education, 23*(8), 1302–1316.

Guskey, T. R., & Passaro, P. D. (1994). Teacher efficacy: A study of construct dimensions. *American Educational Research Journal, 31*(3), 627–643.

Hamachek, D. (1999). Effective teachers: What they do, how they do it, and the importance of self-knowledge. In R. P. Lipka & T. M. Brinthaupt (Eds.), *The role of self in teacher development* (pp. 189–224). Albany, NY: State University of New York Press.

Hansen, D. (2011). *Teacher and the world: A study of cosmopolitanism as education.* London: Routledge.

Hansen, D. T. (2001). *Exploring the moral heart of teaching: Toward a teacher's creed.* New York, NY: Teachers College Press.

Hargreaves, A. (1998). The emotional practice of teaching. *Teaching and Teacher Education, 14*(8), 835–854.

Hargreaves, D. H. (1994). The New Professionalism: The synthesis of professional and institutional development. *Teaching and Teacher Education, 10*(4), 423–438.

Harris, B. (2007). *Supporting the emotional work of school leaders.* London: Sage.

Hobson, A., Malderez, A., Tracey, L., Homer, M., Ashby, P., Mitchell, N., … Tomlinson, P. (2009). *Becoming a teacher: Final report.* London: Department for Children, Schools and Families.

Holmes Group. (1986). *Tomorrow's teachers: A report of the Holmes Group.* East Lansing, MI: Holmes Group.

Huberman, M. (1995). Networks that alter teaching. *Teachers and Teaching: Theory and Practice, 1*(2), 193–221.

Kelchtermans, G. (2009). Career stories as gateways to understanding teacher development. In M. Bayer, U. Brinkkjaer, H. Plauborg & S. Rolls (Eds.), *Teachers' career trajectories and work lives* (pp. 29–47). London: Springer.

Korthagen, F. A. (2004). In search of the essence of a good teacher: Towards a more holistic approach in teacher education. *Teaching and Teacher Education, 20*, 77–97.

Korthagen, F., & Vasalos, A. (2005). Levels in reflection: Core reflection as a means to enhance professional growth. *Teachers and Teacher Education, 19*, 787–800.

Loughran, J. J. (2004). Learning through self-study. In J. J. Loughran, M. L. Hamilton, V. K. LaBoskey & T. L. Russell (Eds.), *The international handbook of self-study of teaching and teacher education practices* (Vols. 1 & 2, pp. 151–192). Dordrecht: Kluwer Academic Publishers.

Louis, K. S. (1998). Effects of teacher quality worklife in secondary schools on commitment and sense of efficacy. *School Effectiveness and School Improvement, 9*(1), 1–27.

Meijer, P. C., Korthagen, F. A. J., & Vasalos, A. (2009). Supporting presence in teacher education: The connection between the personal and professional aspects of teaching. *Teaching and Teacher Education, 23*(2), 297–308.

Moore Johnson, S. (2004). *Finders and keepers: Helping new teachers survive and thrive in our schools.* San Francisco, CA: Wiley.

Moos, L., Day, C., & Johansson, O. (Eds.). (2011). *How school principals sustain success over time: International perspectives.* Dordrecht: Springer.

Nieto, S. (2003). *What keeps teachers going?* New York, NY: Teachers College Press.

Nias, J. (1989). *Primary teachers talking: A study of teaching as work.* London: Routledge.

Nias, J. (1996). Thinking about feeling: The emotions in teaching. *Cambridge Journal of Education, 26*(3), 293–306.

Nias, J., Southworth, G., & Campbell, P. (1992). *Whole school curriculum development in primary schools*. London: Falmer Press.

Noddings, N. (1992). *The challenge to care in schools*. New York, NY: Teachers College Press.

Noddings, N. (2003). *Happiness and education*. New York, NY: Cambridge University Press.

Palmer, P. J. (1998). *The courage to teach: Exploring the inner landscape of a teachers' life*. San Francisco, CA: Jossey-Bass.

Palmer, P. (2004). *A hidden wholeness*. San Francisco, CA: Jossey-Bass.

Palmer, P. (2007). *The courage to teach: Exploring the inner landscape of a teacher's life*. San Francisco, CA: Wiley.

Paterson, L. J. (1991). *An evaluation of the Scottish pilot projects in the Technical and Vocational Education Initiative*. Edinburgh: Centre for Educational Sociology, University of Edinburgh.

Robinson, V., Hohepa, M., & Lloyd, C. (2009). *School leadership and student outcomes: Identifying what works and why. Best Evidence Synthesis Iteration (BES)*. Auckland, New Zealand: New Zealand Ministry of Education.

Rodgers, F. R., & Raider-Roth, M. B. (2006). Presence in teaching. *Teachers and Teaching: Theory and Practice, 12*(3), 265–287.

Rosenholtz, S. J. (1989). *Teachers' workplace: The social organization of schools*. New York, NY: Longman.

Russell, T. (2007). How experience changed my values as a teacher educator. In T. Russell & J. Loughran (Eds.), *Enacting a pedagogy of teacher education: Values, relationships and practices* (pp. 182–191). London: Routledge Falmer.

Sachs, J. (2003). *The activist teaching profession*. Buckingham: Open University Press.

Schön, D. A. (1983). *The reflective practitioner*. London: Jossey-Bass.

Schutz, P. A., & Zembylas, M. (Eds.). (2009). *Advances in teacher emotion research: The impact on teachers' lives*. London: Springer.

Seligman, M. (2002). *Authentic happiness*. New York, NY: Free Press.

Sockett, H. (1993). *The moral base for teacher professionalism*. New York, NY: Teachers College Press.

Sumsion, J. (2002). Becoming, being and unbecoming an early childhood educator: A phenomenological case study of teacher attrition. *Teaching and teacher education, 18*(7), 869–885.

Tonnies, F. (2001). *Community and civil society*. Cambridge: Cambridge University Press.

Trier, J. D. (2001). The cinematic representation of the personal and professional lives of teachers. *Teacher Education Quarterly, 28*(3), 127–142.

Van Den Berg, R. (2002). Teacher's meanings regarding educational practice. *Review of Educational Research, 72*(4), 577–625.

Vanderlinde, R., & van Broak, J. (2010). The gap between educational research and practice: Views of teachers, school leaders, intermediaries and researchers. *British Educational Research Journal, 36*(2), 299–316.

Walker, P. J. (1996). Taking students by surprise: Some ideas on the art of inspiring students. *New Academic, 5*, 12–16.

Woods, P., Jeffrey, B., & Troman, G. (1997). *Restructuring schools, reconstructing teachers*. Buckingham: Open University Press.

Zembylas, M. (2003). Emotional teacher identity: A post structural perspective. *Teachers and Teaching: Theory and Practice, 9*(3), 213–238.

CHAPTER 18

WHO I AM IN HOW I TEACH IS THE MESSAGE: SELF-UNDERSTANDING VULNERABILITY, AND REFLECTION[☆]

Geert Kelchtermans

ABSTRACT

The person of the teacher is an essential element in what constitutes professional teaching and therefore needs careful conceptualisation. In this chapter the author argues for this central thesis, presenting a wrap up of his theoretical and empirical work on the issue over the past decade. These studies have been inspired – both conceptually and methodologically – by teacher thinking-research as well as the narrative-biographical approach to teaching and teacher development. The result is an empirically grounded conceptual framework on teacher development and teacher professionalism. Central concepts are 'professional self-understanding' and 'subjective educational theory' as components of the personal interpretative framework every individual teacher develops throughout his/her career. This personal framework results from the reflective and

☆This article was first published in 2009, in *Teachers and Teaching: Theory and Practice*, *15*(2), 257–272. Reprinted with permission from the publisher, Taylor & Francis Ltd, www.tandfonline.com.

From Teacher Thinking to Teachers and Teaching: The Evolution of a Research Community
Advances in Research on Teaching, Volume 19, 379–401
ISSN: 1479-3687/doi:10.1108/S1479-3687(2013)0000019021

meaningful interactions between the individual teacher and the social, cultural and structural working conditions constituting his/her job context(s). As such the framework is the dynamic outcome of an ongoing process of professional learning (development). Furthermore, it is argued that the particular professionalism or scholarship of teachers is fundamentally characterised by personal commitment and vulnerability, which eventually have consequences for the kind of reflective attitudes and skills professional teachers should master.

Keywords: Teaching; professional practice; self-understanding; subjective theory; emotions in teaching

> Ring the bells that still can ring
> Forget your perfect offering
> There is a crack in everything
> That's how the light gets in
>
> – L. Cohen, 'Anthem'

TEACHING AS ENACTMENT OF SCHOLARSHIP

The debate about the qualification of the teaching job is not new. In the past, several authors have argued that teaching was a 'profession', or at least a 'semi-profession', whereas others contended that it was more appropriate to conceive of teaching as a 'craft' (i.e., Pratte & Rury, 1991). And recently Loughran and Russell (2007) have held a plea to understand teaching as a discipline in its own right. At least two issues become apparent in these discussions. On the one hand, the question of the social status of teaching, and more in particular, the social and public acknowledgement that what teaching contributes to the community (society) is important, and that the ability to enact this demands the mastery of a particular set of knowledge, skills and attitudes. Although this qualification may sound to educationalists a mere sociological concern of classification, it is of course not without importance whether teaching is recognised as socially important and grounded in a particular form of expertise. The social status of a job has immediate consequences for the recruitment of student teachers, the retention of experienced teachers, but also for the way policy makers treat the field (Kelchtermans, 2007a). Think for example of the policy on scripted curricula and teacher proof materials in parts of the United States, as an exponent of the belief that the teacher as such doesn't really matter and can be replaced by strict instructions, behavioural performance, standards for output and quality control. An illustration of the dramatic consequences of this policy can be found in Achinstein and Ogawa (2006).

The second – educationally more challenging – issue in the debate is the question about what makes up the content of that particular discipline or profession. If a particular kind of expertise – knowledge, skills and attitudes – is needed to teach, what are they and how are they developed? And what do they imply for the person who enacts them?

In this chapter, I will limit myself to one element in the answer to that question, namely the fact that teaching is done by somebody. Teaching is an act, or teaching is enacted by someone. It matters who the teacher is. 'The teacher as a person is held by many within the profession and outside it to be at the centre of not only the classroom but also the educational process. By implication, therefore, it matters to teachers themselves, as well as to their pupils, who and what they are. Their self-image is more important to them as practitioners than is the case in occupations where the person can easily be separated from the craft' (Nias, 1989, pp. 202–203). So, the importance of the sense of self to the teaching job is far from a new idea and may even sound like stating the obvious. Yet, exactly because of its almost self-evident and taken for granted character, any attempt to conceptualise teaching needs to include a concept of the teacher as a person or his/her sense of self.

Before developing the issue of the teachers' self, two remarks need to be made. Firstly, although I emphasise in this chapter the person of the teachers, that doesn't change my more fundamental conception of teaching being an inter-personal and relational endeavour. Teaching implies a relationship of responsibility for a group of pupils or students. And to take up the image of the classic 'didactic triangle', teaching involves also the subject matter, the curriculum. It is against the background of this general frame – the triangular relationship of teacher, students and curriculum – that my arguments on teachers' sense of self need to be understood.

Secondly, I do subscribe to the project of acknowledging the particular expertise that is enacted in teaching and thus constitutes the professional quality of teachers and teaching. Rather than speaking about a 'discipline of teaching', I prefer the image in what Loughran (2006), following Shulman (1999), labels as 'scholarship of teaching'. This scholarship – he argues – rests on at least three key attributes: becoming public; becoming an object of critical review and evaluation of the members of that community; and, members of that community beginning to use, build upon and develop those acts of mind and creation (see also Loughran, 2006, p. 81).

This perspective of scholarship may keep us from getting stuck in the pitfall of individualism and a romantic over-emphasising of idiosyncrasy. At the same time it defines an agenda for (student) teachers to work on, in order to develop and improve that scholarship.

As such the scholarship refers on the one hand to a system of know-how that is or can be shared among the professionals in the field, and on the other hand to the particular professionalism of individual teachers (as the 'enacter' of that scholarship). After explaining briefly the two research traditions that have inspired my research, I will elaborate on the central concepts of self-understanding and subjective educational theory, as the domains in teachers' personal interpretative framework. This conceptual clarification brings me to a discussion of the commitment and vulnerability that characterise teaching and teachers, all of which has consequences for the way teacher professional development and more in particular the reflective attitudes and skills in it are to be understood.

HOW I TEACH IS THE MESSAGE

Thinking of teaching as an act automatically implies its observation by others. More than three decades ago Lortie (1975) coined the term 'apprenticeship of observation' to capture the fact that the teaching act is always being watched and experienced by students. In other words, the experience of 'being taught' implies complex processes of sense-making. In the students' experience, the teaching can be engaging or rather boring, challenging or repetitive, etc. Its meaning for the learners is never fully predictable, nor are the outcomes of the process. Furthermore, teaching implies visibility and thus – to quote another image from Lortie – is like 'living in a fishbowl' (Lortie, 1975). This visibility reflects the relational and interactive nature of teaching. One's actions while teaching are being looked at, evaluated and made sense of.

In line with this, Russell (1997) has argued that 'how I teach is the message' constitutes a central principle in the pedagogy of teacher education. In my reading, the principle firstly refers to the issue of credibility: if one wants student teachers to accept, 'believe' and thus understand what is being taught, the way this message is transferred to them is critical for its credibility ('teach as you preach'). Secondly, however, the principle also implies that for student teachers it is not only important to rationally see and understand the message that is conveyed, but also to personally experience what particular forms of teaching actually do to them as learners. The awareness and analysis of those experiences adds to their developing insights in the learning processes that take place in learners/ students and thus enhances their skill of getting into their students' skin while teaching (empathy), anticipating the possible impact of their teaching acts on learners.

In my opinion, however, the argument still needs to be taken a step further. Implicit in the claim 'how I teach is the message' is the acknowledgement of teaching as a relational, social and public act. The teacher (educator) wants to be seen by the students in a particular way, but at the same time his/her ideas about him/herself as a teacher (educator) are influenced by what others – in this case their students – think about him/her. The way teachers understand themselves as teachers thus matters, yet this to a large extent is influenced by how others see him/her or what others say about him/her as a teacher (educator). That's why I want to argue that 'who I am in how I teach is the message'. And that's why a teacher's self-understanding is of key importance in the scholarship of teaching.

TAKING A NARRATIVE-BIOGRAPHICAL APPROACH

My research on teachers, their learning and growth throughout their career (starting with initial teacher education), has been strongly influenced by the so-called 'teacher thinking' research and the tradition of biographical and narrative approaches in social and educational research.

Since the mid-1980s of last century, research on teachers and teaching has become strongly influenced by the developments in cognitive psychology and more in particular the growing understanding how people's actions are influenced by their cognitions. In order to understand (but also to influence or train) teachers' actions, one needs to identify and analyse their 'thinking' (cognitive processes and representations) (i.e., Clark & Peterson, 1986). This 'teacher thinking' research developed into different strands of research and methodologies. One of them was the narrative approach (Carter & Doyle, 1996; Casey, 1995–1996; Clandinin, 2006; Gudmundsdottir, 2001). Since 'narrative is the discourse structure in which human action receives its form and through which it is meaningful' (Polkinghorne, 1988, p. 135), narratives were considered to be a powerful way to unravel and understand the complex processes of sense-making that constitute teaching.

Teachers' talking about their professional lives and practices is very often spontaneously framed in narrative form. They use anecdotes, metaphors, images and other types of storytelling to recall, share, exchange or account for their experiences in classrooms and schools. Storytelling is the natural way through which people make sense of the events, situations and encounters they find themselves in: 'Humans are storytelling organisms who, individually and socially, lead storied lives. The study of narrative, therefore, is the study of the ways humans experience the world' (Connelly & Clandinin, 1990, p. 2; see also Clandinin, 2006).

A different research tradition (mainly in sociology and anthropology), that became intertwined with these narrative developments in research on teaching, is the *biographical perspective* (i.e., Goodson, 1984, 1992; Krüger & Marotzki, 1996). Central to this approach is the idea that human existence is fundamentally characterised by temporality. People have a personal history. Their life develops in time, between birth and death. Interpretations, thoughts and actions in the present are influenced by experiences from the past and expectations for the future.

Building on this tradition, as well as the narrative turn in the teacher thinking-research (Elbaz, 2006), I developed a cycle of biographical interviews, aimed at stimulating teachers to recall the experiences throughout their career and eventually resulting in the reconstruction of their career stories (or professional biographies) (Kelchtermans, 1994). Over the last two decades I have used this method to collect data from teachers in different stages of their careers (student teachers, new teachers, experienced teachers, nearly retired teachers) or in different positions in schools (principals, remedial teachers, ...) (see also Kelchtermans, 1993, 1999, 2005; Kelchtermans & Ballet, 2002a, 2002b). These narrative-biographical data were the basis for my interpretative reconstruction of these teachers' thinking about themselves and their teaching and eventually resulted in the theoretical frame on teachers' professional development that I am presenting below.

PERSONAL INTERPRETATIVE FRAMEWORK: SELF-UNDERSTANDING AND SUBJECTIVE EDUCATIONAL THEORY

Based on my narrative-biographical research, I have argued that throughout their careers teachers develop a *personal interpretative framework*: a set of cognitions, of mental representations that operates as a lens through which teachers look at their job, give meaning to it and act in it. This framework thus guides their interpretations and actions in particular situations (context), but is at the same time also modified by and resulting from these meaningful interactions (sense-making) with that context. As such it is both a *condition for and a result of* the interaction, and represents the – always preliminary – 'mental sediment' of teachers' learning and developing over time.

The metaphor of a *pair of glasses* provides a good way to capture its constructive, interactionist, dynamic, contextualised and narrative nature. People who wear glasses are most of the time not consciously aware that they do so. If the glasses provide a clear view or fit correctly, one tends to forget about them. However, when one's perceptions become hazy or when the frame starts to irritate or – even more importantly – when others comment that the frame is out-dated, then one becomes aware of the glasses, of the way they 'frame' reality and thus influence what one sees and how one is 'seen' (evaluated, appreciated) by others. This awareness then triggers a response, including a critical examination of the lenses (or better of one's eyes in order to adapt the lenses) or eventually going to get a new frame. All of these actions are often afterwards commented on in vivid stories, for example elicited by others' comments on how nicely the new frame fits, how 'cool' one looks ... In a similar way the developments in the personal interpretative framework of teachers can be looked at. Within the framework two different, yet interconnected domains need to be distinguished: the personal self-understanding and the subjective educational theory.

The Professional Self-Understanding

The first domain in the personal interpretative framework of teachers is their conception of themselves as teachers. Nias was right when she observed and labelled teachers' 'persistent self-referentialism': the fact that when talking about their professional actions and activities, teachers cannot but speak about themselves (Nias, 1989, p. 5). And as such their sense of self is very prominent in their accounts about their practice (a practice enacted by them as singular person). This again reflects and illustrates the interpersonal character of teaching and its impact on the sense of self teachers develop. I have, however, purposefully avoided the notion of 'identity' because of its association with a static essence, implicitly ignoring or denying its dynamic and biographical nature. Instead I have used the word '*self-understanding*'. The term refers to both the understanding one has of one's 'self' at a certain moment in time (*product*), as well as to the fact that this product results from an ongoing *process* of making sense of one's experiences and their impact on the 'self'. By stressing the narrative nature the possible essentialist pitfall in conceptualising 'identity' can be avoided. In this view, we should not look for a 'deep', 'essential' or 'true' personal core that makes up the 'real' self. The narrative character implies that one's self-understanding only appears in the act of 'telling' (or in the act of explicit self-reflection and as such 'telling oneself'). As such the intersubjective nature of the self-understanding is immediately included in the concept itself, since the telling that reveals the self-understanding always presupposes an audience of 'listeners'.

My analysis of teachers' career stories resulted in the identification of five components that together make up teachers' self-understanding: self-image, self-esteem, job motivation, task perception and future perspective.

The *self-image* is the descriptive component, the way teachers typify themselves as teachers. This image is based on self-perception, but to a large degree also on what others mirror back to the teachers (i.e., comments from pupils, parents, colleagues, principals, etc.). The self-image is therefore strongly influenced by the way one is perceived by others.

Very closely linked to the self-image is the evaluative component of the self-understanding or the *self-esteem*. Self-esteem refers to the teacher's appreciation of his/her actual job performance (how well am I doing in my job as a teacher?). Again the feedback from others is important, but that feedback is filtered and interpreted. Feedback from some is considered more relevant, valuable or important than that of others. The person defines particular individuals or groups as more 'significant others' (i.e., Nias, 1985). To most teachers, students are the first and most important source of feedback, since they are the ultimate 'raison d'être' for teachers and their teaching. Or even stronger, it is only the presence of pupils and students that makes the teacher a teacher; that allows him/her to enact teaching.

Self-esteem further refers to the fact that emotions matter a great deal in teaching as well. Positive self-esteem is crucial for feeling at ease in the job, for experiencing job satisfaction and a sense of fulfilment, for one's wellbeing as a teacher (Bullough, 2008). Those positive self-evaluations, however, are fragile, fluctuate in time and have to be reestablished time and again. That's why negative public judgements, which for an outsider look almost trivial, may have a devastating impact on teachers (i.e., Kelchtermans, 1996, 1999, 2005).

The self-esteem as the evaluative component has to be understood as intertwined with the normative component of self-understanding: the *task perception.* This encompasses the teacher's idea of what constitutes his/her professional programme, his/her tasks and duties in order to do a good job. It reflects a teacher's personal answer to the question: what must I do to be a proper teacher?; what are the essential tasks I have to perform in order to have the justified feeling that I am doing well?; what do I consider as legitimate duties to perform and what do I refuse to accept as part of 'my job'? The task perception reflects the fact that teaching and being a teacher is not a neutral endeavour. It implies value-laden choices, moral considerations (i.e., Fenstermacher, 1990; Hargreaves, 1995; Oser, Dick, & Patry, 1992). The task perception encompasses deeply held beliefs about what constitutes good education, about one's moral duties and responsibilities in order to do justice to students. When these deeply held beliefs are questioned – and the risk that this happens is always present (see below) – teachers feel that they themselves as a person are called into question. Evaluation systems, new regulations, calls for educational change that differ from or contradict teachers' task perception will deeply affect their self-esteem, their job satisfaction, etc. The emotional impact is very strong because teachers feel that their moral integrity as a person and a professional are called into question. Seeing these deeply held beliefs being called into question may even result in turnover, burnout, etc. (i.e., Achinstein & Ogawa, 2006; Ballet & Kelchtermans, 2008; Hargreaves, 1995; Kelchtermans, 1996, 1999; Nias, 1996). Research on beginning teachers' micropolitical literacy, for example clearly documents how teachers develop a way of reading (making sense of) situations in terms of the working conditions they consider crucial for doing a good job and – in line with this – how the development of effective strategies and tactics for negotiating, navigating, influencing and controlling their working conditions is definitely part of their development as professionals (Kelchtermans & Ballet, 2002a, 2002b).

The *job motivation* (or conative component) refers to the motives or drives that make people choose to become a teacher, to stay in teaching or to give it up for another career. Again, it is rather easy to understand that the task perception as well as the working conditions that allow a teacher to work and act according to that personal normative programme are crucial determinants for the job motivation. It is important to note, however, that the motives for working as a teacher may develop over time. Especially with secondary school teachers, I often found shifts in their motivation. Most of them first of all got into teaching because of their love for and interest in their subject discipline. Over time, however, several of them came to understand that their work, presence, actions were also meaningful to their students for other reasons than just being a qualified source of subject matter knowledge. Meaning something as a person to youngsters who are struggling with their life project, their individual identity, with growing up; in other words being important to them in a broader educational sense, became a very motivating factor in their careers as well as a source for job satisfaction and positive self-esteem.

Finally, self-understanding also includes a time-element: the *future perspective* reveals a teacher's expectations about his/her future in the job ('how do I see myself as a teacher in the years to come and how do I feel about it?'). This component explicitly also refers to the dynamic character of the self-understanding. It is not a static, fixed identity, but rather the result of an ongoing interactive process of sense-making and construction. It thus also indicates how temporality pervades self-understanding: one's actions in the present are influenced by meaningful experiences in the past and expectations about the future. The person of the teacher is always somebody at some particular moment in his/her life, with a particular past and future. This 'historicity' deeply characterises every human being and should therefore be included in our conception of professional self-understanding (and thus in our thinking of what it means to be a professional teacher, enacting the scholarship of teaching).

These five components of self-understanding can be distinguished analytically, but are all intertwined and refer to each other. This way self-understanding is both an encompassing (integrative) and an analytical (differentiated) concept. As such it does justice to the dynamic nature and the contextual embeddedness of teachers' sense of self and still provides an analytical conceptual tool to unravel the way the 'self' pervades all aspects of teaching. That is why I would argue: 'who I am in how I teach is the message'.

Teachers' narrative accounts of their experiences are not just informative about how they think about themselves. Rather they construct that self-understanding in the interactive act, at the same time (implicitly or explicitly) inviting the 'audience' to acknowledge, confirm or question and contradict the statement. Narrative accounts revealing one's self-under-standing are moments of *interactive sense-making*. Because the issue at stake is not a neutral statement, but one's self and the moral choices and emotions it encompasses, the narrative accounts always entail an aspect of *negotiation* (seeking recognition or acknowledgement). The value-laden choices in the task perception, for example can be contested, questioned, but this task perception also offers strong possibilities for negotiating shared under-standings and shared moral and political choices among colleagues.

The Subjective Educational Theory

By the *subjective educational theory* I mean the personal system of knowledge and beliefs about education that teachers use when performing their job.[1] It thus encompasses their professional know-how, the basis on which teachers ground their decisions for actions. Knowledge refers to more or less formal insights and understandings, as derived from teacher education or in-service training, professional reading, etc. Beliefs refer to more person-based, idiosyncratic convictions, built up through different career experiences. If juxtaposed like this the knowledge and belief suggest two different categories of information, but in teachers' thinking they are much more mixed and intertwined and may be better conceived of as the extremes of a continuum.[2] The actual border between knowledge (grounded in and based on research or collective and explicit experiences over time) and more personal beliefs (based on individual experience, single cases, 'hear say') is not always that clear.

The subjective educational theory reflects the teacher's personal answer to the questions: 'how should I deal with this particular situation?' (= what to do?) and 'why should I do it that way?' (= why do I think that action is appropriate now?). 'Using' or 'applying' one's subjective educational theory thus demands first of all a process of *judgement* and deliberation, an interpretative reading of the situation before deciding on which approach may be most appropriate. This ability to read, judge and then act is essential for competent teaching or is a vital indication that one masters the 'discipline of teaching' (Loughran & Russell, 2007).

The *content* of the subjective educational theory is largely idiosyncratic and based on personal experiences. Formal knowledge (e.g. from the curriculum of teacher education programmes or in-service training) only takes root in the subjective educational theory if (student) teachers have experienced that 'it works for them' or 'is true for their practice'. The same applies to the beliefs, for example suggestions or rules of thumb inherited from more experienced colleagues. The epistemological status of the subjective educational theory is that its content 'holds true' for the teacher involved. Whether or to what extent this claim of truth is justified beyond one's own situation is not the teacher's immediate concern.

Here lies an important agenda for teacher education or initiatives for professional development. The content of the subjective educational theory is largely idiosyncratic, based on personal experiences and therefore potentially incomplete, one-sided or simply wrong (even if it 'works' for the teacher involved). Making the implicit educational theory explicit through reflection is of crucial importance if teachers want to develop the validity of their professional know-how, refine or extend it. Only if its content is made explicit, others can comment, question, elaborate, contradict and thus contribute to furthering its validity. Or put differently, this ongoing process of framing and reframing allows teachers to better specify and ground their knowledge (Argyris, Putnam, & McLain-Smith, 1985; Schön, 1983).

Yet, even if its validity, its 'truth' is better grounded, 'using' that subjective educational theory is never simply applying a rule, but still always demands that the teacher *judges* whether a particular situation warrants the use of a particular rule or technique. This judgement about good or appropriate action inevitably raises the question of the norm: good or appropriate in relation to what norm? (or for whom?). Enhancing the validity of subjective educational theory thus cannot suffice with making teachers give up 'unproven' beliefs and replace them by 'proven' truth or theory. The process of judging remains essential (and for example deciding that in this particular situation the most appropriate action is to make an exception of what normally is the rule). This illustrates the link between self-understanding (more in particular the component of task perception) and the subjective educational theory, with the first encompassing the personal programme of goals and norms (the 'what?'), and the latter consisting of the knowledge to achieve them (the 'how to?').

Since teaching is highly contextual and since the judgement of the particular situation is an essential part of teaching, the explicit reflection and sharing of what one would do or has done and why remains a necessary and powerful learning situation for (student) teachers. The content of the subjective educational theory can in principal be made explicit through purposeful reflection (Mandl & Huber, 1983), yet the form or language in which it is explicated can be different. Some teachers use metaphors or images that capture both a type of a situation, as well as the strategies for action and their justification (see also Bullough & Knowles, 1991; Elbaz, 1981), others formulate principles or rules of thumb (i.e., Loughran, 2006).

To sum up, I want to repeat that professional self-understanding and subjective educational theory always need to be considered as two interwoven domains in the personal framework teachers develop and use to interpret and make sense of the professional situations they find themselves in. For research this implies that the research lines on teacher identity on the one hand and on teachers' professional knowledge on the other would benefit from an integrated approach, rather than continue to develop as largely separate fields of study (see for an example of the latter Beijaard, Meijer, & Verloop, 2004).

COMMITMENT AND VULNERABILITY

Typical for narrative self-accounts is that they all reflect the intersubjective nature of teaching (and thus of oneself as a teacher): the way one narratively understands oneself includes the presence and role of the others. Those others are not just a sociologically relevant category of reference persons, but – especially the pupils/students –are the ones that ultimately justify one's sense of oneself as a teacher, because of one's ethical responsibility. This ethical commitment, together with the curricular agenda, sets the scene for teachers' professional actions.

Yet, this conceptualisation of the personal interpretative framework in terms of 'enactment' and 'agenda' may run into another pitfall: an activist bias. Teaching/being a teacher is too exclusively thought about as a matter of intentional and purposeful action. This way, however, important aspects of teaching are neglected, ignored or downplayed. The aspect I want to stress here is the fact that teaching – because of its relational and ethical nature – is also and importantly characterised by *passivity*, by being exposed to others and thus being vulnerable.

Bullough (2008) argues that teaching means standing for something, for a particular idea of what constitutes a good life: a meaningful, valuable life. Teaching implies taking a stance, choosing for a particular set of values and norms (goals) and engaging in their pursuit. This moral commitment, with its emotionally and personally engaging consequences is an inherent part of teaching and therefore of teaching as a discipline. As a result, however, teaching is fundamentally characterised and constituted by *vulnerability* (Kelchtermans, 2005, 2008). Vulnerability in that sense is not so much to be understood as an emotional state or experience (although the experience of being vulnerable definitely triggers intense emotions), but as a structural characteristic of the profession.

There are at least three elements that make up vulnerability in teaching. A first element lies in the fact that teachers are not in full control of the conditions they have to work in (regulations, quality control systems, policy demands). Teachers' working conditions are to a large extent imposed on them: they work within particular legal frameworks and regulations, in a particular school, with a particular infrastructure, population of students, composition of the staff. One could say that this is a formal or political vulnerability, which raises the agenda of power to influence and define one's working conditions. The 'times of performativity' teachers are living in (with its exclusive emphasis on effectiveness and efficiency, based on strict standards and output measurement) definitely intensifies this experience of vulnerability (i.e., Ball, 2003; Kelchtermans, 2007a, 2007b).

Secondly, vulnerability refers to the experience that teachers can, only to a very limited degree, prove their effectiveness by claiming that pupils' results directly follow from their actions. All teachers realise that student outcomes are only partially determined by their teaching. Equally or sometimes even more decisive are personal factors (motivation, perseverance, etc.) or social factors, that are often very hard to influence, change or control. It is not only difficult to prove to what extent a teacher can argue that students' results are his/her own achievement, but equally difficult to know when a result of teachers' actions possibly may occur and become visible at all. Very often teachers are not allowed to witness when the seed of their efforts finds fertile ground to develop. That is why the quality control systems, being based only or primarily on students' test scores are felt by so many teachers as an unfair evaluation of their work, doing injustice to their specific working conditions. This creates ambivalence among the teachers. Teachers with a high internal locus of control may experience high job satisfaction when student outcomes are good. On the other hand, when pupils' learning outcomes are poor, they may tend to blame themselves and feel frustrated and inefficacious. Teachers with a high external 'locus of control' often ascribe student outcomes to factors beyond their efforts and often beyond their control. This may then have a negative impact on their personal feelings of professional competence ('I can't make a difference') and thus have a depressing effect on their motivation and eventually on their sense of self-esteem. During their career teachers find themselves challenged to properly balance between internal and external locus of control, between a satisfying sense of efficacy and a realistic acknowledgement of one's limited impact (Kelchtermans, 1993), between exhausting personal commitment and cynical disengagement (see also Huberman, 1989).

Finally, and this is the most fundamental meaning of the concept 'vulnerability': teachers cannot but make dozens of decisions about when and how to act in order to support students' development and learning, but they don't have a firm ground to base their decisions on. Even when the justification for teachers' decisions can be explicitly stated, with reference to a certain idea (argument) of good education in general and good education for this pupil here and now, that judgement and decision can always be challenged or questioned. And still, it is this capacity to judge, to act and to take responsibility for one's actions which constitutes a key part of teachers' professionalism. There is no escape: the particular scholarship of teaching (professionality) demands that one endures this vulnerability. Vulnerability is the fundamental condition a teacher 'finds himself/herself in'. The expression is important: it reveals the inevitable element of passivity, of exposure that characterises teaching. It is not something one 'makes happen'. Although in much research, training and analysis the emphasis is on acting, planning, designing, there is also this passive dimension of undergoing, surprise, puzzlement, powerlessness.

Yet, at the same time, it is this committed judging and caring action that opens up the 'educational space' in the relationship between teachers and students. In that relationship not everything is fixed, roles and positions are not fully defined or prescribed, the careful judgement can be wrong, etc. In other words, the scholarship of teaching contains a fundamental *paradox*: one has to engage in knowledgeable, thoughtful and purposeful action in order to achieve as good as possible predefined goals, yet at the same time this committed and purposeful action allows things to happen, events to literally take place, educationally meaningful experiences to appear for students. Or to put it differently, in teaching there is always at the same time happening both more and less than one had planned for. Acknowledging this is not an alibi for lousy lesson plans, careless interventions or technically bad teaching performance. On the contrary, only carefully prepared and professionally enacted teaching allows the unforeseen and meaningful to happen. The passivity that characterises the educational relationship is thus also a positive reality. Since not everything can be planned for, authentic interaction between people can take place and that interaction can have deeply meaningful educational value just because it 'happened', it 'took place'. This truth is poetically captured in Cohen's image of the cracks which – while in a sense destroying the ambition of perfection or the solidity of unquestionable expertise – at the same time open up new perspectives, allow enlightening experiences to take place.[3]

This dimension of passivity, of exposure and vulnerability should be acknowledged and thoughtfully conceptualised in the scholarship of teaching. Professional teachers then incarnate the paradox of on the one hand taking a stance, speaking out for normative ideas and values and in line with that designing educational conditions that must help students to learn and to develop their individual capacities and identities as much as possible, while at the same time knowing that their purposeful action doesn't fully capture, direct or predict what will happen.

REFLECTION AND NARRATIVITY

Throughout the discussion of teaching as enacted scholarship, with the central role of the personal interpretative framework, it has become clear that this conceptualisation also impacts the meaning of reflection and reflectivity in teaching and teacher development.

Few educationalists will deny the importance of reflection in teaching and teacher development. Since the early 1980s – especially with the publication of Schön's seminal book on the reflective practitioner (1983) – the term has never left the hit-parade of trendy educational concepts. I am using the term 'reflection' here in a very broad sense to refer to both the skill and the attitude of making one's own actions, feelings, experiences the object of one's thinking. Yet, there is a need for caution. Very often we see that reflective skills and practices are being used in a predominantly instrumental and technical way. Teaching as enacted scholarship demands a concept of reflection that is both deep and broad enough to encompass its moral, political and emotional dimensions (Hargreaves, 1995).

Broad Reflection: Beyond the Instrumental and the Technical

Both the agenda of research on teaching and of teacher education (initial and in-service) are often dominated by instrumental concerns: finding the appropriate means to achieve the desired ends. Through reflective analysis one strives to acquire knowledge and skills in order to improve the effectiveness of one's teaching. Or the reflection may be driven by a concern for technical problem-solving. This thinking (and the research based on it) remains embedded in what Schön (1983) called a rational, instrumental and technical approach to reflection. A lot of research aimed at the development of 'knowledge for practice' (Cochran-Smith & Lytle, 1999) also echoes this idea. Of course, technical issues are neither irrelevant nor illegitimate. Teachers do need a solid knowledge base and the mastery of a broad range of teaching skills (Korthagen, 2001). Teachers live and work under the pressure of day-to-day practice. They must maintain the smooth functioning of the classroom and the school. This pressures them to ask for simple, quick-fix solutions, because schooling has to go on (Hopkins, 2001).

The dominant concern with technical questions is probably to some extent an unintended side effect of the success of formal models for reflection, like the widely used ALACT model (Action/Looking back on the action/Awareness of essential aspects/ Creating alternative methods of action/Trial – Korthagen, 2001, p. 44). These models have proven to be very useful in guiding and supporting the development of reflective skills during the process of becoming a teacher, just because of their formal character. They can be applied independently from decisions on what counts as good teaching, but can therefore easily be limited to instrumental interests of effectiveness.[4]

Yet, at the same time there is more to teaching than questions of effectiveness and efficiency. As argued above, teaching always implies an engagement in relationships of responsibility with students, colleagues, parents, etc. and thus involves also *moral, political and emotional dimensions* (Hargreaves, 1995). Reflective practice should be broad enough to encompass all four dimensions (and their interconnections).

Broad Reflection: Encompassing the Moral, the Political and the Emotional

The Moral in the Technical
Teaching is 'a profoundly moral activity' (Fenstermacher, 1990, p. 132): firstly, because it contributes to the creation and recreation of future generations; and secondly, because teachers constantly make small but *morally* significant judgements in their interactions with children, parents and one another (Hargreaves, 1995, p. 14). What seem to be technical decisions on teaching strategies, on the use of instructional materials, or on interventions for classroom management, are moral decisions in their consequences (Nias, 1999; Oser et al., 1992). The moral dimension in teaching fundamentally refers to the question of what is educationally in the best interest of the students and thus what I should do as teacher/teacher educator? (see also Greenfield, 1991). There is, however, no agreement about what is best for the students and what actions might best achieve that purpose (see above the issue of vulnerability).

The Political Behind the Moral
Issues and dilemmas in teaching that look moral at first sight often hide questions about power and interests. Who benefits from what I/we as a teacher/teachers do? In whose interests are we working? Who is actually determining the what? – and why? – questions in my/our work? These are not only matters of values and norms, but refer to the *political* dimension of teaching and teacher development. *Power* and *interests* are words that still

carry a strong taboo for many teachers and teacher educators. Many teachers feel uncomfortable when these issues are brought up as linked to their work. The political is often still considered as something improper, marginal, just an unfortunate aspect of their particular working conditions or at best a peripheral phenomenon that does not really belong to teaching. This denial makes it more difficult for teachers to see the intrinsically political nature of their work and its fundamental relevance to their effectiveness, job satisfaction and the quality of learning opportunities for their pupils (Kelchtermans, 1996).

These political issues go beyond the level of the individual teacher/teacher educator and his/her group of students (class). They also include context issues at the level of the school as an organisation (for instance, relationship with heads of department, management staff, etc.) and at more central levels of educational policy (for instance, issues of decentralisation; quality control). Discussions about values, goals and teaching procedures can, in fact, carry a strong political agenda that is sometimes disguised as technical or moral.

The Emotional in the Heart of the Relationship
Hardly any teacher or teacher educator will deny that *emotions* play an important part in their work. As with the political – it is still often hard for teachers to see that emotions are not simply a matter of personality or idiosyncratic teaching style, but constitute a fundamental aspect of the job. Emotions have to be acknowledged as part of educational practices, driven by moral commitment and care for others for whom one feels responsible. They reflect teachers' experience of their job situation and commitment and such constitute one dimension of teachers' professionalism (Hargreaves, 1995; Kelchtermans & Hamilton, 2004; Nias, 1996).

DEEP REFLECTION: MOVING BEYOND THE ACTION LEVEL

A concept of reflection that does justice to the specificity of the teaching profession does not only need to be broad or wide in its content, but also deep enough. By this 'depth' I mean that it should move beyond the level of action to the level of underlying beliefs, ideas, knowledge and goals – in other words to the personal interpretative framework with its self-under-standing and subjective educational theory.

Only in this way can teachers' thinking become genuinely *critical*. By examining and unmasking the moral and political agendas in the work context and their impact on one's self-understanding, one's thinking and actions, reflection can open up perspectives for empowerment and for reestablishing the conditions for teaching and learning that allow for pedagogical processes to take place in which people can regain the authorship of their selves (see also Zembylas, 2003a, 2003b).

Critical and deep reflection further implies a *contextualised* approach in which the particularities of one's working context are carefully taken into account, whilst also being fundamentally questioned. Reflection should aim at understanding one's actions in the context of that particular school or institute, at that particular time, in that particular social, political and cultural environment (Goodson, 2001). Experiences and actions have to be looked at and understood in their context. Without this deep and critical character, reflection runs the risk of being just another procedure, a method or coping strategy that confirms and continues the status quo.

PERSPECTIVES FOR PRACTICE: THE PROMISE OF THE NARRATIVE

Teaching as enacted scholarship implies not only a technical agenda of effectiveness (achieving the curriculum goals), but also a complex relationship with others, characterised by moral responsibilities, political interests and emotional experiences. Furthermore, apart from the activist dimension of intentional and purposeful action, there is also the reality of being exposed to others, of passivity.

Taking all of this seriously means that the scholarship of teaching is a *risky* endeavour (see also Loughran, 2006). Finding oneself confronted with opinions and practices that differ from or even contradict one's own opinions and deeply held beliefs. This can be very discomforting. Yet, without these discomforting experiences, deep reflection – in which the content of one's personal interpretative framework is thoroughly challenged and questioned – will far less often be triggered. And without deep reflection, one's personal scholarship cannot be developed, nor the scholarship of teaching in general (as a publicly reviewed set of knowledge to build on). In order to achieve this, teacher education as well as in-service training need to provide spaces to engage in *discomforting dialogues*. Perhaps the most fundamental contribution of the narrative and biographical perspective to this lies in the fact that it provides a different language that allows for the non-technical dimensions of teaching and being a teacher to be conceptualised, talked about, shared and critically challenged. Moral dilemmas, emotional experiences and political struggles can find a place there and thus be acknowledged as fundamental to the experience of teaching and to the scholarship of teaching.

NOTES

1. I am aware that the phenomenon I am referring to has been labelled differently by other authors, like 'subjective theory' (Mandl & Huber, 1983); 'implicit theory' (Clark & Peterson, 1986), 'practical knowledge' (Elbaz, 1981), 'personal practical knowledge' (Clandinin, 1986), etc. and that adding another label may contribute to a further proliferation of concepts rather than contributing to synthesis and theory building. Yet, this risk is outbalanced by the advantage that subjective educational theory as a label explicitly includes some of its essential characteristics: it is an ordered, more or less systematic whole 'theory' of knowledge and beliefs, constructed by the person involved (subjective) about 'education'.

2. Several authors have introduced concepts to stress the holistic, integrative nature of this 'knowledge': gestalts (Korthagen, 2001), images (Elbaz, 1981; Clandinin, 1986).

3. With thanks to Dr Cornelia Löhmer for pointing me to Cohen's line.

4. This remains true even though – for example – the ALACT model clearly emphasises the importance of taking into account not only the teachers' but also the pupils' perspective, and not only thoughts but also feelings (Korthagen, 2001, p. 210).

REFERENCES

Achinstein, B., & Ogawa, R. (2006). (In)Fidelity: What the resistance of new teachers reveals about professional principles and prescriptive educational policies. *Harvard Educational Review, 26*(1), 30–63.

Argyris, C., Putnam, R., & McLain-Smith, D. (1985). *Action science. concepts, methods, and skills for research and intervention.* San Francisco, CA: Jossey-Bass.

Ball, S. J. (2003). The teacher's soul and the terrors of performativity. *Journal of Education Policy, 18*(2), 215–228.

Ballet, K., & Kelchtermans, G. (2008). Workload and willingness to change: Disentangling the experience of intensified working conditions. *Journal of Curriculum Studies, 40,* 47–67.

Beijaard, D., Meijer, P. C., & Verloop, N. (2004). Reconsidering research on teachers' professional identity. *Teaching and Teacher Education, 20*(2), 107–128.

Bullough, R. (2008). The writing of teachers' lives: Where personal troubles and social issues meet. *Teacher Education Quarterly, 35*(4), 7–26.

Bullough, R., & Knowles, G. (1991). Teaching and nurturing: Changing conceptions of self as teacher in a case study of becoming a teacher. *International Journal of Qualitative Studies in Education, 4,* 121–140.

Carter, K., & Doyle, W. (1996). Personal narrative and life history in learning to teach. In J. Sikula, T. J. Buttery & E. Guyton (Eds.), *Handbook of research on teacher education* (2nd ed., pp. 120–142). New York, NY: Macmillan.

Casey, K. (1995–1996). The new narrative research in education. *Review of Research in Education, 21,* 211–253.

Clandinin, D. (1986). *Classroom practice: Teacher images in action.* London: Falmer Press.

Clandinin, J. (Ed.). (2006). *Handbook of narrative research methodologies.* Thousand Oaks, CA: Sage.

Clark, C., & Peterson, P. (1986). Teachers' thought processes. In M. Wittrock (Ed.), *Handbook of research on teaching* (3rd ed., pp. 255–296). New York, NY: Macmillan.

Cochran-Smith, M., & Lytle, S. L. (1999). Relationships of knowledge and practice: Teacher learning in communities. *Review of Research in Education, 24,* 249–305.

Connelly, F., & Clandinin, D. (1990). Stories of experience and narrative inquiry. *Educational Researcher, 19*(4), 2–14.

Elbaz, F. (1981). The teachers' practical knowledge: Report of a case study. *Curriculum Inquiry, 11*(1), 43–71.

Elbaz, F. (2006). Studying teachers' lives and experience: Narrative inquiry into K-12 teaching. In J. Clandinin (Ed.), *Handbook of narrative inquiry: Mapping a methodology* (pp. 357–382). Thousand Oaks, CA: Sage.

Fenstermacher, G. (1990). Some moral considerations on teaching as a profession. In J. Goodlad, R. Soder & K. Sirotnik (Eds.), *The moral dimensions of teaching* (pp. 130–151). San Francisco, CA: Jossey-Bass.

Goodson, I. (1984). The use of life histories in the study of teaching. In M. Hammersley (Ed.), *The ethnography of schooling* (pp. 129–154). Driffield: Nafferton Books.

Goodson, I. (Ed.). (1992). *Studying teachers' lives.* London: Routledge.

Goodson, I. (2001). Social histories of educational change. *Journal of Educational Change, 2,* 45–63.

Greenfield, W. D. (1991). The micro-politics of leadership in an urban elementary school. In J. J. Blase (Ed.), *The politics of life in schools* (pp. 161–184). Newbury Park, CA: Sage.

Gudmundsdottir, S. (2001). Narrative research on school practice. In V. Richardson (Ed.), *Handbook of research on teaching* (4th ed., pp. 226–240). Washington, DC: AERA.

Hargreaves, A. (1995). Development and desire: A post-modern perspective. In T. R. Guskey & M. Huberman (Eds.), *Professional development in education: New paradigms and perspectives* (pp. 9–34). New York, NY: Teachers College Press.

Hopkins, D. (2001). *School improvement for real.* London: Routledge.

Huberman, M. (1989). The professional life cycle of teachers. *Teachers College Record, 91*(1), 31–57.

Kelchtermans, G. (1993). Getting the story, understanding the lives: From career stories to teachers' professional development. *Teaching and Teacher Education, 9*(5/6), 443–456.

Kelchtermans, G. (1994). Biographical methods in the study of teachers' professional development. In I. Carlgren, G. Handal & S. Vaage (Eds.), *Teacher thinking and action in varied contexts. Research on teachers' thinking and practice* (pp. 93–108). London: Falmer Press.

400 GEERT KELCHTERMANS

Kelchtermans, G. (1996). Teacher vulnerability: Understanding its moral and political roots. *Cambridge Journal of Education, 26*(3), 307–323.

Kelchtermans, G. (1999). Teacher career: Between burnout and fading away? Reflections from a narrative and biographical perspective. In R. Vandenberghe & M. Huberman (Eds.), *Understanding and preventing teacher burnout. A sourcebook of international research and practice* (pp. 176–191). Cambridge: Cambridge University Press.

Kelchtermans, G. (2005). Teachers' emotions in educational reforms: Self-understanding, vulnerable commitment and micropolitical literacy. *Teaching and Teacher Education, 21*, 995–1006.

Kelchtermans, G. (2007a). Teachers' self-understanding in times of performativity. In L. F. Deretchin & C. J. Craig (Eds.), *International research on the impact of accountability systems* (Teacher education yearbook XV) (pp. 13–30). Lanham, MD: Rowman & Littlefield Education.

Kelchtermans, G. (2007b). Professional commitment beyond contract. Teachers' self-understanding, vulnerability and reflection. In J. Butcher & L. McDonald (Eds.), *Making a difference: Challenges for teachers, teaching, and teacher education* (pp. 35–53). Rotterdam: Sense Publishers.

Kelchtermans, G. (2008). Study, stance, and stamina in the research on teachers' lives. A rejoinder to Robert V. Bullough, Jr. *Teacher Education Quarterly, 35*(4), 27–36.

Kelchtermans, G., & Ballet, K. (2002a). The micro-politics of teacher induction: A narrative-biographical study on teacher socialisation. *Teaching and Teacher Education, 18*(1), 105–120.

Kelchtermans, G., & Ballet, K. (2002b). Micropolitical literacy: Reconstructing a neglected dimension in teacher development. *International Journal of Educational Research, 37*, 755–767.

Kelchtermans, G., & Hamilton, M. L. (2004). The dialectics of passion and theory: Exploring the relation between self-study and emotion. In J. Loughran, M. L. Hamilton, V. Kubler LaBoskey & T. Russell (Eds.), *The International handbook of self-study of teaching and teacher education practices* (pp. 785–810). Dordrecht: Kluwer Academic Publishers.

Korthagen, F. (2001). *Linking practice and theory: The pedagogy of realistic teacher education.* Mahwah, NJ: Lawrence Erlbaum.

Krüger, H.-H., & Marotzki, W. (Eds.). (1996). *Erziehungswissenschaftliche biographieforschung* [Biographical research in education]. Opladen: Leske & Budrich.

Lortie, D. (1975). *The schoolteacher: A sociological study.* Chicago, IL: University of Chicago Press.

Loughran, J. (2006). *Developing a pedagogy of teacher education. Understanding teaching and learning about teaching.* London: Routledge.

Loughran, J., & Russell, T. (Eds.). (2007). *Enacting a pedagogy of teacher education.* London: Routledge.

Mandl, H., & Huber, G. (1983). Subjektive Theorien von Lehrern [Subjective theories of teachers]. *Psychologie in Erziehung und Unterricht, 30*, 98–112.

Nias, J. (1985). Reference groups in primary teaching: Talking, listening and identity. In S. Ball & I. Goodson (Eds.), *Teachers' lives and careers* (pp. 105–119). London: Falmer Press.

Nias, J. (1989). *Primary teachers talking: A study of teaching as work.* London: Routledge.

Nias, J. (1996). Thinking about feeling: The emotions in teaching. *Cambridge Journal of Education, 26*(3), 293–306.

Nias, J. (1999). Teachers' moral purposes: Stress, vulnerability, and strength. In R. Vandenberghe & M. Huberman (Eds.), *Understanding and preventing teacher burnout: A sourcebook of international research and practice* (pp. 223–237). Cambridge: Cambridge University Press.

Oser, F., Dick, A., & Patry, J. (Eds.). (1992). *Effective and responsible teaching*. San Francisco, CA: Jossey-Bass.

Polkinghorne, D. (1988). *Narrative knowing and the human sciences*. Albany, NY: State University of New York Press.

Pratte, R., & Rury, J. (1991). Teachers, professionalism, and craft. *Teachers College Record, 93*(1), 59–72.

Russell, T. (1997). Teaching teachers: How I teach is the message. In J. Loughran & T. Russell (Eds.), *Teaching about teachers: Purpose, passion and pedagogy in teacher education* (pp. 32–47). New York, NY: Falmer Press.

Schön, D. (1983). *The reflective practitioner: How professionals think in action*. London: Temple Smith.

Shulman, L. (1999). Taking learning seriously. *Change, 31*(4), 10–17.

Zembylas, M. (2003a). Caring for teacher emotion: Reflections on teacher self-development. *Studies in Philosophy and Education, 22*(2), 103–125.

Zembylas, M. (2003b). Interrogating 'Teacher identity': Emotion, resistance, and self-formation. *Educational Theory, 53*(1), 107–127.

PART III
CONTEMPORARY
INTERNATIONAL SCHOLARSHIP

The research strands identified in the first part of this book find full expression in the contemporary international scholarship featured in Part III. Most of this section comes from ISATT's new regions and newest members, but some originates with long-term members who have written specifically about teaching and teacher education challenges their countries face.

We begin with Chapter 19 authored by European editor, Maria Assunção Flores, who hosted ISATT's Braga Conference in 2011. Flores writes about "Be(com)ing a Teacher in Challenging Circumstances: Sustaining Commitment or Giving Up in Portugal?" We then move on to South Africa to become acquainted with "Teachers Dealing with Failure in a Low Socio-Economic Status School in South Africa," which is Chapter 20. It was contributed by doctoral student, Carola Steinberg, who has now been officially conferred her doctorate. Her work was solicited by new regions editors, Samuel Oyoo, Tara Ratnam, and David R. Goodwin. Following that is a work from Kyrgyzstan. Chapter 21 is authored by Cholpon Musaeva and is titled "The Necessity of Providing Guidance for Reflection in Inservice Teacher Training Programs in Kyrgyzstan." In Chapter 22, Samuel Ouma Oyoo, Regional Representative for Africa and New Regions Editor of this book, takes readers to this home country and tells about "Enhancing and Sustaining Teacher Effectiveness as the 'Trojan Horse' in Successful Science Education in Kenya." David R. Goodwin, another of the new regions editors, follows with his chapter (Chapter 23), "Blending Traditional and Constructivist Teaching: How One Teacher Goes About It in a U.S. Middle School Mathematics Classroom." From there, we cross the ocean to China and a work contributed by Xiao Han and Zhuo Feng. Their chapter, Chapter 24, is titled "School-Based Instructional Research (SBIR): An Approach to Teacher Professional Development in China." We then conclude Part III with two chapters from India: Chapter 25 and Chapter 26.

The first one, Chapter 25, authored by Tara Ratnam, India's National Representative and new regions editor, has to do with "Engaging India's Social History to Understand and Promote Teacher Change." The second chapter, Chapter 26, which was commissioned by Tara Ratnam, is titled "Curriculum Reform in a Non-Threatening Collaborative Environment: An Indian Initiative" and was written by Jayshri Kannan.

This concludes Part III and prepares readers for Part IV, Advances in Teacher Education.

CHAPTER 19

BE(COM)ING A TEACHER IN CHALLENGING CIRCUMSTANCES: SUSTAINING COMMITMENT OR GIVING UP IN PORTUGAL?[☆]

Maria Assunção Flores

ABSTRACT

This chapter draws on a larger study on beginning teachers and on their experiences of becoming a teacher in unprecedented challenging circumstances in Portugal. The aim is to look at the ways in which changes in policy and school context, as well as in personal and professional context, impact teachers' professional identity over time. Two beginning teachers' accounts are used to illustrate the key influencing factors that have impacted the development of professional identities. Four main themes emerged: (a) the influence of context, both at a policy and social level and at a school level; (b) the importance of relationships in teaching, particularly with students and colleagues; (c) the emergence of inner tensions resulting from the mismatch between strong beliefs and reality; and (d) the role of emotions in (re)defining teachers' practice of

☆An earlier version of this chapter was presented at the Annual Meeting of the American Educational Research Association (AERA), Vancouver, BC, Canada, April 13–17, 2012.

From Teacher Thinking to Teachers and Teaching: The Evolution of a Research Community
Advances in Research on Teaching, Volume 19, 405–425
Copyright © 2013 by Emerald Group Publishing Limited
All rights of reproduction in any form reserved
ISSN: 1479-3687/doi:10.1108/S1479-3687(2013)0000019022

teaching and teachers' identity development. The chapter concludes with the discussion of the findings and their implications.

Keywords: Teacher identity; beginning teachers; tensions; emotions; teaching context

Be(com)ing a teacher is a multidimensional, idiosyncratic, and context-specific process (Calderhead & Shorrock, 1997; Flores, 2001; Flores & Day, 2006; Hauge, 2000) which implies an interplay between different, and sometimes conflicting, perspectives, beliefs, and practices. A sense of professional identity is, therefore, crucial to becoming and being a teacher. It constitutes a "continuing site of struggle" (MacLure, 1993, p. 313), which is located in a given social and cultural space (Coldron & Smith, 1999) and it is dependent on teachers' views of themselves and of the contexts in which they work. Bullough (1997) argues that "midst the diversity of tales of becoming a teacher and studies of the content and form of the story, two conclusions of paramount importance to teacher educators emerge: prior experience and beliefs are central to shaping the story line, as is the context of becoming a teacher" (p. 95).

Unlike some other countries from where the International Study Association on Teachers and Teaching (ISATT) members hail, teacher surpluses and unemployment are experienced in the teaching profession in Portugal in the early years of career. This has implications for the recruitment of teachers and for new teachers' job security. Added to this, more recently, there has been a profound financial and economic crisis that has affected every sector of Portuguese society and led to increases in unemployment, salary cuts, and higher taxes. All of these have impacted teachers and the teaching profession. Also, recent changes at a policy level have directly impacted teachers' work. These shifts have resulted in the restructuring of initial teacher education programs (at the master's degree level), the introduction of an exam on knowledge and competencies for all entrants into the teaching profession; the introduction of a probationary year; new mechanisms for teacher evaluation; new protocols for school governance; reduction in the school curriculum; introduction of national exams from the primary school upward; and so on. In addition, more pressure is placed on schools and teachers to increase teaching standards and student achievement. All these have affected schools and teachers' work in a multitude of ways, each bearing implications for teachers' professional identity.

This chapter draws on a larger study on beginning teachers and their experiences of being educators in challenging situations. The aim is to look at the ways in which changes in policy and school context, as well as in personal and professional context, affect teachers' professional identities longitudinally.

DEVELOPMENT OF PROFESSIONAL IDENTITY: WHAT DOES THE RESEARCH LITERATURE SAY?

There is a growing body of literature on teacher identity. It has evolved as a specific research area over the last two decades (Beijaard, Meijer, & Verloop, 2004; Pillen, Beijaard, & den Brok, 2012). Research on this topic has attracted the attention of a number of researchers in order to shed light into the nature and process of becoming and being a teacher and the ways in which it occurs over time, in particular during the transition from student teacher to new teacher. Learning to teach "goes beyond the mere application of a set of acquired techniques and skills. Not only does it imply the mastery of practical and more technical issues, but it also encompasses the construction of knowledge and meaning in an ongoing dialogue with the practice" (Flores, 2001, p. 146). A sense of identity is, therefore, crucial in understanding how student teachers learn and develop as practicing professionals.

The process of be(com)ing a teacher entails the (trans)formation of the teacher's identity, a process described by Sachs (2001a) as being negotiated, open, and shifting. She states that "for teachers this is mediated by their own experience in schools and outside of schools as well as their own beliefs and values about what it means to be a teacher and the type of teacher they aspire to be" (Sachs, 2001a, p. 154). During the first years in teaching, teachers develop their professional identities by "combining parts of their past, including their own experience in school and in teacher preparation, with pieces of their present" (Feiman-Nemser, 2001, p. 1029). Through this process, they develop "a sense of purpose for teaching and being a teacher" (Rex & Nelson, 2004, p. 1317). Thus, professional identity is neither a stable nor a fixed entity. It is not a "taken-for-granted process nor a product (...) It is a space of struggle and conflict, and of construction of ways of being a teacher" (Nóvoa, 1992, p. 16).

Most studies on teacher identity over the past decade have dealt with the contexts and influences that shape new teachers' professional identity (Flores, 2001, 2006a; Flores & Day, 2006). The research has included the tensions and accompanying feelings and coping strategies in beginning teachers' professional identity development (Pillen et al., 2012), the role of emotions in student teachers' professional identity formation (Timostsuk & Ugaste, 2010), and the development of self-image as teacher (Sutherland, Howard, & Markauskaite, 2010). Also receiving research attention have been the metaphors that explore new teachers' professional identities (Thomas & Beauchamp, 2011) and the images of teachers as professionals and their projections of a future identity (Hamman, Gosselin, Romano, & Bunuan, 2010; Thomas & Beauchamp, 2007). Further topics of inquiry have included the ways in which novice teachers perceive teaching and teacher education (Ezer, Gilat, & Sagee, 2010), perceptions of new teachers' professional identity to their decisions to leave the profession (Hong, 2010), the negotiation of identity resulting from tensions between views of teaching and beliefs, and the practice of teaching (Smagorinsky, Cook, Moore, Jackson, & Fry, 2004) and beginning teachers' narrative identity work in a peer group (Estola, Uitto, & Syrjälä, 2012).

In their review, Beijaard et al. (2004) identified four characteristics of professional identity: (a) it is not a fixed or stable entity, rather it is a dynamic process involving the (re)interpretation of experiences; (b) it entails the interaction between the person and the context; (c) it consists of a set of sub-identities that more or less harmonize; and (d) the identity development implies teacher agency. Therefore, teacher identity "should not be seen as stable – something that people have – but as, "something that they use, to justify, explain and make sense of themselves in relation to other people, and to the contexts in which they operate" (MacLure, 1993, p. 312).

The development of professional identity is understood as a process integrating one's personal knowledge, beliefs, attitudes, norms and values, and the professional demands from teacher education institutions and schools (Beijaard et al., 2004). Flores and Day (2006) identified key mediating influences on shaping and reshaping new teachers' identities over time: personal biography; training trajectory and the pre-teaching identity relating to images, beliefs, and implicit theories about teaching and being a teacher; and the contexts of teaching (i.e., classroom practice, school culture, leadership).

These factors are complex and interconnected and they influence in different ways new teachers' professional identity development. As other research has noted, sometimes discontinuities, fragmentation, turbulence, and change emerge in the struggle to construct and maintain a stable identity (Day, Kington, Stibart, & Sammons, 2006). Similarly, Soreide (2006), drawing upon her study of five Norwegian teachers, argues that teacher identity is multifaceted and constructed and that it entails the negotiation between multiple selves. Research has also shown that beginning teachers struggle to develop their professional identity during the first year in the profession, a process which is gradual, complex, and often problematic (Thomas & Beauchamp, 2011).

In their study of 182 beginning teachers, Pillen et al. (2012) found that tensions in teacher professional identity relate to an unbalanced personal and professional side of becoming a teacher and to conflicts between teachers' aspirations and the reality. The authors also found that these tensions were often accompanied by feelings of helplessness, anger, and an awareness of shortcomings. Further to this, most beginning teachers tried to cope with tensions by talking to a significant other or by searching for a solution themselves, which lends support to earlier empirical work (Flores, 2004a, 2006b). Also, Timostsuk and Ugaste (2010) concluded that negative emotions exercised the strongest influence on student teachers' professional identity and that supervisors neglected the role of positive emotions as a support for learning. In addition, the most positive emotions had to do with situations involving students.

Empirical studies have also shown the key influence of workplace conditions in new teachers' morale and career choice commitment (Weiss, 1999), the importance of space and place in the construction and negotiation of beginning teachers' subjectivities (lisahunter, Rossi, Tinning, Flanagan, & Macdonald, 2011), and the role of micro-political literacy on new teachers' professional development (Kechtermans & Ballet, 2002). For instance, the staff room is recognized as an important site of professional learning and new teachers "are required to read, understand, negotiate, reconstruct, reproduce, resist, or reconstitute what is acceptable and what is not within this space" (lisahunter et al., 2011, p. 34).

Research has also pointed to the importance of long-term, secure employment at school with access to effective mentoring for beginning teachers so that they can move from a "survival" to a developing competency in the early years (Pietsch & Williamson, 2010). Adopting an approach which combines the narrative-biographical and the micro-political perspectives in the study of teacher socialization, Kelchtermans and Ballet (2002) concluded that micro-politics play an important role in teachers' views of their early teaching experiences.

Professional identity development entails the interaction between the individual and the environment or context (Beijaard et al., 2004; Korthagen, 2004). It implies, therefore, the analysis of the relationships between structures and individual agency (Day et al., 2006). Day et al. (2006) contend that teachers will define themselves not only through their past and current identities as defined by personal and social histories and current roles but through their beliefs and values about the kind of teacher they hope to be in the inevitably changing political, social, institutional and personal circumstances. (p. 610)

THE STUDY: AN OVERVIEW

The larger study from which this work was drawn aimed to analyze the ways in which the professional identities of new teachers developed over time in different school settings through interactions among personal, professional, and contextual factors. The overarching intent was to look at the ways in which changes in policy and school context, as well as in personal and professional context, impact upon teachers' identity over time.

In this chapter, I focus specifically on the key mediating influences on the development of teachers' professional identity from the perspective of two teachers who have participated in previous empirical work reported elsewhere (see Flores, 2001, 2004a, 2004b, 2006a, 2006b, 2012a; Flores & Day, 2006). Tom and Mary (pseudonyms) started to work as first year teachers in 1999, after having completed a 5-year teaching degree in physics and chemistry. Their programs included 4 years of full-time study and 1 year of practicum in a school. They participated in the larger research alongside 12 other new teachers (see also Flores, 2004b).

Data reported in this chapter were collected through semi-structured interviews using a narrative approach (Clandinin, Pushor, & Orr, 2007; Elliot, 2005). In this work, the contexts and influences of the development of teachers' professional identity are discussed and illustrated through the accounts of Tom and Mary, two new and now more experienced teachers who have participated in a longitudinal study for more than a decade. Within the context of the wider study, novice teachers were asked to reflect on their past experiences as students, student teachers, and beginning teachers. They were interviewed twice a year during their first 2 years of teaching. During this period of time, written reflections and reports were also part of the field texts that were collected. Later, reflections about their work as teachers in different schools were collected as writing samples and through semi-structured interviews. Data reported in this chapter draw only from the interviews conducted in 1999, when both teachers were first year teachers, and in 2009, 10 years later. The interviews lasted between an hour and a half and two hours each. Each interview was tape-recorded and transcribed verbatim. Data were analyzed according to an inductive process and substantive themes were identified as they emerged. Data analysis included a vertical analysis and a cross-case analysis (Miles & Huberman, 1994). For the purpose of this chapter, a general overview of some of the key themes in Tom and Mary's accounts is offered and illustrated through their voices. Emerging themes, similarities and differences, and their implications are discussed at the conclusion of this chapter.

TWO BRIEF NARRATIVE ACCOUNTS

Tom: Feeling Like an Outsider in His School

Tom is a teacher of physics and chemistry. He completed a 5-year teaching degree at a university and now has a permanent teaching position at a secondary school in northern Portugal, the campus he attended as a student. Before securing his permanent post, Tom worked in several other schools due to the teacher mobility that is so rampant in Portugal during teachers' early years of career. Tom told me that he never thought of becoming a teacher. He attributed this choice to "destiny" when I first interviewed him in 1999, in his first year of teaching:

> Well, all I can say is ... it was destiny. I had never thought of becoming a teacher and somehow I entered a teaching degree. It was destiny ...

However, Tom concurrently held strong beliefs about what being a teacher meant. His vision included the personal and the professional and strong principles regarding the teacher-student relationship. Being a good person, care, motivation, and being there for the students were key elements in his depiction of being a good teacher when he entered the teaching profession in 1999:

> I think being a good teacher and being a good person are linked realities. There was this teacher who talked to me a lot, who cared about his students ... and in fact (I have already told him this) because of him, because he cared, I became keen on learning and I was able to do my degree.

Ten years later, when I interviewed him, the person of the teacher remained very much present in Tom's account. The same qualities of being a teacher were reiterated in 2009. Tom continued to stress the key importance of being there for the students, of student motivation and the developing productive relationships with them. These, along with being a good person, were, for Tom, core qualities of being a good teacher. However, his first-hand experiences had challenged his ideal image. I turn to Tom's 2009 explanation:

> I thought that being a teacher has to do with transmission of knowledge to students and having a good relationship with them. And also being a person there for them. For me being a good teacher also related to being a good person. I had this idea from the very beginning; you have to have personal qualities to be a good teacher. But from my experience, it doesn't matter after all, because students don't pay attention to what you say, they don't listen to you, they don't care, I have lost this image of being a teacher. I am really tired and I am willing to get out of here as soon as possible.

Although Tom's foundational beliefs about being a teacher are still very present in his account a decade later, disappointment and lack of motivation have set in. These are, in turn, related to a number of workplace conditions, namely, the relationship with colleagues and school administration. In Tom's account below, distance and lack of trust in colleagues, associated with the existence of an individualistic culture at school, are recurring elements:

> For me, the most negative thing in schools is colleagues. I think teachers are a strange professional group. I wasn't expecting such things. My mother told me not to go to a factory but I think that teaching is even worse. Teachers care about themselves only, there is a very individualistic culture here ...

The theme of negative feelings about his relationship with his colleagues also surfaced when he was a first-year teacher in 1999. At that time, his expectations did not play out in reality. He thought that "teachers would have fun in the staff room" and that teachers would do more collaborative work. However, the reality of schools and of staff rooms was quite different, he found, which lead to his disappointment in his image of teaching and teachers' work:

> I was already acquainted with this school, because I did my secondary education practicum [here] ... and now I am allowed to go places [in the school] I have never been before. I thought that it would be very different, you know. You notice a sort of distance among teachers ... and this is also the case with the teachers teaching the same subject. And I thought it would be different. I mean, the group of teachers teaching Physics and Chemistry doesn't work as a team. I think that the group could have a different dynamic in terms of work ... Of course, it depends on the subject leader ... When I was younger I thought that teachers would have fun in the staff room, and that they would talk to one another all the time, but the reality is quite different.

Distance, lack of trust, and individualism among teachers were emphasized in Tom's account. Ten years later, Tom is even more discouraged.

He is very critical of what he describes as power relations and competitiveness in his school context, particularly in regard to school administration and to his colleagues:

> My experience in different schools has taught me that people want power. I am a teacher, I don't need to fight for power, but it seems to me that power is all that people want. People want to be better than others. They compete for that. People want to have roles at school such as head of departments and so on… I don't need that. Those who are close to people with power have benefits… and this makes me angry. I didn't know that teaching was like that, I thought that I would be learning with my colleagues.

Also of relevance in Tom's account was the influence of the policy and social context of Portugal. Tom highlights the lack of professional and social recognition of the teaching profession which impacted him, his motivation, and his job satisfaction. He also questioned the role of the media in the deterioration of the image of teachers and teaching. He additionally was very critical of recent policy initiatives related to teacher evaluation (a rather bureaucratic, summative system) and school governance (head teachers [principals] are not elected anymore, but appointed by the school council), for example. These reforms, according to Tom, have affected in many ways the professional interactions among teachers as well as the school climate, including the relationship between teachers and school administrators:

> With the recent policy on teacher evaluation things have got worse in school, teachers compete with one another and they only care about themselves. And this is getting worse with the new policy on school governance, as the head teacher [principal] is now appointed and he has now more power. Conflicts have become bigger.

And Tom added:

> My lack of motivation has to do with policy initiatives and the lack of recognition of teachers' work and also with students' lack of motivation.

Here, Tom calls into question the outcome-led orientation of teaching and the competiveness among teachers, in part due to the existence of a quota within the new Portuguese teacher evaluation system, and he argues about what being a teacher is all about: "And I ask: what does it mean to be a good teacher? It seems that nobody cares …"

In this way, inner tensions emerged in Tom as he talked about his views about teaching and being a teacher and what he actually sees and does. Students' lack of motivation and behavior were identified by him as critical issues needing immediate attention. In Tom's opinion, this has to do not only with recent government initiatives but also with the ways in which policies have been put into place:

> Then you have the policies from central government and parents... all they want is for students to move to the following year even if they know nothing... I think that students need to be accountable, they need to be responsible for what they do, they have to invest in their learning (...) What disappoints me is the lack of rigor in teaching. It has become less demanding. Students feel that they don't need to work and it is up to the teacher to do their job... they just don't care.

Tom also admits that recent changes in the policy context in Portugal and in his school context have affected him as a teacher in many ways. Of particular note are his relationships with colleagues and school leadership, which are more and more distant and marked by conflicts. Increasingly, he feels like an outsider. For him, students continue to sit at the core of teaching as a profession. His devolving relationships with them is a recurrent element in Tom's discourse, even when he talks about the gaps between his idealistic image of teaching and being a teacher and what he actually thinks and does. These tensions became exacerbated over time, due to students' reported lack of motivation and investment in their learning. In spite of these multiple challenges, Tom still finds that teaching is sometimes enjoyable and rewarding:

> Teaching was not initially my vocation, but the most important thing for me is the kids and the relationship with them, especially when they are interested in learning something. I feel happy and I enjoy being in the classroom, I enjoy teaching and time flies... Some of them are complicated, I have to admit. But looking back on my years of teaching, the most important things are the students. I have good memories ....

Despite this, Tom's feelings of fatigue and frustration outweigh his good experiences and "good memories." During his first 10 years of teaching, the policy and social environment of Portugal as well as his immediate school climate seemed to undermine his sense of professionalism and motivation, which affected, in turn, his professional identity. Despite teaching in the school where he used to be a student and where he taught as a first year teacher, the account Tom shared with me was marked by disappointment, low morale, and feelings of wanting to give up:

> I am really tired. Actually I am thinking of going back to university to do another degree... teaching is not what it was anymore.

The feeling of being frustrated with his career became more prevalent and intensified in Tom's accounts over time. His negative emotions were associated with a decrease in motivation and job satisfaction. The gap between expectations and reality produced inner tensions that have affected his professional identity as a teacher. Tom is close to abandoning the profession, doing another degree, and beginning a new occupation:

> I thought that teaching and being a teacher would be different... I feel disappointed. I started to do what others do. I don't want to be upset about what is going on here. But I am tired and I am giving up.

When asked about how he sees himself as a teacher in the near future, he emphatically replied:

> I don't see myself in teaching in the next few years. If I am strong enough I will do another degree and move to another job... I am leaving teaching, I cannot stand it anymore (...) I am leaving...

Mary: Struggling to Sustain Motivation and Hope

Like Tom, Mary is also a teacher of physics and chemistry in a secondary school in northern Portugal. She used to be a good student and she decided to do a master's degree in chemistry during her early years of teaching. Mary largely decided to become a teacher due to employment opportunities and the social status the profession offered. When I interviewed her in her first year of teaching, in 1999, she stated that:

> I believe that the choice of a career has to do with social status ... I mean, my parents belong to the lower-middle class and are not very well-off, but they could afford to pay for my instruction. There was a fear of lack of professional employment opportunities, so I decided to become a teacher ... even though teaching was not something that I really wanted to do ...

Mary's intrinsic motivation as a student and her investment in learning, as readers will soon see, were key elements in her vision and experiences as first year teacher. Being a student, for her, was as a better experience than being a teacher when she started teaching in 1999:

> I always enjoyed studying very much. I was really motivated at school ... I can even tell you that I would rather go on being a student now, than being a teacher. I always enjoyed studying a lot, so I had always a strong motivation, which is something many students don't have nowadays.

Ten years later in 2009, Mary continued to try to keep herself motivated, but uncertainty also emerged in her narrative account. This uncertainty was associated with her beliefs and experiences of teaching and being a teacher in different schools. For Mary, her reality did not match her expectations, particularly where social status and recognition of the teaching profession were concerned:

> The idea that I had about teaching has changed. I saw teachers as very important professionals, they would be there for you, they would know a lot and they would be there to do their teaching and would be respected. And I have noticed that the reality is not like that. There is no such respect and students don't look at me as a very important person, they have access to other kinds of information and other sites to learn.

Mary is keenly aware of the changes in the teaching profession over the past decade and of the tasks that are expected from teachers. She stresses the lack of social recognition, in part, due to policies that have affected teaching and teachers' work. She refers namely to the new teacher career statute and to the new scheme for teacher evaluation which have introduced more competitiveness among teachers leading to demonstrations on the part of the teachers (see Flores, 2010, 2012b). Mary points to the lack of trust in teachers and the role of the media in the deterioration of the social image of the teaching profession, which she experiences as demanding, stressful, increasingly bureaucratic, and consuming of her time and energy. Thus, keeping a balance between home and work is more and more critical:

> Sometimes I think of changing my career. The lack of trust in teachers especially through the media makes me sad. I think teaching is one of the professions that imply doing work at home. I spend hours and hours working at home. Luckily my husband is a teacher too and he understands that. He also has work to do.

And she goes on to say:

> Nobody understands how much time teachers work. People get home and they spend time with their families, whereas teachers have always work to do.

On the top of that, Mary claims that government initiatives have contributed to teachers' lack of motivation and public criticism. The lack of trust in teachers, in her view, is a negative factor affecting teachers, especially those who take their job seriously:

> Government initiatives have been negative. Instead of motivating teachers, it made teachers unmotivated. (...) You feel unmotivated especially if you want to do a good job. There are teachers that are not affected by policies as they don't care enough. For teachers who take their job seriously it is a problem, because the lack of trust in teachers affects them. Teachers' work is more and more under criticism. Everybody complains...

All these have affected Mary's sense of professionalism despite her strong beliefs about what it means to be a teacher. After 10 years in teaching, she continues to stress the key role of teacher-student interactions and she admits that she has moved from a more distant to a closer relationship with her students over the years:

> For me the most important part in teaching is the relationship with my students. This is the dimension that has changed the most over the last years. At the beginning I had a more distant relationship with students. I tried not to be strict but now my relationship with them is closer. But at the same time I keep on thinking "Am I doing the right thing?" Maybe I am not a good example for my students? And I try to relate to them always thinking about the good example that I should offer them. I think this is my biggest change.

Being a role model, "being there for the kids," and the need to educate them for success are elements of paramount importance in Mary's image of being a teacher. Mary is very demanding of herself in this regard and sometimes she questions her "good example." She also reiterates the contribution of teachers to the development of society and to students' growth. Care, self-motivation, and the teacher as a person and as a professional are prevalent in her account as readers will see in the following interview excerpt from 2009:

> I think being a teacher is of great importance to society as we spend more time with students than their parents. You have to be a model for them. You have to teach them but you also have to care about them. I have to be motivated and be there for my students. Of course they are looking at the way I teach but they also looking at my example, and I have to be careful. And this has to do with who I am, and how much I care about them. You have to educate them at all levels.

Having a closer relationship with her students is a key element in Mary's depiction of being a teacher. She admits that her students are "the best part in teaching:"

> As for the relationship with the students, my idea is that it is even better because it is much closer than the one I had with my teachers. And sometimes it is great to talk to students about the situations in which they are living. This is the best part in teaching, I mean, the close relationship with students.

The importance of relationships also emerged as a key theme in her view of teaching and being a teacher, not only with students but also with her colleagues. And she recalls the support and guidance from a colleague who made a difference in her life as a teacher. Mary stresses her friendly relationship and what she has learned from her fellow teacher. She sees herself as a critical friend:

> There is a colleague of mine who is really important to me. I met her in a school. She has made a difference in my life as I have learned a lot from her. She has a view of teaching

similar to the one I would like to have. So talking to her was a great experience, I think she has a perspective on life that is better than mine, and I have learned from how she relates to students, the idea that students have to be involved in their own learning, and so on. She told me about many situations she has lived with her students. I always try to learn something from her in order to integrate it in my own teaching. And this has been a great experience in my professional learning.

Also of relevance to Mary is the influence of school leadership, in particular in the context in which she is working. The support she gets from the school leadership team and their person-centered, value-oriented qualities sit at the forefront of her description of the school:

I think good leadership is a key to school success. My previous schools were problematic in this regard, there was lack of organization and unsupportive leadership ... This school is different. It works better because it seems that they have more autonomy, they know what they are doing. They think about their students and their staff at the same time. And there is a good atmosphere here and I think everybody does his/her best. The leadership team is very supportive... especially in terms of relationships among people. You feel like working here because you feel supported. You know that you have to do your job and that you are accountable but it works ...

Still, Mary's future in teaching does not come across as promising in 2009 as it was in 1999. She refers to the changes in the teaching profession and their effects on teachers' futures. These reforms are associated with policy initiatives, in particular, teacher evaluation and the teacher career statute, issued in 2007 in Portugal:

I don't want to think about my future. I guess I am sad. I was doing a job – the coordinator role – and now another person will do that because of the new teacher career statute. And I did a good job, people said. This is sad ...

But hope is also present in Mary, despite the increase in bureaucracy and control over teachers' work. She adds that:

As for my future in teaching, I can say that it is very dark at the moment, especially with recent changes in policy in regard to teacher evaluation and so on. My hope is that things will get better. I think that working conditions are worse now and there is too much paperwork.

So, Mary admits that she is struggling to keep her heart in teaching. She claims that sometimes she feels good in being a teacher and sometimes she feels unmotivated and disappointed. Again, students are the key element in her motivation and willingness to continue in teaching. Pride, job satisfaction, success, and enjoyment are used to describe her best moments in being a teacher and remaining motivated despite everything else swirling around her:

> There are moments that I feel good and other moments that I feel really bad. I go through these two stages always: there are times that I am motivated and other times where I am completely unmotivated and disappointed. So I think that it would be good if I leave teaching and do another job that would allow me greater job satisfaction. I would be recognized for my effort. This was the ideal situation. I would be recognized and I would have success and at the same time I would do teaching because I enjoy being with students ... I feel proud when my students have the best results in the national exams.

DISCUSSION AND CONCLUSIONS

These two brief accounts of Tom and Mary excerpted from a larger decade-long study are illustrative of the struggles and tensions in the development of the professional identities on the part of beginning teachers and the ways in which they were reconstructed and deconstructed over time. Despite differences in school context and in professional trajectories, these two teachers' accounts reveal a number of core themes that help us to better understand the ways in which their images and beliefs about teaching and being a teacher and their practice have been challenged and changed in different school contexts.

As the existing literature has demonstrated, professional identity development is influenced by personal, social, and cognitive response and it implies an "ongoing and dynamic process which entails the making sense and (re)interpretation of one's own values and experiences" (Flores & Day, 2006, p. 220). As such, the two accounts instantiated the transition of beginning teachers as they became more experienced in their school contexts. This resulted in (new) understandings and experiences that affected their professional identities. Four main themes can be pinpointed: (a) the influence of context, both at a policy and social level and at a school level; (b) the importance of relationships in teaching, particularly with students and colleagues; (c) the emergence of inner tensions resulting from the mismatch between strong beliefs and reality; and (d) the role of emotions in (re)defining teachers' practice of teaching and teachers' identity development.

It is clear that, for Tom and Mary, context made a difference, particularly to the interactions among teachers and between teachers and school leadership. School climate and particularly collaboration and collegiality are important workplace conditions (Kelchtermans, 2006) that, along with school leadership, have implications for new teachers' learning and development (Flores, 2004a; Williams, Prestage, & Bedward, 2001). Research shows that the employment context in which beginning teachers work has an impact on the development of their professional knowledge and on their commitment, self-confidence, and self-image as teachers (Pietsch & Williamson, 2010).

Both teachers spoke at length about the broader policy and social context. On the one hand, Mary and Tom identified a number of policy initiatives, namely, the new scheme for teacher evaluation and the teacher career statute (which has introduced issues of hierarchy and differentiation in teachers' career) and changes in school governance (i.e., head teachers [principals] are not elected anymore, but appointed by the school council). These policies and the ways in which they were implemented in schools clearly affected the two teachers' levels of motivation and their professional identities. Added to these is the negative image of teaching and of teachers portrayed in the media, which, according to both participating teachers, has contributed to the deterioration of the public image of teaching. As Sachs (2001a) suggests, teachers' professional identity is not straightforward, rather it is reestablished and negotiated as "there would be incongruities between the defined identity of teachers proposed by systems, unions and individual teachers themselves and that these will change at various times according to contextual and individual factors and exigencies" (p. 155).

Relationship in teaching was also one of the core themes in both Tom and Mary's narrative accounts. They both referred to the importance of relationships, particularly with colleagues and students, in their development as teachers. Not surprisingly, guidance and learning from colleagues seen as critical friends along with support from school leadership were at the forefront of Mary's more positive attitude toward teaching and, more specifically, reflective of her school context. Conversely, Tom was very critical of his school climate and leadership and the way new policies were implemented in his school. Power, competitiveness, and conflict were recurring elements in his depiction of his school ethos. This has led Tom to a more distant and, sometimes, alienated position focusing his attention on his classroom practice and in particular on his students.

However, this was not without its own set of problems. Tom recognized that students are the key element in his profession and in particular his relationship with them. He admitted that he has "good memories" but, at the same time, he claims that students' lack of motivation and lack of investment in their learning do not encourage him to remain in teaching. Mary also highlighted students and her relationship with them as a core element in her profession. She has great expectations and sometimes high demands where her work as a teacher is concerned. She sees herself as a role model for her students, not only as a teacher but also as a person. And she stresses that being with her students is the "best part of teaching," even though sometimes she feels sad for not being able to fulfill her role as a teacher in the manner she ideally would like.

Another central theme emerging from the two narrative accounts related to the values and beliefs in regard to what it means to be a teacher. Both Tom and Mary held strong beliefs in this regard, despite practice spurning their images. This lends support to earlier work which has pointed to conflicts between desire and reality (Pillen et al., 2012). The ideal image of (good) teaching and of being a (good) teacher does not match the reality and this leads to the development of inner tensions that, in turn, cause negative and sometimes contrasting emotions and feelings: happiness and frustration, joy and sadness, anger and love, and giving up and gaining hope. Despite Mary's negative emotions from time to time, she is not thinking of giving up teaching. This is in sharp contrast to Tom's decision to leave the teaching profession as soon as he is able. The contradictions between beliefs and practices and inner tensions were tied to their shifting identities from beginning teachers to more experienced teachers and grounded in the changing contexts of teaching.

A growing body of literature points to emotion as a significant and ongoing part of being a teacher. This includes the emotional impact of climate of the school and classroom practices (Flores & Day, 2006). For instance, Timostsuk and Ugaste (2010) concluded that negative emotions exercised the strongest influence on student teachers' professional identity and that the most positive emotions were related to pupils. This was most certainly the case of Tom and Mary as well. Similarly, Pillen et al. (2012) identified feelings of helplessness, anger, and an awareness of shortcomings when new teachers experience tensions in their practice. Research also has shown that the teachers who leave the profession suffer from the most emotional burnout (Hong, 2010).

Teaching is very demanding emotionally and teachers do experience a wide range of positive and negative emotions, especially when social recognition, trust, respect, and professional practice are challenged. As Day et al. (2006) stress, an "ongoing part of being a teacher is the experiencing and management of strong emotions" (p. 612). The influence of positive or negative emotions most definitely played a key role in (re)shaping teachers' understanding of teaching and in (re)constructing their professional identities in my longitudinal research with Tom and Mary. Of importance in understanding their shifting identities were the role of conflicting experiences in different contexts and their emergent inner tensions, their beliefs and motivations for becoming a teacher and to remain in the teaching profession, and their making sense of flesh-and-blood learning experiences in their school milieus (especially with students and colleagues).

Empirical work on identity is essential to teachers' education and development. It is influenced by conceptions and expectations about what a teacher should be able to know and do (Beijaard et al., 2004), and it entails the double-loop transaction between biographical and relational dimensions (Lopes & Pereira, 2012). Thus, standards and social expectations may lead to conflicts with teachers' personal desire, and diminish their experiences of good teaching (Beijaard et al., 2004; Korthagen, 2004).

The ways in which Mary and Tom in this work understood their roles and tasks and the nature of teaching itself led to a (re)construction of their professional identities in their shifting contexts of teaching. In a nutshell, their understandings of what it means to be a teacher were challenged – and altered – as they negotiated their institutional roles in their workplaces. As Sachs (2001b) puts it:

> Teacher identity stands at the core of the teaching profession. It provides a framework for teachers to construct their own ideas of "how to be," "how to act" and "how to understand" their work and their place in society. Importantly, teacher identity is not something that is fixed nor imposed, it is negotiated through experience and the sense that is made of that experience. (p. 15)

Clearly, the narrative accounts I report in this chapter emphasize the importance of changing contexts of teaching in defining, justifying, and transforming teachers' identities. But my work with Tom and Mary has also highlighted the key role of personal beliefs in (re)shaping teacher professional identity and teacher response to the institutional and situational constraints of the workplace. Listening to teachers' narratives and their restorying of them may provide important information that will enable the ISATT community and those beyond to better understanding teachers' professional worlds and lived experiences and the values surrounding teaching and being a teacher. This may contribute to more informed decision making about teacher education and induction and help to better support and sustain teachers' motivation and commitment to teaching once they enter school contexts presumably for the long term.

REFERENCES

Beijaard, D., Meijer, P. C., & Verloop, N. (2004). Reconsidering research on teachers' professional identity. *Teaching and Teacher Education, 20,* 107–128.

Bullough, R. V. (1997). Practicing theory and theorizing practice. In J. Loughran & T. Russell (Eds.), *Purpose, passion and pedagogy in teacher education* (pp. 13–31). London: Falmer Press.

Calderhead, J., & Shorrock, S. (1997). *Understanding teacher education. Case studies in the professional development of beginning teachers.* London: Falmer Press.

Clandinin, D. J., Pushor, D., & Orr, A. M. (2007). Navigating sites for narrative inquiry. *Journal of Teacher Education, 58*(1), 21–35.

Coldron, J., & Smith, H. R. (1999). Active location in teachers' construction of their professional identities. *Journal of Curriculum Studies, 31*(6), 711–726.

Day, C., Kington, A., Stibart, G., & Sammons, P. (2006). The personal and the professional selves of teachers: stable and unstable identities. *British Educational Research Journal, 32*(4), 601–616.

Elliott, J. (2005). *Using narrative in social research: Qualitative and quantitative approaches.* London: Sage.

Estola, E., Uitto, M., & Syrjälä, L. (2012, April). *Narrative identity work of beginning teachers: Finnish example.* Paper presented at the Annual Meeting of the American Educational Research Association (AERA), Vancouver, BC, Canada.

Ezer, H., Gilat, I., & Sagee, R. (2010). Perception of teacher education and professional identity among novice teachers. *European Journal of Teacher Education, 33*(4), 391–404.

Feiman-Nemser, S. (2001). From preparation to practice: Designing a continuum to strengthen and sustain teaching. *Teachers College Record, 103*(6), 1013–1055.

Flores, M. A. (2001). Person and context in becoming a new teacher. *Journal of Education for Teaching, 27*(2), 135–148.

Flores, M. A. (2004a). The impact of school culture and leadership on new teachers' learning in the workplace. *International Journal of Leadership in Education, 7*(4), 297–318.

Flores, M. A. (2004b). *The early years of teaching: Issues of learning, development and change.* Porto, Portugal: Rés-Editora.

Flores, M. A. (2006a). Being a novice teacher in two different settings: Struggles, continuities, and discontinuities. *Teachers College Record, 108*(10), 2021–2052.

Flores, M. A. (2006b). Induction and mentoring. Policy and practice. In J. R. Dangel (Ed.), *Research on teacher induction* (pp. 37–66). Lanham, MD: Rowman & Littlefield.

Flores, M. A. (2010). Teacher performance appraisal in Portugal: The (im)possibilities of a contested model. *Mediterranean Journal of Educational Studies, 15*(1), 41–60.

Flores, M. A. (2012a, April). *Be(com)ing a teacher in challenging circumstances: Giving up or sustaining commitment?* Paper presented at the Annual Meeting of the American Educational Research Association (AERA), Vancouver, BC, Canada.

Flores, M. A. (2012b). The implementation of a new policy on teacher appraisal in Portugal: How do teachers experience it at school? *Educational Assessment Evaluation and Accountability, 24*(4), 351–368.

Flores, M. A., & Day, C. (2006). Contexts which shape and reshape new teachers' identities: A multi-perspective study. *Teaching and Teacher Education, 22*(2), 219–232.

Hamman, D., Gosselin, K., Romano, J., & Bunuan, R. (2010). Using possible-selves theory to understand the identity development of new teachers. *Teaching and Teacher Education, 26,* 1349–1361.

Hauge, T. E. (2000). Student teachers' struggle in becoming professionals: Hopes and dilemmas in teacher education. In C. Day, A. Fernandez, T. E. Hauge & J. Moller (Eds.), *The Life and work of teachers. International perspectives in changing times* (pp. 159–172). London: Falmer Press.

Hong, J. Y. (2010). Pre-service and beginning teachers' professional identity and its relation to dropping out of the profession. *Teaching and Teacher Education, 26,* 1530–1543.

Kelchtermans, G., & Ballet, K. (2002). Micropolitical literacy: Reconstructing a neglected dimension in teaching development. *International Journal of Educational Research, 37,* 755–767.

Kelchtermans, G. (2006). Teacher collaboration and collegiality as workplace conditions. A review. *Zeitschrift Fur Pedagogik, 52,* 220–237.

Korthagen, F. (2004). In search of the essence of a good teacher: Towards a more holistic approach in teacher education. *Teaching and Teacher Education, 20,* 77–97.

lisahunter, Rossi, T., Tinning, R., Flanagan, E., & Macdonald, D. (2011). Professional learning places and spaces: The staffroom as a site of beginning teacher induction and transition. *Asia-Pacific Journal of Teacher Education, 39*(1), 33–46.

Lopes, A., & Pereira, F. (2012). Everyday life and everyday learning: The ways in which pre-service teacher education curriculum can encourage personal dimensions of teacher identity. *European Journal of Teacher Education, 35*(1), 17–38.

MacLure, M. (1993). Arguing for Yourself: Identity as an organising principle in teachers' jobs and lives. *British Educational Research Journal, 19*(4), 311–322.

Miles, M., & Huberman, M. (1994). *Qualitative data analysis: An expanded sourcebook* (2nd ed.). Thousand Oaks, CA: Sage.

Nóvoa, A. (1992). Os professores e as histórias da sua vida. In A. Nóvoa (Ed.), *Vidas de Professores* (pp. 11–30). Porto, Portugal: Rés-Editora.

Pietsch, M., & Williamson, J. (2010). "Getting the pieces together": Negotiating the transition from pre-service to in-service teacher. *Asia-Pacific Journal of Teacher Education, 38*(49), 331–344.

Pillen, M., Beijaard, D., & den Brok, P. (2012). Tensions in beginning teachers' professional identity development, accompanying feelings and coping strategies. *European Journal of Teacher Education,* i-first, 1–21. doi: 10.1080/02619768.2012.718758

Rex, L. A., & Nelson, M. (2004). How teachers' professional identities position high-stakes test preparation in their classrooms. *Teachers College Record, 106*(6), 1288–1331.

Sachs, J. (2001a). Teacher professional identity: Competing discourses, competing outcomes. *Journal of Education Policy, 16*(2), 148–161.

Sachs, J. (2001b, September). *Learning to be a teacher: Teacher education and the development of professional identity.* Conferência convidada proferida no Congresso da ISATT, Faro, Portugal, September 21–25.

Smagorinsky, P., Cook, L. S., Moore, C., Jackson, A. Y., & Fry, P. G. (2004). Tensions in learning to teach. Accommodation and the development of a teaching identity. *Journal of Teacher Education, 55*(1), 8–24.

Soreide, G. E. (2006). Narrative construction of teacher identity: Positioning and negotiation. *Teachers and Teaching: Theory and Practice, 12*(5), 527–547.

Sutherland, L., Howard, A., & Markauskaite, L. (2010). Professional identity creation: Examining the development of beginning preservice teachers' understanding of their work as teachers. *Teaching and Teacher Education, 26,* 455–465.

Thomas, L., & Beauchamp, C. (2007). Learning to live well as teachers in a changing world: Insights into developing a professional identity in teacher education. *Journal of Educational Thought, 41*(3), 229–243.

Thomas, L., & Beauchamp, C. (2011). Understanding new teachers' professional identities through metaphor. *Teaching and Teacher Education, 27,* 762–769.

Timostsuk, I., & Ugaste, A. (2010). Student teachers' professional identity. *Teaching and Teacher Education, 26,* 1563–1570.

Weiss, E. M. (1999). Perceived workplace conditions and first-year teachers' morale, career choice commitment, and planned retention: A secondary analysis. *Teaching and Teacher Education, 15*(8), 861–879.

Williams, A., Prestage, S., & Bedward, J. (2001). Individualism to collaboration: The significance of teacher culture to the induction of newly qualified teachers. *Journal of Education for Teaching, 27*(3), 253–267.

CHAPTER 20

TEACHERS DEALING WITH FAILURE IN A LOW SOCIO-ECONOMIC STATUS SCHOOL IN SOUTH AFRICA

Carola Steinberg

ABSTRACT

This chapter explores the emotional struggles and professional dilemmas of teachers as they deal with the on going failure of their learners in a poorly resourced school serving a low socio-economic community in South Africa. The chapter illustrates the resilience of teachers who are torn between conflicting impulses: the desire for their learners to do well while simultaneously wanting learners' failure to be acknowledged and the pressure to conform to curriculum demands while simultaneously wanting to teach and assess in ways that are more authentic to themselves and appropriate to the social context.

Keywords: Teachers' emotions; assessment; accountability; emotional labour

This story from South Africa illustrates the 'emotional labour' (Hochschild, 1983) of teachers in a primary school that serves children from a low-level socio-economic community. Hlubi, Mathoto and Joyce work in a primary school

From Teacher Thinking to Teachers and Teaching: The Evolution of a Research Community
Advances in Research on Teaching, Volume 19, 427–442
Copyright © 2013 by Emerald Group Publishing Limited
All rights of reproduction in any form reserved
ISSN: 1479-3687/doi:10.1108/S1479-3687(2013)0000019023

where all teaching takes place in ex-shipping containers large enough to fit 30 children compactly, but are typically filled to overflowing with 50 learners. In Joyce's words, the children 'come from shacks' and 'the social economic thing around us is very, very, very poor.' The research examines the dilemmas and struggles that teachers face as they deal with multiple and conflicting demands concerning what is right and appropriate for their learners and their situations and what their country expects of youth in terms of their academic performances. This chapter emanating from a new region (South Africa) of the International Study Association on Teachers and Teaching (ISATT) adds to what is known about the emotional turmoil teachers experience when dealing with the failure or potential failure of the students they serve.

In South Africa, national learner achievement is consistently low, as is evident in the results of the Annual National Assessments (Department of Basic Education [DBE], 2011), the low position of South Africa on international tests such as Progress in International Reading Literacy Study (PIRLS), Trends in International Mathematics and Science Study (TIMSS), and Southern and East Africa Consortium for Monitoring Educational Quality (SACMEQ) (Fleisch, 2007; Van der Berg et al., 2011) and the constant media focus on low passing rates. In fact, at least 60% of teachers in South Africa work in schools where failure is chronic. Even when the learners progress as individuals, they still look collectively weak on the Annual National Assessments. This failure is structurally endemic because of deep historical and economic inequalities beyond the control of teachers (Shalem & Hoadley, 2009). Yet, the public debate in the media focuses on what teachers should do to improve the scores and how teachers should be better regulated so that the scores improve, narratively smoothing the deep historical connections between and among poverty, race and low achievement. For committed teachers, this is a humiliating situation in which to be. They work hard, they take responsibility for their learners' results and yet they are vilified by the public media as 'incompetent teachers' and 'blamed for poor results' (*Sunday Independent*, 09.12.2012). This generates a sense of public failure, making teachers 'almost embarrassed to say' what they do and exacerbates teachers' deep insecurities about their effectiveness (Steinberg, 2013). This vicious circle further adds to the complexities of teachers' work in low socio-economic status schools in South Africa.

CONCEPTUAL FRAMEWORK

Before I present my case study from South Africa, I briefly describe the conceptual frame I used to analyse teachers' emotions. I used three concepts to make visible and analyse what was going on in the emotional world of teachers in relation to assessment. Following Nussbaum (2001), emotions are defined as 'cognitive-evaluative' (p. 23). By this, I mean that emotions are inextricably intertwined with our thoughts, beliefs and moral values and express the judgements we make regarding events and people that touch our lives. In Nussbaum's (2001) words, emotions are 'forms of evaluative judgement that ascribe to certain things and persons outside a person's own control great importance for the person's own flourishing' (p. 22). According to her, emotions 'direct us to an important component of our well-being and register the way things are with that important component' and thus 'emotions are acknowledgements of our goals and their status' (p. 135). Yet in spite of the object's importance, we cannot control it, and so 'the emotion records that sense of vulnerability and imperfect control' (p. 43). Analysing the teachers' expressed emotions thus enabled me to describe situations from their perspective by analysing which 'objects' were significant to the teachers and how the 'objects' were related to teachers' value system and purposes. Following Turner (2007), I also looked at how 'emotional arousal' (p. 81) operates in institutional settings. He claims that 'emotions are embedded in social structure and culture' in a two-way process: 'emotions are systematically generated under sociocultural conditions and, once aroused, they have effects on these conditions' (p. 66). Turner's (2010) conceptual scheme shows how 'emotions generated in micro-level encounters are often the fuel for either change of, or commitment to, meso and macrostructures and their respective cultures' (p. 171). He argues that love/loyalty/strong positive emotions are 'symbolic media', which, like the symbolic media of money, power or knowledge, are distributed by institutional domains (p. 173) and, once acquired, can be used to accumulate not only more positive emotions but also more of other symbolic media. Thus, positive emotions are a valued resource both intrinsically and socially. Yet, like money and knowledge, positive emotions are distributed unequally, so that the 'distribution of positive and negative emotional energies among members of a population will generally correspond to the distribution of other resources such as money, power, prestige, influence and love' (p. 175). Turner's theory enables a perspective on how the emotions of teachers both affect and are affected by the institutional structures in which teachers live and work. When teachers experience strong positive emotions within (and thus towards) their educational systems, schools, and classrooms, all is fine, but when these emotions become primarily negative, the relationships and motivation to work start to break down.

In addition to this understanding of the function and impact of emotions, I used two concepts that helped me to make the emotions more visible for research purposes, namely, emotional rules and emotional labour. The concept of 'emotional rules' is derived from Hochschild (1979, 1983), although she termed it 'feeling rules'. Adding insights from Theodosius (2008), Winograd (2003), Zembylas (2005) and Turner (2007), I describe emotional rules as the implicit, socially constructed expectations of how emotions can be expressed, given and received in social encounters. These expectations are implicit rules which are aligned with hierarchy and social status, culture and ideology and possession of knowledge, wealth and power (symbolic media). The rules can be weighted in such a way that the lower status person does not receive a 'just share' of the positive emotions exchanged in the encounter. For professionals, the emotional rules of the job are intertwined with professional norms and identity. It is worth excavating teachers' emotional rules because these enable increased awareness of emotional dynamics and it may also become possible to challenge emotional rules that inhibit a transformation of educational practice or institutional culture. When Hochschild (1983) coined the term 'emotional labour', she used it to point out a previously unnoticed form of exploitation of labour: the emotional work of friendliness demanded of service workers without them receiving any additional payment in return. The concept can be extended to teachers because the complexity of their professional positions will inevitably involve them in labouring emotionally at work in ways that go unrecognised by their employers. Yet for professionals, emotional labour is less about exploitation and more about self management, because professionals need the intrinsic motivation engendered through positive emotions in order to do their work with commitment. As Hargreaves (1998) argues, teaching is an 'emotional practice' (p. 835). So I followed Theodosius (2008) and Archer (2000) by expanding the concept to include a component of agency. In this understanding, emotional labour includes an 'inner dialogue or conversation' (Archer, 2000, p. 195), that is a 'ceaseless discussion' around the emotions which are aroused by the human needs for physical well-being, performative achievement and a sense of self-worth (p. 199). The process for resolving the tensions that arise between these different needs involves 'discernment', 'deliberation' and 'dedication', that is, it involves emotionally and cognitively discerning the conflict, deliberating the various priorities and dedicating a preferred course of action (Archer, 2000, pp. 230–241; Theodosius, 2008, pp. 101-102). Thus, as much as it is emotional labour for a salary, it is also a labour for self and can be used in empowering ways to benefit self and the moral purposes that teachers want to fulfil alongside learners.

The elaboration of these three concepts – emotions, emotional rules and emotional labour – gave me a language to make teachers' emotions more visible for the purposes of research and analysis.

DATA COLLECTION AND ANALYSIS

Data were collected through seven school-based focus group interviews with 19 teachers. The teachers were selected as a purposive sample according to the following criteria: they were committed to their work of enabling learner achievement, engaged in professional development, and working in functional public schools. They came from a range of ethnic and class backgrounds. They were not teachers who were particularly recognised for their 'organizational citizenship behaviour' (Oplatka, 2007) or remembered as 'heroic' teachers (Jansen, 2011). But they all wanted to be teachers, took their professional work seriously and, on the whole, enjoyed teaching. The schools represented a wide socio-economic range, with the most well-to-do school being long established and well resourced, situated in an upper middle class area, while the poorest school was operating in classrooms made of shipping containers and surrounded by densely packed small houses and shacks.

The focus-group interviews asked about teachers' emotions regarding various 'objects' within assessment (for example, its value, memories, policy, learners, marking, report writing, accountability), lasted between 1 and 2.5 hours and were analysed in great detail using the qualitative analysis software *Atlas.ti*. The codes used for categorising data were initially generated from the literature review and then augmented by issues that arose from the interview data. For this chapter, I am focussing on data that were coded 'dealing with failure', which is a code that arose from the data towards the end of the analysis process. Three of the seven focus groups had long conversations about the extent of the failure of their learners, what that meant for the nation and how they were attempting and struggling to deal with the failure. For this chapter, I am using only the data that came from the focus group which taught in the poorest school – the M group, which consisted of Hlubi, Mathoto and Joyce. Their discussion of learner failure spread over 68 (from a total of 220) interview responses, constituted just under a third of the interview. They returned to the discussion of failure at four points during the interview, in response to different questions (concerning the value of assessment, childhood memories of being assessed, assessment policy and their relationship with education officials). It was thus an important issue to them.

This work presents a 'thick description' (Geertz, 1993) of dealing with failure through the conceptual lens of emotional rules and emotional labour. The first selection of data presents an excavation of the emotional rule regarding failure that was vividly expressed in this group yet was common to teachers across all the focus groups. The second selection of data illustrates the emotional labour, that is the 'incessant discussion' and, in this case, spoken 'inner conversation' (Archer, 2000) that Hlubi, Mathoto and Joyce engaged in so as to deal with the 'object' (Nussbaum, 2001) of learner failure.

TEACHERS' 'EMOTIONAL RULES' FOR DEALING WITH FAILURE

Like the teachers in other focus groups, regardless of socio-economic context, the teachers in the container classroom primary school experienced themselves as interdependent with the achievement of their learners. When their learners developed and produced good results, it made them happy and motivated to continue. When their learners produced weak results, they began to doubt themselves and their teaching. As Mathoto said when justifying why assessment was important: 'You are going to assess yourself as the teacher, how much did the learner learn from you? Then if you realise that some learners did not understand well, then you assess yourself and it gives you feedback to redo it'. Her colleague Hlubi elaborated on this idea:

> I feel embarrassed and bad if my learners are not performing the way I wanted them to perform. Because the main aim of teaching them is to ensure they are well developed, they are well educated. But if they do badly in my assessment, I get confused, and say, "What went wrong? Or where did it go wrong?" Then I start to think again and see what I can adjust, so that they can make ... a little bit of achievement.

This emotional interdependence of the teachers' sense of self with learners' failures and successes is the reason why they have such a great need to deal with learner's failure when it occurs.

In terms of the policy context in which these teachers work, it is worth noting that education policy regulates the decisions that teachers can make regarding whether to pass or fail learners. Assessment policy (Department of Education, 2001, p. 20) prescribes that children cannot 'stay in the same phase' for longer than one extra year, so that children can 'progress with their age cohort'. 'Decisions about progression' are to be based on 'the recorded assessment tasks' as well as 'the advice of teachers, learners, parents and education support services'. It is preferred that when learners 'need more time to achieve the Learning Outcomes', they 'need not be retained in a grade for the whole year', but should receive a 'learner support strategy'. National policy thus emphasises learner promotion over retention, and department officials have ways and means of ensuring that the policy emphasis is implemented.

Because Hlubi, Mathoto and Joyce were responsible for the results of their learners, and because, like all human beings, they prefer to feel good, it gave them an intrinsic, personal, vested interest in enabling positive learner achievement. Thus, it came as an initial surprise to me that they were strongly opposed to the learner progression policy presented earlier. They were happy to fulfil their aim of developing and educating their learners, but they did not want their learners to be undeservedly promoted, to be 'pushed' and their marks 'polished' (Hlubi's words), so learners could move into a higher grade without earning the right to be there. They believed that covering up failure was not doing their learners any favour and was in fact adding to the failure of South African learners as exposed by the PIRLS, TIMSS and SACMEQ results. As Joyce argued,

> If you get a zero, it's a zero! And a fail must be called a fail! They must stop saying a fail is 'not competent.' They're just trying to come up with modernised English here. A fail is a fail.

Her colleague, Hlubi, agreed with her wholeheartedly:

> In terms of fail, let it be a fail. Whether I'm using a red pen, a black or a green pen - if it's a fail, it's a fail. We cannot put flowers on something that is not good.

These South African teachers did not want failure to be whitewashed by a change of terminology to 'not competent' or 'did not meet the requirements' or by denying the failure and 'pushing learners through to Grade 10' (Hlubi). They wanted learners to repeat and have a chance to improve their understanding. They wanted the reality of failure at the primary school level to be recognised, so that it could be remedied before South African learners failed the international tests at the secondary level. As Hlubi argued,

> If we say 'let's push the learner up a grade, maybe he will do something good and improve higher up', even though the learner is not doing well, then we are killing the nation. We are not only killing the kids in our school, we are killing the nation as a whole. It gives us the results which show that South Africa is not performing at the end of the day.

Of course, Hlubi, Mathoto and Joyce wanted their learners to be successful, but not at the expense of pretending that failures did not exist.

They understood that the policy of progression had been formulated 'because we are addressing the imbalances of the past', but they thought it was being done 'with the wrong culture and doing the wrong things' (Hlubi). For them, success became meaningful when failure is acknowledged. Without a clear delineation of failure, they saw no possibility of clearly delineating success either. As Hlubi concluded, 'We are not loving our kids in such a way. Let a child know if he has done wrong. Let wrong be wrong and right be right'!

The teachers' need to recognise failure is clearly a strongly held belief, but is not yet an emotional rule, as it does not tell them how to feel about failure or what currency of feeling is owed in the situation. Yet as a belief, it encompasses teachers' core values of fairness and responsibility. In Turner's (2007) language, the belief about recognising failure expresses one of the social factors that have the most impact in shaping emotional rules: the expectation of what is a 'just share' that should be received from an encounter. Maybe the implicit emotional rule is simply a variation on the emotional reality that we feel bad when we think we have failed and we feel good when we think we have succeeded, that is something like: when learners pass, the learners and teachers can rejoice; when learners fail, the learner and the teacher should feel a degree of shame. What the teachers' belief about a fail being a fail is then saying about emotions, is that these feelings of elation or shame need to be appropriately deserved. Success is achieved (and thus appropriately deserved) when prior effort has been made. Teachers need to put effort into teaching and learners need to put effort into learning before experiencing the elation of success. I would thus formulate the emotional rule as follows: *Feelings of elation at success and shame at failure need to be appropriately deserved. The elation of success requires that effort be put into teaching and learning.*

There is a disjuncture between the policy norm of favouring learner promotion over retention as compared with the teachers' belief that failure needs to be acknowledged as such and the resulting emotional rule. At stake is a differing conception of fairness. The policy considers learner promotion as fair when teachers ensure learner progress by providing additional, on-going support for weak learners. Yet for the teachers, learner progress is fair when learners are judged on their effort and results. There is also a difference in causal attribution – the policy attributes the responsibility for learners' passing grades to teachers, whereas the teachers, while not denying their responsibility, place ultimate responsibility at the feet of the learners. Teachers want learners to make the effort so as to deserve their 'just share' of positive success emotions. Emotionally, it is only when effort is made that the elation of success is appropriately deserved.

TEACHERS' 'EMOTIONAL LABOUR' OF DEALING WITH FAILURE

In this section, I use Archer's notion of an inner conversation that follows the process of 'discernment', 'deliberation' and 'dedication' as a way of making visible the process of emotional labour of Hlubi, Mathoto and Joyce when confronted with the failure of their learners. Although these teachers from a poor school and community insisted on the need to acknowledge failure as shown earlier, it was still exceedingly painful for them to confront the failure, especially when they saw the failure of their learners as a symptom of the failure of the nation's youth. All of the focus groups in the larger study touched on the national failure and, in three of the groups, it became a topic for lengthy discussion. What I want to emphasise here is how the pain and soul-searching of the teachers became ever more emotionally draining as the communities served by the school dropped lower in socio-economic status.

For Hlubi, Mathoto and Joyce teaching in the container school, the situation of learner failure felt desperate, although they never actually used that word.[1] Their desperation was apparent in the intensity of their voices and in the stories they told of how they were looking for ways to improve their teaching and learning situation. Hlubi was the first to 'discern' the problem by describing how they felt 'confused', 'demoralised' and 'criticised' by the government officials who visited their school and expected them to meet administrative standards that they were unable to live up to and did not quite see the sense of. They felt harassed by the demand that assessments needed to be written on exactly the same day in all parallel classes, giving them no space to 'work at the pace of the learners'. They resented being labelled as 'lazy'. They wanted time for teaching and time for learning, without being forced into a situation where they have to 'always assess, assess, or give [their students] work and assess without teaching them'. They experienced the department as 'putting out a lot of pressure' and themselves as 'becoming emotionally out of control' (Hlubi's words).

The subsequent 'deliberation' of the group involved discussing the various factors that made them so anxious – the curriculum policy and its pacing of lessons, their insecurity about ways of teaching and classroom management, and the lack of learner motivation. Regarding curriculum policy, Joyce explained it as being designed '*for* us', meaning that 'the involvement of teachers was not there', and thus, though it might serve the 'well-developed schools', it 'was not designed for these learners at this school'. The policy, she continued, did 'not take into consideration learners sitting underneath a tree and overcrowding'. This lack of consideration for learners in poor schools showed itself primarily in the pacing of the curriculum. Joyce found it an impossible task to do oral assessments, which required her to listen to the reading and pronunciation of each of the 50 children in her class, in order to assign a formal grade. She also found the lesson plans in the 'Foundations for Learning' series 'not practical for us' because they were 'too lengthy' and did not allow her to 'go at my pace, teaching these learners until I see that they have grasped it'. Mathoto agreed that expecting learners to participate at those levels is like 'killing them and burying them' and what she wanted instead was to 'prepare a lesson at the learners' level, so that you give them a foundation'. Hlubi also struggled to fit enough teaching into his lessons because the lesson plans used were at such a 'high pace, and a hungry child cannot grasp quickly like a child who is okay in [his/her] stomach'. No matter how much they tried, these three South African teachers could not get the learning pace of the children in their classes to match the national norm. Mathoto spoke for all three when she wished she could 'make sure that I hide that assessment book where no one would ever find it' so they would no longer spend so much time assessing. What they wanted was to spend more time on teaching and co-creating knowledge with their students instead.

The three teachers also deliberated their responsibility for the failure. Compared to teachers in more well-resourced schools, they felt less able to alleviate the slow progress and low skill level of their learners. They wanted their learners to 'learn and use that knowledge' so that 'we are building a better nation' (Mathoto), but were faced with the problem of how exactly to 'ensure that our learners are taking the right road' (Hlubi).[2] They felt that curriculum policy prohibited them from teaching according to a culturally familiar and effective model[3] and that their cramped teaching spaces prevented them from fulfilling the policy expectations of group work and other interactive pedagogical methods. The gap between their own learning history and the pedagogy as set out by curriculum policy made them feel very insecure about their teaching and classroom management.

Intensifying this deliberation was the sense that the department is 'killing the teacher's part of assessment' because when learners were not motivated to make an effort, 'there's no indication in the policies as to how we are supposed to discipline the learners who didn't do the work' (Hlubi). They understood that 'pushing' learners up the grades resulted in assessment losing its function as a disciplining and motivating agent. An indication of how desperate they felt came through Hlubi when three times he raised and deliberated on a taboo subject: the issue of corporal punishment. He knew that enacting corporal punishment would land him in jail, but sometimes he wished he could use it as a threat and as a way to motivate learners as it had been used on him when he was a grade 5 student. He personally recounted how being 'beaten a little bit'

> assisted us and motivated us to read, to work hard and to do the schoolwork properly, so to avoid this kind of punishment. And it fortunately worked for me, because ultimately I became an educator. Because I came from there, I know that if you want to work hard, you need to be beaten a little bit so that you exercise the extra amount of working.

When comparing his childhood experience with his current experience as a teacher, he thought it 'unfortunate' that 'that kind of discipline, which is called corporal punishment' is no longer available, because its absence

> demoralises the standard of learning of our kids, because they have decided not to do their schoolwork, because they know no one is going to discipline them.

The effectiveness of hitting children to encourage motivation is hotly debated, but the point of highlighting Hlubi's recruitment of corporal punishment in the cause of assessment is to show how desperately Hlubi is looking for anything that will 'energise' the children to work harder and to 'exercise the extra amount of work'. His problem is that 'really, the new ways we are assessing is good, but it does not work properly for us' and 'there's no indication in the policies as to how we are supposed to discipline the learners who didn't do the work, who are playing'. In the low socio-economic context of his container school, Hlubi feels he needs a drastic intervention to make assessment work properly to generate learner achievement. And, for him personally, being beaten was something that worked. So now he sometimes tries 'to scare them. I don't beat them. I scare them by saying that I'm going to beat you and I'm going to tell your father that you are not doing your work'! But the threat of corporal punishment does not help. The reality, as Joyce described in her response to Hlubi, is that 'the children, if they get a zero for their class work, there's no problem, it's just one of those things. They don't care. A zero is just a number'.

Children who, as Hlubi noted, have hunger pangs in their bellies, obviously have more pressing concerns to worry about than a zero as a grade. In a school where children are extremely socially disadvantaged and policy does not allow for learners to repeat a class, good grades are no longer a motivator for learning and thus assessment does not operate as a disciplining force. Yet when the learners' results are bad at a school and at national level, what happens? Hlubi answered this question succinctly: 'Whenever there's a poor result, the national government blames the teachers'.

In their process of deliberation, the teachers in the socio-economically poor school needed to do intense emotional labour in order to maintain a fine balance. On the one hand, they must remain patient and creative with the slow progress of the learners, which is necessary for teachers to gain the 'intrinsic reward' (MacIntyre, 1982) of learner achievement. On the other hand, they must somehow manage to be up to date with the pacing demands of the curriculum and the accountability demands of the department officials, which is necessary for the 'extrinsic reward' (MacIntyre, 1982) of departmental approval. It is not surprising that this balancing act generated insurmountable tension and that the teachers easily 'get emotionally out of control' (Hlubi).

The third step of the emotional labour process – the resolution and renewed 'dedication' for how to handle the situation – remained unexpressed in this conversation. I found nothing in the interview that could be interpreted as a dedication for how to alleviate low learner achievement or lessen the emotional pain around learner failure. The only thing they could do was to tenaciously hang on and continue teaching. Hlubi, Mathoto and Joyce were stuck in a triple bind. They wanted their learners to succeed, but for reasons of poverty and class overcrowding, their lesson pacing could not keep up with the national curriculum standards. Their insecurity regarding their pedagogical practices diminished their pleasure in teaching. And by having to 'progress' all learners, they lost the motivating and disciplining function of assessment. This left them in a desperate state of affairs. They would like to dedicate themselves to learners experiencing the 'love' of learning, but what was happening felt more like 'killing' learning. The emotional labour that Hlubi, Mathoto and Joyce were doing just to continue teaching every day while living with this over-whelming sense of failure was immense.

In spite of their on going and painful emotional labour, Hlubi, Mathoto and Joyce had not given up – they continued to take responsibility for the achievement (or lack of it) of learners in their classes. They also had moments when they thoroughly enjoyed teaching and assessment. But because the general level of achievement of their learners was low, and they were constantly getting into trouble with department officials for not having records ready on time, they felt they were being blamed. Indeed, if they accepted this blame and turned it into self-blame, it would overwhelm them completely. So they diverted the blame away from themselves by blaming policy for being inappropriate to their school. Yet blaming policy prevented them from recognising their work as a valid interpretation of policy in context. This left them frustrated in multiple ways.

But I did find other moments of dedication in the words of these teachers. Although Hlubi, Mathoto and Joyce did not receive enough satisfaction from high learner achievement, they did remain determined to be teachers. At a practical level, there was the security of a steady job. As Joyce laughingly said at the beginning of the interview, 'You won't get retrenched because the job doesn't get finished. Kids are born day in, day out. So whenever I see a woman pregnant, I say, there comes my job'. At a deeper, more personal level, they experienced teaching as having emotional compensations and rewards though their interaction with the children, quite separate from assessment. When learners 'express themselves' and 'we interact' (Mathoto), when learners 'are performing' and we 'see their reasoning' (Joyce), when we see their 'creativity and understanding' (Hlubi), then they received pleasure and moral rewards. The teachers also 'learned a lot of things from these learners' (Joyce); they had the opportunity to 'solve other people's problems' and in doing so found solutions for their own (Mathoto), and they loved it 'when the learners come to you and hug you' (Mathoto). Their pleasure in teaching resonates with the emotional rules for being a teacher that Winograd (2003) highlights: teachers love their work and the children they teach. And finally, at a community level, the three teachers had hope for the future. This did not appear during the course of the interview, but afterwards, when Hlubi took me on a stroll around the school grounds. Hlubi had been with the school since the beginning. He was there when it started as a community initiative. He was there through the years of struggling to get it registered with the department. And he was there when it recently received funds from the business sector building a small brick school hall, with the promise of grade 1 classrooms to follow. Hlubi was proud of what the school had achieved – the recognition from the department, the increasing number of container classrooms to satisfy community demand for attendance and the support from outside the community. The fact that parents chose this school for their children also gave him hope. If so many parents sent their children, then they must be satisfied with the school and the teachers, a satisfaction which softened the teachers' struggles with failure. With the community backing them up, Hlubi and his colleagues trusted that things would continue to get better.

CONCLUSION

This story of teachers' emotional rules and labour in a school with few resources in a low socio-economic community in South Africa illustrates the amazing resilience of teachers like Hlubi, Mathoto and Joyce. Compared to their colleagues with more able learners in better resourced schools, teachers such as Hlubi, Mathoto and Joyce in poorly resourced schools experience more desperation and less efficacy, more fear and less satisfaction. Nevertheless, their deliberations illustrate how they uphold the ethical choice of continuing their efforts to enable learner achievement. And, even when they feel stuck in situations of failure shaped by long-standing historical inequities, they continue their work with hope for the future. In spite of the vulnerability (Kelchtermans, 1996) they experienced in the face of difficult work, student failure and pressure from departmental policy, these teachers drew inspiration from the children they teach and continued feeling a sense of satisfaction from doing something of value for learners.

I used interviews that asked teachers about their emotions in relation to various 'objects' of assessment (Nussbaum, 2001) with an understanding that emotions are aroused within and distributed by institutional domains (Turner, 2007). I then analysed the data through the lens of emotional rules (Hochschild, 1983; Zembylas, 2005) and emotional labour (Archer, 2000; Hochschild, 1983; Theodosius, 2008). The approach I have outlined enabled this story to be told in a detailed and intimate way from the perspective of a particular group of teachers operating in a particular context. Yet, I trust that the expressed emotions resonate across contexts to other scholars internationally and enable insights into other, both similar and different, contexts in which teachers diligently work to enable learner achievement.

NOTES

1. Even though their conversation had a strong emotional undertone, these three teachers did not use many emotion words. They tended to tell stories and present arguments that illustrated their predicaments, without naming the emotions evoked. So occasionally I needed to infer the emotions, rather than being able to present

them as part of a quotation. But I did send the teachers copies of this chapter, and Hlubi's comment on the chapter dealing with emotional rules and labour of assessment, from which this story is drawn, was that 'It makes sense; it's a true reflection of what teachers are going through'.

2. Another group of teachers in a school surrounded by poor communities experienced the same problem. Thobile said, 'Last year we had so many learners who could not go to high school, because their work was just zero. And to our surprise, most of that group were able to run away from us to high school. We only have 20 who are back with us this year because they cannot proceed to high school. But I'm telling you, we still have the same problems. We don't know what to do. The very same learners in the same class, they fail.

3. Here is a vivid description of that model: 'There was this Biology teacher. He liked using rote ... we call it memorising ... rote learning, singing. In grade 10, there was this picture of a tooth, with brackets and labels. And with this diagram we used to sing a song and dance. It was rote learning; it was playing. That method worked for me, because I still remember those words today. The first one was enamel, then it was dentine, and then it was gum. Then we'll be going around greeting each other: "enamel, dentine, and the gum". Twisting our tongues. I still remember those. It was nice. Not everything that was done in the olden days was bad. Even when it comes to our language, SePedi, we used to memorise, sing these things, and then if it was time for exams, you will start singing and writing. And that's how we managed to pass. And the other important thing is, we still remember those words even today (bangs hand on table for emphasis). We can still use them today. It was fun. Yes, there were times of teachers beating us, but other times it was fine because we were singing and dancing about what we were doing in class'.

ACKNOWLEDGMENT

Great thanks is extended to my doctoral supervisor, Professor Yael Shalem, who provided conceptual rigour and emotional support for this work.

REFERENCES

Archer, M. S. (2000). *Being human: The problem of agency*. London: Cambridge University Press.

Department of Education, Republic of South Africa. (2001). *National policy on assessment and qualifications for schools in the general education and training band*. Pretoria, South Africa.

Department of Basic Education (DBE), Republic of South Africa, Pretoria. (2011). *Report on the Annual National Assessments of 2011*. Pretoria, South Africa.

Fleisch, B. (2007). *Primary education in crisis: Why South African schoolchildren underachieve in reading and mathematics*. Cape Town, South Africa: Juta & Co.

Geertz, C. (1993). *The interpretation of cultures*. London: Fontana Books.

Hargreaves, A. (1998). The emotional practice of teaching. *Teaching and Teacher Education*, *14*(8), 835–854.

Hochschild, A. R. (1979). Emotion work, feeling rules, and social structure. *The American Journal of Sociology*, *85*(3), 551–575.

Hochschild, A. R. (1983/2003). *The managed heart: Commercialisation of human feeling*. Berkeley, CA: University of California Press.

Jansen, J., with Koza, N. Toyana, L. (2011). *Great South African Teachers*. Johannesburg: Pan Macmillan and Bookstorm.

Kelchtermans, G. (1996). Teacher vulnerability: Understanding its moral and political roots. *Cambridge Journal of Education*, *26*(3), 307–325.

MacIntyre, A. (1982). *After virtue: A study in moral theory*. London: Duckworth.

Nussbaum, M. C. (2001). *Upheavals of thought: The intelligence of emotions*. Cambridge: Cambridge University Press.

Oplatka, I. (2007). Managing emotions in teaching: Towards an understanding of emotion displays and caring as non-prescribed elements. *Teachers College Record*, *109*(6), 1374–1400.

Shalem, Y, & Hoadley, U. (2009). The dual economy of schooling and teacher morale in South Africa. *International Studies in Sociology of Education*, *19*(2), 110–134.

Steinberg, C. (2013). *Teachers' emotions towards assessment: What can be learned from taking the emotions seriously?* Unpublished doctoral dissertation. University of the Witwatersrand, South Africa.

Theodosius, C. (2008). *Emotional labour in healthcare: The unmanaged heart of nursing*. London: Routledge.

Turner, J. H. (2007). *Human emotions: A sociological theory*. London: Routledge.

Turner, J. H. (2010). The stratification of emotions: Some preliminary generalizations. *Sociological Inquiry*, *80*(2), 168–199.

Van der Berg, S. et.al. (2011). *Low quality education as a poverty trap*. A report by the Social Policy Research Group, Department of Economics, University of Stellenbosch, funded by the Programme to Support Pro-Poor Policy Development, A partnership between the Presidency, Republic of South Africa and the European Union.

Winograd, K. (2003). The functions of teacher emotions: The good, the bad and the ugly. *Teachers College Record*, *105*(9), 1641–1673.

Zembylas, M. (2005). *Teaching with emotion: A postmodern enactment*. Greenwich, CT: Information Age Publishing.

CHAPTER 21

THE NECESSITY OF PROVIDING GUIDANCE FOR REFLECTION IN INSERVICE TEACHER TRAINING PROGRAMS IN KYRGYZSTAN

Cholpon Musaeva

ABSTRACT

In this chapter, the author argues that only raising awareness about teaching techniques in short-term inservice teacher training programs is not sufficient. She calls for inclusion of practical guidance for systematic reflective practice that will help teachers become autonomous in the long term. As many developing countries are still deprived of formal teacher development faculty at educational institutions who can support teachers' growth in-house, she suggests that inservice teacher training programs incorporate guidance for teacher reflection to assist practitioners' ongoing learning when they return to their school settings.

Keywords: Reflection; inservice teacher training; teacher's professional development; awareness raising; teacher change

To be afforded the opportunity to participate in an inservice course in most developing countries is a stroke of good luck for those teachers fortunate

From Teacher Thinking to Teachers and Teaching: The Evolution of a Research Community
Advances in Research on Teaching, Volume 19, 443–456
ISSN: 1479-3687/doi:10.1108/S1479-3687(2013)0000019024

enough to be selected. Due to social, geographical, and financial constraints, many teachers are still unaware of innovations that could enhance their teaching and make their practices more psychologically rewarding and up-to-date. However, there is no guarantee that even those lucky teachers who have experienced short-term inservice teacher training programs will be able to sustain their continuing professional development after completion of the course.

This chapter is based on a study conducted in Kyrgyzstan, a country that was part of the former Soviet Union. In the following sections, I discuss two major findings that arose from my field-based work. The first is that teachers' awareness of techniques and strategies for effective teaching is a critical step in boosting their confidence and self-esteem which, in turn, fuels quality professional development. The second finding shows that equipping participants with discrete teaching techniques, approaches, and knowledge, while useful, does not guarantee and is not sufficient to enhance teachers' further development. After sharing my two findings, I discuss how incorporating guidelines for reflective practice into short-term inservice teacher training programs encourages ongoing systematic professional development. Such a course of action narrows the distance between teacher training and teacher development. Often considered as two poles on a continuum, initial training and subsequent teacher development programs in developing countries struggle to be both cost effective and of practical value. I conclude this chapter with a discussion about a program which included awareness raising methods, techniques, beliefs, knowledge, and practices but did not include practical guidance for reflection in supporting teachers' continuous professional growth.

TEACHER TRAINING AND TEACHER DEVELOPMENT

In the literature, training and development are generally contrasted. Bailey (2006), on one end of the continuum, cites Freeman who defines *training* as a "strategy for direct intervention by the collaborator (defined by Freeman as 'someone who helps the teacher learn'), to work on specific aspects of the teacher's teaching" (as cited in Bailey, 2006, p. 67). On the other end of the continuum, *development,* according to Bailey's (2006) interpretation, is a "strategy of influence and indirect intervention that works on complex, integrated aspects of teaching [that] are idiosyncratic and individual" (p. 67). Head and Tailor refer to training as being based on the knowledge of the topic to be taught, and to development as centered on "the learning atmosphere which is created though the effect of the teacher on the learners, and their effect on the teacher" (as cited in Bailey, 2006, p. 68). The research team states that development is about people skills and awareness of their attitudes and behaviors. However, due to practical reasons, reducing the distance between training and development by complementing teachers and supporting their systematic reflective practices in a short-term training course emphasizing rudimentary, intuitive, and vague reflections are unlikely to bring about changes that will positively impact "life in classrooms" (Jackson, 1968).

There are various types of reflection in the professional and academic literature. This study adopts a type of reflection that Hoover called "a learned activity … it is a carefully planned set of experiences that foster a sensitivity to ways of looking at and talking about previously unarticulated beliefs concerning teaching" (as cited in Farrell, 2001, p. 36). Farrell (2001) suggests that deepened sensitivity to one's approach to teaching needs to be a component introduced by the end of training courses in order to raise participants' awareness of the ways to reflect independently after the session is complete.

CONTEXT OF THE STUDY

This study is based on a three-month inservice teacher training course conducted in Bishkek, Kyrgyzstan, a city where English is a foreign language and citizens have limited exposure to English. Most of the teachers of English lack pedagogical knowledge, skills, and beliefs about facilitative teaching due to several factors. First, English language departments preparing teachers largely focus on linguistic instruction with little or no space for examining theory and practice of teaching a foreign language in their curricula. Consequently, only the strongest students have a solid command of English post-graduation. The graduates, however, usually do not have knowledge and skills about teaching and learning (including teaching skills and sub-skills, lesson or course planning, assessment, the nature of the learner, the learning process, classroom management, working with materials, syllabus, curriculum, motivation, facilitation, etc.). Second, graduates are generally not motivated to become teachers, especially those who major in foreign languages. They plan to use their language skills in better paid corporate or multinational organizations. Comparatively, the socioeconomic status of teachers is low and the workload is heavy. So, if English Language teachers are offered jobs with higher salaries in other fields, they willingly leave teaching.

RATIONALE

As Lev Tolstoy (1967) stated, good teaching is "not a method but an art" (as cited in Schön, 1983, pp. 65–66). That art is not a mere set of techniques and frameworks, rather a whole myriad of multifaceted aspects of competencies such as values, beliefs, knowledge, skills, and practices. To achieve that level of professionalism, it requires inborn abilities and hard work via mediated, experiential, and reflective learning. The learner who is trained, and used to top-down information transmission method needs guidance on ways to reflectively learn.

In Kyrgyzstan, the in-house coaching, supervision, and induction of novice teachers at universities are poorly developed; they exist either only in documents or a surface level. Teachers are mostly left to their own devices. Some undergo short-term inservice training programs or workshops; others blindly follow text-books never questioning the curriculum or objectives of their teaching. At the same time, they cannot be blamed for their complacence; they are unaware of other forms of learning. Without support, teachers generally learn and teach according to the traditional model. Furthermore, there is no guarantee that even those teachers who experience short-term training programs on teaching skills will continue to grow after the course is over. This is because courses are largely based on information transmission, mostly on techniques, frameworks, and discrete elements of teaching. Though awareness-raising is fundamental and integral to further development, simply learning new skills unfortunately does not lead to their further development. Moon (2004) asserts that reflective and experiential learning supports awareness-raising as central to self-directed professional growth. After the course is over, teachers need to be able to take responsibility for their further learning by noticing, thinking, selecting, reflecting, and acting. Integral to internally directed growth is the integration of both top-down and bottom-up paradigms in the teacher development course.

This study suggests that inservice teacher training programs integrate a component that will guide teachers on how to reflect either during or after the course. This integration rather than separation is likely to be effective because both top-down and bottom-up strategies promote teacher learning, and the approach seems viable for developing countries with no induction programs. The purpose of this study then is to better understand (a) the role of awareness in teaching skills in teacher's professional growth, and (b) an awareness-raising approach to improve the quality of teachers' teaching.

METHODOLOGY

The professional development course consisting of sessions on classroom management, teaching vocabulary, grammar, speaking, listening, reading, and writing skills, and including written and oral assessment was conducted once a week for 4–5 hours. It was offered by an independent training school twice a year and was meant for teachers seeking improvement and change in their teaching skills. Teachers themselves willingly initiated and attended the course because it was not a compulsory.

The course incorporated different interaction patterns and used experiential learning principles in the form of demonstration lessons where the participants first experienced all the techniques as students in the sessions, and then analyzed and discussed them from a teacher perspective. After each session devoted to particular skill and/or content, the participants were encouraged to try the discussed techniques and frameworks with their students and to write about their lesson procedures and difficulties and successes in their reflective journals.

The six female Kyrgyz teachers of English working at universities in the capital of The Kyrgyz Republic involved in this research study were selected from the participants of a three-month inservice teacher training course. They had been interviewed and selected to participate in this training course. Three teachers had three months experience and three teachers had six or more years of experience. The reasoning behind the selection of novice and relatively experienced teachers was to examine whether experience makes a difference in learning and incorporating new skills into their teaching, and to see whether their reflection is deeper than that of novice teachers.

The data in the qualitative research study were collected and analyzed using coding and classification to aid in the analysis. Two 30-minute to 60-minute informal interviews were conducted with each participant. Non-participatory classroom observations also took place at the beginning and at the end of the training program. For every participant, two to four lessons were observed. Journal entries capturing communication between the course trainers and the participants were collected at the end of the course as well.

Transcriptions of the audiotaped interviews, videotaped lessons, and field notes and transcriptions of diary entries were pooled together. From the amassed evidence, participants' recurring concerns were identified which, in turn, became the study's main themes. These themes were analyzed by comparing and making sense of the material accessed gained through the research tools described above to understand (a) how the participants made sense and use of awareness of teaching knowledge and skills to which they had been introduced, and (b) whether this type of awareness was sufficient enough to promote autonomous continuous teacher growth.

FINDINGS

Data analysis across participants suggested that they shared certain common experiences. Irrespective of their age and experience, all six participants experienced more or less similar feelings, doubts, and struggles while incorporating new techniques in their lessons.

Benefits

The participants' journal entries, their discussions during the training sessions, and the discussions with me clearly showed that the teachers benefited from the course in terms of their competency based proficiency in certain teaching skills and practical knowledge. They became aware of the existence of alternatives to the traditional way of teaching and were exposed to new ways of teaching, and thus were cognizant of how much they knew and how much more they needed to learn.

One of the novice teacher participants, for example, noted in her journal entry (Words in bold indicate participants' raised awareness):

> After our discussion in the first session I **understood** that I always conduct the traditional lessons (including "Who is absent?" "What is a date today?" etc.). I don't want to conduct my lessons this way. I **found out** in the learning teaching book that there are 3 kinds of teachers. After reading the book I think that I am an *explainer* teacher who knows [her] subject matter well, but has limited knowledge of teaching methodology. But I want to be the *enabler* teacher. I hope that I'll be *the enabler* teacher day-by-day, step-by-step, of course with the help of you.

After she had had a demonstration lesson and discussed classroom management strategies including different interaction patterns the same participant quoted above had the following to say to me in an interview:

> **At the beginning of this course** I had some questions, but **now** I am working on them, I'm trying to change them. **Earlier-before** coming to this course before the beginning of the lesson I **never asked** students about their problems or difficulties with homework. **Now** I ask them if they have any problems, I give them a minute. And I'm working on dividing group into two groups or small group or pair work. I like this way very much because

students will be able to communicate with each other and they can express their opinions. **Now** I know that it is one of the effective ways to learn.

The main themes that emerged from the six teachers' journal passages, discussions, and lesson observations had to do with learning new games and activities to explain grammar; motivating and involving learners; creating opportunities for students to speak English in class; dealing with mixed ability groups of students; giving instructions; and learning new techniques and frameworks to make lessons interesting. The participants' awareness was also raised by the demonstration classes. The classes exposed them to new ways of instruction and a new environment. Their discussions and interaction with the course trainers through journal exchanges were beneficial. The researcher's observations of the classes and discussions also indicated raised awareness. As one of the novice teacher-participants noted in her journal:

As for first impressions? ... We played a game, and I **understood** that we should play games more because the students were happy and everyone was involved. I promised them another game next week.

Another novice teacher-participant wrote in her journal:

After our last session on vocabulary I had to work on MPF (Meaning, Pronunciation and Form). But **before** coming to this course when I worked on vocabulary, I only wrote the words with their translations on the board. **But now** I try to use vocabulary techniques (I choose one which [relates] to my theme). I **liked** MPF because by using it the students will be able to pronounce the words in correct way and be ready to answer. And I think if they touch the things, they will understand the words and what they mean. Thank you.

In an interview, one of the experienced participants emphasized the following:

Before coming to this course my students **did not use** to work in pairs, groups. **Now** they work in pairs and groups. **Earlier** for listening I **used to** play the tape immediately without telling them what they will do, and there wasn't any post listening. **Now** with my students I follow all the stages of the pre, during, and post listening model. It's **important** to prepare students using pictures, creating situations, use background knowledge of students, elicit and pre-teach vocabulary. Also the post- production stage is **important.** It gives students a chance to use their background knowledge to make up stories, dialogues, etc.

These excerpts from the participants' journals and discussions clearly showed that they learned new techniques and frameworks, and how and why to use them. Furthermore, all of the participants learned new techniques and frameworks and tried using some of them in their classes in their own ways. They were not able to use all the learned skills at the same time, so their focus was on an issue or a set of issues that was important to them. A field note entry from the beginning of the lesson taught by one of the participants suggests that her attention and focus was limited.

The teacher had a class with the first year university students whose proficiency level was basic. The teacher began the class in a friendly manner. For a warm-up activity to introduce the topic of the lesson "Clothes" she used the game "Hangman" (Fig. 1).

T: *I have some pictures for you* (T showed pictures and stuck them on the board, drilled pronunciation: "blouse," "trousers." When Ss saw the picture of trousers/pants, one of them said: *"pants"* but T ignored it. The pictures were small and not visible, and she put the pictures close to each other. It would probably be a good idea to teach or elicit from Ss collocations with "A pair of …" "pants/trousers/pyjamas/ glasses")

(Eventually T presented 20 words by sticking pictures on the board by drilling pronunciation. After she put all the pictures on the board, she tried eliciting spelling of the words, but by that time the Ss forgot the words. However, she worked on spelling and wrote them on the other side of the board. After that she said: *Let's repeat all these words.* Then she divided the group into two: A and B, and gave instructions)

T: *Here are two pictures. You need to find differences.*

(Then she tried asking a concept check question to check if the Ss understood the instructions)

T: *What should you do?*

T: *You have to find differences and write in your notebooks. You have 7 minutes.*

(Though it was a wonderful information gap activity, she did not mention how many differences they needed to find and what language to use for description … While Ss were working by speaking mostly Russian, the T was not monitoring, but busy writing a crossword puzzle (which was the next activity) on the blackboard).

Fig. 1. Field Note Entry.

This example indicates that the teacher learned techniques and could describe and analyze their benefits, but when she taught a face-to-face lesson with students, there were quite a few gaps of which she was still unaware. By the end of the class, everyone was happy. She incorporated many elements she learned from the given training course by using pictures, games, handouts, board, group work, etc. It was obvious that she had put much effort into the preparation of this lesson. It was varied in terms of materials and tasks: an interesting warm up, a wonderful information gap activity and a crossword puzzle, for example. However, she lacked proficiency in managing them because she was more focused on providing activities. For example, if the target of the lesson was vocabulary development (where close monitoring is important), her attention probably should not have been directed to the crossword puzzle on the board when students were doing the activity. She also could have incorporated certain words in the hangman game, which were related to clothes. This would have been meaningful and helpful to students' "communicative competence" (Hymes, 1966). It seems at this introductory stage it is quite normal for a participant to be concerned with more discrete aspects of teaching, rather than considering the overall flow of the lesson.

Reflection

The analysis of the data also revealed that the course trainers' journal responses to the participants promoted a particular type of rudimentary reflection. The teachers started to understand the reasoning behind different classroom management strategies, such as pair work and group work, giving clear instructions, etc. They began using some elements of different techniques for teaching/eliciting vocabulary; the Presentation, Practice, Production (PPP) framework for teaching grammar; and the Pre-During-Post (PDP) framework for teaching perceptive skills, which were discussed in the course.

Participants internalized certain aspects of the course content in ways unique to each individual. They focused mostly on issues that sparked their personal and professional interests. For example, the majority of the participants loved the pre-teaching vocabulary technique using pictures. However, while observing these lessons, I witnessed that two of the teachers overused this technique by pre-teaching more than 20 words. Each time they showed the picture, drilled the pronunciation in chorus or individually, or both, and so forth. It was obvious that in the beginning the students were excited and involved due to newness of the whole process, but after the 15–16th word they were tired of drilling the words, and when the teachers tried to elicit spelling of the words after sticking all the pictures on the blackboard, the students found it difficult to remember the words, not to mention their spelling.

Most of the teacher participants perceived that fun equaled learning, possibly forgetting about the pedagogical purposes of the lessons. One teacher was extremely creative and always sought materials from different sources. Once, she found games from the internet that fit the theme of her lesson and played them with her students. However, it could be argued that none of the tasks really served any pedagogical purpose. Yes, the students and the teacher were happy and excited, but it is questionable where learning actually occurred in the class.

As can be seen from the examples presented above, teachers showed behavioral change and could reflect on certain practical aspects they learned in the training course. However, this change occurred at a surface level, and course learning was transferred selectively. Even toward the end of the course the participants struggled to incorporate some of the course elements into their teaching and in their journals they asked for advice.

The example that follows shows a sincere desire to make improvements.

> Dear Trainer,
> I'm asking for your advice. I have students from the 1st course and 2nd course (first and second year students). In some groups the level of knowledge is good, but there are some groups of the 2nd course in which the students' level is low. They are beginners .... So, what should I do? I cannot explain from the beginning, because they are 2nd course students and also I have a (syllabus) which I must follow ... I know that it is not their fault. The problem they said is that they had teachers changing very often [last year]. I don't know what to do. Please give me advice.

The professional developer replied to this journal entry by suggesting that she form groups so that strong students and weak students work together, so that stronger students could help weaker ones. The teacher did assign different tasks to different students accordingly. The participant replied to the trainer's suggestion in the following way:

> I'm grateful for your advice. At first, I tried mixing strong students with weak students, but I didn't see the progress ... I saw that weak students just repeated what was said by the strong students without any understanding ... Then, I decided to give different tasks and homework. Now I can see for sure that it works better. I see the progress both of strong and weak Ss. Thank you very much! ☺

The participant's comments show that her willingness to explore the advice indicates that positive change and development is possible.

This kind of training course is an initial stage that raises teachers' awareness of areas of instruction they need to improve. However, for further professional growth, Dewey (1933) argued that teachers need three attributes of reflection: open-mindedness, responsibility, and wholehearted-ness (as cited in Farrell, 2007, p. 2). By the end of the inservice course, these participants were excited about the new teaching techniques which were an alternative to the traditional way of teaching. However, they lacked alternatives and had limited knowledge of underlying principles and rationale behind the strategies and techniques they were using. This deeper kind of knowledge could empower them to be *open-minded* in a professional sense. Where *responsibility* is concerned, they were still struggling with new assumptions about teaching. They borrowed the activities, used them in their classes, and were happy to see how their students enjoyed this way of teaching. However, they were not ready to look deeply at the consequences of them yet as they had not brought them fully into their sense of knowing and their repertoires of experience. *Wholeheartedness* "implies that teachers can overcome fears and uncertainties to critically evaluate their practice in order to make meaningful change" (Farrell, 2007, p. 2). While the teachers in this study had overcome some of their anxieties, they were not at the point at which they could critically and creatively engage in a reflective turn (Schön, 1991) on their practices. Some were still trying to find recipes to resolve dilemmas of practice (i.e., A. Berlak & Berlak, 1981/2012; Korthagen & Kessels, 1999).

DISCUSSION

The findings of this study make three contributions to what is known about teaching and teacher education locally, regionally, and internationally. First, awareness raising as a form of training is necessary for teacher learning, but not sufficient for continuous and autonomous development (Day, 1993). As Pennington (1995), for example, rightly stated, "[t]eacher change and development requires an awareness of a need to change" (p. 705). It is indeed a prerequisite for initiation of learning, but it is not the only thing that is needed. Second, courses aimed at transmission of knowledge and skills inform teachers about different issues, encourage them to be creative, but, at the same time, make them receivers of knowledge who expect solutions from outsiders. They act as curriculum implementers not curriculum makers (Clandinin & Connelly, 1992; Craig & Ross, 2008). They wait for guidance, new materials, lesson plans, etc. to come from someone else. They do not yet see themselves and each other as sources of knowledge, insight, and action. Workshops and training courses, they believe, are the only places to encounter new ideas. This is unfortunate because due to the low socioeconomic conditions in the country they might not have another opportunity to attend training programs and workshops. Third, authentic growth happens only when the teacher engages himself or herself, prepares, performs, and evaluates his or her actions using a self-initiated and self-directed systematic process of reflection (Dewey, 1933; Loughran, 2006; Lyons, 2010).

In my work, the six teacher participants transferred and internalized information selectively. Bailey (2006) explained that they were choosy about the advice they were given and then decided if they would process it at all.

> [T]eachers take in only those aspects of the available input which are accessible to them. *Accessible input* refers to those types of information which the teachers are prepared to attend to because of a high awareness and understanding of the input coupled with favourable attitudes such as preexisting interest in or positive attitudes towards the form of input or the person giving the input, a strong recognition of a need for input or change, or a strong feeling of discomfort at a pre-existing clash of values. (as cited in Bailey 2006, p. 65)

If we situate the type of teacher training I have described here in the larger international landscape of teacher development process, it would be akin to what Korthagen and Vasalos (2005) label "a quick fix," which is

> a rapid solution for a practical problem – rather than shedding light on the underlying issues. While this may be an effective short-term measure in a hectic situation, there is a danger that one's professional development may eventually stagnate. (p. 48)

Though a basic reflection activity was incorporated that fostered the understanding of fundamental practical concepts and skills, it was far from sufficient. It is obvious that a deeper, systematic type of reflection is required.

The hope now is to enable teachers to develop through self-initiated and self-directed inquiry leading to *double-loop learning* (Argyris & Schön, 1978) after the completion of the training program. Such reflection would allow teachers to learn from their experiences, connect that learning with past experiences, and to apply that learning in new situations in more productive ways. In the future, this will be achieved by including a component on reflection to raise teachers' awareness about and provide some models of ways to reflectively learn. However, it would be overambitious to aim for the deep reflection. Schön (1983) highlighted in the practitioner-resident's interaction. Schön (1983) analyzed this in terms of reflection-in-action: "oscillat[ing] between the unit and the total ... and between involvement and detachment" (p. 102). This was possible because the practitioner and resident knew the functions of the discrete constituents of a system as well as "the larger relationships on which the qualities of the whole idea will depend" (*ibid.*, p. 102). Competence and an adequate knowledge base were presupposed. In the under-resourced and underdeveloped English language education system in Kyrgyzstan, competence and an adequate knowledge base of teachers is not a given. Hence, including an aspect on reflection in an inservice training course would be a beginning step. More lofty goals for reflection will come later. For now, an awareness of systematic reflective strategies will provide teachers with opportunities for internally directed learning rather than having them wait for an outsider to assist them to grow. This way the teachers will come to know their idiosyncrasies and develop in their own distinctive manners.

CONCLUSION

For most of the teachers in the study, reflection was not a consciously planned systematic activity that enhanced the quality of their teaching and learning. However, collaboration with other teachers, access to professional and academic literature and other resources, along with raised awareness of the importance of reflection and guidance on the ways of systematic reflection, would slowly lead to increased teacher autonomy and self-growth. This study reinforces the notion that effective teacher growth can be stimulated by reflection. In order to grow and change personally and professionally, teachers need to know that reflection assists practitioners to examine and evaluate themselves and their teaching practices. It is vitally important because it sustains teachers in their careers (Clandinin, 2010) and is therefore important. Teachers also need guidelines on how to be reflective probably toward the end of the training program or as a post-training workshop focusing on self, pair and collective models of engaging in reflective practice. Incorporating a component on reflection in short-term inservice teacher training courses prevent teachers' professional stagnation in Kyrgyzstan and other developing countries where educational establishments lack in-house teacher development and induction programs.

REFERENCES

Argyris, C., & Schön, D. A. (1978). *Organizational learning: A theory in action perspective.* Reading, MA: Addison-Wesley.

Bailey, K. M. (2006). *Language teacher supervision: A case-based approach.* Cambridge: Cambridge University Press.

Berlak, A., & Berlak, H. (1981/2012). *Dilemmas of schooling: Teaching and social change.* London: Routledge.

Clandinin, D. J. (2010). Sustaining teachers in teaching. *Teachers and Teacher Education, 16*(3), 281–283.

Clandinin, D. J., & Connelly, F. M. (1992). Teacher as curriculum maker. In P. W. Jackson (Ed.), *Handbook of research on curriculum: A project of the American Educational Research Association* (pp. 363–461). New York, NY: Macmillan.

Craig, C., & Ross, V. (2008). Cultivating the image of teachers as curriculum makers. In F. M. Connelly (Ed.), *Sage handbook of curriculum and instruction* (pp. 282–305). Thousand Oaks, CA: Sage Publications.

Day, C. (1993). Reflection: a necessary but not sufficient condition for professional development. *British Educational Research Journal, 19*(1), 83–93.

Dewey, J. (1933). *How we think.* Buffalo, NY: Prometheus Books.

Farrell, T. S. C. (2001). Tailoring reflection to individual needs: A TESOL case study. *Journal of Education for Teaching: International Research and Pedagogy, 27*(1), 23–38.

Farrell, T. S. C. (2007). *Reflective language teaching: From research to practice.* London, UK: Continuum.

Hymes, D. H. (1966). Two types of linguistic relativity. In W. Bright (Ed.), *Sociolinguistics* (pp. 114–158). Mouton: The Hague.

Jackson, P. (1968). *Life in classrooms.* New York, NY: Teachers College Press.

Korthagen, F. A., & Kessels, J. P. (1999). Linking theory and practice: Changing the pedagogy of teacher education. *Educational Researcher, 28*(4), 4–17.

Korthagen, F., & Vasalos, A. (2005). Levels in reflection: Core reflection as means to enhance professional growth. *Teachers and Teaching: Theory and Practice, 11*(1), 47–71.

Loughran, J. J. (2006). *Developing a pedagogy of teacher education: Understanding teaching and learning about teaching.* Abingdon UK: Routledge.

Lyons, N. (2010). *Handbook of reflection and reflective inquiry: Mapping a way of knowing for professional reflective inquiry.* New York, NY: Springer.

Moon, J. (2004). *A handbook of reflective and experiential learning: Theory and practice.* New York, NY: Routledge Falmer.

Pennington, M. C. (1995). The teacher change cycle. *TESOL Quarterly, 29*(4), 705–731.

Schön, D. A. (1983). *The reflective practitioner: How professionals think in action.* London, UK: Ashgate Publishing Limited.

Schön, D. A. (1991). *The reflective turn: Case studies in and on educational practice.* New York, NY: Teachers College Press.

Tolstoy, L. (1967). On teaching the rudiments. In L. Wiener (Ed. & Trans.), Chicago, IL: University of Chicago Press.

CHAPTER 22

ENHANCING AND SUSTAINING TEACHER EFFECTIVENESS AS THE 'TROJAN HORSE' IN SUCCESSFUL SCIENCE EDUCATION IN KENYA

Samuel Ouma Oyoo

ABSTRACT

This chapter links ideas about a key issue and a major factor in successful implementation of effective science education in Africa. It presents the Kenyan case as a prototypical African country. While located in the sub-Saharan region, Kenya shares similar national development plans and dreams as well as socio-economic conditions as most African countries. In this work, the current status of science education in Kenya [Africa] is explained, and a blueprint for successful science education relevant to any country in Africa is presented. This chapter argues for contextual and practical approaches to enhancing science teacher effectiveness. It is anticipated that discussions of this work will generate debate within and about science education in Africa and hopefully ignite cross border research on teachers and the teaching of science. Also, the question of

From Teacher Thinking to Teachers and Teaching: The Evolution of a Research Community
Advances in Research on Teaching, Volume 19, 457–477
ISSN: 1479-3687/doi:10.1108/S1479-3687(2013)0000019025

quality science education in Africa and elsewhere will be raised locally and internationally.

Keywords: Teachers; teaching; science education; Africa; Kenya; effectiveness

Science is a high status subject in Kenya because of the many job and training opportunities available to graduates in science-related professions. Its high status has also been achieved from its deliberate sale by the government as a necessary ingredient of a fully industrialised economy (Republic of Kenya, 1998). Science education, as currently conceived, arguably started in Kenya after independence in 1963, since formal education was not widely available in Kenya prior to independence. The system of education in Kenya prior to independence was discriminatory and fell exclusively in the domain of a minority non-indigenous population of the country. Due to the non-universal, non-compulsory nature of formal education at the time, a very small number of privileged indigenous students attended school. Access to science was therefore limited only to a few school attendees; science is therefore relatively new in the national school curriculum. Apart from the discriminatory school education inherited at the time of the country's independence, teaching approaches in use best fitted with what could be termed a 'cookbook' approach to the teaching of science (Swift, 1983). The science syllabi, on the other hand, were of the 'traditional' variety where students were taught the basic principles of science and good thinking skills through standard topics and experiments. The main aim was to prepare youth for further studies in science, but it was also hoped that they would be able to apply the skills they learned in science in everyday situations. This primary aim remained the same even when the first post-independence system of the education (Republic of Kenya, 1964–1965) changed to the current one where learners attend eight years of primary school, four years of secondary school and those who are selected to join universities take at least four years to complete an undergraduate degree, hence its name, the 8-4-4 system of education (Bogonko, 1992; Republic of Kenya, 1981).

At its inception in 1985, the good feature of the 8-4-4 system of education was the fact that it gave all school children a chance to learn science as a compulsory subject using a common syllabus for the first 12 years of schooling; that is, from the primary school level right to the end of secondary education. In the primary schools, the subject was, and still is, taught as a single subject called science, while the secondary school level science is divided into distinct subjects: Biology, Chemistry and Physics in Forms One and Two. At Forms Three and Four, schools could offer the three subjects separately or as two separate topics: physical science and biological science. The syllabi were designed to make each subject '… interesting, real and more meaningful to the learner through the emphasis on the application of knowledge gained to the local environment…' Furthermore, 'project work in the syllabus was intended to create a new dimension in application of knowledge gained, and to add more interest and fun to the subject' (Republic of Kenya, 1992, p. 25). Also included in the science syllabi were issues on how science impinges on society as the following general aims of the physics course, for example, illustrate

- To help the learner discover and understand the order of the physical environment.
- To make the learner aware of the effect of scientific knowledge in everyday life through application to the management and conservation of the environment, the utilisation of resources and production of goods.
- To enable the learner to appreciate the responsibility of the scientist to the society.
- To inculcate in the learner a willingness to co-operate in using scientific knowledge in the society. (Republic of Kenya, 1992, p. 75)

While the overall intention of science education as illustrated by the listed objectives of school physics education included the important aim to enhance learners' understanding of the environment, the achievement of this initial intention has remained elusive. The implementation of the science curriculum has never achieved these aims. The 8-4-4 secondary school science curriculum has therefore had to undergo a number of adjustments or revisions in order to more readily achieve its aims.

As already mentioned, science subjects were previously offered either as three separate subjects, namely biology, chemistry and physics or as two subjects: biological science and physical science. It was expected that only the schools with well stocked laboratories (mainly the National and provincial schools) were to offer the three science subjects separately. Although physical science as a subject has recently been phased out, biological science, instead of Biology, is still offered to students with disabilities, perhaps because of the nature of the practical examination in Biology. Other students without disabilities are now expected to take at least two science subjects between physics, chemistry and biology. While chemistry has been made compulsory in most schools, students are expected to choose between physics and biology as their other secondary school science subject. Many students therefore take chemistry and physics or chemistry and biology examinations at the end of secondary school in order to be granted the Kenya Certificate of Secondary Education (KCSE), which is equivalent to other country's high school diplomas. A small number of students in a small number of schools register for physics and biology. Some students take all the three (pure) science subjects: physics, chemistry and biology, although these are mostly youth from secondary schools with better-equipped laboratories.

In spite of the changes to the science curriculum as so far discussed, the secondary school science curriculum continues to be broad and overloaded. A survey of the new science education curriculum or syllabi currently being used in schools reveals that the order of the topics and the clearer definition of the specific objectives are the only things that may have been revised (see Republic of Kenya, 1992, 2002). The teaching requirements in particular therefore remain the same and similar demands are placed on relatively underdeveloped infrastructure in the less endowed schools, mainly from the rural and poorer regions of the country. With the introduction of pure sciences in all secondary schools, changes now need to be made to allow for the teaching of separate science subjects in all secondary schools. Yet, all along, this has not been affordable in the less endowed schools. This seems to suggest that science education in these secondary schools could be heading toward more problems, and by extension, science education in the country will continue to be challenged because most schools lack the materials and resources to enact the mandated curriculum objectives.

Furthermore, the many curriculum reforms, like the recent phasing out of the physical and biological sciences, have resulted in making 'whole' science available to fewer students in the secondary schools. The consequence of this has been that the students in the less endowed secondary schools have been disadvantaged further, since the access to science has now been reduced. While this might resurrect the question of what the aims of science education in Kenya need to be, it also suggests that reconsideration be given the government's plan to industrialise the economy by the year 2030 (Republic of Kenya, 1996, 1997) through generating a qualified and scientifically literate human workforce. It shows how curriculum changes may work against the development of science education in the country, making curriculum reform hinder both the intended wider access to science education and the success of the plans to industrialise the economy. Apart from the challenges that curriculum changes have posed on the attainment of the aims of science education in Kenya, science education has also faced other problems and challenges, some being the consequence of the government's policy of cost sharing as will now be discussed.

PROBLEMS AND CHALLENGES OF SCIENCE EDUCATION IN KENYA

The Kenyan government's policy of cost-sharing in education has been the major stumbling block to the success of education in the country generally. Under this policy, parents have been left to meet most of the costs of secondary schools, which include general maintenance, physical facilities development, vehicles, electricity, water and other services, as well as personal reimbursement of support staff (Republic of Kenya, 1999). The high level of unemployment in the society overall and the absence of any social security arrangements have rendered most parents unable to cost-share. The government's role has increasingly been limited to provision of teachers' salaries through the Teachers Service Commission (TSC). This accounts for 90% of the expenditures and the government has consequently been unable to allocate more funds to education (Odhiambo, 2003, 2004). As a result, the provision of basic infrastructure for learning and teaching is grossly inadequate in many primary and secondary schools. The science subjects, because of their capital-intensive nature, are the hardest hit in this respect.

In many secondary schools, for example, science laboratories, workshops and equipment are inadequate and curriculum materials such as textbooks are in short supply. The situation is so serious in the poorer regions of Kenya as to make it safe to claim that apart from the enrolled students, such schools lack everything else needed for successful learning of science (Ojwang, 2004). Further, in many schools the number of students in a classroom is higher than a teacher can effectively handle; on some campuses, a class has as many as 65 students. As a result of this, teachers' giving individual attention to students is not possible.

While there is a chronic shortage of teachers for science subjects resulting in very heavy teaching loads for the teachers who can teach these subjects, the shortage of science teachers has been aggravated by the government's freeze in mass employment of teachers that has been in force since 1997. Although as a requirement, all teachers at secondary level are supposed to have two teaching subjects, the new rule that allows all students to register for at least two of the three science subjects with an option between physics and biology is an apparent attempt to reduce the large teaching loads for the existing physics teachers. This would seem to be supported by the phasing out of physical science in all schools and biological sciences in some, because some teachers have been teaching both of their science content areas to large classes.

The need for better leadership in the secondary schools is rarely mentioned, although many science teachers have talked about school principals who are deliberately not keen on the science disciplines. Some school principals have often frustrated science teachers' efforts to improve learning of science subject matter in secondary schools. While some principals have openly discouraged students from registering in certain subjects, notably physics, others have deliberately avoided acquiring even the most basic science equipment. This is despite the fact that parents always have had to pay for the purchase of science equipment and chemicals as part of their cost-sharing of education. In some schools, lack of apparatus and materials for science teaching has apparently been due to the diverting of funds by school principals (Kigotho, 2004). This may be argued considering the amount of money used in extra-curricular activities like drama and sporting activities against the amount of money paid for these activities as laid out in the annual fees structures. This apparent diversion of funds may be the reason no money is often allocated to activities related to science learning such as students' participation in science conferences/fairs or even science trips or study excursions.

The overall outcome through the years in each of the science subjects at the end of the secondary school examinations in Kenya has generally been low. The highest mean score ever attained in each of the subjects in KCSE since its inception in 1989 as presented in Table 1 confirms that on average, quality scores have always eluded Kenyan science candidates.

Table 1. Highest KCSE Mean Scores and When Attained between 1989 and 2006 (Inclusive).

Subject	Biology		Chemistry		Physics	
Gender	Female	Male	Female	Male	Female	Male
HMS %	30.07	33.64	22.31	26.76	38.81	40.57
Year	1994	1996	1992	2006	2006	2006

Source: Oyoo (2008, p. 274).
Note: HMS, Highest mean score.

In none of the three tested science areas has the overall mean score ever reached the 50% mark in any one year over the time period referenced. In spite of these persistently and generally low science outcomes, there has been an apparent bias on the part of the Ministry of Education and the Kenya National Examinations Council to highlight only the relatively lower outcomes of females in comparison to the outcomes of males as the only problem that needs to be addressed. The gravely low mean scores on the National Examinations highlight the need to generally enhance student outcomes in the science subjects. How to improve the level of outcomes in science is a perplexing challenge to education stakeholders in Kenya. Generally the fault has been attributed to students' and teachers' negative attitudes toward science. Teachers in particular have bore the brunt of the blame.

TEACHING OF SCIENCE IN KENYAN SECONDARY SCHOOLS – A REVIEW

Teachers' Inability to Relate Science to Students' Life Situations

In the current science teaching context, science teachers have been criticised for not being intuitive and innovative enough in their teaching. Many science lessons are still chalk-and-talk lectures, in some cases, straight out of the textbooks. The representation of science in the mainly imported course books has also not been a help to the teachers. Mostly, teachers have aimed at teaching the content as represented in these textbooks, an approach that has not been a great help to the students' understanding of science especially with regard to relating it to their immediate environments. To evidence this with respect to school physics, a common comment from Kenyan youth including current as well as former school students is often that

> Physics is not applicable anywhere in my life. I would just be swinging pendulums in class but would not see where it could help me. It is never made applicable in our lives and it just looks like something meant for the classroom.

This has partly been because preparing students to pass the mandated examinations is always foremost in the minds of the teachers and priority is always given to completing the (wide) syllabus. Examples of bad/ unfavourable teaching practices are still common. Student experiences in some science classrooms still bear characteristics of what was typical in the immediate post-colonial years as described by Museveni:

> In some science subjects like chemistry, the teachers would teach badly, introducing new subjects without explaining their genesis and expecting pupils to 'cram' things without understanding them. They would say: 'The symbol for sodium is "**Na**"'. When I asked 'Why not say "**So**" if it is sodium?' they replied: 'You must just take it as it is'. It was only later that I came to learn that symbols were taken from Latin and were internationally recognised. It was really incredible the way some teachers were turning children against their studies, and so unnecessarily. Their attitude was: 'If you want to pass your exam and get a good job, you take it as it is and memorise it'. (Museveni, 1997, p. 12; bold, my emphasis)

This account also illustrates the authoritative nature of some science teaching approaches, which may be traced to poor preparation of lessons and/or the lack of grasp of science subject content matter by some of the teachers. Lack of knowledge of content, perhaps the consequence of experiences during their own schooling (similar to immediately after independence as just described), may be part of the reason many teachers do not teach in ways that relate the science content to students' physical and social environments. This implies that the teaching approaches being used in some schools are not geared to demystifying the sciences.

In some instances, teaching has served to perpetuate the view of science as a mysterious thing to students. This claim is based on this author's experience with a secondary school teacher of chemistry during an introductory lesson in Organic Chemistry:

> On teaching us the properties of the element *Carbon*, the teacher stated that 'Carbon can form a chain' and perhaps to help us visualise how long the carbon chain could be, this teacher said that 'carbon can join to carbon, to carbon, to carbon, to carbon, to carbon... up to *siri guru masawa*'. *Siri Guru Masawa* is a place beyond the horizon, usually formed by the red rays of the sun as it sets over ..., a very large water mass near my rural home. It is alleged (as a local myth) that beyond the horizon, – at S*iri Guru Masawa*, wild animals, in fact man-eaters, live. To have to imagine that carbon can form chains up to such a place made me wonder about carbon. In the process I stopped writing but I was forced to write all words including *Siri Guru Masawa* – In my mind, *Siri Guru Masawa* was not chemistry, yet this teacher did not welcome any questions about this at all.

Another example of a teaching approach lacking in sensitivity to student learners and their backgrounds is evident in the following student's comment about a physics teacher in Kenya:

> Sometimes he does something on the blackboard and we just wonder what he is doing ... Like working out a question he just speaks to himself...We do very few practical

examples and we think he could plan more for us...We are given questions by the teacher and when we look at them and we find that they are too hard and we ask the teacher for help, he does not help.

Use of Practical Work in Teaching Science

In many Kenyan schools, including even some well-resourced secondary schools, full-fledged practical approaches to teaching science are not a common feature; many teachers do very few science demonstrations and almost no classroom experiments. On many campuses, practical work sessions are held just before the national examination, particularly once the schools are aware of which apparatus the candidates would be expected to use in the practical exam. Some teachers do not engage in hands-on work because some chemicals are harmful to students' health. This lack of practical work means that graduates never attain a mastery of the skills necessary for the learning of science.

Gender Issues in Teaching Science

According to some researchers (i.e., Tsuma, 1998), some teachers still hold to the belief that students' science learning abilities are determined by their gender. Hence, teachers have been blamed for discouraging girls from science

> ... by consciously or unconsciously perpetuating long-held myths about girls' inability to cope with these subjects which are deemed more suitable to males. Many teachers discourage girls from continuing with science...by accepting mediocre performance by the girls as opposed to boys ... enforcing the belief that the subjects are designed for boys. (Oyoo, 2004, p. 29)

In one study in the Kenyan context (Oyoo, 2007a) a girl-friendly approach (though not an exclusively girl-specific approach) to the teaching of physics has been characterised. In that approach, teachers attend more to students' social needs in physics/science classrooms during teaching. This is the way that has been associated with the 'feminization' of science by many physics teachers. Meanwhile, physics teaching methods in boys-only classrooms have been markedly different. A typical approach is evident in the following statement made by one teacher at a well-established boys-only secondary school:

> It should be known that physics is a doing subject and the learner has to do more than the teacher does... In physics, pupils should be involved more with exercises and practical [activities]...

Such an opinion is perhaps the result of the widely held belief by Kenyan physics teachers and society as a whole that boys are better able to take responsibility for their learning, including the ability to do things on their own initiative. It is therefore a surprise finding that the academically stronger boys who formed part of the sample in the Oyoo (1999) study gave a higher rating than girls to the 'girl-favourable approach' to physics education. As reported in the study, 'the boys, more than the girls would prefer a teaching approach where physics teachers give students notes, motivate students and smile at the students in class' (Oyoo, 1999, p. 44). While it is the expectation that teachers should know that even between the boys in the physics classrooms there are individual differences, it could be taken that the study revealed neglect of use of the affective domain to enhance teaching physics to male students. The physics teachers, as a result, could be argued to be exercising gender bias against the male students just as they have been blamed generally for the alienation of girls from physics.

Insensitivity to the Linguistic Ability of the Science Learners

English is the language of most school education in Kenya including secondary education. The non-uniform distribution of education resources in Kenya, including the deployment of English teachers, has resulted in students not attaining the required level of proficiency in English at the end of primary schooling. With regard to the role of English language in successful learning of school subjects, the common observation is that students who score poorly in secondary school examinations tend to be those who had low primary school English scores. Hence, proficiency in English is a major contributor to successful learning of most school subjects. This observation has led to the widely held assumption that once the students have attained proficiency in English, they should be able to understand everything taught in the classrooms (Rollnick, 1998, 2000). Consistently lower outcomes in some school subjects, especially the sciences in Kenya, have however shed doubt on the validity of such an assumption. Yet even science teachers have fallen victims of this gross claim; as a result, they have contributed to making science not only difficult but also unattractive to school students through their classroom use of language. This is evident in one Kenyan physics teacher's recollection of how he went through school physics during his school days:

> The first teacher who taught me physics in Form One messed up my life. He could not communicate. I think he was a very bad speaker and he would also assume a lot of

things; yes, just talk, talk, talk and go and he did not involve us in any communication. We didn't have the chance to talk; that was Year One and Year Two. Year Three I was taught by a lady teacher, who would explain every word of the sentence and very exhaustively and I liked it and even now when I meet her I tell her *mwalimu* (teacher) that was good. So I have had those two extremes. Then I think when I was in 'A' level, I was taught by another teacher who was not very keen on explaining the words. So he talked…superficially but in Form Five I had the interest and I could go looking for the meaning of the words myself.

In the aforementioned recollection, it is apparent that the first physics teacher might have assumed that the students had been well prepared in English at the primary school level. Meanwhile, the second teacher taught the way the physics teacher liked. As for the third instructor, the physics teacher forgave him. By Form Five (A level), the student (now teacher) was able to take responsibility for his learning. A question remains as to when or at what level students are best able to take control of their learning. It seems a benchmark level of proficiency in the instructional language and its relationship to successful learning remains elusive (Oyoo, 2007b). Evidence that science teachers' manner of use of language during teaching has the potential of reducing/discouraging enrolments in science classrooms can be construed by the Kenyan physics teacher in reference when he was asked the following additional but apparently leading question:

Question: So from that experience would you say that the teacher who did not communicate well almost made you to opt out of the subject?

Response: Yeah it is true. You know Year [Form] One and Two physics was compulsory and at Year [Form] Three it was optional… So, at the time I could think of quitting physics, the better teacher came.

The foregoing are examples of the not so favourable science teaching approaches that have persisted throughout the life of science education in Kenya. The takeaway point is that some teachers have continued to perpetuate the reputation of the science subjects as being very difficult. The existence of approaches considered unfavourable by students in the secondary schools is itself enough evidence for taking science teachers' work as one reason the students' outcomes in science have continued to be as low as already discussed. It would, however, be an inaccurate and unfair representation of the Kenyan science teaching situation to generalise these claims to all teachers in the secondary schools in the country. As mentioned, variations exist in how schools are endowed with resources for teaching science; these variations impact teaching methods in the different schools. Also not to be ignored is the fact that individual differences also exist between science teachers. It may generally be agreeable that in reality, teaching approaches are never the same between any two teachers and may be expected to vary from teacher to teacher even within the same school following same local and national teaching policies. Since most science teachers in Kenya are relevantly qualified, many factors, some beyond the control of these teachers can be blamed instead. Most of the challenges and problems so far discussed are direct outcomes of the economic policies put in place by the government, especially that of cost-sharing. So the question may be: What is the best approach to science education in Kenya, given the limitations already discussed? Teaching practices and activities that could help turn around Kenyan students and science classrooms will now be discussed. This will be accomplished through focusing on the teaching of school physics, the most challenging science subject in all secondary schools (Oyoo, 2008).

TOWARD EFFECTIVE TEACHING OF SCIENCE IN KENYA: SOME SUGGESTIONS

Teaching has been described as a web of alternatives in which students engage with content, sometimes with the teacher, sometimes with each other and sometimes alone (Ronkowski, 1998). This view of teaching sits well with the argument that effective teaching of science requires multi-pronged approaches (Gunstone & Mitchell, 1998; Harlen, 1999; Leach & Scott, 2000, 2003) in order to make the subject relevant to the student's immediate environment. Thus in Kenya's case, teacher activities which use approaches that make science/physics more accessible and relate it to everyday life would help make teaching more effective. What will be highlighted next are suggestions that help teachers manoeuvre amid formidable curriculum and resource challenges that technically can deter from both effective science education and effective classroom practice.

- In order to counter the foreignness of science as presented in imported textbooks, it would help learners to own the subject more if teachers *used relevant examples for questions and problems during teaching*. The questions can be related to development topics in the locality. Assignments after a lesson can be used to show how the lesson topic relates to real-life situations, and this can be done without taking up any valuable lesson time.
- Another way of making learners to own the subject as well as to relate the content to the students' immediate environment can be when teachers *use a visit or an item of technology in the locality to introduce*

a topic – a teacher entering a class with a charcoal stove should certainly arouse some interest, probably more than entering using standard equipment. Alternatively, a visit can stimulate learning to the extent that on balance, time is saved and subsequent lesson time may be made even more efficient. It is for this reason that school principals need to support school visits to science centres or industries in the schools' neighbourhoods.

- *Using everyday items for experiments and demonstrations:* this is the essence of being innovative in science teaching, for example using freshly prepared orange juice as a source of electricity. We recognise that this suggestion is within the need to be able to improvise as and when necessary, especially because of the general lack of teaching materials for science including chemicals. Improvisation needs to be considered to include the use of our environment to enhance teaching (Carelse, 1983). In this line of argument, Swift (1983) suggests that the teacher should be aware of all potential visual aids in the vicinity. For example black and white wall and metal surfaces in the sunlight to illustrate heat radiation; desk lids and pencils and rulers for illustrating moment of forces; a bicycle, a small stove, power and telephone lines etc.
- Mastery of the skills necessary for the learning of science includes students' ability to manipulate different pieces of apparatus that they may need to use during practical lessons. A means to training students in handling apparatus (practical work) while at the same time managing time during practical teaching would by teachers' use of *circus approach in practical work*. This is where a teacher plans for a number of different short experiments using different pieces of apparatus within one lesson time. This way, it becomes possible for the teacher to cover different practicals or make students use different pieces of apparatus in one session – this approach will also enable effective use of the scarce science teaching resources.
- *Helping with the school science club:* many schools have science clubs or similar out-of-class groups, often working toward a national science congress or other inter-school competition. If the topics illustrated are being covered in lessons, they will help the keener students to develop their knowledge of the topic and perhaps save time that could have been used during the normal lessons for an explanation. Some projects that relate directly to the local situation will help relate science to the students' normal environment and in the process make them see the connection more vividly between science and their everyday living. Alternatively, this can be done through a formal project.
- *Using a project approach:* instead of teaching science/physics topic by topic, the subject matter to be taught is embodied in a practical project,

for example, a design study. The project could be introduced through a study visit and the science/physics topic introduced as needed. Depending on how it is performed by the students, such projects could even replace practical examinations, or internal continuous assessment. At a national level this could also be implemented[1] providing safeguards are taken to restrict the degree of teacher/parent participation in the project.

While the above teacher activities are meant to help the teacher to enhance student understanding of what is taught, teachers rarely question their own practice, yet such questioning would enable them to better their performance as teachers. Such questioning would include aspects of the teacher assessing own lessons taught.

Following up or assessing own lessons after teaching sessions by the teacher is necessary as this provides a reflection on effectiveness of approach as a means to effective learning. This is an aspect of 'professional development', under the action research concept. Action research conceptualised as the act of teachers systematically recording what they do and how the students respond during the lessons, is a relatively untapped form of educational research, which makes teachers to learn from experience. By these records 'teachers help to halt *"epidemics of pedagogical amnesia"*' (Nafziger, 1998, p. 72; italics in original). In practice, teachers never look back on their teaching and its consequences such that the learning that does occur is rarely articulated and shared with others. In fact it is forgotten year-to-year, by the teacher who experienced it. This model could revolutionise teaching and identify favourable approaches in the context of learners in similar environments. This is especially true of cultural appropriateness.

Sensitivity to Equity Issues in Science Teaching as an Aspect of Effective Teaching

Gender sensitive teaching must not be ignored. Neither can the need for sensitivity toward students' linguistic capabilities. In the Kenyan science learning context, changes in how teachers treat female learners would affect how they respond to physics. In the end result, the effective teaching of science requires the teacher to relate to each student in the classroom as individuals who happen to be of different genders. The following assertion by Murphy (1996) is especially relevant to this line of thinking:

> We need to talk in terms of not a pedagogy for girls or boys but a pedagogy being composed of a range of strategies (which include a range of materials and content,

teaching styles, and classroom arrangements/rules) for different groups of students ...
The key issue is for the teacher to understand which strategy is appropriate and effective
in which setting and for which group of students and individuals. (Murphy, 1996, p. 8)

With regard to the language difficulties students may encounter due to inadequate instruction, it might be necessary for teachers to respond to the students' circumstances by lowering the classroom language (Henderson & Wellington, 1998) so that it does not become a barrier to the learning of science. This can be done by being conscious of how word meanings change when used in the science context as well when used as scientific terms (Oyoo, 2012).

In sum, the use of a contextually relevant approach to teaching is necessary, especially when science is taught to learners whose environment is different from what is taken to be conventional (or mainstream) by the scientific community and reflected in textbooks or research contexts. An effective teaching method involves the judicious implementation of the widely recommended approach to science teaching: that is, by connecting science concepts to students' personal, social and physical environments. It is probable that this approach to teaching will both demystify and demythologise science. Now we turn to the next consideration: Why the focus on teachers and teaching?

Secondary School Science Teaching as Central to Effective Science Education

The many challenges and problems of science education in Kenya that have been touched on in this chapter hinge on policies that the government or other interested stakeholders can work to remove from the schooling system. The focus on the teacher and teaching (of science at secondary school level) is essential because of the profound impact teachers and their approaches have on student learning. As has been argued by Schwille et al. (1983)

Teachers, as they interact with students, are the ultimate arbiters of what is taught (and how). They make decisions about how much time to allocate to a particular school subject, what topics to cover, when and in what order, to what standards of achievement, and to which students. Collectively, these decisions and their implementation define the content of instruction. (1983, p. 3)

The problem of poor performance in science education at secondary school level can be traced to the primary level where a good foundation in science needs to be laid. Since the entry requirements into the primary teacher training colleges do not emphasis science, many teacher trainees who possess poor background in science subject matter have gained admission into these colleges. In the Kenyan context (similar to the case in many countries), there is a generalist or non-specialist route to preparing teachers to teach in primary schools. At the primary teachers' colleges in Kenya, teachers study 13 compulsory subjects without specialisation in any of them. It can be argued that many graduates of teacher education programs often leave college without adequate mastery of content as well as relevant methodology for teaching science. Many of them, in turn, are challenged when it comes to laying the necessary foundation in science at the primary school level. Furthermore, no one should blame them for this. Arguably, a long-term solution to this problem may reside in secondary school level teaching of science. Given the centrality of the teacher in all learning as so far presented, the particular role of the secondary school science teacher in the overall success of science education can now be argued.

In Kenya's 8-4-4 system of education, secondary school graduates at Form Four are recruited to be educated as teachers of science at all levels depending on their overall examination outcome on KCSE. How effectively the secondary school science teachers teach science to the secondary school students determines to a certain extent the level of competence in science of secondary school graduates, who themselves are potential science teachers. The secondary school graduates recruited to the primary teacher training colleges, even if without great passes in science at KCSE, as well as those who will join the Diploma colleges and universities to be trained or prepared as secondary school science teachers, will then have a good grounding in science. The secondary school science teacher education recruits/trainees always have had to pass science subjects and mathematics as prerequisites to be accepted into the training institutions as science teacher educators. The secondary school science teachers, by teaching science effectively, will have provided a solid foundation on which the teacher educators at the teacher education institutions (colleges and universities) would build, to produce better and more confident teachers of science for the Kenyan school system. The quality and effectiveness of science teachers at secondary school level therefore remains the major factor in moving successful science education forward in Kenya. This is in line with the argument that the success of a formal science education curriculum is dependent on the quality and performance of science teachers across the school levels (George, 1999, 2000). This in effect suggests that the condition for successful science education depends unequivocally on how effective science teachers educate students in science knowledge, skills, and dispositions.

SUSTAINING EFFECTIVE TEACHING OF SCIENCE IN KENYAN SCHOOLS: THE PROCESS

The Place of (Collaborative) Research and Curriculum Review on Effective Teacher Practice in Science Education

In a review of science education research, Harlen (1999) reveals that the themes that have dominated research in science teaching include: use of practical work, taking into account students' alternative conceptions, emphasis on meta-cognition, relating assessment to content, proper lesson planning, strategic questioning, ability of the teacher to display knowledge of subject matter and use of theories of learning and teaching science. Although the research studies reviewed were exclusively those conducted in the Organisation for Economic Co-operation and Development (OECD) countries, findings in research within these same research themes have always informed pedagogical practices in the teaching of science in Kenya. The problem has been that the dissemination of the findings has often/ mainly been without any attempts to localise them to fit the African milieu, which differs from the 'mainstream' science education terrain. A dire need exists to interpret findings and recommendations from these studies to suit the circumstances prevalent in Africa. Some, though understandably not all, of these circumstances have been mapped in this chapter.

Since field-based research on teachers and teaching in Africa is sparse, this gives way to the raw consumption of findings arising from studies conducted in other contexts. Perhaps the time has come for more collaborative forms of research aimed at connecting what is known in research terms to the African situation. Possibly through theory, practice and policy fruitfully informing one another, a means to enhancing teacher effectiveness and more successful science education in Africa will be discovered. On the local scene, this would begin with wider access to quality science education and resources that would promote rather than hinder its success. A further recommendation would be to make science once again compulsory to all at the secondary school level either by learners taking all the three science subjects separately or combined under the biological science and physical science focus areas.

Initial and Continuing Professional Development of Science Teachers

Initial and continuing professional development of science teachers is also a means to ensure and sustain teacher effectiveness, hence appropriate curricula in higher education would aid in the preparation of relevantly qualified and experienced teacher educators over the long term. Where in-service training or continuing professional development programs are concerned, foci need be on the weak areas as contextually determined in order to respond to the needs of the local milieu. Calloids, Gottelmann-Duret and Lewin (1997) have outlined the following approaches to in-service education:

- In-service days where teachers are gathered locally at special centers to discuss particular topics.
- Short in-service courses lasting up to a week, usually residential in regional centers run by national staff members.
- Longer in-service courses lasting three months or more usually associated with certification and upgrading of qualifications.
- School-based in-service support (otherwise known as on service) during and after school hours, located in schools (p. 125).

Since the financing of (science) education in Kenya is such that funds for these in-service courses are the responsibility of the schools, it is important to consider the most economical approach. It may be true that the cheapest forms of in-service support are almost certainly those which are delivered locally or through school-based sessions and these can be conducted by local amateurs – subject associations and panels (Calloids et al., 1997). However, the most economical approach and the most lasting approach may constitute two different things.

CONCLUSION AND A WAY FORWARD

In sum, this chapter has revealed that Kenya experiences major problems that hinder proper access to and outcomes in science education with other African countries; these include, but are not limited to, lack of resources for teaching science, inadequate laboratory facilities, too few science teachers and large classes (Naidoo & Savage, 1998). An additional factor is the remuneration of school teachers that has been a major source of teachers' dissatisfaction with their work. Hence, it also is an important consideration shaping teachers' general commitment and satisfaction with their jobs. As apparent from the discussion in this chapter, the scenario in the science education field in Kenya has been adversely impacted by the government's economic policies. Paradoxically, the government hopes to improve the country's economy through science education and training (see Republic of

Kenya, 1998) and science education and training requires more of the nation's resources to improve the economy. The reality is that with or without a good science curriculum, the country's economic circumstances remain an important factor in the level of success of science education as well as of the efficacy of science teachers. Curriculum and resource issues aside, it remains a surface-level fact that the cause of the persistent poor outcomes in science as so far discussed can be traced to science teachers' classroom/teaching practices at both primary and secondary school levels. Hence, a great deal has been suggested in this work concerning how a teacher as an individual can and be helped to improve his/her pedagogical practices and become a more effective science teacher.

In this chapter, I have attempted to link my ideas about what I think is a key issue as well as factor in successful implementation of effective science education in Africa by centering on the Kenyan case. Kenya is a prototype African country and shares similar national development plans and dreams as well as socioeconomic context with most African countries. In this work, suggestions of contextual and (not so new) practical approaches meant to enhance and sustain science teacher effectiveness have been discussed. It is hoped that this chapter will generate debate within and about Africa to ignite productive cross border research and other ventures to tackle the whole question of quality science education in Africa and elsewhere throughout the world. This work is a clarion call aimed at 'waking up' all stakeholders across all nations to the current state of affairs of science education.

NOTE

1. It is noted that the implementation of this approach in the primary schools has not been successful as parents would buy ready-made items which they would present for assessment on the pretence that they were made by their children.

REFERENCES

Bogonko, S. N. (1992). *A history of modern education in Kenya (1895–1991)*. Nairobi and London: Evans Brothers (Kenya) Ltd.

Calloids, F., Gottelmann-Duret, G., & Lewin, K. (1997). *Science education and development: Planning and policy issues at secondary level*. Paris: UNESCO.

Carelse, X. F. (1983). *Making science laboratory equipment: A manual for students and teachers in developing countries*. Chichester, NY: Wiley.

George, J. (1999). Worldview analysis of knowledge in a rural village: Implications for science education. *Science Education, 83*(1), 77–96.

George, J. M. (2000). The Caribbean response to Project 2000+: A personal view. Project 2000+ – *Scientific and technological literacy for all*, Symposium 3.4, Limassol, Cyprus.

Gunstone, R. F., & Mitchell, I. (1998). Metacognition and conceptual change. In J. J. Mintzes, J. H. Wandersee, & J. D. Novak (Eds.), *Teaching science for understanding: A human constructivist view*. A Volume in the Educational Psychology Series (pp. 133–163). San Diego, CA: Academic Press.

Harlen, W. (1999). *Effective teaching of science: A review of research*. Edinburgh: Scottish Council for Research in Education.

Henderson, J., & Wellington, J. (1998). Lowering the language barrier in learning and teaching science. *School Science Review, 79*(288), 35–45.

Kigotho, W. (2004, July 22). Heads a law unto themselves. *School & Career*. Retrieved from http://www.eastandard.net/schoolcareer/features/feat01.htm

Leach, J., & Scott, P. (2000). Children's thinking, learning, teaching and constructivism. In M. Monk & J. Osborne (Eds.), *Good practice in science teaching: What research has to say* (pp. 41–56). Buckingham, PA: Open University Press.

Leach, J., & Scott, P. (2003). Individual and sociocultural views on learning in science education. *Science and Education, 12*, 91–113.

Murphy, P. (1996). Defining pedagogy. In P. F. Murphy & C. V. Gipps (Eds.), *Equity in the classroom: Towards effective pedagogy for girls and boys* (pp. 9–22). London, Washington, DC: The Falmer Press, UNESCO Publishing.

Museveni, Y. K. (1997). *Sowing the mustard seed: The struggle for freedom and democracy in Uganda*. London: Macmillan.

Nafziger, D. (1998). The impact and role of science and technology on educational change. In B. Otaala, L. Mostert, J. C. Magnus, C. Keyter & C. Shaimemanya (Eds.), *Issues in education: An occasional publication of the Faculty of Education, University of Namibia and the National Institute for Educational Development* (p. 72). Windhoek: Faculty of Education, University of Namibia.

Naidoo, P., & Savage, M. (Eds.). (1998). *African science and technology education into the new millennium: Practice, policy and priorities* (p. xiii). Kenwyn: Juta.

Odhiambo, G. (2003). *Teacher appraisal and its significance for the development of a quality assurance culture in Kenyan secondary schools*. Doctoral dissertation. University of New England, Australia.

Odhiambo, G. (2004, December). *Appraising teachers in Kenya: Accountability or teacher growth?* Paper presented at the Australian and New Zealand Comparative and International Education Society annual Conference, Melbourne.

Ojwang, A. (2004). Why students perform poorly in sciences. *School & Career*. Retrieved from http://www.eastandard.net

Oyoo, S. O. (1999). *Just a matter of attitude…The making of physics simple but not simpler in Kenyan secondary schools*. Unpublished B.Ed. [Hons.] dissertation. School of Education: University of Nottingham, England, UK.

Oyoo, S. O. (2004). *Effective teaching of science: The impact of physics teachers' classroom language*. Doctoral dissertation. Faculty of Education, Monash University, Melbourne, Australia.

Oyoo, S. O. (2007a, August). *Does a girl-friendly approach to teaching school science exist?* Paper presented at the 2007 DETA Conference, Makerere University, Kampala, Uganda.

Oyoo, S. O. (2007b). Rethinking proficiency in the language of instruction (English) as a factor in the difficulty of school science. *The International Journal of Learning, 14*(4), 231–242.

Oyoo, S. O. (2008). Attention to female students' "lower" outcomes in science as social construction of a negative perception of their ability in school science. *The International Journal of Learning, 15*(11), 271–286.

Oyoo, S. O. (2012). Language in science classrooms: An analysis of physics teachers' use of and beliefs about language. *Research in Science Education, 42*(5), 849–873.

Republic of Kenya. (1964–1965). *Report of the Kenya Education Commission (Ominde Commission)*, Vol. 1. Nairobi: English Press Ltd.

Republic of Kenya. (1981). *Second university in Kenya – Report of the presidential working party* (Mackay Report). Nairobi: Government Printer.

Republic of Kenya. (1992, May). *Secondary education syllabus*, Vol. 7. Nairobi: Ministry of Education/Kenya Institute of Education.

Republic of Kenya. (1996). *Sessional paper no.2 on industrial transformation to the year 2020.* Nairobi: Government Printer.

Republic of Kenya. (1997). *Master plan on education and training 1997–2010.* Nairobi: Jomo Kenyatta Foundation.

Republic of Kenya. (1998). *Master plan on education and training 1997–2010.* Nairobi: Jomo Kenyatta Foundation.

Republic of Kenya. (1999). *Totally integrated quality education and training (TIQET): Report of the Commission of Inquiry into the education system of Kenya – Learning and moving together into the 21st century and the third millennium.* Nairobi: Government Printer.

Republic of Kenya. (2002, April). *Secondary education syllabus, Vol. 2.* Nairobi: Ministry of Education, Science and Technology, Kenya Institute of Education.

Rollnick, M. (1998). The influence of language on second language teaching and learning of science. In W. W. Cobern (Ed.), *Socio-cultural perspectives on science education: An international dialogue* (pp. 121–138). Dordrecht: Kluwer Academic Publishers.

Rollnick, M. (2000). Current issues and perspectives on second language learning of science. *Studies in Science Education, 35*, 93–122.

Ronkowski, S. (1998). *Special topics for teachers – TAs: Strategies to enhance learning.* Retrieved from http://id.www/ucsb.edu/ic/ta/hdbk/ta3-4.html#SEL

Schwille, J. R., Porter, A. C., Belli, G., Floden, R. E., Freeman, D. J., Knappen, L. B., ... Schmidt, W. (1983). Teachers as policy brokers in the content of elementary school mathematics. In L. Shulman & G. Sykes (Eds.), *Handbook on teaching and policy analysis* (pp. 257–273). New York, NY: Longman.

Swift, D. G. (1983). *Physics for rural development: A sourcebook for teachers and extension workers in developing countries.* Chichester, NY: Wiley.

Tsuma, O. G. K. (1998). *Science education in the African context.* Nairobi: Jomo Kenyatta Foundation.

CHAPTER 23

BLENDING TRADITIONAL AND CONSTRUCTIVIST TEACHING: HOW ONE TEACHER GOES ABOUT IT IN A U.S. MIDDLE SCHOOL MATHEMATICS CLASSROOM

David R. Goodwin

ABSTRACT

This chapter is focused primarily on the detailed analysis of a segment of a single classroom exercise involving the use of a worksheet to reinforce the teaching of "surface area" by a seventh grade mathematics teacher and the classroom context in which the exercise occurred. The analysis examines traditional teaching and the engagement and respect for students' own constructive capacities in relation to the individual teacher's consciousness and motivation. The larger issue though is to better understand teaching as a unity in the person as a whole. How does the unity of connection to subject matter, deeper motivation for teaching, and care for student learning manifest in the classroom? This chapter looks at how one teacher goes about it.

Keywords: Qualitative research; case study; microanalysis; consciousness; portraiture; middle school; mathematics; narrative; self; subject matter

From Teacher Thinking to Teachers and Teaching: The Evolution of a Research Community
Advances in Research on Teaching, Volume 19, 479–501
ISSN: 1479-3687/doi:10.1108/S1479-3687(2013)0000019026

This chapter is centered on the deeper aspects of self involved in the teaching of Susan (a pseudonym), a seventh grade mathematics teacher. This chapter articulates a fuller understanding of the depth, complexity, and beauty of teaching taking the consciousness, self, larger life of Susan into account. I try to show the depth and unity of self (and level of understanding) first with a brief biographical sketch of Susan, and secondly, through a detailed analysis of a seven-minute segment of classroom teaching where she is reinforcing her students' conceptual development of "surface area" using a worksheet activity. Her teaching blends traditional and constructivist approaches. The central aim is explore the unity of Susan's teaching which "flows from the heart."

First is a short summary of the qualitative in-depth portraiture methodology. That is followed by a biographical sketch of Susan (a pseudonym) along with a description of the classroom context within which the worksheet exercise occurred. Next is the detailed verbatim transcript of an approximately seven-minute segment of Susan's teaching using the worksheet. Integrated into the segment transcript is a running interpretive analysis to highlight details of Susan's teaching and current consciousness. In the discussion that follows the classroom segment analysis, I discuss the analysis of the teaching segment in relation to the unity (almost a oneness) in Susan's self as a whole. In a closing comment, I suggest that seeing the unity of the person should be prominent in developing sound educational policy to better reflect the deeper realities of teachers and teaching which of course means advocating for the depth and integrity of teachers.

METHODOLOGY

The research I report here stems from qualitative in-depth interview and observation studies to better understand comprehensive teacher growth (Goodwin, 2005). What the larger study includes is an effort to understand how teacher growth, understood holistically as an inseparable unity of the personal and professional – the person as a whole – occurs daily in the classroom during teaching interactions with students and in relation to deeper connection with subject matter, here mathematics. This chapter shows a part of the ongoing analysis. The research takes place in individual classroom contexts using multiple open interviews with individual teachers, in-depth analysis on a case-by-case basis using the analytical methods involved in essentialist portraiture (Goodwin, 1999; Witz, 2006; Witz, Goodwin,

Hart, & Thomas, 2001), and classroom ethnography (Smith & Goeffry, 1968). With Susan, the approximately one-hour unstructured interviews were face-to-face and audio-recorded, involved discussion of life experiences from memory as well as related feeling states, emotionality, imagery, etc. The classroom observations were also audio-recorded and supplemented with handwritten field notes. The complete data set for Susan's class includes twelve 90-minute classroom observations, 15-minute to 20-minute debriefing sessions after each observation, my field notes, multiple face-to-face audio-recorded interviews, audio-recording of all observed teaching sessions, teaching artifacts, and informal discussions with students. All the observation sessions occurred during the teaching of a unit on seventh grade geometry.

The analytical approach to the data included verbatim transcripts along with "microanalysis of and identification with prosodic and other dynamic features of discourse, and empathy with and compassion for the object of study (the person interviewed, her experience, and the overall story in relation to the problem)" (Witz et al., 2001, p. 195). While I am not presenting a portrait in this chapter, the analysis presented in this chapter makes use of the principles of portraiture development where (in this case) the nature and essence of teacher growth as actually experienced by the teacher and how that is manifested in teaching is studied in detail. The standard of such analysis is

> one of *authenticity*, capturing the essence and resonance of the [participant's] experience and perspective through the details of action and thought revealed in context... [requiring a] vigilance to empirical description and aesthetic expression. (Lawrence-Lightfoot & Davis, 1997, p. 12)

In portraiture, while grounded theory data analysis techniques (Corbin & Stauss, 1990) and biographical methods (Smith, 1994) are used (such as in developing biographical timelines which would include significant periods of change and development, role of family, recurring growth aspects and emotional/feeling states, etc.), the ultimate aim in the data analysis in portraiture is to evoke the consciousness and unity in the person as a whole with respect to the phenomenon being investigated. The use of micro-analysis coupled with empathetic and sympathetic identification with the participant by the researcher greatly extends the depth of understanding the consciousness and self (subjective experience) of the participant (Witz, 2006; Witz & Goodwin, 2012). It is in fact through such empathy, identification, and reflection that the researcher becomes able to bring her own conscious-ness and self fully empathically into relation with the consciousness and self of the participant in gaining an understanding of the subjective experience of the participant (Witz & Lee, 2013).

BIOGRAPHICAL SKETCH OF SUSAN

At the time of the interviews and observations, Susan was in her mid-30s. She began her mathematics education career teaching high school mathematics. After several years, she resigned from her position to devote herself to raising her children. A few years passed and then she was approached by a principal, whom she respected, to teach 7th grade middle school mathematics. She was in her fifth year of teaching middle school when I met her.

Susan grew up with her younger sister in rural Missouri. Her dad was a truck delivery driver and her mom worked at a local convenience store. She was the first in her family to go to college. Susan characterized her family and community growing up as "compact." Everyone knew each other. Day-to-day life was up-close and personal. When she married her high school sweetheart, for example, 12 of her high school teachers came to the wedding. The nearest urban environment, about 30 miles away, felt impersonal, threatening, and uncomfortable. Susan only gradually became acclimated to the nearby urban landscape when she went to college. She had planned to return to her home town and teach in the same high school she had attended, but there were no openings. Consequently, she now teaches and lives with her own family in an urban center. Her parents and extended family, including her younger sister, sweetly refer to her as the "city-slicker."

Susan loves mathematics; she always has. Everywhere she looks she sees numbers, forms, and structures – she gets excited when, from experience, she "can describe that mathematically." While she became interested in computer technology in college, her central focus remained on mathematics and teaching. Her dad was good at math and he encouraged her. Susan grew up liking school; she worked well with her teachers growing up, was trusted, and often asked to help out. When in the 6th grade, her mathematics teacher noticed how proficient she was at mathematics and also supported her. This attention persisted through high school. Her teachers put her in with a group to be monitored and supported with advanced classes. At times, her friends kidded her about her teaching some of the math classes. Mathematics became a source of confidence for her. She often tutored her friends. She enjoyed learning and sharing her learning, helping others who struggled in middle and high school. Susan even felt wronged by teachers who were not giving their all.

It became clear to Susan in high school that she wanted to become a teacher: "...I was good at going to school, good at photocopies, good in technology, so why don't I become a teacher ... I love math." In college, she focused on mathematics and computer technology. She loves working with computers but her depth of interest in learning mathematics overshadowed her fascination with the new technology being introduced in the mid-1990s. She had thought about pursuing higher mathematics and did well in the upper level math courses, but she "never felt confident enough" to pursue becoming a mathematician.

Susan began teaching integrated algebra in high school but soon realized that she wanted to be more creative in her teaching approach. Creativity was not encouraged in her high school teaching; she thought there was an "overemphasis on direct teaching." So, when she weighed the needs of her growing family with the rather traditional high school mathematics teaching she was expected to replicate, it was not a difficult family decision to quit and focus on her children and home for the next several years. Soon after accepting the offer to teach middle school, Susan recognized it was the perfect place for her to share her love of mathematics and her desire to be a creative math teacher.

Susan's aspiration to be a teacher, not just a learning manager, has been realized in middle school. Mathematics and the teaching of math have become one. At the time of the interviews, she was teaching 7th grade math in a traditional classroom setting. The year after my observations were completed, she was teaching in a fully computerized classroom. Now she is in another public school position helping high school students who struggle with mathematics. In each of these periods of her professional work there is an expansion of her inner intelligence and awareness to engage her students in mathematics learning. She knows that learning mathematics will really help them know more about the world.

In this account, it is evident that Susan's teaching and larger life "flows from the heart." Her energy for teaching and love of mathematics grows out of a deep feeling of "connection" with her students at the level of heart. Her interactions growing up were wrapped in interconnectedness that was taken-for-granted in family and belonging to community. Building connection personally, as the teacher, through mathematics is serving her students and is what makes her work as a teacher real. Susan remembers always being the teacher, always taking a leadership role. She actually does not remember a time when she was not the teacher/learner in her family, with her younger sister, and in school. She knows she was not that good at all things: "I always had to work at it." But she "was successful." Her life as a devoted teacher expresses a unity in her life as a whole. Her love of learning, mathematics, technology, taking the lead, helping her friends, becoming the teacher, and raising a family, all show a deepening committed life with total dedication to education.

THE "SURFACE AREA" WORKSHEET

The sense of Susan as "all heart" guided the analysis of the "surface area" teaching segment discussed below. Coming to know and identify with Susan this way (as involving the heart; what she was doing as "flowing from the heart") truly facilitated intuitive and spontaneous awareness on my part to the depth in her teaching at a micro level while still trying to keep her person intact. But first are some general comments to briefly characterize Susan's general classroom organization and context as background for the "surface area" worksheet activity.

General Classroom Organization

The classroom organization Susan had developed during the school year included placement of the desks with a "U" corridor between them to be easily rearranged to help with cooperative learning in small groups of three or four. Students needing more attention were placed along the "U" corridor so she could easily make use of proximity (see Appendix A). Classroom procedures to help each student keep track of work completed included using a large three-ring binder which was updated weekly during "house cleaning." Much effort was put into developing a routine structure where students could see what they have done and what they were doing, their successes, needed improvements, test results, and homework assignments. She made sure parents also saw the accumulated work as well. Students typically graded homework in small groups, sharing what they came up with, and making corrections while Susan walked around the room checking progress, etc.

Susan made use of what I called "procedural care" in teaching mathematics, reflected in the general pattern of instruction which involved both hands-on individual and small group activity and traditional (or more direct) instruction, as well as in the compiling of their notebooks. She typically (though not necessarily always in this order) provided some traditional instruction on the concept, gave examples and work with the formula if part of the lesson, asked questions, engaged students in their answers, responded to student questions; then she would back away and allow student interaction on the task or problem to be solved sometimes individually and sometimes in small groups. Susan would indicate how much time they have: that is, 2 minutes, 4 minutes, etc. Then she refocused collective attention on what they have been doing and connects that or asks the students to connect that to the next part of the lesson/activity. She made time for questions and discussion to conclude the lesson or hands-on activity. This general cycle of instructional practice varied in time spent, Susan's intuitive sense of where students were with the work, her attention to individual students, her sense of the progress on the activity as a whole, while making on-the-fly adjustments. She also used humor and some of her own math struggles to connect at a more equal level with her class. Her students have been more or less working in this way over the past five months or so. Susan intends that they learn the classroom process and her organizational scheme. This organization of the class and the related learning process becomes then part of what it means for students to learn math and for Susan to teach it.

The Day of the "Surface Area" Worksheet Activity

Susan had been ill during part of the week prior to the "surface area" worksheet assignment. On the day she returned, her students told her how bored they had been with the substitute teacher and how happy they were that she (Susan) was back. Because she had been out, Susan felt behind and thought she needed to cover "surface area" more to reinforce what was covered the class period before the substitute teacher came, which included the mini cereal box activity. That mini cereal box activity involved removing the wrapped contents inside (to be eaten at the end of the assignment as a snack), cutting the box apart carefully, laying it flat, drawing it on graph paper, measuring it, seeing the opened up box as a "net," and then calculating the "surface area." The activity was done in groups of three or four but each student had a mini cereal box.

The class today started out with five "Getting Started" geometry math problems (finding the area of a rectangle, triangle, etc. with given dimensions). About 10 minutes later, the students got out homework, note pages, and extra credit to turn in. After that, they began their "housecleaning:"

organizing their prior work in their notebooks. Students then began grading their homework in small groups – paired shoulder partners. This was an interactive activity where they traded papers, discussed, and made corrections. What follows is an excerpt from my observation notes:

> [Susan] is continually monitoring the activity and moving quickly through the grading. She allows for brief moments of chatter, then she over-talks the din – the students quiet back down. All students are focused on the grading of each other's homework papers – getting the work done ... all student interaction at this point appears at what I call a normal level, in-context type of engagement with each other and with homework. Susan is walking around the classroom observing what the students are doing in each group and interacting with students both "as needed" and interrupting to point something out, providing clarification and encouraging discussion of the homework answers. (Observation #5)

The homework is finished, handed back, and then they wrapped up their "Getting Started" questions.

The descriptions and characterizations so far are external and only at very general levels. It does not capture what Susan is actually doing in teaching mathematics – the deeper resonance of the heart in fostering connection.

The "Surface Area" Worksheet Activity Transcript with Running Interpretive Comments

What follows is a verbatim transcript of a 7-minute segment of class time (Observation #5, mid-February) that my friend and colleague Klaus Witz and I worked on together over a couple of days. The running interpretive and analytical comments are in italics. A completed student example of the "surface area" worksheet referred to in the transcript is shown in Appendix B. The transcript starts at 46:20 minutes into the 90-minute class. Standing at the head of the class, Susan projects a blank copy of the "surface area" worksheet from a document camera onto a Smart Board©. Her 27 students just finished grading and turning in their "Getting Started" activity. There was some general student chatter when the bell Susan uses to signal it is time to begin a new activity goes off. [*Transcript notation guide*: S = Susan; **Drx**, etc. are student pseudonyms; **Student1**, 2, etc. = unnamed individual students in the classroom; time is noted as (minutes:seconds); (s = seconds); parentheses "( )" demarcate descriptive comments to clarify or add information to parts of the transcript; an accent "'" is used to indicate emphasis on a syllable of the word in speech; "< >" is used to indicate common "throw away phrases" such as <you know>; commas are used to indicate hesitations and shifts in prosodic flow as experienced in ordinary discourse, and "[ ]" are used to provide information not pertaining directly to the interpretation of the transcription.]

S: (46:18) (Bell timer goes off at front of the classroom.) Dinner's ready. (In loud teacher voice:) I need you quiet. (6.0s pause) Ok (to a student). Ok, now (class getting quiet). This would be (stretched out:) item-m-m twelve. Please put item twelve on here so the next time we're organizing [putting their work into their notebooks], you're not asking me what item this is. (direct:) This is item twelve.

> In the above, Susan is calling to the students, letting them know that they are now transitioning to a new activity. She indicates that they are going to do something important: "I need you quiet." She also refers to work they had just finished, "organizing" their individual mathematics 3-ring binder notebooks where they kept all their work together and organized. This activity also has to do with how Susan sees organization in mathematics, keeping ideas and definitions straight, ordered. She conceptualizes and relates to mathematics as a content area that cannot be understood unless there is organization to the learning. The notebooks and the emphasis on staying organized reflect that approach.

Student chatter: (46:37).

> Susan stands waiting, looking over the class, giving students time to settle down and begin the new activity.

S: (46:43) C'mon. Okay-y-y, starting at the top (elongated:) there-e-e, ahm, Chrx, (voice softens:) would you read for me that first sentence up there at the top?

Chrx: (carefully with deliberate enunciation:) The figure below is called a net. A net is a flat two dimensional shape that can be folded to form a three-dimensional figure.

S: (47:00) (talking quickly, not so loud, even tone, students are quiet:) Ok, we've already dealt with 'nets. <You know>, we started with a three-dimensional figure. We cut our, our cereal box open. We laid it flat to create a net. Ahm, I've given you dimensions of nets and you guys have created your own, and tried them, cut them out and folded them to see if they work or don't work. So-o-o, (slower:) this is kind of a 'review. We've already 'covered some of this, and this should go through real quick, right here, this first part. Then (quickly again:) we're going to talk about surface area. Okay, (slowed speech:) question number one. (no pause, maintaining high teacher voice:) Madx would you read question number one please?

Susan does not go on to the next item on the worksheet as she begins describing the cutting up of the mini cereal box activity. She stops, recalls what they had done before during the prior week, and talks about the hands-on experience as a whole. She is activating prior knowledge, specific activities that were completed along with specific content, i.e., "nets." But, there is much more. By stopping and speaking to what they have done and been exposed to, she is allowing them to recall their experiences in a more holistic way. She is giving respect to their individual activity space (aspect of inner continuous field of knowing).[1] Directly above, she has not really told them anything new, but she is giving them freedom to think about what they have done already, reminding them of that freedom: "I've given you dimensions of nets and you guys have created your own, tried them,..." Then, she gets them ready for the new idea "surface area." In going through the review, she is providing them words in association with calling up their prior awareness and memory of what they have actively accomplished, recognizing their own individual activity space in learning about nets. And, she is clearly indicating a conceptual connection between "nets" and "surface area."

The worksheet is written up in a very traditional way that suggests a usual way of teaching surface area: "cut up the object," "lay it out flat," "compute the area of each piece," and "add them all up." The traditional way this might be taught then would be to just follow the series of discrete steps and then get the steps reinforced by doing the worksheet. But Susan is approaching the role of the worksheet differently. She has a more continuous model of what she wants them to do and learn (related to her total understanding at that time). She has an idea of where she wants them to go and she is preparing them to get there. In working this way, she is creating levels of activity and involvement which will be integrated into the experience of the current lesson. Instead of taking them quickly through discrete steps, she is working with their individual continuous fields of knowing, acknowledging and respecting her students and their current activity space. She is still doing the discrete steps but she is giving them some freedom in the process. She is taking her students carefully through the process again in this "reinforcing" and relearning experience. Susan is aware that her students are working both individually and collectively at the same time.

After introducing the concept, "... then we are going to talk about surface area," she quickly calls on Madx to read Q1 on the worksheet, no waiting.

Madx: (47:28) (low voice, even, steady, quick:) Suppose that you fold the net into a figure. What three-dimensional figure would be formed?

S: (no pause, expectant matter-of-fact, objective, lowered tone:) Ok. What is it going to make me Madx when I fold this figure?

Madx: Ahm, ahm, (unsure:) rectangular thing?

S: Ok, rectangular what?

Student1: (low voice near microphone, 0.5s before Madx:) Prism.

Madx: Prism?

S: (47:42) Prism. Ok. (direct:) Write that down. (2.0s pause) It's going to make me a rectangular prism. It's going to make me a Kleenex box. Ok.

> Susan evokes again the memory of the cutting up activity with the cereal box and creates an equivalence between the Kleenex box and a rectangular prism. She is giving the category and an instance of the category. She calls up a mental image and gives it a name. Prior to doing that though, she states very directly: "Write that down." The statement above, "...suppose you fold the net into a figure...," is recreating the entire cutting up activity with the cereal boxes and in making a box activity when given the dimensions of the nets in two quick sentences. Each time, she is referring to student memory and relating that to the current structured review activity. She is addressing them at different levels of mind: being directed to write it down (which emphasizes the importance of the category); describing the cereal box activity as a whole in two sentences; describing the cereal box activity in about 8 sentences earlier; helping students to realize that they are talking in numerous ways about one thing: that there are different levels of mastery over the concepts of rectangular prism and surface area.

Student2: (47:50) It's hot in here.

S: I know it. I'll ???. (inaudible due to student chatter that starts up right away at "I know it," Susan says something about talking to Maintenance, inaudible.)

Student chatter: (about heat:) "It goes back and forth," one student to another: "it's a Kleenex box," (???-inaudible).

> The sun was shining brightly in the east windows this morning heating up the room. The students have had trouble before on warm winter days due to poor ventilation. Maintenance has tried to adjust the air flow but the building and system is old. So, for about 11 seconds Susan lets the students be off task. At this point, the students are not being pushed. There are no unsolved problems to engage them, nor is she pushing them to perform. She is letting them write down the name ("rectangular prism"); they are all catching a breath; it feels like a transition to Q2 on the worksheet. Susan waits and gives them time, assessing readiness to continue.

S: (48:01) (loud, over-talking the student chatter:) Ok, now (1.5s pause, looking around the room:) question two-o-o-o. Drx, would you read question two please?

> Susan is treating students as adults when she asks Drx to read Q2: she is asking him to make a contribution to the activity. As noted already, Susan has been describing what they are doing using different levels of mind and continuing to indicate to her students that what they are doing is important by her tone, cadence of speech, emphasis, calling to get their attention, and verbal pacing to keep focus. She is indicating as well that Drx's reading of Q2 is important and that reading too is important to this learning process. Of course, Susan is also using student reading to help the class stay focused and attentive. In

this way, she is treating students as equals where all the aspects of the current worksheet activity has relevance and requires their attention.

Drx reads in a way that seems to register his sense of being a part of this work (the lesson). He reads Q2 with seriousness, care, and purpose.

Drx: Question two is: Find the area of each of the six faces of the three-dimensional figure.

S: (48:15) Ok. (clearly enunciates each word:) Find the area of the six (slight 1.0s pause for emphasis:) faces. (1.0s pause) Ok, we're gonna go ahead, ahm, (2.0s pause), so this, you notice they actually put a dark line in there, showing you this is where this face starts and this is where <you know> one ends and one starts. Would you please go ahead and 'number for me to prove to me, how you found the area. So, number the boxes. For example, this one (points to it), (**Student1**: Ah ha), you're showing me your work. You're proving to me how you got the answer. That box there, that face, has an area of twelve. Please do that on all the other faces there. Please number them (voice rising to continue speaking)...

About 1 second after Drx stops reading, Susan calls the students' attention to her and basically repeats Q2. What follows is: she is letting the students become more involved with their own activity space in terms of their overall engagement with the activity, but also in terms of numerous cognitive jumps in her descriptions. She puts emphasis on "faces"; she shifts attention to the "dark line" on the worksheet drawing of the net; she clearly states how they are to show their work to her and the meaning of doing that - indicating that this is "proving to me" that they know what they are doing; she points out the area of 12 on one of the faces. In each phrase, she is giving more clarity to the task and trying to keep the students focused on the work. Susan sees such attention and focus on the steps in the task as leading to a deeper, fuller engagement with the concepts she is teaching. That happens at this micro-level of classroom learning management. One student says loudly, "ah ha," perhaps indicating he is getting it. She continues, playing into the experience of their getting it, but she is also doing her job: repeating, clarifying, and confirming everything.

For the next 9-11 seconds, a student asks about listing the areas of the faces, and she responds "yes." That student and most of the class are catching on to what they are to do with the activity, what is to be accomplished, so it seemed at this point from observation notes.

Student1: (48:57) (interrupting:) So you kind of like, twelve comma, and on?
S: (low tone:) You are just going to list them, yes.

Student1: Ah, ok.

S: (louder to whole class:) Ok, now go to the second face there and start numbering it.

Student2: (49:06) But there's like, (**Student3**: Would it be like…), I don't know what that line is either, … (inaudible) (other content-related chatter inaudible)

S: You need to (more inaudible student chatter)

S: (49:12) (louder:) You need to do all the faces, you'll do one through three, how many one, two, three, four, five, six. (slightly lower tone, spoken evenly, no change in pitch:) On each face, you're going to number each face. I tried to make it a little darker so you could see. They have it on there, darkened in.

> Some of the students want more clarification. Noticeable in the chatter is some desperation about what to do next by some students. From the observation notes, most students seemed to know what they were doing but some were not quite sure how to proceed. At this point though, the engagement of the whole class with the lesson was starting to unravel. Susan notices this, as she surveys the chatter, and focuses in on some individual students with questions and starts to clarify more. Other students still have questions.

Student3: Like that? Like this one? (**S** looks to him, nods.) Ok.

Student4: With the next face, you like, ah, or would it be like you would you start counting at one?

S: You'd start counting at one.

Student4: Oh!

S: (49:37) (to the whole class:) I don't want the total area. I want the area of (strong emphasis:) 'each' face. That's what the question asked me, (1.0s pause) the area of (stronger emphasis:) 'each face.

> Here, Susan is re-emphasizing what she wants from them and is working to keep students focused on one single activity, not to move ahead, trying to stay in control. Susan is emphasizing the words she wants students to continue to pay attention to. With each phrase "area of each face" (repeated) calling their attention to the object, the net which has "faces" (surfaces) that make up the 3-D object (Kleenex box or the mini cereal box they cut up and laid out flat). She wants them to recognize the component parts of the object and to integrate that into their current activity space and overall conception. She is also teaching them to pay attention to each question and what each question is specifically asking about.

Student5: So, what, how would it be, like, so that, (**S** interrupts)

S: You've got to list them, twelve comma, however many, whatever else is needed.

Student5: ...(inaudible)... 12 tall?

S: (49:54) (to Student5:) Yes. (2.5s pause) Ok. Now, what's, what's our label going to be on those, that twelve? That is twelve what?

> Now Susan is regaining their focus and letting the class know that there is more going on than just making a list: "... twelve what?" She is letting them know that they need to keep track of more than just counting and listing the "areas of each face." There is another important concept that they have discussed before that puts "area" into a mathematical context, a needed specification. She gives (respectful) wait time to hear from the students (about 11 seconds go by before she talks again).

Student6: Inches squared?

Student7: Centimeters!

Student8: Units.

Student9: We don't know what it is.

Student8: Units!

S: (50:07) (without special emphasis:) So, we'd say units. So, it's actually twelve units (1.0s pause, with emphasis:) squared. Twelve squares, you could say. <Ok>, so if it is area, you could say it's (in measured, even voice:) twelve square units. (4.0s pause) Remember we used the "u" for units when we don't know what the measurements are. Ok. (elongated:) Question (3.0s pause) three here in a minute. I want to let you finish those up (listing the area of the faces).

> At the end here, she is becoming more natural in tone, more gentle as she moves the class to the next question, Q3. She has noticed the students as a whole are working on finishing the task at hand – like they are in their own worlds doing it and she is comfortable with giving them the time. She stops herself with a 3 second pause (reflection) and decides to let them finish before going on to Q3.
>
> Susan has been talking through each aspect of the worksheet at many levels. She is showing part of her system of instruction that the students have experienced with her for the last 5 months. The students are also recognizing that they are learning by being involved in her system this way. This is a current collective consciousness – the students' recognition of the teaching approach brings along security and confidence that each step in the lesson is a necessary one. They are at this moment learning by doing it her way and they feel good about it. This is seen in the way they interact with her, their even tone in questioning, how they comfortably interact with her even when unsure of what to do next. On the one hand, she is being very direct with the class. On the other hand, she is giving them freedom in how they go about it, respecting them as persons with their own individual activity space.

S: (50:49) (sweetly:) Gerx, could you go ahead and read question three for me?

Gerx: Alright. Add the areas of the six faces. The total area is called the *'surface area'* (in italics on worksheet).

> Gerx reads this exactly as she wants it read. He seems to be working with Susan's teaching approach (system). He read beautifully with emphasis on "surface area." [Gerx is never trouble in class. He does his work but he is not that motivated.] Here, he is reading in a way that shows he is engaged in the activity. He is playing along with the worksheet review and seems to be enjoying it. He is getting what Susan is trying to convey. [In the four prior class observations, I noted Gerx as fairly low key when it came to class participation, but here, he is "letting himself shine."] He reads Q3 like he is aware of himself in the stoplight and takes it seriously.

S: Ok. So once you have, all of those, 'counted and you've got them listed, then right here I need you to (with emphasis:) add them, it says to add, and this is going to be called our surface area. (quickly transitioning:) Now, using our matheneze, (emphasizing:) our math language, when we do surface area, so we don't have to write surface area, over and over, we use "S" "A." You mathematicians, when you use SA, I know that means surface area. If you just put a regular "A," I'll think you are just talking about 'area and those are two different things. (1.5s pause) Ok.

> Here, Susan goes back through emphasizing immediate past experience and tying that to a new idea, "surface area," and their current activity space. She is making a conceptual shift with the reference to surface area and distinguishing it from "area." She is saying they need to be clear in their communication and use of language. She brought "surface area" up at the beginning of the worksheet activity description, but now she returns to it clearly, with strong emphasis. She is making the conceptual shift vivid and emphasizing correctness in communication. She is also exaggerating in reference to "using our matheneze, our math language." She is tying her students' work on surface area to something even more general, their math language and the need for clarity.

Student9: (inaudible...) if you have to write, SA equals ... (inaudible)
S: (51:37) You need to write down the work.

Student10: SA?

S: (51:41) (to the class:) SA stands for surface area. So for question three, you are going to put SA and you are going to show me your addition. So, write this plus this plus this and then give me the answer. (5.0s pause) That is, again, our SA is our matheneze, it's our language. Instead of having to write out (even tone, slight emphasis:) "surface area is," we use SA as shorthand.

In a usual more direct way of teaching, the teacher would give a certain amount of information, specific steps, and procedures. Then the student would give back to the teacher the various points, answers, with the steps taken into account etc., as defined by the worksheet or set of problems. But, Susan is doing more. She is training them to have a verbal aspect integrated with mathematics activity. She is giving them more words and how that language fits into this lesson. In this sense, she is continuing to fill their mathematics activity space, their world actually, by giving a language structure to the mathematics conceptual structure on which they have been working. She is saying that by doing this integration of math and language, they are being like mathematicians.

Student10: Whoaaa.

Student11: (speaking to student 10, with serious tone:) I just told you how to find the surface area.

Student9: What?

Student10: What?

Student11: (to Student 10:) The next question is to explain how to find the surface area of the box. (exasperated tone:) I just told you.

S: (52:13) (to Student 11:) Maybe he's trying to see if you are paying attention (with a smile). (4.0s pause) This is the ahh mixed work, it's, it's kinda like the reading and writing, mixed with reading. (7.0s pause) Derx, I want you to read that question (Q4) to me again. What does it say to do?

Derx: Explain how you can find the surface area of the box.

S: <Ok>, now I want us to be doing content skills. So, what did we do first to find the surface area? Gerx?

Gerx: We like split it up into different parts.

S: And what are those parts called?

Gerx: Ahh?

S: Comparative (tone goes down:) faces. Ok. So, we had our (tone goes back up:) 'faces.

(Student chatter.)

S: (low voice:)Yeah.

Gerx: (deliberate, almost dictated, even tone:) We counted up, the area in each of the faces.

S: (52:53) (elevated tone:) So, the first thing we did was counted up the area in each of the 'faces, (8.0s pause) (lowered tone:) and then what did we do? We got them all at, we got them all counted up, and figured out this one's worth 12 and this one's worth,

Gerx: (interrupting, same deliberate tone:) and then we added them all up to find the surface area.

> Over the last 2 minutes, there does not seem to be the same common focus. Susan is giving students latitude, but she is also going back through what they have been doing over the last 8 minutes or so. Yet, with all the questions coming from students to her and to each other, she also knows they are working on this, that they are sharing information with each other. They have freedom to ask about and explore their current consciousness (awareness) of what they are learning and practicing in their activity space – continuous field of knowledge. Students are connecting the lesson (the external aspects) with their own inner awareness of how they are coming to understand the lesson.

S: (53:19) Ok. So then we added them all up to find the surface area. So when I get a surface area question, and you say "I don't get it," I'm going to say "Hmmm." You probably need to go back to that class work and maybe read what we wrote down on question four, because you just told yourself exactly how to do it... [The lesson continues for about another fifteen minutes and ends with students calculating the surface areas for a rectangular prism and a cylinder.]

> Besides letting her students know the importance of what they are doing and how they can clarify confusion that might arise in the future, that they can go back to what was just accomplished to solve problems, she also makes reference to what she has been trying to get them to learn and realize: "You just told yourself exactly how to do it." This is exactly what she has been focused on for this lesson. She wants them to experience a deepened awareness of their individual activity space and the sense of their constructive capacity for independent learning. The whole lesson here reflects that higher order awareness. The procedural care Susan gives to this lesson indicates her authentic connection to their "getting it" which the students also feel.

DISCUSSION

Throughout the lesson, Susan was not just referring to memory, to specific things or events. She was being more global with the class, more in line with letting them be persons. She was guiding the class for sure, but she was letting each student live in their personal activity space (respectful of their continuous field of knowing). Susan is working carefully with the steps and procedures in finding "surface area" and referring to students' memory of how they first worked with the concept. She is operating in a way that does not rely on memory of specific things alone though. Rather, she is focused on her students' awareness of prior experience, asking them to feel it as a whole. In approaching the worksheet, Susan was trying to "bring it all into play ... I went into the traditional teacher mode to connect to everything we had done" (Follow-up discussion notes). She was showing them levels of discourse with respect to conceptualizing the concepts and how their "matheneze," talking, and thinking/reflecting about it integrates with activity. She lets them make the integration. Students were being directed to work more or less at the same speed in how they structured their experience as well, for example, the number of seconds given to consider the question, definition, or experience of "matheneze." In that time-related sense, similar levels of experience were occurring across the class. What is the interconnectedness? What is the logic here? Susan has each individual student structuring on their own, at the same speed and level of experiencing, keeping their attention focused on each step where each step is a conceptual enlargement. But, students are individuals doing that inner structuring on their own too, and she reminds them that they are doing it for themselves; it is becoming part of them, part of who they are.

Susan has been massaging and reworking the existing curriculum and creating new lessons as needed, in her view, to better support math learning. She also involved her family in trying the new lessons out. Such activity and commitment involves her whole person. She is rechanneling her life energies into her teaching world to benefit her students and her classroom life. We see at the micro level in the aforementioned instance by the way she allowed students time to work on the task at hand (within their own activity space engaging their continuous field of knowing). Her students see that Susan is giving her whole self. They trust her and are willingly attentive to the process. This form of collective awareness in the classroom is what she seeks to develop in them – organization and seriousness in learning math. This is not an abstraction – she is teaching her students to see math as knowledge (subject matter) they can actually use to better understand the world. For Susan, this is a whole life, whole-family activity filled with beauty and truth. The students are evolving in the classroom and being exposed to the complexity of the concepts under discussion, "nets," "surface area," "rectangular prism," and "matheneze." Susan is enabling her students to identify with the whole learning process but at the same time she is not asking them to give up their freedom. She sees freedom built into the subject matter itself. Knowing how to conceptually deconstruct a "Kleenex" box, for example, into a system of mathematical concepts that apply to all instances of the category (rectangular prism) is substantial, complex, and liberating.

This analysis suggests a moral/ethical unity at the core of the activity and Susan's teaching in general, a consciousness that strives for connection that "flows from the heart." In discussing an early draft of the micro-analysis with her, I asked her about the worksheet experience. She said that she wanted

> to make sure that the work they [her students] had done before on area, nets, and surface area showed back up, ..., [she wanted them to] make those connections, ..., to giving students experiences of it all, to feel how it comes together, to imagine the flow, and put it into words. (Observation 5 worksheet follow-up discussion notes)

CONCLUDING COMMENT

The larger issue which motivated this study in the beginning is to better understand the nature and beneficence of individual teacher growth as a unity in the person as a whole (Goodwin, 1999, 2005) and how that plays out and develops in the classroom in relation to subject matter involvement. In schooling and society-at-large, subject matter areas like Mathematics, Science, the Arts, Literature, and areas of educational work like school Counseling and Teaching, are important ways individuals become inspired, develop as persons, construct meaning in day-to-day living, and deepen a sense of life fulfillment (Witz, 2000). Certainly constructivist teachers aim to enhance students' fundamental engagement with educational processes (Gordon, 2009; Richardson, 1999) that include subject matter learning. The same can be said of more traditional teachers. Either way, such engagement is inseparably related to the teacher, her own connection to subject matter, higher values, deeper motivation to teach, and caring for children's development, the unity of which is at the core of teaching mastery.

There is little doubt that a more nuanced understanding of the great wonder and complexity of teaching case-by-case which takes the teacher's life (Goodson, 2008; Goodson & Numan, 2002), voice (Clandinin & Huber, 2005), "best-loved self" (Craig, 2011), and consciousness (Witz & Goodwin, 2012) seriously is fundamental to educational improvement at the classroom and school level. This understanding is central to "rais[ing] the quality of advocacy" (Stake & Rosu, 2012, p. 57) in developing educational policy.

NOTES

1. "Activity space" and "continuous field of knowing" as terms make use of holistic language to represent conceptual development in children as involving motor/sensory activity, interpretation, imagination fused with the current consciousness at many levels of generality and life experience. The analytical reference to a child's or group's activity space takes into account the unity of the person and the dynamics of being active and engaged. The dynamic and complex individual knowledge structuring engaged by the teacher is an expansive realm in the consciousness of the child that involves in some way the whole of the child. The suggestion here as well is to recognize children's learning experiences and the teacher's actions as unified and coherent to better understand and appreciate the intrinsic nature of conceptual development happening naturally in the classroom. In the segment under analysis, Susan recognized and appreciated the complex dynamics and prior experience/knowledge as part of the collective classroom experience. That larger whole, with respect to learning mathematics in this case, may in an important sense be characterized by individual "continuous field of knowing" that also have shared qualities as suggested by Cooley's adolescent primary group mind, a "sphere of intimate association" (Cooley, 1956, p. 24). The conceptual development of and meaning of subject matter knowledge involves the person as a whole, unbroken, interrelated, evolving, and with changing inner structuring assimilating and reacting to current experience. Of course, all this needs to be investigated carefully.

REFERENCES

Clandinin, J., & Huber, M. (2005). Shifting stories to live by: Interweaving the personal and professional in teachers' lives. In D. Beijaard, P. Meijer & G. Norine-Dershimer (Eds.), *Teacher professional development in changing conditions* (pp. 43–59). Dordrecht, The Netherlands: Springer.

Cooley, H. H. (1956). *Two major works: Social organization. Human nature and the social order.* Glencoe, IL: Free Press.

Corbin, J., & Stauss, A. (1990). Grounded theory research: Procedures, canons, and evaluative criteria. *Qualitative Sociology, 13*(1), 3–21.

Craig, C. (2011, April 8-12). Teacher education and the best-loved self. A paper delivered at the ISATT Symposium on International Trends in the Study of Teaching/Teacher Education: Disseminating Research for the Public Good, *American Educational Research Association annual conference*, New Orleans, LA.

Goodson, I. (2008). *Investigating the teacher's life and work.* Rotterdam, The Netherlands: Sense Publishers.

Goodson, I., & Numan, U. (2002). Teacher's life worlds, agency and policy contexts. *Teachers and Teaching: Theory and Practice, 8*(3/4), 269–277.

Goodwin, D. (2005). Comprehensive development of teachers based on in-depth portraits of teacher growth. In D. Beijaard, P. Meijer & G. Norine-Dershimer (Eds.), *Teacher professional development in changing conditions* (pp. 231–243). Dordrecht, The Netherlands: Springer.

Goodwin, D. R. (1999). *A qualitative study of the personal and professional growth of teachers involved in collaborative educational action research projects.* Unpublished doctoral dissertation, University of Illinois, Urbana-Champaign, IL.

Gordon, M. (2009). The misuses and effective uses of constuctivist teaching. *Teachers and Teaching: Theory and Practice, 15*(6), 737–746. doi: 10.1080/13540600903357058

Lawrence-Lightfoot, S., & Davis, J. H. (1997). *The art and science of portraiture.* San Francisco, CA: Jossey-Bass.

Richardson, V. (1999). Teacher education and the construction of meaning. In G. A. Griffin (Ed.), *The education of teachers: Ninety-eighth yearbook of the National Society for the Study of Education* (pp. 145–166). Chicago, IL: The University of Chicago Press.

Smith, L. M. (1994). Biographical method. In N. Denzin & Y. Lincoln (Eds.), *Handbook of qualitative research* (pp. 286–305). Thousand Oaks, CA: Sage.

Smith, L., & Goeffry, W. (1968). *The complexities of an urban classroom: An analysis toward a general theory of teaching.* New York, NY: Holt, Rinehart, and Winston, Inc.

Stake, R., & Rosu, L. (2012). Energizing and constraining advocacy. In N. Denzin & M. Giardina (Eds.), *Qualitative inquiry and the politics of advocacy* (pp. 41–58). Walnut Creek, CA: Left Coast Press, Inc.

Witz, K. (2000). The 'academic problem.' *Journal of Curriculum Studies, 32*(1), 9–23.

Witz, K. (2006). The participant as ally and essentialist portraiture. *Qualitative Inquiry, 12*(2), 246–268.

Witz, K., & Goodwin, D. (2012). A single "consciousness-and-'I'" from childhood to old age: Consciousness in the study of human life and experience III. *Qualitative Inquiry, 18*(8), 699–710. doi: 10.1177/1077800412452852

Witz, K., Goodwin, D., Hart, R., & Thomas, S. (2001). An essentialist methodology in education-related research using in-depth interviews. *Journal of Curriculum Studies, 33*(2), 195–227.

Witz, K., & Lee, H. (2013). "The self," "I," and "a single-consciousness-and-'I'": Consciousness in the study of human life and experience V. *Qualitative Inquiry, 19*(6), 419–430. doi: 10.1177/1077800413482095

APPENDIX A: CLASSROOM VIEWED FROM THE FRONT TO SHOW THE "U" DESK CONFIGURATION

APPENDIX B: STUDENT ARTIFACT SHOWING THE FIRST PAGE OF "SURFACE AREA" WORKSHEET

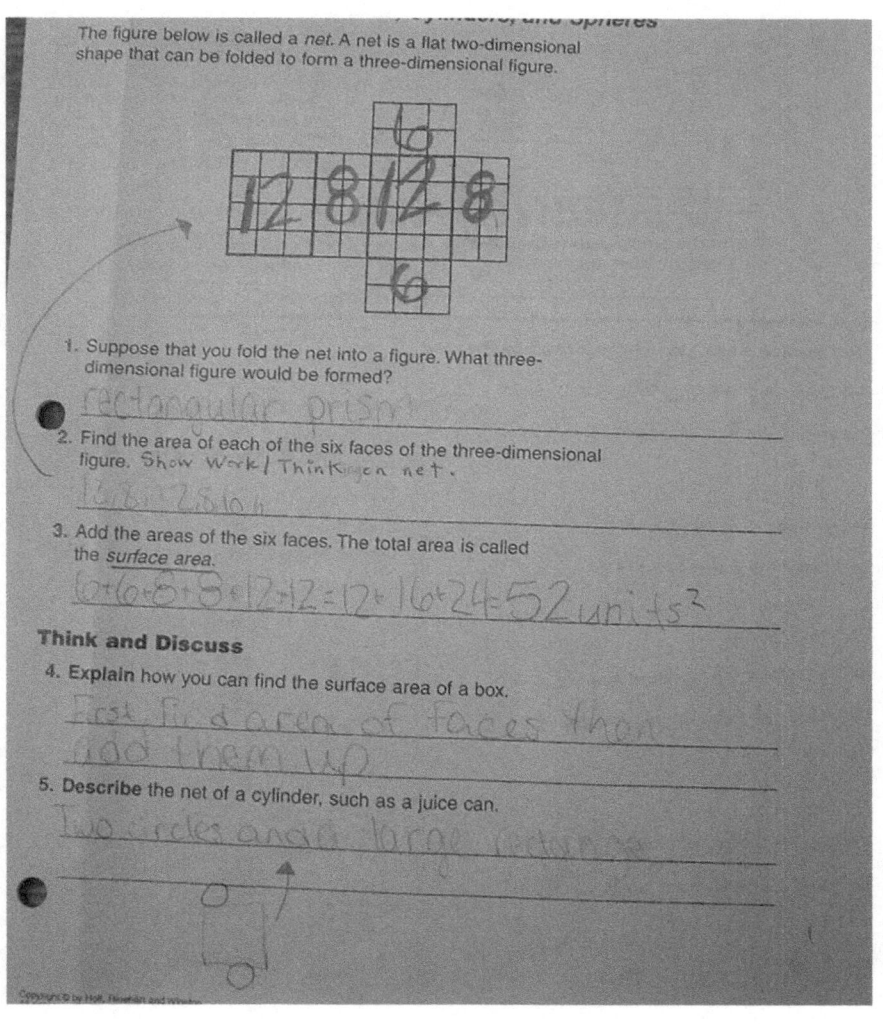

The figure below is called a *net*. A net is a flat two-dimensional shape that can be folded to form a three-dimensional figure.

1. Suppose that you fold the net into a figure. What three-dimensional figure would be formed?

   rectangular prism

2. Find the area of each of the six faces of the three-dimensional figure. Show Work / Think on net.

3. Add the areas of the six faces. The total area is called the *surface area*.

   6+6+8+8+12+12 = 12+16+24 = 52 units²

Think and Discuss

4. Explain how you can find the surface area of a box.

   First, find area of faces than add them up

5. Describe the net of a cylinder, such as a juice can.

   Two circles and a large rectangle

CHAPTER 24

SCHOOL-BASED INSTRUCTIONAL RESEARCH (SBIR): AN APPROACH TO TEACHER PROFESSIONAL DEVELOPMENT IN CHINA

Xiao Han and Zhuo Feng

ABSTRACT

The Chinese system of education is shifting from an examination orientation to a more creative approach in order to increase educational quality. The New Curriculum in China requires not only changes in content and form, but also sets higher expectations for teachers' instructional strategies and quality course design. Against this policy backdrop, China developed and implemented the School-Based Instructional Research (SBIR) model to improve teachers' professional knowledge and development. In this ISATT anniversary chapter, our discussion revolves around the theme of SBIR, including its origin, progression, process, elements, and methods. To end, we summarize the expectations and prospects for SBIR in the Chinese educational context.

Keywords: SBIR; in-service teacher development; reflective practice; China

From Teacher Thinking to Teachers and Teaching: The Evolution of a Research Community
Advances in Research on Teaching, Volume 19, 503–525
Copyright © 2013 by Emerald Group Publishing Limited
All rights of reproduction in any form reserved
ISSN: 1479-3687/doi:10.1108/S1479-3687(2013)0000019027

INTRODUCTION

With the in-depth study of teachers' knowledge pioneered by the International Study Association on Teachers and Teaching, researchers and theorists as well as teachers themselves have become more concerned about teachers' practical knowledge. In China, we have become increasingly aware that teachers' practical knowledge as held, expressed, and used by teachers plays a key role in their professional development. The profession of teaching, we aver, does not build on strict, scientific, conclusive principles but on practical knowledge gleaned through lived experiences. It has long been an international trend to study teachers' knowledge from the inside-out based on their experiences and classroom practices. In recent years, with the implementation of quality education and the New Curriculum, China not only changed the instructional content and media, but more importantly, it called for a new model of school culture that acknowledged that teachers' professional lives are changing. China has increasingly used School-Based Instructional Research (SBIR) to study teachers and their practical knowledge. The concept of "SBIR" has its specific origin in China. It can be traced to Chinese thinker and philosopher, Confucius, and his notion of "Dao (道)." One aspect of the meaning of Dao (道) is "experiences."

In China, examination-oriented education focusing on students' academic performance has existed for decades. It places a heavy burden on students and much pressure on teachers and parents as well. Educational reform aimed at changing an examination orientation to quality education focusing on all-round development including physical, mental, and ethical characteristics to meet students' needs and learning styles has intensified. China started to enact China's New National Curriculum Reform (CNNCR) on basic education in 2001. Compared to the previous curriculum reform, this reform stresses a revolutionary change in instructional concepts, including curriculum function, curriculum structure, curriculum content, instructional model, curriculum evaluation, and management. For example, the New Curriculum reform emphasizes transforming teaching and learning from the traditional examination-oriented approaches of rote memorization, lecture, and drill to more student-centered approaches in which students have space to develop their creativity, openly express their ideas, collaborate with each other, and learn by doing that emphasizes holistic development (Dello-Iacovo, 2009). In fact, educators in China have long been enlightened by Confucius's thoughts on individualization (因材施教). According to Confucius, first, we must understand different characteristics of the students by carefully observing and understanding them, and offering them targeted education to avoid blindness; and second, we should pay attention to students with certain talents while setting basic requirements for them, accommodating their individual differences. The reform aims at achieving a favorable process of quality education by changing teachers' instructional modes and students' learning methods (Guan & Meng, 2007) from teacher-centered to student-centered. These transformations pose a huge challenge for teachers' traditional instructional approaches.

To some extent, quality teachers play a key role in the success of CNNCR. Undoubtedly, access to high-quality programs of professional development is needed to support teachers to reinvent themselves professionally to cope with the transformation in the role of teachers called for by the reforms (Sargent, 2011). The development and implementation of CNNCR requires that a teacher is not only a knowledge transmitter (Darling-Hammond, 1997; McNiff, 1993) but also a researcher who is able to find, explore, and solve problems. Against the background of CNNCR, how to promote teachers' professional quality and what kind of teacher training should be offered have become urgent topics of inquiry in teacher education in China. Teachers are supposed to be prepared as "professionals" so a new model for teacher development in light of the background of basic education reform in China is formed. The model has two parts: one is general knowledge of the new curricula, and the other is methodology leading teachers to integrate advanced methods proposed by new curricula with traditional methods (Guan & Meng, 2007). Therefore, in order to solve the specific problems encountered in the practice of the New Curriculum reform, there is an urgent need to establish a field-based instructional research approach situated in the practical work of schools.

In-service teacher training in China has traditionally been lecture-centered, theory-orientated, and experience-led. It is unlikely to provide a context in which teachers are able to apply instructional theories into practice. Such an approach has not been effective for various contemporary reasons as Gu and Yang (2003) discuss below:

> There are many forms of current in-service teacher professional development, which includes short time curriculum training, unit workshops, and teaching observation and deliberation, and so forth. All of these forms are faced with the question of transforming from theory to practice. In fact, most of the teachers in these training programs are not able to apply theory into their daily practice. This has become an insolvable "chronic disease." (Gu & Yang, 2003, p. 1–2)

Under these circumstances, and based on the concept of teachers' practical knowledge, a unique model of teachers' professional development generated in the school context has arisen. That is SBIR, the theme around which our ISATT anniversary chapter coheres.

SBIR is a problem-centered instructional research activity which is based on the needs of schools and particularly teachers. It fully utilizes various kinds of resources inside and outside the school including the guidance and cooperation of external people and organizations. Specifically, SBIR refers to research activities that are carried out by teachers based on their own practices. It aims to advance teachers' practical capacities and to provide them with sustainable professional development. After reviewing the literature, we could not find a direct English translation of the term, School-Based Instructional Research (校本教研). The phrase is a unique term used in teacher education programs in China. SBIR, to a great extent, is similar to the concepts of action research (Gibson, 1985), narrative inquiry (Clandinin & Connelly, 2000), classroom-based research (Taber, 2007), practitioner-based enquiry (Murray, 1992), teacher as researcher inquiries (McNiff, 2002), reflective practitioner (Schön, 1983, 1987, 1991), and reflective teaching (Bartlett, 1990).

Currently, SBIR is exhibiting many advantages over the teacher-centered training models as an effective way of cultivating in-service teachers and has become one of the most important channels of teachers' continuing education in China. With its implementation, schools develop their unique characteristics in promoting teachers' professional development programs. Professor Lingyuan Gu (2005) pointed out that SBIR causes a profound change both in instructional and research strategies, and in teachers' learning and experiencing styles. Teaching should not be a lonely profession. The joy and pain of teaching need to be shared in a group. Through four dialogues: dialogue with themselves, dialogue with their peers, dialogue with the theory, and dialogue with practice, teachers are able to look for differences and begin to conduct instructional research (Gu, 2005).

BACKGROUND

Since the 1960s, the need to improve teachers' professional status has become increasingly urgent and the concept of teacher professionalization is largely agreed upon around the world. With the advance of teachers' professionalization, teachers' professional development has received more attention and has been gradually recognized as the core and the only way to achieve teacher specialization.

Concerning teachers' professional development, there are two kinds of orientations: an intellectual-technical orientation and a practical-reflective orientation. Intellectual-technical orientation believes that knowledge and skills are the important base and premise of teachers' specialization because teachers' professional development is affected mostly by accumulating knowledge and skills, especially subject and pedagogical knowledge, and instructional skills. It is concerned more with "what knowledge is essential for teaching." As research on teacher knowledge deepens, people gradually realize it is "what do teachers know" that affects teachers' professional development. So scholars began to focus on teachers' practice and everyday lives, in which they realize that there is a kind of special knowledge existing between theory and practice that fundamentally affects teachers' everyday classroom teaching and learning. The emphasis on teachers' practical knowledge forms the practical-reflective orientation of teachers' professional development.

In discussing the nature of knowledge in teaching and teacher education, Fenstermacher (1994) also raised questions to explain who is "the knower" (Dewey & Bentley, 1949), and what is "the known" in teacher knowledge research. By answering and analyzing these questions, Fenstermacher (1994) identified two types of knowledge (Schön, 1987), TK/F (teacher knowledge: formal) and TK/P (teacher knowledge: practical). Fenstermacher showed particular interest in the knowledge produced by practical teachers as he claimed that the type of practical knowledge is "not only different from formal knowledge but perhaps more powerful for understanding and advancing teaching" (Fenstermacher, 1994, p. 47).

The first type of knowledge, formal knowledge, is produced and known by researchers. It represents a type of teacher knowledge and skills that teachers should know and be able to do – the much-applauded knowledge base for teaching in practice. This view is based on the assumption that knowledge that informs teaching comes from authorities outside the profession itself. It represents a limited epistemological formal perspective that is grounded in conventional social and behavioral sciences, and generated through "studies of teaching that use conventional scientific methods, quantitative and qualitative; these methods and their accompanying designs are intended to yield a commonly accepted degree of significance, validity, generalizability, and intersubjectivity" (Fenstermacher, 1994, p. 8).

The second type of knowledge, teachers' practical knowledge, is based on the belief that teachers possess the knowledge of teaching as a result of their preparation and experience. Fenstermacher defined this type of knowledge as "how to do things, what the right time or place to do them is, and how to interpret the events related to one's actions." The researchers seeking this type of teacher knowledge believe that teachers possess abundant knowledge about teaching that researchers do not know from their own experience and action (Clandinin, 1985; Cochran-Smith & Lytle, 1993; Elbaz-Luwisch, 1983; Schön, 1983, 1987). The teachers are not passive consumers of knowledge; they are producers and users of their own knowledge as well.

John Dewey (1938), an outstanding American educational philosopher of the 20th century who remains very influential in China, pointed out that education as life and life as a continuum of experience. He viewed teachers as minded professionals and their knowledge as a sense of knowing carved of experience. For Dewey, interaction (the personal and the social), continuity (past, present, and future), and situation (place) were integral to his concept of experience and his developing ideas about practical knowledge. In China, Dewey was called the "second Confucius." Confucius was also looking for the most tolerant and richest form of human existence, which was called "experience" by Dewey and "Dao (道)" by Confucius (Grange, 2004). Confucius said, "By three methods we may learn wisdom: first, by reflection, which is noblest; second, by imitation, which is easiest; and third, by experience, which is the bitterest." Confucius's educational thoughts emphasize lifelong learning as does Dewey's philosophy of education.

In this chapter, in describing and reflecting on teachers' SBIR currently espoused in China for teacher professional development, we concur with the claim that teachers develop personal practical knowledge conceptualized by Clandinin (1985) based on Dewey's theory of experience. Teachers' personal practical knowledge, as stated by Clandinin and Connelly (1994), is:

> In the person's experience, in the person's present mind and body and in the person's future plans and actions. It is knowledge that reflects the individual's prior knowledge and acknowledges the contextual nature of the teacher's knowledge. It is a kind of knowledge, carved out of, and shaped by, situations; knowledge that is constructed and reconstructed as we live out our stories and retell and relive them through the process of reflection. (p. 125)

The definition embodies Dewey's criterion of experience (1938): interaction, continuity, and situation. Teacher knowledge is revealed through their accounts of experiences which are individually continuous and situated in cultural and social contexts. Teachers are regarded as knowers who can continually construct and reconstruct knowledge within themselves and in classrooms and schools. Dewey (1938) emphasized the integral nature of the knower and the known, and the importance of learning through experience.

Practical knowledge, which focuses on teachers' experiences, actions, and reflections, is teachers' "lived experiences," in Dewey's words. The connection between education, experience, and life is "organic" and a "permanent frame of reference" (Dewey, 1938, p. 25).

In studying teachers' personal practical knowledge, Craig formed the concept of knowledge communities (1995a, 1995b, 2001, 2003, 2007a, 2007b), which happens to be consistent with the Confucian notion of learning as an aesthetically ordered process that draws on the diverse perspectives and understandings of the members in the learning communities. She (Craig, 1992) found teachers brought with them different stories and versions of storied experiences to different people that form their communities of knowing. According to Olson and Craig, "teachers belong to multiple knowledge communities and they take different experiences and different versions of their experiences to different communities of knowing for interpretation" (Olson & Craig, 2001, p. 671). They make meanings of their experiences and provide insights in them. The sharing and interpreting of stories shape the understanding of their narrative knowledge. The different perspectives teachers share would be impossible to know if only through personal reflection (Craig, 2001). Another important component in the reflective inquiry process while teachers develop their personal practical knowledge is "collaborate and share." Some teachers form Teacher Research Communities or Critical Friends Groups where they are involved and engaged in relational conversations which feature dialogue, analysis, and reflection (Craig, 2003). Through questions, comments, and feedback, discussions within the groups helps them explain experiences, see alternative perspectives, and make connections between theory and practice (Lyons, 1998).

One should not ignore Schwab's Practical (1969, 1971, 1973, 1983) which contributed to and helped change the landscape of education. The classroom is a practical place with many variables and teachers have tacit knowledge to handle them on a daily basis. It is important to surface this tacit understanding and bring it to a level of awareness that permits reflective or deliberative consideration. When arguing for teacher's integral role in curriculum, Schwab (1983) also spoke to the necessity of teachers' reflective practice:

> Teachers will not and cannot be merely told what to do … There are thousand ingenious ways in which commands on what and how to teach can, will, and must be modified or circumvented in the actual moments of teaching. Teachers practice an art. Moments of choice what to do, how to do it, with whom and at what pace, arise hundreds of times a school day, and arise differently every day and with every group of students. No

command or instruction can be so formulated as to control that kind of artistic judgment and behavior, with its demand for frequent, instant choices of ways to meet an ever varying situation. Therefore, teachers *must* be involved in debate, deliberation, and decision about what and how to teach.... (p. 245)

Schön (1983, 1987, 1991), one of the most important theorists on reflective inquiry, articulated and developed the theories of reflective practice in which most people in different disciplines are unknowingly engaged. His thoughts were derived from Dewey's theory of experience. He develops such concepts as knowing-in-action, reflecting-in-action, and reflecting-in-practice. He assumes that competent practitioners usually know more than what they say in their practice. They exhibit a knowing-in-practice, most of which is tacit. They are also able to think about and reflect on their intuitive knowing in the midst of action (reflection-in-action) and use this capacity to cope with the unique and uncertain situation of practice.

Teachers' practical knowledge develops from teachers reflecting on action and experience (Schön, 1983). By participating in reflective inquiry like SBIR, teachers are more likely to frame and reframe the pedagogical problems and solve them by trying different ways. They analyze their past teaching and projected on their future practice. Schön's description of reflection-in-action further clarifies what reflective practitioner does in the process of active reflection and reflective conversation with the situation:

> When someone reflects-in-action, he becomes a researcher in the practice text. He is not dependant on the categories of established theory and technique, but constructs a new theory of the unique case. His inquiry is not limited to a deliberation about means which depends on a prior agreement about ends. He does not keep means and ends separate, but defines them interactively... because his experiment is a kind of action, implementation is built into his inquiry. Thus reflection-in-action can proceed, even in situations of uncertainty or uniqueness, because it is not bound by the dichotomies of Technical Rationality. (Schön, 1983, p. 68)

The "back-talk" and "reflective conversation" are ideas of Schön (1987) when he describes how a reflective practitioner responds to problems arising in a complex situation with an ill-defined and problem-solving process in which boundaries are shifting with variations and uncertainties. Practitioners must be involved in reflective conversation with the puzzling and uncertain situations, frame and reframe the problems, and make sense of uncertain situations which initially make no sense. They may find a way to solve a problem or may get into uncertainty again and try something else. The conversation with the situations is meaningful, reflective, and constructive. Also, when facing situation's back-talk, practitioners need to reflect-in-action to construct the strategies of action.

THREE ESSENTIAL ELEMENTS OF SBIR

Individual teacher reflection, teachers interacting in knowledge communities, and expert researchers' guidance are the three key elements of SBIR. They form multilevels of dialogues, as illustrated in Fig. 1.

First Dialogue: Self-Reflection – Dialogue within Teachers Themselves

Teacher reflection refers to the ability to critically examine his/her own behavior and teaching practice. For a teacher, reflection is a decisive element in his /her professional development. Teachers examine their own teaching through various forms of self-reflection to improve understanding of their teaching activities and keep an active mentality of inquiry. According to Calderhead and Gates (1993), successful and effective teachers tend to actively and creatively reflect on the important things in their career, including their instructional objectives, classroom environment, and professional competency. American psychologist Posner (1989) proposed that teachers' growth formula is: growth = experience + reflection. Posner wrote: "reflection with no experience is sterile and generally leads to unworkable conclusions, while experience with no reflection is shallow and at best leads to superficial knowledge" (Posner, 1989, p. 22). That is, reflections move teachers' behaviors from experience to theory, and from being spontaneous to being conscious. Obviously, reflection is not a general sense of "looking back," but that of reflecting, pondering, exploring, and solving the problems from all aspects of the teaching process. The approach

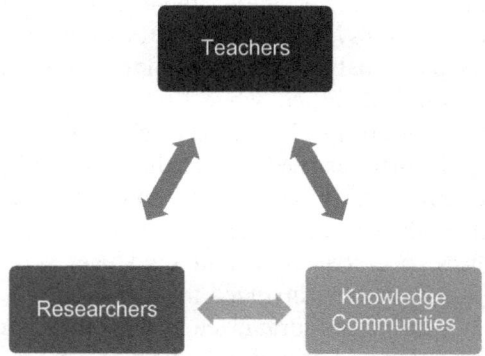

Fig. 1. Three Essential Elements of SBIR.

is research-based and practice-intensive. It constitutes the basic form of SBIR.

According to the instructional process, self-reflection in teaching practice should be divided into three stages, reflection before teaching, reflection in teaching, and reflection after teaching. By reflection before teaching, teachers predictably analyze new teaching activities in virtue of previous teaching experience. It forms the basic ideas of instructional design. Reflection in teaching refers to teachers' ability of monitoring problems in teaching process by identifying and reacting to them in a timely manner. This kind of reflection shows teachers' wit. In reflection after the teaching, teachers go back and analyze, summarize the problem in the teaching process, which is a critical process.

Teachers in self-reflection are in the process of (1) discovering the problem; (2) analyzing the problem; (3) selecting programs; (4) taking actions; and (5) summarizing assessment. The primary method of reflection is to write journals and educational autobiography.

Second Dialogue: Peer Coaching – Dialogue between Teachers and Colleagues

In peer coaching, two or more teachers take the initiatives and cooperate with each other to continuously and actively enhance self-improvement through a variety of methods (Zhu & Zhang, 2007). The quality and effectiveness of teachers' peer coaching is an important factor affecting the outcomes of SBIR. An empirical study conducted by Joyce and Showers (1982) showed that the interaction between teachers by observing and advising each other's classrooms enables them to apply the knowledge into everyday classroom teaching. They carried out a comparative study on two groups of teachers participating in a three-month in-service training. One group interacted with each other, while the other group did not. It was found that in the former group 75% of the teachers were able to consciously and effectively apply their learned knowledge and skills to their routine instruction, while only 15% of the latter group performed in the same way. More studies such as the one conducted by Singh and Shifflette (1996) also found that teachers' peer coaching and guidance were obviously more effective than if they were only involved in workshops.

Peer coaching has two types, organized and spontaneous. In the former, schools purposefully plan and organize the peer coaching; spontaneous peer coaching refers to teachers' active cooperation with their peers in teaching and research activities to form knowledge communities (Craig, 1995a, 1995b). The specific forms of peer coaching include collaborative lesson planning, classroom observation, after-class assessments, etc. Through these activities, teachers share experiences, find their weaknesses, improve teaching quality, and ultimately realize the goal the professional development. It can be said that peer coaching and cooperative knowledge communities formed among teachers are important indicators of SBIR.

Third Dialogue: Professional Guidance – Dialogue between Theory and Practice

The so-called professional guidance, by its very nature, is a dialogue between theory and practice, and the reconstruction of the relationship between theory and practice. In SBIR, college teachers, researchers, exemplary school teachers, and principals act as facilitators and guide teachers as they carry out research activities and help them improve their teaching, thus leading them to professional growth. Although SBIR is school-based and teacher-based and concerned with the problems within the school, it is not entirely confined to the school context. The participation of professional researchers is indispensable. Without their participation, SBIR could become stagnant and possibly result in formality and mediocrity (Zhang & Pu, 2008).

In terms of its activities and their purposes, current SBIR in China has the following three forms: (1) academic special report; (2) theoretical counseling seminars; and (3) on-site instructional guidance (Lv, 2008).

In sum, self-reflection, peer coaching, and professional guidance operate relatively independent of one another. But they are also complementary, relating to each other through mutual penetration and reinforcement. Only by fully playing their respective roles and focusing on their integration can they contribute to the construction of SBIR and promote the professional development of teachers.

IMPLEMENTATION OF SBIR

In practice, there are a variety of specific methods for enacting SBIR as described by Yin (2009). These include: narratives, case studies, journals, blogs and portfolios, self-study, etc. Below, we describe and explain some of them with a few examples and two tables.

Narratives

Put simply, narrative refers to activities where teachers tell stories about teaching events in written or oral format, reflecting on a certain lesson unit or part of a unit. By doing this, the process of SBIR is transformed into the process of telling instructional stories in which teachers story and restory (Connelly & Clandnin, 1990) what happens in their teaching, how they cope with questions and challenges, and what the results are and how they evaluate it. Undoubtedly it is the process of personal practical reflection that can improve teachers' daily practice. Below is an example of narrative in which an elementary math teacher vividly describes the process of how her students learn to brainstorm and design and draw a table to record data.

Squares Are Not Enough. How Do We Do?

I remember that the students in my class were very interested and enthusiastic about learning statistics. After learning the statistics knowledge, I required that they complete the statistics chart in the book by filling in their favorite sports. Originally I intended to assign them an exercise to strengthen their knowledge about statistics, but I didn't expect that there were so many kids that liked swimming – 25 in total. However, the squares could only represent 20 people even if the kids used 1 square to represent 2 people. Then they were anxious and worried. "What do we do?" The classroom quieted down. Suddenly, the little smart Feng Fan proudly said, "That's easy? Just add 3 squares above and paint 2 and a half of them." At this time, the squad leader Lu Haojian disagreed, "That won't work. There's no more room to add additional squares." "Then do we have a better way to do it?" I asked. The students started to think… "I know, I know. Since one square can represent 2 units, I can also use it to represent 3 units," Zhang Ke stood up and said. Then another kid stood up, "I think we can also use 1 square to represent 4 units." Then Feng Fan was so upset that he jumped up and said, "Bad idea! Bad idea!" "Why is it bad?" I asked. He said, "5 people loved running. How can we paint them? Too much trouble." At this time, Wang Yasong stood up. He said slowly, "I think the best way is to use 1 square to represent 5 people because the numbers are 5 by 5. For example, use 1 square to represent 5 people since 5 likes running; 10 people like jumping rope, so we use 2 squares; 25 people like swimming so we use 5 squares. It's easy and convenient to use 1 square to represent 5 people." All the kids nodded and agreed. I confirmed their thoughts, then took this opportunity to guide them, "Please think about how to decide the number of things that a square can represent." The students actively began their discussion. A while later many students raised their little hands.

"I feel it has to do with the number of things. Just use 1 square to represent 1 thing if the number is small."

"I want to first figure out the characteristics of the number of things, and then decide how many things a square can represent."

"Yes! I think we need to first figure out the maximum and the minimum numbers, and then make the decision."

"Yes, I think we should also consider which way is more convenient to paint the square."

"You all have great ideas! Do you want to design a statistics chart of your own? Please choose one of the following tables and design a chart with your partners." I took the opportunity to assign them the learning task.

I was surprised and moved by the creativity and thinking ability demonstrated by the students in this class. In math learning, the children will encounter various kinds of problems. When dealing with these problems, teachers should not always clear all the "obstacles," but let the children learn to think and find the ways to solve the problems. We need to provide opportunities and create conditions for children during the class by consciously speaking less and have them talk more, thus enabling them to solve real-life math problems through their own efforts.

Case Study

A case is a typical example of a problem solving situation and the methods used to solve these problems. Case study is a research method where teachers analyze, discuss, exchange ideas, and communicate about typical teaching examples to improve their professional capacity. The process of case study involves case presentation, analysis and discussion, design, reflection and evaluation. Below is a case fragment where a middle school teacher taught students to differentiate the words "cook" and "cooker."

Case Fragment: How to Teach English Words Vividly with More than One Way

I pay great attention to the context of the use of the word when teaching the meaning of an English word. For example, when I taught words "cook" and "cooker [cookware]" I showed a few pictures and some kitchenware to the students. Through the intuitive perception of the pictures and kitchenware, the students could clearly and explicitly understand the meaning of the two words without becoming confused from the very beginning. And the students' understanding of the two words would be further deepened by the sentence such as "He is a good cook; he has many cookers." This teaching strategy is simple and effective, and can expand students' knowledge as well.

Class Observation

Class observation refers to the recording, analysis, and study of the classroom environment by observing the teaching process. Based on the results, students' learning is improved and teachers' professional development is promoted. Classroom observation consists of three stages: the discussion and meeting before class, the observation and recording in class, and analysis and feedback after the class. This constitutes a process of determining the problem, collecting information, and solving the problem. Based on classroom observations, teachers recognize, understand, and grasp the true meaning of classroom teaching, clarify the focus of teaching practice, and create new teaching improvement strategies following the data collection and analysis. Professor Yunhuo Cui (2007), for example, breaks classroom observation into 4 dimensions, 20 perspectives, and 68 observation points, which we have summarized in Table 1.

Journal

Through writing entries in journal, a teacher describes and inquiries into his/her teaching practice. Journals usually explain emergent happenings and teaching puzzles. As a reflective tool, writing in journals is a simple and

Table 1. Cui's 4 Dimensions, 20 Perspectives, and 68 Observation Points of Class Observation.

Dimension	Perspective	Example of Observation Points
Student learning (L)	(1) Preparation (2) Listening (3) Interaction (4) Autonomy (5) Accomplishment	For example, in "autonomous," "how much time can students control? How many students are involved? How about the involvement of students from low-income families?"
Teacher instruction (I)	(1) Link (2) Demonstration (3) Dialogue (4) Guidance (5) Wit	For example, in "link," "do these links develop around instructional goals?"
Curriculum characteristic (C)	(1) Goal (2) Content (3) Implementation (4) Assessment (5) Resource	For example, in "goal," "what criteria by which the goal is identified (curriculum standards/students/textbook)? Does the goal fit the students?"
Classroom culture (C)	(1) Thinking (2) Democracy (3) Creativity (4) Love (5) Characteristics	For example, in "characteristics," "does the design of the whole class have unique characteristics (links/teaching material/introduction/teaching strategies/guidance/dialogue)?"

effective task. Below is a small excerpt from journal entry written by a teacher in China that has to do with how he can encourage and help underachieved students improve their learning.

Reflective Journal

By Jiahai Zhao

"Underachieving students" is one of the most difficult "rows to hoe." But I think it is critical to show caring for them. Criticism only produces "underachievers' hostile feelings." Recently, I communicated with praise, and encouraged them more frequently than usual, and also let excellent students help them more during class independent-learning time. Through these efforts, I build up their confidence and improve their learning.

Blog

Teachers' blogs are called educational blogs (edublogs). Taking advantage of the emerging Internet "zero barrier (零壁垒)" blog technology, teachers use text and multimedia to put episodes from their daily classroom life, teaching experiences, lesson planning, classroom records, and courseware online. On the blog platform, teachers can narratively instantiate teaching strategies they hear and observe, and thus improve their reflective practice. Additionally, blog technology fully supports the concept of "dialogue, cooperation, and sharing." Blogs contribute to externalizing teachers' knowledge and achieve the sharing of knowledge. A live example of this is Jin Hai elementary school teachers' blog site at http://www.jha2008.com/Item/365.aspx

Portfolios

Teacher growth portfolios present a collection of the work of individual teachers. These portfolios reflect teachers' professional growth process and provide a full display of their ethics, teaching, research, and continuing education experiences. The portfolio contains a self-introduction, ideas about instructional design, a description of the teachers' teaching record, instructional research and cases, reading notes and reflections, student work samples, and awards they have received. Portfolios cause teachers to self-evaluate and self-reflect; they encourage them to actively pursue professional development. Table 2 presents table of contents of a teacher's portfolio in China.

Table 2.   The Contents of a Teachers' Portfolio in China.

Teachers' Growth Portfolio Catalogue		
The Preface – Education Ambition		

Section One: Planning and learning

1. Personal information	2. Personal professional development plan	3. Learning and training records (a variety of training records, the selected reading notes, reflections, education narrative, etc.)

Section Two: Research

1. Teaching materials (excellent instructional design, wonderful courseware, public teaching)		2. Table that records involved research activities

Section Three: Research and reflection

1. Instructional research (teaching experience, quality analysis, paper analysis)		2. Educational essays, teaching reflection (a selection of one reflective paper once a week)

Section Four: Achievements and summary

1. Honorary titles (copies of the certificates)	2. Student counseling award (copy of the certificate)	3. Yong teacher guidance

Section Five: Evaluation and management
Class management information

Section Six: Life and features

Projects

Teacher-research projects are also an important part of SBIR. Through participation, teachers increase their professional knowledge. A basic process in instructional research, in general, includes (1) select subject area; (2) determine participants; (3) establish research project; (4) implement research plan; (5) analyze and process research data; (6) complete research project; and (7) evaluate research results. Instructional research fits teachers' learning methods. It evolves from practice to theory and back again. It is a process of coming from life and back to life, ultimately enhancing teachers' professional development.

THE PROCESS OF SBIR

Zhang and Pu (2008) summarized the processes of SBIR and stated that there are three possible processes to address classroom challenges, which we summarize in Fig. 2.

Process 1: The teacher discovers problem in teaching – teacher reflection – data collection – solve the problem – discover new problem – teacher reflection.
Process 2: The teacher discovers problem in teaching – teacher reflection – data collection – unable to solve problem – teacher and researcher cooperation – solve the problem.
Process 3: The teacher discovers problem in teaching – teacher reflection – data collection – unable to solve problem – teacher and researcher cooperation – unable to solve the problem – education experts seminar – propose agreeable program – teacher tests by practice – revise the program – solve the problem.

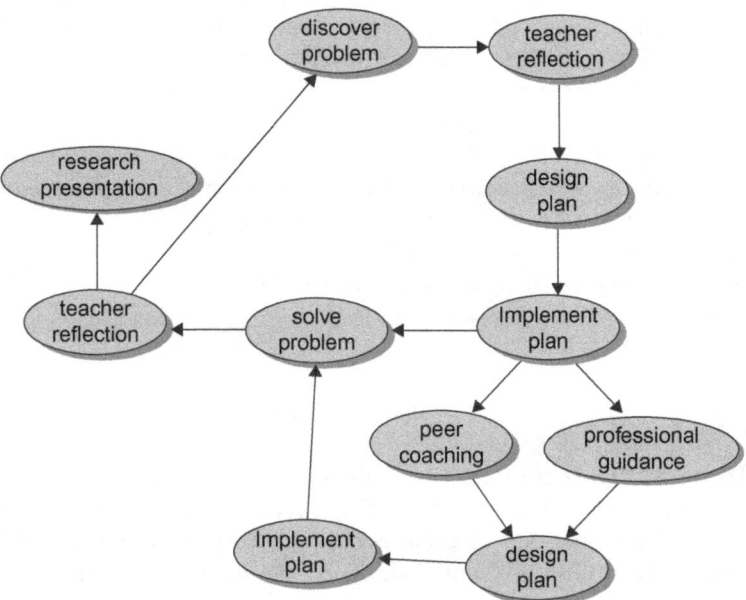

Fig. 2. The Process of SBIR.

AN EXEMPLAR ILLUSTRATING
THE PROCESS OF SBIR

Research Topic of the Exemplar

How to organize students to carry out effective cooperative learning in math instruction
    Lesson Topic: Have a Guess
    (The lesson is from the third grade math experimental text book edited by Beijing University)

Original Lesson Delivery ("I" is the teacher of this lesson)

My teaching goal is (1) students know the probability of events occurrence by doing experiments; and (2) students are able to list the size of the probability of event occurrence.
    Activity 1: Showing dials
    (1) show dial 1 (two colors); (2) talk about the possibility of which color the pointer will stop if turning the dial; (3) explain the reason; and (4) prove by testing. Then show dial 2, 3, and 4. Repeat the same process. At last, students conducted the activity of talking about it.
    Activity 2: Throwing paper cups
    (1) Guess what would happen after throwing the paper cups; (2) in small groups, each student repeatedly throws cups for 5 times, and record the results; (3) group report; (4) ask students what they discovered through the data; and (5) students communicated and provided feedback.
    Activity 3: Touching balls (omitted)
    Activity 4: Probability of precipitation (omitted)
    Activity 5: Throwing pushpin (omitted)

Problems Found

The lesson of "Have a Guess" was implemented on the basis of students' existing knowledge of probability. The purpose was to let the students experience the probability of event occurrence through doing experiments, and listing the results of them. I designed the activities of showing dials, throwing paper cups and pushpins etc. to engage students. Overall I paid attention to every student and achieved the learning objectives. However, the class rhythm and group activities were slow; the requirements for group activities were vague. These were the aspects that I need to improve in my future teaching efforts.

Peer Coaching

The teachers who observed the class commented that the lesson reached the goal of making students explore and understand that there were many probabilities in life through carefully designed learning activities. They concluded that: (1) the teacher was very affectionate, used simple mathematical terminologies, and paid attention to every student. So the students were very active and motivated to participate in the activities; (2) activities were designed creatively and intuitively with important and difficult points highlighted; and (3) group work focused on cooperation and collaboration.

The teacher observers also suggested that the lesson be improved in the following ways: (1) the teacher could make clear the requirements before the activities so the students would not rush to start the hands-on activities; (2) to improve the effect of group cooperative learning, the teacher could set time limits to avoid wasting time; and (3) the teacher could lecture less and guide more.

Professional Guidance

The researcher in the Department of Teaching and Research commented: (1) the curriculum standards for this lesson require that students have initial understanding of the uncertainty of events and probability through the activities. Teachers are only the organizer and participant of the lesson. The teacher understood the content well and the teaching was appropriate; (2) the teacher transformed the teaching and student learning strategies. It was experiential teaching; (3)the teacher arranged the activities well and clearly. The classroom atmosphere was easy; and (4) the role of the teacher in the teaching process is positioned appropriately, creating a relaxed and harmonious atmosphere in the classroom.

The researcher also commented about the weaknesses of the teaching: (1) the arrangement of the activities was not well implemented, and (2) the requirements for group learning were unclear; the researcher also pointed out that (3) there could be more positive comments about student performance.

The Re-Delivery of the Same Lesson (Omitted)

Teacher Reflection
With the help of expert reviews and colleagues, I (the teacher of the class) revised the lesson and taught it again. Through this teacher research, I learned that (1) requirements and objectives of the activities should be stressed before the class. Otherwise the students would be confused about what to do and the lesson would be ineffective; (2) the process should be regulated. As the group was dispersed, there would be interference factors. Teachers should make demands and group check to ensure the classroom efficiency; (3) in group work, I should have given the students appropriate time. The group work would be "strained" if the time was too tight; on the other hand, it was a waste of time if making the students feel too relaxed; and (4) to discover the problem in time to "make points to explain overall questions."

DISCUSSION

First, SBIR is focused on the teacher as a reflective practitioner and "teacher as researcher." It connects teachers' instructional activities with their research activities. Teachers are encouraged to conduct research while teaching, and acquire sensitivity to problems and a habit of conducting classroom research. They learn how to cope with their students, how to cooperate with colleagues, and how to make their teaching more effective and successful. SIBR is an effective way to become a "teacher as researcher." Teachers obtain a deep understanding of their professional growth and knowledge through this layered approach.

Second, SBIR promotes teachers' practical knowledge and wisdom. Wisdom is inseparable from practice and practical wisdom often exists in individual teachers in the form of tacit knowledge. SBIR emphasizes teachers' reflective practice and teachers gain new insights into their personal assumptions and their instructional philosophy. SBIR also provides teachers with a way to inquire into the complex professional knowledge landscapes (Clandinin & Connelly, 1996) in which they live and work. In this process, through various ways of communicating, sharing with colleagues and peers, and reflective practice, teachers' tacit knowledge surfaces, is transformed into personal practical knowledge, and their practical wisdom is promoted.

Third, SBIR causes teachers to be active rather than passive. Teachers' professional development spans teachers' professional careers. It has both individual and community dimensions to it. One of the important functions of SBIR is to stimulate an awareness of teachers' initiatives and show their active participation in their career development. In SBIR activities, teachers' professional development is rooted in their instructional practice and is meant to resolve the problems that emerge in their practices. In short, it meets teachers' felt needs. To a great extent, SBIR awakens teachers' consciousness of, and attitude toward, research and inspires their passion for teaching and learning (Zhang & Pu, 2008).

CONCLUDING REMARKS

In China, we have a great deal of experience in conducting SBIR. The practice of SBIR has played a critical role in helping teachers: (1) understand the concept of China's New Curriculum, (2) improve instructional strategies, (3) reflect on personal professional practice, and (4) achieve professional growth. SBIR has proven itself to be an effective model of in-service teacher training and teacher professional development. However, the SBIR approach is not our ultimate goal. Our ultimate aim is to make SBIR part of the teaching culture, a way of life for teachers, and a value-based approach to teacher education. In China, we want to integrate SBIR into our thoughts and action (Gu, 2007). Only when it is instantiated can the nature and meaning of teachers' professional development be realized. Stated differently, teachers should not only use SBIR to inquire into their practices, but also take it into their professional lives as well. That is to say, SBIR should no longer be a supplement to the teaching profession. It should reflect Chinese teachers' professional life space and embody the nature of a teacher as a person and as a practitioner. In this inquiry space, teachers experience their responsibilities and understand the value and meaning of their existences; in this way of life, the teacher, by virtue of his/her own strength, is tightly connected with students; co-constructing the meaning of the world and more fully understanding their personal rationale for their ideas and actions. They no longer mimic others and repeat their experiences; they create their own world of reason and sensibility. Only in this world will they experience peace of mind. Perhaps it is in this way of life, the SBIR achieves its original meaning (Zheng, 2004).

REFERENCES

Bartlett, L. (1990). Teacher development through reflective teaching. In J. C. Richards & D. Nunan (Eds.), *Second language teacher education* (pp. 2002–2214). New York, NY: Cambridge University Press.

Calderhead, J., & Gates, P. (Eds.) (1993). *Conceptualizing reflection in teacher development* (p. 123). London: The Falmer Press.

Clandinin, D. J. (1985). Personal practical knowledge: A study of teachers' classroom images. *Curriculum Inquiry, 15*(4), 361–385.

Clandinin, D. J., & Connelly, F. M. (1994). Personal experience methods. In N. K. Denzin & Y. S. Lincoln (Eds.), *Handbook of qualitative research*. Thousand Oaks, CA: Sage Publications.

Clandinin, D. J., & Connelly, F. M. (1996). Teachers' professional knowledge landscapes: Teacher stories – Stories of teachers – School stories – Stories of school. *Educational Researcher, 25*(3), 24–30.

Clandinin, D. J., & Connelly, F. M. (2000). *Narrative inquiry: Experience and story in qualitative research*. San Francisco, CA: Jossey-Bass.

Cochran-Smith, M., & Lytle, S. L. (1993). *Inside/outside: Teacher research and knowledge*. New York, NY: Teachers College Press.

Connelly, F. M., & Clandnin, D. J. (1990). Stories of experience and narrative inquiry. *Educational Researcher, 19*(5), 2–14.

Craig, C. (1995a). Knowledge communities: A way of making sense of how beginning teachers come to know. *Curriculum Inquiry, 25*(2), 151–172.

Craig, C. (1995b). Safe places on the professional knowledge landscape: Knowledge communities. In D. J. Clandinin & F. M. Connelly (Eds.), *Teachers' professional knowledge landscapes* (pp. 137–141). New York, NY: Teachers College Press.

Craig, C. (2001). The relationships between and among teacher knowledge, communities of knowing, and top down school reform: A case of "The Monkey's Paw.". *Curriculum Inquiry, 31*(3), 303–331.

Craig, C. (2003). *Narrative inquiries of school reform: Storied lives, storied landscapes, storied metaphors*. Greenwich, CT: Information Age Publishing.

Craig, C. (2007a). Illuminating qualities of knowledge communities in a portfolio-making context. *Teachers and Teaching: Theory and Practice*, 617–636.

Craig, C. (2007b). Story constellations: A narrative approach to contextualizing teachers' knowledge of school reform. *Teaching and Teacher Education, 23*(2), 173–188.

Cui, Y. (2007). Classroom observation: A new paradigm. *Exploring Education Development, 9*(B), 38–41.

Darling-Hammond, L. (1997). *The right to learn*. San Francisco, CA: Jossey-Bass.

Dello-Iacovo, B. (2009). Curriculum reform and 'Quality Education' in China: An overview. *International Journal of Educational Development, 29*, 241–249.

Dewey, J. (1938). *Education and experience*. New York, NY: Collier Books.

Dewey, J., & Bentley, A. F. (1949). *Knowing and the known*. Boston, MA: The Beacon Press.

Elbaz-Luwisch, F. (1983). *Teacher thinking: A study of practical knowledge*. London: Croom Helm.

Fenstermacher, D. (1994). The knower and the known: The nature of knowledge in research on teaching. *Review of Research in Education, 20*(1), 3–56.

Gibson, R. (1985). Critical times for action research. *Cambridge Journal of Education, 15*(1), 59–64.

Grange, J. (2004). *John Dewey, Confucius, and global philosophy*. Albany, NY: State University of New York Press.

Gu, L. (2005). School-based instructional research: The driving force that led the teachers. *Modern Education*, 6.

Gu, L. (2007). School-based instructional research: From system construction to classroom focus. *People's Education, 19,* 45–47.

Gu, L., & Yang, Y. (2003). School-based action research on teachers' professional development. *Exploring Education Development, 6,* 1–7.

Guan, Q., & Meng., W. (2007). China's new national curriculum reform: Innovation, challenges and strategies. *Frontiers of Education in China, 2*(4), 579–604.

Joyce, B., & Showers, B. (1982). The coaching of teaching. *Educational Leadership, 40*(l), 4–8.

Lyons, N. (1998). Constructing narratives for understanding: Understanding portfolio interviews to scaffold teacher reflection. In N. Lyons (Ed.), *With portfolio in hand: Validating the new teacher professionalism* (pp. 103–119). New York, NY: Teachers College Press.

McNiff, J. (1993). *Teaching as learning: An action research approach.* London and New York, NY: Routledge.

Murray, L. (1992). What is practitioner based enquiry? *British Journal of In-service Education, 18*(3), 191–196.

Olson, M. R., & Craig, C. J. (2001). Opportunities and challenges in the development of teachers' knowledge: The development of narrative authority in knowledge communities. *Teaching and Teacher Education, 17*(6), 667–684.

Posner, G. (1989). *Field experience: Methods of reflective teaching.* New York, NY: Longman.

Sargent, T. C. (2011). New curriculum reform implementation and the transformation of educational beliefs, practices, and structures in Gansu Province. *Chinese Education and Society, 44*(6), 47–72.

Schön, D. A. (1983). *The reflective practitioner: How professionals think in action.* New York, NY: Basic Books.

Schön, D. A. (1987). *Educating the reflective practitioner.* San Francisco, CA: Jossey-Bass.

Schön, D. A. (1991). *The reflective turn: Case studies in and on educational practice.* New York, NY: Teachers College Press.

Singh, K., & Shifflette, L. M. (1996). Teachers' perspectives on professional development. *Journal of Personal in Evaluation in Education, 10*(2), 145–160.

Schwab, J. J. (1969). The practical: A language for curriculum. *School Review, 78,* 1–23.

Schwab, J. J. (1971). The practical: Arts of eclectic. *School Review, 79,* 493–542.

Schwab, J. J. (1973). The practical 3: Translation into curriculum. *School Review, 81,* 501–522.

Schwab, J. J. (1983). The practical 4: Something for curriculum professors to do. *Curriculum Inquiry, 13*(3), 239–265.

Taber, K. S. (2007). *Classroom-based research and evidence-based practice: A guide for teachers.* London: SAGE Publications.

Zhang, C., & Pu, D. (2008). *The model of school-based instructional research and teacher' professional development.* Sichuan, China: Sichuan Science and Technology Press.

Zheng, J. (2004). From practitioner to researcher: The change of teachers' roles. *People's Education, 2,* 32–33.

Zhu, N., & Zhang, P. (2007). Analysis on school-based instructional research model of teacher's peer coaching. *Education Science, 23*(6), 16–20.

Yin, X. (2009). Summary of SBIR in elementary and middle schools. *Journal of Tianjin Normal University, 10*(4), 27–31.

CHAPTER 25

ENGAGING INDIA'S SOCIAL HISTORY TO UNDERSTAND AND PROMOTE TEACHER CHANGE

Tara Ratnam

ABSTRACT

This chapter examines the problem of teacher education as it unfolds in the Indian context. It focuses on the historical and cultural context in which teachers' attitudes and identities develop. Attention is particularly paid to contextual factors that frame teachers' actions beyond individual intentions. Possibilities for breaking these frames and engaging in new alternatives for action are imagined. An historical approach is employed to understand teachers' current pedagogical beliefs and action, and its future orientation.

Keywords: Teacher education; change; alternative perspective; teacher beliefs and identities; cultural context; historical analysis

Teacher education has tended to focus mainly on subject matter and related methods and child psychology in a universalist frame and neglected the widely varying sociocultural context in which teachers' attitudes and identities develop. In this chapter, I attempt to illuminate the problem as

From Teacher Thinking to Teachers and Teaching: The Evolution of a Research Community
Advances in Research on Teaching, Volume 19, 527–553
ISSN: 1479-3687/doi:10.1108/S1479-3687(2013)0000019028

it unfolds in the Indian context. Since India is one of ISATT's New Regions, this is an opportunity to contribute to the wider dialogue on teacher education by inviting educators globally to better understand our situation.

In India, the challenge of teacher education has assumed a perennial dimension in an ever elusive effort to keep it abreast of the changing demands placed on it by the rapidly changing social situation (i.e., Pandey, 2011). While the progressive teacher education discourses revolve around acknowledging teachers' "experiential knowledge" in promoting their learning, preparing teachers as facilitators of learning and to be responsive to the demands of inclusive education (National Council for Teacher Education [NCTE], 2009), teacher education practice remains conventional and seems to have little impact on promoting teachers' agentive power (Batra, 2009; Majumdar, 2011; Ratnam, 2008).

Why are teachers not motivated to change? What promotes or hinders their development? It is important to raise these basic questions anew, because without finding satisfactory answers to them, we are unlikely to develop the deep insights required for rethinking teacher education avoiding the pitfalls of essentialist assumptions that seem to pervade mainstream teacher education practice. The Western essentialist model of teacher education, developed to match the sense of certainty, progress, and authority associated with the discipline of natural science in the Modern age, was implanted in colonies like India. The introduction and expansion of mass education in the newly independent nations after mid-20th century, aided by agencies such as the United Nations Educational, Scientific and Cultural Organization (UNESCO) (i.e., Govinda, 1999) also adopted these approaches as the norm. However, this model fails to take into account the indigenous cultural ethos of India, the larger picture within which the deep-rooted tradition of values, attitudes, and practices develop (Professor J. Tharu, personal communication, December 25, 2012). I argue that it is very essential to know where teachers come from, their position in history and society in order to understand their preconceptions about teaching and learning, and also what helps or hinders their development. I take as a premise the uniqueness of the tradition in India with a cultural history of several thousand years. There are elements in this ancient tradition of thought that relate to knowledge, its discovery and elaboration, and also the means of teaching. The quite complex understanding of teaching and learning articulated then is epitomized by the well-known phrase, guru–shishya (preceptor–disciple) relationship. The modernist colonial education, which was dominant from the mid-19th century, was largely focused on the instrumental goal of maintaining social stability. Its bureaucratic control over the definition and dissemination of knowledge relegated teachers to the position of implementers of an alien curriculum. Although this precipitated a break with tradition in some ways, there were also elements of tradition relating to education which survived and were reinforced. Thus there are tacit and collective aspects of teachers' epistemological beliefs developed historically and culturally that are part of the worldview of educators broadly, especially those of teachers. These need to be investigated and understood since some of the conflicts and resistances to reform found today seem to have roots there. As will be seen in the fuller discussion that follows, there are both positive and negative aspects of Indian tradition from the perspective of the reform needed in the 21st century. Although there is evidence to show the presence of dialogic practices and relationship of the Socratic kind between the *guru* and *shishya* in traditional India, it was the cultural capital of the few. The present Indian context with its democratic concerns of equity and social justice stands in contrast to it. This opposition creates a tension between the centralizing forces of the dominant culture, on the one hand, and the diverging voices of those sections of society on the other, who, until recently, were excluded, and who need inclusive attention. While this concern for inclusive education forms part of the current teacher education discourse as mentioned earlier, teacher education has not been effective in linking this theory to teachers' practice. A "delivery of knowledge" approach to teacher education has not been successful in establishing this connection. What is needed is a better understanding of the mediation of culture in the development of teachers' sense of the self, their thinking, and practice. This need forms the rationale for my focus on history and its links to teachers' developmental trajectories.

THEORETICAL AND METHODOLOGICAL ORIENTATION

The dominant thinking in teacher education practice today exposes a Cartesian dualistic understanding of learning and development. It separates the knower from the known and establishes a direct link between "knowing" and "doing" in an "application-of-theory" model (Korthagen & Kessels, 1999) of teacher education. This unproblematic view of teacher education as transfer of skills reduces teacher education to "teacher training" (Widdowson, 1984), an exercise in changing teacher behavior to norm with established standards that are assumed to be universally applicable across contexts.

The dissatisfaction with such a mechanistic view of teacher education is a motivation to look for an alternative perspective that holds more potential to address the problem of teacher education, one that recognizes both "history and agency of subjectivity" (Grumet, 1987). This emphasis on history and agency is because, although teachers as individuals are differently disposed and their activities are meaningful to them, their practice shows remarkable similarities in their individual responses to similar institutional demands (Ratnam, 2006). This collective aspect in individual teacher's decision-making needs attention in studies of teacher thinking in order to emphasize the contribution of the more socially sourced interaction between individual and collective experience that mediates their beliefs and shapes their development. The cultural pattern observed in teachers' practice points to the need of a conceptual and methodological framework that sees historical and social factors, on the one hand, and individual agency, on the other, as interrelated levels. This relational ontology sees persons as agentive beings who develop by being embedded in cultural contexts and in relation to others. Such a view of human development gets articulated in Vygotsky-inspired sociocultural approaches (i.e., Cole, 1995; Cole & Levitin, 2000; Ellis, Edwards, & Smagorinsky, 2010; Engeström, Engeström, & Santio, 2002; Max, 2010; Wertsch, 2000). I use insights from Lev Vygotsky and Michael Bakhtin to underline the importance of history in understanding teachers' pedagogical beliefs and action here and now and its future reorientation in the Indian context.

Vygotsky (1981) points out that instrumental form of behavior is the product of historical development. Cultural tools are created and transformed in ongoing activity. Therefore, both the activities in which people engage and the tools of mediation carry history and culture. Going by this, we can think of a teacher culture taking shape over time socially (Berger & Luckman, 1966) in practice as teachers respond to their cultural role expectations and institutional demands. In turn, teacher culture, in its "sedimented" form provides tools that mediate teachers' thinking and action in both facilitative and constraining ways. There is a dialectic relationship between history and emerging actions of teachers. In this dialectical process, there is always a continuing "nexus of relations with past and future generations" (Stetsenko, 2009, p. 6), because teachers' pedagogical activities in the present build on previous practice while their unique contribution to it in the present paves the way for future. Bakhtin's (1986) notion of "great time" helps capture this continuity in time of teacher's developmental trajectory. According to him,

> ... there can neither be a first nor a last meaning; it always exists among other meanings as a link in the chain of meaning, which in its totality is the only thing that can be real. In historical life, this chain continues infinitely, and therefore each individual link in it is renewed again and again, as though it were being reborn. (Bakhtin, 1986, p. 146)

The notion of great time shows how teachers' developmental trajectories take shape appropriating meaning from their cultural past, from "other people's contexts" (Bakhtin, 1981, p. 294). It provides a framework to characterize the tacit and collective aspects of teachers' epistemological beliefs developed historically and culturally. In terms of methodology, this suggests that we need "to remove ourselves in time from the phenomenon under investigation" (Bakhtin, 1986, pp. 3–4) and enter "great time" to unearth its roots in the distant past. Therefore, in understanding teachers' observed behavior here and now in India, I break through the boundaries of their own time to see their practice as a continuation of the past and essentially related to it. This historical perspective on pedagogical approaches can help illuminate

(a) the cultural contextual factors that frame teachers' actions beyond individual intention and
(b) the possibilities for breaking these frames to imagine new alternatives for action.

DATA SOURCES AND ANALYSIS

The discussion here is based on secondary data in the form of documentary and other information compiled for an ethnographically oriented longitudinal study (Ratnam, 2006) involving my work with teachers located in the Indian ESL context at the pre-university level. For the purposes of this chapter, the sources of data chosen from the study are documents, literature, conversation with Sanskrit scholars, educationists, in-depth interviews of teachers (T-int), and class observations (Cl Ob) of both traditional Sanskrit and ESL teaching and field notes.

At issue in the Indian educational context is the conflict between the dominant transmissive pedagogical practice and the perceptions and needs of culturally diverse students. In the reigning hierarchy of castes of traditional India, the "lower"[1] sections were excluded from access to knowledge by design and not due to lack of resources. Mass education, now powerfully endorsed by the Right to Education Act (RTE 2009), challenges this exclusive elitist view of education. There is also the principle that what students bring to school as their knowledge and their expectations must be recognized. However, the transmissive monologic teaching, with its built in exclusion of responses (Voloshinov, 1973), seems to fail to set up the necessary interaction between the "hierarchically alien" second language that the students must learn and their spontaneous "native word" (Illich, 1981) which is required to make learning meaningful. So the question for my investigation at the historical level is, "What is the dynamics by which monologic aspects of teaching have evolved historically and dominate the present-day teachers' implicit beliefs and practice in India?" This has been undertaken by examining the cultural systems of meaning within which pedagogical relationships and communication are embedded. Since my concern here is with understanding teachers' epistemological beliefs and practice, the categories for my historical analysis are: (a) *the evolution of teacher-learner role relationship* using three types of hierarchical relationships salient in our context, that is, father–son, caste, and adult–child, (b) *archetypes of knowledge, teaching, and learning*, followed by (c) *the evolution of transmissive pedagogy*. The historical periods analyzed include *Traditional* and *Modern* (the British colonial times) India, linking them to the more recent *Independent* (post-1947) India. For analytical convenience, while discussing the evolution of transmissive pedagogy in traditional India, I have used the division of ancient Indian education into four periods made by Altekar (1934)[2], viz., Early Vedic[3] Period (up to about 2000 BCE); Late Vedic and Brāhmanic Period (c. 2000 BCE to 1000 BCE); Upanishadic,[4] Buddhist, and Sūtra[5] Period (c. 1000 BCE to c. 1 CE); and the Age of Smritis,[6] Purānas,[7] Commentaries, and Bhakti[8] (c. 1 CE to c. 1800 CE).

THE EVOLUTION OF TEACHER–LEARNER ROLE RELATIONSHIP

From a cultural perspective, teacher–learner relationship forms one of the components of the system of relationships in which they are involved (Pianta et al., 2005). Psychoanalytic studies (i.e., Basch, 1989; Kakar, 1991; Littner, 1989) support the idea that the teacher is not a new person whom the learner encounters in school, but someone toward whom the child unconsciously directs hopes, fears, and wishes that were developed in earlier contacts with parents and other people of significance (Basch, 1989, p. 773). This phenomenon, which is called "transference" in psychoanalytic language, helps in understanding the attitudinal context of the classroom in which unconsciously internalized identities of teachers and learners shape their expectations of and reactions to each other. What are the cultural frameworks of relationships that can be seen to contribute to the shaping and reshaping of teacher and learner identities in the Indian context? The embedded nature of teacher–learner role relationship is analyzed below, under the three salient relationships mentioned earlier, followed by how it has evolved over time.

(a) *Father–Son Relationship*: The present teacher–learner relationship is linked to the past through the archetypal image of *guru–shishya*. It is important to recognize the close association of the Vedic guru with the figure of the father in order to understand the embedded nature of this relationship and the salient position of authority of the guru over his disciple in it. The early sages, who revealed and stored the Vedic knowledge in hymns, were also teachers imparting this knowledge to their *shishyas* (Mookeriji, 1969). Guru, according to *Yājnavalkyasmriti* (1.34),[9] is one who performs the sacraments (*Samskāras*) and imparts the Veda. The relationship between the *guru* and the *shishya* was similar to the one between father and son, with the guru displaying the same concern and responsibility toward the *shishya*, as a father would for his son's moral, spiritual, and intellectual learning (Sanskrit scholar, Sri K. S. Varadachar, personal communication, December 27, 2005). It also entitled him to the authority that went with it.

Just as it was the *guru*'s *dharma* or obligation to mold the *shishya*'s character and impart the sacred knowledge known to him (*Āpasthambadharmasūtra 1.1.1.2* and *1.1.1.14*), the *shishya* was also bound by duties toward his preceptor (*Prashnōpanishad 6.8*) as to a father (*Manusmriti 2.171*). Respect and obedience to the teacher has received great attention in the Epic (e.g., *Ramāyana*) and *Smriti* (e.g., *Parāsarasmriti, Manusmriti*) literature. His student life (*brahmacharya*) was regulated on the principles of morality and service to the teacher. This was marked ritually by the *Upanayana*,[10] an offering of sacred fuel to the *guru* (*Mundakōpanishad 1.2.12, Chandogyōpanishad 4.6.1*) indicating his willingness to serve him and his sacred fires. The teacher, in turn, would put his hand on the heart of his disciple and pray that there should be a perpetual and perfect accord between them (*Hiranyakeshiyagrihyasūtra 1.5.11*), thus emphasizing the sacred nature of the *guru–shishya* relationship and the importance of the empathetic union between them for teaching and learning to take place.

In this ideal *guru–shishya* relationship, the *guru*'s authority is derived from his spiritual orientation. The *shishya* was enabled to develop calmness (*shānta*), self-restraint (*dānta*), self-denial (*uparata*), patience (*titiksu*), and being collected (*samāhita*), qualities seen as absolutely essential to be able to receive the highest knowledge of the "Self" or the *brahman*[11] (i.e., *Subālōpanishad 9.14*). Thus, morality was considered the foundation of spirituality. The above analysis shows the paternal, moral, and spiritual nature of the guru's authority over his disciple. This needs to be examined further against the norms governing other relationships in Indian society such as caste and adult–child relationships to understand how the subsequent image of teacher–learner received cultural legitimacy and became a thing taken-for-granted.

(b) *Caste Hierarchy*: Caste seems to be one of the foremost among the social relationships shaping teacher–learner relationship. The asymmetrical social relations of power deriving from the dominant/superior "upper" castes and subordinate/inferior "lower" castes and the *brahminic*[12] effort to reify and naturalize it have received considerable attention elsewhere (Ratnam, 2006). Suffice it to mention here that caste hierarchy in its sedimented form in the collective psyche is at the basis of the tendency to view all other social relationships, including that of teacher and learner, through a hierarchical lens.

(c) *Adult–Child Relationship*: In the Indian society, adults, be it father, mother, guru, elders in the community or older siblings, have power over the child by virtue of their superior knowledge and experience and so they are expected to be treated with respect by the child. For instance, in a study of school children, Sarangapani (2003) found that "elders should be respected" was a natural and indisputable value held by children. Her study also illustrates the point that multiple-layered dyadic relationships marked by patterns of authority over children shape the identities of teachers and learners and "deepen the institutional authority of the teacher to a taken-for-granted, subconscious level of the psyche" (*ibid.*, p. 117). It is important to recognize these a priori structures of relationships, because they form the cultural source from which the authority of the teacher derives its legitimacy making it naturally acceptable.

The Evolution of Teacher–Learner Relationship

The asymmetry in the relationship between the *guru* and *shishya* along with notions such as respect, authority, and obedience can be characterized in at least two ways. From a dualistic point of view, this could be seen as *guru*, the knower, and *shishya*, the ignorant. Here, the *shishya* who receives the knowledge that the *guru* has will eventually merge with him by moving into his epistemic position. In this monologic relationship, respect and obedience would mean unquestioning compliance with the *guru*'s knowledge and authority. Alternatively, the difference between the *guru* and *shishya* can be conceptualized dialogically, where the *shishya*'s distinctiveness is used by the *guru* to motivate dialogue through asking questions, responding, agreeing, disagreeing, and so on, thus enabling the learner to develop his own "learning stance" (Littner, 1989). Here, respect to the *guru* would be shown through reflective appropriation of the *guru*'s word rather than by imitating it.

There is plenty of evidence to show that a dialogic relationship was the preferred ideal in Vedic, Upanishadic, and Buddhist times. The spiritual quest of self-realization could hardly be envisaged as something that a *guru* could transmit externally except in a dialogic relationship marked by difference and dialogue. Monologic and dialogic instructional strategies will receive more detailed attention in the next section which deals with knowledge, teaching, and learning. Here, the focus is limited to pointing out the changes arising from repeated sense making of the archetypal image of *guru–shishya* relationship and the accompanying discourse of authority, respect, and obedience in accommodating the flux of time and social circumstances.

Kakar (1991, p. 42) characterizes the Upanishadic guru (who is like a Vedic *guru*) as human, intelligent, "astute and compassionate, demanding from the disciple the exercise of his reason rather than exercises in submission and blind obedience." In this Vedic and Upanishadic view, the *guru* holds a revered position as a "sage" (Lannoy, 1971) who has experienced self-realization (*Brahman*). His role is one of a mediator, enabling the disciple to discover for himself the knowledge of the *Brahman*. This is not far from the facilitative role given to the *guru* by the philosopher, Shankara (Vivekachudamani), and the Buddha (*Baudadarshana*, in *Sayana's Sarvadarshanasangraha*). They could be seen to be in accord with Bakhtin (1990, p. 87) when he asks, "In what way would it enrich the event if I merged with the other, and instead of two there would be only one? And what would I myself gain by the other's merging with me?" The dialogic relationship between the *guru* and *shishya* can be seen here as marked by respect for the other owing to the mutually enriching experience; each provides the other from their distinct individual location, "accent," or "voice." For instance, Shankara portrays the *guru* as one who gazes with empathy at his dissonant *shishya*, assuring him of a safe environment that communicates care (*Vivekachudamani*, slōka 41) and respect. The *shishya* is considered a *Vidwan* or knowledgeable (*ibid.*, slōka 43), thus affirming his self-worth, and is expected to invest in the process of learning (*ibid.*, slōkas 51–55).

The Vedic image of the *guru* as sage evolved into a mystical one with the rise of the Bhakti cults (Kakar, 1991; Lannoy, 1971). From facilitating the acquisition of knowledge sought by exclusive disciples, the *guru* was now expected to become the "conduit to Brahman" (Kakar, 1991, p. 42) by providing spiritual liberation to the populace, which looked up to him as god incarnate. Implicit faith, that is, *bhakti* and devotion replaced knowledge (*jnāna*) and reason in the interaction between the *guru* and his disciples. In keeping with this shift, the discourse of respect and obedience took on the meaning of unquestioned devotional surrender to the *guru*/god. The authority of the Bhakti *guru* is thus attributed to his mystical power rather than his power to reason. The disciple's salvation lay in merging his whole being with that of the *guru* (Babb, 1987). Kakar (1991, pp. 41–44) points out that a shift in the dominant image of the *guru* from *jnāna* to *bhakti guru*, which caused his moving from "man to god," was accompanied by a complementary change in the position of the *shishya* from "man to child," who could renounce adult categories of rational inquiry. The pedagogical consequence of this change in the role of the *guru* from a knowledge facilitator to that of an emotional "healer" (Kakar, 1991, p. 45) will be picked up in the next section. Here, the point that needs to be stressed is that it is the archetype image of Vedic *guru–shishya* reinscribed and infused with the *Bhakti* cult meaning that seems to pervade the collective psyche even today and is resonated in the daily prayers that commonly form part of the ritual beginning of the day in school in which the *guru* is considered to be the trinity of Hindu Gods, *Brahmha*, *Vishnu*, and *Maheshwara*.

The hierarchical *guru–shishya* relationship continued to hold through colonial times but due to a different dynamics. The image of the modern teacher took shape in an institutionalized and bureaucratic context with the teacher himself/herself having to submit to an external authority, which also regulated the curriculum s/he was to teach. Although this impinged upon the teacher's sense of professional autonomy, it did not change his/ her traditional authoritative position inside the classroom, for the alien curriculum that the teacher was to transmit in the classroom was linked with examinations. It made learners submit naturally to teachers' controlling authority as something good and in their interest (Sarangapani, 2003). This hierarchical teacher–learner relationship that the Indian collective uncon-scious has helped construct dominates present-day classrooms (Cl Ob). The foregoing analysis shows that the archetype of the present teacher–learner relationship can be traced to the ancient Vedic ideal of *guru–shishya* relationship, itself embedded in other structured hierarchical relationships notably caste, father–son, and child–adult relationship prevalent in the wider Indian society. The dominant social hierarchical structure of power relationships in which the adult (superior knower) exercises authority over the child (ignorant) who submits to it has framed the teacher–learner relationship through transference. Figure 1 represents how this relationship has evolved over time.

The asymmetrical relationship of power and knowledge has been sustained at the subconscious level as a way of restoring equilibrium whenever it is disturbed by the changing social climate. The foregoing analysis has illustrated this compensating tendency at work tacitly during the Bhakti and colonial periods, and its continuing impact on the present.

The teacher–learner role relationship has organic links with teachers' epistemic views and practice, although they are treated separately here for analytical purposes. In the next section, therefore, epistemological views that have evolved inherently with the evolving *guru–shishya* relationship and their impact on teachers' practice are examined.

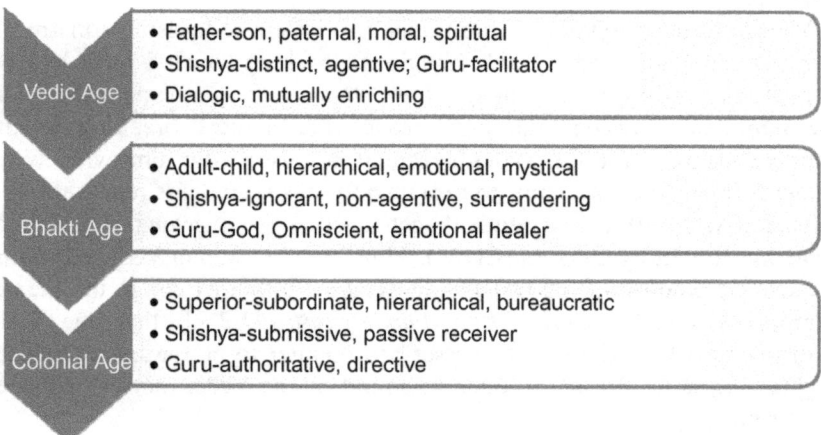

Fig. 1. The Evolution of Teacher–Learner Role Relationship.

ARCHETYPES OF KNOWLEDGE, TEACHING, AND LEARNING

From a cultural historical perspective, teachers' epistemological views are seen as embedded in the larger societal cultural schema. Linking teachers' beliefs to the surrounding cultural motifs, a process which cultural anthropologists call "contextualizing" (i.e., Shweder & LeVine, 1984), provides a "frame of reference" within which teachers' actions appear "rational" (*ibid.*). Hence, in this section, the cultural archetypes of knowledge, teaching, and learning that have a bearing on teachers' beliefs and action will be examined.

Traditional Indian learning emphasized memorization through constant rehearsal (*abyās*). Concerns with preserving the primordial *Veda* in its pristine form made its oral transmission the primary focus of Vedic education (Altekar, 1934). Systematic linguistic and kinesthetic devices have been developed for the accurate preservation and transmission of the Vedic *mantras*.[13] Besides, great value and potency is attached to the sound of the sacred words (Agrawala, 1953; Mitra, 1964). Consequently, learning the sacred text involves more than merely knowing to recite the words, its proper vocalization with controlled "stress, pitch, and rhythm" (*ibid.*) and the accompanying "somatic component" (Ong, 1982). It requires listening intently to the *guru*'s deliberate recitation pronouncing every syllable and word according to the rules regulating accents and stress and intoning after him.

Methods exemplifying this traditional oral system of transmission are still prevalent in Vedic and *Āgamic* (religious) teaching which I have had the opportunity to observe. It consists of two stages, *adhyayana* and *āvartané*. In the *adhyayana* session, the *guru* recites the mantra breaking it into manageable units and the students recite it in unison after him twice. When students falter, the *guru* stops to explain and makes students repeat till he is satisfied. After *adhyayana*, students get together for *āvartané* or practicing what was taught by the *guru* (Cl Ob). Thus, the first step in Vedic education is correct recitation of the text taught. There are injunctions in the literary compositions called *sūtras* (e.g., *Jaiminiyasūtra 1.2.32*) that the Vedic mantras must be recited in the prescribed manner to be rewarding and the slightest lapse in uttering a letter or sound of the Vedic mantra will spell utter ruin.

It is improbable that today's teachers would establish a conscious link between these myths and their own implicit belief that the first step in teaching reading to ESL students is to make them learn to "pronounce correctly" (T-int). However, it makes sense to see this belief as having been shaped by the remote oral culture inherited unconsciously. The ESL teachers' general practice of reading the text aloud or "model reading" as it is commonly called, followed by students taking turns to read parts of the text with the teacher intervening to correct their pronunciation (Cl Ob), has an uncanny resemblance to the practice of Vedic *guru* although it lacks the purpose as well as the mystical resonance of the Vedic recitation. However, as far as the teachers are concerned, it just seems the "way things are done" (Shotter, 1978, p. 70).

The description of the oral Vedic education provided so far carries images of a mimetic *abyās* culture, where teaching consists of transmission of text and learning memorizing it in the way received from the *guru*'s lips. This transmissive pedagogy is in keeping with a purpose that was validated by the religious, political, and literary needs of a particular historical context (Mookerji, 1969). However, even in those times, it did not form the whole of Vedic education. The pursuit of the highest truth through an insight into the inner meaning of the Veda made the contemplation and comprehension of its meaning a vital aspect of learning, envisaging a different method of instruction. There are several references in ancient literature of the futility of learning the Veda, which lacks a focus on its interpretive understanding (i.e., *Nirukta 1.18*). Education as appropriation of "second-hand information" (Buchmann & Schwille, 1983, p. 30) of accumulated cognition (Dewey, 1916), which provides access to cultural thoughts is characterized as *aparāvidya* (*Mundakōpanishad 1.1.4*). However, acquiring this *aparāvidya* as mere information, as an end in itself, fails to lead one toward *parāvidya* or self-realization, which is seen as the ultimate goal of education and which, according to *Mundakōpanishad* (3.1.6), is the highest stage of Vedic wisdom, the science of sciences wherein the knowledge of all else lies implicit. The celestial sage Nārada, for instance, was unable to achieve this transformative experience even after amassing the knowledge of all the extant sciences, because, according to his new *guru*, Sanathkumāra, he had acquired them as mere "words" (*Chandogyō-panishad 7.1.1–5*) without the internal development of the word's meaning (Vygotsky, 1987).

The knowledge of *Brahman* cannot be conceptualized within a transmissive framework. Doubt and dialogue are essential aspects of a pedagogy that seeks to advance *parāvidya*.[14] For instance, Shankara who focused on inquiry into *Brahman* (*brahma-jijñāsa*) in education imagined his *guru* as following "a questioning approach." Hirst (2005), who has examined Shankara's questioning approach in detail, avers that "much of the repertoire of the aims and techniques of good questioning may already be found in his Thousand Teachings as well as his major commentaries" (p. 147). Shankara's questioning techniques are open-ended, meant to generate discussion (*samavāda*), and to enable learners not only speak from their current state of knowing, but also risk moving beyond (*Upadeshasā-hasri*). Thus empathy for the learner is shown in being sensitive to their learning needs both cognitive and affective.

There are three pedagogic processes leading to transformative knowledge mentioned in *Brihadaranyakōpanishad* (4.5.6): listening (*shravana*), reflecting (*manana*), and thinking through the consequence of action (*nidhidhyāsana*). The interacting processes of *shravana, manana,* and *nidhidhyāsana* show that although the Vedic *guru* has an important role in instruction, his mediation invites much thinking and active contribution to the teaching–learning process from the learner. For instance, in one of the Upanishads, Varuna, the father and preceptor of Bhrigu, leads him toward self-realization by repeatedly urging him to reflect on the content of his instruction. Bhrigu goes back to his father each time with a different answer that indicated the progressive refinement in his thinking and understanding till he finally experienced the nature of the "Self" (*Taittariyōpanishad, Bhriguvalli, 1–6*). An acknowledgment of the critical potential in the learner and their intellectual struggle to reach higher understanding through reflective appropriation of the social interaction in the classroom is reflected particularly in the growing area of Writing Portfolios (i.e., Rutledge, 2006; Song & August, 2002; Wigglesworth & Storch, 2012). The principle under-lying the portfolio approach can be seen to be similar to the Upanishadic pedagogic principle used, for instance by Brighu's father/*guru*, Varuna, mentioned above. Both aim at providing a context of "continuity" (Kegan, 1982) in order to allow time and support for critically reevaluating held beliefs, exploring alternatives, and developing new understanding.

What is the archetype of knowledge, teaching, and learning that emerges from the above analysis of Vedic education? It would seem that analytically it has two separate components: one, verbatim memorization of texts as transmitted by the *guru*; and two, transformative learning in a dialogic *guru–shishya* relationship. These two pedagogical models which speak to different conceptions of learning, one imitative and the other, dialogic, seem to pose a paradox. Seen synchronically, these practices might seem to be in conflict. However, seen on a developmental cline, they appear compatible. Memorization, as has been pointed out, did not form the whole of Vedic education. It formed the main part of instruction in the earlier years of education when children's facility for such learning is supposed to be at its peak. Dialogic ways of expounding the meaning of the memorized texts received increased emphasis as the mind matured toward greater individuation in thinking. The two aspects of Vedic education can thus be viewed as forming different stages in learning.

Taken as a whole, the archetype of knowledge, teaching, and learning represented by the Vedic education shows it to be dialogic. It remains to be seen as to how it is that the mimetic aspect has got isolated from this robust *abyās* culture and has come to dominate the present educational scene. This question is examined in light of the larger changes in the social and curricular preoccupations of the subsequent ages.

THE EVOLUTION OF TRANSMISSIVE PEDAGOGY

As mentioned earlier, here I use the classification of traditional Indian education into four periods made by Altekar (1934). He views the *Early Vedic* period as a creative period of hymnal activity and the Vedic collections (*Samhitā*) its product, as belonging to a later time. Therefore, there was a difference in the way the Veda was studied in the early Vedic period and late Vedic period onward. The early Vedic Period was marked by creative flexibility to allow freedom to refine the hymns (*ibid.*). So, learning can be seen as characterized by both imitation and improvement. The curriculum included teaching the principles of prosody to encourage the development of the skills of versification. Grammar and etymology were still unknown. This is a significant point, which will be picked up again in what follows.

Considerable changes in the curriculum took place in the *Late Vedic* and *Brahmanic Period* owing to historical reasons. With the spread of Āryans in India, intrusions coming from a mixing of civilizations led to the beginning of an evolution in the Vedic Sanskrit language of the Āryans. It is against this background that concerns with protecting the sacred hymns from the corrupting influences of other language and cultural thought began to develop. This resulted in the canonization of the Vedic hymns in the *Samhitā* collections. From creativity, the emphasis in teaching and learning shifted to knowledge transmission, which was by now regarded as received and, therefore, not open to any changes. Theories about the importance of the sound in reciting the Veda and about its ineffectiveness if mispronounced that began to be popularized through mythical stories can be seen as part of the effort to preserve the Veda in its pristine form (Altekar, 1934, p. 122; Thapar, 2000, p. 197). This impulse for meticulous oral preservation can be seen to be the beginning of the rote *abyās* culture, that is, of memorizing the mantras verbatim through repeated practice or *abyās*.

Another notable outcome of the differentiation of the spoken language from the Vedic dialect was the development of a gap between the fast developing vernaculars of the learners and the language of the Vedic education. This is not very different from the present-day problem of home–school language and cultural gap in teaching culturally diverse students (i.e., Banks et al., 2005; Cummins, 2000; Mohanty, 2006). Efforts were made to bridge this gap. Lists of Vedic Sanskrit words (*Nighantus*) were compiled for students to learn and speculations about grammar and etymology started to develop. With the passage of time, grammar came to be regarded as the most important of the sciences ancillary to the Veda (Yadav, 2005). Students, who were keen on learning the Veda, undertook to master grammar as a preparation for it. So, *grammar teaching* as well as *memorization* seems to have acquired significant pedagogical attention with the development of home–school language gap and the canonization of the Veda. Both of these pedagogical features as being essential aspects of language learning are echoed in the beliefs of ESL teachers today (T-int). *Text explication*, another pedagogical feature necessitated by the home and Vedic language gap, has also come to stay (Cl Ob).

By the time of the *Upanishadic*, *Buddhist*, and *Sūtra Period*, the original texts in the Vedic language were becoming increasingly unintelligible, leading to the development of *sūtra* literature, to convey the Vedic thought in summary forms. Around the same period, Upanishadic literature was attempting to resurrect the spirit of the Vedic thought by exemplifying, as has been illustrated earlier, various strategies to mediate the meaning of the text for its unique appropriation by the learner. For, the students in this period were not only expected to memorize the Veda, but also know its meaning. However, as Kane (1941, p. 358) points out, in spite of these precepts, the students, who learned the Veda as a cultural tradition, never cared to know its meaning. There were reasons for this. In India, the Upanishadic and Buddhist periods were creative periods with remarkable achievements in the realm of philosophy, literature, grammar, philology, astronomy, medical science, sculpture, and so on (Agrawala, 1953; Altekar, 1934). This diversification in knowledge captured the interest of many, who, after the initial instruction in grammar and some Vedic hymns, branched off to specialize in other secular and scientific fields (*ibid.*). So, the number of students who pursued Vedic learning for their own sake, much less with the elevated goal of self-realization, was probably becoming less.

In keeping with this changing trend, there was a simultaneous readjustment in the nature of exhortations that shaped the new cultural beliefs, viz. the mere memorizing of the Vedic texts confers sanctity and removes all sins (Kane, 1941). In these attempts to preserve the word, if not the thought, a shift in tendency from meaningful *abyās* to rote learning of the Veda can be seen.

The tendency to rote learn the knowledge transmitted by the guru uncritically became the dominant trend in the latter part of the *Age of Smritis, Purānas,* and *Commentaries* with the growth of *Bhakti* cults and the popular inclination to follow blind faith over reason as has been explained earlier. However, apart from this popular vernacular movement, the critical traditions continued to hold in the exclusive circles of scholarly learning in Sanskrit. The importance attached to learning grammar continued, as it formed the foundation for further studies. Both in ESL and Sanskrit learning today grammar is believed to be very important, although teachers and students seem to fail to pursue it with the rigor of the earlier days that seems to have enabled them to acquire the language proficiency necessary for further studies through it.

The beginnings of this decline in effective teaching and learning of grammar can be noticed during the British *"Modern"* period. The progressive child-centered pedagogy advocated by the modern system of education was in conflict with its own prescribed rigid curriculum backed by a rigorous examination system, which was associated with certification and securing employment. The washback effect of this on classroom was a single-minded focus on learning the contents of the prescribed textbooks. This goal was achieved by using traditionally available tools of text explication and memorization. However, this was an alienating exercise, particularly for the culturally diverse students who had no such prior learning experience. The replacive curriculum which was discontinuous with the indigenous cultural ethos (Nurullah & Naik, 1962) upset the synchrony between the *word* and its *meaning.* Much of what was learned was mechanical as teaching did not create zones of knowing for its meaningful appropriation. These practices have continued in independent India as Kumar (2005, p. 87) points out, "The norms of pedagogy that evolved under colonial rule did not weaken with the coming of national independence. Sitting in a classroom today one can still observe the distinct features of teaching that are related to the colonial legacy." My class observations, where teaching and learning are separated by teachers' monologue and rote teaching for examination (i.e., see the Appendix) causes me to concur with this point made by Kumar.

DISCUSSION

The historical analysis shows that the archetype of the present teacher–
learner relationship can be traced to the ancient Vedic ideal of *guru–shishya*
relationship, itself embedded in other structured hierarchical relationships
prevalent in the wider Indian society. The dominant social hierarchical
structure of power relationships in which the adult (superior knower)
exercises authority over the child (ignorant) who submits to it, has framed
the teacher–learner relationship through transference. This asymmetrical
relationship of power and knowledge has been sustained at the subconscious
level as a way of restoring equilibrium whenever it is disturbed by the
changing social climate. The foregoing analysis has illustrated this
compensating tendency at work tacitly during the Bhakti and colonial
periods, and its continuing impact on the present. With respect to
knowledge, teaching, and learning, it is the *abyās* culture with views of
knowledge as received, teaching as transmission, and learning as memorization through incessant practice or *abyās*, which formed only an aspect of
Vedic education, which seems to have provided the archetype for guiding
teachers' practice generation-after-generation up to the present through
changing social climates[15] as the following figure (Fig. 2) shows.

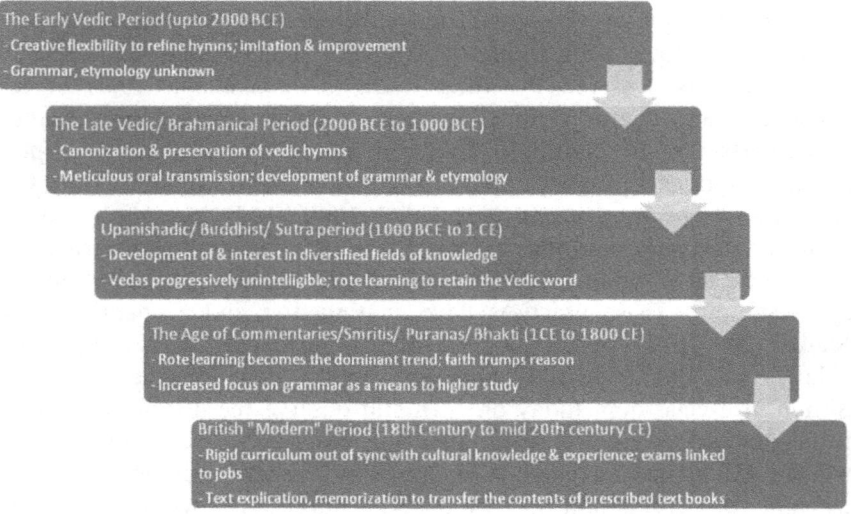

Fig. 2. The Evolution of Transmissive Pedagogy.

However, this unbroken flow of the mimetic culture, as the analysis and Fig. 2 representing it show, is not "a process of deliberate continuity" (Thapar, 2000, p. 195), for there has been a compensatory selective process at work of what is desired knowledge and pedagogical means in having to constantly adjust to the changing needs of changing times. Although there is evidence to show the presence of dialogic practices and reciprocal relationship between the *guru* and *shishya* in the Vedic times, monologic practices within a dualistic teacher–learner relationship was adopted more and more to cope with the dissonances of successive ages such as differentiation of the spoken language from the Vedic dialect in traditional India, the popular quest for salvation in the traditional Bakhti period, the alien curriculum of the colonial times, the universalization of education in independent India, and the commercial competition of the global free market age. Yet the instructional strategies of the more remote Vedic education, such as initiating, doubt, critical reasoning, and reflective appropriation of meaning that show an awareness of the learning process (i.e., Bruner, 1996; Vygotsky, 1987), are also the ones advocated by the current educational and teacher education discourses as pointed out earlier, albeit without much success. The historical analysis I have undertaken with respect to the Indian situation seems to have an explanation for this.

The analysis points to the complex history behind the present symptoms of teacher inertia. Teachers' present practice which is shaped by their implicit beliefs does not develop individually but is seen to be derived from a sphere of historical Indian existence beyond their immediate experience. Teachers emerge along with the world and reflect the historical emergence of the world. For instance, the beliefs that the teacher is the knower, with superior authority, who should be obeyed and not contradicted; correct pronunciation and grammar are important components of learning; teaching is passing the content of the text; and learning is memorizing the given answers are commonly held among teachers. These beliefs reflect history, the dynamics through which they have developed, and the "power of compensation" (Jacobi, 1968, p. 10) they exert to restore the disequilibrium created by the changing social conditions without being visible to consciousness (Jung, 1959). The tacit working of the cultural schema can be seen in the gaps between teachers' espoused and implicit beliefs that their practice mirrors. For instance, teachers claim that they are "democratic" in their relation with students and do not consider themselves "superior" to their students, but their implicit belief gets articulated in practice, "*I will ask them [students] to list the questions and will reply in the end. I collect all the questions beforehand to see if there are questions I don't know ... . We are allowing them to speak. ... But we know something more than the students that we are in a position to give ... ."* (T-int).

At stake here is the teacher's self or identity as "knower," a cultural image that he/she is unable to surrender. It makes him/her impervious to the deeper epistemological contradictions this gives rise to between his/her espoused theory of action and lived practice. It is the same with the observed differential treatment of students in the classroom. The structured hierarchical relationship prevalent in the wider Indian society seems to be so deeply etched in the collective psyche that it makes teachers' biased behavior seem natural to them. The resulting "symbolic violence" (Bourdieu & Passeron, 1990) in the classroom has damaging consequences for the culturally diverse and disadvantaged students, whose learning seems to be depressed by it. The narrow psychological view of learning that teachers historically hold makes them believe that individual ability and effort are all it takes to succeed. For instance, it is a common thinking among them that, *"If students have interest and put in effort, they should be able to learn and pass the examination"* (T-int). This seemingly deficit view of learners blinds teachers to the social segregation and educational exclusion that has put the culturally diverse students at a disadvantage from the beginning. It also makes them neglect to notice their own implicit beliefs that guide their practice in ways that are insensitive to the learning needs of these children. Viewing the learning problems of the disadvantaged students in psychological terms "misrecognizes" (Bourdieu & Passeron, 1990) its social and historical nature. A similar "genesis amnesia" (*ibid.*) seems to ail Indian teacher education where teachers are viewed as deficient in an input–output model of teacher education: *"We have given them all the input, through Resource Books, training, and supplementary materials. We have shown them what exactly they have to do in the classroom. They should learn to do it. They just make excuses"* (a teacher educator). Such assertions from teacher educators reflect a lack of awareness of where teachers and they themselves come from. By and large, teachers have been socialized into a transmissive pedagogy with conceptions of teaching as telling. However, they are currently being exhorted to transform themselves into facilitators of learning without a parallel redefinition of teacher learning, thus erasing their beliefs and identity as teachers. All the teachers I interviewed in my study seemed committed to the same transformative goals of teaching as those stated in the curriculum. However, their practice, which was traditionally transmissive, went against their intentions and teachers seemed unaware of this divide (T-int). A transmission model of teacher education fails to address this disjuncture, because it divorces knowledge from teachers' tacit beliefs shaped by the mediation of history and culture. However, from a cultural–historical perspective, it is only in the light of teachers' historically and collectively held beliefs that meaningful understanding and learning are possible.

CONCLUSION

Engaging with history helps challenge the naturalized deficit view of learners by teachers and of teachers by teacher educators by illuminating the social constructions that render "psychological processes historically contingent" (Cole, 1998, p. 89). A deficit view obstructs the construction of a robust response to the problem of teaching and teacher education. The urgent need of the hour in Indian teacher education and I would argue elsewhere as well is to prepare teachers for inclusive education. Culturally diverse students are disadvantaged. They have endured sustained exploitation by successive sociopolitical formations manifesting inequality through changing discourses of caste, bureaucracy, and market in keeping pace with changing social contexts. As a result, they paradoxically have been denied literacy even when access is provided to them (Ilaiah, 1996). To be certain, these students are not without talent. However, teachers seem to miss identifying them. An Indian teacher, who is able to place the problem of the socially disadvantaged learners in historical perspective, would perhaps refrain from blaming the learners for their poor school achievement and instead, ask himself/herself, "What am I doing that contributes to this failure?" (Allen & Hermann-Wilmarth, 2004, p. 214). When such questioning becomes part of teachers' thinking, a heightened self-awareness can open up new possibilities for practice. The primary challenge of teacher education then seems to be that of fostering "historical consciousness" (Giroux, 1997) and enabling teachers to reflectively reclaim their "unthought known" (Bollas, 1987), of the "borders" that constrain their understanding and influence their action against reason and intention, so that these borders "may be substituted by, translated into different borders" (Bakhtin, 1986, p. xix).

The historical adaptations in teaching and teacher education in response to the changing social demands in India seem to betray a conservative interest belying the progressive concerns espoused in education. My historical inquiry into the Indian situation is a step toward illuminating the nexus between cultural history and cognition in mediating teacher learning and change, in order to point out how essential this understanding is for reforming teacher education in India.

NOTES

1. Terms such as "upper" and "lower" with reference to caste do not represent the author's personal values, but the way they are used in the common cultural discourse.

2. I have modified Altekar's last division, viz. the Age of Smritis, Purānas, and Commentaries (c. 1 CE to c. 1200 CE), to accommodate Bhakti period, which runs parallel with it and extends up to about 1800 CE. This is because Bhakti period holds a very important position in marking the way teacher–learner role relationship and pedagogy have evolved.

3. A period in history during which the Vedas, the oldest scriptures in Hinduism, were composed.

4. Upanishads are philosophical texts concerning the nature of ultimate reality, viz. *Brahman*.

5. Aphoristic compositions summarizing Vedic teaching.

6. A class of Hindu sacred literature derived from the Vedas, containing social, domestic, and religious teaching.

7. A genre of important Hindu, Jain, and Buddhist religious texts consisting of narratives of the history of the universe from creation to destruction, genealogies of kings, heroes, sages, and demigods, and descriptions of Hindu cosmology, philosophy, and geography.

8. A tradition of Hindu monotheism that spread throughout India during the medieval ages as a popular movement.

9. The texts in Sanskrit are referred to conventionally by mentioning their name with the author (e.g., *Mundakōpanishad* means the Upanishad by Mundaka) and the number of the chapter and its subsection for locating the particular sloka/mantra or verse (e.g., 3.1.6., where "3" indicates the main *Adhyaya* (chapter)/*prashna* (question), "1" the *kandha/pāda* (sub-section such as a quarter)/*patāla* (sub-question), and "6" the *slōka/sūtra/mantra* (hymn/verse). Therefore, a separate bibliography for the Sanskrit material used here is not warranted. All the *slōkas* referred to in this study have been sourced from original Sanskrit texts. A taped copy of these *slōkas* is available with the author. Diacritical marks are used for Sanskrit words to denote longer vowels by '¯', ā as in "path," ī as in "peel," ū as in "tool," and ō as in "oats."

10. Sacred thread ceremony to mark the point at which boys began their formal spiritual education.

11. *Brahman* is the ultimate essence of material phenomena, including the original identity of human self, whose nature can be known through the development of self-knowledge.

12. *Brahmins* were the uppermost in the caste hierarchy.

13. Oral mnemonic devices such as samhita, pāda, krama, jata and gana pātās were handed down as part of knowledge, facilitating systematic and accurate oral transmission (Sri K. S. Varadachar, personal communication, December 27, 2005).

14. Theories of conceptual change (i.e., Pintrich, Marx, & Boyle, 1993) point to the importance of challenging the existing view of learners to create the disequilibrium necessary for change.

15. It must be noted that this is the archetype representation of the culture of the dominant group. The data in this study shows however, that all the teachers, regardless of their group affiliation, seem to have appropriated these cultural mores and beliefs having been socialized into it in school. This study has not posed explicit questions to teachers on their caste affiliation. However, it has captured the symbolic violence and exclusion that the culturally diverse students face in the classroom based on data from class observations.

REFERENCES

Agrawala, V. S. (1953). *India as known to Panini: A study of the cultural material in the Ashtādyāyi*. Lucknow: University of Lucknow.

Allen, J., & Hermann-Wilmarth, J. (2004). Cultural construction zones. *Journal of Teacher Education, 55*(3), 214–226.

Altekar, A. S. (1934). *Education in ancient India*. Benares: The Indian Bookshop.

Babb, L. (1987). *Redemptive encounters*. Delhi: Oxford University Press.

Bakhtin, M. M. (Ed.) (1981). *The dialogic imagination: Four essays* (M. Holquist, Ed., C. Emerson & M. Holquist, Trans.). Austin, TX: Texas University Press.

Bakhtin, M. M. (1986). *Speech genres and other late essays* (C. Emerson & M. Holquist, Eds., V. W. McGee, Trans.). Austin, TX: Texas University Press.

Bakhtin, M. M. (1990). *Art and answerability: Early philosophical essays (M. Holquist & V. Liapunov, Eds., V. Liapunov & K. Brostrom, Trans.)*. Austin, TX: Texas University Press.

Banks, J., Cochran-Smith, M., Moll, L. C., Richert, A., Zeichner, K., LePage, P., ... McDonald, M. (2005). Teaching diverse learners. In L. Darling-Hammond, J. Bransford, P. LePage, K. Hammerness & H. Duffy (Eds.), *Preparing teachers for a changing world: What teachers should learn and be able to do* (pp. 232–274). San Francisco, CA: Jossey-Bass.

Basch, M. (1989). The teacher, the transference, and development. In K. Field, B. Cohler & G. Wool (Eds.), *Learning and education: Psychoanalytic perspectives* (pp. 771–787). Madison, CT: International University Press.

Batra, P. (2009). Teacher empowerment: The education entitlement-social transformation traverse. *Contemporary Education Dialogue, 6*(2), 121–156.

Berger, P. L., & Luckman, T. (1966). *Social construction of reality*. Hammondsworth: Penguin.

Bollas, C. (1987). *The shadow of the object*. London: Free Association Books.

Bourdieu, P., & Passeron, J. (1990). *Reproduction in education, society and culture* (R. Nice, Trans.). London: Sage.

Bruner, J. (1996). *The culture of education*. Cambridge, MA: Harvard University Press.

Buchmann, M., & Schwille, J. (1983). Education: The overcoming of experience. *American Journal of Education, 92*(1), 30–51.

Cole, M. (1995). Socio-cultural-historical psychology: Some general remarks and a proposal for a new kind of cultural genetic methodology. In J. V. Wertsch, P. Del Rio & A. Alvarez (Eds.), *Sociocultural studies of mind* (pp. 187–214). Cambridge, UK: Cambridge University Press.

Cole, M. (1998). Cognitive development and formal schooling: The evidence from cross-cultural research. In L. C. Moll (Ed.), *Vygotsky and education* (pp. 89–110). Cambridge, UK: Cambridge University Press.

Cole, M., & Levitin, K. (2000). A cultural-historical view of human nature. In N. Roughley (Ed.), *Being humans: Anthropological universality and particularity in transdisciplinary perspectives* (pp. 64–80). New York, NY: de-Gruyter.

Cummins, J. (2000). This place nurtures my spirit: Creating contexts of empowerment in linguistically-diverse schools. In R. Phillipson (Ed.), *Rights to language: Equity, power and education* (pp. 249–258). Mahwah, NJ: Lawrence Erlbaum Associates, Inc.

Dewey, J. (1916). *Democracy and education.* New York, NY: Macmillan.

Ellis, V., Edwards, A., & Smagorinsky, P. (Eds.). (2010). *Cultural-historical perspectives on teacher education and development: Learning teaching.* London: Routledge.

Engeström, Y., Engeström, R., & Santio, A. (2002). Can a school community learn to master its own future? An activity-theoretical study of expensive learning among middle-school teachers. In G. Wells & G. Claxton (Eds.), *Learning for life in the 21st century: Sociocultural perspectives on the future of education* (pp. 211–224). Oxford, UK: Blackwell Publishers.

Giroux, H. A. (1997). *A pedagogy and the politics of hope.* Boulder, CO: Westview Press.

Govinda, R. (1999). *Reaching the unreached through participatory planning: School mapping in Lok Jumbish, India.* Paris: IIEP.

Grumet, M. R. (1987). The politics of personal knowledge. *Curriculum Inquiry, 17*(3), 319–329.

Hirst, J. S. (2005). A questioning approach: Learning from Shankara's pedagogic techniques. *Education Dialogue, 2*(2), 137–169.

Ilaiah, K. (1996). *Why I am not a Hindu.* Calcutta: SAMYA.

Illich, I. (1981). Taught mother language and vernacular tongue. In D. P. Pattanayak (Ed.), *Multilingualism and mother-tongue education* (pp. 1–39). Delhi: Oxford University Press.

Jacobi, J. (1968). *The psychology of Jung* (R. Manheim, Trans.). London: Routledge & Kegan Paul.

Jung, C. G. (1959). *The archetypes and the collective unconscious* (R. F. C. Hull, Trans.). London: Routledge & Kegan Paul.

Kakar, S. (1991). *The analyst and the mystic.* New Delhi: Viking Penguin.

Kane, P. V. (1941). *History of Dharmaśāstra (ancient and mediaeval religious and civil law)* (Vol. II). Poona: Bhandarkar Oriental Research Institute.

Kegan, R. (1982). *The evolving self: Problem and process in human development.* Cambridge, MA: Harvard University Press.

Korthagen, F., & Kessels, J. (1999). Linking theory and practice: Changing the pedagogy of teacher education. *Educational Researcher, 28*(4), 4–17.

Kumar, K. (2005). *Political agenda of education* (2nd ed.). London: Sage.

Lannoy, R. (1971). *The speaking tree.* New York, NY: Oxford University Press.

Littner, N. (1989). Reflections of early childhood family experiences in the educational situation. In K. Field, B. Kohler & G. Wool (Eds.), *Learning and education: Psychoanalytic perspectives* (pp. 825–849). Madison, CT: International Universities Press.

Majumdar, M. (2011). Politicians, civil servants or professionals? Teachers' voices on their work and worth. *Contemporary Education Dialogue, 8*(1), 33–66.

Max, C. (2010). Learning-for-teaching across educational boundaries: An activity-theoretical analysis of collaborative internship projects in initial teacher education. In V. Ellis, A. Edwards & P. Smagorinsky (Eds.), *Cultural-historical perspectives on teacher education and development: Learning teaching* (pp. 212–240). London: Routledge.

Mitra, V. (1964). *Education in ancient India.* New Delhi: Arya Book Depot.

Mohanty, A. K. (2006). Multilingualism of the unequals and predicaments of Education in India: Mother tongue or other tongue? In O. Garcia, T. Skutnabb-Kangas & M. E. Torress-Guzman (Eds.), *Imagining multilingual schools* (pp. 262–283). Clevedon: Multilingual Matters.

Mookerji, R. K. (1969). *Ancient Indian education.* Delhi: Motilal Banarsidas.

NCTE (National Council for Teacher Education, New Delhi). (2009). *National curriculum framework for teacher education towards preparing professional humane teachers.* New Delhi: Member-Secretary, NCTE.

Nurullah, S., & Naik, J. P. (1962). *A students' history of education in India.* New Delhi: Macmillan & Co.

Ong, W. J. (1982). *Orality and literacy: The technologizing of the word.* London: Methuen.

Pandey, S. (2011). *Professionalization of teacher education in India: A critique of teacher education curriculum reforms and its effectiveness.* Retrieved from http://www.icsei2011/Full%20Papers/0007.pdf

Pianta, R., Howes, R., Burchinal, M., Bryant, D., Clifford, R., Early, D., & Barbarin, O. (2005). Features of pre-kindergarten programs, classrooms, and teachers: Do they predict observed quality and child-teacher interactions? *Applied Developmental Science, 9*(3), 144–159.

Pintrich, P. R., Marx, R. W., & Boyle., A. (1993). Beyond cold conceptual change: The role of motivational beliefs and classroom contextual factors in the process of conceptual change. *Review of Educational Research, 63*(2), 167–199.

Ratnam, T. (2006). *Developmental trajectories of ESL teachers: A sociogenetic approach.* Unpublished Ph.D. dissertation, The English and Foreign Languages University (TEFLU), Hyderabad, India.

Ratnam, T. (2008). Communities of teachers for educational change. *42nd annual IATEFL conference,* The University of Exeter, Exeter, April 7–11.

Rutledge, I. (2006). Learning logs. *Home Education Magazine.* Retrieved from http://www.homeedmag.com/HEM/231/learninglogs.html

Sarangapani, P. M. (2003). *Constructing school knowledge: An ethnography of learning in an Indian village.* New Delhi: Sage.

Shotter, J. (1978). The cultural context of communication studies: Theoretical and methodological issues. In A. Lock (Ed.), *Action, gesture and symbol: The emergence of language* (pp. 43–78). London: Academic Press.

Shweder, R., & LeVine, R. (1984). *Culture theory: Essays on mind, self and emotion.* New York, NY: Cambridge University Press.

Song, B., & August, B. (2002). Using portfolios to assess the writing of ESL students: A powerful alternative? *Journal of Second Language Writing, 11*(1), 49–72.

Stetsenko, A. (2009). Personhood: An activist project of historical becoming through collaborative pursuits of social transformation. *New Ideas in Psychology, xxx,* 1–10.

Thapar, R. (2000). *Cultural pasts: Essays in early Indian history.* New Delhi: Oxford University Press.

Voloshinov, V. (1973). *Marxism and the philosophy of language* (L. Matejka & I. R. Titunik, Trans.). New York, NY: Seminar Press.

Vygotsky, L. S. (1981). The instrumental method in psychology. In J. V. Wertsch (Ed.), *The concept of activity in Soviet psychology* (pp. 134–143). White Plains, NY: Sharpe.

Vygotsky, L. S. (1987). *The collected works of L. S. Vygotsky. Vol. 1. Thinking and speech* (R. W. Rieber & A. S. Carton, Eds., N. Minick, Trans.). New York, NY: Plenum Press.

Wertsch, J. V. (2000). Vygotsky's two minds on the nature of meaning. In C. D. Lee & P. Smagorinsky (Eds.), *Vygotskian perspectives on literacy research* (pp. 19–30). Cambridge, UK: Cambridge University Press.

Widdowson, H. G. (1984). The incentive value of theory in teacher education. *ELT Journal, 38*(2), 86–90.

Wigglesworth, G., & Storch, N. (2012). What role for collaboration in writing and writing feedback. *Journal of Second Language Writing, 21*(4), 364–374.

Yadav, B. (2005). Decline of Sanskrit. *Economic and Political Weekly, 40*(53), 5537–5539.

APPENDIX

(a) Sample Excerpt: Teacher Monologue

Teacher*: [reads] I estimated he had a four-day beard. [explains] He is looking at the beard. "Estimated" means? As he is a barber, he knows. He can estimate, means he can make out, judge that it is four days' beard. [reads] "…the four days taken up by the latest expedition in search of our troops." [explains] the barber is talking about "our troops." "Our troops" means, what was he? What was the barber? He was also a rebel. So he is talking about his troops. "Expedition" means what?, a journey, in search of the rebels.*

(b) Sample Excerpt: Teaching to Examination

Teacher*: So, who was the professor who studied linguistics? If they [in the examination] ask, "who was the professor?" you have to say, Dr Christopher Boehm. Who was the professor who studied linguistics?*

Students*: (chorus) Dr Christopher Boehm.*

Teacher*: Who was Dr Christopher Boehm? If they ask, "Who was Dr Christopher Boehm?"*

Students*: (chorus) Anthropologist.*

Teacher*: Anthropologist and linguist.*

Students*: [repeat] Anthropologist and linguist.*

CHAPTER 26

CURRICULUM REFORM IN A NON-THREATENING COLLABORATIVE ENVIRONMENT: AN INDIAN INITIATIVE

Jayshri Kannan

ABSTRACT

This chapter explores teachers, administrators, and subject area specialists collaborating in a nonthreatening environment leading to curriculum reform in India. It draws on teacher experiences that emerged from a 2007–2012 curriculum renewal project in the Nagaland Board of School Education. In order to illustrate the transformation, a case study about the growth of two teachers who participated in the curriculum development project is featured. This work takes into account the collaborative settings, the nature of teacher learning opportunities these settings provided, and the pace at which learning occurred for each of the two teachers. Though originally tried out in the context of an English language curriculum, the bottom-up approach of broad-based collaboration reform described herein may be relevant to other disciplines and other countries.

Keywords: Collaboration; Indian education; curriculum development; case study; transformation; ELT

From Teacher Thinking to Teachers and Teaching: The Evolution of a Research Community
Advances in Research on Teaching, Volume 19, 555–566
ISSN: 1479-3687/doi:10.1108/S1479-3687(2013)0000019029

Education in India falls under the control of both the Union Government and the states. This means some responsibilities lie with the Union whereas others reside with the states. Most state board examinations in the country have been criticized for being based on rote learning rather than problem solving. The Nagaland Board of School Education (NBSE) took the simple first step in redesigning the entire English Language Teaching (ELT) curriculum by inviting this author to spearhead the Curriculum Renewal Project.

The NBSE-ELT project began in the year 2008 with a study conducted in three districts of Nagaland. Nagaland is one of the tribal states in the North East of India (89% tribal). The population of the state is only around 2 million and the number of students passing out of school each year is about 20,000. These students are distributed over 11 districts of Nagaland. Even here the maximum numbers of students are in the Kohima and Dimapur districts. In this curriculum development project, teachers represented all districts with the maximum number of participants coming from Kohima and Dimapur. The project involved different stakeholders in the curriculum renewal process, particularly teachers, who contribute significantly to the understanding of teaching and learning in the classroom from an insider's perspective (Crossley & Vulliamy, 1996; Pope, 2012).

In Phase 1 of the project, teachers, numbering anywhere between 30 and 60, attended workshops. In the second phase, material production was the focus. The several in-service programmes that had been organized as part of the project gave rise to the creation of materials for the series of books entitled *Orchids* for classes 9, 10, 11, and 12. As for the third phase, it involved editing the documents and publishing them as classroom materials. It was in this phase that support tools like CDs, sample papers, criteria for listening and speaking examinations, and new curriculum and teacher support books were produced. The fourth phase centered on the study of the impact of this new curriculum on the professional development of the teachers (Ponte, Ax, Beijaard, & Wubbels, 2004). The areas of concern in this study were the following: What kind of environment will lead to teachers implementing newer ideas? Will having teachers experience the process of teaching/learning, test item development, collecting feedback, collaborating, taking examinations, group/self-evaluations lead to the development of an informed new curriculum? What kind of insights do teachers gain when they become test takers? (i.e., Rudduck, 1988). Phase 5 of the Nagaland reform project focused on the impact of the curriculum through classroom observations. In 2009–2010, the English Course "A" curriculum for Nagaland Board of School Education was changed. The shift of emphasis was from prescriptive teaching–learning techniques and the view of teacher as implementer (Clandinin & Connelly, 1992) to a more accommodative insider-oriented view of language teaching–learning with the teacher positioned as a curriculum maker (Clandinin & Connelly, 1992; Craig & Ross, 2008). This necessitated a shift in teaching methodologies and approaches to testing.

RATIONALE

The need for the study arose in 2007 from an interaction with teachers and school administrators in the districts of Dimapur, Kohima, and Mokok-chung who met with teachers and principals from other districts in and around those regions. The rationale for the NBSE-ELT project emerged from this Phase 1 study.

The complexities of this curriculum reform project in India emerged from various sources (Hargreaves, 1996). The initial conditions that framed the study were the following: (a) teachers were dissatisfied with the present content and techniques but were unaware of recent research; (b) learner test scores were declining or were lower than expected in some areas; (c) teachers did not have access to teaching resources or did not know how to use the old materials to enhance understanding; (d) teachers had heard of technology to enhance learning but did not have access to it; (e) teachers and others wanted the content of the program to relate to contemporary problems and issues; (f) teachers were looking for ways to increase cognitive academic language proficiency by engaging in interdisciplinary work in which students were engaged; (g) students had lost faith in the previous curriculum as a way to make life more meaningful; and (h) administrators, parents, and teachers had concerns about implementation – that is, how the curriculum would be lived. Many were caught in conflicts between and among belief systems, agendas, and values which became manifested in feelings of anger, guilt, and frustration. This caused curriculum reform to be a personal and social issue as well. The NBSE-ELT project therefore was driven by the desire to draw on the teacher's experience and empowering teachers with as many language teaching methods and techniques as possible in order to work toward discovering their own implicit and explicit thoughts and beliefs about teaching (Ellis, 1998; Larsen-Freeman & Anderson, 2010).

RESEARCH TOOLS AND PROCEDURES

Four independent questionnaires were circulated, and the data was collected and tabulated at different stages of the project. The first study was conducted in 2007 with 102 teachers. This data was collected before the curriculum change workshops began to understand the needs of the state curriculum. A second study was done in 2010 with 52 teachers. The teachers had used *Orchids* class 9 texts for a year and had just started using the *Orchids* class 10 texts. Hence, most of the feedback was based on *Orchids* class 9 teaching. The third study was based on the questions and interviews to understand which aspects of the new curriculum had nudged teachers to reflect on the process of teaching and learning. Also, the teachers were asked about changes they experienced both in the areas of personal beliefs and their practices of teaching English.

Questionnaires were generated based on the discussions before and after the implementation of the new curriculum with all the stakeholders, members of NBSE, the teachers and principals of schools. A set of four

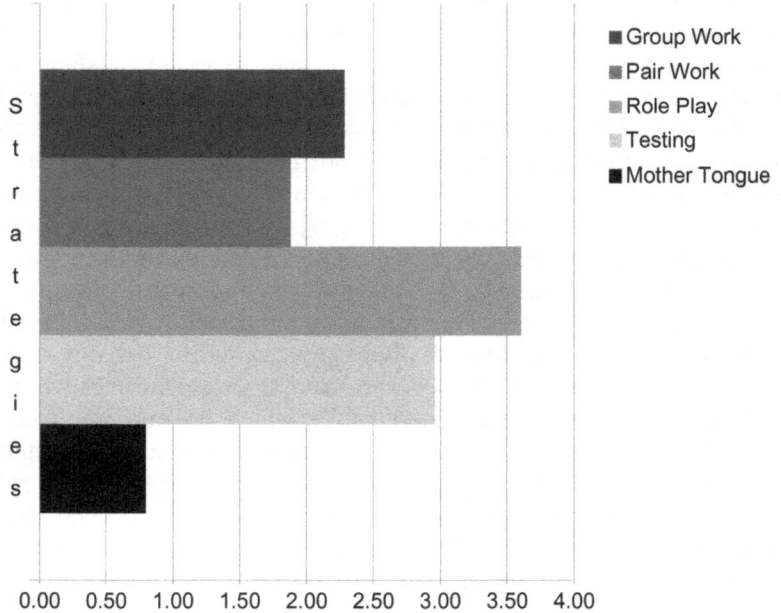

Fig. 1. Teachers' Changing Comfort Level Based on Strategies Used in the Classroom.

questionnaires related to shifts in classroom dynamics before and after the introduction of the new materials (*Orchids* 9, 10, 11, and 12), effectiveness of the new curriculum, and changing beliefs of teachers before and after the project was circulated. Based on the data obtained, themes were selected and information pertaining to each theme was compiled based on the frequency of the response. Bar diagrams were generated for each theme as demonstrated in Fig. 1.

Interviews were carried out to obtain insights into teachers' and principals' perceptions of collaborative teacher development. The interviews provided a comprehensive overview of all possible outcomes. All interactive interviews were recorded and transcribed verbatim. Notes were simultaneously taken during the interviews. At the end of each day of interviewing, the resource persons gathered to share insights and revelations. These notes were all combined a week later. Some interesting revelations were the challenges the new curriculum posed in class 9 and the encountering of the same challenges in class 10. Also, the teachers who did not attend the workshop expressed a desire to interact with subject matter experts.

TWO CASE EXAMPLES

In order to illustrate the transformation, case studies on the growth of two teachers were created. These cases focused on participation in the curriculum development process in the various collaborative settings where they worked, on the nature of teacher learning opportunities these settings presented, and the pace at which learning occurred in each. What follows is a brief description of the participants.

Among (a pseudonym) was a Naga teacher from the 9th study teacher training group. Among had been a strong student himself, but he did not participate much in workshop discussions. Questions such as the following ones were never answered by Among: (1) What kind of assessment do you think will make your learners proficient in English? (2) Why do you think your students need a new pattern of testing? (3) Where is the problem coming from in assessment: Teacher attitudes? Learner attitudes? Adherence to administrative procedures? (4) What do we tend to test largely in our English question papers? Accuracy? Fluency?

Among, however, did very well in the material development workshops where the framework and testing parameters were given. He developed tasks following the guidelines. But when faced with questions concerning what should be tried, Among waited for other teachers to arrive at a consensus.

Yet, Among worked diligently. He took copious notes during the training sessions and maintained his files well. He studied the examples given during the material development workshop sessions before devising tasks. I knew Among would be able to use the curriculum effectively, but I was worried about his understanding of the material.

James (a pseudonym) was a second Naga teacher from the 9th study teacher training group. James was keen on acquiring more degrees. He had not decided which courses to opt for. His test items were frequently fragmentary and incomplete. He was unhappy with devising listening test items. He was displeased with functional grammar items. He was upset with literature items as well. He posed questions about everything: every underlying principle, every fact presented. "How did it ..." was his favorite question. James even complained that there was not enough time for feedback during the workshop and not enough direction as to how to prepare test items. But never were James's questions reactive or combative. Despite his unhappiness with the process, his questions were well thought out and well-structured. His questions, in turn, improved the quality of our workshop discussions; he had in-depth knowledge and sought understanding when he felt it was absent. He excelled at devising "what" questions. I knew James understood the material, but this unfortunately was not evident in the test items he devised.

SUPPORT TO TEACHERS

In order to enhance Among's understanding of ELT and to help James apply all that he was beginning to understand, the teachers were encouraged to maintain journals that we called "suitcases." The teachers were asked to jot down thoughts they had brought to the workshops and to reflect on what they were taking back to their classrooms once the various workshop sessions were completed.

The notes the teachers created were discussed and brainstormed as there were many questions that arose. In his journal, Among tended to jot down facts. As for James, he noted the questions that came to his mind as the training sessions unfurled. Both Among and James relied on the handouts to provide them with facts.

Some questions James noted, for example, were: "If learners were given an opportunity to use the language, the classes would get noisy and wouldn't this be frowned upon by administrators and other subject teachers?" "If fluency is made more important than accuracy, how will learners know their errors?" "If terminology teaching and testing is not done in grammar, how can functional grammar alone improve their language proficiency?" "Should formative assessment be done formally? Are we not already doing it?" "How can we test speaking skills in large classes?" James found solutions to most of these questions from his colleagues at the workshop. But some of his queries were still left unanswered.

The teachers were then divided into groups (Stenhouse, 1972) to devise test questions which they knew could become part of the textbooks. The resource persons monitored the group activities. We pushed Among to go beyond the factual level in designing test items. James was challenged to complete his items without breaking them into too many questions. The groups exchanged their test questions and reviewed them. The resource person then created a test using the items the teachers created. The test makers (the teachers) then became the test takers in an authentic setting.

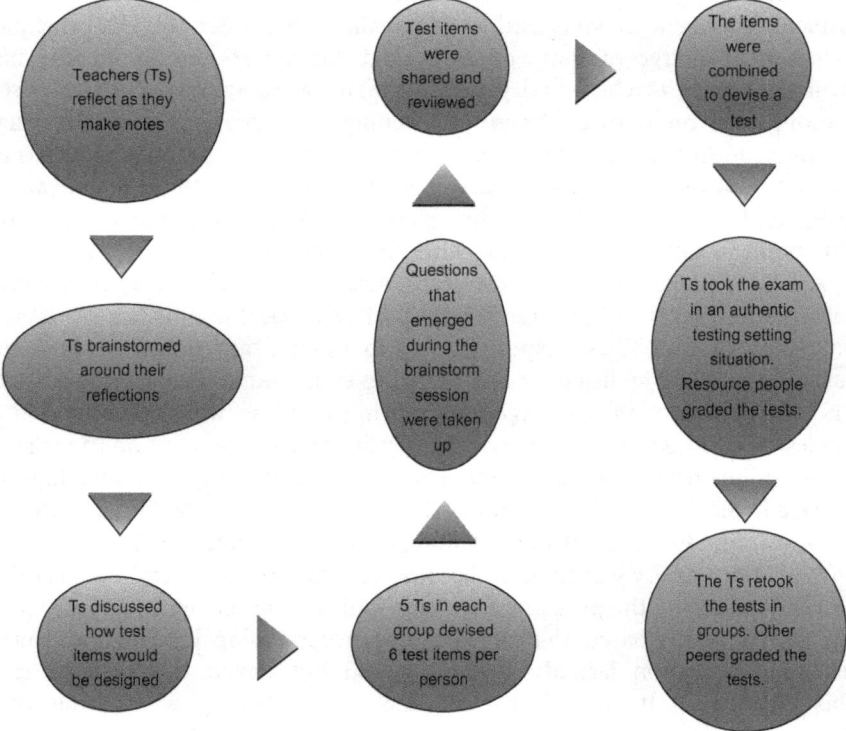

Fig. 2. Teachers' Professional Development Journey.

The answer sheets were graded and scores were shared. The teachers then went back to their groups and retook the test. Each group had to answer one whole test. The method of approaching the work was left up to them. They were even allowed to talk to other groups. At this stage the time allotted to complete the task was cut to almost half, although this also was not so rigidly adhered to. The whole process is illustrated in Fig. 2, which appears on the previous page.

CASE STUDY FINDINGS

Among's test items were now informed by his own and others' answers to the questions. Earlier Among would adhere to the format suggested at the workshop, but now he had new test item types with assessment scales attached to them, which he wanted to discuss at the workshop. Among told us (Interview, 2012) that he also had initiated a discussion with his school principal to begin teaching and testing at the Primary School. His principal put him in charge of that endeavor, and Among started to prepare his primary school teachers and generated many work samples for their use. Among also built up a library of listening and speaking texts. He very proudly showed us the titles. In a state where access to resource materials is almost nonexistent, Among's personal initiative is sure to go a long way. Nagaland has very limited internet access and Among and most others, to this point in time, are unfamiliar with resources on the web.

As for James, his test items were now less sketchy. He introduced information gap activities. Earlier his preferred speaking tasks were either role play or individual responses. As no other State Board in India is teaching and testing listening and speaking skills, James became innovative and learned through exchange and sharing of ideas with other teachers. James, in contrast to Among, is computer literate, and he went on to register for an online teacher development program. That, in turn, motivated him to engage in teacher research (Hammersley, 1993; Kirkwood & Christie, 2006).

During the first part of the test that Among and James took, James said that his test anxiety was reduced because they had become familiar with the test design during the process of devising and writing the items. It was when the scores were shared that Among began expressing his opinions such as: "This question lacked clarity"; "I did not devise this task to test this objective." It was clear that James and Among were using this discussion time for support and as an opportunity to develop their own professional judgement, confidence, and insight (Day, 1993). During one of the workshops held in Kohima, for example, James said one thought kept running through his head. After students have taken a test and their test anxiety is behind them, what they have studied remains fresh in their minds. He felt that in Naga's schools, because of the obsession with grades, the opportunity at this point for the teacher to tap into informal or practical knowledge to support learning was being overlooked.

Among said that in his group they learned to share their viewpoints, and then restate what they all agreed upon. He also went on to say that some of his teammates appreciated many of his ideas. This, in turn, made him to recognize others' contributions to the school environment and outside it too. Among also admitted that this was the first time he had worked in teams where evaluation was the topic of discussion. He admitted that he was very nervous and unsure of how he would react if he were humiliated. Dismissing this thought, he said he realized that he was not the target at all. He had come to know that learning was the focus (Day, 1993).

DISCUSSION AND CONCLUSION

Phase 1 of the project focused on the needs analysis and meetings to establish directions for needed reform. Based on these meetings, Phase 2 was developed to orient and ready teachers in the areas of Teaching ELT, the process of producing teaching and learning materials, and understanding curriculum change. Master staff developers were also identified amongst the trainees.

Some responses of the teachers in the initial phase were that training sessions on academics of language skills were of great value, but when it came to functional grammar the teachers were unsure of what would work best for them (Ellis, 1998). Where teaching methods were concerned, it was agreed by all that learner-centric classrooms would lead to improved language proficiency amongst learners. However, the idea of creating a nonthreatening atmosphere made the teachers feel as if they were losing control. Regarding evaluation, the move from testing only content to including content and process was understood by the teachers to be the need of the hour. But when it came to the testing and teaching of listening and speaking, the teachers were not sure how to proceed. After the teachers were exposed to some of the existing practices in other countries, a consultative meeting was held to arrive at a feasible approach applicable to Nagaland. The process took a week of full-day consultation and resulted in a format which is now in use in Nagaland.

Once the teachers returned to their classrooms they continued to express their concerns regarding the need for support to conduct the listening and speaking tests throughout the year. They were also concerned about the inadequacy of resources from which they could devise test items. To this point in time, the collaboration between the subject experts, NBSE, and teachers has proven rewarding. Principals now have an understanding of the kind of support teachers require to conduct the listening and speaking tests. Also, resource material was sent on loan for one year so test items could be written. Sample test questions were sent for the first six months in the case of listening and speaking exams.

Phase 3 involved editing the materials the teachers had produced in Phase 2. The teachers had been divided into a listening and speaking group, a reading group, writing group, a grammar group, and a literature group. As outlined in Fig. 2, a minimum of five teachers in each group wrote about six test items each. The questions devised by the listening and speaking groups and the reading group were used in the textbook. These areas were completely new to the teachers, and so presumably they had fewer preconceived notions attached to them. Where the test items produced by the literature, grammar, and writing groups were concerned, only 10% of them were usable. The literature tasks had only "where" questions. They had no extrapolations or inferential questions. The functional grammar tasks were left half done, and the writing tasks did not focus on the writing process at all. But as years rolled on and as the teachers conducted trial runs of the test items in their classrooms, there was a noticeable difference in the quality of materials produced. When it came to classes 11 and 12, almost 60–70% of the teacher-designed test items could be used in the textbooks. The time required for yearly meetings became gradually reduced. What began with a month's training was now decreased to 15 days and eventually reduced to a week for class 12. All the materials were new and suited to local conditions. Such materials were not culled from the Internet, from teacher guidebooks, or other locally available materials. When it came to choosing selections for the literature reader, the teachers developed materials of their own. They did so by changing the genre in some cases and by rewriting Nagaland folktales and Nagaland achievers stories in their own way. In class 9, the focus was language reinforcement in the Nagaland social context. In class 10, the teachers felt the learners were now ready for academic language acquisition. This led to the introduction of theme-based learning and tasks which required the skills of comparing, classifying, synthesizing, evaluating, and inferring to solve them. Classes 11 and 12 became more demanding as new ideas, concepts, and language were presented simultaneously and formal grammar work became greatly reduced.

The NBSE-ELT Project has not only resulted in new learning materials for NBSE but has also produced new assessment procedures. In the course of the project, over 200 NBSE school teachers received professional development in syllabus design and production of learning materials. This is perhaps the first time in the recent history of education in Nagaland that classroom teachers played a lead role in curriculum change. From the beginning, the project was teacher-driven. Nagaland also became the first school board in India to test Listening and Speaking in Board examination in addition to Reading, Writing, Literature, and Grammar.

The transformation has been captured in this case study research project (Stenhouse, 1978) involving two Naga teachers. Indeed, both Among and James learned and benefited in their own ways. Both of them actively constructed knowledge for themselves and engaged in cooperative problem solving during the curriculum development process. The outcomes of the evaluation process kept them actively engaged in their learning. They also developed increased competence, motivation, confidence, and control over their learning. Through this work, we see in an up-close way how the removal of fear and authority and how understanding social, historical and cultural forces, leads to participatory learning on the part of teachers – and, eventually, their students.

REFERENCES

Clandinin, D. J., & Connelly, F. M. (1992). Teacher as curriculum maker. In P. W. Jackson (Ed.), *Handbook of research on curriculum: A project of the American Educational Research Association* (pp. 363–461). New York, NY: Macmillan.

Craig, C., & Ross, V. (2008). Developing teachers as curriculum makers. In F. M. Connelly (Ed.), *Sage handbook of curriculum and instruction* (pp. 282–305). Thousand Oaks, CA: Sage.

Crossley, M., & Vulliamy, G. (1996). Issues and trends in qualitative research: Potential for developing countries. *International Journal of Educational Development, 16*(4), 439–448.

Day, C. (1993). Reflection: A necessary but not sufficient condition for professional development. *British Educational Research Journal, 19*(1), 83–93.

Ellis, R. (1998). Teaching and research: Options in grammar teaching. *TESOL Quarterly, 32*(1), 39–60.

Hammersley, M. (1993). On the teacher as researcher. *Educational Action Research, 1*(3), 425–445.

Hargreaves, A. (1996). Transforming knowledge: Blurring the boundaries between research, policy, and practice. *Educational Evaluation and Policy Analysis, 18*(2), 105–122.

Kirkwood, M., & Christie, D. (2006). The role of teacher research in continuing professional development. *British Journal of Educational Studies, 54*(4), 429–448.

Larsen-Freeman, D., & Anderson, M. (2010). *Techniques and principles in language teaching.* Oxford, UK: Oxford University Press.

Nunan, D., & Pierce, B. N. (1997). Standards for teacher research: Developing standards for teacher research in TESOL. *TESOL Quarterly, 31*(2), 365–367.

Ponte, P., Ax, J., Beijaard, D., & Wubbels, T. (2004). Teachers' development of professional knowledge through action research and the facilitation of this by teacher educators. *Teaching and teacher education, 20*(6), 571–588.

Pope, M. (2012). Anticipating teacher thinking. *Research on teacher thinking: Understanding professional development* (Vol. 19).

Rudduck, J. (1988). Changing the world of the classroom by understanding it: A review of some aspects of the work of Lawrence Stenhouse. *Journal of Curriculum and Supervision, 4*(1), 30–42.

Stenhouse, L. (1972). Teaching through small group discussion: Formality, rules and authority. *Cambridge Journal of Education, 2*(1), 18–24.

Stenhouse, L. (1978). Case study and case records: Towards a contemporary history of education. *British Educational Research Journal, 4*(2), 21–39.

PART IV
ADVANCES IN TEACHER EDUCATION

In this section, we focus on the theme, the advancement of teacher education, a research strand that is central to ISATT's mission. Three chapters are featured. Chapter 27 is authored by European editor, Anneli Lauriala, and deals with "Changes in Research Paradigms and Their Impact on Teachers and Teacher Education: A Finnish Case." Chapter 28 is a collaborative, international enterprise. It is a reprint of an Association of Teacher Education (ATE Yearbook) chapter authored by John Loughran (Australia), Fred A. J. Korthagen (The Netherlands), and Tom Russell (Canada). Titled "Teacher Education that Makes a Difference: Developing Foundational Principles of Practice," its principles are drawn from the authors' teacher education programs in their home countries. The third part of this section is a chapter commissioned by The Middle East editors, Freema Elbaz-Luwisch and Lily Orland-Barak. Contributed by Michal Zellermayer and Edith Tabak, Chapter 29 focuses on "The Sustainability and Nonsustainability of a Decade of Change and Continuity in Teacher Education."

CHAPTER 27

CHANGES IN RESEARCH PARADIGMS AND THEIR IMPACT ON TEACHERS AND TEACHER EDUCATION: A FINNISH CASE

Anneli Lauriala

ABSTRACT

This chapter explores the idea of paradigm shifts and the changes that have taken place in the field of teaching and teacher education over the past four decades. The work unpacks how teachers, their practices, their professional development, and their education are conceived in the positivist and interpretive paradigms. The study of teaching and teacher education is likewise shaped by the ontological and epistemological underpinnings associated with different research methods and the paradigms with which they are associated. To demonstrate the influence of paradigms, this chapter concludes with a rich example of how the interpretive tradition has shaped a teacher education program in northern Finland.

Keywords: Teacher education; paradigm shift; interpretive paradigm; Finland

From Teacher Thinking to Teachers and Teaching: The Evolution of a Research Community
Advances in Research on Teaching, Volume 19, 569–595
ISSN: 1479-3687/doi:10.1108/S1479-3687(2013)0000019030

This chapter addresses the changes that have taken place in research paradigms over the course of four decades, specifically from the 1970s until now. The assumption is that shifts or turns in research paradigms have meant changes not only in the aims, foci, and methods of research, but also in teachers' positioning and roles in research, in teacher competencies, as well as in methods and contents of teacher education programs, and in how we understand the relationship between research and practice.

Furthermore, shifts in research paradigms are reflected in school policies and decision making as well as in teachers' levels of autonomy and self-determination. The positivist paradigm in education dominated in Finland until the 1980s, when qualitative research gradually became a more common and scholarly accepted way of knowing in educational research. This work will specifically focus on describing the change from the positivist to the interpretive paradigm in Finland, and discuss the meaning and impact of this paradigmatic turn on teachers and teacher education. This shift has been called the linguistic turn, implying the giving of voice to teachers and appreciating their subjective experiences and meanings. These research trends in Finland have greatly benefitted from the work done within the International Study Association of Teachers and Teaching (ISATT). ISATT can be seen as a forerunner of the principles that scaffold contemporary Finnish teacher education – such ideas as the teacher-as-a-researcher and the reflective practice approach to teaching and teacher education. This chapter addresses the following research questions:

- How has a teacher's role and position in research studies and the teacher–researcher relationship changed along with the change from positivist to interpretative paradigm? How do these approaches affect teacher action and teacher competencies?
- How is teacher knowledge created and what is the nature of this kind of knowledge?
- What is the relationship between research and practice in teacher education?

This work concludes with an example of a teacher education curriculum from the University of Lapland, Finland. That curriculum was constructed to correspond with the core assumptions underlying the teacher-as-researcher and reflective practitioner approaches to teaching and teacher education. Relationships between these approaches and interpretive methods of research on education as well as scholarship conducted by the ISATT community of researchers will be interwoven throughout this work.

PARADIGMS

In literature, there are at least 20 different definitions for the term "paradigm." It has been defined as the basic belief system or worldview that guides the investigator, not only in choices of method but in ontologically and epistemologically fundamental ways (Guba & Lincoln, 1994). According to Guba and Lincoln (1994), "paradigms... have consequences for the practical conduct of inquiry, as well as the interpretation of findings and policy choices..." (p. 112). They additionally can be seen as related to different views of education: technological, humanistic, and emancipatory perspectives. Further to that, they shape the evaluation criteria for teaching and learning. The positivist and qualitative paradigms will now be compared.

Within the qualitative research paradigm, I will concentrate mostly on the interpretive approach, which I believe is closely associated with the basic tenets of ISATT. The critical paradigm is likewise important when thinking about the challenges of education today and the need to develop prospective teachers into transformative intellectuals. For example, the critical perspective is at work when preservice teachers engage in reflection on their beliefs and actions in ways that account for the social, political, and cultural context of their work (i.e., Zeichner, 1994). However, the critical paradigm has difficulty making its way into schools because of a priori theoretical commitments to inequities and hegemonies in the education system. The interpretive paradigm, in constrast, lets experience as opposed to theory lead the way. The upshot of this is that more rhetoric than tangible achievement has been produced where critical reflection and teacher education are concerned (Kaasila & Lauriala, 2012).

Positivistic Paradigm

Characteristic to positivism is the striving to find generalizations, law-like accounts that enable action to be predicted and controlled (Calderhead & Gates, 1993). Research in the positivist tradition is concerned with things that can be publicly observed and tested (Kerlinger, 1973). Although positivism in its original form has died, the so-called neo-positivism has influenced education research and research on teacher education since the 1970s (Giroux, 1981). According to the positivist worldview, scientific knowledge should be objective – value-free and context-free. In education, this means we cannot formulate alternative visions to the status quo; the positivistic research does not see beyond "what is." By glorifying the present, positivism rejects the future. In Finland, positivist–empirical research dominated in the 1960s, although it never totally eliminated hermeneutic or historical educational research. The backlash against positivism in educational research increased during the 1970s. It took wings at the Nordic Symposium of Educationists in Lund, Sweden, in 1972 (i.e., Paivansalo, 1980, p. 234) and spread more widely at the Annual Meeting of Finnish Educationists in Helsinki in the end of 1970s.

Relationship Between Research and Practice
In the positivistic approach to research, the function of research is to predict and control educational phenomena, which is an instrumental stance. The emphasis in research on teaching and teachers was on teachers' external behavior, which was studied as related to student achievement. Classroom life was "divided" into measurable variables (atomism) and in each research investigation only some features (i.e., variables) were under study. In the search for causal dependency among individual factors, assumed to work independently, separately, a myriad of factors, their interdependence, and the complexity of teaching/learning situations and overall bustle of classroom life were not paid attention to. The complexity, wholeness of teachers' work, and its cultural, social, and personal aspects were ignored, as were teachers' own intentions, aims, and beliefs. Positivistic research provided objective knowledge in fragmented bits.

Consequences for Teachers and Teaching
Positivist tenets based on rationalistic approaches to teaching developed in the beginning of the 19th century in the context of behaviorism. The behaviorist influence tried to transform theories of learning into methods for efficient teaching (i.e., Laursen, 1994). The aim was to make teaching effective. This process–product research movement of the 1980s did not, however, yield much evidence on the relationship between teacher behavior and student achievement (i.e., Elbaz, 1983), and the findings, explanations obscured more than they revealed of social conditions, practices, and interests (Popkewitz, 1984, p. 193). Thus, the positivist research failed to bring about better teaching or better learning outcomes. Teachers often experienced the research findings, presented in the form of statistical probabilities, as insignificant, trivial, and far removed from the everyday concerns of the classroom. This may explain why some teachers to this day disregard educational research and theory. To summarize, the positivist research paradigm – applied to education – was flawed in its underlying rationale, and it failed to bring about changes in teaching and classroom life.

Teachers were objects of study, and the researcher–teacher relationship was hierarchical and distant. Often they did not meet face-to-face. The role of the teachers was that of a passive recipient of the knowledge created by researchers. The underlying theory-into-practice relationship was that teachers were to adopt and implement external, objective knowledge that others had predetermined for them (Ojanen & Lauriala, 2006).

School Innovation and School Policy
In the behaviorist tradition, school development and innovation are achieved through top-down models. Innovations are developed outside of schools, according to a research–develop–deliver model. The teacher's role is to mechanically and uniformly adopt and apply innovations developed by experts. As a consequence, innovations seldom proceeded in the expected way. They did not significantly influence life in classrooms (Jackson, 1968), which is typical of top-down reforms (Lauriala, 1998a). They ignored the fact that teachers filter innovations through their personal practical knowledge (Clandinin, 1985). Hence, if they do not find the innovations relevant to their practices, they do not enact (i.e., implement) them. Process–product kind of research has shown clearly that prescriptive generalizations about teaching that are not based on the study of classrooms are "dangerously untrustworthy" (McIntyre, 1988, p. 101). In school policy, the positivist tradition took control of teachers by mandating curricula and prescribing how they were to teach.

In Finland, the planning of teaching was strongly influenced by the Tyler model of curriculum design, which was believed to be based on a behavioristic (input–output) conception of learning (Malinen, 1992). Teachers were viewed as technicians who delivered educational ends developed and decided upon by experts outside of school. Teachers were also subjected to an external evaluation system that aimed to maximize efficient and effective delivery of the curriculum and to standardize educational outcomes. This meant that pedagogical action was externally regulated and evaluated. Many studies, however, have shown that teachers did not use the written curricula in the way curriculum planners had intended (i.e., Clark & Peterson, 1986; Kosunen, 1994).

Positivism and Teacher Education
In teacher education, the positivistic research paradigm and the behaviorist perspective existed simultaneously and emphasized a technical approach to teaching skills and methods. This continued in Finnish teacher education in the 1980s. Focus was placed on finding, modeling, and conveying effective

teaching methods or techniques and on fostering behavioral competencies and characteristics of performance-based teacher education (i.e., Zeichner, 1983). Where evaluation was concerned, behaviorism led to the development of a system that assessed teachers' abilities according to certain knowledge, dispositions and performances thought to be necessary for effective teaching, which, in turn, created individualism and competition among teachers and teacher candidates. Although the concept of teacher-as-researcher was launched in the educational literature in Finland in the 1970s (Malinen, 1974), it still involved training in the analytical skills needed to plan for instruction, to adapt general principles to one's own teaching, as well as skills in teaching technology (Korpinen, 1998). This, of course, mirrors ideas presented by researchers in the early phases of the ISATT movement (Pope, 1993).

According to behaviorism, the learning of pre-service teachers is based on apprenticeship and craft traditions, and socialization into the dominant norms of the school and teacher culture (i.e., Feiman-Nemser & Floden, 1986; Lauriala, 1998b; Zeichner, 1983). Teachers' inner world – their thinking, intentions, goals, values, and personalities – was largely ignored. In Finland, the training schools (demonstration schools) in which the practice teaching mainly took place continued the positivistic–empirical stance until the 1980s. The stance then spilled over to the schools where the practice continued even longer. Students became accustomed to prescribed outcomes and "right" methods, and it took time to alter this orientation to student teaching.

Interpretive Paradigm

There are many forms of interpretive approaches. These include qualitative, case study, participant observation, symbolic interaction, phenomenologi-cal, narrative, and constructivist/interpretive study (Guba & Lincoln, 1994). However, what is important is their common aim to look for, describe, and understand human action on the basis of individual (and also collective) meaning making, to understand people's subjective, inner world, and its impact on their action. The basic tenet of the interpretive perspective is that human (social) action is meaningful and that one cannot begin to understand what happens in classrooms and schools if one does not attempt to interpret situations in teachers' and children's own terms. Accordingly, the interpretive paradigm assumes that a teacher's subjective school-related knowledge determines for the most part what happens in the classroom (i.e., Halkes & Olson, 1984; Pope, 1993). Education is understood as an intentional activity, which implies that it is guided by the actors, that is teachers' consciousness: beliefs, conceptions, and values. Hence, research into teachers' perceptions and thinking is needed if we are to understand or change their action. Furthermore, interpretive research values context sensitivity. In other words, it privileges understanding a phenomenon in all its complexities and within a particular situation and context (i.e., Maykut & Morehouse, 1994, p. 13).

Teachers' dispositions, beliefs, and ideas are seen as most significant not only for understanding their actions, but also for helping to make sense of students' learning motivation and achievements. The origin of the ISATT organization, which began as the International Study Association on Teacher Thinking, was based on this presupposition. Teachers' inner worlds have been represented via different theoretical concepts, such as teacher understandings, practical knowledge, personal practical knowledge, teacher conceptions, beliefs, cognition perspectives, craft knowledge, image, script, schema, subjective theories, and dilemmas (Pope, 1993). Besides teachers' telling and writing, interpretive research in teaching relies on participant observation, especially in interactionist and ethnographic approaches to study. It assumes the nature of the classrooms as socially and culturally organized environments for learning. Research concerns participants' experiences and meaning making, the sociohistorical backdrop of schooling, subjective meaning, and its relation to the ecological circumstances of action; that is the micro-cultures and micropolitics of classrooms (i.e., Woods, 1979, 1990). Typical questions of the interactionist–interpretive research stance include: What is happening in a particular situation and what do the actions mean to the teachers and students involved in it? What kind of individual strategies or cultural patterns can be found in these actions? Interpretive and ethnographic studies have managed to capture life and interaction in classrooms through probing the life-worlds of teacher and students in said classroom. The research approach has made visible the invisibility of everyday life. Situated practice is described and details specific to local situations are made public.

Relationship Between Research and Practice
The ontological assumption underlying the interpretive paradigm is that the world is real, but that individuals vary in their perceptions and experiences of it. Hence, in teacher research, the aim is to describe, interpret, and understand a teacher's work/life-world, to characterize and understand ways in which the teacher makes sense of his/her experiences of it and, in

turn, how the teacher attempts to adjust the educational environment within schools and classrooms based on the changing phenomena he/she perceives. Instead of focusing on generalized knowledge, interpretive research is "striving for understanding particular individuals' perspectives through case studies and ethnographies that focus particularly on the language and interaction of participants" (Calderhead & Gates, 1993, p, 13). Teachers' practical/personal practical knowledge is described as qualitatively different from academic, subject matter, or formal theoretical knowledge (Clandinin, 1985; Elbaz, 1991; Lauriala, 2004; Webb & Blond, 1995). A group of scholars and researchers, who originated ISATT, also understood by the end of the 1970s that it was time to turn to the teacher as an active agent in educational situations, if we were to enhance their professional development and improve teaching practice. The ultimate hope was that as our understanding of teachers' thinking improved, it would inform teacher education practices in the future (Calderhead & Gates, 1993). This shift spread widely in the 1990s in Finland, and ISATT can be regarded as one of the main architects and influencers of this trend. This chapter presents one attempt to instantiate these principles in teacher education.

Teacher's Position in Research
Along with the linguistic turn, the role of the researcher changed and became one of the "passionate listener, participant" actively engaged in facilitating the "multivoice reconstruction of her own construction as well as those of the other participants" (Guba & Lincoln, 1994, p. 115; see also Lauriala, 1997, p. 62). It became important to achieve intersubjectivity between researcher and teachers through sharing thought processes and taking each other's perspective into account. For researchers, it became critically important to create the conditions so that teachers would share what they had on their minds (Lauriala, 1997).

A researcher's active involvement was needed so s/he could understand others' perspectives and gain access to their personal knowledge. Needless to say, the researcher needed to develop rapport, trust, and identification with the teachers involved. "Truth" was not created by the researcher, following scientific, rigorous rules, but intersubjectively was reached between the researchers and those being researched. Indeed, the research process (i.e., interviews; discourses) offered the possibility of creating new language and knowledge (Mercer, 1995). Also, constructions (accounts/ findings) are assumed to be created, elicited, and refined through interaction between and among researcher and teacher respondents, which some refer to the principle of "reciprocity" (i.e., Clandinin & Connelly, 1994, p. 424).

Intersubjectivity inherently involved the valuing of teachers and their experiences, and it implied empowering teachers: giving them a voice. Teachers were understood to have something to contribute and were thought to have undergone experiences worthy of talking about. All in all, their opinions were of interest to the researcher. Instead of the former rational, objective, and distant stance, the researcher's role became a sensitive one, respectful of teachers and appreciating their feelings and cognitive orientations (i.e., Lauriala, 1997; Woods, 1992).

Teacher's Role in School Decision-Making and Innovation Activities
While teacher autonomy in school decision-making has diminished in the United States, Great Britain, and Australia, for example, over the last two decades, the trend has been exactly the opposite in Finland. The bodies that formerly used to dictate and control teaching no longer play those roles, and teachers are increasingly expected to define for themselves their norms of practice. In 1985 centrally developed curricula in Finland was supplanted by municipal, local curricula, which set in motion a dynamic process of curriculum development (Atjonen, 1988). In 1994 *Core Curriculum for Basic Education* appeared and each school was expected to create its own curriculum. That curriculum would describe the educational principles and actions of the school, based on the overarching principles of the core curriculum. In this process, teachers were seen as active agents in educational situations; they not only delivered mandated curriculum, but interpreted, made, and cocreated it alongside students (i.e., Clandinin & Connelly, 1992; Craig & Ross, 2008; Kosunen, 1994). The autonomy given to schools and teachers did not always lead to changes at the classroom level. However, by engaging collectively in curriculum development, teachers started to talk together about educational issues and to value discussions, often involving parents, that were carried out widely in schools. School-based curriculum work also fueled collaborative teaching in schools. Finnish teachers learned to talk together about professional matters, which broke, to some extent, the norms of privacy embedded in the teacher culture. However, it was not easy to assist teachers in their decision-making, to help them become active agents in their work and development, especially since they had become accustomed to being told – at least, to that point in time – what to do and how (Lauriala, 1997). Because change is emotionally laden, less positive emotions of teaching such as guilt, shame, anger, jealousy, envy, and fear also surfaced in the innovative work (i.e., A. Hargreaves, 2002; Lauriala, 1997). It involved much more than simply

changing status or formally declaring teachers to be autonomous (Lauriala, 2002). For teachers to take ownership and to commit themselves to change, they needed to reflect on their own experiences (Rudduck, 1988). In this regard, research-based teacher education has recently expanded to include teachers' roles in school decision-making, action, and development, and how to become more active and autonomous, which signals the overall empowerment of teachers.

The greater autonomy given to teachers may be seen – at least partially – to be influenced by the fact that the School Reform, Comprehensive Education Curriculum of 1972 (POPS) had not succeeded in the expected way – and, after 20 years of being rolled out in the schools, its basic aims had not been realized. The failure confirmed the teachers' decisive role in the realization of innovations. It also set in motion grassroots innovations started by individual teachers working in cooperation with university researchers in the County of Oulu and elsewhere and supported by the National Board of Education. This was an attempt to instantiate the hopes and ideals of comprehensive schools (Lauriala, 1997; Lauriala & Syrjala, 1995).

Rethinking the Theory-Practice Relationship
As presented earlier, the interpretive approach focuses on subjective meaning making and language, instead of observable, objective behaviour. This change is defined as the linguistic turn and the narrative tradition. It altered how we understand the generation and nature of teacher knowledge, that is, knowledge on and for teaching. What was new and apt to give more value to teachers was the view that knowledge is also created in practice and that teachers are knowledge producers. In other words, teachers generate knowledge and personal theories, test and modify them in and through their action, and they use personally preexisting theories and beliefs to explain and plan their teaching. The nature of this knowledge has also become better understood through research done by ISATT members over the past 30 years. Teachers' knowledge has been characterized as largely knowledge-in-action, tacit knowledge, created in classrooms in close connection to students. It is practical and has caring and moral dimensions. Thus, it is not value-free. Teachers' work is full of moments, situations, and decisions involving moral and ethical issues and dilemmas (Elbaz, 1992). This further confirms the view that models of teaching are not universally applicable. They necessarily have to be adapted and modified for particular classes and situations (Calderhead & Gates, 1993).

Teacher Reflection

Reflectivity became a trend in teacher education in Finland in the 1980s and 1990s (Ojanen, 1998). It became important that teachers themselves (as well as others) were aware of their knowledge, which gave way to their articulating and sharing it, and hence, to the idea of teachers' voice. Taking into account the norms of teacher culture had, to this point in time, not been acknowledged. To break the pattern of inherited teacher socialization, it became important to cultivate a new culture of talking and sharing during formal teacher education, and to continue doing so into teachers' later professional lives. As Elbaz (1991) has argued, teacher thinking researchers have always been concerned with "voice" because it gives teachers and prospective teachers the power to define their own reality and the power to care for and sustain one's self and others (i.e, Fine, 1994). Furthermore, having a voice implies that teachers have developed a language in which to give expression to authentic concerns (Elbaz, 1991). Teacher voice links teacher action and reflection, an idea that sits at the heart of the teacher as a reflective practitioner approach. The reflective approach to teaching involves reflectively monitored action, guided by practical consciousness, which the teacher agent can, at least to some extent, explicate and decide for him/herself (Giddens, 1984; Laursen, 1994). Instead of privileging external knowledge, it emphasizes accepting and respecting teachers' experienced knowledge and honoring the voices of teachers (i.e., Elbaz, 1990; Featherstone, Munby, & Russell, 1997).

Teachers' pedagogical autonomy and freedom to decide about their practice are ideas grounded in the complexity of the myriad of the factors present in classroom life, which makes each teaching/learning situation unique, one demanding unique and authentic action by the teacher. Hence, good practice is not ready-made; pedagogical decisions must be made that involve pedagogical tact and improvization of actions (Schön, 1983; van Manen 1991). It has been stated that teaching practice is wiser than the theoretical models trying to rationalize it (Laursen, 1994; van Manen, 1991), which means the research–practice relationship generated partly in and from practice.

As suggested earlier, teacher knowledge is not value-free. Pedagogy includes the ability to distinguish between what is good and what is not good for the child (van Manen, 1991). Good pedagogy involves love and care for children, a deep sense of responsibility, moral intuitiveness, self-critical openness, and thoughtful maturity. A good pedagogue (teacher) considers how particular situations appear from the child's point of view, including how the child experiences his/her world at school. A good teacher also possesses interpretive intelligence which allows him/her to pedagogically understand children's needs.

Interpretive Research and Teacher Education

As described, the interpretive approach produced linguistic turn, a shift in focus from external behaviour and methods to verbal representations, a change from a focus on controlling behavior to understanding behavior. Similarly, in teacher education, attention is paid to preservice teachers' talk and writing, through which they will become aware of, share and analyse, and construct and reconstruct their views and perspectives. Throughout their careers, teachers develop "a set of personal cognitions, mental representations, that operates as a lens through which teachers look at their job, give meaning to it and act in it" (Kelchtermans, 2007, p. 40).

The interpretive approach has also meant changes in the conceptions of teacher learning and teacher knowledge, which likewise is reflected in Finnish teacher education (i.e., Clark, 1986; Kremer-Hayon, 1986). Teacher learning is understood as experiential, situated learning, which undermines the possibility of objective, general knowledge in teaching: If we accept that teacher learning is experiential, teachers need to reflect and interpret their experiences to become more knowledgeable, expert teachers (i.e., LaBoskey, 1993).

Finnish teachers have a great deal of freedom in decision-making and their actions are not controlled by external authorities, which enables them to be flexible and act in situationally appropriate ways. Using inquiry-oriented approaches and interpreting one's experiences are thought to be fundamental to teacher growth in Finnish teacher education at the moment. Teacher education in Finland is no longer dominated by showing, telling, and guided practice, but more and more it is based on the prospective teacher as researcher approach, which involves researching practice and constructing personal, principled knowledge, and strategies (i.e., Loughran, 2007).

The reflective practice approach described above can be seen as connected to the basic ideas of a progressive developmentalist humanistic approach to teacher education (Lauriala, 1998a; Zeichner & Liston, 1990). The approach includes following features and principles:

- The teacher is a naturalist, possessing an attitude and skill of eager, alert observation (Zeichner & Liston, 1990), an active interpreter of classroom events, one who is a keen observer of children, their development, and their individual and personal needs, to pupil diversity (Elbaz, 1992).

■ A teacher's self is involved; hence, his/her personal development is emphasized (i.e., Beijaard, Meijer, & Verloop, 2004; Kelchtermans, 2007; Lauriala & Kukkonen, 2005; Zeichner, 1983). Accordingly, education is seen as enabling "full realization" of self or "full potential" of an individual (which is already there but not evident) to emerge. This principle pertains to students and teachers and is the core idea of humanistic education (Rogers, 1983).

INTERIM SUMMARY

Where ontological assumptions are concerned, the paradigmatic shift from positivist to interpretive approach has meant a move from a view that there is a "real" reality which consists of facts, which the researcher is able to capture to a view of research as a means to co-construct reality, which, in turn, implies a relational reality. From a theory–practice point of view, they mutually inform one another rather than theory dominating and determining practice through a one-way flow of information. Also, where knowledge is concerned, positivist research has never been able to adequately describe how new knowledge is discovered (Maykut & Morehouse, 1994, p. 13). In contrast, interpretive research focuses on unfolding "new" knowledge and highlighting individual and social processes of knowledge construction. In terms of research aims, this can be seen as a move from predicting and explaining to describing, interpreting, understanding, and making conscious changes, transformations, and situations. The shift from positivism to interpretivism has meant a move from causality to intentionalism, from correspondence to coherence, from products to processes, meanings, and social life. While the research questions traditionally used to be "Which teacher behaviors are positively correlated with student gains on tests of achievement?" they have now changed to an interpretive or meaning-making perspective: "What does this situation and events mean to teacher/students; and what personal intentions, goals, biographies do they have, that need to pay attention when trying to understand their actions, classroom interactions, and in the pursuits to improve school and enhance learning and school development?"

Also, the researcher role has changed from the traditional role of hierarchical, undemocratic, distant, neutral observer, external expert, and bystander to an emphatic listener and interpreter, who generates communicative relationships and initiatives dialogues with the teachers. It also means a shift from facelessness to face-to-face situations. It additionally means a move to participatory inquiry, to researcher as full participant/ negotiator who does not make all decisions, but who creates and maintains democratic relationships with the researched, whether they be teachers or students.

Whereas findings in the positivistic research tradition were seen as value-free, general, universal, context-free, and independent from the researcher, they are, in the interpretive approach subjectivist, created findings that are situationally relevant and local in terms of explanation. A major justification for the shift can be found in Stenhouse's words. Stenhouse emphasized that

> it is difficult to see how teaching can be improved or how curricular proposals can be evaluated without self-monitoring on the part of teachers. A research tradition which is accessible to teachers and which feeds teaching must be created if education is to be significantly improved. (Stenhouse, 1975, p. 165)

Furthermore, it is now widely recognized that when trying to make changes in schools, it is important to pay attention to teachers' concerns, their circumstances, and day-to-day contingencies, which may also reveal the hidden side of the school (i.e., hidden curriculum) (Jackson, 1968; Lauriala, 1992). It also has to be acknowledged that to promote professional development we must be better informed about teachers' subjective world and the meanings they themselves regard as meaningful through giving voice to teachers as constructors and agents.

The interpretive paradigm implies that as knowledge develops and changes, it is dynamic by nature. In addition, research may be a catalyst for unfolding even deepest feelings or experiences that respondents so far may have been unaware of. Stories, when told, may resonate with those of others, become reinterpreted, and further developed. Hence, knowledge is shared, refined, reconstructed, and truth is relative, pragmatic, and negotiated. The above suggests that there is not a wide gap between the interpretive stance and the critical stance. This is because "the question 'how do things work?' is also a question of how to change those things. The study of 'what is' has reformist as well as descriptive qualities" (Popkewitz, 1984, p. 184). When preservice teachers perceive and become aware of the factors and processes guiding (often underlying) schooling and classroom life, they have a possibility of unearthing issues that may constrain teachers' and students' action, which may lead to a felt need to change the situation.

A brief overview of teacher education in Finland will now be introduced, followed by the exemplar from the University of Lapland, which illustrates how the interpretive paradigm now shapes its teacher education program.

DEVELOPMENT OF TEACHER EDUCATION IN FINLAND

Structural reforms for teacher education in Finland during recent decades have included centralizing teacher education in the universities (1974) and adding a Master's degree program to the primary school teacher diploma (1979). The intent of both of these tertiary reforms was to expand the theoretical knowledge basis of teacher education. Since 1979, the education of teachers has consisted of a four-year program. However, since the Bologna Agreement, teacher education now consists of a three-year Bachelor's degree program, followed by a two-year Master's degree program. Teacher education takes place in 10 teacher education departments attached to eight universities located in different parts of Finland. Since the 1990s, each university has established its own priorities because of the greater autonomy that has been granted universities (i.e., Lauriala & Syrjala, 1995). In addition to university-based study, practice teaching plays a central role in all teacher education programs. Practice teaching is accompanied by lectures and exercises in seminars or smaller groups, as well as independent study. The state maintains 11 practice or training schools (so-called normal schools) that belong administratively to the universities and work in sustained interaction with their respective Departments of Teacher Education.

When teacher education became the responsibility of universities in 1974, emphasis was placed on the psychologically and behaviorally oriented scientific bases of teacher education. This trend was also reflected in the Master thesis studies undertaken by prospective teachers as part of their education (Lauriala & Syrjala, 1995).

Although each department of teacher education determines their own curriculum, and each university is expected to develop its own teacher education program, the curricula are also nationally coordinated to assure sufficient coherence. National-level coordination of degree programs in Teacher Education and Educational Sciences was introduced in Finland in 2003–2004, and was coordinated by the Ministry of Education and called Vokke. The main task of the Vokke project was to coordinate teacher education and expert programs in the educational sciences (See

Jakku-Sihvonen & Niemi, 2006). A need has been expressed by the National Board of Education for joint models to be developed. These models are to be shared so that others can learn from them.

Although these were accepted principles of Finnish teacher education in the 1990s, it has taken time to proceed from rhetoric to full-blown implementation. Actually, a lot of rhetoric continues to exist. Still, the teacher as researcher stance has not been realized in many countries. However, Finland is a country where the image of teacher as researcher, like reflectivity, is lived. This may be one of the key factors which explains the high quality of teaching and "the Finnish miracle" in PISA (Program for International Student Assessment) (i.e., Estola, Lauriala, Nissila & Syrjala 2006).

The Role of Research Studies in Teacher Education

When Finnish teacher education expanded to include a Master's degree in education, all preservice teachers were to carry out research. Initially, the research methods that were used reflected the quantitative paradigm. However, these research studies were regarded by M.Ed. students, and often also by their teacher educators, as worthless. Students seemed to see them as unrelated to their pedagogical studies and unlikely to benefit them or their students in future work. Hence, motivation and commitment were low. Concurrently, studying quantitative research methods took up a lot of time in the teacher education program, detracting from pedagogical and didactic studies. A commonly expressed fear was that teachers were no longer equipped with the competencies they needed in their practical work.

In an attempt to solve this problem, we at the University of Oulu started a project to combine research work with practical school experiments that were carried out as collaborative enterprises by students, their coordinating class teachers in the training schools, university researchers, and their teacher education supervisors. This formed a major deviation from the traditional positivistic research paradigm (Lauriala, 1997; Lauriala & Syrjala, 1995).

The research base has lately been emphasized not only in the teaching profession and the development of teacher education (Jakku-Sihvonen & Niemi, 2006), but also in the areas of school decision-making and guidance. From a Finnish perspective, the research base takes into account three aspects:

- Teaching is based on the latest research.

- Teaching is conducted according to the latest findings and insights of research on learning.
- Learning in teacher education is based on the teacher-as-researcher approach.

THE TEACHER EDUCATION MODEL AT THE UNIVERSITY OF LAPLAND

The Model and Its Rationale

Basic assumptions surrounding teacher education at the University of Lapland are the same as those in other Finnish universities. Like the other universities, we have developed our own teacher education model which is based on the student-teacher-as-researcher approach. After working over 20 years as a teacher educator, I am now in a position to put into practice all that I have learned about teacher learning, knowledge, and teacher professional development during my years in ISATT circles. From my first positive experience at the ISATT conference in Surrey, England, in 1991, I've been keenly following the development of ideas within ISATT through books, the *Teachers and Teaching: Theory and Practice* journal, and attending biennial conferences held at cities dotted around the world. These have confirmed my conception of the importance of building a teacher education curriculum around the idea of students as active constructors of their pedagogical knowledge and their personal teacher identities.

The emphasis in constructing and conducting the program has been on *the connection of theory and practice,* so that pedagogical studies and learning of research methods/approaches are combined. Research and practice are understood as being interrelated and mutually influencing each other. To enact and concretely carry out the teacher-as-researcher approach, each practicum involves learning about and practicing one research approach/methods in authentic contexts (i.e., classrooms and schools). The program contents and research methods are fitted together to form a vertically unfolding continuum. The guiding principles throughout the program are the reflective practitioner and the student-teacher-as-researcher approaches. The entire teacher education program is understood as a reflective process, the focus of which varies from phase to phase.

We see reflective practice as a means by which teachers can develop a greater self-awareness about the nature and impact of their performance, an awareness that creates opportunities for professional growth and development (i.e, Osterman & Kottkamp, 1993). Meta-cognitive processes and skills are seen as the cornerstone of professional learning in and after teacher education (Calderhead, 1988).

Reflective practice, as defined in our teacher education curriculum, involves review, research, and reformulation. However, it is not easy to attain the higher, critical levels of reflective thinking that address wider societal and global issues. Research has indicated (Handal, 1991; Kaasila & Lauriala, 2012) that student teachers' reflections often remain at the action level without reaching the higher or critical levels (Zeichner & Liston, 1987). However, their striving to justify their practice is enhanced through continuous writing (pedagogical portfolios, essays) and collective discussions in pedagogical seminars, which can be regarded small educative communities. Reflective practice takes place both on both individual and social, and community levels.

The new teacher education curriculum provides students with opportunities to become acquainted with different research approaches during their five-year teacher education: ethnography, interactionist studies, phenomenology, phenomenography, action research, and narrative research. Along with these approaches, they learn various types of tools thought to be essential in their future work. These include student interviews, participant observation techniques, reflecting on their own experiences, and participating in school development activities. They also make portfolios that capture their experiences and write in their personal reflective journals. It is noteworthy that in different phases, the foci of their inquiry vary, and in each practicum phase the preservice teachers collect data of and analyze particular aspects of children's lives, learning, and their own actions in response to said children's experiences (Loughran, 2007).

Identity Work as Part of Student-Teacher-As-Researcher Approach

Following Meijer (2011) and many others, we regard the development of professional identity as central in teacher education, and view it as: (a) an ongoing process of interpretation and reinterpretation of experiences; (b) implying both person and context; (c) consisting of sub-identities that more or less harmonize with each other; and (d) demanding an active role of a student teacher (i.e., Lauriala & Kukkonen, 2001; Meijer, 2011). Identity formation is one key issue in the teacher education which student teachers are guided to reflect throughout their education. Through writing and joint discussions that knit together dialogue about theory and their own experiences, the student teachers are given a voice and feel a sense of empowerment. They become more aware of their identities and begin to reconstruct them to achieve a better balance between different parts of their identities, and thus increase their professional well-being (Lauriala & Kukkonen, 2001).

During preservice education, student teachers develop an internal work orientation, which includes developing a professional identity and constructing one's own personal practical theory of education. In our teacher education context, identity is understood to revolve around narratives that are shaped and reshaped by ongoing experiences (Beauchamp & Thomas, 2009). To understand preservice teachers' identity work, it is important to know how they construct narratives from their experiences. These narratives are approached through digital pedagogical portfolios that include students' autobiographies. Identity development, in our teacher education program, is a process of deep reflection and self-evaluation, where past, present, and future identities enter into a dialogue with one another, which leads to one's awareness of a tension or gap between the actual and the ideal state of identity (Kaasila & Lauriala, 2010). This is one of the key promoters of professional learning (Lauriala & Kukkonen, 2001). Preservice teachers' future-oriented talk is regarded as an essential part of this identity work, in which they engage during teacher education (Urzua & Vasquez, 2008). It means giving voice to neophyte teachers with an eye focused on their future professional development as well. Metacognitive processes and critical reflection are used to prevent students from uncritically implementing their images of practice acquired through past and present experiences in schools (Calderhead, 1988). As Loughran (2007) has argued, the authority of one's own experience is a critical aspect of the student-teacher-as-researcher approach, which provides possibilities for learning embedded in student teachers' teaching and learning experiences. Thus student teachers can develop more meaningful and sustained ways of focusing on their learning about teaching. To summarize, the interpretive approach is present in our preservice teacher education because:

- Preservice teachers' own beliefs, personal histories, and interests are paid attention to.
- Teacher learning is understood as experiential, thus analyzing, interpreting, and reflecting on one's experiences are important, metacognitive skills.

- Preservice teachers are also made aware of their prior experiences, school memories, and unconscious beliefs.
- Teacher educators aid them to gradually build their personal pedagogical theories, professional identity, and professional knowledge.

Reflective Processes in Professional Development of Student Teachers

Our program on reflective practice in teacher education means developing reflective capabilities and dispositions in the midst of preservice teacher education activities (Zeichner, 1994).

Reflection is understood, according to Dewey, as active and continuous. It takes careful consideration of one's conceptions, views, and knowledge while keeping in mind its foundations and consequences (Schön, 1987). To foster reflection, it is also important to understand and explore barriers to reflection. For example, negative experiences, lack of motivation and time, the expectations of others and the self, and fear of failure can possibly block reflective processes. In our research, we have found many students who told about negative memories (i.e., as a learner of mathematics) and how – by becoming aware of these noneducative experiences and sharing them – they felt liberated and were able to find more adequate and satisfying ways of acting in the future (Kaasila & Lauriala, 2012). By the end of our program, we want our students to reach the level of broad reflection and to take on issues encompassing the moral, the political, and the emotional. We want them to reflect in their situations and contexts "What is educationally in the best interest of the students and thus what should I as a teacher to do?" (i.e., Greenfield, 1991, p. 162). This query, for us, denotes the highest level of professionalism (Hargreaves, 1993).

Also, collaboration and community, co-constructing of pedagogical knowledge, and developing professional language are aimed at aiding the development of critical reflection. We know that preservice teachers' peers can facilitate change in their beliefs and practices. These kinds of collaborative practices, which we call pedagogical seminars, are currently emphasized in Finnish research-based teacher education (Kaasila & Lauriala, 2010).

To enhance reflective skills, we think it is important to provide processes and practices through which student teachers can analyze and assess their own actions. Thus, they collect data and analyze particular aspects of children's learning, classroom interaction, and their own teaching with their foci changing from one practicum to another. Student teachers are guided to:

- Recognize what they are doing, assess that knowledge, as well as give grounds and justify their actions.
- Articulate, talk aloud about their experiences, methods, practices and values, and aims (digital pedagogical portfolios, pedagogical seminars).
- Participate in teachers' talking together, collective reflection, developing of professional language, and thereby sharing of professional (often silent, tacit) knowledge, constructing, reconstructing, and co-constructing of knowledge (pedagogical seminars).

Integrating Theory, Practice, and Research Studies in University of Lapland

The basic rationale of the teacher education program developed at the University of Lapland can be seen as a coherent model of professional development; it embraces both continuity and progression as is apparent in Fig. 1.

The progression demands paying attention to different content, different foci, and different theoretical justifications underlying reflection and the methods of inquiry used (D. Hargreaves, 1993). The ultimate aim of our teacher education programme at the University of Lapland is for practice to become praxis – that is, a form of practice that is ethically informed and guided by critical reflection on practice traditions and one's own practical actions. At the end of their studies, prospective teachers will have developed their personal practical knowledge in the classroom and the school as its wider society (Clandinin, 1985).

PARTING STATEMENT

This chapter focusing on changes in research paradigms compared and contrasted the positivist and interpretivist paradigms and their shaping influences on the role of the teacher, the knowledge held and expressed by teachers, the nature of how practice is conceived, how teachers' professional development occurs, and the tools most likely to aid prospective teachers as they embark on careers in schools. The work exemplifies how the interpretivist worldview has pervaded the University of Lapland teacher

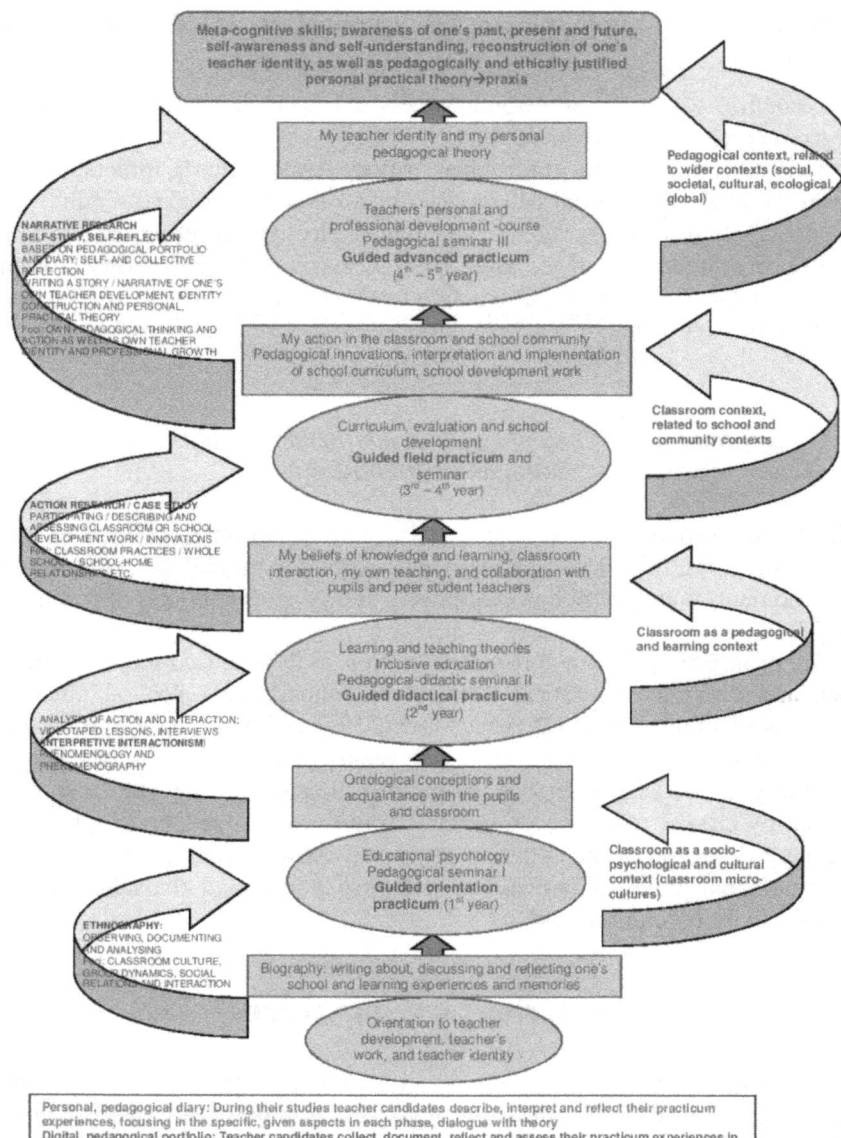

Fig. 1. The Teacher Education Model at the University of Lapland, Finland.

education program and altered the theory–practice relationship by interrupting the hierarchical flow of information. Lastly, the chapter suggests that this orientation, which has been greatly influenced by the ISATT organization and its members, may – in no small part – be critical to Finland's success on international comparison tests.

REFERENCES

Atjonen, P. (1988). Kunnan opetussuunnitelma koulun kehittämisessä [Local curriculum in the development of school-based curricula]. *Kasvatus, 19*(3), 190–197.

Beijaard, D., Meijer, P. C., & Verloop, N. (2004). Reconsidering research on teachers' professional identity. *Teaching and Teacher Education, 20*, 107–128.

Beauchamp, C. & Thomas, L. (2009). Understanding teacher identity: an overview of issues in the literature and implications for teacher education. *Cambridge Journal of Education, 39*(2), 175–189.

Calderhead, J. (1988). The development of knowledge structures in learning to teach. In J. Calderhead (Ed.), *Teachers' professional learning* (pp. 51–64). London: The Falmer Press.

Calderhead, J. & Gates, P. (1993). Introduction. In J. Calderhaed & P. Gates (Eds.), *Conceptualizing reflection in teacher education* (pp. 1–22). London: Falmer Press.

Clandinin, D. J. (1985). Personal practical knowledge: A study of teachers' classroom images. *Curriculum Inquiry, 15*(4), 361–385.

Clandinin, D. J., & Connelly, F. M. (1992). Teacher as curriculum maker. In P. W. Jackson (Ed.), *Handbook of research on curriculum* (pp. 363–461). New York, NY: Macmillan.

Clandinin, D. J., & Connelly, F. M. (1994). Personal experience methods. In N. K. Denzin & Y. S. Lincoln (Eds.), *Handbook of qualitative research* (pp. 413–427). Thousand Oaks, CA: Sage Publications.

Clark, C. (1986). Ten years of conceptual development in research on teacher thinking. In M. Ben-Beretz, R. Bromme & R. Halkes (Eds.), *Advances in research on teacher thinking* (pp. 7–20). Lisse, Netherlands: Swets & Zeitlinger.

Clark, C., & Peterson, P. (1986). Teachers' thought processes. In M. C. Wittrock (Ed.), *Handbook of research on teaching* (3rd ed., pp. 225–296). New York, NY: MacMillan.

Craig, C., & Ross, V. (2008). Cultivating teachers as curriculum makers. In F. M. Connelly (Ed.), *Handbook of curriculum and instruction* (pp. 282–305). Thousand Oaks, CA: Sage Publications.

Elbaz, F. (1983). *Teacher thinking: A study of practical knowledge*. London: Croom Helm.

Elbaz, F. (1990). Knowledge and discourse: The evolution of research on teacher thinking. In C. Day, M. Pope & P. Denicolo (Eds.), *Insight into teachers' thinking and practice* (pp. 15–42). London: The Falmer Press.

Elbaz, F. (1991). Research on teachers' knowledge: The evolution of a discourse. *Journal of Curriculum Studies, 23*, 1–19.

Elbaz, F. (1992). Hope, attentiveness, and caring for difference: The moral voice in teaching. *Teaching and Teacher Education, 8*, 421–432.

Estola, E., Lauriala, A., Nissila, S.-P. & Syrjala, L. (2006). The antecedents of success: The Finnish miracle of Pisa. In C. Craig et al., (Eds.), *American Teacher Education Yearbook* (pp. 189–206). Lanham, MD: Rowman & Littlefield.

Featherstone, D., Munby, H., & Russell, T. (1997). *Finding a VOICE while learning to teach.* London: The Falmer Press.

Feiman-Nemser, S., & Floden, R. (1986). The cultures of teaching. In M. Wittrock (Ed.), *Third handbook of research on teaching* (pp. 506–525). New York, NY: Collier-MacMillan.

Fine, M. (1994). Working with hyphens. Reinventing self and other in qualitative research. In K. Denzin & Y. Lincoln (Eds.), *Handbook of qualitative research* (pp. 70–82). London: Sage.

Giddens, A. (1984). *The constitution of society.* Cambridge, England: Policy Press.

Giroux, H. (1981). *Ideology, culture, and the process of schooling.* Philadelphia, PA: Temple University Press.

Greenfield, W. D. (1991). The micro-politics of leadership in an urban elementary school. In J. J. Blase (Ed.), *The politics of life in schools* (pp. 161–164). Newbury Park, CA: Sage.

Guba, E., & Lincoln, Y. (1994). Competing paradigms in qualitative research. In N. Denzin & Y. Lincoln (Eds.), *Handbook of qualitative research* (pp. 105–117). London: Sage.

Halkes, R., & Olson, J. (1984). Introduction. In R. Halkes, & J. Olson (Eds.), *Teacher thinking: A new perspective on persisting problems in education.* Proceedings from the first symposium of the International Study Association on Teacher Thinking (pp. 1–6). Lisse: Swets & Zeitlinger.

Handal, G. (1991). Promoting the articulation of tacit knowledge through the counselling of practitioners. In H. K. Letiche, J. C. vander Wolf & F. X. Plooij (Eds.), *The Practioners' power of choice in staff development and inservice training* (pp. 71–84). Amsterdam: Swets & Zeitlinger.

Hargreaves, A. (2002). Teaching in a box: Emotional geographies of teaching. In C. Sugrue & C. Day (Eds.), *Developing teachers and teaching practice* (pp. 3–25). London: Routledge Falmer.

Hargreaves, D. (1993). A common-sense model of the professional development of teachers. In J. Elliott (Ed.), *Reconstructing teacher education* (pp. 86–92). London: The Falmer Press.

Jackson, P. W. (1968). *Life in classrooms.* New York, NY: Teachers College Press.

Jakku-Sihvonen, R., & Niemi, H. (2006). The Bologna process and its implementation in teacher education. In R. Jakku-Sihvonen & H. Niemi (Eds.), *Research-based teacher education in Finland. Reflections by Finnish teacher educators. Finnish Educational Research Association. Research in Educational Sciences* (25, pp. 17–30). Turku: Painosalama Oy.

Kaasila, R., & Lauriala, A. (2010). Towards a collaborative, interactionist model of teacher change. *Teaching and Teacher Education, 26*(4), 854–862.

Kaasila, R., & Lauriala, A. (2012). How do pre-service teachers' reflective processes differ in relation to different contexts? *European Journal of Teacher Education, 35*(1), 77–88.

Kerlinger, F. (1973). *Foundations of behavioral research.* New York, NY: Holt, Rinehart and Wilson.

Kelchtermans, G. (2007). Professional commitment beyond contract: Teacher's self-understanding, vulnerability and reflection. In J. Butcher & L. McDonald (Eds.), *Making a difference. Challenges for teachers, teaching and teacher education* (pp. 35–54). Rotterdam, Netherlands: Sense Publishers.

Korpinen, E. (1998). Tutkiva opettaja ja opettajankoulutus [Researching teacher and teacher education]. In S. Ojanen (Ed.), *Tutkiva opettaja [Researching teacher]* (Vol. 2, pp. 21–30). Tampere: Tammer-Paino.

Kremer-Hayon, L. (1986). Reflection and professional knowledge. In C. Day, M. Pope & P. Denicolo (Eds.), *Insight into teachers' thinking and action* (pp. 57–70). Lewes: Falmer Press.

Kosunen, T. (1994). Making sense of the curriculum: Experienced teachers as curriculum makers and implementers. In I. Carlgren, G. Handal & S. Vaage (Eds.), *Teachers' minds and actions. Research on teacher thinking and action* (pp. 247–259). London: The Falmer Press.

LaBoskey, V. (1993). A conceptual framework for reflection in preservice teacher education. In J. Calderhead & P. Gates (Eds.), *Conceptualizing reflection in teacher development* (pp. 23–38). London: Falmer Press.

Lauriala, A. (1992). The impact of innovative pedagogy on teacher thinking and action: A case study of an in-service course for teachers in integrated teaching. *Teaching and Teacher Education, 8*(5/6), 523–536.

Lauriala, A. (1997). *Development and change of professional cognitions and action orientations of Finnish teachers.* Acta Universitatis Ouluensis, Scientiae Rerum Socialium, E27. University of Oulu, Oulu.

Lauriala, A. (1998a). Reformative in-service education for teachers (RINSET) as a collaborative action and learning enterprise: Experiences from a Finnish context. *Teaching and Teacher Education, 14*(1), 53–66.

Lauriala, A (1998b). Socialization for teaching, interactionism and the possibility of change within schools. In M-L. Laherand, A. Liimets & R. Liimets-Sorokin (Eds.), *The Educational science as an integrative science and integration issues in education* (pp. 79–85). Tallinn: TPU Kirjastus.

Lauriala, A. (2002). Teacher autonomy and pedagogy. In T. Kuurme & S. Priimägi (Eds.), *Competing for the future: Education in contemporary societies* (pp. 127–144). Tallinn, Estonia: TPU Kirjastus.

Lauriala, A. (2004). Teacher knowledge and learning in a context of change. In M.-L. Husso & T. Wallandingham (Eds.), *Teacher as researcher - pictures and perspectives of professionalism. Journal of Teacher Researcher*, 2004. Jyväskylä: Tuope.

Lauriala, A., & Kukkonen, M. (2001). Evolving professional identity: An awareness of self-discrepancies as a spur for learning. *Teaching and Learning in Higher Education: New Trends and Innovations.* University of Aveiro, Portugal.

Lauriala, A., & Kukkonen, M. (2005). Teacher and student identities as situated cognitions. In P. M. Denicolo & M. Kompf (Eds.), *Connecting Policy and Practice – Challenges for teaching and learning in schools and universities* (pp. 199–208). Abingdon: Routledge.

Lauriala, A., & Syrjala, L. (1995). The influences of research into alternative pedagogies on the professional development of prospective teachers. *Teachers and Teaching: Theory and Practice, 1*(1), 101–118.

Laursen, P. F. (1994). Teacher thinking and didactics: Prescriptive, rationalistic and reflective approaches. In I. Carlgren, G. Handal & S. Vaage (Eds.), *Teachers' minds and actions. Research on teacher thinking and action* (pp. 125–136). London: The Falmer Press.

Loughran, J. (2007). Encouraging a student teacher as researcher stance in teacher education. In J. Butcher & L. McDonald (Eds.), *Making a difference. Challenges for teachers, teaching and teacher education* (pp. 221–233). Rotterdam, Netherlands: Sense Publishers.

Malinen, P. (1974). Opettaja tutkijana [Teacher as researcher]. *Kasvatus*, 5(6), 349–351.
Malinen, P. (1992). *Opetussuunnitelmat koulutyössä [Curricula in school work]*. Helsinki: Valtion painatuskeskus.
Maykut, P., & Morehouse, R. (1994). *Beginning qualitative research. A philosophical and practical guide.* London: The Falmer Press.
McIntyre, D. (1988). Designing a teacher education curriculum from research and theory on teacher knowledge. In J. Calderhead (Ed.), *Teachers' professional learning* (pp. 97–114). London: The Falmer Press.
Meijer, P. (2011). The role of crisis in the development of student teachers' professional identity. In A. Lauriala, R. Rajala, H. Ruokamo & O. Ylitapio-Mäntylä (Eds.), *Navigating in educational contexts: Identities and cultures in dialogue* (pp. 41–54). Rotterdam: Sense Publishers.
Mercer, N. (1995). *The guided construction of knowledge. Talk among teachers and learners.* Clevedon: Multilingual Matters Ltd.
Ojanen, S. (1998). Miksi tarvitaan tutkivaa opettajaa? [Why do we need a researching teacher?]. In S. Ojanen (Ed.), *Tutkiva opettaja [Researching teacher]* (Vol. 2, pp. 11–17). Tampere, Finland: Tammer-Paino.
Ojanen, S. & Lauriala, A. (2006). Enhancing professional development of teachers by developing supervision into a conceptually-based practice. In R. Jakku-Sihvonen & H. Niemi (Eds.), *Research-based teacher education in Finland. Reflections by Finnish teacher educators* (Vol. 25, pp.71–88). Finnish Educational Research Association. Research in Educational Sciences.Turku: Painosalama Oy.
Osterman, K. & Kottkamp, B. (1993). *Reflective practice for educators: Improving schooling through professional development.* Newbury, CA: Corwin.
Pope, M. (1993). Anticipating teacher thinking. In C. Day, J. Calderhead & P. Denicolo (Eds.), *Research on teachers' thinking. Understanding professional development* (pp. 19–33). London: The Falmer Press.
Popkewitz, T. (1984). *Paradigm and ideology in educational research. Social functions of the intellectual.* London: The Falmer Press.
Paivansalo, P. (1980). Kasvatuksen tutkimuksen kehityspiirteista ja niiden taustatekijöista maassamme. [On the characteristic features and background factors of the development of educational research in Finland]. *Kasvatus*, 4, 232–238.
Rogers, C. (1983). *Freedom to learn for the 80s.* Columbus, OH: Charles E. Merrill.
Rudduck, J. (1988). The ownership of change as a basis for teachers' professional learning. In J. Calderhead (Ed.), *Teachers' professional learning* (pp. 205–222). London: The Falmer Press.
Schön, D. (1983). *Reflective practitioner.* London: Temple Smith.
Schön, D. (1987). *Educating the reflective practitioner: Toward a new design for teaching and learning in the professions.* San Francisco: Jossey-Bass.
Stenhouse, L. (1975). *An introduction to curriculum research and development.* London: Heinemann.
Urzua, A., & Vasquez, C. (2008). Reflection and professional identity in teachers' future-oriented discourse. *Teaching and Teacher Education*, 24, 1935–1946.
van Manen, M. (1991). *The tact of teaching.* Alberta, Canada: The Althouse Press.
Webb, K., & Blond, J. (1995). Teacher knowledge: The relationship between caring and knowing. *Teaching and Teacher Education*, 11, 611–625.
Woods, P. (1979). *The divided school.* London: Routledge & Kegan Paul.

Woods, P. (1990). *Teacher skills and strategies*. Lewes: Falmer Press.

Woods, P. (1992). Symbolic interactionism. In M. LeCompte, M. Millroy & J. Preissle (Eds.), *The handbook of qualitative research in education* (pp. 337–404). San Diego, CA: Harcourt Brace & Company.

Zeichner, K. M. (1983). Alternative paradigms of teacher education. *Journal of Teacher Education, 34*(3), 3–9.

Zeichner, K. M. (1994). Resarch on teacher thinking and different views of reflective practice in teaching and teacher education. In I. Carlgren, G. Handal & S. Vaage (Eds.), *Teachers' minds and actions: Research on teachers' thinking and practice* (pp. 9–27). London: The Falmer Press.

Zeichner, K. M., & Liston, D. (1987). Teaching student teachers to reflect. *Harvard Educational Review, 57*(1), 1–22.

Zeichner, K., & Liston, D. (1990). Traditions of reform in U.S. teacher education. *Journal of Teacher Education, 41*(2), 3–20.

CHAPTER 28

TEACHER EDUCATION THAT MAKES A DIFFERENCE: DEVELOPING FOUNDATIONAL PRINCIPLES OF PRACTICE ☆

John Loughran, Fred A. J. Korthagen and Tom Russell

ABSTRACT

Teacher education has long been criticized for having little apparent impact on practice. Despite the fact that the teacher education literature is replete with examples of alternative or restructured programs designed to better align teacher education practices with the anticipated demands and expectations of school teaching, principles of practice seem strangely absent. Principles of practice for teacher education programs must be at the heart of any attempt to construct a meaningful and relevant program that might realistically respond to the expectations, needs, and practices of student teachers. In this chapter, the authors develop a set

☆An early version of this research was published in 2006 in *Teaching and Teacher Education*, Volume 22, Issue 8. This chapter was first published in 2008 in *Imagining a Renaissance in Teacher Education* (edited by C. Craig & L. Deterchin). Reprinted with permission from the publisher, Rowman & Littlefield.

From Teacher Thinking to Teachers and Teaching: The Evolution of a Research Community
Advances in Research on Teaching, Volume 19, 597–613
Copyright © 2013 by Emerald Group Publishing Limited
All rights of reproduction in any form reserved
ISSN: 1479-3687/doi:10.1108/S1479-3687(2013)0000019031

of foundational principles based on teacher education programs in Australia, Canada, and the Netherlands, in order to initiate a renaissance of teacher education based on fundamental principles to guide the development of responsive teacher education programs that genuinely make a difference.

Keywords: Preservice teacher education; teacher education curriculum; teacher effectiveness; teaching effectiveness; teaching practice; evidenced-based practice

Claims that traditional teacher preparation programs do not adequately prepare beginning teachers for teaching have long been familiar in the research literature, as are calls for change (Lanier & Little, 1986). Responding productively has been difficult, not least because teacher educators themselves have had little voice in the literature in comparison to university researchers, law makers, and policy analysts (Fenstermacher, 1997). Consider how difficult it must be to determine how to respond constructively and coherently to issues as broad and complex as the perceived mismatch between teacher preparation and the reality of schools (Barone, Berliner, Blanchard, Casanova, & McGowan, 1996; Sandlin, Young, & Karge, 1992), the fragmented nature of teacher preparation programs (Bullough & Gitlin, 2001), overreliance on theory transfer through lectures despite obvious limitations and inadequacies (Ben-Peretz, 1995; Carlson, 1999; Clandinin, 1995), the persistence of teacher education practices that are generally counter-productive to teacher learning (Wideen, Mayer-Smith, & Moon, 1998), and traditionally trained teachers becoming teachers who teach in a traditional manner (Stofflett & Stoddart, 1994).

For many teacher educators, these challenges are very real in their daily work. Recognizing and acknowledging the difficulties is one thing, but responding is quite another; many of the authors noted above hoped to create an agenda for change within the community of teacher educators of which they themselves were members. As the report by Cochran-Smith and Zeichner (2005) makes clear, part of the problem involves the complex methodological issues associated with trying to establish an empirical basis for effective teacher education. We need a serious rethinking of the nature of teaching about teaching and that is encapsulated in views about and approaches to a pedagogy of teacher education (Korthagen, 2001; Loughran, 2006; Russell & Loughran, 2007).

With the emergence of self-study of teacher education practices (Hamilton, Pinnegar, Russell, Loughran, & LaBoskey, 1998; Kosnick, Beck, Freese, & Samaras, 2006; Loughran, Hamilton, LaBoskey, & Russell, 2004; Samaras,

2006), a productive avenue for such rethinking has become available. Self-study of teacher education practices has allowed teacher educators to begin to demonstrate their individual responses to the dilemmas, issues, and concerns of teacher education by highlighting in detail the complex nature of teaching and learning about teaching that is rarely apparent to those not involved on a day-to-day basis. A growing range of self-study reports illustrate how teacher educators have been working to address these concerns in their own practice, their programs, and their institutions (Loughran, 2005).

The field of self-study represents one positive way of beginning to create more coherent, meaningful, and applicable responses to the vagaries and contradictions of teacher preparation and has led to new ways of teacher educators beginning to share their attempts at developing a pedagogy of teacher education. However, without a strong foundation from which to build a pedagogy of teacher education, the deeper understandings of practice necessary to achieve genuine educational change may still not be fully grasped. To better capture the opportunities created through the research outcomes of self-study and other teacher education research, we propose seven foundational principles that can improve the quality of teacher education practices, programs, and structures.

A BASIS FOR PRINCIPLES

Teacher education programs are embedded in institutional contexts that are important in shaping not only what happens, but also why and how. In the three institutional contexts through which our understanding of principles has emerged (Monash University in Australia, IVLOS in The Netherlands, and Queen's University in Canada), we conceptualized our teacher education programs as case studies. The three cases from three different continents were interrogated with the question: *What central principles are apparent that are intended to respond to the expectations, needs, and practices of teacher educators and student teachers?*

As this research question suggests, our attempt to see beyond specific contexts is one way of creating possibilities for generalizing across the three programs in ways that allow our research efforts to speak to one another in meaningful ways. The three programs lend themselves to comparison because each has had an end-on model (postgraduate teacher preparation) for a considerable period of time, originally with the common organizational features of curriculum method subjects, educational foundational subjects, and school teaching practicum.

Each of the programs has been extensively researched (Brouwer & Korthagen, 2005; Hermans, Créton, & Korthagen, 1993; Kessels & Korthagen, 1996; Koetsier & Wubbels, 1995; Koetsier, Wubbels, & Korthagen, 1997; Korthagen, 1985; Korthagen & Kessels, 1999; Korthagen & Russell, 1995; Korthagen, Kessels, Koster, Lagerwerf, & Wubbels, 2001; Loughran, 1996, 1997, 2002; Loughran & Russell, 1997; Northfield & Gunstone, 1983, 1997; Russell, 1995, 2002; Upitis, 2000; Vedder, 1984; Vedder & Bannink, 1987) and our meta-analysis of these research studies combined with analysis of a variety of program documents generated a strong base from which to extract underlying program features that might lead to principles of practice. There were three criteria for constructing a principle:

1. On the basis of the materials under study, it was evident that the staff of the teacher education program considered the principle to be fundamental, in the sense that without this principle the program would lose its essential nature.
2. The principle could not be considered as self-evident. The principle should differentiate the approach followed in the program from several others in the world.
3. The principle could be recognized in many practices throughout the entire program.

It is not the intention of this chapter to fully outline the methodology and individual program features and contexts from which the underlying principles were derived (see Korthagen, Loughran, & Russell, 2006). The principles presented here were developed by focusing on paradigmatic examples (Freudenthal, 1978) of good practice. One feature that gave direction to our method was the notion of *naturalistic generalizability* (Stake & Trumbull, 1982), which means that an aim of our study was to support the transfer of our findings to other contexts, such that they might also contribute to *catalytic validity*, that is, the degree to which the research can lead to transformations of practice (Lather, 1991).

ARTICULATING PRINCIPLES OF PRACTICE FOR TEACHER EDUCATION

From our analyses of the three cases we derived seven principles of student teacher learning and program change that we consider fundamental and foundational to teacher education practices. Central to these principles is the importance of creating real opportunities for learning from experience, for student teachers and teacher educators alike. We briefly outline each of the principles below and conclude the chapter with a discussion of several implications of applying such principles in teacher education more generally.

Learning about Teaching Involves Continuously Conflicting and Competing Demands

Teacher education is inevitably inadequate (Northfield & Gunstone, 1997) and cannot fully prepare teachers for their entire careers. In accord with views of professional learning, teacher education needs to focus explicitly on encouraging participants to learn through experience in ways that help them build their professional knowledge. In so doing, there is a need to recognize and respond to a range of conflicting and competing demands. Those learning to teach inevitably struggle with the need to be both learners of learning and learners of teaching at the same time. What students experience as learners of teaching can dramatically shape their understanding of practice. Teacher education practices must continually make explicit the dual roles of learning about learning and learning about teaching so that both perspectives are always at the forefront of students' analysis of their experiences.

As Lortie (1975) pointed out, the *apprenticeship of observation* has a lasting impact on students' understanding of practice and certainly maintains a strong influence on students' learning about teaching. This is hardly surprising for students rarely have access to the pedagogical reasoning of their teachers and what they construct as images of teaching unwittingly carries little about the underlying thinking that shapes the teaching and learning experienced. Hence teaching will appear simple and straightforward rather than driven by a multitude of questions, choices, and decisions that collectively make teaching highly problematic. Because of the competing demands of learning about learning and learning about teaching, the apprenticeship of observation can easily "spill over" into teacher education (as Goodlad [1990] suggested) and mask the complexity of "good practice."

Creating opportunities for student teachers to recognize and respond to the competing demands in their learning to teach is one way of helping them to learn in meaningful ways through experience and to see that the better they manage these competing demands, the more likely they are to develop richer understandings of the complex nature of teaching and learning.

Learning about Teaching Requires a View of Knowledge as a
Subject to be Created Rather Than as a Created Subject

Teaching as telling has had a lasting influence on both teachers and teacher educators and partly explains the perceived "unhelpfulness" linked to approaches to teaching about teaching in many schools of education (Russell, 1999). The practice of teaching as telling, whether performed intentionally or not, also detracts from and discounts the significance of experience in learning. An outcome of teaching as telling is that theory is imparted to student teachers in an "unquestioned manner," generally ignoring issues about the nature of theory and in the way it is developed in teachers.

Like Freudenthal (1978), we see knowledge as a subject to be created by learners themselves which can be facilitated through a process of guided reinvention. This means that theory development as a consequence of student teachers' learning from their own situations has greater individual significance. Also, developing personal knowledge offers a vision for ongoing professional growth and autonomy in practice. One way that this approach to knowledge creation can be encouraged in teacher education is through the one-to-one (Korthagen et al., 2001) which gives student teachers opportunities to learn on the basis of their own experiences and the concerns they develop through such experiences. They learn not so much by being taught by their teacher educators but by structured reflection on their experiences and discussions with peers. Thus student teachers begin to create their own professional knowledge as their learning through experience is overtly supported and valued, but not made complicated through issues such as maintaining order in the classroom.

Learning about Teaching Requires a Shift in Focus from
the Curriculum to the Learner

Teacher educators teach teaching. If student teachers are to "see into" teaching in sophisticated ways and to be better informed about the nature of practice, then they need to better understand the dynamics of a teaching situation – what is involved in planning the teaching, doing the teaching, and reflecting on the teaching. One way of doing this is through student teachers experiencing teaching practice being both constructed and deconstructed so that their learning about teaching is purposefully linked to their experiences of learning and teaching (Segall, 2002).

Principle 3 builds on principle 2 and challenges the assumption in teacher education that the university-based components concentrate almost solely on the theoretical underpinnings of teaching while the school practicum is the site in which teaching is practiced. When we teach teaching there is a constant need to "not tell the class" about an issue but to make the issue a part of the teaching episode itself. It is not hard to see how "teaching as telling" can create major problems in terms of mixed messages about teaching and learning that can detract from developing deeper under-standings of practice. This issue establishes why it is so important to teach the students, not the curriculum, and how crucial it is to link theory and practice through experience. The learning of student teachers is obviously considerably more meaningful when it is *embedded in their experiences* of learning to teach. Teacher educators need to be actively creating situations where this can occur as a natural part of teacher preparation.

Learning about Teaching is Enhanced through (Student) Teacher Research

Principles 2 and 3 create an impetus for principle 4, which depends on challenging traditional practices and trusting that student teachers can not only learn about practice through their own experiences, but also do so by researching their own practice. Just as teacher research and practitioner inquiry (Cochran-Smith & Lytle, 1990, 2004; Lytle & Cochran-Smith, 1991; Zeichner & Noffke, 2001) have been important in encouraging teachers to learn about, and better value, their knowledge of practice, so they are important in learning about teaching.

By embarking on formalized processes in researching practice, student teachers are able to better grasp issues surrounding the perceived distinctions between theory and practice that so often confront them in their emerging roles as beginning teachers. In one sense, by adopting a student teacher as researcher stance, there is the overt expectation that student teachers will actively seek out, and therefore more wholeheartedly explore, problems of practice that are rooted in their needs, their concerns, and their expectations for their own professional learning. By actively researching their own practice, they are more likely to come to "see into" pedagogic situations differently and reframe (Schön, 1983) their practice.

Trusting student teachers to adopt a student-teacher-as-researcher stance is one way of giving permission for them to place more faith in the development of the authority of their own experiences (Munby & Russell, 1994), which contrasts starkly with teacher educators or school practicum supervisors telling them what their problems are, how to resolve them, and what their practice should look like. Establishing a student-teacher-as-researcher expectation in teacher education is important for creating a sense of ownership in learning about teaching that goes beyond the technical aspects of practice alone. When student teachers purposefully collect and analyze data from their own experiences, the outcomes are twofold. First, the individual learning for the student-teacher-researcher is often powerful in its own right. Second, that which they choose to document and share with their peers is more likely to influence their colleagues' learning because of the added value of identifying with similar issues, concerns, and practices. Being in a similar situation makes a major difference to the nature of the learning that results. Student teachers learning by researching their own practice is a crucial component in learning about teaching and offers an explicit way to counterbalance the tendency in traditional teacher education programs to accentuate the gap between research-based knowledge and practice.

Learning about Teaching Requires an Emphasis on those Learning to Teach Working Closely with Their Peers

Research literature draws attention to the importance of collegiality as a crucial factor in shaping teachers' understandings of classroom practice (Hagger, Burn, & McIntyre, 1993). Putnam and Borko (1997) capture the essence of the need for a focus on collegiality.

> Just as students need to learn new ways of reasoning, communicating, and thinking, and to acquire dispositions of inquiry and sense-making through their participation in classroom discourse communities, teachers need to construct their complex new roles and ways of thinking about their teaching practice within the context of supportive learning communities. (p. 1247)

Learning about teaching is enhanced by explicitly collaborative and collegial approaches to "unpacking" teaching and learning. The school practicum is clearly a time when this may be most advantageous, but such an approach need not be limited to school teaching experience. One aspect of collaboration that can accentuate learning about practice involves the way that standing back from experience and looking for patterns in accounts of teaching experience can be used as a catalyst for learning from and through experience.

By working closely with their peers, student teachers have direct access to others' perspectives on the process of learning to teach. This matters because almost everywhere else they turn, they see teaching as an individual and isolated process. They rarely see two teachers at work in the same room at the same time, yet they are well aware that learning is enhanced through sharing and collaboration. Hence learning about teaching can create a "clash of identities" as the expectations of individualism and isolation confront the experiences of collaboration and collegiality. Creating serious prospects for learning about teaching to be viewed as "optimal" through collaboration is then a platform from which views of learning about teaching more generally might be challenged to enhance approaches to articulating professional knowledge of practice.

Peer-supported learning (Tigchelaar & Melief, 2000) is a mechanism for student teachers to not only structure their own reflection, but also to help each other reflect. Through the process of learning how to support each other's reflection, student teachers can gain insights into their own practices and into the process of reflection. When student teachers develop their skills of peer-supported learning, benefits can extend to their guidance of their own students in school. This fifth principle shifts the emphasis in learning to teach from the traditional reliance on *vertical* relationships to endorsing and valuing *horizontal* relationships (Galesloot, Koetsier, & Wubbels, 1997).

Learning about Teaching Requires Meaningful Relationships between Schools, Universities, and Student Teachers

Northfield and Gunstone (1997) remind us that "teacher educators should maintain close connections with schools and the teaching profession" (p. 49). Although it is difficult to disagree with this view, the worlds of school and university can be very different and distinct places. Yet in teacher education, each relies heavily on the other for support, and cooperation is crucial. One major difference between the work of school teachers and the work of teacher educators can complicate understandings and expectations of each institution. Teachers are mainly concerned with the intricacies of *teaching itself*, which is both similar to and different from *teaching about teaching*, and it can be argued that these similarities and differences are not always fully grasped by both and can play out in unusual ways in student teachers' learning about teaching.

The type of close cooperation necessary to support quality learning about teaching requires recognition of three different perspectives: (a) the individual learning to teach, (b) the teacher in the school setting, and (c) the teacher educator in the university setting. Each requires careful consideration in constructing the relationships central to teacher education programming. Despite their naturally different perspectives, experienced teachers in schools and teacher educators in universities will have occasions to discuss the development and progress of the student teachers for whom they are responsible, yet it would seldom be the case that conversations about the experiences and expectations of learning to teach would involve all three together. Unfortunately, both experienced teachers and teacher educators tend to respond to the need for school–university relationships as being driven by their own program needs and concerns and student teachers' voices are strangely mute.

Student teachers' perspectives need to be sought actively and responded to positively in building up the relationships so crucial to quality in learning to teach (Goodlad, 1990). Cook-Sather (2002) captures this point and builds a strong link to principle 5 when she argues that student teachers' voices must be attended to in order to provoke a "conceptualization of teaching, learning, and the ways we study them as more collaborative processes" (p. 3). We maintain that the issues inherent in learning about teaching cannot be understood appropriately if a student teacher perspective is not adequately represented by student teachers themselves.

> Close cooperation is needed, not only in the sense of school-university partnerships, but also in three-way cooperation among teachers in schools, teacher educators in universities, and those who are learning to teach. While school-university cooperation is often seen as the broad goal, it is easy to overlook the teacher candidate who is passing through the program structure en route to a classroom of her or his own. Ironically, if we were to view the temporarily present teacher candidate as the one with the most to gain from closer cooperation, that goal might be much more readily achieved. The problems that teacher education has faced for a long time, may be well due to the fact that this sixth principle has only recently been taken seriously in the organization of teacher education programs. (Korthagen et al., 2006, p. 1035)

Learning about Teaching is Enhanced when the Teaching and Learning Approaches Advocated in the Program are Modeled by the Teacher Educators in Their Own Practice

Segall's (2002) analysis of the experiences of social studies methods course students at a Canadian university provides compelling evidence of the importance of modeling in teacher education. Segall highlighted the importance of breaking away from a technical–rational approach to teaching about teaching based on the "how to," the "what works," and the mastering of the "best" teaching methods (Aronowitz & Giroux, 1985, cited in Segall, 2002, p. 13). What Segall made abundantly clear was that for student teachers' deeply held views and assumptions about teaching to be challenged adequately, and for them to consider alternative approaches and be able to contextualize theory within practice and practice within theory, modeling pedagogical episodes that foster such challenges is crucial. Such modeling is not common in teacher education (Lunenberg, Korthagen, & Swennen, 2007). In the absence of such challenges, it seems unrealistic to expect a transformation of teaching practices in schools.

It is not unusual to hear stories about teacher educators who advocate innovative practices to their student teachers but fail to model those innovative practices. Russell (1999) boldly questions this situation by asserting that "universities generally, and university-based teacher educators particularly, have no right to recommend to teachers any teaching practices that they have not themselves used successfully at the university" (p. 220).

Student teachers need opportunities to experience and learn about how experienced teachers and teacher educators take risks and develop new teaching approaches in their own practice as a fundamental form of modeling the development of pedagogical understanding: "Making the pedagogical reasoning for practice clear, explicit, and understandable for student teachers is an important aspect of modeling teaching in teacher education" (Korthagen et al., 2006, p. 1036). However, although modeling offers ways of looking into practice, it should not be confused with attempts to simply demonstrate particular teaching procedures. Everything done in teacher education models something – the intended and the unintended.

> [Modeling needs to be] conceptualized as embracing the possibilities for critique and interrogation in learning about teaching experiences, no matter how they arise; be they planned or unplanned. Modeling of this form means that teaching itself is continually being questioned so that both the subtleties and complexities of practice might be viewed and reviewed in order to shed light on pedagogical reasoning, thoughts and actions. This view of modeling carries with it the hope that as students of teaching see their teacher educators teach in this way that they will be encouraged to risk doing the same. As a consequence, there is a greater likelihood that the holistic, nonlinear and personal nature of teaching might be better illuminated while at the same time the notion that knowledge of practice must inevitably be tacit may be challenged. (Loughran, 2006, pp. 39–40; see also Lunenberg et al., 2007)

This approach to modeling offers student teachers a variety of ways of seeing for themselves the complexity of teaching while capturing the essence of teaching as a problematic activity, something that needs to be experienced to be understood and something that goes hand in hand with the confidence necessary to manage the uncertainty of practice.

CONCLUSION: PRINCIPLES WORKING TOGETHER

In their exhaustive analysis of North American research on the effectiveness of teacher education, Cochran-Smith and Zeichner (2005) find no clear evidence that certain approaches in teacher education are more effective than others. However, Brouwer and Korthagen (2005) offer an alternative view of that conclusion:

> [Our research results] present empirical evidence that more specific principles guiding the practices within a program may lead to clear and positive outcomes in the graduates of such a program. This suggests an urgent need for identifying such principles, especially principles that support the link between experience and theory in ways that are responsive to the expectations, needs and practices of teacher educators and student teachers.

The seven principles we offer in this chapter resonate in many ways with teacher education programs across the globe. We believe that the principles fit together in such a way that their sum matters more than the individual principles alone and that, in considering the development of teacher education from a principled base, some of the concerns and issues raised by Cochran-Smith and Zeichner (2005) can be addressed.

The principles proposed in this chapter have a necessary interconnection that is illustrated in Fig. 1. The principles can be grouped into three elements that we see as fundamental to teacher education: (a) views of knowledge and learning that direct the practices of the teacher educators, (b) program structures and specific practices, and (c) the quality of staff and organization.

This perspective on the seven principles acknowledges that simply changing a principle in one component without simultaneously addressing the other components reduces the power and effectiveness of the principles as a whole.

> For example, if teacher educators make the important step from building on *episteme* to developing *phronesis*, as when they start to see knowledge about teaching as a subject to be created instead of an already created subject (principle 2), this will require helping student teachers to become a strong community of learners in which they work and learn closely together (principle 5). This in turn has consequences for the way teaching practices are organized, which points towards the importance of principle 6. In other words, we believe it is the coherence across the three components ... that will make a difference. (Korthagen et al., 2006, p. 1037)

In working from this position about the principles and the manner in which they relate to one another, it becomes clear that program change in teacher education must be viewed as an in-depth process that does not happen in a meaningful way overnight. As Russell (1999) reminds us, "it is

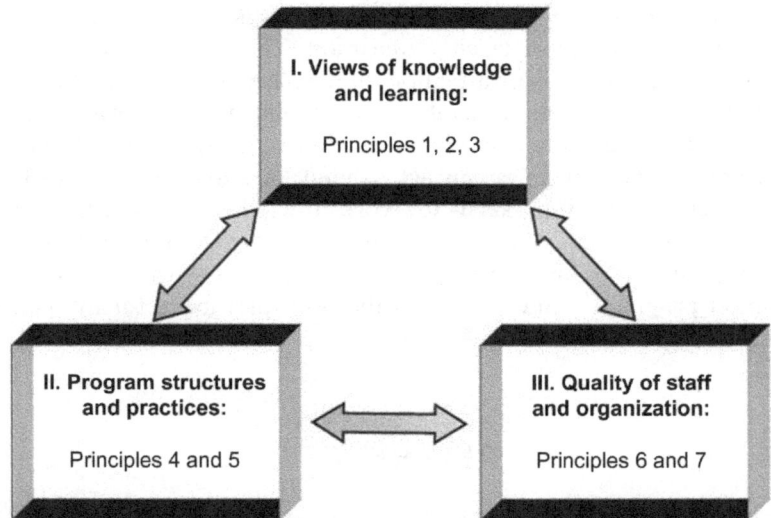

Fig. 1. Clustering Seven Principles into Elements of Programs and Program Change.

far too easy to propose early changes that fail to give the innovation a clear chance" (p. 221). In contrast, considerable progress was made in the 15-year approach to the bridging the gap between theory and practice played out in the IVLOS program in The Netherlands (see Brouwer & Korthagen, 2005; Korthagen & Kessels, 1999).

For program structures and practices to change, both how we think about teacher education and how we practice teacher education must change. Without such changes, the structures may look different and the way the constituent parts of teacher education are put together may be new, but the essence of student teachers' experiences of teaching and learning about teaching will still be traditional. Change is a long-term process, and at the heart of such change is the development of a pedagogy of teacher education driven by and constructed as a result of teacher educators accepting more responsibility for the nature of the total teacher education program experience.

The three aspects of Fig. 1 are often viewed in isolation. This diminishes the likelihood that teacher education programs and practices can be genuinely responsive to the needs, concerns, and expectations of those learning to teach. Considering change in the holistic manner suggested by the seven principles and their interrelationships is one way of more fully embracing a pedagogy of teacher education. The principles we offer here indicate one way of focusing attention on the place of experience in learning about teaching. The seven principles also provide a way of considering what a common language for the development of a pedagogy of teacher education might entail. The principles can act as guidelines and possibilities for all those teacher educators keen to work toward reconstructing teacher education from within. For teacher educators, it may be helpful to reflect on two questions: "How can I work with the principles in my own teacher education program?" and "What do the principles mean for my personal teacher education practices?"

REFERENCES

Aronowitz, S., & Giroux, H. (1985). *Education under siege: The conservative, liberal, and radical debate over schooling.* South Hadley, MA: Bergin & Garvey.

Barone, T., Berliner, D. C., Blanchard, J., Casanova, U., & McGowan, T. (1996). A future for teacher education. In J. Sikula, T. Buttery & E. Guyton (Eds.), *Handbook of research on teacher education* (2nd ed., pp. 1108–1149). New York, NY: Macmillan.

Ben-Peretz, M. (1995). Curriculum of teacher education programs. In L. W. Anderson (Ed.), *International encyclopedia of teaching and teacher education* (pp. 543–547). Oxford, UK: Elsevier Science.

Brouwer, N., & Korthagen, F. (2005). Can teacher education make a difference? *American Educational Research Journal, 42*(1), 153–224.

Bullough Jr., R. V. ,& Gitlin, A. (2001). *Becoming a student of teaching: Linking knowledge production and practice* (2nd ed.). London: RoutledgeFalmer.

Carlson, H. L. (1999). From practice to theory: A social constructivist approach to teacher education. *Teachers and Teaching: Theory and Practice, 5*(2), 203–218.

Clandinin, D. J. (1995). Still learning to teach. In T. Russell & F. Korthagen (Eds.), *Teachers who teach teachers* (pp. 25–31). London: Falmer Press.

Cochran-Smith, M., & Lytle, S. (1990). Research on teaching and teacher research: The issues that divide. *Educational Researcher, 19*(2), 2–11.

Cochran-Smith, M., & Lytle, S. (2004). Practitioner inquiry, knowledge, and university culture. In J. J. Loughran, M. L. Hamilton, V. K. LaBoskey & T. Russell (Eds.), *International handbook of self-study of teaching and teacher education practices* (Vol. 1, pp. 601–649). Dordrecht, The Netherlands: Kluwer Academic Press.

Cochran-Smith, M., & Zeichner, K. M. (Eds.). (2005). *Studying teacher education: The report of the AERA panel on research and teacher education.* Mahwah, NJ: Lawrence Erlbaum.

Cook-Sather, A. (2002). Authorizing students' perspectives: Toward trust, dialogue, and change in education. *Educational Researcher, 31*(4), 3–14.

Fenstermacher, G. D. (1997). Foreword. In J. Loughran & T. Russell (Eds.), *Teaching about teaching: Purpose, passion and pedagogy in teacher education* (pp. viii–xiii). London: Falmer Press.

Freudenthal, H. (1978). *Weeding and sowing: Preface to a science of mathematical education.* Dordrecht, The Netherlands: Reidel.

Galesloot, L. J., Koetsier, C. P., & Wubbels, Th. (1997). Handelingsaspecten bij wederzijds leren van ervaren docenten [*Aspects of acting in reciprocal learning of experienced teachers*]. *Pedagogische Studiën, 74,* 249–260.

Goodlad, J. I. (1990). *Teachers for our nation's schools.* San Francisco, CA: Jossey-Bass.

Hagger, H., Burn, K., & McIntyre, D. (1993). *The school mentor handbook.* London: Kogan Page.

Hamilton, M. L., Pinnegar, S., Russell, T., Loughran, J., & LaBoskey, V. (Eds.). (1998). *Reconceptualizing teaching practice: Self-study in teacher education.* London: Falmer Press.

Hermans, J. J., Créton, H. A., & Korthagen, F. A. J. (1993). Reducing the gap between theory and practice in teacher education. In J. T. Voorbach (Ed.), *Teacher education 9, Research and developments on teacher education in the Netherlands* (pp. 111–120). De Lier, The Netherlands: Academisch Boeken Centrum.

Kessels, J. P. A. M., & Korthagen, F. A. (1996). The relationship between theory and practice: Back to the classics. *Educational Researcher, 25*(3), 17–22.

Koetsier, C. P., & Wubbels, T. (1995). Bridging the gap between teacher training and teacher induction. *Journal of Education for Teaching, 21*(3), 333–345.

Koetsier, C. P., Wubbels, T., & Korthagen, F. A. J. (1997). Learning from practice: The case of a Dutch post-graduate teacher education programme. In M. I. Fuller & A. J. Rosie (Eds.), *Teacher education and school partnerships* (pp. 113–132). New York, NY: Edwin Mellen Press.

Korthagen, F. A. J. (1985). Reflective teaching and preservice teacher education in the Netherlands. *Journal of Teacher Education, 36*(5), 11–15.

Korthagen, F. A. J. (2001). Building a realistic teacher education program. In F. A. J. Korthagen, with, J. Kessels, B. Koster, B. Langerwarf, & T. Wubbels (Eds.), *Linking practice and theory: The pedagogy of realistic teacher education* (pp. 69-87). Mahwah, NJ: Lawrence Erlbaum Associates.

Korthagen, F. A. J., & Kessels, J. P. A. M. (1999). Linking theory and practice: Changing the pedagogy of teacher education. *Educational Researcher, 28*(4), 4–17.

Korthagen, F. A. J., Kessels, J., Koster, B., Lagerwerf, B., & Wubbels, T. (2001). *Linking practice and theory: The pedagogy of realistic teacher education.* Mahwah, NJ: Lawrence Erlbaum Associates.

Korthagen, F. A. J., Loughran, J. J., & Russell, T. (2006). Developing fundamental principles for teacher education programs and practices. *Teaching and Teacher Education, 22*(8), 1020–1041.

Korthagen, F., & Russell, T. (1995). Teachers who teach teachers: Some final considerations. In T. Russell & F. Korthagen (Eds.), *Teachers who teach teachers: Reflections on teacher education* (pp. 187–192). London: Falmer Press.

Kosnick, C., Beck, C., Freese, A., & Samaras, A. (Eds.). (2006). *Making a difference in teacher education through self-study: Studies of personal, professional, and program renewal.* Dordrecht, The Netherlands: Springer.

Lanier, J., & Little, J. (1986). Research on teacher education. In M. Wittrock (Ed.), *Handbook of research on teaching* (3rd ed., pp. 527–569). New York, NY: Macmillan.

Lather, P. (1991). *Getting smart: Feminist research and pedagogy within the postmodern.* New York, NY: Routledge.

Lortie, D. C. (1975). *Schoolteacher*. Chicago, IL: University of Chicago Press.

Loughran, J. (1996). *Developing reflective practice: Learning about teaching and learning through modeling*. London: Falmer Press.

Loughran, J. (1997). Teaching about teaching: Principles and practice. In J. Loughran & T. Russell (Eds.), *Teaching about teaching: Purpose, passion and pedagogy in teacher education* (pp. 57–69). London: Falmer Press.

Loughran, J. (2002). Effective reflective practice: In search of meaning in learning about teaching. *Journal of Teacher Education, 53*, 33–43.

Loughran, J. J. (2005). Knowledge construction and learning to teach about teaching. In D. Beijaard, P. C. Meijer, G. Morine-Dershimer & H. Tillema (Eds.), *New directions in teachers' working and learning environment* (pp. 27–41). Dordrecht, The Netherlands: Springer.

Loughran, J. J. (2006). *Developing a pedagogy of teacher education: Understanding teaching and learning about teaching*. London: Routledge.

Loughran, J. J., Hamilton, M. L., LaBoskey, V. K., & Russell, T. (Eds.). (2004). *International handbook of self-study of teaching and teacher education practices*. Dordrecht, The Netherlands: Kluwer Academic Publishers.

Loughran, J., & Russell, T. (Eds.). (1997). *Purpose, passion and pedagogy in teacher education*. London: Falmer Press.

Lunenberg, M., Korthagen, F., & Swennen, A. (2007). The teacher educator as a role model. *Teaching and Teacher Education, 23*(5), 586–601.

Lytle, S., & Cochran-Smith, M. (1991). Teacher research as a way of knowing. *Harvard Educational Review, 62*(4), 447–474.

Munby, H., & Russell, T. (1994). The authority of experience in learning to teach: Messages from a physics method class. *Journal of Teacher Education, 4*(2), 86–95.

Northfield, J. R., & Gunstone, R. F. (1983). Research on alternative frameworks: Implications for science teacher education. *Research in Science Education, 13*, 185–192.

Northfield, J. R., & Gunstone, R. F. (1997). Teacher education as a process of developing teacher knowledge. In J. Loughran & T. Russell (Eds.), *Teaching about teaching: Purpose, passion and pedagogy in teacher education* (pp. 48–56). London: Falmer Press.

Putnam, R. T., & Borko, H. (1997). Teacher learning: Implications of new views of cognition. In B. J. Biddle, T. L. Good & I. F. Goodson (Eds.), *International handbook of teachers and teaching* (pp. 1223–1296). Dordrecht, The Netherlands: Kluwer Academic Publishers.

Russell, T. (1995). Returning to the physics classroom to re-think how one learns to teach physics. In T. Russell & F. Korthagen (Eds.), *Teachers who teach teachers* (pp. 95–109). London: Falmer Press.

Russell, T. (1999). The challenge of change in teaching and teacher education. In J. R. Baird (Ed.), *Reflecting, teaching, learning: Perspectives on educational improvement* (pp. 219–238). Cheltenham: Hawker Brownlow Education.

Russell, T. (2002). Guiding new teachers' learning from classroom to experience: Self-study of the faculty liaison role. In J. Loughran & T. Russell (Eds.), *Improving teacher education practices through self-study* (pp. 73–87). London: RoutledgeFalmer.

Russell, T., & Loughran, J. (Eds.). (2007). *Enacting a pedagogy of teacher education: Values, relationships and practices*. London: Routledge.

Samaras, A. (2006). *Self-study of teaching practices*. New York, NY: Peter Lang.

Sandlin, R. A., Young, B. L., & Karge, B. D. (1992). Regularly and alternatively credentialed beginning teachers: Comparison and contrast of their development. *Action in Teacher Education, 14*(4), 16–23.

Schön, D. A. (1983). *The reflective practitioner: How professionals think in action.* New York, NY: Basic Books.

Segall, A. (2002). *Disturbing practice: Reading teacher education as text.* New York, NY: Peter Lang.

Stake, R. E., & Trumbull, D. (1982). Naturalistic generalizations. *Review Journal of Philosophy and Social Science, 7*(1/2), 1–12.

Stofflett, R. T., & Stoddart, T. (1994). The ability to understand and use conceptual change pedagogy as a function of prior content learning experience. *Journal of Research in Science Teaching, 31,* 31–51.

Tigchelaar, A., & Melief, K. (2000). Peer supported learning for students on paid practice: Student teachers learn to supervise one another. In G. M. Willems, J. H. J. Stakenborg & W. Veugelers (Eds.), *Trends in Dutch teacher education* (pp. 185–195). Apeldoorn, The Netherlands: Garant.

Upitis, R. (Ed.). (2000). *Who will teach? A case study of teacher education reform.* San Francisco, CA: Caddo Gap Press.

Vedder, J. (1984). *Oriëntatie op het beroep van leraar [Orientation towards the teaching profession].* Lisse, The Netherlands: Swets & Zeitlinger.

Vedder, J., & Bannink, P. (1987). *The development of practical skills and reflection at the beginning of teacher training.* Paper presented at the meeting of the Association of Teacher Education in Europe, Berlin.

Wideen, M., Mayer-Smith, J., & Moon, B. (1998). A critical analysis of the research on learning to teach: Making the case for an ecological perspective on inquiry. *Review of Educational Research, 68*(2), 130–178.

Zeichner, K. M., & Noffke, S. (2001). Practitioner research. In V. Richardson (Ed.), *Handbook of research on teaching* (4th ed., pp. 298–330). Washington, DC: American Educational Research Association.

CHAPTER 29

THE SUSTAINABILITY AND NONSUSTAINABILITY OF A DECADE OF CHANGE AND CONTINUITY IN TEACHER EDUCATION

Michal Zellermayer and Edith Tabak

ABSTRACT

This chapter revolves around a decade of change and continuity in teacher education in one of the largest colleges in Israel. Through the action research method, field work collected over a decade was used to characterize how the particular School of Education transitioned from a craft orientation to a community of practice and then morphed to a collaborative community whose reach is continuing to unfurl. The work provides first-hand insights into the cyclical process of change and the conditions that prompt it. The live exemplar shows both sustainable and nonsustainable practices and how each, in its own way, contributes to "knotworking" within the organization and further fuels change efforts.

Keywords: Change; teacher education; teacher education programs; Israel

From Teacher Thinking to Teachers and Teaching: The Evolution of a Research Community
Advances in Research on Teaching, Volume 19, 615–635
Copyright © 2013 by Emerald Group Publishing Limited
All rights of reproduction in any form reserved
ISSN: 1479-3687/doi:10.1108/S1479-3687(2013)0000019032

This qualitative action research study focuses on a three-phase process in one of the largest teacher-education colleges in Israel. It began with a four-year government-supported experimental project in elementary teacher education and continued with the restructuring of the entire college and the establishment of undergraduate and graduate schools. It picked up again during the construction of a new MTeach program, a collaborative project of the two schools. The purpose of our study is to better understand this process of change. More specifically, it aims

- to use the cyclical action research design in order to retrospectively describe and reflect on the evolutional aspects of the change process; and
- to construct a future oriented theory of change.

THEORETICAL FRAMEWORK

Our conceptualization of the change process that we participated in draws on sustainability theory in education (Fullan, 2005; Hargreaves & Fink, 2005), the notion of Communities of Practice (CoP) (Wenger, 1998) and its criticism (Hughes, Jewson, & Unwin, 2007; Jahreie & Ottesen, 2010), the work of Deleuze and Guattari (1987) and particularly that of Engeström (2005, 2006, 2007, 2009), who distinguishes among Craft, Community of Practice, and Collaborative Community.

Our review of this theoretical work begins with Fullan (2005), who employs constructs of "complexity" and "sustainability" derived from the study of other complex dynamic systems in the analysis of systemic, successive, and longitudinal change in education. Fullan (2005) defines sustainability as "the capacity of a system to engage in the complexities of continuous improvement consistent with deep values of human purpose" (p. ix), while creating horizontal and vertical relationships. It explains real change as a nonhierarchical, horizontal evolution, energized through collaboration and various elements in a system, that creates conditions for self-transformation and learning. It therefore has a vested interest in communities, their daily practices, and their learning processes.

What are the conditions for successful change in educational organizations? Hargreaves and Fink (2005) associate sustainable change with "leadership and improvement [that] preserves and develops *deep learning* for all that spreads and lasts, in ways that do no harm to and indeed create positive benefit for others around us, now and in the future" (p. 17). Sackney and Walker (2006) further posit that sustainable leadership develops the notion of "knowledge ecology," according to which, to know is to participate in a network of relationships among people, material, artifacts, and activities. According to them, sustainable leadership "does not claim to institutionalize new ideas nor attempt to contain or to control knowledge" (Sackney & Walker, 2006, p. 9). Instead, people are encouraged to engage with outside stakeholders, and a partnership implies the use of information from various external sources for the development of new communities of inquiry, reflection and lifelong learning.

To summarize, organizational change theorists note that the world of human activity is increasingly dominated by longitudinal, dialogic relationships of collaboration between multiple agents and emergent activities. Their work reveals that in order to succeed, change agents must recognize the temporality and flexibility of such relationships and accept that organizations are hybrid, weekly bounded, rhizomatic forms of life.

An important counterpart to this theory is Wenger's (1998) work on Communities of Practice and the connection between participation and reification. Recently, however, this work has been under attack by those who perceive Wenger's theory as relatively simplistic. Some perceive it as too benign, avoiding power issues, and neglecting discursive processes of conflict, instability, and power negotiations (Lea, 2005). Others see it as a closed theory with a clear center of gravity, that focuses too heavily on reproductive systems and too little on transformative processes. They also argue that this CoP is invested in people and their membership or lack of membership rather than on semiotic social spaces with no stable boundaries (Gee, 2005).

The most interesting criticism of CoP was that of Yrjo Engeström (2007), who sees a different model of learning emerging, one in which learning is equally inevitable, but largely amorphous. Engeström (2009) promotes the idea of knotworking, whereby "collaboration between the partners is of vital importance yet takes shape without rigid predetermined rules or a fixed central authority" (p. 44). Influenced by the work of Deleuze and Guattari (1987) on the rhizome as a metaphor for nonhierarchical, horizontal structures which form multi-directional connections, Engeström (2007) uses a similar botanical metaphor, the mycorrhizae (the symbiotic association between a fungus and the roots of a plant), to conceptualize knowledge as socially constructed through a process of negotiation in contextualized, collaborative learning environments.

In mycorrhizae-like activities, actors are typically defined by a shared activism which relies on both improvisation and persistence; developing connections in a dynamic and expanding process while retaining a stabilized and durable structure. Through knotworking "the participants disperse outward to pursue their various trails and to expand the scope of the mycorrhizae, but also return and come together in various ways to contribute to the forging of the runaway object" (Engeström, 2009, p. 12).

An important phenomenon in mycorrhizae-like activities is that of runaway objects. Runaway objects can be small and dormant yet highly unpredictable and emancipatory, with the potential to escalate to a global scale of influence and controversy. Because we live in a world in which on a daily basis small events escalate and become global revolutions (for example, the recent events in the Arab world), we believe that it is appropriate for us to use this extremely powerful metaphor to describe the more modest change projects that we led.

The above metaphors enable Engeström to distinguish between three types of organizations: craft, communities of practice for mass production, and collaborative communities with social and peer production. In craft organizations, each individual practitioner is focused on his or her own object or fragment of an object as they develop from novices to masters. They are commonly held together by externally imposed or tradition-based coordination. In mass production, team members who form communities of practice cooperate for the purpose of solving problems. However, the teams, often facilitated by process managers, run into trouble and find their limits when faced with objects which require critical questioning of the division of labor, rules, and boundaries of the team and the wider organization. Like Lave and Wenger's (1991) notion of Legitimate Peripheral Partici-pation (LPP), Engeström too refers to learning as motion that creates movement. In craft organization, the motion creates a movement from periphery to center, while "mass production" is defined by linear movement (typified by project management structures). Engeström compares the forms of movement associated with social and peer production to pulsation and swarming.

An extension of Engeström's work to the field of teacher education (Yamazumi, 2007) that describes school–university partnerships highlights three important concepts enabling the sustainability of agency in these entities: *Boundary crossing* refers to work and learning in which actors step outside their customary domains of authority and expertise to find new ideas and solutions together with other actors; boundary crossing typically entails risks and requires efforts at building a shared language between actors. *Co-configuration* refers to work and learning conducted in distributed multiactor partnerships for building and nurturing a shared complex object that has a long life cycle and requires constant reconstruction. *Negotiated knotworking* refers to partially improvised forms of intense collaboration between partners that are otherwise loosely connected but engage in solving problems and rapidly designing solutions when required by their common object; in knotworking, there is no fixed single center of authority and control.

The focus on social production does not mean that individual agency disappears, rather that the individual faces new challenges in attaining the position of an "agentive subject" (Engeström, 2009). The individual gains authority and agency by becoming recognized in, and supported by, a community. Engeström believes that communities are becoming increasingly open in character with weaker boundaries as a result of people's involvement in multiple actual and virtual communities.

According to sustainability theory, one can only understand change when one is in the double role of participant and observer. Unlike participant observers who are normally expected to stay somewhat detached from the situation that they observe, action researchers maintain a high level of involvement in the situation that they are attempting to change. In order to distance themselves from the situation they are studying, they often resort to theory for interpreting their observations. We found that Engeström's ideas could help us to create a coherent story of the last decade; thus, we adopted his language to describe the changes and transformations that we experienced as members and leaders of the communities that will be described below.

METHODOLOGY

The participants of this study are teacher educators of our college who took part in the different action research cycles. As researchers we were both active participants and observers of the henceforth described situations.

Data were collected during the last 10 years from:

1. Transcripts of audiotapes of conversations that took place during regular weekly faculty meetings.
2. Online conversations among the participants.
3. Interviews with each of the participating teacher educators at the end of each academic year.
4. Reflective diaries written by the researchers.
5. Official documents produced by the Ministry of Education, and reports written by the College to the Ministry's committee for the restructuring of teacher education colleges.

The retrospective data analysis was written on the basis of our experiences as leaders of the change processes that we describe and from the point of view of our present positions as heads of the two largest schools in our college – the Graduate School (Michal) and the Undergraduate School of Education (Edith). It consists of:

1. The identification of the participants' concerns and their sources.
2. The construction of an action research story consisting of three action cycles. Each cycle comprises the classical sequence of *concern, plan, action, and reflection.*
3. Theory grounded understandings gained through dialectical comparison of data and theory.
4. The construction of a practice-based change theory.

THE ACTION RESEARCH STORY

Pre-2001 Craft – Personal Object

In this section, we describe the situation in our college at the onset of the action research, our concerns, and why we decided to start a new teacher education project. We joined the College in the 1990s as part of a system in which lecturers were hired on the basis of their disciplinary specializations by the heads of the relevant departments and felt accountable mainly to them. Teaching was the only thing expected of us and we were accountable only to the department head. In interviews that we conducted for this study, we found out that we were not alone. Yael, a science education specialist, had the same experience:

> Other than N. (the department head) I knew nobody. I came to teach my course and left without even entering the teachers' lounge.

There were no staff meetings, no discussions of teaching, and no thinking about commitment to teacher education, as Gila informed us:

> I did not conceive of myself as a teacher educator. As a psychology specialist, I taught as was done in the psychology department. When students started to tell about their teaching experiences, I would silence them politely. I did not understand how it related to me and why they interrupted my teaching with such anecdotes.

The lecturers were not aware of the context of their teaching and, as a consequence, there was a large gap between the theoretical courses and the practicum, as well as between the lecturers and the teacher educators. The lecturers never visited the cooperating schools and never engaged in professional conversations with the clinical staff. They considered themselves to have higher academic status than the clinical staff. Individual lecturers aimed mainly to advance their own teaching, with no regard for the teaching practicum. A sociology lecturer's reflection on her career at the college bears evidence of this phenomenon as well:

> I have been a staff member of this College for the last 20 years and only this year, upon my retirement, did I visit a cooperating school for the first time. I was overwhelmed by the complexity of the work that is being done there and the important contribution of the student mentors. I had never seen them as my collaborators or even considered their work before.

Nor did the lecturers relate to other courses that their students took at the college or even the demands of the Ministry of Education, and most of them had no interest in research on teacher education. As a result, the students did not find the disciplinary courses relevant to their work in schools and developed a negative attitude toward theory and research. There was a disconnection between theory and practice, between disciplinary knowledge and teacher education, as well as between school teachers and teacher education in the College curriculum.

The students practiced with teachers who were identified by their clinical supervisors as master teachers. These cooperating teachers engaged the students as their assistants. From them, the students learned that practice was mainly instrumental, based on practical recipes and ad hoc solutions to problems that emerged during the practicum, and based on the relationship with a particular cooperating teacher. They often encountered conflicting views about educational theories and teaching methods from their clinical supervisors and cooperating teachers and had to make an impossible choice between them. Reflection was mostly emotional with no effort to construct one's own theory of teaching.

The student teachers' disciplinary knowledge developed as a part of their relationship with particular lecturers in a particular discipline in a small number of specialized courses which often failed to adequately link theory with practice and in which specialized content area knowledge was unconnected to the world of classroom teaching. In addition, preservice teachers were subjected to a variety of theoretical constructs and learning environments that did not relate closely to the classroom practice they experienced in their practicum and to the learning environments that they were expected to construct for their pupils.

To summarize, the following features characterized the craft culture in our college: Individualism – individual faculty members followed their personal aims in teachings; Territorialism – clear distinctions among the disciplines, and between them and teacher education; Hierarchical subordination – subordination of the faculty members to the department heads; Vertical communication – formal authority following hierarchical structure; Oligarchy and tradition – the curriculum and syllabi remained unchanged for many years.

At the beginning of the 21st century, it became apparent that craft culture was no longer satisfactory and that the college curriculum needed to change. In addition, the college suffered from the steadily dwindling number of applicants for the elementary school program as well as from the declining status of the teaching profession in the country.

Cycle 1: Breaking Away and Creating a Community of Practice (2002–2006)

The first phase of the change process was a four-year (2002–2006) government-supported experimental project initiated by the head of the elementary school program, who decided to break away from the program that she managed and to develop an alternative one. She invited the two of us, together with a relatively small number (24) of faculty members who had been studying together for three years, to join the project and work together as a community of practice in order to co-construct an integrated curriculum for elementary teacher education. This community included us, along with faculty members representing the various elementary school disciplines, teacher educators, and clinical supervisors.

The project initiator obtained the support of the College and the Ministry of Education by convincing them that the project was a proactive response to the public concern about schooling, on one hand, and to the new priorities in the government's policy concerning teacher preparation, on the other. Her proposed plan was to construct and experiment with an innovative alternative learning environment for elementary teacher education that would enhance the quality of teaching and learning in the teaching practicum as well as in the college courses, and to generate learning among teacher educators. The proposal for the project focused on five key predetermined principles:

■ The design of a multigenerational professional development program for student-teachers, teachers, and teacher educators, implemented through partnerships between the college and the cooperating schools.

- The creation of an integrated three-year pre-service curriculum.
- Research as an integral part of the program for students and faculty.
- A multitrack orientation, inviting students from three separate divisions – Early Childhood, Elementary School, and Special Education – to study together.
- A technologically rich learning and teaching environment.

During the four years of the project, we formed a fairly well-bounded community of practice with clear boundaries and membership criteria. As a member, it was understood that one was expected to work toward the realization of the aforementioned principles. This commitment on the part of both faculty members and their students resulted in a sense of solidarity among those of us who shared the same concerns about teacher education and the same vision for the future as well as clear boundaries between us and those who were left out. There was a clear sense of elitism.

I (Michal) was invited by the initiator and the coordinator of the project to serve as the professional developer and research facilitator for the other members. It was made clear to me from the start that the team needed my support as well as the time, place, and intellectual capacity to collaboratively inquire into their practice. The coordinator assumed that there was general agreement among the project members about the importance of learning from experience. I introduced them to sociocultural theory and it became their common theoretical framework to discuss the importance of authentic, problem-based social interaction among students and between students and their teachers, and the significance of dissonance and mistakes for transformational learning. Indeed, part of the discussion in the community was devoted to collaborative analysis of data collected during mutual observations of students' field practices. I enjoyed the special status of mentor, facilitator, and model for the rest of the faculty's change from novice researchers toward mastery. At the weekly faculty meetings, much time was devoted to uncovering the participants' epistemological conceptions and educational worldviews. We argued about the essence of knowledge and knowing, and about the essence of teaching and learning. We engaged in discussions about our aim and about what was worth doing; we dealt with moral issues such as which schools are suitable for a student-teacher practicum? Or, who are suitable student-teachers? We compared and contrasted various epistemologies. Issue often emerged during our discussions and we examined them in depth.

The same kind of facilitation was offered by the clinical supervisors to the student teachers as well as to their cooperating teachers in the partnership schools, inviting them to become legitimate peripheral participants in the innovative teacher education process. Instead of assigning individual students to individual master teachers, we sent teams of students to partnership schools in order to participate with the teachers and principal in their efforts to establish professional learning communities. Our purpose was to create a teaching education curriculum whereby the college and the partnership schools would develop a reciprocal relationship. However, this did not work. We now believe that the partnership initiatives were not sustainable because of the disparity in activities between the two sites of activity.

For example, in the college, because of the simultaneity of planning and teaching, one could say that the project was constructed during its implementation. Through reflection and inquiry, we attempted to make adjustments, revise, abandon old strategies and develop new ones that would improve learning for our students, for their students, and for ourselves as teacher educators. Through our work, a fairly large repertoire of practices was created to enable the implementation of each of the above principles. In the schools, the clinical supervisors attempted to reinforce the same kind of collaborative curriculum planning that was based on the big ideas and practices that we developed in the college. Yet the schools resisted being shaped by us.

Another principle that did not materialize was an integrated teacher education curriculum oriented to the needs of diverse populations in Israeli elementary schools that would enable inclusion of children with special needs in regular classrooms. Apparently, this was too big a goal for our project because it depended on the collaboration of faculty members outside the project. At the time, the college consisted of subject-matter oriented departments and age-related divisions, while the special education program had an agenda of its own. Therefore, the concept of curriculum integration met with considerable resistance from members of the college faculty who had not participated in the project. They were worried about the potential reduction of subject-matter content knowledge, about the consensus among the project participants regarding social constructivism, and about the loss of academic freedom for themselves. In addition, the Special Education and Early Childhood divisions were relatively strong in terms of numbers of students and academic level and did not share the hardships that the Elementary School division faced. They were not interested in collaborating with the project in curriculum integration. So our community of practice remained encapsulated within its own boundaries. Although it presented its work publicly in academic circles and to the Ministry of Education, the change process that it started did not affect the rest of the College. These difficulties, which were never critically discussed among the project members, together with the termination of financial support for the project, led the College management to end the project.

A year after the project ended, it was replaced by a more aggressive reorganizational change mandated by the Ministry of Education, according to which the age-related divisions would be replaced by a comprehensive school of education, which would become one of four schools catering to the various populations of students in the college: undergraduate student-teachers, graduate students who were practicing veteran teachers, in-service students, and music education students. I (Michal) am now head of the Graduate School and Edith (the former department head) is head of the undergraduate School of Education (Table 1).

The School of Education configured above is an academic entity comprising a common core of education studies for all its 1,800 teacher education students, as well as practicum age-related cohorts and school discipline specialization departments. Altogether, there are approximately 500 part- and full-time lecturers and 50 clinical supervisors. Among the faculty in this newly configured School of Education are Edith and me. This story of continuity and change will continue with what Edith says, and then return to my (Michal's) telling interspersed with our shared interpretation.

Edith: As head of the new School of Education, my first concern was how to build on the principles that guided the project in the new school. However, while trying to implement and disseminate the main principles of the project within the school of education, I began to hear concerned voices.

Table 1.   The New School of Education.

Specializations & Disciplines / Age-related practicum	Early Childhood	Special Education	Elementary School	High School
Early childhood	X			
Special education		X		
Mathematics			X	X
Biology			X	X
English			X	X
Jewish studies	X			
Arts	X	X		
Literature			X	X
Bible			X	X
Hebrew Language				X

Many of the lecturers and clinical supervisors were afraid that they would be forced to adopt the principles of a project that did not respect them enough to invite them to join in. They were fiercely critical of the project. One said that

> It created an oppressive, noninclusive environment in which an elitist language was developed and clear boundaries separated them [the community of practice] and us, the other teacher educators who were not allowed to participate in the experimental program.

Another critic said that

> The students in the project paid too high a price for the ambitions of the project leaders, too many of them left the project because of its high demands. Although as a result of a very intensive training the students in the project were considered as more skilled and better trained, they felt "outsiders" and the other students in the College didn't consider them part of their social context.

In addition, one of the school's faculty members claimed that

> There is no real evidence of deep learning in the cooperating schools, and most of them are not interested to develop a partnership with a college, because of the elitist language of the project.

Finally, the former members of the project protested that

> The project was initiated by a central authority. The key principles were established a priori and little freedom was given to new participants who joined the project.

Moreover, they felt that practice in the project was based on constantly modeling the authority's mastery, and new practices were not considered legitimate.

In other words, they protested against the unidirectional tutoring by the faculty toward mastery that reflected the transition of the student practicum and the clinical supervisors from marginal to full participation.

It was obvious that new conditions needed to be developed so that the entire faculty of the School of Education could develop their own vision. Unlike the a priori plan with clear guidelines and principles that characterized the project, we, at the new School of Education, set out with a much smaller aim: to develop an inclusive framework in which all staff members could participate in the development of a new culture of teacher education that would answer the various interests and the different purposes of the participants.

Cycle 2: Toward a Collaborative Community

The first stage of the plan included the design of office space for all the heads of the different academic departments in the school that gave each of them privacy, as well as a common meeting room that helped them feel a sense of community. Instead of competitors, they became neighbors. If previously they each had their own personal secretaries, now the secretaries shared an office and each one served all of the academic programs. One provided services for students, another for academic staff, etc. As the heads of the different academic departments became friendly neighbors, they also attended school meetings and the courses for all students in the school. The fifty staff members from all disciplines decided on weekly two-hour meetings for that purpose.

They began by setting up plenary meetings in which student management, a central issue for the new school, became one of the first topics of discussion. Apparently, there were significant differences among faculty members regarding procedures of student counseling and registration. For example the coordinator of the early childhood program said that she was too busy to deal with student counseling. She expected the secretaries to deal with the 300 students in the program, most of whom she did not know personally, while she would be consulted only regarding exceptional students. She was therefore very interested in developing clear and unified procedures that could be handled by the administrative staff so that they could make decisions without her. The coordinator of the special education program, on the other hand, said that she expected to be personally involved in student counseling because of their different individual academic needs. This disagreement was opened for discussion at the weekly meeting where most of the faculty supported the idea that student management required a more flexible, student-tailored kind of procedure.

This was the beginning of a significant change in the relationship between the academic and administrative staff that was characterized by more horizontal communication, which was ongoing and open-ended. Without the interference of the school head, the coordinators of the academic program set up personal, informal meetings with the secretaries to discuss the issue of student management and to begin an on-going relationship with them.

Another task that needed to be dealt with right from the start was integrative curriculum making. The faculty needed to establish guidelines for curriculum planning for the school. Influenced by the experimental project that several of us had participated in prior to the establishment of the school, we suggested focusing on big ideas that would lead the curriculum and would be accepted by the entire faculty. In accordance with our social constructivist philosophy, we suggested a focus on the Zone of Proximal Development (ZPD). Some of the other faculty members asked us to exemplify how this could be implemented in their work, and to center on a particular learning task where this idea would be implemented. After a long discussion, we decided on the topic of scaffolding students' academic writing, and particularly the writing of the final project. This task required identifying a particular research question which emerged from the practicum, reading theoretical material and reflective analysis of data collected during the practicum year.

During the first academic year, the weekly meetings focused on developing understandings and personal interpretations of the ZPD. The staff members read and reflected on their own learning and noted the ways that they applied this idea to their practice. For example, the clinical supervisors said that when the students read their notes they could identify questions that the children had raised that could provide clues to their ZPD. They discussed these questions with their students and helped them plan so that they would respond to the children's needs. In this way, while scaffolding children's work on their school projects, the student teachers felt that that they were actually developing ideas for their own practicum. One clinical supervisor said that through the students' inquiry, she could now hear the children's voice, and this was a significant change for her.

At the end of this first year, when we attempted to summarize what we learned, Iris and a group of lecturers claimed that "integration will be possible when we get to know the different domains that we teach." In the second year, following Iris' suggestion, the plenary meetings were devoted to the lecturer's presentations of their syllabi and to discussions on the ways that they attempted to realize their pedagogical creed. It soon became clear that most of them found it difficult to conceptualize the guiding principles of their own teaching. They needed to step outside their customary domains of authority and expertise in order to theorize their own teaching in a language that would be understood by the rest of the staff members. In order to help them do that, we decided to focus on one syllabus – on learning theories and curriculum planning – and to build on ideas from that syllabus for their presentations.

The participants' presentations revealed diverse pedagogical creeds and varied beliefs about teaching and learning. All of them were legitimized as valuable for curriculum planning. Aviva, a veteran lecturer commented:

I now understand that integration means allowing a conversation among different voices, understanding the tensions and conflicts among them, and managing paradoxes.

The result was less defensive discourse, making room for differences of opinion and challenging existing beliefs and attitudes.

A Shared, Collective, Dispersed, or Distributed Leadership Approach
While dealing with the big ideas such as the ZPD and the integrative curriculum and their implications for teaching and learning at the meetings, the heads of the academic departments in the school felt the need to form small groups to discuss the curriculum of each particular specialization. These meetings were both focused and open-ended. They were open-ended in that they allowed each academic program to realize its academic autonomy and focused because the participants took care to preserve the common core. Soon it was decided that the meetings would alternate between focusing on the common core and on developing each program. The early childhood people decided to study story retelling and its implications for developing preschool literacy, the elementary school staff focused on developing rich technological environments, and the high school on how to create and sustain partnerships. What emerged was a landscape with a two-way traffic of ideas from the center (the general faculty meetings) to the periphery and from the periphery (where the activities of the different programs took place) to the center. This traffic enriched both the center and the periphery.

Our analysis of this process shows that it was difficult for us to attend exclusively to big ideas that would include the interests of all stakeholders. What was created instead was a kind of "milieu" in which rather than adopting ideas and objects developed by the center, new ones (runaway objects) were being improvised in the periphery of the department as small and marginal innovations. These innovations were then transported by the participants back to the center and disseminated during the general meetings in which they were discussed and transformed, to be carried back to the periphery by the participants, thus creating a culture of "suburbia" in which local experiments were carried out in schools or among department members.

An interesting example of this process is the initiative of one clinical supervisor that took place during the third year. Her student-teachers trained in a weak junior high school with children from low-income families, many of whom were new immigrants from the former Soviet Union and Ethiopia. It was the student-teachers who immediately identified a large group of eighth-graders who could not read or write in Hebrew and presented their concern to the clinical supervisor, Anat. It was understood that this was an at-risk group who, without support, would soon drop out of school, and although this was not part of her training program, Anat decided to organize an intervention for them. She first consulted with a language and literacy specialist from the School of Education, who came to visit the school and observed the children. Subsequently, she gained the principal's support for launching a special program for them. The program was first run by Anat and her student-teachers, and later enlisted the collaboration of the cooperating teachers.

This innovation was not preplanned but developed in response to contextual conditions in one particular practicum site. It was not initiated by the School's head or even the head of the upper school department, but by an individual clinical supervisor who took upon herself challenges, attaining the position of an "agentive subject." When Anat, a novice clinical supervisor, shared her story with her colleagues at the plenary meetings, she became recognized in, and supported by, the larger collaborative community.

In contrast to the partnership relationships of the community of practice described in the second research cycle, the school–university partnerships were not coordinated by the head of the School of Education, but led by the clinical supervisors who identified opportunities for collaboration, enlisted help from the academic staff and the schools, and coordinated the relationship with cooperating teachers, etc.

The partnerships became hybrid spaces for work and learning energized by distributed multi-actor (student-teachers, clinical supervisor, cooperating teachers, college lecturer, school principal, and parents) initiatives where shared complex objects were constructed. When the problem was identified, building the object became the collaborative mission of all the actors involved. It was understood by the different actors that the language and reading problem would become a great obstacle for the children who, unless they made progress, would not be able to participate in classroom learning, and this would create discipline problems for the teachers. These objects would then have lives of their own and would require constant reconstruction.

Thus the boundary crossing and knotworking activity in the partnerships was constructed around an authentic problem and resulted in a plan constructed by the student-teachers and the cooperating teachers for each day of the week, in which each one of them contributed her expertise to the relationship, creating a space whereby differences and contradictions such as those between theory and practice, school and academia, lecturers and clinical supervisors, and interns and specialists became less and less significant.

As a result of the partnership activity, we saw transformation in the college as well. The staff members formed a milieu that did not simply consist of "teamwork" in the usual sense of a small, homogeneous, and bounded community. Rather, "it was an informal group that spanned a wide range of competencies and knowledge bases, and that shifted constantly to accommodate the evolving nature of knowledge projects" (Adler & Heckscher, 2006, p. 44). In other words, faculty members who originally identified themselves with a particular discipline came together to create a new academic territory, which could not be easily defined or bounded within the college, nor was it included in the regular academic program.

Moreover, the various academic programs felt that they had the autonomy to identify their own particular needs and to attend to them. The processes that they developed became simultaneous, multidirectional, and often reciprocal. Thus in both sites – the college and the partnerships – mycorrhizae-like, hybrid, poorly bounded relationships with the center were developed.

From the success of these activities, we learned that sustainability does not require that the relationship to the center should hold, or even that the agentive activities of the academic programs necessarily need to be interconnected. In order for them to sustain they required "a reflexive form of coordination among spontaneous local activities that is flat (nonhierarchical) in character while at the same time being based on a comprehensive summary view of things" (Engeström, 2006). Under such coordination they learned to negotiate and balance multiple parallel loyalties, both mutually enriching and at times hostile to one another.

Cycle 3: Expansion – The MTeach Program in Progress

The Graduate School was invited by the Ministry of Education to submit a proposal for a new MTeach program, which would offer a professional teacher education program to university graduates in the school disciplines. Since in our data, the voices that dominated the conversations in the School of Education were those of the education teachers, rather than the content-area specialists, our concern was how to empower the latter so that they could lead this new MTeach project. Another concern relates to the conflict of interest created between our two schools: the School of Education and the Graduate School. We worried that the new program prepared by the Graduate School would compete with the School of Education for the same population of university graduates seeking teaching certificates. How could we consolidate between the interests of the two schools?

We devised a proposal in which MTeach students would take theoretical and research courses at the Graduate School and do their practicum under the supervision of the School of Education. Our assumption was that this proposal offered the best of what the two schools had to offer. The MTeach program opened at the beginning of the 2011 academic year; we have documented its implementation.

CONCLUSION

Our study shows that when innovations die, they may still spread when adapted and diffused in different settings by others. In addition, it illustrates how unpredictable and emancipatory transformations can be spurred by runaway objects. As Engeström explains, runaway objects differ radically from "projects" which begin big and often end up as partial failures or disappointments. They have a tendency to begin small without a plan and escalate to events that affect the entire system. Finally, based on our experience, our study makes distinctions among craft culture, communities of practice, and collaborative communities in terms of the sustainability potential of these entities.

Our analysis, influenced by Engeström's writings, shows the advantages of our evolving collaborative community over the project's community of practice in the following areas:

- It is more inclusive and more tolerant of differences, allowing for more integrative discourse that is multidimensional and multi-vocal.
- It supports the notion of good neighbors, such as was developed among the department heads in the School of Education.
- It is more horizontal in terms of power relationships, with a system of distributed, ad hoc shared responsibilities, based on complementary needs of the various participants.
- It takes shape without rigid predetermined rules or principles and proceeds with weaker ties to a fixed central authority, thus allowing the periphery to develop autonomous context-bound innovative practices in hybrid spaces.
- In these hybrid spaces, there is accountability to peers or those below in the hierarchy, rather than to one's formal superiors.
- It brings values into the realm of public discussion, so that they can become common orienting and motivating elements for all members of the community.

- There is a reciprocal learning relationship between the center and its peripheries that is not imposed but is built into the operating principles of the social activity.
- Rather than following the direction of a formal coordinator, there is sporadic incidence of local leadership that rises to the occasion.

The literature on teacher education includes many descriptions of change projects, but only a small minority focuses on systemic, longitudinal processes. The present study is a retrospective account of an ongoing change process initiated 10 years ago by a relatively small group of Elementary School teacher educators. Its main purpose is to understand how, despite crises, this process evolved into bigger and more complex developments, and, on the basis of this understanding, to form a future-oriented theory of action.

Several theoretical resources guided our analysis:

First, Sustainability Theory and its implications for educational leadership call attention to the significance of an enactivist orientation to change that embraces deep learning. Our study shows that the persistence of this orientation in varied forms and contexts during the different phases of the change process in our college contributed to its sustainability.

This qualitative action research illustrates the cyclical process of change and identifies the conditions that activate it. It describes three cycles of change – from craft to a community of practice, from a community of practice to a collaborative community, and the expansion of that process. It demonstrates how each cycle evolved from the former, while lessons were learned about the implementation of innovation in teacher education. Our concern about the implications of craft culture in our college drove us to break away from the main college curriculum in order to develop a local experimental project in elementary teacher education. This project expired but enabled larger innovative practices in which the entire School of Education began a transformation toward a collaborative community. Today, five years later, we are beginning to expand this process while building a collaborative Graduate School and School of Education MTeach program and carefully observing the process.

Second, the metaphors of rhizome and mycorrhizae with horizontal and vertical relationships enabled us to understand how a project evolves notwithstanding its crises, and how its key principles intertwine, expand, and transform the whole system, creating new organizational entities. For example, as a rhizome that refers to a horizontal underground stem, the key project principles "folded in" when the experimental project was discontinued, ready to reemerge when conditions were right. This happened when new guidelines of the Ministry's committee for the restructuring of teacher education colleges mandated us to establish the College of Education and once again while planning the MTeach program. The mycorrhizae metaphor illustrates that innovative practices begin by knotworking, when the relevant people get together for a limited time period in order to support the innovation and then disperse again. While knotworking, the participants cross boundaries created by institutions, school disciplines, and specializations, and by status and level of expertise, to create a hybrid space of agency. This kind of activity may explain the sustainability potential of the present integrative curriculum developed by the School of Education and the activity in its partnerships.

Third, our increasingly deeper understandings and self-awareness were enhanced by the cyclical process of action research. This point, in our view, lies at the very heart of action research, which often leads to transformations resulting from newly made connections and experimental actions conducted to seek new ways and forms of becoming. As a result of this awareness, we are now able to harness top-down government policies in order to activate internal transformations in our undergraduate and graduate programs.

Fourth, when each cycle of action research is a phase of change that evolved from the former in a cyclical process, a practice-based theory is constructed. Our present theory is that engaging in an evolving course of action is inevitably a future-oriented experience. We appreciate the importance of being involved in a process of becoming in which there is no predetermined limit on what we may become or how we may engage with problems and create events. We understand that in order to sustain, we must preserve the fluidity of the communities that we lead. Furthermore, we must "make room for persistent communicative engagements from below that are not reducible to us as central authorities" (Yamazumi, 2007, p. 28), and are carried on with the occasional leadership of others who choose to do so.

REFERENCES

Adler, P. S., & Heckscher, C. (2006). Towards collaborative community. In C. Heckscher & P. S. Adler (Eds.), *The firm as a collaborative community: Reconstructing trust in the knowledge economy*. Oxford: Oxford University Press.

Deleuze, G., & Guattari, F. (1987). *A thousand plateaus: Capitalism and schizophrenia*. Minneapolis, MN: University of Minnesota Press.

Engeström, Y. (2005). Knotworking to create collaborative intentionality capital in fluid organizational fields. In M. M. Beyerlein, S. T. Beyerlein & F. A. Kennedy (Eds.), *Collaborative capital: Creating intangible value* (pp. 307–336). Amsterdam: Elsevier.

Engeström, Y. (2006). Development, movement and agency: Breaking away into mycorrhizae activities. In K. Yamazumi (Ed.), *Building activity theory in practice: Toward the next generation* (pp. 1–41). Osaka: Center for Human Activity Theory, Kansai University.

Engeström, Y. (2007). From communities of practice to mycorrhizae. In J. Hughes, N. Jewson & L. Unwin (Eds.), *Communities of practice: Critical perspectives* (pp. 41–54). London: Routledge.

Engeström, Y. (2009). The future of activity theory: A rough draft. In A. Sannino, H. Daniels & K. Guttierez (Eds.), *Learning and expanding with activity theory* (pp. 303–328). Cambridge: Cambridge University Press.

Fullan, M. (2005). *Leadership and sustainability: System thinkers in action.* Thousand Oaks, CA: Corwin.

Gee, J. (2005). Semiotic social spaces and affinity spaces. In D. Barton & K. Tusting (Eds.), *Beyond communities of practice* (pp. 214–231). Cambridge: Cambridge University Press.

Hargreaves, A., & Fink, D. (2005). *Sustainable leadership.* San Francisco, CA: Jossey-Bass.

Hughes, J., Jewson, N., & Unwin, L. (Eds.). (2007). *Communities of practice: Critical perspectives.* London: Routledge.

Jahreie, C. F., & Ottesen, E. (2010). Construction of boundaries in teacher education: Analyzing student teachers' accounts. *Mind, Culture, and Activity, 17*(3), 212–234.

Lave, J., & Wenger, E. (1991). *Situated learning: Legitimate peripheral participation.* Cambridge: Cambridge University Press.

Lea, M. (2005). Communities of practice in today's higher education: Useful heuristic or educational model? In D. Barton & K. Tustin (Eds.), *Beyond communities of practice* (pp. 180–197). Cambridge: Cambridge University Press.

Sackney, L., & Walker, K. (2006). *Leadership for Knowledge Communities.* Paper presented at the Commonwealth Council for Educational Administration and Management (CCEAM) Conference, Nicosia, Cyprus. Retrieved from http://www.topkinisis.com/conference/CCEAM/wib/index/outline/PDF/SACKNEY%20Larry.pdf. Accessed on August 19.

Wenger, E. (1998). *Communities of practice: Learning, meaning and identity.* Cambridge: Cambridge University Press.

Yamazumi, K. (2007). Human agency and educational research: A new problem in Activity Theory. *Action: An International Journal of Human Activity Theory, 1,* 19–39.

PART V
GROWTH IN COMMUNITY

Part V also consists of three chapters. The Growth in Community theme is first taken up by Slovenian coauthors, Barbara Šteh and Marjet Šarić, in Chapter 30, "Two European Reflections on Professional Development in the ISATT Community: Looking Backward, Moving Forward." Next comes Chapter 31, the Asia Pacific editors' contribution to the volume. In "Self and Community: The Impact of ISATT on the Professional Learning, Teaching, and Research of Members in the Asia-Pacific Region," authors Issa Danjun Ying, Amanda McGraw, and Amanda Berry present the results of the extensive research project they conducted in their region. Finally, the conclusion of the section and the book is reached with Chapter 32. In that chapter, Xiaohong Yang from China, a new ISATT member, takes up the topic, "Back to the Future from a Chinese Perspective: A Philosophical Reconstruction of Ideas Gleaned from the Fifteenth ISATT Conference."

CHAPTER 30

TWO EUROPEAN REFLECTIONS ON PROFESSIONAL DEVELOPMENT IN THE ISATT COMMUNITY: LOOKING BACKWARD, MOVING FORWARD

Barbara Šteh and Marjeta Šarić

ABSTRACT

This chapter consists of two reflective accounts from Slovenia. Both accounts are connected with Barica Marentič Požarnik, who in Part I of this 30th anniversary volume directly linked her personal professional development to the International Study Association on Teachers and Teaching (ISATT) during its emergent years as an organisation. In this chapter in the fifth and closing section, Marentič Požarnik's counterparts follow in the footsteps that their senior colleague and mentor planted and make tracks of their own. They crystallise how ISATT has affected their professional development and influenced their lines of research as they - and ISATT - press towards the future.

Keywords: Mentoring; ISATT; community; dissemination; Slovenia

From Teacher Thinking to Teachers and Teaching: The Evolution of a Research Community
Advances in Research on Teaching, Volume 19, 639–668
ISSN: 1479-3687/doi:10.1108/S1479-3687(2013)0000019033

This chapter presents two reflective accounts from ISATT members who reside in Slovenia. It joins together three generations. Barica Marentič Požarnik has been a mentor to Barbara Šteh, who later found herself in the role of a mentor to Marjeta Šarić. For both individuals, Barica Marentič Požarnik is an inspiration. Readers will recall that in Part I of this 30th anniversary volume, Marentič Požarnik connected her career development to the International Study Association on Teachers and Teaching (ISATT) during its emergent years as an organisation. In this work, Barbara Šteh and Marjeta Šarić link their development to Barica Marentič Požarnik and to what has now known as ISATT. The larger portion of the chapter revolves around Barbara Šteh's attendance at a decade of ISATT conferences and traces key ideas of presenters whose scholarship affected her research agenda, her pedagogical practice, and her professional growth. As for the second portion of the chapter, it is written by doctoral student, Marjeta Šarić. In her reflective analysis, Šarić presents the background of her doctoral research work, followed by a discussion of the ways in which ISATT influenced her line of research. Both individuals demonstrate the shaping effects of ISATT as a professional study association at the introductory stages of career.

BARBARA ŠTEH'S PERSONAL ACCOUNT

In the first part of this chapter, I reflect on the ISATT conferences I attended between 1999 and 2009. During my decade of participation, many topics have captured my interest and contributed to my professional growth. In this reflective chapter, I address each biennial conference separately. I highlight main ideas and conference presenters who impacted my research inquiries, my teaching practice, and my personal professional development. Before I begin, though, let me introduce myself and share some of my background.

Personal Biography

In 1989, I graduated in psychology from the Faculty of Arts, University of Ljubljana, Slovenia. In the first year after graduation, I worked in the field of market research and I soon found out that this area is not at the centre of my professional aspirations. A grammar school job followed: in the first year I worked as a counsellor and psychology teacher; later only as a teacher. In that period I acquired a sense pedagogic and andragogic knowing and passed the teacher certification exam. In the academic year 1992/1993, I participated in the project 'Teachers Teaching Teachers' under the leadership of the Kempler Institute from the Netherlands. In November 1993, I was offered employment at the Department of Educational Sciences of the Faculty of Arts in Ljubljana as an educational psychology teaching assistant. I have been employed there ever since.

In 1998, I obtained my master's degree in the area of educational psychology. My master thesis was titled 'Mutual Influence between Teachers' and Learners' Conceptions of Knowledge and Learning' and I was supervised by Professor Barica Marentič Požarnik. In my thesis work, I studied issues such as (a) What are prevailing teachers' conceptions of learning, knowledge and teaching?; (b) What is the quality of their teaching?; (c) What are the connections between the levels of conceptions, teachers' goals and their actual work in class? In December 2000, I completed my doctoral degree. My dissertation was titled 'The Quality of Learning and Teaching in the Frame of the Secondary School Programme'. I completed my terminal degree also under the supervision of Professor Barica Marentič Požarnik.

In October 2005, I became an assistant professor. I gave lectures and seminars in educational psychology and experience-based learning for students of pedagogy and andragogy. Above all, I like the teaching part of being a professor. My teaching includes active and experience-based teaching methods (i.e., video self-confrontation) and I have mentored numerous students. Since January 1994, I have led workshops and in-service seminars for teachers at all levels, mentors and educational advisors.

A Decade of Membership in the ISATT Community

Ninth Biennial Conference, 1999, Dublin, Ireland: Developing Teachers and Teaching Practice – International Research Perspectives

When I attended my first ISATT Conference in Dublin in 1999, I was already full of ideas of the influence of conceptions of learning, teaching and knowledge of a person on that person's learning and teaching (Dolk, Korthagen, & Wubbels, 1995; Fox, 1983; Gow & Kember, 1993; Vermunt, 1993). I had already completed my master's degree on the topic of mutual influence between concepts of learning and knowledge and the way teachers and students act.

In my research program to that point in time, I had successfully combined quantitative and qualitative research approaches. I built on the assumption that research methods have to be adapted, in a flexible and well-considered way, to address particular problems and situations, and that there are no barriers to the joint use of quantitative and qualitative research procedures. On the contrary, such procedures are even desired in many studies (Miles & Huberman, 1994; Sagadin, 1991). In the 1999 paper titled 'Observations on the Teacher's and the Student's Role in the Context of Secondary School Curricular Reform', Barica Marentič Požarnik and I used a quantitative/ analytic and qualitative/interpretative research method to obtain a more authentic insight into what is actually happening in secondary school classrooms (Marentič Požarnik & Šteh, 1999). In this respect, our work was reinforced at the conference by Günter L. Huber's presentation that concluded with the following thought by Cizek, '... qualitative and quantitative researchers should not so concerned with methodological hegemony, but help producers and consumers of their research make sense of it' (Huber & Schrodi, 1999, p. 14). However, the most feedback we received had to do with the significance of the qualitative methodology. What was reinforced for me at the Dublin Conference was the role qualitative research plays in enabling insight into a person's subjective experience. This correspondingly influences his/her actions (phenomenological approach). To this point in time in Slovenia, qualitative research methods were considered inferior. For me, the support I received from fellow ISATT members was highly significant in my personal and professional development as a researcher.

Qualitative methods, as foreshadowed, were used in many of the presented papers. I learned about case studies, participant observation, classroom interaction, analysis of unfinished sentences, in-depth interviews, focus group interviews, stimulated recall interviews, use of metaphorical images and language, etc. all of which presents a considerable digression from scientific neutrality and the dominant positivist research orientation. I particularly recall the problem of the neutral scientist's position that was presented in Nola Oliver's (1999) conference contribution. Oliver high-lighted the fact that being committed to qualitative research is not enough because fixed ways of interpreting the world can still prevent us from really hearing and understanding stories told by individuals about their position and involvement in the study. We should be aware of and deal with this challenge. It is one that researchers in the educational research arena repeatedly face.

I was also influenced by the work on metaphorical language. I was, for example, impressed by Andy Hargreaves' keynote lecture, 'Teaching in a Box: Emotional Geographies of Teaching' (Hargreaves, 2002). In his talk, he emphasised that emotions are not only necessary and favourable but they also form the basis of quality learning and teaching. How to establish the right amount of closeness in interactions with colleagues, students and parents is an important issue for any teacher. Hargreaves clearly showed that we need to dedicate more attention and give more 'room' to emotions as we engage in both the teaching and researching processes.

In addition to Andy Hargreaves' 'Emotional Geographies of Teaching' lecture, I would also like to highlight the paper, 'Responsive Choreography', by Kathryn A. Noel and Robert B. Macmillan (Noel & Macmillan, 1999, p. 90). Noel and Macmillan said that effective teachers engage in detailed planning of their lessons, but they also read students' needs, and respond to their (mis)understanding and feelings. For the authors, '…"responsive" coupled with "choreography" portrays how these teachers used knowledge and skills to create a powerful dance of learning for students' (Noel & Macmillan, 1999, p. 91). Similarly, in his keynote lecture, Peter Woods (2002) spoke of creative teaching and learning as well as researching. To be creative, Wood said it is necessary to be autonomous and take into account the voices of those involved, both of which present challenge. In another keynote speech, Milbrey McLaughlin (2002) stressed the importance of connections between researchers, curriculum planners and teachers in the development of schools. For McLaughlin, all three levels of knowledge are intertwined in mature schools: knowledge 'for practice' (knowledge of researchers, curriculum developers), knowledge 'of practice' (knowledge of teachers who start researching what is happening at their schools) and knowledge 'in practice' (knowledge of teachers as a result of reflecting on their own practice in class, leading them to implement changes). Solutions cannot be externally imposed on a school; studies (portfolio development, critical friend relationship, etc.) conducted within a school context are essential.

By the late 1990s, Douwe Beijaard and Nico Verloop (1999) had already shifted the focus of their research from teacher knowledge in practice towards studying teachers' knowledge of their professional identities. They were inquiring into changes along the career span and arguing that a teacher's sense of identity should be taken into account when introducing innovations to schools.

At the conclusion of the first ISATT Conference I attended, the response I received about my research and the feeling of being included in the ISATT community were important for me. At the 1999 Dublin Conference, I did not feel like an alien from another planet as I often feel in my home academic environment. Despite coming from different countries and diverse cultures, we spoke the same language and shared common values.

The teacher was integral to all of the presentations I heard. In fact, most conveyed teachers' experiences in their own voices, using their own terms.

Tenth Biennial Conference, 2001, Faro, Portugal: Connecting Policy and Practice – Challenges for Teaching and Learning in Schools and Universities
Similar to reforms that were taking place elsewhere in the world in the 1990s, there was a pervasive focus on school organisation and curricula at all levels of pre-university education in Slovenia from 1995 to 2000. Although we could learn from the experiences of others, many authors warned of the failure of 'top down' reforms and reforms 'from the outside' (i.e., Altrichter & Posch, 1991; Fullan, 1993), our reforms were not much different. Encouraged by the many contributions and questions about what is actually happening in practice, my mentor Barica Marentič Požarnik and I presented our paper, 'What is Actually Happening in Secondary Classrooms? The Rhetoric and Reality of Curricular Reform' (Šteh & Marentič Požarnik, 2005a) at the 2001 ISATT Conference in Faro, Portugal. Our paper presented some of the results of my doctoral thesis. My dissertation work revealed major discrepancies between the high-level aims of school reform and prevailing classroom activities, on one hand, and between teachers and students' perceptions of the same processes, on the other hand. It became obvious that teachers need support in raising awareness to these discrepancies, especially between aims and teaching/assessment strategies, and they need more opportunities to experience and to try out new teaching approaches, while reflecting upon and discussing the implications of them. This is extremely difficult in circumstances when efficiency and school improvement are given highest priority where the judgment of the quality of teaching and learning is concerned. This was also emphasised in the keynote speech, 'How Performance Audit Prevents Teachers from Evaluating Their Teaching' which was delivered by John Elliott (2001). He problematised the introduction of an evaluation model where the attainment of external standards is constantly checked, and teachers become less and less satisfied, since they are given more and more responsibility while their powers are simultaneously reduced. Elliot indicated that this inevitably leads to professional identity crises. The same phenomenon occurs to researchers in the field of education, said Elliot. For scholars, the criteria for promotion deter them from engaging in participatory research with teachers. Such research is frequently construed by others to be a deviation from the academic discipline and hence, results in less psychic, monetary and positional recognition. Concurrently, trust between the researcher and

the teacher dissipates. John Elliott (2001) stressed that we should pay attention to the difference between (a) efficiency (the use of resources to achieve a certain output) and effectiveness and (b) school improvement and school development.

I also found the findings of Ingrid Carlgren and Kirsti Klette (2001) on the outcomes of reforms in Nordic countries (Sweden, Norway, Finland and Denmark) in the 1990s interesting. As they listened to teachers, it became evident to the researchers that both too much and too little freedom can present teachers with problems. I learned that we should not forget that, together with autonomy, teachers need support at all levels. These would range from appropriate norms and quality training to support networks where teachers exchange their knowledge and experiences. The significance of context was confirmed in 'David's Story: A Reform Enthusiastic Teacher in Dutch Secondary Education Whose Enthusiasm is Strongly Decreasing Due to Context-specific Factors Related to School Organizational and Current Governmental Policies' presented by Klaas Van Veen (Van Veen & Sleegers, 2001, p. 1). Again, two points can be gleaned from Van Veen's presentation: how important it is to listen to teachers when introducing innovations and how important stories can be from both research and educational perspectives. When included in the research process, teachers enable us to reach deeper understandings, and become aware of teachers' thoughts and feelings in certain contexts and situations. In reference to this, Raija Erkkilä and Maarit Mäkelä (2005) pointed out that the narrative-biographical interview is a two-way process, which only too rarely shines light on the role of researchers who, when listening to various stories, face their own experiences and emotions and change accordingly. Also, Hannu L. T. Heikkinen (2001) shared a part of his own story when he became 'a narrative teacher educator' and demonstrated how he used the portfolio method to ascertain the shifting personal and professional identities of teachers.

My own teaching practice was influenced by the contributions of Norwegian authors (Haugstveit, 2001; Oygarden, 2001; Sjolie, 2001), who caused me to reflect on my assessment practices as I strive to help my students achieve certain educational goals. We often overlook the primary (pedagogic) purpose of assessment: that students can develop strategies of self-regulated learning, participate in the setting of criteria, and gain competences in self-assessment and peer assessment. Moreover, we should be aware that assessment always involves ethical issues. To assign a fair grade, we have to take the student's integrity into account in a way that encourages him/her to go on.

To sum up, the key ideas on which the 2001 Faro Conference focused and which interested and influenced me were teachers' identity (i.e., Beijaard, 2001; Heikkinen, 2001; Lauriala & Kukkonen, 2005), teachers' voices (i.e., Elliott, 2001; Van Veen & Sleegers, 2001), narrative approaches to teaching and research (i.e., Erkkilä & Mäkelä, 2005; Heikkinen, 2001; Pritzker, 2001; Van Veen & Sleegers, 2001) and the role of portfolios and reflection in professional development (i.e., Craig, 2001; Haugstveit, 2001; Mansvelder-Longayroux & Verloop, 2001; Vaisanen, 2001).

Eleventh Biennial Conference 2003 in Leiden: New Directions in Teachers' Working and Learning Environment
One of the key objectives of the reform that took place in Slovenia from 1995 to 2000 was, as in other countries, to improve the autonomy and professional responsibility of schools and teachers (Principles of Curricular Reform [Izhodišča kurikularne prenove], 1996). However, Slovenian teachers received contradictory messages. On the one hand, they were supposed to become more autonomous in teaching, while on the other hand, their teaching was increasingly controlled by standards, external high-stake tests and also by regulations concerning classroom assessment, discipline, etc. and school inspection. This was anything but a liberal education policy. At the same time, teachers were not consistently supported in their professional development. As a result, the question of how teachers themselves experienced and understood the intentions of the reforms arose. Hence, in the evaluation study carried out between 2000 and 2002 (Marentič Požarnik, Kalin, Šteh, & Valenčič Zuljan, 2002) in Slovenia, the main aim was to gain insights into the professional autonomy and responsibility of teachers in the process of school reform from their personal perspectives. Barica Marentič Požarnik and I presented some of our results at the conference in Leiden, the Netherlands, in the paper 'Teachers' Perception of Their Professional Autonomy in an Environment of Systemic Change' (Šteh & Marentič Požarnik, 2005b). The results we shared at the conference showed considerable discrepancies between the intentions and rhetoric of the reform and teachers' perceptions. Teachers' perceptions of autonomy are mainly congruent with the 'weak' conception (which may be in line with official intentions) and only partly conform to the idea of a 'new professionalism' (Niemi & Kohonen, 1995). Only 31% of teachers understood autonomy in terms of professionalism and responsibility, which is not surprising in light of our Slovenian context at the time and increases in external control. As was the case elsewhere in the world, the question arose as to how to create a space for teachers' autonomy and professional development.

Similarly, Lynne M. Hannay (Hannay, Bray, & Telford, 2005) pointed out a potential dichotomy in highflying reforms where, on the one hand, student scores on external tests become the key criteria for school improvement, which can be in opposition to the conceptions of practitioners who see school improvement in increased loyalty, forming learning communities, and the process of changing, on the other hand. In her conclusion she recalled an old Fullan (1981) maxim, namely it is individuals who change and not school buildings and that in all great reforms it is necessary to ensure a certain balance between 'teacher passion, purpose, and capacity' and 'student engagement in learning' as well as between pressure and support (Hannay et al., 2005, p. 270). Hannay et al. continued by stating that 'pressure for improved student achievement on high-stakes testing can be raised only if support is equally raised' (Hannay et al., 2005, p. 270). In the paper session *Evaluation and Teacher Learning* (Craig, 2003; Mayer, 2003), it was very clearly pointed out that only setting professional standards will not lead to quality teaching and that it is crucial to respect teachers' voices in all phases of the reform process.

In his keynote speech, Les Tickle (2003) asserted that what teachers need is an anthem. To this end, he modified the lyrics of the well-known song *The Wall* by Pink Floyd, which we used to sing enthusiastically in our school years:

> We don't need no constant inspection;
>
> We don't need your curriculum controls.
>
> Dark sarcasm to the teachers;
>
> Minister, leave us all alone.
>
> Hey, minister, leave us all alone. (Tickle, 2003, p. 4)

Considering the current political interventions in the field of education in Slovenia, the aforementioned lyrics are even more relevant now than they were over 10 years ago.

In his keynote address, *Knowledge construction and teaching teachers*, John Loughran (2003) challenged us with questions of how to find out whether our teaching practice conforms to our beliefs and whether we ask ourselves how our students' view our teaching. When I reviewed my notes, I was reminded that, despite collecting feedback from students and engaging in discussions, I only rarely reflect on my teaching practice. Sometimes, we can slip into a routine teaching pattern that may have been previously successful, but this may not be most appropriate for the group of students with whom we are currently working. For me, two parts of Loughran's speech were of key importance: the significance of constant reflection of my own practice and how essential it is for students as future teachers (or educational advisors) that I constantly inform them of the aims and approaches of my teaching. This becomes their educational material and a source of professional knowledge that provides them with opportunities to both reflect on and research teaching. Therefore, it is important to make our teaching as explicit as possible both to ourselves and to our students.

In another plenary speech titled 'Practice, Theory and Person in Lifelong Professional Learning', Fred Korthagen (2005) pointed out the significance of teachers' reflecting on their personal teaching experiences during the process of their education and offered his well-known onion model of core reflection. Korthagen told audience members that it is important to highlight our beliefs and conceptions; however, our feelings, needs, desires, etc. also influence our way of teaching and our way of handling certain teaching situations. We must therefore highlight these non-rational sources of behaviour in the process of reflection. Accordingly, during the process of reflection, we must dig deep and also ask ourselves 'Who am I (in my work)?' and 'What inspires me?' Since then, I have had a thought of Hamacheck (as cited in Korthagen, 2005) imprinted in my mind, which I have subsequently shared with my students, 'Consciously, we teach what we know; unconsciously, we teach who we are' (p. 93). That is exactly the point Jean Clandinin (2003) stressed in her keynote speech at Leiden. She stressed that a teacher's professional knowledge is not separated from his/her life. Clandinin informed us that 'a teacher's identity is understood as the unique embodiment of his/her story to live by, a story shaped by the landscape past and present in which she/he lives and works' (p. 8). When studying narrative stories, Jean Clandinin focused on the moments of tension which trigger shifts in awakening to children's cultural, family or institutional stories (Clandinin, 2003; Clandinin & Huber, 2005). I was also touched by a paper written by Per F. Laursen (2005). His empirical study was based on observations in classrooms and semi-structured interviews. It clearly showed that excellent teachers do not have the same personalities and dispositions but are able to teach in accordance with the qualities they happen to have. In fact, some of them have had to change jobs to allow themselves to teach in ways consonant with their personalities and belief systems. Moreover, all of them stressed that development of their competences is not a matter of certain personal traits, but a result of hard work. Many problems in teaching and learning arise from incongruities between our thinking, feeling, wanting and doing (Korthagen, 2005; Korthagen & Vasalos, 2005). On the path towards high-quality professional development, it is thus necessary for teachers to examine these incongruities in themselves and also to encourage students to do the same.

These were important challenges for my professional development as a teacher, and they motivated me to reflect on my own practice, and also to participate in two workshops on core reflection in Slovenia (in October 2008 and November 2009), led by Fred Korthagen. The workshops brought me face-to-face with myself and my own practice and, consequently, supported me and gave me fresh insights and new energy as I returned to my professional work. I was faced with both my strengths – core qualities (interest in others, flexibility – ability to listen to students and at the same time to keep in mind and follow the key learning goals, deriving satisfaction from a student's advancement, etc.) – and my limitations (expecting too much from students or myself at times, and consequently setting requirements too high, impatience, etc.). I was relieved to find that destructive beliefs that repeatedly occur in the form of a voice telling me what I should/cannot do can be transformed into a positive belief if I allow myself to simply be with my students. With a focus on core reflection, I can give them a lot and at the same time learn from them. I felt genuine satisfaction and confirmation after hearing a participant at one of the workshops in 2012, who at the closing evaluation said, 'You brought me great relief, as finally somebody told me that I am allowed to be what I am and to follow this [maxim] in my pedagogical work'. Therefore, the key issue of the education of teachers or other professionals is how to support the development of their competencies in a way that aligns with who they are as human beings as well as what moves them forward and inspires them to work (Meijer, Korthagen, & Vasalos, 2009).

Looking back on the 2003 Conference, I felt directly addressed by Kari Smith's (2005) keynote lecture when she cited an anonymous source who e-mailed her to state what it meant to be a teacher. In those words, I also found my own beliefs – because these are also my core qualities, as Korthagen (2005) refers to them: '(t)o be a teacher is to learn to talk and how to keep quiet, and to learn to keep quiet and how to talk'; '(t)o be a teacher is to sometimes think and say nothing, but never to say anything without thinking' and '(t)o be a teacher is to listen to the thoughts behind the words, and to listen to words without thoughts' (Smith, 2005, p. 95).

With this understanding comes the awareness that good teachers are varied and that quality teaching is also varied. How then should we evaluate teaching? Among others, Kari Smith analytically answered the questions 'who evaluates what for what purposes' and 'who evaluates what, with which tools'? Today, well over 10 years later, in the Slovenian and international educational context as well, there is a tendency to establish standards and attain accountability. We too often forget that this tendency does not always fit with quality professional development for teachers.

In various other articles presented at the 2003 Leiden Conference, the importance of remembering the central purpose of education was stressed through paying attention to how to stimulate the learning and professional development of teachers. This should be our guide when contemplating school and curricular reform, evaluating educational programmes and teaching, as well as every time we teach students or student teachers.

Twelfth International Conference 2005 in Sydney: Challenges for the Profession – Perspectives and Directions for Teachers, Teaching and Teacher Education

In 2005 at the 12th ISATT Conference in Sydney, Australia, my colleague, Jana Kalin, and I presented some of the empirical results of an evaluation study of school reform in Slovenia. That study clearly showed that only autonomous teachers can creatively act in practice. It is they who introduce and test novelties and thus develop their skills. This, in turn, leads them to greater autonomy where professionalism and personal responsibility are concerned (Kalin & Šteh, 2007). All these can take place on the basis of a very clear vision of the school mission and culture, which enables a connection between all participants and their development. Thus, a community can be formed in which individuals can make progress in their confrontation with the challenges of everyday practice. The question of how to support them and how to establish the learning community arises.

In her keynote lecture in Sydney, Jennifer Gore (2007) pointed out that all teachers can provide quality teaching if they focus on supporting quality learning of their students. This, in turn, creates a quality learning environment and allows students to learn what is meaningful to them. Gore claimed that the following four questions could be used as support: 'What do I want my students to learn'? 'What does this learning mean to them'? 'What do I expect from them – how well should they do it'? 'How do we support teachers without making them fear challenges'? Models are welcome, both in quality teaching and quality reflection, Jennifer Gore told audience members. However, each of us must find his/her own way and act in accordance with oneself. In the next keynote lecture, Geert Kelchtermans (2007) stated that good teachers are distinguished by their dedication to their subject matter and their genuine interest in students. Kelchtermans (2007) stressed that 'who I am as a teacher is the message' (p. 39) we send to our students. Hence, it is really important for quality teaching that a teacher has significant self-understanding (self-image, self-esteem, job motivation, task-perception and future perspective). Christopher Day (Day et al., 2005), in his presentation, added the importance of consistency between a teacher's work and his/her private life, which allows the teacher to attain satisfaction. Satisfied teachers are more efficient in their teaching.

The conference's closing session stressed that the way to quality does not lie in a safe pathway, but in taking risks in both teaching and research. In the latter, we often forget to discover quality as opposed to surfacing weaknesses. A recurrent question I ask myself concerns the degree to which I have courage to pursue new paths.

Thirteenth Biennial Conference 2007 in St. Catharines, Canada: Totems and Taboos – Risk and Relevance in Research on Teachers and Teaching

Given the topic of quality teachers that perennially surfaces at ISATT meetings, my colleague, Jana Kalin, and I began in 2006 to analyse the quality of the education program offered by the Department of Educational Sciences of the Faculty of Arts where we teach. Thus, at the 13th Biennial ISATT Conference held in St. Catherines, Ontario, Canada, in 2007, we presented some of our findings. The key question driving our research was whether university teachers, by virtue of our influence and the challenges to which we draw attention, manage to make students aware of their conceptions of learning, knowledge and teaching. We wondered whether we can help them develop conceptions based on the idea of active and constructive learning, and thus grow to be independent learners who can manage their own learning. This, for us, was the basis for their further professional development and one of the criteria for evaluating the quality of university studies. Among other things, Kalin and I wrote in our conclusion:

> Students have a lot to tell us about the quality of the studies if we care to ask them. The question is whether we are prepared to listen to them or whether their reactions may prompt us to profound changes in our own teaching when we are convinced of our indisputable superiority. (Šteh & Kalin, 2008, p. 195)

Our work clearly pointed out that we have to take seriously their messages, that we should not underestimate them and that they desire a more active role in the study process.

To a certain extent, we listened to their ideas concerning more active inclusion in the study process, but the question still remains whether we are truly ready to accept them as partners and how much all students are prepared for this more active and responsible role (Šteh & Kalin, 2012). It seems that teachers themselves send mixed messages on the key roles of both the teacher and student in the study process, as well as on what students should know for exams. How can we convince higher education teachers to sit at the same table and learn each other's views, expectations and requirements and form a common vision around which we will strive within the boundaries of our academic community? To what extent do we succeed in promoting and developing students' in-depth approach to their studies? Do we assist them in creating their own conceptions? It depends on prevailing university teachers' approaches to teaching (information transmission/teacher-focused approach or conceptual change/student-focused approach). That was the empirical finding that keynote speaker, Keith Trigwell (2008), shared at the Brock University Conference. Jana Kalin and I continue to seek students' views on teacher quality and to analyse experiences that are meaningful for students. To us, this feedback can inform future teaching, especially if we are ready to accept constructive feedback as a challenge to improve our teaching. A good indicator may be that in 2011, a team of six members from the Department of Educational Sciences at the Faculty of Arts in Ljubljana and three members from the equivalent department at the Faculty of Philosophy in Belgrade started working collaboratively on the project 'Ensuring Quality of University Studies: The Students' and Teachers' Roles and Responsibilities'. This has served as a catalyst for many fruitful discussions and allowed us to see our own teaching practices via new windows of understanding.

Keith Trigwell (2008) found that teachers with a conceptually changed/ student-focused approach are more satisfied, and only satisfied teachers can create circumstances where students can find satisfaction as well. In his keynote lecture, Joel Spring (2007) also provocatively pointed out that within the frame of the philosophy of equal opportunities, we should start advocating for the importance of creating opportunities for each individual to live a happy and satisfying life instead of equal opportunities for education. Moreover, we should not neglect the fact that this global world is not equal and that the earlier mentioned thesis can play an important role in raising awareness in the consumer-rich environment: To what are we striving for and does it significantly contribute to our quality of life? Certainly, a completely different situation exists in social environments where education has never been accessible to all due to gender, poverty, ethnicity and the like. The latter was emphasised in the keynote address by Shannon Moore (2008). She quoted Tomaševski (as cited in Moore, 2008), pointing out that the right to education should be at the centre of our efforts, because it is the cornerstone of all other human rights. Currently, this is a major issue in the 'European crisis' and not only in the so-called third world. If most Slovenian elementary school students, for example, had excellent or very good grades and enrolment in grammar school programs and universities was on the rise, I could agree with Joel Springer's thesis. However, pronounced stratification has taken place and, judging from government measures, the danger exists that the quality of public schooling will fall and that university studies will be accessible only to the wealthy.

At the Brock University Conference in St. Catherines, Canada, we mostly dealt with teacher identity (i.e., Day, 2007; Fisher & Egemann, 2007; Kompf & Fulton, 2007; Nissilä, 2008), teacher satisfaction (i.e., Day, 2007; Van Veen, 2007) and the role of colleagues and collaboration in teachers' professional development (i.e., Ingvarsdottir, 2007). It was again pointed out that researchers can profit enormously from the personal stories of teachers and that teachers themselves can learn a lot from them (i.e., Hansen & Mulholland, 2007; Jónsdóttir, 2007; Kitchen, Kosnik, & Beck, 2007; Kompf & Fulton, 2007, etc.).

Fourteenth Biennial Conference 2009 in Rovaniemi, Finland: Navigating in Educational Contexts – Identities and Cultures in Dialogue

Between 2006 and 2008, six colleagues from my department formed a team to conduct the research project, 'Levers of Successful Co-operation Between the School and the Home: Modern Solutions and Perspectives' (Kalin et al., 2008). The shared endeavour was encouraging to me and supported my research work. At the 14th Biennial Conference in Rovaniemi, Finland, Jana Kalin and I presented some of the project findings in our paper, 'The Importance of Respecting Teachers' and Parents' Differences in Navigating Mutual Relationships' (Kalin & Šteh, 2009). In our research, it became evident that co-operation and communication between teachers and parents is crucial to developing a culture of dialogue and problem solving in an atmosphere of respect and acceptance of differences. In addition, methods and forms of co-operation need to be adapted to particular circumstances and the needs of all parties involved. An essential starting point is granting each other freedom and autonomy while remaining interdependent and sharing common goals. While this helps build trusting relationships between researchers, teachers and students, we recognised that we often overlook the importance of these foundations in the communities in which we are active.

Säde-Pirkko Nissilä (2009), in her 2009 ISATT Conference contribution, also stressed the importance of dialogue. In her case, dialogue fuelled professional development programs for higher education teachers. The higher education teachers who were included in Nissilä's research stressed the importance of reflection, collective support and practice.

Also interesting at the Rovaniemi Conference was the finding of Sanne F. Akkerman and Paulien C. Meijer (2011), namely the increased number of publications dealing with teacher identity in SSCI (Social and Science Citation Index) journals in the past two decades. Since 2008, teacher identity has surpassed such topics as teacher knowledge, teacher competencies and teacher beliefs as the basis of professional development. Audience members learned that increasingly research focus has turned to the role of emotions, passion, commitment and courage in teaching (Beauchamp & Thomas, 2009; Day, 2004; Kelchtermans, 2005; Palmer, 1998 in Akkerman & Meijer, 2011). Continuing this research trend, the authors offered a dialogical conceptualisation of teacher identity, which is particularly useful as an analytical framework in studying the professional development of teachers. For Akkerman and Meijer, a way to come to an understanding of the complexity of teacher identity 'is to look more carefully at the doubts, dilemmas and uncertainties that teachers experience, implicitly within their normal work routines, or perhaps more explicitly when faced by educational innovations or career transitions' (Akkerman & Meijer, 2011, p. 318).

Crisis also accompanies our lives, stressed Paulien C. Meijer (2009) in her keynote address in Rovaniemi, Finland. But crisis, Meijer also told us, represents an opportunity for growth. However, we should be aware that the transformative learning process is demanding, emotional and sometimes even threatening. A transformative focus on learning, in Meijer's (2009) words, 'requires teacher educators to also raise dilemmas and crises, in order to create opportunities for transformative learning'. She continued to explain: 'This implies a different stance to many deep-rooted assumptions in teacher education, in particular the issue of safety in learning' (Meijer, 2009, p. 5). A constant ISATT theme over the 1999-2009 span of biennial conferences, I was reminded, has been striking a balance between pressure and support for teachers and also those who study teaching.

Interim Remarks

In the first part of this chapter, I have highlighted some of the ideas and contributions that at certain points of time have been important to my professional path because they both challenged me and instilled confidence in me. Undoubtedly, somebody else with her/his own core qualities and challenges of life would have highlighted other things; all of us look at the world through our own lenses (but sometimes we have to change our glasses in order to improve our sight). Over the aforementioned decade, the ISATT community has made many important contributions to the research literature and the conduct of schooling in respective members' countries. There are, of course, many other sessions that could be featured - my ISATT conference experiences have been limited by the sessions I chose to attend. The three or four concurrent sessions that I did not attend will undisputedly influenced other ISATT members.

Reflecting back on my research path, I see that I was first oriented towards detecting conceptions of learning, knowledge and teaching in both teachers and students and instantiating what is happening in classrooms. This led to my interest in how teachers experience autonomy within the constraints of school reform, and later to co-operation between teachers and parents for the purpose of improving student learning. I was convinced of the value of qualitative research even before I joined the ISATT community, although in this regard, the ISATT community has greatly helped me acquire the necessary self-confidence to continue on - even though the positivist paradigm has a stranglehold grip on educational research in my home country and many others as well. Underestimation and discrimination of the value of qualitative methodology in psychology and pedagogical research is still dominant in Slovenia; however, there are many more individual researchers who bravely make use of qualitative research procedures since I first began my life in higher education under the supervision of Professor Barica Marentič Požarnik. In the department where I teach, I am happy to see a marked increase in the number of diploma theses where the qualitative research methods have been used.

With a team of co-workers, I am once again carrying out an analysis of the quality of university studies in the department where I teach. I am now looking at the challenges this presents to our professional development. I ask myself how to, on one hand, encourage dilemmas and critical self-reflection in colleagues, students and myself and, on the other hand, ensure appropriate support in an expanding comfort zone that will lead to transformative learning. I see the crucial question is how to foster quality dialogue and make it become an integral part of the milieu in a specific educational institution and wider community (between researchers, teachers, students, etc.) and not only a characteristic of individuals and smaller 'islands' of people within this community.

I recognise that a defined space ensures my autonomy as researcher and teacher, but I also need other researchers and teachers who work with me and each other to strive towards achieving common goals. In this respect, I would like to point out a thought of Hafdis Ingvarsdottir expressed at the Brock ISATT Conference in 2007 in Canada, 'Autonomy gives you the freedom to fly, while alliance provides wings'. The ISATT community has been a good ally to me. It has given me wings. I find further support in the thought of the late Janez Bečaj (2009), who taught me during my student years. Namely, our goals set the direction of our activities, while the essence is in nurturing the processes that we believe will lead us in the chosen direction, even if the path is long.

MARJETA ŠARIĆ'S PERSONAL ACCOUNT

In this second part of this chapter focusing on ISATT's significant shaping effects on Slovenian scholars, I (Marjeta Šarić), like Barbara Šteh before me (and Barica Marentič Požarnik [Chapter 3] before her), tell of my association with ISATT. I begin by introducing my doctoral research and then trace the influence ISATT has had on me.

Doctoral Research Topic

In preparing my doctoral proposal, I decided to focus on the ways in which professional reflection helps teachers to recognise and cope with the emotional aspects of their work. Teachers' work is not only intentional systematic arrangement of optimal conditions for learning. Besides intelligent decision making, it involves emotional aspects. The emotional aspects of teaching are becoming more and more acknowledged (i.e., Hargreaves, 2005; Schutz, Cross, Hong, & Osbon, 2007; Schutz & Zembylas, 2009; Sutton & Wheatley, 2003; Winograd, 2003). Furthermore, it is impossible to strictly separate cognitive and emotional processes because they are deeply intertwined, as is recognised from different research fields: neuropsychology (Immordino-Yang & Damasio, 2007; Phelps, 2006), developmental and educational psychology (Pianta, Hamre, & Stuhlman, 2003; Sutton & Wheatley, 2003) and cognitive and social-constructionist psychology (Niedental, Krauth-Gruber, & Ric, 2006). The teaching profession is strongly influenced by interpersonal relationships and involves much personal engagement of teachers. This implies emotional responses from both professional and personal perspectives, recognising that there are strong links between those two sides in teaching. Nias (1990) vividly illustrates the characteristics of teaching profession:

First, it involves affect as well as cognition and practical activity. The day-to-day work of classroom teaching involves emotional highs and lows; as an occupation it is felt as well as experienced. Second, it calls for a large number of cognitive, practical and interpersonal skills, and to do it well requires that these be carried to a high level of 'balance', a form of craft performance which at times becomes artistry. (p. 205)

Nias continues with describing other characteristics, among them those on an experiential level which include 'mental and physical exhaustion, constant self-examination, and self-doubt..., warmth, acceptance, exhilaration, self-extension, fulfilment, and the satisfactions...' (p. 205). All these qualities suggest intense personal involvement in teaching. The question arose as to how do teachers recognise and cope with such a demanding job. Another query followed: Are there ways to encourage and support teachers in their everyday challenges as described above? My questioning led me to two rather different areas. The first one was the study of emotion in order to understand the scope and variability of teachers' emotional responses to their demanding job. The second area was reflection in the context of teachers' professional development. The central question was formed when bringing those two areas together, namely how emotional experiences of teachers are dealt with and what role does structured supervision play in this process.

The first line of inquiry, the study of emotion, is currently a rapidly growing field with many different theoretical approaches. As a psychologist, I started with the psychological literature, where there is no clear consensus of what the study of emotion actually is. There is a lack of a generally accepted common definition of the concept of emotion – the whole issue of the journal *Emotion Review* [October 2012, Vol. 4(4)], for example, is devoted to this problem. As a working solution I decided to accept the general multi-component definition which defines emotion by enlisting its components: 'subjective feelings, expressive motor behaviour, cognitive appraisals and styles, physiological arousal, and the readiness to take particular action as to the component process' (Niedental et al., 2006, pp. 6-7).

Becoming Acquainted with ISATT Members and Their Research

At different times during my research work, certain themes kept resurfacing spontaneously and in uninvited ways. The one I would like to mention here is vulnerability, not only of teachers but my own as well: the concept of vulnerability of teachers I have met before, especially while studying the literature of Kelchtermans (1996, 2005). Kelchtermans (2005) expands

the concept of vulnerability beyond its experiential aspect to a wider understanding of vulnerability as 'a structural condition that teachers find
themselves in' (p. 988). He suggests that the experience of vulnerability has
its source in lack of perceived control and as such is mediated by micropolitical, social and structural contexts that teachers experience (Kelchtermans, 2005). While this conception of vulnerability contributes to a better
understanding of teachers' profession, it is also an example of how difficult it
is to delineate experiential processes only as an emotion because they carry
other aspects of experience with them. The actual work with teachers
provided me with concrete examples and allowed me to deepen my
understanding of the vulnerability they felt. Their openness to talk about
emotional and other personal issues they encounter in their workplace has
had a great impact on me, one being my increased awareness of my own
vulnerability. To expose my own vulnerable issues, there are the frustrations,
struggle and feelings of 'I don't belong here' that have coloured my attitude
towards my academic work. My first and so far only ISATT Conference
in Rovaniemi in 2009 provided me with much needed confidence. There
I encountered a broad scope of different and (for me) unusual research
approaches and ideas. I was inspired by the readiness for encountering
uncertainty in the research work. All these helped me to widen the aperture of
the lens that I had on my own research study. However, while the
vulnerability issues keep returning, I just try to continue with the work,
supported by my mentor Barbara Šteh and by the knowledge, inspiration
and fresh ideas of the researchers I met at the ISATT Conference.

In designing my research approach I was encouraged by the ISATT
philosophy, which has extended the boundaries of what can be done.
Examples presented by ISATT members and other researchers at the ISATT
2009 Conference as well as in the journal *Teachers and Teaching: Theory and
Practice* encourage me to follow a research line, which is not traditional in
Slovenian psychological and pedagogical fields. In my country, quantitative
research approaches prevail and detailed statistical analysis is preferred in
the collection and analysis of empirical data. Qualitative approaches are
rarely used in research; they are mostly viewed as an addition to the
quantitative analysis of data. Despite the dominant research climate, I
decided to design my doctoral study as an attempt to encourage teacher
professional development in ways that are meaningful to them. It is very
important for me that deep relationships develop for research participant
and researcher to the mutual benefit of both parties. All things considered,
I decided to conduct a case study and I selected four teachers with whom
I individually conducted eight supervision sessions in an approximately

six-month period. The supervision was based on the five phase ALACT model of reflection, named after the first letters of the five phases (action, looking back on the action, awareness of essential aspects, creating alternative methods of action, and trial), and core reflection developed by Korthagen and his colleagues (Korthagen & Vasalos, 2005; Korthagen, Kessels, Koster, Lagerwerf, & Wubbels, 2001).

In the data collection period, I also acquired a deeper, experiential understanding that boundaries between professional and personal are not tight and rigid but rather permeable. Because the personal side is usually overlooked and neglected in the scientific literature, I was fascinated and encouraged by an article written by Meijer et al. (2009), which highlights the interconnectedness of various aspects of teachers' lives. It is one of the examples that really influenced my search for meaningful academic work. Teaching and reflection on teaching are not only rational processes but permeate a person's whole being. This is highlighted in another recent article on teacher reflection by Hoekstra and Korthagen (2011) where they presented a case of one teacher and her transformation in both professional and personal ways. The authors reported that the supportive supervisory sessions helped the teacher to increase awareness on her own thought patterns, beliefs, feelings, needs, values and their relationship to her behaviour. This suggests that problems and difficulties in teachers' work have roots in teachers' personal issues as well (i.e., fears, insecurities, ideals) and in order to be successful in teacher's learning, these have to be dealt with on the personal level.

The connection between professional and personal in teachers' work clearly manifested itself in the data of my doctoral study. To illustrate, I present some excerpts from the on-going analysis of transcripts. In this presentation of data, the emotions per se are not the main issue; my intention here is focused on how these emotionally coloured issues were dealt with in the course of a supervision session. Two selected excerpts show how inner processes were triggered by the supervision sessions with teachers. One of these processes, also mentioned by Hoekstra and Korthagen (2011), is increased awareness of certain aspects of one's own inner cognitive and affective approaches. At the beginning of third supervision session, when we reviewed what had happened after the previous session, a teacher reported how she became aware of the pattern of her emotional reaction to the students' behaviour:

Teacher (T): Because, before (previous supervision session) I wanted to "hit my head against the wall," when the student got on my nerves, although I kind of expected it, because he has done that before many times.

Her preconception of how things should be with this student caused her to be 'stuck' in her reactions ('wanted to hit her head against the wall'). This was followed by a detailed description of her looking at her own response tendencies, how automatic they were and how she could observe herself in these automatic responses. She recognised that it was her own expectations and beliefs that prevented her from acting differently:

> T: The biggest step was, well, that in me, in my head, I recognized I could do that *(react differently)* earlier, but it was funny to look at myself, to have that striving to be how I imagine myself to be. And it seems to me that many times I have that-
>
> Supervisor (S): Yes, go on.
>
> T: That I imagine one thing - how it's supposed to be, or I have, how to say this, some manner, some way how this has to be and then I am so blind, I don't know at all ...
>
> S: Yes.
>
> T: To give up a little, or maybe take another perspective or take a wider look.

This wider look provided the teacher with a much wider spectrum of possible reactions to the student's difficult behaviour. She could spontaneously decide what to do in her classroom in a given moment. Aware of this, she stayed connected to herself and to the student as well.

The teacher also increased self-knowledge in a way that heightened sensitivity towards what was going on inside of her, even outside the scope of specific problems that were dealt with in the supervision sessions. The following passage is excerpted from the beginning of the second last session:

> T: You know, when you're in such a distress, and I remembered our first sessions, well, now that I thought about it and all those problems, well, I realize how much relationships mean to me, even though I might have not been aware of it, I have many times, when I felt, uhm, not very good, I have later realized that I hadn't made that connection. And I need it, some kind of two-way flow, to somehow resonate with people, otherwise there is this obstacle, something is not right, but I didn't know what was wrong.

The last excerpt I present is from the conclusion of the second supervision session. It is significant in the way it shows the difficulties teachers have in expressing and communicating inner experiences.

> S: (Summarizes the teachers explanations of an event, offers another interpretation [could it be that...] and checks whether it is congruent with her observation).
>
> T: Umm, yes.
>
> S: Is this acceptable for you? *(Another check)*
>
> T: Yes, it is a fully logical interpretation to me.

S: How do you feel about this interpretation?

T: *(Relieved laughter.)* At the moment really good.

S: Is it okay?

T: Such a burden has been lifted. What a relief. Suddenly I feel ... less guilty. *(Laughter, bodily change.)*

S: It's easier for me too.

T: It really is *(emphasized)*, I cannot say how much.

S: Yes. Well, okay.

In this interaction, there are many exchanges that are worthy of attention. First, I would like to emphasize the teacher's statement: 'I cannot say how much', which she expressed in a very assertive way. There are, of course, many possible meanings for this statement; however, the most straightforward one may be the difficulties we have in capturing our immediate experiences in words and descriptions. Our concrete emotional experience in any given moment is dynamic, evolving and changing. It has the potential to bring new meanings to the situation as a whole. If this concretely felt sense is carried forward, in Gendlin's meaning (Gendlin, 1996), it has the potential to bring new conceptualisations of the situation at hand, and as such is not yet available to be described in words because it is still so new, so unknown, so fragile. This is the place, however, from which new ways of perceiving, interpreting, interacting and so forth can arise. The first impression is that this difficulty in communicating inner experiences can pose a considerable obstacle to research studies where time is of the essence. On the other hand, I consider this rather exciting, for it is a sign that we have come close to the very core of teachers' inner lives. In usual circumstances, these core levels are hidden more-or-less deep in the unconscious and it takes feelings of personal safety as well as curiosity to look at and be cognisant of whatever arises from those deep levels.

The research I describe in my personal account is still on-going and there remains much work to do. This second portion of this chapter describes some aspects of my research on teachers' emotions and the role that reflection as part of structured supervision plays in teachers' recognising and coping with emotions. In the process of designing and working on the doctoral thesis, I have struggled with many challenging issues. Nevertheless, I try to view those struggles as opportunities for learning. One of the important lessons that I have learned, largely through the influence of ISATT and its members, is that the holistic approach to teaching appreciates teachers in their own terms at all levels of their being.

FINAL COMMENTS

In this chapter, we (Marjeta Šarić and Barbara Šteh) have mapped how each of us came in contact with ISATT together with our older colleague and mentor Barica Marentič Požarnik who encouraged us to join ISATT member. Her modelling, along with our attendance at biennial meetings and our vicarious interactions with members/authors through the *Teachers and Teaching: Theory and Practice* journal and other publications, has sustained us during our early years of career. With great anticipation, we look forward to our continued association.

REFERENCES

Akkerman, S. F., & Meijer, P. C. (2011). A dialogical approach to conceptualizing teacher identity. *Teaching and Teacher Education, 27*(2), 308–319.

Altrichter, H., & Posch, P. (1991). Učitelji raziskujejo svoj pouk [Teachers research their instruction]. *Vzgoja in izobraževanje, 22*(2), 12–22.

Bečaj, J. (2009). Cilji so vedno v oblakih, pot pa je mogoča le v resničnosti [Goals are always in the clouds but the path can only be in reality]. *Vzgoja in izobraževanje, 40* (jubilee number), 27–40.

Beijaard, D. (2001, September). Teachers' professional identity and how it shaped during teacher education: An analysis of the concept and some research examples. In *ISATT 10th Biennial Conference, Conference Programme and Book of Abstract: Connecting policy and practice: Challenges for teaching and learning in schools and universities* (pp. 50–51). Faro, Portugal: University of Algarve, Campus de Gambelas.

Beijaard, D., & Verloop, N. (1999, July). *Domains and development of professional identity: A teacher knowledge perspective.* Paper presented at the 9th ISATT conference, Dublin, Ireland.

Carlgren, I., & Klette, K. (2001, September). Reform policy, teacher autonomy and the mission of schooling. In *ISATT 10th Biennial Conference, Conference Programme and Book of Abstract: Connecting policy and practice: Challenges for teaching and learning in schools and universities* (p. 54). Faro, Portugal: University of Algarve, Campus de Gambelas.

Clandinin, D. J. (2003). Stories to live by on landscape of diversity: Interweaving the personal and professional in teachers' lives. In B. H. J. Smith (Ed.), *New directions in teachers' working and learning environment* (pp. 7–8). Leiden, The Netherlands: ICLON, Leiden University.

Clandinin, D. J., & Huber, M. (2005). Shifting stories to live by: Interweaving the personal and professional in teachers' lives. In D. Beijaard, P. C. Meijer, G. Morine-Dershimer & H. Tillema (Eds.), *Teacher professional development in changing conditions* (pp. 43–59). Dordrecht: Springer.

Craig, C. (2001, September). Investigating school portfolios: What teachers know and how they know it. In *ISATT 10th Biennial Conference, Conference Programme and Book of Abstract: Connecting policy and practice: Challenges for teaching and learning in schools and universities* (p. 36). Faro, Portugal: University of Algarve, Campus de Gambelas.

Craig, C. (2003, June). The influence of context on teachers' knowledge, communities of knowing and school context. In B. H. J. Smith (Ed.), *New directions in teachers' working and learning environment* (pp.43–44). Leiden, The Netherlands: ICLON, Leiden University.

Day, C. (2007, July). Identity, well-being and effectiveness: The emotional context of teaching. In *ISATT 13th Biennial Conference, Totems and Taboos: Risk and relevance in research on teachers and teaching, conference program* (p. 11). St. Catharines, Canada: Brock University.

Day, C., Sammons, P., Kington, A., Stobart, G., & Hadfield, M. (2005, July). Profiling variations in teachers' work, lives and effectiveness: The VITAE project. In *12th International Conference ISATT, Challenges for the profession, perspectives and directions for teachers, teaching and teacher education: Conference program* (p. 93). Sydney: Australian Catholic University.

Dolk, M., Korthagen, F. A. J., & Wubbels, T. (1995, August). *What makes teachers teach the way they teach? Instruments to investigate aspects of teachers' gestalts*. Paper presented at the 6th European conference for research on learning and instruction, The Netherlands.

Elliott, J. (2001, September). How performance audit prevents teachers from evaluating their teaching. In *ISATT 10th Biennial Conference, Conference Programme and Book of Abstract: Connecting policy and practice: Challenges for teaching and learning in schools and universities* (p. 63). Faro, Portugal: University of Algarve, Campus de Gambelas.

Erkkilä, R., & Mäkelä, M. (2005). Confronting the person in biographical interviews. In P. M. Denicolo & M. Kompf (Eds.), *Connecting policy and practice: Challenges for teaching and learning in schools and universities* (pp. 223–227). London: Routledge.

Fisher, R., & Egemann, J. (2007, July). The unexplored continent of Canadian colleges. In *ISATT 13th biennial conference, Totems and Taboos: Risk and Relevance in Research on Teachers and Teaching, Conference Program* (p. 15). St. Catharines, Canada: Brock University.

Fox, D. (1983). Personal theories of teaching. *Studies in Higher Education, 8*(2), 151–163.

Fullan, M. (1993). *Change forces: Probing the depths of educational reform*. London: The Falmer Press.

Gendlin, E. (1996). *Focusing-oriented psychotherapy: A manual of the experiential method*. New York: Guilford Press.

Gore, J. (2007). Improving pedagogy: The challenges of moving teachers towards higher levels of quality teaching. In J. Butcher & L. McDonald (Eds.), *Making a difference: Challenges for teachers, teaching and teacher education* (pp. 15–33). Rotterdam, The Netherlands: Sense Publishers.

Gow, L., & Kember, D. (1993). Conceptions of teaching and their relationship to student learning. *British Journal of Educational Psychology, 63*(1), 20–23.

Hannay, L. M., Bray, C., & Telford, C. (2005). The dichotomy between large-scale reform rhetoric and the perception of school-based practitioners. In D. Beijaard, P. C. Meijer, G. Morine-Dershimer & H. Tillema (Eds.), *Teacher professional development in changing conditions* (pp. 257–272). Dordrecht: Springer.

Hansen, P. J., & Mulholland, J. A. (2007, July). *Professional biography and story-lines as tools for understanding vulnerability in early career male elementary teachers*. Paper presented at ISATT conference, St. Catharines, Canada: Brock University.

Hargreaves, A. (2002). Teaching in a box: Emotional geographies of teaching. In C. Sugrue & C. Day (Eds.), *Developing teachers and teaching practice, international research perspectives* (pp. 3–25). London: Routledge Falmer.

Hargreaves, A. (2005). Educational change takes years: Life, career and generational factors in teachers' emotional responses to educational change. *Teaching and Teacher Education*, *21*(8), 967–983.

Haugstveit, T. B. (2001, September). How do teachers think about educational assessment? Interviews with six primary school teachers. In *ISATT 10th Biennial Conference, Conference Programme and Book of Abstract: Connecting policy and practice: Challenges for teaching and learning in schools and universities* (p. 64). Faro, Portugal: University of Algarve, Campus de Gambelas.

Heikkinen, H. L. T. (2001, September). Telling stories in teacher education: A narrative-biographical view on portfolio work. In *ISATT 10th Biennial Conference, Conference Programme and Book of Abstract: Connecting policy and practice: Challenges for teaching and learning in schools and universities* (p. 78). Faro, Portugal: University of Algarve, Campus de Gambelas.

Hoekstra, A., & Korthagen, F. (2011). Teacher learning in a context of educational change: Informal learning versus systematically supported learning. *Journal of Teacher Education*, *62*(1), 76–92.

Huber, G. L., & Schrodi, F. (1999, July). *Logical minimization as a tool for research on teacher thinking*. Paper presented at the 9th Biennial Conference of the ISATT, Dublin, Ireland.

Immordino-Yang, M. H., & Damasio, A. (2007). We feel, therefore we learn: The relevance of affective and social neuroscience to education. *Mind, Brain and Education*, *1*, 3–10.

Ingvarsdottir, H. (2007, July). Autonomy and alliance – Two dimensions in teacher development. In *ISATT 13th Biennial Conference, Totems and Taboos: Risk and Relevance in Research on Teachers and Teaching, Conference Program* (p. 11). St. Catharines, Canada: Brock University.

Izhodišča kurikularne prenove [Principles of Curricular reform]. (1996). Ljubljana: Nacionalni kurikularni svet.

Jónsdóttir, L. M. (2007, July). Stories of beginning teachers' journey to become the teachers they initially intended to become. In *ISATT 13th Biennial Conference, Totems and Taboos: Risk and Relevance in Research on Teachers and Teaching, Conference Program* (p. 6). St. Catharines, Canada: Brock University.

Kalin, J., Govekar-Okoliš, M., Mažgon, J., Mrvar, P., Resman, M., & Šteh, B. (2008). *Vzvodi uspešnega sodelovanja med domom in šolo: Sodobne rešitve in perspektive* [Levers of successful co-operation between the school and the home: Modern solutions and perspectives] (Research report). Ljubljana: University of Ljubljana, Faculty of Arts.

Kalin, J., & Šteh, B. (2007). Teachers facing the challenges of daily practice in a school reform. In J. Butcher & L. McDonald (Eds.), *Making a difference: Challenges for teachers, teaching and teacher education* (pp. 157–172). Rotterdam, The Netherlands: Sense Publishers.

Kalin, J., & Šteh, B. (2009). The importance of respecting teachers' and parents' differences in navigating mutual relationships. In *Papers from the ISATT 2009 conference: Navigating in educational contexts: Identities and cultures in dialogue* (p. 16). Rovaniemi, Finland: University of Lapland.

Kelchtermans, G. (1996). Teacher vulnerability: Understanding its moral and political roots. *Cambridge Journal of Education*, *26*(3), 307–324.

Kelchtermans, G. (2005). Teachers' emotions in educational reforms: Self-understanding, vulnerable commitment and micropolitical literacy. *Teaching and Teacher Education*, *21*(8), 995–1006.

Kelchtermans, G. (2007). Professional commitment beyond contract: Teachers' self-understanding, vulnerability and refection. In J. Butcher & L. McDonald (Eds.), *Making a difference: Challenges for teachers, teaching and teacher education* (pp. 35–53). Rotterdam, The Netherlands: Sense Publishers.

Kitchen, J., Kosnik, C., & Beck, C. (2007, July). Marisa's induction: A life history study of a new teacher. In *ISATT 13th Biennial Conference, Totems and Taboos: Risk and Relevance in Research on Teachers and Teaching, Conference Program* (p. 6). St. Catharines, Canada: Brock University.

Kompf, M., & Fulton, G. (2007, July). Inside-out views of teachers' lives and careers. In *ISATT 13th Biennial Conference, Totems and Taboos: Risk and Relevance in Research on Teachers and Teaching, Conference Program* (p. 11). St. Catharines, Canada: Brock University.

Korthagen, F. (2005). Practice, theory and person in life-long professional learning. In D. Beijaard, P. C. Meijer & G. Morine-Dershimer (Eds.), *Teacher professional development in changing conditions* (pp. 79–94). Dordrecht: Springer.

Korthagen, F., Kessels, J., Koster, B., Lagerwerf, B., & Wubbels, T. (2001). *Linking practice and theory: The pedagogy of realistic teacher education.* Mahwah, NJ: Lawrence Erlbaum Associates.

Korthagen, F., & Vasalos, A. (2005). Levels in reflection: Core reflection as a means to enhance professional growth. *Teachers and Teaching: Theory and Practice, 11*(1), 47–71.

Lauriala, A., & Kukkonen, M. (2005). Teacher and student identities as situated cognitions. In P. M. Denicolo & M. Kompf (Eds.), *Connecting policy and practice: Challenges for teaching and learning in schools and universities* (pp. 199–208). London: Routledge.

Laursen, P. F. (2005). The authentic teacher. In D. Beijaard, P. C. Meijer & G. Morine-Dershimer (Eds.), *Teacher professional development in changing conditions* (pp. 199–212). Dordrecht: Springer.

Loughran, J. (2003). Knowledge construction and learning to teach. In B. H. J. Smith (Ed.), *New directions in teachers' working and learning environment* (pp. 5–6). Leiden, The Netherlands: ICLON, Leiden University.

Mansvelder-Longayroux, D., & Verloop, N. (2001, September). The portfolio as a tool for the professional identity formation of student teachers. In *ISATT 10th Biennial Conference, Conference Programme and Book of Abstract: Connecting policy and practice: Challenges for teaching and learning in schools and universities* (p. 51). Faro, Portugal: University of Algarve, Campus de Gambelas.

Marentič Požarnik, B., Kalin, J., Šteh, B., & Valenčič Zuljan, M. (2002). *Strokovna avtonomija in odgovornost pedagoških delavcev* [Professional Autonomy and Responsibility of Teachers] (Research Report). Ljubljana: MŠZŠ.

Marentič Požarnik, B., & Šteh, B. (1999). Observations of teacher's and student's role in the context of secondary school curricular reform. In *ISATT Book of Abstracts of 9th Biennial Conference* (p. 73). Dublin, Ireland: St. Patrick's College.

Mayer, D. (2003, June). Professional standards for teachers: professional learning or teacher evaluation? In B. H. J. Smith (Ed.), *New directions in teachers' working and learning environment* (pp. 44). Leiden, The Netherlands: ICLON, Leiden University.

McLaughlin, M. (2002). Sites and sources of teachers' learning. In C. Sugrue & C. Day (Eds.), *Developing teachers and teaching practice, international research perspectives* (pp. 95–115). London: Routledge Falmer.

Meijer, P. C. (2009). The role of crisis in the development of teachers' professional identity. In *14th Biennial Conference of ISATT, Navigating in educational contexts: Identities and cultures in dialogue, Abstracts* (p. 5). Rovaniemi, Finland: University of Lapland.

Meijer, P. C., Korthagen, F. A. J., & Vasalos, A. (2009). Supporting presence in teacher education: The connection between the personal and professional aspects of teaching. *Teaching and Teacher Education, 25*(2), 297–308.

Miles, M. B., & Huberman, A. M. (1994). *Qualitative data analysis.* Thousand Oaks, CA: Sage Publications.

Moore, S. A. (2008). Social justice and education in "A World Fit for Children?" In J. A. Kentel & A. Short (Eds.), *Totems and taboos, risk and relevance in research on teachers and teaching* (pp. 17–29). Rotterdam, The Netherlands: Sense Publishers.

Nias, J. (1990). *Primary teachers talking.* London: Routledge.

Niedental, P. M., Krauth-Gruber, S., & Ric, F. (2006). *Psychology of emotion: Interpersonal, experiential and cognitive approaches.* New York: Psychology Press.

Niemi, H., & Kohonen, V. (1995). *Towards new professionalism and active learning in teacher development.* Reports retrieved from the Department of Teacher Education in Tampere University, Tampere, Finland.

Nissilä, S. P. (2008). Towards equity and self-awareness in teacher education. In J. A. Kentel & A. Short (Eds.), *Totems and taboos, risk and relevance in research on teachers and teaching* (pp. 213–228). Rotterdam, The Netherlands: Sense Publishers.

Nissilä, S. P. (2009). Identity, pedagogical awareness and interaction in HE teacher education. In *14th Biennial Conference of ISATT, Navigating in educational contexts: Identities and cultures in dialogue, Abstracts* (pp. 14–15). Rovaniemi, Finland: University of Lapland.

Noel, K. A., & Macmillan, R. B. (1999). Responsive choreography: Reconceptualizing teaching and learning. In *ISATT Book of Abstracts of 9th Biennial Conference* (pp. 90–91). Dublin, Ireland: St. Patrick's College.

Oliver, N. (1999). Confessions of a reforming bean-counter: An anthology of self-indulgent tales. In *ISATT Book of Abstracts of 9th Biennial Conference* (p. 99). Dublin, Ireland: St. Patrick's College.

Oygarden, B. (2001, September). How do pupils develop self-assessment skills in classroom context? Self-assessment in oral and written dialogues with teacher. In *ISATT 10th Biennial Conference, Conference Programme and Book of Abstract: Connecting policy and practice: Challenges for teaching and learning in schools and universities* (p. 63-64). Faro, Portugal: University of Algarve, Campus de Gambelas.

Phelps, E. A. (2006). Emotion and cognition. *Annual Review of Psychology, 24*(57), 27–53.

Pianta, R. C., Hamre, B., & Stuhlman, M. (2003). Relationships between teachers and children. In W. M. Reynolds, G. E. Miller & I. B. Weiner (Eds.), *Handbook of psychology, volume 7, educational psychology* (pp. 199–234). New Jersey: Wiley.

Pritzker, D. (2001, September). Narrative chain as a starting point for development of thought processes in teacher education. In *ISATT 10th Biennial Conference, Conference Programme and Book of Abstract: Connecting policy and practice: Challenges for teaching and learning in schools and universities* (p. 78). Faro, Portugal: University of Algarve, Campus de Gambelas.

Sagadin, J. (1991). Kvalitativno empirično pedagoško raziskovanje [Qualitative empirical educational research]. *Sodobna Pedagogika, 40*(7–8), 343–355.

Schutz, P. A., & Zembylas, M. (Eds.). (2009). *Advances in teacher emotion research: The impact on teachers' lives.* New York: Springer.

Schutz, P. A., Cross, D. I., Hong, Y. I., & Osbon, J. N. (2007). Teacher identities, beliefs, and goals related to emotions in the classroom. In P. A. Schutz & R. Pekrun (Eds.), *Emotion in education* (pp. 223–241). San Diego, CA: Academic Press.

Sjolie, G. (2001, September). How to study pupil assessment as part of professional competence? Methodological challenges in a classroom study of teacher competence in primary school. In *ISATT 10th Biennial Conference, Conference Programme and Book of Abstract: Connecting policy and practice: Challenges for teaching and learning in schools and universities* (p. 63). Faro, Portugal: University of Algarve, Campus de Gambelas.

Smith, K. (2005). New methods and perspectives on teacher evaluation, Who evaluates what and for which purposes? In D. Beijaard, P. C. Meijer, G. Morine-Dershimer & H. Tillema (Eds.), *Teacher professional development in changing conditions* (pp. 95–114). Dordrecht: Springer.

Spring, J. (2007, July). An alternative to global education policies. In *ISATT 13th Biennial Conference, Totems and Taboos: Risk and Relevance in Research on Teachers and Teaching, Conference Program* (p. 5). St. Catharines, Canada: Brock University.

Šteh, B., & Kalin, J. (2008). The changing students conceptions in evaluating teacher effectiveness in higher education: Facing challenges and taboos. In J. A. Kentel & A. Short (Eds.), *Totems and taboos, risk and relevance in research on teachers and teaching* (pp. 183–197). Rotterdam, The Netherlands: Sense Publishers.

Šteh, B., & Kalin, J. (2012). Students' views on important learning experiences: Challenges related to ensuring quality of studies. In N. Popov, C. Wolhuter, B. Leutwyler, G. Hilton, J. Ogunleye, & P. Almeida (Eds.), *International perspectives on education, BCES conference books* (pp. 291–297). Sofia: Bulgarian Comparative Education Society (BCES).

Šteh, B., & Marentič Požarnik, B. (2005a). What is actually happening in secondary classrooms? The rhetoric and reality of curricular reform. In P. M. Denicolo & M. Kompf (Eds.), *Connecting policy and practice: Challenges for teaching and learning in schools and universities* (pp. 99–106). London: Routledge.

Šteh, B., & Marentič Požarnik, B. (2005b). Teachers' perception of their professional autonomy in the environment of systemic change. In D. Beijaard, P. C. Meijer, G. Morine-Dershimer & H. Tillema (Eds.), *Teacher professional development in changing conditions* (pp. 349–363). Dordrecht: Springer.

Sutton, R. E., & Wheatley, K. F. (2003). Teachers' emotions in teaching: A review of the literature and directions for future research. *Educational Psychology Review, 15*(4), 327–358.

Tickle, L. (2003, July). *The crucible of the classroom: A learning environment for teachers, or a site of crucifixion?* Paper presented at the meeting of ISATT, Leiden, The Netherlands.

Trigwell, K. (2008). Quality teaching: Some insights from higher education research. In J. A. Kentel & A. Short (Eds.), *Totems and taboos, risk and relevance in research on teachers and teaching* (pp. 31–40). Rotterdam, The Netherlands: Sense Publishers.

Vaisanen, P. (2001, September). Professional growth group and portfolio as tools for student-teacher development. In *ISATT 10th Biennial Conference, Conference Programme & Book of Abstract: Connecting policy and practice: Challenges for teaching and learning in schools and universities* (pp. 103–104). Faro, Portugal: University of Algarve, Campus de Gambelas.

Van Veen, K. (2007, July). *Rethinking the concept of teachers as professionals: Implications for teachers' working conditions, teachers training and professional development, and social*

BARBARA ŠTEH AND MARJETA ŠARIĆ

discourse. Paper presented at ISATT conference, St. Catharines, Canada, Brock University.

Van Veen, K., & Sleegers, P. (2001, September). *Caught between a rock and a hard place: Orientations and emotions of a reform enthusiast teacher in a context of change.* Paper presented at 10th Biennial Conference of the ISATT, Portugal.

Vermunt, J. D. H. M. (1993). Constructive learning in higher education. In J. K. Koppen & W. D. Webler (Eds.), *Strategies for increasing access and performance in higher education* (pp. 143–156). Amsterdam: Thesis Publishers.

Winograd, K. (2003). The functions of teacher emotions: The good, the bad, and the ugly. *Teachers College Record, 105*(9), 1641–1673.

Woods, P. (2002). Teaching and learning in new millennium. In C. Sugrue & C. Day (Eds.), *Developing teachers and teaching practice, international research perspectives* (pp. 73–91). London: Routledge Falmer.

CHAPTER 31

SELF AND COMMUNITY: THE IMPACT OF ISATT ON THE PROFESSIONAL LEARNING, TEACHING, AND RESEARCH OF MEMBERS IN THE ASIA-PACIFIC REGION

Issa Danjun Ying, Amanda McGraw and Amanda Berry

ABSTRACT

In this chapter, the relationship between self and community is addressed through inquiring into the impact of the International Study Association on Teachers and Teaching (ISATT) on the professional learning, teaching, and research of members specifically in the Asia-Pacific region. The authors employ qualitative methods, primarily self-study and narrative inquiry, and use descriptive statistics derived from survey responses to support their claims. The work not only speaks to ISATT's significant

From Teacher Thinking to Teachers and Teaching: The Evolution of a Research Community
Advances in Research on Teaching, Volume 19, 669–701
ISSN: 1479-3687/doi:10.1108/S1479-3687(2013)0000019034

shaping effects but also to historical and contemporary challenges the organization faces as it moves toward the future.

Keywords: ISATT; professional learning; professional communities; Asia-Pacific region

A key purpose of International Study Association on Teachers and Teaching (ISATT) is to enhance the quality of education through improved teaching and professional learning opportunities. If social processes are inherently linked to effective thinking and learning, how can a large international association composed of members from diverse geographical settings and with diverse perspectives really have impact? This chapter explores and examines this key issue.

This chapter draws upon a multilayered research study conducted by Issa Danjun Ying (Hong Kong Institute of Education, China), Amanda McGraw (University of Ballarat, Australia), and Amanda Berry (Leiden University, the Netherlands). The research aims to investigate the impact of ISATT on members in the Asia-Pacific region specifically with the hope of gaining insight into the organization's influence globally. As researchers, we conducted a survey of members, interviewed a small sample of key members in the region who had sustained involvement in ISATT, and reflected on their own connections to the Association. Reflections from new members were also included to provide different voices from the region. Our inquiry predominantly employed qualitative methods including self-study (Hamilton, 1998; Pinnegar & Hamilton, 2009) and narrative inquiry (Clandinin & Connelly, 2000; Connelly, Clandinin, & He, 1997; Georgakopoulou, 2006a, 2006b) and also drew upon quantitative data gained through the survey responses (Robson, 2002).

Key questions we address are listed below:

1. In what ways does our participation in ISATT impact on our professional learning, teaching, and research?
2. What issues related to teacher learning and identities emerge through our own narratives and email exchanges both as project researchers and ISATT members in the Asia-Pacific region?
3. What potential do dialogical processes have for enhancing professional learning across diverse geographical settings?

In the first part of this chapter, we present a profile of the ISATT membership in the Asia-Pacific region and identify issues that emerged from the online survey which members were invited to complete. In the second part of this chapter, we illustrate notions of self and community by focusing on the personal–professional experiences of three ISATT members from the Asia-Pacific region. In the third part of this chapter, we present our insights from working together on this ISATT project, a collaborative study that explored our professional learning and collaboration.

CREATING AND SUSTAINING COMMUNITY

This section presents a profile of ISATT membership in the Asia-Pacific region and the results of a survey that we conducted to explore how members' participation in ISATT impacted on their professional learning, teaching, and research. The survey included 10 questions in total, focusing on participants' ISATT membership, their reasons for being ISATT members, memories associated with ISATT conferences, the nature of their participation in ISATT, and suggestions for further development of ISATT in the future. Two of the survey questions were open questions, which invited members to explain why they became a member of ISATT and to describe some significant moments in their experience of ISATT. Members were also encouraged to elaborate on their answers for closed questions or questions with rating scales.

We used Survey Monkey, an electronic survey method, which enabled members to click on the web link of the survey rather than fill in a hard copy. As members were busy in their profession and had a range of commitments, we hoped this user-friendly method could boost the response rate. We sent the survey link to 74 members and 37 responded, therefore the response rate was 50%. The major findings of the survey are presented below.

A Glimpse into ISATT Membership in the Asia-Pacific Region

The ISATT membership in the Asia-Pacific region has some unique features. By the time we did the survey in early May 2012, there were 74 members in total from 39 institutions in 13 different regions and countries (Table 1). Relatively, it is a small group in ISATT, but it is important to note that the number of ISATT members in this region has grown quickly in recent years. For example, only 5 members joined ISATT before 2001 and in the next 8 years from 2002 to 2009, 18 members joined. However, the number increased strikingly with 51 new members from 2010 to 2012. This

Table 1. ISATT Membership in Asian-Pacific Region.

Areas	Members	Institutions
Australia	27	9
Mainland China	3	2
Hong Kong	8	4
India	8	6
Japan	3	2
Macau	1	1
Malaysia	1	1
New Zealand	13	6
Pakistan	2	2
Singapore	4	2
Sri Lanka	1	1
South Korea	1	1
Taiwan	2	2
In total	74	39

was largely due to ISATT's regional conference activity in Hong Kong and India. For 37 out of the 74 members who responded to our survey questions, about 95% of members work in higher education. About 68% of them have been members for 1–4 years, 27% for 5–10 years, and only 5 % for more than 10 years.

Consequently, the respondents represent a comparatively "young" sample of the member group but full of diversities.

Reasons for Joining ISATT

There are various reasons why members joined ISATT. Most of those surveyed liked to network with colleagues from other parts of the world and updated themselves on professional matters. Following are some of the reasons why members first joined the Association:

To network, make a difference in education

Want to meet more professionals in the field of teacher education around the world

It promised to be a diverse international group of educators

To keep up to date with recent research in the field of education

I wanted to connect with the larger group of teacher educators in the world, and know what is happening outside, and this is my first attempt at it. Since I belong to what is basically different from mainstream education, I also want to learn the techniques of research, so that I can look at my own work with new eyes. This will help me in handling my data and learning to present it to others, giving as well as receiving information.

I joined as I thought it was a good organisation to be a part of as the focus on teaching and teachers underpins my research. I thought it would enable me to meet with like minded researchers and keep up to date with the latest developments in the field.

– Excerpts from survey participants' responses.

Some members joined ISATT because they enjoyed learning and sharing at the ISATT conferences and decided to stay afterward.

I attended the conference in Australia that was sponsored by my own university. I was excited by the guest lecturers and the topic of the papers presented.

– An excerpt from survey participants' responses.

A number of members were recommended to attend the ISATT conference by their colleagues or PhD supervisors.

It was recommended by my supervisor. I attended the conference, and I felt it strongly connected with my Ph.D. study. Also, people were so nice and the conference made me feel like being in a big family.

Colleagues suggested the conference as an ideal forum to present new research so registered for conference and became a member in 2011.

A colleague recommended that I join. She gave me copies of the [*Teachers and Teaching: Theory and Practice*] journal to read when I was starting my doctoral studies and I immediately saw a connection between to my own teaching and learning interests.

It was coincidental I went to the conference [after seeing] a poster. Then I met Michel Huberman and some other scholars with whom I had some deep scholarly conversations. I thought this could be a place for me to learn continually.

Cheryl Craig introduced me to ISATT at the Castle "self-study" conference in East Sussex, UK. I share ISATT's concerns about giving voice to teachers and understanding their thinking and practice as mediated by the context in which their work is embedded.

I liked the objectives of ISATT. I must include my engaging interaction with Ms. Daniela Hotolean and Prof. Cheryl Craig at Hyderabad, India. It was a moment of moments. I think teaching is an art. I was looking for a solid platform for teacher education. I have been involved in such things in India.

I was introduced to the organisation by a fellow colleague and felt it was a highly reputable professional body to belong to at the time when I was involved in ITE programmes.

An encounter with Paulien [Meijer] and Cheryl [Craig] at the Second East Asian Conference on Teacher Research in Hong Kong [regional conference] convinced me of the high profile of ISATT and I thought it would provide me the opportunities I need for my professional development.

A colleague (Ruth Kane) introduced me to the Teachers and Teaching journal and to ISATT when I had just completed my Ph.D. A key focus in my research is teacher beliefs in intercultural situations, so the international focus of the journal and ISATT in general. Its emphasis on teacher thinking and beliefs hit my "spot."

– Excerpts from survey participants' responses.

Some members were attracted to the conference by the nature of the research presented or by journal articles and books published by members. Some found the ISATT website attractive, especially the objectives of ISATT and decided to come along to the conference. Other reasons included shared academic/research interests with other members and the relevance of the conference topics to their own work.

My academic interest lies in teachers' thinking and curriculum studies and so I find ISATT goes along well with my academic pursuit and thus my joining the ISATT.

It's related to my work in Teacher Education. The aims of ISATT are aligned to my research agenda.

I appreciate the quality and the breadth of the research done by its members. I did/do also intend to be a contributor.

My research interests are related to ISATT's research focuses.

I joined as I thought it was a good organisation to be a part of as the focus on teaching and teachers underpins my research. I thought it would enable me to meet with like-minded researchers and keep up to date with the latest developments in the field.

– Excerpts from survey participants' responses.

Participating in ISATT

As noted in the survey (Table 2), about 57% of members have been to ISATT conferences once or twice, only 16% attended ISATT conferences more than three times, and about 27% have never attended an ISATT conference. This was not surprising since the rapid increase of members in this region only occurred in the last three years, that is, from 2010 to 2012, as a result of ISATT's targeted development in the region.

When members were invited to describe their participation in ISATT (Table 3), about 8% reported that they did not find the conferences very useful or interesting; however, the majority participated in ISATT conferences (67.6%) and enjoyed the conferences (56.8%). They appreciated

Table 2. ISATT Conference Participation.

How Many Times Have You Been to ISATT Conferences?		
Answer Options	Response Percent	Response Count
a. 1–2	56.8%	21
b. 3–5	10.8%	4
c. 6 or more	5.4%	2
d. Never	27.0%	10
Answered question		37

Table 3. Members' Participation in ISATT.

How Would You Describe Your Participation in ISATT? Please Tick the Statements That Apply to You? You Can Tick More Than One.		
Answer Options	Response Percent	Response Count
a. I sometimes read material published by ISATT (e.g., the journal, website material, newsletters, books);	56.8%	21
b. I closely read material published by ISATT (e.g., the journal, website material, newsletters, books);	43.2%	16
c. I have attended ISATT conferences but have not found them useful or interesting.	8.1%	3
d. I find ISATT conferences useful and interesting.	56.8%	21
e. I have presented at one or more ISATT conferences.	67.6%	25
f. I actively network with others at ISATT conferences.	24.3%	9
g. I have worked with fellow ISATT members on collaborative research projects.	27.0%	10
h. I talk with fellow ISATT members about my pedagogy.	40.5%	15
Others or add a comment to elaborate on your response to this question if you wish:		13

the conference focus on teaching and learning and its recognition of both the teaching and research roles of teacher educators.

> ISATT is an important conference for me as it places teachers and teaching -and more recently teacher education – at the forefront of research.

> I appreciate the focus on teaching and learning in various contexts. Many journals tend to include articles written by academics only, rather than by practising teachers. There is

always something of interest in every journal. There would appear also to be a unique focus on the identity of teachers, which suits my interests.

ISATT provides a forum that recognises both the teaching and research roles of teacher educators, which is unlike many other conferences – which typically emphasis one or the other aspects. ISATT is also more of an international conference – no particular dominance of any one country – which makes it more interesting and more balanced than many other so-called international conferences, and is helpful in developing my understanding of the contextual similarities and differences for teacher educator/ academics internationally.

– Excerpts from survey participants' responses.

Sharing and networking are quite active among ISATT members. Materials published by ISATT were quite popular: about 43% of members read ISATT publications closely and about 57% read them sometimes. Some members felt closely connected with ISATT, and some new members were looking forward to participating in the ISATT conference in the near future. However, some members had mixed feeling about ISATT and felt disappointed by some keynote speeches.

Impact of ISATT from Members' Perspective

Figure 1 indicates that the impact of ISATT mainly on members' research and their thinking about teaching and/or research, and professional learning.

The impact of ISATT extended when about 78% of members reported that they shared their experiences of ISATT with colleagues and/or students

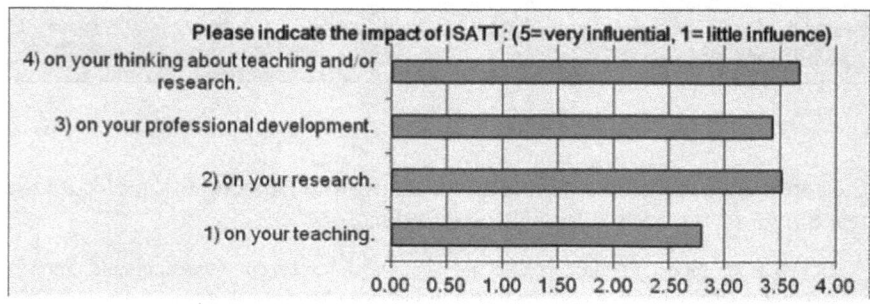

Fig. 1.   The Impact of ISATT on Members' Thinking, Teaching, Research and Professional Development.

and encouraged them to join ISATT. This was the way in which a number of members joined ISATT. Members also shared ISATT publications with colleagues/students.

> I have talked with the staff at my institute and have encouraged them to read the research published and to become members.
>
> I encouraged my first tow doctoral graduates to present in 2011 in Portugal. It was a most regarding experience for them and for me.
>
> There have been a couple of key journal articles that I have shared widely with others – colleagues and students. One of those is Rodgers and Raider-Roth's article on presence. I went to the ISATT conference in Portugal last year with two colleagues and we talked during and after the conference about issues raised at presentations we enjoyed. ... We plan to present collaboratively at the conference in Belgium.
>
> – Excerpts from survey participants' responses.

Some members promoted ISATT membership within their own professional communities and shared their experiences of participating in ISATT due to their strong sense of belonging to this community. For example,

> I promote membership, and honour my own membership and contributions to ISATT work. I invite my colleagues and graduate students to join ISATT by sharing with them conference news and ISATT websites.
>
> I have spoken to them about the sense of belonging that isatt provides and the advantages of belonging to a community with shared interests, where there's support for growth professionally and socially.
>
> – Excerpts from survey participants' responses.

When members were asked to recall some significant moments, they reported that they enjoyed networking and getting to know people in ISATT, sharing and discussing with other members. They also reported that reading ISATT publications is stimulating as these are relevant for study, research, and teaching.

> Through reading of the publication, *Teachers and Teaching: Theory and Practice*. It has given me new ideas about my research on teacher education.
>
> Reading the paper given by a presenter at the Australian conference, opened up a new research pathway for me.
>
> – Excerpts from survey participants' responses.

A member reported that ISATT helped him/her build identity as a researcher.

2011 conference was my first international conference experience so was really significant for me in my feelings about my developing identity as a researcher, a teacher educator, and as an academic.

– An excerpt from survey participants' responses.

Some members described their moments at length when they were invited to describe any significant experience in association with ISATT. For example:

ISATT has been a powerful influence on my development as a researcher and teacher-researcher. I attended ISATT for the first time in 2003 (Brandenburg, R., 2003, July. *Self-study in the tertiary environment: restructure, reconnection, reflection and re-visioning.* Paper presented at the International Study Association of Teachers on teaching Conference, Leiden. The Netherlands). This was also my first international conference and my first research paper that focused on my Ph.D. studies. I was trialing Korthagen's ALACT framework for reflection and felt encouraged when he referred to my research in his keynote address. We maintained contact. By invitation, in 2008 he visited Australia and conducted a two day joint – university workshop on reflection, and now in 2012, we have co-written a paper based on research ethics with multiple international authors which is to be presented at an international conference in August. This is one example of a connected and collaborative research relationship that was born in ISATT and has continued to develop. ISATT colleagues are generous with time and expertise and provide mentorship that has an 'international flavour' – meaning that multiple perspectives about learning and teaching can be unpacked, understood and appreciated.

I attended a conference in 2010 at the Hong Kong Institute of Education and the ISATT Executive was there – actually, they were the reason I went. They participated in a number of group seminar presentations and I was so impressed by their thoughtfulness, their attempts to create dialogue, their inclusiveness and by the way they sought critical feedback. I am not a fan of academic conferences where people present in factory-like systems for 15–20 minutes at a time. I learn very little and come away frustrated. The ISATT Executive members modeled a different, more meaningful approach. While I had been a member for some time prior to this, this was my first direct experience of ISATT. Prior to arriving in Hong Kong, I was asked to have dinner with the Executive members. I was made to feel a part of the association and for me the personal and emotional connections between people, make a difference to my learning.

The Rodgers and Raider-Roth article titled 'Presence in Teaching' (2010) also had an impact on my teaching. I have used that piece with my students and it inspired a workshop I created with a local playwright. Reading it also led me to visit Carole Rodgers in the US and observe her teach. Korthagen's work on core reflection and teacher education has also been influential.

Professional colleagues that I work closely with are also members of ISATT.As a group we have similar research interests and together we reflect deeply on our practice. Together we talk about ISATT conferences and share readings we believe others might be interested in.

– Excerpts from survey participants' responses.

Some members appreciated that ISATT provided opportunities for networking with more experienced scholars and researchers. A member described two significant moments as follows:

1. There are only 2 ISATT members from Taiwan. I contacted that professor. We planned to work on the collaborative research project. Unfortunately my proposal was not accepted. It was a great experience because I had the chance to contact that professor.

2. I attended the conference in 2011. It was a great experience, particularly the session on journal article writing and submission."

– An excerpt from survey participants' responses.

These significant experiences and moments told in small narratives reveal how members became connected with ISATT and developed a sense of belonging.

Suggestions to ISATT Development in the Future

Members have made some suggestions about ways to improve the experiences of ISATT in the future. Issues related to the roles and responsibilities of ISATT were raised. For example,

I'm not sure that ISATT intentionally aims to be collaborative, friendly and inclusive – or whether that is just a product of the nature of the people who have gravitated toward the association. I wonder what could be achieved, if this was an intentional focus. I would like to see ISATT define more explicitly the sorts of research methodologies it favours. I think that its identity in this respect could be less muddy. At the Portugal conference there was such a mix of approaches (qualitative and quantitative) and presentation styles. There was the production line approach as well as 'round table' interactive sessions. As a narrative researcher, only certain sessions appealed to me and had me thinking. I think that ISATT could more clearly define what it thinks effective practices are, rather than try to be all things to all people.

ISATT can build up a group of experts who can train teachers for tomorrow. It should take lead role in 3rd world countries where teaching in general hasn't yet reached the expected professional height.

– More frequent contact among members

– More cemented in group bond

– More activities in different fields

Given an opportunity, I could take part in different committees."

– Excerpts from survey participants' responses.

Some were concerned with the location of the conference, the length of presentations, and the cost of traveling:

> I really want to be able to travel to more of the ISATT conferences, but as noted earlier these tend to be based in Europe. It is very expensive and time consuming to get there. Only having a 15-minute presentation slot at the conference is another prohibitive factor. I'm sure we could have longer paper presentations so people get more of a sense of where their work connects with others. It might also be easier to persuade my institution to provide funding if I was doing something more substantial when I arrived.

> The reality is that when you live on the opposite side of the world to where the majority of the conferences are held the cost in flying there ... can be prohibitive. My university grants us $2000 for travel/accommodation plus conference registration is partially covered but this rarely gets close to the overall expense of a conference for ISATT.

>   – Excerpts from survey participants' responses.

Some comments are even more critical:

> I wonder if conference organising committees are chronically trapped in a mode of dated protocols while they sing songs about aspirations for the future in their posters. What values are being advocated to the younger generation in the way that the old ruts of academic hierarchy are reinforced in the conference proceedings? I think ISATT can do better in addressing critical issues of teachers' roles and responsibilities in a true sense of becoming educators, instead of becoming an organisation of mutual back-scratching.

> Keynote speakers need to be aware of their audiences and to provide real food for thought and not something you might hear at a preservice or graduate lecture. Keynote presenters should not treat their moment as sages on the stage and as a boys' club. Need to lift the caliber.

>   – Excerpts from survey participants' responses.

Other suggestions are briefly summarized as follows:

- Invite keynotes on cutting edge with new material.
- Post possible collaboration topics or network.
- Why not having a conference in Hong Kong?
- Not affordable for young researchers.
- Include some articles about language teachers.
- Provide some specific mentors.
- Opportunities to network.
- More activities that provide opportunities of dialogue between members.
- To be more specific with methodology.
- More seminars or workshops for novice researchers.
- Provide platform for discussion.
- More local (Asia-Pacific) activities in between biannual conference.

>   – Excerpts from survey participants' responses.

Finally, one member expressed his experiences of ISATT as a poem:

> ...
> Before you search for a reason
> I meditate near the Banyan tree.
> Your restlessness remain blotted
> In a cup of tea.
> I am what I am becoming
> As a song
> Of several blood images.
> It burns my pain
> And reduces all anxious thoughts to ashes.
> You teach me how a river turns into a gutter.
> You grapple for meaning
> I beg for food ....
> In a packed classroom
> Near the bank of River Dulong.

> – An excerpt from survey participants' responses.

Interim Summary

This section examined the data collected from the survey and aimed to explore the views of ISATT members in the Asian-Pacific region and the impact of ISATT on members' teaching, research, and professional learning. It seems that most members in this region at the time the survey was conducted were keen to share their experiences of teaching and research with colleagues, including colleagues in the broader ISATT community. The majority of the respondents reported that they "fed back" their experiences of ISATT to colleagues and students. Indeed, quite a number became ISATT members due to the recommendation of their supervisors or colleagues. This is one of key factors in creating and sustaining ISATT as a community.

PERSONAL THREADS AND PROFESSIONAL TIES

In this second part of the chapter, we illustrate notions of self and community through a focus on the personal–professional experiences of two long-standing members, Associate Professor Ora Kwo, University of Hong Kong, and Professor John Loughran, Monash University. We conducted individual interviews with Ora and John to learn about how each experienced their induction into the ISATT community, the unfolding of their association over time and some insights about possible future directions for ISATT as a professional organization. Together these voices helped us gain a deeper perspective on the notion of community in ISATT.

Connecting with ISATT

Each of the two members expressed their initial motivation for coming to ISATT as an opportunity to meet and learn from colleagues who shared a common professional interest, that is, teaching and teacher education. In addition, each member emphasized the importance of being able to hear about ideas and from people whom they could not easily access in their home countries. For Ora, it was the chance to connect with others "beyond her own organisation." For John, it was a chance to connect with European, non-English speaking colleagues.

> John: I wanted to know about Europeans and their work. I couldn't access that work through the normal journals because few of them wrote and published in English. At the conference, I could listen to their ideas, for example, colleagues from Norway and Denmark.

Accessibility and Openness

Both members highlighted the value of being able to listen first-hand to high-profile education academics speak about their work. This was as much the case in the organized lectures as in the informal meetings in or between conference sessions. John described an attraction of the conference as the high-profile keynote speakers who made themselves accessible and available throughout the conference, especially to junior academics such as himself. Ora recalled feeling "touched" by the humility and openness of a well established academic keynote speaker who began by saying, "I am nervous … …" While the initial ISATT experiences of these members was many years ago, it seems that the spirit of approachability and openness continues to exist.

Opportunities to Speak and Be Listened to

Each member spoke with appreciation about the ISATT conference as a place where it is possible to "express your ideas freely and have them taken seriously by others, no matter whether English is your second (or third or fourth language), or whether you are a beginning or junior academic." Ora described how she felt "at home" during the conferences and that she felt free to show her opinions and concerns. She saw the best presenters (both key note and in sessions) as those prepared not only to share their ideas but also listen to participants, using sessions to encourage discussion and debate rather than simply reporting their own research. John confirmed this sense of the ISATT conference as an open and encouraging forum for discussion and debate of all members.

Similar to the notion of accessibility above, ISATT seems to be a place where participants have an opportunity to speak and be listened to. The conference culture appears to offer space where sharing of ideas is valued and where participants make an effort to connect with each other as people, and with each others' ideas, as scholars. In this book's closing chapter, Yang, a new Asia Pacific member from China offers the metaphors of "bag" and "bridge" to describe the differences between "the physical and psychological distances inhibiting dialogical approaches" (bag), and "efforts to narrow down the distances and to share, understand and sympathize" (bridge).

Developing Deeper Connections

After several years, both John and Ora took on leadership roles within the ISATT organization, which gave them access to new people and new opportunities for their own learning, and for supporting the learning of colleagues. Both John and Ora are former members of the Executive committee and reviewers for the ISATT journal, *Teachers and Teaching: Theory and Practice*. John recalled being invited to join the Executive group, as an ex officio, at a public meeting of ISATT in 1997. He explained that,

> In fact, it was the best thing to keep someone like me around, to keep me in the organisational part. Maybe that was deliberate on the part of Chris Clark and Christopher Day. They could tap into the way I think and operate. I was on executive until 2003 or 2005. I ended up being on the journal. That gave me more a sense of ownership or belonging to the conference, but because I had goals, things to do.

Apart from these more formal positions, both John and Ora now see their role as nurturing and supporting the next group of scholars within the organization. For this task, they use their own formal and informal networks both within and outside of ISATT. Ora encouraged colleagues to come along with her to the conference, taking ISATT as a platform to support and cultivate younger scholars in the same way she had experienced herself. John also encouraged colleagues to attend, but lamented that in his new role of Faculty Dean he no longer has the time to keep a strong connection with ISATT. He feels that his work on the journal is one way of keeping him somewhat connected with the organization.

ISATT as a Community

John and Ora expressed their different ideas about the notion of ISATT as a community. Ora felt that the extent to which ISATT participants experienced a sense of belonging or community was dependent on their own initiatives. As she worded it, "ISATT is what you make it." As for John, he found it difficult to think of ISATT as a community because the conference is a biennial event, so the sense of continuity with people and ideas is hard to maintain. The changing group of participants and the shifting nature and focus according to different participants made it feel to him more like a network or organization. He wondered whether the term "community" might be more appropriate to describe those who belong to the Executive or Journal or perhaps those who already are affiliated with one another with the various regions, if we were to extend his thinking.

Impact on Thinking

John identified the strong connection and impact that ISATT had on his ideas about teaching and teacher learning. Initially, he was attracted to the conference by its central focus on "teacher thinking," and the valuing of teacher knowledge. These ideas have remained central in his work, albeit in more refined and complex ways.

> John: I think that those ideas around Teacher Thinking – where ISATT started – is one of those ideas that still exists in my head, around terms like complexity and problematic and sophisticated – all those sorts of things that go back to the idea of teacher thinking that tried to value what teachers know and try to do, even if teachers don't know they're doing it. I think I'm still saying the same things now, just in different language. I've refined my language around the ideas.

John recognizes his own contribution now, as a senior member of ISATT, in terms of continuing to "seed" ideas about the importance of recognizing and valuing teacher knowledge, for example through practitioner research and self-study. He considers ISATT as a place where such ideas should be more firmly embedded.

While John took a more explicitly strategic approach to his involvement in ISATT, Ora never considered herself as one who purposefully tried to shape the organization or "feed in" particular ideas. She enjoyed attending the sessions and meeting different colleagues and from time to time there was a special moment or person who impacted her thinking.

> Ora: I met Michael Huberman at the sixth biennial conference in Surrey in 1991. It was the first ISATT conference I attended. I found myself entering a rather long and engaging conversation with Michael Huberman about my doctoral work in progress. At that time, I was not aware that he was a well-known and widely cited scholar. I enjoyed his responses to my questions, warmed by his genuine interest in what was bothering me. It was only later that I came to learn more from his writing. He accepted my nomination to be invited to my university as a Visiting Scholar, but then he was far too occupied with multiple commitments to be able to come as planned. We had to engage in a long haul of effort re-arranging dates. I was continually impressed by his humble stance with patient correspondence and sincerity. Though we never succeeded with the plan, I learned other dimensions of a scholar's virtues. Whether or not humility is a valued virtue in the ethos of ISATT, I am content to have met someone I aspire to learn from.

Working Toward the Future

Both members expressed similar ideas about the increasingly difficult position that teachers find themselves in when they begin to take their work seriously. Teachers relatively low occupational status, the "outside" perception that teaching is "easy" work, and more and more demands and pressures of accountability, distract teachers from a proper focus on education. Teachers are encouraged to support the development of their learners as autonomous individuals, and yet teachers themselves experience little opportunity to act with agency, given the external controls that dominate education, all over the world, but particularly in China, a part of the Asia Pacific region.

In line with these critical ideas about the empowerment of teachers, Ora expressed her concern that ISATT should be careful not be become too "cozy;" a place where people stay within their comfort zones of culture, academic knowledge or collegial groups. She explained that "ISATT should involve more commitment, not to reinvent, but to pursue good studies and research to address some global issues, rather than to decorate." This may involve reshaping the structure or activities of ISATT so as to more directly target the real and urgent educational issues, such as educating children of poverty.

> Ora: Education is a privilege for few, not reaching all. Schooling doesn't equal to education. Students need opportunities and good teachers to be educated and enriched ... ISATT could become an open space to dialogue, to bring educators together to roundtables, not to listen to each other, but to 'hatch' each other. ISATT should be creative to look for some new ways that integrate from the 'floor', more than the 'stage'.

Interim Summary

Looking across the set of experiences that comprise these members' experiences of ISATT, the themes of voice and inclusion strongly emerge. Each valued opportunities to have his or her own voice heard and respected, and his or her ideas discussed. These themes are applicable not only to how members recalled their own participation in ISATT but also to their everyday work as teachers and with teachers. Clearly, an important future goal for ISATT will include how to pay close attention to practices of inclusion in all aspects of the work of the organization, from the structure and nature of conference sessions, through the presentations of keynote speakers, to making genuine opportunities for relationship building between all colleagues. At the same time, ISATT must maintain a diligent focus on the pressing problems of education – and be courageous in addressing these.

SELF WITHIN COMMUNITY: COLLABORATIVE RESEARCH AS A PATCHWORK OF DIGITAL NARRATIVES ACROSS TIME AND PLACE

When we were invited to edit and write a section in this text about ISATT, we saw it as an opportunity to learn about the level of impact that an international association such as ISATT can have on its members. We were also eager to work collaboratively on a research project.The fact that great oceans separated each of us (Issa Ying lives in Hong Kong, Mandi Berry in the Netherlands, and Amanda McGraw in Australia) did not seem an issue. We had never worked together; in fact we barely knew one another and yet from our first email messages there was a sense of connection and a willingness to share, take responsibility, cooperate, and respect new ideas. It is worth noting that all of our thinking occurs across time zones and with the assistance of technology. We have never, during this project, met face-to-face. I (Amanda McGraw) write this with a frozen image in mind of Mandi Berry in mid-flight, hitting a volleyball (her photo ID on Skype), and Issa Ying standing smiling before a large building, a book in her hands. This third section of our chapter aims to capture significant moments in our journey as we worked together as ISATT members across long distances and in doing this, we will draw attention to key aspects that have enabled us to work collaboratively as researchers. These include the use of technology to construct and learn through disparate narratives; how meaning and engagement relies on personal and professional interconnections; and how important the ongoing development of relationships is to thinking and working effectively together. Our storytelling during this time reveals interesting insights into ISATT and its impact on us as teacher/researchers. What is revealed through our disparate narratives will also be discussed. Finally, we examine the implications of what we have learned through this project, for ISATT as an international organization that can potentially foster research connections across geographical boundaries.

While there is a growing interest in the use of technology for collaborative research purposes, mainly in the fields of management and business (Kimiloglu, Ozturan, & SencerErdem, 2012), a focus on the use of technology to support collaborative educational research is limited. As a research group, we have talked at different times about whether our activities constitute us as a "community of practice" (Wenger, 1998) and we wonder like others (Johnson, 2001; Palloff & Pratt, 1999) whether communities of practice can be built and sustained in virtual worlds. While our group members were selected by ISATT Executive (and we have never been told why we were selected[1]), it has emerged through discussion that the three of us have a number of shared research interests, principles, and practices. Given that membership of ISATT draws us together at one level, we have found that by sharing our stories and being purposely engaged in this project, rich intersecting experiences have emerged and personal connections have developed. These have informed our decision making and actions. The relational connections and the respect and care shown at times when our outside lives interrupted the flow of work, have enabled us to focus and refocus purposefully on the task set by ISAAT's Executive. The nature of the task was not absolutely clear or strictly bound, and this has meant that we have used technology as a tool to help us negotiate meanings, develop concepts, revise our thinking, offer feedback and set new directions. Partway through the project, as inevitably happens, the ground shifted and new organizational structures were set by ISATT. This created tension for us as we not only owned and were committed to our initial ideas but also our research was underway (and had been approved by a university ethics committee). If communities of practice are, as Wenger (1998) suggests, self-evolving, situated, human constructs where the negotiation of meaning is constant, then we believe we have become a community of practice.

From our first interactions via email we began to focus practically on the task of researching the impact of ISATT on members in the Asia-Pacific region. We prepared a submission to ISATT for a Collaborative Research Grant; wrote an ethics application to have our research approved through the University of Ballarat; developed survey and interview questions; made "to-do" lists; and so on. These documents, which are examples of "reification," cover a range of processes including designing, making, clarifying, naming and describing (Wenger, 1998). Without reification, participation can lack purpose and shared meaning. Wenger (1998) suggests that the concept of reification is about giving form to our experience through objects. These objects, he argues, become a focus for the negotiation of meaning between people and work to shape our experience in tangible ways. Reification also includes processing tools so the technology we use also works to shape and reshape our collective activity and understandings. For Wenger (1998), material objects are only the tip of the iceberg; what are also significant are the personal contexts and broader meanings that sit behind them. These meanings are generated, shared, negotiated, and debated through participation and interaction. It is evident that this collaborative research experience is effective because the dimensions of reification and participation intertwine. While we work together formalizing, classifying, and conceptualizing our knowledge and understandings in public documents; we also articulate our emotions, reflect on experiences, and share significant stories.

Even in early messages, we tell our personal stories as a way of capturing significant experiences with ISATT and also to build relational connections. Our language is purposeful and exploratory; open and suggestive; polite and familiar. As we move through the year our language continues to be like this. I (Amanda McGraw) include in this piece some of our email exchanges that not only illustrate the ideas discussed but also foreground our actual voices and show that dialogue is "mutually accomplished" (Freebody, 2003). It is through the interactions that the most interesting connections are revealed: how meaningful professional experience can be imbued with intimate emotional and visual memories; how people centered our professional decision making can be; how new ideas emerge through dialogue that is nonthreatening and where participants take shared responsibility; and how influential key educational mentors are to the professional development of early career researchers.

We begin with our first email messages. Email addresses have been blotted out to preserve our privacy.

Sent: Sunday, January 29, 2012 9:58 PM
To: Issa
Cc: ████████████████████████████████
Subject: ISATT Edited Book Update
Dear Issa,

Perhaps we could begin by thinking about what we would like to see included in our section as well as suggest some relevant themes/ideas to play with. Perhaps we could also consider our own experiences and perceptions of ISATT as a starting point. What are your experiences Issa? I have been a member for about 10 years but I would say for most of that time I have been a silent member. Helen Hayes, who at that time was supervising my doctorate, suggested I join ISATT and introduced me to the journal. Helen has since passed away from cancer and in some ways I connect the Association with her. She loved ISATT and went to a few of the conferences. She was a very thoughtful, reflective, quietly perceptive person and in some ways I think about the Association in the same way. There is a small group of us here at the University of Ballarat who are members and I had heard through them about the wonderful ISATT conferences – how friendly the Association members are and how there are opportunities for meaningful discussions. In 2010 I heard that ISATT was going to have a presence at the East Asian International Conference on Teacher Education Research and I decided to go. The ISATT seminars were my favourite part of the conference – I felt as though the speakers were talking my language: we had similar concerns, research interests, questions about practice and thinking – and probably more importantly for me, similar research sensitivities. Last year I attended the conference in Braga and while the Association is certainly diverse, I do feel as though there are interesting connecting points that make me feel as though I belong. And that I can be challenged. As I'm writing this message, I'm wondering whether down the track we could also use our email correspondence of part of the text! What do you think? Our email exchanges could act as a sequential narrative that could hold the piece together and make the connections clear. What do you think about that as an idea?

Looking forward to hearing from you (and Mandi when she comes on board). Amanda
From: Issa < ████████████████ > [mailto: ████████████████]
Sent: Wednesday, 1 February 2012 8:42 PM
To: ████████████████████████████
Cc: ████████████████████████████████████
Subject: Re: FW: ISATT Edited Book Update
Dear Amanda,

It is so interesting to read your story of encountering ISATT, which reminded me of my first conference experience with ISATT. My supervisor strongly recommended it, so I applied for it. No surprise, I stay with it. I will write separately about it. I will copy your experience and make it a separate file and put it in the shared folder. I will also put some comments and questions there. I would like to test whether this way of communication works.I cc a copy this email to Mandi Berry to keep her informed.

Mandi, welcome to this email loop and please feel free to respond when you are ready. Wish you a smooth transfer to the new institution and a prosperous year ahead!

Best regards,

Issa

From: mandi berry <█████████████████> [mailto:█████████████████]
Sent: Thursday, 2 February 2012 10:24 AM
To: ████████████
Cc: ████████████████████
Subject: Re: FW: ISATT Edited Book Update

Hi Amanda and Issa,

Thanks for getting this started and i look forward to working with you! I have now accepted your drop box folder sharing invitation. As you may know, i am moving to live and work in Leiden, Netherlands from Feb 10th so my contact will be a bit messy until mid-March. So I am very grateful that you can get the ball rolling without me, at least initially.

I really like your suggestion about inviting members to share their stories, perhaps some structuring questions will be useful but also encourage members to free write if they wish. I'm sure if we invite all listed members that we will not have everyone responding to us, so it would be worth sending out the invitation, just to see what happens. And if there are specific people that we wish to hear from, then we might send a special invitation to request a contribution.

I am not very experienced as an ISATT member – having attended only 3 conferences – Faro, Portugal; Rovienmi, Finland; and Braga, Portugal. There are a handful of members at Monash in the Faculty of Education, and typically we would take along new teacher educators to this conference as a way of helping them to find their 'peer group'. John Loughran encouraged me to attend, having recommended this group as talking about aspects more specific to teacher education, compared with bigger, broader conference groups, like AERA. It is certainly a friendly and 'intimate' conference, which makes it very easy to be able to talk with any colleagues – not just those I already know.

Amanda's idea of including our own discussions as part of how the chapter comes together sounds a very lovely one.

Please keep me posted!

Best wishes,

Mandi

As we encountered new demands and our ideas developed, we found we needed to search for new technologies to support our communication. We quickly set up a communal Drop Box that allowed us to collaboratively draft documents. This was Issa Ying's first time using Drop Box and she now has four other communal Drop Boxes she shares with other colleagues. We also set up a Wiki but found that we never used it. Our conversations have mainly taken place via email; however, we also used Skype at times when we needed to explore more complex ideas synchronously and make immediate decisions. Mandi Berry has written about her use of email for research purposes in another context (Berry & Crowe, 2009) where the focus was on the use of technology to support self-study. Like others (Freese, Kosnik, & LaBoskey, 2000; Hoban, 2004), Berry and Crowe (2009) saw that the value of using email for research purposes lay not only in its capacity to shape thinking through reflection but also to make thinking visible and public. In email communication we can shift sometimes quite quickly between different voices: internal, fragile voices; directional, authoritative voices; practical, objective-driven voices; and voices where we show personal care and concern. Email is both a social process and a personal experience. One of the most intriguing aspects of our communication via email has not only been how we move freely between public and private voices but also how through the expression of reflective thoughts, we reveal surprising interconnections between our experiences, ideas, and values. We write to one another in moments squeezed between work commitments, in the early or late hours of busy days, and in private, quiet times when writing is fuelled by vivid visual memories and shaped by a strange, ill-formed sense of audience on the other side of the world. We are taken by our references to the weather – on one side of the world it is snowing; elsewhere it is hot and dry. There are blizzards, storms, and heat in the background of most correspondences. Also interspersed, are family, and career moments – children completing exams, a mother diagnosed with a major illness, visits to overseas conferences, flus, stress, and news of publications! While we share these experiences in snippets, possibly because of the transient nature of email, they indicate that even as we work on pragmatic matters, our desire to make meaning of our complex, sometimes difficult professional worlds, involves attention to our personal histories, our situated contexts, and present perspectives. Greene (1986) suggested some time ago that the self cannot be actualized through private wonderings; connectedness is required. She advocated a "dialogical" self-reflection in teacher education (Greene, 1978). Reflecting on experience through email is at once personal and communal. And it can challenge our conventional notions of narrative needing to be sustained and linear.

In face-to-face conversations and interviews and in written accounts like journal entries, we tend to create more unified narratives that are sequenced in fairly linear ways. Our narrative story-telling through email, is more fragmented. Walker (2005) suggests that email and text messaging nurtures a kind of "distributed" narrative. Distributed narratives, according to

Walker (2005), are stories that cannot be experienced in a single session; they are fragments of narrative that come together not as a self-contained whole or as a "thing," but as connections. What is interestingly revealed through our correspondences is not what we learn through formal ISATT presentations, collaborations and publications, but how interesting the personal "backstories" are and the connections that exist between them.If life narratives function as "sites" for learning (Goodson, Biesta, Tedder, & Adair, 2010), what can be learned about the impact of ISATT from looking at our narrative fragments and the connections that exist between them?

From: mandi berry < ██████████████ > [mailto: ████████████████]
Sent: Sunday, 30 September 2012 8:00 PM
To: ██████████████
Cc: ████████████████████████
Subject: Questions to consider

Hi Amanda and Issa,

I don't have any strong singular memories of ISATT that have been significant. More than anything I enjoy catching up with colleagues and finding research connections with those present. Having said that I have not made any formal collaborations from meetings at the conference. Maybe through this project I'll remember something though …….

Mandi

From: Issa < ██████████████ > [mailto: ████████████████]
Sent: Tuesday, 2 October 2012 11:53 AM
To: ██████████████
Cc: ████████████████████████
Subject: Re: Questions to consider

Hi Amanda and Mandi,

It seems that we are having very interesting dialogues via emails.

As for me, I was introduced to ISATT by my doctoral supervisor, too. While I was studying in HKU, I could be funded to join one or two conferences. When I asked my supervisor which one I should go for, she suggested ISATT. She said she had been to many conferences and ISATT was the one that she kept attending. It was a small conference, but it was a good one and I could learn a lot from it. My first ISATT was in 2007, which became an unforgettable experience for me. My trip to ISATT 2007 was not an easy one. There was a new policy just started in that year that a visa was needed even when you transferred your flights in the US. I was not aware of that till I went to the airport to check in my flight. I was told that I could not go because I didn't have the visa for transferring the flight in the US. I made lots of phone calls and had to cancel my flight at the airport and booked a direct flight to Toronto almost at a full price for the following day. I nearly wanted to give it up as there were so many changes that I had to make and I had to pay for the extra cost myself. However, I was glad that I made the trip after I attended the conference. My impression of ISATT started with its preconference. I found it very inspiring to listen to others' proposal presentations and the comments from more experienced researchers. I could feel that more experienced people were helping those green hands. When the conference started, I did enjoy some presentations and felt connected. I had opportunities to make friends during those social events and share my research with them. To look back, some important links were made at that time though I realized it later. ... Another impression was that ISATT valued teachers' stories as teacher knowledge, which was my interest as well. For me, ISATT 2007 was an important event for my Ph.D. study and career development to some extent. Today, when I am recounting it, I can't help thinking, what if I gave up that trip at the airport in 2007? Lots of things could be different. It seems that decisions at those critical moments were important. But what impacted on my decision making? I am still pondering ...

Best

Issa

From: Amanda McGraw < ███████████████ > [mailto: ███████████
███████████]
Sent: Monday, 1 October 2012 9:30 AM
To: ███████████████
Cc: ██
Subject: Re: Questions for you to consider

Hi Mandi,

I actually have a memory associated with ISATT that includes you! In 2011 I went to the seminar that you contributed to on teacher educators crossing boundaries between universities and schools. The session was memorable for me for a couple of reasons. I was a 'boundary crosser' for four years. When I started working in teacher education I was also working in a school as an Assistant Principal. I could relate on a personal level to both the value of doing this sort of work as well as to the challenges.

The other thing I remember is your metaphor of the sheep dog and the image of the paddock you had in the background. I can't really remember the exact meaning you attached to the image but I do remember being able to relate to the idea of being fenced into two different worlds as well to ideas for creating bridges. Metaphors seem to speak to me like nothing else can.

Another thing I remember is your passion and enthusiasm. I also remember thinking: it's interesting that she's chosen to speak from the floor and not from the stage (where the others were seated). She's visually showing that those 'fences' around what's expected from presenters at conferences also need to be broken down.

That was my first ISATT conference in Braga and I went expecting more boundaries to be broken and to hear more examples of meaningful research. While there were a few sessions that really had me thinking, I was disappointed by some of the sessions.

Amanda

From: mandi berry <████████████████> [mailto:████████████████]
Sent: Saturday, 6 October 2012 5:50 PM
To: ████████████████████████
Cc: ████████████████████████████
Subject: Re: Questions to consider

Hi Amanda,

I said I would write back regarding your memory and what it sparked in me and here it is. That ISATT session – a symposium – represented my efforts to bring together teacher educator/researchers from The Netherlands and Australia around the ideas of identity construction and boundary crossing. I figured it was a chance to try to connect my worlds – oz and NL- and also to try to set up some kind of opportunity for sharing of ideas, encourage teacher educators to meet each other etc. Also one of the 'big names' in the field of border crossing work, Sanne Akkerman, would be at the conference and I thought it would be a good networking opportunity for these teacher educators to draw on her work, meet her, etc. And for me to meet her too ;) So I put myself as discussant.

Anyway, I liked the idea of the session a lot as an opportunity and as a concept, the teacher educator as boundary crosser. As I thought about it more, I linked it with the idea of the Aussie boundary rider, who goes around checking the fences and repairing etc. Except in this case, the boundary rider is not someone who actually maintains the boundaries but moves across and within them, understands the differences/uniqueness of each space; trying to create openings rather than build separateness. That was the point I wanted to get to, but wasn't quite sure how.

As I said, I liked the metaphor a lot, and still do, but didn't completely work it through in a way that I felt completely satisfied with. The session itself turned out rather strangely, too many different agendas in the presentation and then I felt extremely dissatisfied with what I had done as discussant. Couldn't quite hit the nail on the head as I had wished to. Maybe my own sense of being a boundary rider between two countries was what I was trying to figure out at the time.

I spoke from the floor because there was no room on the stage. That's funny how it can get interpreted differently. And I feel uncomfortable on the stage also – especially since in that session, I felt like I had nothing of real value to say beyond a cool metaphor.

So it's interesting to hear what you have to say about being a participant in a session. Having been an AP there is another interesting layer about identity negotiation. And that it spoke to you.

I love the idea that you raise about boundaries to be broken at ISATT – your expectations of such and how things transpired for you.

Maybe that is what we can work towards with our own session next year?

Mandi

From: Amanda McGraw <████████████████████████>
[mailto:████████████████████████] On Behalf Of Amanda
McGraw <████████████████████>

Sent: Monday, 8 October 2012 11:36 AM
To: ███████████████
Cc: ██
Subject: Re: Questions to consider

Dear Mandi and Issa,

Thanks for your response Mandi – it was not only honest and thoughtful but it raises issues that I think we can all relate to in relation to being involved in presenting research ideas with and to others. In some ways the stories behind the scenes are more interesting than the research itself! Maybe that's the value of us including our own stories in this section – and trying to do it authentically. Perhaps it's the backstory that I can focus on in this section – what lies behind the main narrative. … I like that!

There's an interesting backstory behind the paper I presented at the ISATT conference too. I had written a piece some time ago about being involved in the Core Reflection experience that Korthagen and Vasalos ran for us at Warrenmang – you were there Mandi for some of the time, although we didn't talk to each other. It was a piece that had frustrated me for some time – I found it to be a fascinating professional learning experience and I wanted to explore the impact it had on me. I decided to return to that piece and present it at the ISATT conference – this in itself was a big decision because the piece is very personal and it involves other professional colleagues – Fred Korthagen has read the piece but writing in this way about the work of someone so well respected is no easy thing.

Anyway, that morning the bus to take us from our hotel didn't arrive and it was pouring with rain. I arrived at the session wet and late – and there were about 8 people there. The other papers were very different and involved hard data and scientific approaches so mine seemed out of place and no one there knew Korthagen anyway. I was pleased it was over but when I went out to have a coffee, the best thing happened. One of your ex-colleagues from Monash (Elly I think her name is) hunted me down. I didn't recognise her but I did make a connection to her at Warrenmang and an experience I shared with her I wrote about in my paper. She had wanted to come to the presentation but she too had arrived late and missed it. Anyway, we had a really interesting conversation about what happened there and my writing challenges – so for me it was worthwhile in the end.

Issa – your story about getting to the ISATT conference is also an interesting backstory.

I'm still thinking about the boundary metaphor – Mandi and Issa, do you feel at the boundaries of ISATT? I'm just wondering whether an association like ISATT has a shifting core and then layers of involvement that emanate out from there. And what factors lead to different levels of involvement and ownership?

The thing that puzzles me most is the sheep dog. Where did I get that idea/image from????

Amanda

Alterio and McDrury (2003) use the term "backstory" to describe implicit, previous stories that shape the main narrative. The stories behind our attendance at ISATT conferences and behind the presentations we (Mandi, Issa, and Amanda) were involved in are revealing, and perhaps as Nymark (2000) suggests, their value is that such stories have the potential "to tap into the unconscious, qualitative phenomena that pervade organisations" (p. 54). The influence of respected others is clear for the three of us who were all introduced to ISATT and urged to attend its conferences by our doctoral supervisors. For early career academics in particular, having a "defining community" (Taylor, 1989) is crucial. Being with others who share a common language as well as concerns, vulnerabilities, and values enables academics to flourish, define their goals and interests, and deepen their understandings through dialogue and reflection. Those feelings of belonging expressed to some extent by each of us become more important as academics shape and reshape their evolving identities in increasingly individualistic and highly competitive work environments.

While ISATT does not include fostering research collaborations and communities of practice in its stated purposes, many members in the Asia-Pacific region believe that ISATT is a friendly association that encourages participation. When more experienced researchers welcome and actively invite early career researchers and new members to participate, they not only enhance the professional learning of members but also build new opportunities to revitalize the Association. The opportunity to be involved in this collaborative research project is a prime example of an initiative instigated by ISATT that intends to build research capacity in early career researchers, mentoring links and new networks. In this instance it has worked effectively on a number of levels. Not only have we worked productively and cohesively but also through our dialogue and storytelling we have expressed more intimate details of our involvement in ISATT that relate to professional identity, personal tensions, and emotional impact. Connecting points include the personal doubts and uncertainties that can surround our research actions; how personal connections enhance meaning-making during conference presentations; how memory is influenced by visual and metaphorical elements; and how thinking is sustained by ongoing narrative connections. As ISATT moves into a new era where thinking and communication is possible across geographical boundaries, we would suggest the Association intentionally create and support more opportunities for purposeful, collaborative activity.

We conclude this section by including a later exchange where we reflect on our involvement in this research project and what we have personally gained.

From: Berry, A. [mailto: ███████████████████]
Sent: Wednesday, 21 November 2012 9:50 PM
To: Amanda McGraw; Issa Ying
Subject: RE: ISATT Book–Contract Negotiations and Possible ISATT Book Sessions at the Ghent Conference

Hi Amanda,

Initially I was quite concerned about what was going to happen with this project. I had attended the ISATT book meeting in Braga, Portugal, and it seemed that there was no real consensus on what had to be done, how and for what purpose. I left in a mist of concerns and ideas ... what would we/I do? At the time also, I was a sole author of the chapter. Some months later, I had an email that informed me there were now three of us working together on this chapter, me together with Amanda and Issa. I was happily relieved that I was not the only person who was going to put together the Asia Pacific section, but was still very much wondering what we would do and how we would do it. But, my worries soon shifted – were relieved – it seemed that as soon as you two came on board, that the project exploded with fire and energy! Issa was off and running with ideas about what could be done and Amanda was alongside with creative expansions of these starting points. Quickly, it seemed, we had a proposal developed for funding, an outline of a project and a team of workers. The energy of both of you, Amanda and Issa, inspired me to stay on board and work towards this goal of completing the work. The purpose of the task had now shifted for me somewhat, in that I was completing something with my team, and I respected the ideas and commitment of the team, compared to doing something for ISATT which up until that time had been a rather disaffecting experience. So that's an interesting insight that things became more relevant and motivating when they were locally connected and imbued with the energy of the collaborators.

Mandi

From: Amanda McGraw
Sent: Tuesday, 27 November 2012 11:05 AM
To: Issa
Cc: ███████████████████████████
Subject: RE: ISATT Book–Contract Negotiations and Possible ISATT Book Sessions at the Ghent Conference

Dear Mandi and Issa,

It's really interesting how many common connections there are in our experiences.

In some ways ISATT took a risk asking people to work collaboratively on this project and I imagine in some places there would be leaders taking control. One of the things I've really liked about this experience is that it has truly been collaborative. Somehow we've been able to work together, recognise and rely on one another's strengths and stick with the project even though we've all had a difficult year.

The personal/professional connections are interesting.Issa has been juggling massive workloads and new professional roles, Mandi has not only moved jobs but moved

ISSA DANJUN YING ET AL.

countries and I have had a challenging year emotionally as well as professionally. I remember feeling guilty that I wasn't contributing as well as I could have at the time when my mother was ill. For a large part of this year I've almost felt like I've been travelling between different worlds – the multiple worlds of work, supporting my daughter who not only went on exchange to Thailand, but spent a term on King Island (a wild and rugged island just off Tasmania, Issa), and then trying to contend with my Mother's changing domestic world where nothing is clear anymore.

Our work has taken place in a virtual world – and for me, that has been one of the reasons I think it has worked so well. Communicating virtually has meant we've been able to talk in our own time (and in airports, classrooms, homes at night); we've been able to get glimpses of one another's home lives and interests (I'm thinking of waving to Issa's son in the background of a Skype conversation and seeing Mandi in action on the volleyball court) and we don't get to look at one another's faces in the corridor and feel really guilty that we haven't met the latest deadline!

Having to (largely) write our thoughts via email has been interesting for me.Writing in this way is still informal and conversational – but it is probably more reflective and thoughtful because you have the chance to stop and think and usually the thinking is happening in a quiet moment. Like in *this* moment. It's Tuesday morning and I'm working from home and there have been thunder storms all night. Everything is still and quiet outside and every now and again I hear distant rolling thunder. It's perfect thinking weather.

Another thing that I find interesting is our fairly organic way of working together. Applying for the Collaborative Grant forced us to tie down some ideas, strategies and focus questions; and even though the ground has shifted and we've been asked to change our focus, we've been able to continue to do things our way and make decisions ourselves based on emerging ideas. I've never been absolutely clear about what we're doing – I think that Mandi makes this point too. That would probably stress some people out – but I've been happy to go with the flow and I think that's because I trust you both.You are both capable and reliable and so I feel that things won't fall in a heap. I also think there's an absence of ego in our relationship – and that probably helps too. I wonder if things would be different if there was a male in the team …….

Amanda

From: Issa Ying [▮▮▮▮▮▮▮▮▮▮▮▮▮▮▮▮▮▮]
Sent: Tuesday, 27 November 2012 12:13 PM
To: Amanda McGraw
Cc: ▮▮▮▮▮▮▮▮▮▮▮▮▮▮▮▮; Amanda McGraw
Subject: Re: ISATT Book–Contract Negotiations and Possible ISATT Book Sessions at the Ghent Conference

Hi Amanda,

I just sent Thomas to his school and am on my way to my office. It is raining and cold for people living in HK, 13 C, which might not be cold at all for Mandi perhaps.

I will have a busy day today: 5 hours for intensive individual speaking assessment, 5 students per hour, and then 3 hours for group speaking assessment for 36 students ... I left home at 7:30am and will be back home around 8pm or 8:30pm.

It is such a great joy to read your long email on this rainy day. I can't help laughing when you write about "ego" and ask, what if there was a male member in our group?

This has been an opportunity for me to keep contact with others in this community and push myself to continue to work in the field that I am interested in, apart from the opportunity of publication. I have also learned a lot from you and Mandi, such as your ways of thinking, writing up all sorts of documents for various purposes, and the use of Survey Monkey. I enjoy our cooperation very much, especially when we all worked hard to apply for the project grant and construct the survey questions!

I do agree there are certain shared concepts, understanding, flexibility and trust among us.

Issa

Working on this project has been a positive experience of conducting collaborative research across geographical boundaries. We have learned that technology can be used as an effective tool to construct and learn through disparate narratives; how meaning and engagement relies on personal and professional interconnections; and how important the ongoing development of relationships is to thinking and working effectively together. The project has not been without its professional and personal tensions but in many ways these have imbued the experience with depth and challenges that have extended our thinking. Our mutual engagement with the initial task set by ISATT and with connected tasks that we then established ourselves were fuelled by respectful, caring relationships, a shared sense of accountability as well as shared professional experiences related to ISATT. We would suggest that as ISATT moves into the future, it continues to tap into the qualitative phenomena that pervade the Association; that it surfaces the backstories of members and searches for shared meanings. Promoting the use of technology to foster collaborative inquiries is a powerful way to engage in such endeavors.

NOTE

1. We have since learned that representatives from ISATT's different regions were chosen with attention paid to stage in career, race and ethnicity, and gender.

REFERENCES

Alterio, M., & McDrury, J. (2003). Collaborative learning using reflective storytelling. In N. Zepke, D. Nugent & L. Leach (Eds.), *Reflection to transformation* (pp. 40–57). Palmerston North: Dunmore Press Ltd.

Berry, A., & Crowe, A. R. (2009). Many miles and many emails: Using electronic technologies in self-study to think about, refine and reframe practice. In D. Tidwell, M. Heston & L. Fitzgerald (Eds.), *Research methods for the self-study of practice* (pp. 83–98). London: Springer.

Clandinin, D. J., & Connelly, F. M. (2000). *Narrative inquiry: Experience and story in qualitative research*. San Francisco, CA: Jossey-Bass.

Connelly, F. M., Clandinin, D. J., & He, M. F. (1997). Teachers' personal practical knowledge on the professional knowledge landscape. *Teaching and Teacher Education, 13*(7), 665–674.

Freebody, P. (2003). *Qualitative research in education: Interaction and practice*. London: Sage.

Freese, A., Kosnik, C., & LaBoskey, V. (2000). Three teacher educators explore their understandings and practices of self-study through narrative. In J. Loughran & T. Russell (Eds.), *Exploring myths and legends of teacher education* (Vol. 1, pp. 75–79). *Proceedings of the third international conference of the self-study of teacher education practices*, Queen's University, Herstmonceux Castle, East Sussex, UK.

Georgakopoulou, A. (2006a). The other side of the story: Towards a narrative analysis of narratives-in-interaction. *Discourse Studies, 8*(2), 235–257.

Georgakopoulou, A. (2006b). Thinking big with small stories in narrative and identity analysis. *Narrative Inquiry, 16*(1), 122–130.

Goodson, I. F., Biesta, G. J. J., Tedder, M., & Adair, N. (2010). *Narrative learning*. Oxon: Routledge.

Greene, M. (1978). *Landscapes of learning*. New York, NY: Teachers College Press.

Greene, M. (1986). Reflection and passion in teaching. *Journal of Curriculum and Supervision, 2*(1), 68–81.

Hamilton, M. L. (Ed.). (1998). *Reconceptualising teaching practice: Self-study in teacher education*. London: Falmer.

Hoban, G. F. (2004). Using information and communication technologies for the self-study ofteaching. In J. J. Loughran, M. L. Hamilton, V. K. LaBoskey & T. Russell (Eds.), *International handbook of self-study of teaching and teacher education practices* (pp. 1039–1072). Dordrecht: Kluwer.

Johnson, C. M. (2001). A survey of current research on online communities of practice. *Internet and Higher Education, 4*, 45–60.

Kimiloglu, H., Ozturan, M., & Sencer Erdem, A. (2012). Collaborative research: Opinions and information technology utilization potential. *Management Research Review, 35*(12), 1134–1152.

Nymark, S. (2000). *Organisational storytelling*. Oslo: Foglaget Ankerhaus.

Palloff, R., & Pratt, K. (1999). *Building learning communities in cyberspace: Effective strategies for the online classroom*. San Francisco, CA: Jossey-Bass.

Pinnegar, S., & Hamilton, M. L. (2009). *Self-study as a genre of qualitative research: Theory, methodology and practice*. Dordrecht: Springer.

Robson, C. (2002). *Real world research* (3rd ed). New York, NY: Wiley.

Taylor, C. (1989). *Sources of the self: The making of the modern identity*. Cambridge: Cambridge University Press.

Walker, J. (2005). Distributed narrative: Telling stories across networks. In M. Consalvo, J. Hunsinger & N. Baym (Eds.), *The 2005 association of Internet researchers annual* (pp. 91–103). New York, NY: Peter Lang.

Wenger, E. (1998). *Communities of practice: Learning, meaning, and identity*. New York, NY: Cambridge University Press.

CHAPTER 32

BACK TO THE FUTURE FROM A CHINESE PERSPECTIVE: A PHILOSOPHICAL RECONSTRUCTION OF IDEAS GLEANED FROM THE FIFTEENTH ISATT CONFERENCE

Xiaohong Yang

ABSTRACT

This chapter draws extensively on the keynote speech delivered by António Nóvoa, Rector of the University of Lisbon, at the fifteenth biennial ISATT conference held in Braga, Portugal, in 2011. Nóvoa's talking points frame this reflective response. Like António Nóvoa, the author probes the meaning of the phrase, back to the future, *as the increasingly global world presses forward in time and ISATT as a professional organization celebrates its thirtieth anniversary. The reflective work links the researcher's life experiences with those of his daughter and students and weaves in understandings he has gleaned from*

From Teacher Thinking to Teachers and Teaching: The Evolution of a Research Community
Advances in Research on Teaching, Volume 19, 703–723
ISSN: 1479-3687/doi:10.1108/S1479-3687(2013)0000019035

other sessions and scholars who also helped to shape the contours of his knowing at his first ISATT meeting.

Keywords: Reflection; ISATT; community; future

The fifteenth ISATT Biennial Conference of the International Study Association on Teachers and Teaching (ISATT) was held at the University of Minho, Braga, Portugal, in 2011. ISATT's 2011 conference theme, *Back to the Future: Legacies, Continuities and Changes in Educational Policy, Practice and Research,* resonated not only "with the venue of the conference – the historic city of Braga" (Flores, 2011) but also with my colleagues – a professor, his adult daughter, and four young graduate students attending from the historic country of China, a country energetically emerging as a new global player.

This was our first time as Chinese nationals to feel the impact of globalization in an international milieu. Everything about the global economy – technology, human capital emigration, internationalization of education, and different language usages – presented itself in varied cultural hues at the conference. Forced to move out of, and then back into, our culture-specific perspective in an effort to understand perspectives of other cultures and to find our own position in the international arena, we gained a great deal in terms of knowledge, skills, and attitudes in our interactions with educators and scholars from all around the world. In fact, a new horizon emerged in our understanding of education in general, and education in China in particular.

Although it is beyond the scope of this chapter to present a panoramic view of the 2011 ISATT conference, this chapter does present a philosophical reconstruction of particular ideas shared, discussed, and digested in the author's personal interactions during the four days at Braga. In this chapter, the keynote speech by Professor António Nóvoa, Rector of the University of Lisbon, both frames – and fuels – my thinking.

Nóvoa's speech, *Teachers: How Long Until the Future?,* was presented in four parts: (a) From the inside, (b) activity is the road to knowledge, (c) the risks of dialogue, and (d) education as a public space. Professor Nóvoa did not focus on educational policy, practice, or research, rather he gave his full attention to foundational ideas. He challenged all participants to reflect actively and deeply by posing provocative questions that arose from his perspective as a historian and philosopher of education. In this work, I use Professor António Nóvoa's speech as a source of reflection and integrate his message with other learnings I gleaned from my first ISATT conference experience.

TEACHERS: HOW LONG UNTIL THE FUTURE?

The title of Professor Nóvoa's keynote speech echoed beautifully the theme of ISATT 2011, both in terms of the words chosen and the paradox intended. The word "future" in the theme seems odd when positioned after "back to," which, in our usual temporal schemata, should refer to the past rather than to the future. The expression of "how long until the future" is also paradoxical. The term "how long" is pointless, if "the future" refers to some definitive time in the future. Similarly, the word "until" is meaningless if "future" refers to that part of the time continuum designated by the words "past" and "present" that always remains elusive to us. The paradoxical nature of these expressions is further spotlighted and deeply felt when it finds its counterpart in the following two quotes excerpted from António Nóvoa's keynote speech:

> As an educator, I spent half of my life fighting for some ideals, and the other half of my life fighting against the false appropriations of these ideals and the way they are wrongly applied. (Gabriel Compayré, 1889, p. 43)

> Although progressive rhetoric is everywhere, progressive practice is much harder to find. We are in the unlovely position of being seen both as pillars of the establishment and as zealots of the constructivist insurrection and, thus, we find ourselves defending the indefensible while also demanding the unrealizable. (Labaree, 2003, p. 5)

The two quotes, one from a French theorist and historian of education living at the turn of nineteenth century, and the other from an American educational theorist and historian teaching presently at Stanford University, seem to constitute an asynchronous dialogue focusing on a fundamental paradox of education that underlies major problems in the field that transcend time and cultures.

The paradoxical life of Gabriel Compayré is an indicator of a universal social disposition seeking security and coziness in ideals readymade as magic solutions and fashions rather than as intuitive insights and promises to take up challenge. Yet with no intuitive exploration and promises to change for the better, ideals as crystallized explorative efforts in education tend to lose their cutting edge and their capacity to transform practice and to be transformed in return through empirical evidence. As such, they are likely to collapse into distorted and empty progressive rhetoric.

Labaree's insight into the paradoxical opposition of progressive rhetoric and practice seems to be an effort "to [squeeze] the universe into a ball, to roll it towards some overwhelming question" (Eliot, 1917, pp. 3–8). It reminds us of the fundamental paradox of the social roles of teachers – teachers as "pillars of the establishment" and as "zealots of the constructivist insurrection" (Labaree, 2003, p. 5). Caught between incommensurable social demands, the ideal teacher would be one with a miraculous capacity to show respect for inherited ideals by reconstructing them through deconstruction. Viewed in this light, Compayré fought to defend the right to reconstruct inherited ideals in explorative practice in the first half of his life. In the second half of his life, he battled against the disrespect of his lifetime ideals, which had become fragmentary and rhetorical. Here the perennial question arises: How can we as teachers achieve the kind of insight that helps steer us clear of "false appropriations" and "wrong applications" and work toward reconstruction?

To this perplexing query, Professor Nóvoa replied: "Let each one be situated through the knowledge of the others, knowing that no one can avoid their own journey with their own dilemmas and turbulence." The combination of the words, "situated" and "through," rather than "in," is directed at the coziness of progressive rhetoric, which is situated *in* "the knowledge of the others" rather than *in* their own journeys with their personally felt and deeply lived "dilemmas and turbulence." The knowledge of the others, like a nautical chart, helps us only when we set out on a voyage, predicting what we might encounter and providing a repertoire of strategies and tactics to choose from when we find ourselves in difficult situations. It is the fight we wage that will lead us through the knowledge of the others to a better future. However, progressive rhetoric will lead only to stagnation without a sense of history.

FROM THE INSIDE

As is evident in the above discussion, the fundamental paradox of teachers' social roles places teachers in an unlovely position (Labaree, 2003, p. 5). Professor Nóvoa described that place as one of "lowly status" where teachers "engage in a difficult practice that looks easy" (Nóvoa, in press, p. 2). Above teachers in the educational hierarchy are national and international consultants, teacher educators, educational researchers, educational administrators, publishers, and technology gurus, all of whose demands and requirements encroach on the life space of frontline teachers. The practitioners, as "pillars of the establishment" (Labaree, 2003, p. 5) engaged in a quasi-profession, face external pressures in their daily work arising from accountability demands, research findings, best practices, the dictates of professional developers, and so forth.

The effects of these outsider perspectives on teachers have been documented and were discussed in many ISATT presentations, including one made by Cheryl Craig of the University of Houston who is the current Secretary of ISATT. In her paper, she illustrated this point with the American case of literacy teacher Daryl Wilson:

> When Daryl's campus became involved with a readers' and writers' workshop approach to literacy instruction, he grieved the fact that he no longer would be able to teach the Holocaust unit of study he had developed over a period of years, alongside his personal travels to Israel and the Jewish Concentration Camps in Europe. With his school's hiring of a readers' and writers' literacy expert, new units of study were collaboratively developed and all of the teachers' previous curriculum development—one might say, their scholarship—was purged. Daryl, as Department Chair, mourned this loss—and the associated loss to his students who, to his way of thinking, were not connecting to the new foci of study with the same enthusiasm and intellectual engagement as previous students had related to his Holocaust unit.

Craig continued to write:

> In my research with Daryl, I saw his self-directed agency as a teacher who viewed teaching through the teacher-as-curriculum-maker lens (Clandinin & Connelly, 1992) being suppressed as the view of teacher-as-curriculum-implementer (Clandinin & Connelly, 1992)—doing what he was told to do—took precedence in his school context, especially administratively where teaching tended to be seen as something to be determined, regulated, and monitored by others. Also, other teacher participants in the same study lamented Daryl's loss—laying it alongside their corresponding regrets—and discussing what had happened to the literacy department at Yaeger—and Yaeger's students—often. One female colleague of Daryl's, for example, said the approach made her feel captive like a "butterfly under a pin" (Craig, 2012). Another mentioned that what had happened had metaphorically "pulled [teachers] through knotholes" in trees, presumably reshaping their practices in ways acceptable to those in charge—that is, consultants, administrators, school district/state agency personnel and policy makers, but at the expense of the personal practical knowledge (Clandinin, 1986; Clandinin & Connelly, 1985) of the teachers enacting them. (Craig, 2011a, p. 61)

In contrast to this outsider perspective on the teaching profession, Craig (2011a) introduced an inside perspective of education offered by Joseph J. Schwab, an American educationalist and biologist who lived between 1909 and 1988. Craig summarized Schwab's perspective in this way:

In Schwab's early writing, he outlined the distinctive properties of human nature. The "human person," he observed, is a "self-moving living thing" that is able to "produce itself," to "develop itself," and to create a "personal history" that is non-replicable. (Schwab, 1964, p. 8, cited in Craig, 2011a)

Craig (2011a) went on to say:

Schwab favored education through the growth metaphor as Dewey (1938) before him did. He boldly declared that people are not only products of their education, but products of the choices their selves make (Schwab, 1960/1978, p. 218). Schwab (1971) furthermore added that flexible inquirers such as teachers—that is, those interacting in complex milieus—are the result of "intelligent rebellion and self-education after [they] are trained ..." (Schwab, 1971, p. 23). Even amid prescription and shared practices and procedures, Schwab found important spaces where the self makes choices.

She (2011a) continued:

Schwab also stalwartly supported teachers and gave unwavering support to their "... looking at their own practices and the consequences of them ..." (Schwab, 1959/1978, p. 168). He additionally emphasized that teachers have "different bents" (Schwab, 1983, p. 241) and, hence, their strengths and reflections on practice will necessarily differ... For him, the teacher was the "fountainhead of the curricular decision" (Schwab, 1983, p. 245). Students "are better known by no one [else] but the teacher," Schwab said, because the teacher is the only one who actively "tries to teach them"; he/ she is the only one "who lives with them for the better part of the day and the better part of the year." (Schwab, 1983, p. 245, cited in Craig, 2011a)

To conclude her analysis, Craig wrote:

To Schwab's way of thinking, recognizing that teachers are "agent[s] of education, not of its subject matter" (Schwab, 1954/1978, p. 128) is the only conceivable road to sustained improvement of practice because:... only as the teacher uses the classroom as the occasion and the means to reflect upon education as a whole (ends as well as means), as the laboratory in which to translate reflections into actions and thus to test reflections, actions, and outcomes, against many criteria is he [sic] a good ... teacher (Schwab, 1959/ 1978, pp. 182–183, as cited in Craig, 2011a).

The tension between the view of teacher-as-curriculum-implementer and the view of teacher-as-curriculum-maker (Clandinin & Connelly, 1992; Craig & Ross, 2008) is found not only in the Western world, but perhaps is even more prevalent in China, where the collective cultural bent and a blind trust in Western-style science and technology makes it harder for teachers to engage in "intelligent rebellion and self-education after [they] are trained" (Schwab, 1971, p. 23). Even in my country's present effort to shift the teaching focus from knowledge transmission to interest in learning and the abilities of autonomous-learning and cooperative learning, we have to adopt a top-down strategy relying on a small number of outside educational experts.

The paradox of the Chinese situation is that we want to apply Schwab's conception of human being as "self-moving living thing" to cultivate students with the ability to "produce [himself/herself]" (Schwab, 1964), to "develop [himself/herself]," and to create a "personal history through the choices he/she makes;" yet the teachers commissioned to carry out the tasks are not given adequate space and support to do what they are supposed to do. In our present efforts to transform our teaching, we need to be like the teacher Schwab (1954/1978) described in *Eros and Education*. As Craig explains:

> He (Joseph Schwab) wants something more for his students than the capacity to give back to him a report of what he himself has said. He (Joseph Schwab) wants them to possess a knowledge or a skill in the same way that he possesses it, as a part of his best-loved self ... He (Joseph Schwab) wants to communicate some of the fire he feels, some of the Eros he possesses, for a valued object. His controlled and conscious purpose is to liberate, not captivate the student. (Schwab, 1954/1978, p. 124–125, as quoted in Craig, 2011a, p. 64)

Without the Schwab-like fire of Eros, teachers are not able to act as "flexible inquirers" (Schwab, 1971) and the "fountainhead[s]" (Schwab, 1983) of the curricular decisions. Thus, the inside perspective will remain subjugated to the outsider perspective. Here, critically important questions rise to the fore: How can a teacher acquire Schwab-like knowledge or skill as part of "his/her best-loved self, part of the fire he feels, and part of the Eros he possesses?" What will it take for the outsider view to willingly surrender its dominant position to achieve balance with the insider view?

ACTIVITY IS THE ROAD TO KNOWLEDGE

Schwab-like knowledge or skill as part of one's best-loved self is the product of the process of self-production, self-development, and the creation of personal history through explorative efforts in unknown territories, as well as through personal decision making amid the dilemmas one encounters. It no longer is ready-made knowledge or skills determined by others. Instead, it is a crystallization of the activities in which one has engaged, the problems one has solved and the experiences one has reflected upon. Such explorative activities require one to take an adventurous plunge into the making of history where vision and mission become welded together in the fire of passion.

Education for growth demands an inside view of education, which uses the knowledge of others as a space for interaction between the teacher and his/her students. It is a life space where students are guided by their teachers to create knowledge. This space is where both the teacher and the students act as masters of their own teaching and learning. This life space provides opportunities for co-learning activities through reconstructing formal knowledge. In stark contrast, the outsider view, which transmits others' knowledge, denies the teacher his/her right to engage in constructive rebellion and self-education. Furthermore, it undercuts his/her role as the master/mistress of his/her own teaching, depriving him/her of the opportunities to learn and grow in a personally driven way.

In his speech, Professor António Nóvoa employed quotes from George Bernard Shaw and Michel Serres to show the devastation that the outsider view has caused the teaching profession. Both offered insights as to how teachers could productively respond. The statements Nóvoa focused on were the following:

> He who can, does; he who cannot, teaches. (Shaw, 1900/1971, p. 784)

> Activity is the only road to knowledge. (Shaw, 1971, p. 792)

> Men are wise in proportion, not to their experience, but to their capacity for experience. If we could learn from mere experience, the stones of London would be wiser than its wisest men. (Shaw, 1900/1971, p. 792)

> No departure, no learning. Yes, depart, divide yourself into parts. (Serres, 1991, p. 28)

> All learning involves a journey with the other and towards alterity. (Serres, 1991, p. 86)

The sarcastic tone of the first quote from the Irish playwright Shaw aroused a blast of guffaw among the audience, while the quotes that followed caused audience members to be deathly silent. Sitting among professors from various cultures, I felt the power of philosophical insight sweeping across the fully-packed auditorium and started reflecting on those quotations.

My daughter later divulged that Professor Nóvoa's highlighting of George Bernard Shaw's views on experience and the capacity for experience struck a chord deep in her heart and provided her with a new understanding of life. At the time of the conference, she had been a college teacher for three years. She was successfully teaching in her own way, yet without the passion of a successful teacher. She felt confused by this; however, Professor Nóvoa helped her name the tension she was experiencing. Hearing the keynote address also helped her acknowledge her lack of conscious effort to reflect on her experiences and to transform her past experience into a new capacity for growth.

Shaw's focus on the capacity for experience might distinguish "doing" from "teaching." The former (doing) is deeply rooted in purposeful activity through an uncertain path requiring courage, intelligence, decision, and power. The latter (teaching), according to the outsider view, is simply a matter of transmitting knowledge with nothing uncertain – and certainly nothing personal – at stake.

Shaw, with his preoccupation with the capacity for experience, emphasizes the preconditions for gaining knowledge and wisdom whereas Serres, with his attention to "departure" and learning, stresses the ongoing reconstruction of self through one's reflective capacities. Serres's emphasis is evident in his desire to segment the word, "depart," into "de" and "part," and to later assert the necessity of "divid[ing] yourself into parts." This directs our attention to the most important moment in our journey of learning: the moment of decision when the learner is torn between others and their varying alternatives. Each of the others – indeed, each point of view – might lead him/her down a different road, ultimately making him/her a different self.

In addition to the aforementioned quotations, Professor Nóvoa listed on his PowerPoint slides the following lines to spur further thinking:
Reflection:

- A sequence of ideas with consequences in practice.
- Estrangement→ Entrenchment→ Estrangement.

Nóvoa's comment *on reflection* is an effort to link the capacity for experience of Shaw with the departure of Serres. This echoes Dewey (1985) who Nóvoa quoted as saying:

> Thought or reflection ... is the discernment of the relation between what we try to do and what happens in consequence (p. 151) ... The starting point of any process of thinking is something going on; something which just as it stands is incomplete or unfulfilled. Its point, its meaning lies literally in what it is going to be, in how it is going to turn out ... Reflection also implies concern with the issue—a certain sympathetic identification of our own destiny ... the flagrant partisanship of human nature is evidence of the intensity of the tendency to identify ourselves with one possible course of events, and to reject the other as foreign ... all thinking involves a risk ....The conclusions of thinking, till confirmed by the event, are, accordingly, more or less tentative or hypothetical .... Tentative means being tried out, feeling one's way along provisionally. (pp. 154–155)

According to Dewey, reflection on what one is trying is not only foundational to the making of knowledge but also to the making of one's self-identity and, therefore, the mapping of one's destiny. The direction the event is going to take interacts with the way our values and goals are orientated. This demonstrates how Shaw's emphasis on doing complements Serres's focus on departure as something indispensable in learning.

The "flagrant partisanship of human nature" referred to in Dewey (1985) finds paradoxical expression in Nóvoa's model of *estrangement* to *entrenchment* and back again. It captures the essential stages in the development of self through explorative practice. In the psychological literature on self, self concept is believed to consist of various schemas. Cross and Makus (1990, p. 728) explain:

> Some refer to the individual's here-and-now experiences, while others refer to past or future experiences ... (They)lend structure and coherence to the individual's self-relevant experiences. They are constructed creatively and selectively from one's past experiences in a particular domain.

When an individual identifies himself with one possible course of events among several alternatives and tries to push in that direction, he "invests the particular alternative with self-relevant meaning, claiming the desired end state as his or her own and making it part of the self" (Cross & Markus, 1990, p. 729). Continuing their explanation, they state:

> The splitting of the universe into "me" and "not-me" is a continual, ongoing project. Some actions and domains are permanently designated as "me." It is in these areas that one develops self-schemas. Other actions and domains gain or lose their residence status within the boundaries of the self depending on situational and environmental contingencies.

Self-schemas often refer to future experience as the "possible self," representing "what individuals could become, would like to become, or are afraid of becoming ... they are motivational resources that are invoked by the individual, alone or in interaction with other possible selves, in the course of willful action" (Cross & Markus, 1990, p. 730–731). Professor Nóvoa's model of estrangement to entrenchment and back to estrangement represents a dynamic course of self-production, self-development, and the creation of a personal history that unfurls as our lives unfold. This led to his comment on lifelong learning:

> Lifelong learning ... I wish to avoid the "capitalization of the self" and the pressure of "salvation narratives" that look at teachers as a kind of social redeemers ... to reveal the richness and complexity of teaching through a "knowledgeable activity." (Nóvoa, in press, p. 5)

Nóvoa's commentary on lifelong learning seems to imply that the issues involved in learning have bearing not only on the individual but also on the society as a whole. According to Flint and Needham (2007), in the rapidly changing globalized economy and knowledge society, there exist two contrasting forms of discourse of lifelong learning. What is described as "capitalization of the self" is one interpreting lifelong learning "as a means to improve competitiveness and productivity regarding what is done in practice within a global economy," while teaching through a "knowledgeable activity" might be regarded "as opening the possibility of the identity of human beings belonging together with the movement of difference" (2007, p. 85).

The two contrasting discourses are illustrative of the conflict between two different visions of education: education as a private good (formed by the self-interested actions of individual consumers) versus education as a public good (formed by the social aims of reform movements). In his review of the history of American school reform, David Labaree (2011) points out:

> In short, the vision of education as a private good has consistently won out over education as a public good. At the same time, consumers have pushed the system in contradictory directions because they want sharply different benefits from it. Throughout the history of American education, some consumers have demanded greater access to school in order to climb the social ladder while others have demanded greater advantage from school in order to protect themselves from these same social climbers. Obligingly, the school system has let us have it both ways, providing access and advantage, promoting equality and inequality (retrieved from http://www.stanford.edu/~dlabaree/).

Caught between these conflicting visions of education and demands for sharply different benefits, what should the teacher do to defend his or her position of teacher-as-curriculum-maker while making his learning "a journey with the other and towards alterity"?

THE RISKS OF DIALOGUE

All learning, as Michel Serres (1991) asserts, necessarily involves "a journey with the other and towards alterity." It is even more the case with teachers who live in a world consisting of various social groups with different interests such as education reformers, policymakers, education consumers of low social statuses and education consumers of high social statuses. Whether as curriculum-implementer or curriculum-maker (Clandinin & Connelly, 1992; Craig & Ross, 2008), the teacher finds himself/herself situated in the eye of a storm, facing a swirl of incompatible social discourses – each trying to sweep him in its direction. As a co-traveler, the teacher must learn how how to work with others, trying to share experiences and expectations through dialogue in an effort to reach consensus by reconstructing one's self.

Dialogue, as a step to open up oneself to another, requires both commitment and courage. Professor Nóvoa quoted Arjun Appadurai (1949) as saying,

> The first risk of dialogue is that the other party may not understand what you mean. The risk of misunderstanding is inherent to all human communication. The second risk of dialogue is exactly the opposite, and that is the risk that we may in fact be understood too clearly. This paradox is partly based on the worry that the other party may see through our surface expressions and understand motives or intentions which we prefer to conceal. (p. 6)

Nóvoa (in press), paraphrasing Appadurai (2006), continued:

> But the deeper risk of being fully understood is the risk that the other party will actually see our deepest convictions, our foundational opinions and even our doubts. The reason why this is a risk is that dialogue is not about everything. To be effective, dialogue must be to some extent about shared ground, selective agreement and provisional consensus. All dialogue is a form of negotiation and negotiation cannot be based on complete mutual understanding or a total consensus across any sort of boundary or difference. The negotiation of the right parts of our humanity with each other is both prudent and sufficient to build a contingent and evolving framework for conviviality. (Nóvoa, in press, p. 6)

Misunderstanding in dialogue signals differences in social backgrounds, life experiences, values, and life goals, which squelch our opportunities to reformulate our experiences in ways that take into account the perspectives of those around us. The fear of misunderstanding prohibits us from moving out of an arrogant coziness of our own experience, which, according to Dewey (1985), can be overcome through communicative effort. As Dewey put it, "The experience has to be formulated in order to be communicated. To formulate requires getting outside of it, seeing it as another would see it, considering what points of contact it has with the life of another so that it may be got into such a form that he can appreciate its meaning" (p. 8). Viewed properly, cases of misunderstanding might offer opportunities for deeper reflection outside the constraining boundaries of our narrow self and lead to a reconstruction of personal experience.

Being understood "too clearly" by our partner in discourse offers an even better opportunity to know and reshape the self, for it indicates that our partner is one with richer experience and greater wisdom, from whom the one with less experience and less wisdom might gain enlightenment. The fear "to be understood, too clearly" arises from narrow-mindedness that is preoccupied with competiveness for immediate benefits and from a consequential absence of persistent pursuit of inner growth. Lacking also is confidence in the unlimited possibilities of one's self. In Confucius's words, a person who loves to learn "frequents the company of men [sic] of principle that he may be rectified" (1995, p. 69). Such discursive action offers a test of one's inner strength, along with opportunities for the negotiation of "the right parts of our humanity" (Appadurai, 2006).

The ISATT 2011 conference embodied the conviviality advocated by Arjun Appadurai by creating co-learning spaces where participants actively engaged in sharing their experiences, communicating their ideas and negotiating new meanings. On a final note, of the 12 symposia I attended, the one titled *Teacher Learning That Matters: International Perspectives,* which was presented about a book (Kooy & van Veen, 2011) bearing the same title. It was organized in such a unique way that it was possible for each participant's voice to be heard, respected and discussed. The symposium reported the results of a joint project involving six scholars from The Netherlands, Canada, Australia, USA and China. Professor Klaas van Veen from Leiden University in The Netherlands, acting as the Chair, declared at the beginning that each symposium presenter would be given only five minutes to present. He added that the major part of the time would involve voluntary attendee participation in one of the six focus groups, each taking up one of the six themes in the joint project.

The group I joined in consisted of seven veteran professors, including Professor Paulien Meijer from IVLOS/Utrecht University and Chair of ISATT, and Professor Christopher Day from University of Nottingham and Editor of *Teachers and Teaching: Theory and Practice.* We had a very heated discussion about critical moments that work as heuristics to transform learning and teacher identity. I sat in an aisle seat and was surprised to see that a professor from New Zealand close to me remained in a kneeling position throughout the group discussion. When it was time for representatives to share with all participants what each group had achieved in their discussions, the first one who seized the opportunity to speak was a professor from Australia. She spoke for us of all when she expressed her deeply-felt gratitude to the Chair for the wonderful space for dialogue in which she found the best part of her humanity awakened, nourished and developed. The last speaker in the joint meeting was Qiuyuan Tang, a graduate student from China under my guidance, who later wrote a narrative reflecting the growth she had achieved in the dialogical life space of ISATT 2011:

> On the last day of the ISATT conference, we were a few minutes late. After entering the room, we separated, as our [professor] had told us, to sit dispersed ... This would

provide opportunities for us to communicate with others instead of just among the members [from China]. That was very effective. I surveyed the room quickly and chose a seat near the platform ... next to David Goodwin, a professor from Missouri State University, USA, whose presentation I had attended on the first day. He chose the aisle seat, so I greeted him and sat next to his bag which was in the chair between us. At that time, the subject of the presenter was community. She had listed some of her understandings about community, which stimulated my thinking. I had a desire to talk with David, but the bag between us seemed to separate us psychologically and physically. I wanted to shorten the distance .... As he had chosen the aisle one, the easiest way was for me to just put his bag on my side and sit next to him as it did not seem convenient for him to put the bag on my side .The better way was to ask David to move and then the bag would be on his side. I ... struggled ... because I am the kind of person who does not readily inconvenience others. I prefer to wait for [suggestions] to be offered ... Maybe the small request could hardly be called inconvenience ... However, for me, it was. But I decided to change my definition of inconvenience. I tried[to re-frame] inconvenience as ... invitation. And then it worked out well. I said hello to Dr. Goodwin and told him that I would like to invite him to sit next to me. He nodded with a smile and I realized, at that very moment, that it was not a terrible thing to ask for what you want if it does not cause major inconvenience.

My student's journal entry continued:

... Stimulated by the contents of the presentation, I had a strong desire to ask this question: What's the aim of the ISATT meeting? Why do they sponsor the ISATT conference? Do they just provide a platform to communicate and exchange ideas among professors and teachers from different parts of the world? And, for what purpose? As for me, I thought that, through the exchanges and interactions during the ISATT meeting, the experienced professors should pass the baton to the young professors to encourage them to grow faster. If they succeed at doing so, then ISATT can ensure its positive role in improving teachers and teaching. But I wonder if they have done this well enough??? So I shared my doubts with David and explained why I have these doubts. I told him: professors and teachers coming here are eager to learn from each other. But how do they make contact in such a short time? As much as I am trying to make contact, it was hard for me to meet people, not to mention becoming a member of their community. How about other young teachers? Professors? Is there anyone who can be the bridge between the two communities, if we consider the young and experienced teachers and professors two communities?

Qiuyuan Tang went on to write:

Luckily, David encouraged me ... and he suggested that I share my thoughts with the others. Then we engaged in a discussion of community ... David first gave a general introduction of my questions to audience members in the session and then he invited me to share my specific concern. I think that he acted as a bridge between the other members and me at that time.

My student's story continued to unravel:

During the discussion, I raised further questions: A community must have certain common features and a distinct culture. What are the common features among us or what is the culture? What can the organizers do to cultivate the distinctive culture of ISATT? We still seem to be individuals ... We just have a conference every two years. It is long time in-between. What other ways are there for teachers/professor to communicate with each other besides email or Facebook? Are there any other regional activities or any other people responsible for organizing activities? During our discussion, I found others in our group who shared the same doubts as me.

Tang's journal entry ended this way:

When it was time to share with other groups what we had discussed, David and the other group members encouraged me to speak as their representative, which I found very moving. Therefore I was the last person who had the chance to share my thoughts with all the participants by the end of the last symposium. The questions were as follow: "I assume that the group next to us is a community of experienced professors, while my group is a community of young teachers. Other groups stand for different kinds of communities. If I want to be a member of the community of the experienced teachers or other communities, how do I do so? Apart from active and hard work, is there another bridge for us? Are there other people who would like to serve as bridges?

I received friendly applause and some comments from one of the organizers, although I forgot what she said. Most importantly, my speech later led to fruitful action. After the symposium, Dr. Klaas van Veen, Professor at Leiden University, the Netherlands, who with Dr. Mary Kooy from Canada who co-chaired the symposium, responded to my email message. He said that he would like to do something like that. Also, David Goodwin shared his research with other members of our Chinese team. I keep in contact with Klaas, and the story continues ... It takes time.

The gist of Tang's narrative can be summed up in two important metaphors: bag and bridge; the first, symbolic of the physical and psychological distances prohibiting dialogic exchanges; and the latter, symbolic of efforts to reduce distance and to share, understand and sympathize. The bag is something that is found everywhere: between Tang and Goodwin, Tang and her Chinese colleagues, Tang's group and other groups and, between Tang and the Chair of the symposium. The bridge is something like the initiative approach of Tang, Goodwin's introductory effort, the conversation among the groups and the Chair's commitment to address the felt problem. The effort to replace bags with bridges is an attempt to reexamine and reconceptualize life, society and the world in a new light. This helps to open up new spaces for dialogue about shared ground and for negotiation of the right parts of our humanity with each other.

The episode I have just described is illustrative of the following comment António Nóvoa offered about dialogue:

Collaboration is not a "salvation narrative," but a "construction"

→ Connecting biography and social context;
→ Connecting life history and political history;
→ Connecting the individual and the social.

By connecting the individual and the social, dialogue in collaborative social discourse helps participants move beyond their own experiences and perspectives. It makes it possible for them to overcome narrow-mindedness and competitiveness. It gives their lives a new sense of meaning that leads to the building of a contingent and evolving framework of conviviality (Appadurai, 2006, in Nóvoa, 2011).

My student, Qiuyuan Tang, has since embarked on a new job as a volunteer teacher of the Chinese language in Tennessee, USA. From Tennessee, she sent me a letter. In it, she talked not only about her experience of ISATT 2011 but also about the new light that it shed on her understanding of life. Qiuyuan Tang wrote:

> This very morning it occurred to me that as a volunteer teaching Chinese in Tennessee, I am a cultural bridge between China and America. What should I do to make myself strong enough to bear more [weight]? That is another important question for me, which is related to the metaphor of bridges. I love the connotations of the word: bridge. It changes some of my attitudes toward life and the people I meet. Be active and brave enough to be ready to be the bridge for others and find your own bridge.

EDUCATION AS A PUBLIC SPACE

The new vision that Tang gained in her career shows the significance of knowledge making and meaning making through committed exploratory undertakings embedded in social discourse. An open, ongoing and nonauthoritarian social discourse conducive to meaning making depends on the commitments of all parties to work collaboratively so that the position and interests of each is respected and ideas emanating from each are listened to, discussed, questioned, and reconstructed. Only in such social interactions can each turn the knowledge of the other into a source of intellectual nourishment, motivational power and emotional encouragement in his/her individual journey of self-production, self-development and creation of personal history. Without committed efforts to replace bags with bridges in order to create co-learning opportunities, dialogue would be full of risks, and, the public space of dialogue would be a fragmented arena of conflicting interest groups.

Education as a public space involves all stakeholders (students, teachers, parents, school administrators, education experts and policymakers). This would form a striking contrast to the present situation where the voices of policymakers, education experts, school administrators and parents are much louder and more certain than those of the frontline teachers and students. The fragmentation of the public sphere of education leads to all kinds of conflict, as illustrated in Cheryl Craig's case of Daryl Wilson – the teacher suffering from the dictates of the literacy trainer, or in the case of Gabriel Compayré – fighting paradoxically for certain ideals as a frontline teacher in the first half of his life and then against false appropriations and misapplications of these ideals as an education expert in the second half. The unlovely situation of education torn between two conflicting visions of education as reviewed by Labaree is an inevitable consequence of the deterioration of education as public space, when absence of dialogue and displacement of progressive practice by progressive rhetoric undercuts negotiation for shared ground, selective agreement and provisional consensus.

The following is Nóvoa's commentary on the situation:

> In Education, the past always strikes back. We don't need more past. We need more history. Problems of teachers will not be solved only within the school. Prophecies of salvation through the school enclose teachers in unreasonable ambitions, blaming them for the failures of school reform.

António Nóvoa's insights direct our attention to the distinction between the word, "past," and the word, "history." If the past is understood as what we have undergone to the present and history as a reflective reconstruction of the past arising from a search for meaning, then the distinction between "past" and "history" is something comparable to Bernard Shaw's distinction between "experience" and "capacity for experience," or between "the stones of London" and "the wisest men." The transformation of the past into history requires an open, ongoing dialogue where insights are gained, meanings are created and new departures are made possible through reflection, interrogation and reconceptualization involving the collaborative efforts of all stakeholders. Without a dialogical space, there would be no history but only a past that strikes back again and again, leaving all stakeholders struggling in a mire of setbacks, frustrations and disappointments.

In discussing the reconstruction of education as a public space, Nóvoa once again quoted Michel Serres:

> Reborn,
> he knows,
> he has compassion.
> Finally,
> he can teach.
> (Serres, 1991, p. 249)

The word "reborn" emphasizes the importance of a negation of the old self and a departure from it if the teacher really wants to break out of the unreasonable ambitions imposed on him/her by outside experts. To achieve this, teachers have to reject "salvation narratives" and, instead turn to a dialogical life space, where one understands and is understood in return, just as Daryl Wilson did in Craig's (2011b, p. 346) research:

> In the summer months following Daryl and his colleague's two-year stint with the literacy trainer who left "army boot footprints on their practices" (another colleague's expression), Daryl chose to fly to a different state to attend a professional development session led by another literacy workshop expert whose approach significantly differed from that of the first trainer. This second literacy expert challenged the gathered teachers—"in a good way" (Daryl's words)—to develop tension and beauty in their writing products through reflectively drawing on their personal experiences and engaging in the writers' workshop method. As a learner, Daryl returned to his school with drafts of how he wove beauty and tension into his story of running away as a teenager. The workshop enabled him to inspire his students using examples from his own essay. His students subsequently produced quality writing samples, also involving tension and beauty, and emerging from their teen experiences. Daryl additionally combined what he and his students had authored and presented the work to his colleagues in a literacy department meeting. In response, Daryl's peers ... made it clear to him that his teaching example resonated with them—and that it, along with his student work samples, were products to which they—and their students—would aspire. One colleague distinctly noted that his lesson was not a "zinger lesson"—a fail-proof lesson that would work anywhere, anytime—like the ones the initial staff developer used to teach their students or the lessons the teachers routinely carried back with them from their summer training sessions in [other states]. (Craig, 2010, p. 432–433)

Daryl Wilson's new professional development session is not an authoritarian space as was his previous one, but rather a public space where the expert challenges and the teachers respond by developing tension and beauty in their reflective writing on their personal experiences and by authentically engaging in the writers' workshop method. It releases the creative power in Daryl (Craig, 2010), who, by successful rebirth, gains invaluable insights into growth and teaching. Further to this, his power to know and understand is contagious among his colleagues.

EPILOGUE

Ideals embodied in teaching practice, departures that are knowledge making and self-surpassing, and dialogues and bridges in education as a public space are the major ideas I gleaned from ISATT 2011. These thoughts, when clearly reconstructed and properly understood, might help educational stakeholders in China to reframe problems caused by spoon-fed teaching in a new light. When ISATT 2011 was still in full swing, I commented on the odd phrase "back to future" on my blog (54yxhclass.blog.163.com), to which one of my students responded:

> Back to the future, in my understanding, refers to the fundamental truth that education is something orientated to the future and is, by its very nature, designed to bring about a better world. It is something very far from the harsh and cruel reality of our exam-orientated education where children are overloaded with test-orientated exercises and persuaded by their parents into a false belief that better scores lead to better universities and therefore better jobs. What preoccupies our mind is a cozy life instead of a better world, and even coziness, for too many of our generation, becomes something too luxurious to be practical. ... Back to the future, in it I hear a call to me and all youth like me, a call to rebel against the crazy job-hunting, a call to dream, to read books we like to read, and to embark on adventures!

No dream may exist in the life space of the more experienced and practical parents, but that should be no excuse for one to suppose that there are no dreams and no ideals in their children. From what the student wrote, we can conclude that children would not allow the past to strike back again and again. Children, it seems, have dreams and ideals that inspire them to embark on adventures and to make their own personal histories.

"Back to the future" was the clarion call of ISATT 2011 that was issued to all those involved in the public space of education, where the voices from the hearts of the frontline teachers and students, apart from those of policymakers, school administrators, educational experts and parents, should ring loudly, and bridges should be made for our educational institutions to take the dreams of the students as the goals of schools and universities and to work back to the future.

REFERENCES

Appadurai, A. (2006). *Fear of small numbers: An essay on the geography of anger*. London: Duke University Press.

Clandinin, D. J., & Connelly, F. M. (1992). Teacher as curriculum maker. In P. W. Jackson (Ed.), *Handbook of curriculum* (pp. 363–461). New York, NY: Macmillan.

Compayré, G. (1889). *Cours de pédagogie théorique et pratique*. Paris: Librairie Classique Paul Depaplane.

Confucius. (1995). *The confucian analects: The four books*. Changsha, China: Hunan Press.

Craig, C. (2010). "Butterfly under a pin": An emergent teacher image amid mandated curriculum reform. *Journal of Educational Research, 105*(2), 90–101.

Craig, C. (2011a, July). Teacher education and the best-loved self. In *Proceedings of the 15th biennial of the International Study Association on Teachers and Teaching, back to the future: Legacies, continuities and changes in educational policy, practice and research.* Paper presented at 15th Biennial ISATT Conference, University of Minho, Braga, Portugal (pp. 60–68).

Craig, C. (2011b). Developing experience-based principles of practice for teaching teachers. In *Proceedings of the 15th biennial of the International Study Association on Teachers and Teaching, back to the future: Legacies, continuities and changes in educational policy, practice and research.* Paper presented at 15th Biennial ISATT Conference, University of Minho, Braga, Portugal (pp. 342–353).

Craig, C. (2012). Coming full circle: From teacher reflection to classroom action and places in-between. *Teachers and Teaching: Theory and Practice, 16*(4), 423–435.

Craig, C., & Ross, V. (2008). Developing teachers as curriculum makers. In F. M. Connelly (Ed.), *Sage handbook of curriculum and instruction* (pp. 282–305). Thousand Oaks, CA: Sage.

Cross, S. E., & Markus, H. R. (1990). The willful self. *Personality and Social Psychology Bulletin, 16*(4), 726–742.

Dewey, J. (1938). *Education and experience.* New York, NY: Collier Books.

Dewey, J. (1985). *Democracy and education. The middle works, 1899–1924* (Vol. 9). Carbondale, IL: Southern Illinois University Press.

Eliot, T. S. (1917/1963). *The love song of J. Alfred Prufrock. T. S. Eliot: Collected poems 1909–1962.* Orlando, FL: Harcourt, Brace & Company.

Flint, K. J., & Needham, D. (2007). 'Framing' lifelong learning in the twenty-first century: Towards a way of thinking. In D. N. Aspin (Ed.), *Philosophical perspectives on lifelong learning (pp. 85–108).* New York, NY: Springer.

Flores, M. A. (2011). About the conference. In *Proceedings of the 15th biennial of the International Study Association on Teachers and Teaching, back to the future: Legacies, continuities and changes in educational policy, practice and research.* 15th Biennial ISATT Conference, University of Minho, Braga, Portugal.

Kooy, M., & van Veen, K. (2011). *Teacher learning that matters: International perspectives.* New York, NY: Routledge.

Labaree, D. (2003). Life on the margins. *Journal of Teacher Education, 10,* 106.

Labaree, D. (2011).David Labaree homepage, Stanford University website. Retrieved from http://www.stanford.edu/~dlabaree/

Nóvoa, A.(2011). *How long until the future?* Keynote speech at the 15th Biennial of the International Study Association on Teachers and Teaching, Braga, Portugal.

Nóvoa, A. (in press). How long until the future? In M. Flores, A. Carvalho, F. Ferreira, & M. Vilaça (Eds.),*Back to the future: Legacies, continuities and changes in educational policy, practice and research.*

Schwab, J. (1964). Structure of the disciplines: Meanings and significances. In G. Ford & L. Pugno (Eds.), *The structure of knowledge and the curriculum.* Chicago, IL: Rand McNally.

Schwab, J. J. (1954/1978). Eros and education: A discussion of one aspect of discussion. In I. Westbury & N. Wilkof (Eds.), *Science, curriculum and liberal education: Selected essays.* Chicago, IL: University of Chicago Press.

Schwab, J. J. (1959/1978). The 'impossible' role of the teacher in progressive education. In I. Westbury & N. Wilkof (Eds.), *Science, curriculum and liberal education: Selected essays.* Chicago, IL: University of Chicago Press.

Schwab, J. J. (1960/1978). What do scientists do? In I. Westbury & N. Wilkof (Eds.), *Science, curriculum and liberal education: Selected essays* (pp. 184–228). Chicago, IL: University of Chicago Press.

Schwab, J. J. (1971). The practical: Arts of eclectic. *School Review, 79*, 493–542.

Schwab, J. J. (1983). The practical 4: Something for curriculum professors to do. *Curriculum Inquiry, 13*(3), 239–265.

Serres, M. (1991). *Le-tiers-instruit*. Paris: Editions François Bourin.

Shaw, B. (1900/1971). *Collected plays with their prefaces* (1st ed.). London: The Bobley Head.

ABOUT THE CONTRIBUTORS

Beatrice Avalos, Ph.D., is associate researcher at the Centre for Advanced Research in Education, University of Chile. She has journal and book publications on teacher education, educational policy in developing countries and gender issues focussed particularly on Chile and Latin America. She has worked and taught in universities in Chile, Britain, Canada and Papua New Guinea, and carried out consultancy work in Bangladesh and several Latin American countries on issues related to school improvement, teacher professional development and teacher initial education.

Douwe Beijaard, Ph.D., is a Professor of Professional Learning and Dean of the Eindhoven School of Education (ESoE) of the Eindhoven University of Technology, The Netherlands. He previously worked at Wageningen University, Leiden University, and the University of Groningen. He was and is (executive) member of editorial boards of several scientific journals. His current research addresses the professional identity, quality and development of (beginning) teachers.

Amanda Berry, Ph.D., is an Associate Professor at ICLON Graduate School of Teaching, Leiden University, The Netherlands. Her research focuses on the development of teachers' knowledge and the ways in which that knowledge is shaped and articulated through teacher preparation, beginning teaching and in-service learning. She has been an ISATT member since 2007. She enjoys the learning opportunities afforded by the ISATT conferences and the opportunities to meet with international colleagues.

Sephora Boucenna has been a Researcher and a Trainer at the Department of Education and Technology, University of Namur, Belgium, since 1999. She has been organizing and leading workshops and modules in the field of the analysis of professional practices, both for Master's students and for adults through lifelong learning programs. Her research focuses on the analysis of professional activities, specifically the methodologies of collecting and analysing data that give access to teachers' experience. She is also working on the professionalization process of the adults' trainers.

Evelyne Charlier, Ph.D., is a Professor at the University of Namur, Belgium. Her research interests are mainly focused on teacher training and professional development. She is in charge of the Center for In-service Training in the Department of Education and Technology where she supervises a staff of 15 researchers who are investigating thematic areas relating to professionalism, evolution of teachers' identities within school reform contexts and the organizational design of secondary schools to reduce school failure. She considers teaching and learning support as a key element of society

D. Jean Clandinin, Ph.D., is a Professor and Director of the Centre for Research for Teacher Education and Development in the Faculty of Education at the University of Alberta, Canada. She is a former Teacher, Counselor, and Psychologist. She is past Vice President of Division B of AERA and is the 1993 winner of AERA's Early Career Award. Additionally, she is the winner of the Canadian Education Association Whitworth Award for educational research in 1999, the Kaplan Research Achievement Award in 2001, Division B Lifetime Achievement Award from AERA in 2002, the University of Alberta's highest award for research, and Killam Scholar at the University of Alberta in 2004.

Christopher Day, Ph.D., is an Emeritus Professor of Education and leads the Teachers' Work and Lives and School Leadership Research groups in the Centre for Research in Schools and Communities, the University of Nottingham, UK. Prior to this, he worked as a Teacher, Lecturer, and Local Education Authority Adviser. His particular concerns center upon the continuing development of teachers, teacher effectiveness, teachers' lives and work, successful school leadership, learning networks, and action research and change.

Freema Elbaz-Luwisch, Ph.D., is a member of the Faculty of Education at the University of Haifa, Israel. Her interests include auto/biographical writing and narrative inquiry, multiculturalism, and dialogue across difference, the study of educational alternatives, presence, and spirit in teaching. Her most recent book *Autobiography and Pedagogy: Memory, Body and Presence in Teaching* is being published in 2013 by Peter Lang.

Eila Estola, Ph.D., is a Professor of Early Childhood Education at Faculty of Education, University of Oulu, Finland. One of her research interests deals with teachers' narrative identities. She has been developing narrative and action methods for peer groups and prepared others in these methods in different courses as well as worked as a counselor in teachers' groups.

Currently she also is a leader of the research project "From Exclusion to Belonging: Developing Narrative Practices in Day Care Centers and Schools."

Zhuo Feng, Ph.D., is an Associate Professor in the College of Educational Science at Shenyang Normal University, China. Her research interests include teacher knowledge, teacher professional development, and qualitative research.

Maria Assunção Flores, Ph.D., is an Associate Professor with qualification at the University of Minho, Portugal. She received her Ph.D. at the University of Nottingham, UK in 2002. Her research interests include teacher professionalism and leadership, teacher education and professional development, induction and change. She has published books, chapters, and articles in national and international journals. She is a member of various international associations.

David R. Goodwin, Ph.D., teaches Educational Research at Missouri State University, Springfield, USA. He received his Ph.D. in Educational Psychology from the University of Illinois at Champaign-Urbana in 1999. His interests include collaboration in work; holistic understanding of teacher development, teaching, and learning; inquiry in the teaching of research; qualitative research methodology especially in relation to portraiture; participatory educational action research; and the development and unity of the person/self.

Sigrun Gudmundsdottir, who passed away in June of 2003, was a Research Associate in the Department of Education, The University of Trondheim, Norway. Her research interests centered on the knowledge base of teaching. Her work included numerous international publications, including "Pedagogical Models of Subject Matter" in J. Brophy (Ed.), *Advances in Research on Teaching*, and "Values in Pedagogical Content Knowledge" in the *Journal of Teacher Education*.

Xiao Han, Ed.D., is a Curriculum Developer and Graduate Student Success Center Director, in the School of Education, University of St. Thomas, Houston, TX, USA. She has extensive teaching experience in higher education in China. She earned her Doctor of Education in Instructional Technology in Curriculum & Instruction from the University of Houston. Her interests include technology integration in teacher education, online course design and development, and narrative inquiry.

Maher Hashweh, Ph.D., is an Associate Professor of Education at Birzeit University in Palestine. His interests are in science education with an emphasis on student conceptions in science, teacher knowledge and beliefs, research on teaching, teacher professional development, and democracy education. He is a former Dean of Arts and is presently Dean of Education at Birzeit University.

Jukka Husu, Ph.D., is a Professor of Education in the Department of Teacher Education, University of Turku, Finland. His research focuses on teachers' pedagogical knowing, reflection, and ethical judgment in teaching. He has published extensively in internationally refereed journals and edited books. He is a member of the International Editorial Board of *Teaching and Teacher Education*.

Jayshri Kannan has taught English Language in schools and has worked in Publishing Houses as an ELT expert and Resource Person in India. She has travelled extensively throughout India and trained teachers in various aspects of ELT and is additionally engaged with schools in order to incorporate newer practices based on needs of the context. She is the Author of many English Language Teaching books used at different levels in school curriculums across her country.

Geert Kelchtermans, Ph.D., studied educational sciences and philosophy at the University of Leuven in Belgium, where he received his Ph.D. in 1993 with a narrative-biographical study on teachers' professional development. He now works at the same university as a full Professor and Chair of the Centre for Educational Policy, Innovation and Teacher Education. He has widely published on teacher and school development, narrative-biographical methodology, micropolitics in schools and educational leadership. He is currently also a Visiting Professor at the University of Oulu, Finland.

Michael Kompf, Ph.D., is a Professor of Education at Brock University, Canada where he has taught since 1985. His research interests include developmental issues for adult learners and teachers; personal construct psychology; global policies and practices in higher education; and philosophies of inquiry. He has been a member of the International Study Association on Teachers and Teaching (ISATT) since 1985, and has served four terms as a Chair and four terms as an Editor of the ISATT Newsletter. He has published extensively in adult education and the various areas of teacher thinking, and has consulted, presented papers and given lectures throughout North America, the EU and Australasia.

Fred A. J. Korthagen, Ph.D., is a Professor of Teacher Education at VU University in Amsterdam, The Netherlands, specializing in the professional development of teachers and teacher educators. He gives lectures and conducts workshops all over the world, frequently focused on the core reflection approach, which deepens professional learning. Fred has received international awards for his scientific work, for example, from the American Association of Teacher Educators (ATE) and the American Educational Research Association (AERA).

Ora W. Y. Kwo, Ph.D., is an Associate Professor in the Faculty of Education at The University of Hong Kong. Her research interests stem from professional experiences in teacher education, leading to work on critical discourse for professional learning, empowerment and leadership, narrative inquiry, building of learning communities, values embedded in mainstream schooling, and private supplementary tutoring.

Anneli Lauriala, Ph.D., is a Professor of Education who specializes in teacher education at the University of Lapland, Rovaniemi, Finland. Her major research interests are teacher development and teacher identity as well as pedagogical innovations. She has been Finland's regional representative for ISATT since 1997, and she has served as an Associate Editor for ISATT's official journal, *Teachers and Teaching: Theory and Practice* since 2006. She has been involved in and led many school–university projects aimed at reforming pedagogical practices in Finland.

John Loughran, Ph.D., is the Foundation Chair in Curriculum & Pedagogy and Dean of the Faculty of Education, Monash University, Australia. He was a science Teacher for 10 years before moving into teacher education. His research has spanned science education and the related fields of professional knowledge, reflective practice, and teacher research. John was the co-founding Editor of *Studying Teacher Education* and is an Executive Editor for *Teachers and Teaching: Theory and Practice*.

Joost Lowyck, Ph.D., is a Professor Emeritus at the University of Leuven, Belgium and has served as the Chair of the School of Education there. His research focuses on educational technology and instructional design associated with teacher training in The Netherlands and Flanders. He was the Chair of ISATT (1985–1988), a member of the Editorial Board of *Teaching and Teacher Education* (1983–1986), and Director of the Academic Teacher Training Institute, University of Leuven (2001–2006). He also participated as a member and chair in quality assessment of teacher education programs and research in Dutch teacher training institutes.

Barica Marentič Požarnik, Ph.D., is a Professor Emerita in the Faculty of Arts, University of Ljubljana, Slovenia. Her teaching and research are mainly in the areas of active learning, learning styles, experiential learning, teacher education, action research, environmental education and improving university teaching. She is also an organizer and trainer of numerous in-service workshops for teachers, including university staff.

Maria Inês Marcondes is Doctor in Education and Associate Professor and Researcher at the Graduate Program in Education at Pontifícia Universidade Católica do Rio de Janeiro, Brasil. She has edited books, published chapters and articles in national and international journals. She is a member of various international associations such as ISATT and AERA. She is a member of the Editorial Board of the journal *Studying Teacher Education*. Her research interests include teacher education and curriculum studies.

Amanda McGraw, EdD, is a Coordinator of the Graduate Diploma of Education (Secondary) program at the University of Ballarat in Australia. Her research interests include teachers' professional learning, pedagogy in initial teacher education, and literacy learning. She worked for many years as a leader in schools and taught English. She is intrigued by narrative as a method for better understanding what teachers do and think.

Paulien C. Meijer, Ph.D., is professor in the field of teacher learning and development at Radboud University Nijmegen, the Netherlands. Her publications focus on teacher learning in different phases of the professional career. As a Teacher Educator and former Teacher in Social Sciences, she is specifically interested in teacher learning that includes the development of professional identity. Since 2009, she has chaired the International Study Association of Teachers and Teaching (ISATT).

Cholpon Musaeva is an EFL/ESL teacher with seven years of teaching experience in English Language Teaching in Kyrgyzstan and India. Presently she is pursuing a Ph.D. in English Language Education and is working as a Teaching Assistant at the Non-Formal Courses Department at The English and Foreign Languages University, Hyderabad, India. She has participated in a number of short-term teacher development courses for teachers of English including SIT TESOL and Hornby Summer School. She is interested in teacher development, materials production, course design, ESP, EAP, and using 2.0 tools in ELT and teacher development programs.

Lily Orland-Barak, Ph.D., is a Professor in Education and Dean of the Faculty of Education, University of Haifa, Israel. Her research focuses on professional learning, mentoring, and curriculum development in the context of teacher education. She has published numerous articles on these topics, and serves on national and international academic committees and editorial boards. Her recent book *Learning to Mentor-as-Praxis: Foundations for a curriculum in teacher education* (2010), by Springer, was awarded the Division K 2012 "Exemplary Research in Teaching and Teacher Education Award" at the American Educational Research Association (AERA) Meeting in Vancouver, Canada.

Samuel Ouma Oyoo, Ph.D., is a Senior Lecturer in Science Education at the School of Education, the University of the Witwatersrand, Johannesburg, South Africa. He is a graduate of both Nottingham and Leeds Universities, UK and also Monash University, Melbourne, Australia. His research interests are in Education as a general area, but with a focus on issues in learning and teaching school science, especially physics. He is also the author of the article "Language in Science Classrooms: An Analysis of Physics Teachers' Use of and Beliefs about Language," published in the journal *Research in Science Education*.

Tara Ratnam, Ph.D., is an ESL teacher, teacher educator and researcher from India. Her research revolves around teacher learning and change in reflective communities of inquiry. In this pursuit, she focuses on the cultural, historical and institutional forces that mediate teachers' thinking and the resulting tension-laden pathways they negotiate. She is also keenly interested in issues of diversity and in providing socially sensitive learning support to culturally diverse student populations.

Tom Russell, Ph.D., is a Professor in the Faculty of Education at Queen's University, Canada, where he has taught courses in science education since 1977. His research focuses on how people learn to teach and how teachers improve their teaching, with special reference to learning from experience. He is a founding Co-Editor of the journal *Studying Teacher Education*.

Frances O'Connell Rust, Ph.D., is a Visiting Professor and Director of Teacher Education at the University of Pennsylvania Graduate School of Education. During the 2009–2010 academic year, she served as a Visiting Scholar at the University of Illinois-Chicago. From 2007 to 2009, she was a Senior Vice President for Academic Affairs and Dean of Faculty at Erikson Institute. She is a Professor Emeritus at New York University's Steinhardt School of Education where she was a professor of education between 1991 and 2007.

ABOUT THE CONTRIBUTORS

Marjeta Šarić works as a Teaching Assistant in the Department of Educational Sciences, Faculty of Arts, University of Ljubljana, Slovenia. She is working on her Ph.D. Her research interests include emotions in teaching, teacher reflective practice, school culture, and teaching in higher education.

Michael Schratz, Ph.D., is a Professor of Education at the Department of Teacher Education and School Research, University of Innsbruck, Austria, and is presently Dean of the School of Education. He also is a scientific Director of the Austrian Leadership Academy. He has been involved in research projects on educational leadership and policy development and his publications have been translated into several languages.

Barbara Šteh, Ph.D., is an Assistant Professor of Educational Psychology in the Department of Educational Sciences at the Faculty of Arts of the University of Ljubljana, Slovenia. Her research interests include the quality of teaching/learning, implementation of active learning methods, the cooperation between school and parents, teacher autonomy and professional development. She also organizes many workshops and seminars for teachers at all levels and educational advisors.

Carola Steinberg, Ph.D., spent 20 years working as an adult educator before joining the Wits School of Education at University of the Witwatersrand, South Africa as a teacher educator in 1999. She teaches in the Division of Curriculum, specializing in assessment. She has recently successfully defended her doctoral dissertation entitled: "Teachers' Emotions towards Assessment: What can be Learned from Taking the Emotions Seriously?"

Leena Syrjälä, Ph.D., is a Professor of Education at the Faculty of Education, University of Oulu, Finland. For years she has been interested in narrative research on teachers. She has been a leader of the research group "Living Story" where narrative and multidisciplinary approaches have been used in the research on teachers' identities and well-being and in the practice of teacher education.

Edith Tabak, Ph.D., is the Rector of Levinsky College of Education in Tel Aviv, Israel. Previously she served as the head of the School of Education, in charge of curriculum development for both pre and in-service teachers and responsible for the college's relationship with the Partnership schools. She has developed numerous projects in teacher education, in which she documented teacher learning and teacher leadership. Her teaching, research and publications, have been in the areas of teacher education, self-study, action research, and curriculum inquiry.

Kirsi Tirri, Ph.D., is a Professor of Education and Research Director in the Department of Teacher Education at the University of Helsinki, Finland. She was the President of ECHA (European Council for High Ability) for the years 2008–2012, and is currently the President of the International Studies SIG (Special Interest Group) at AERA (American Educational Research Association). Her research interests include moral and religious education, gifted education, teacher education, and cross-cultural studies. She has led Finnish teams of researchers in many national and international research projects.

Auli Toom, Ph.D., is an Adjunct Professor at the Faculty of Behavioral Sciences, University of Helsinki, Finland. Her major research interests are teacher's tacit pedagogical knowing, teacher knowledge, teacher reflection, and teacher education. She leads and coleads research projects on teacher education and university pedagogy. In addition to her research activities, she has worked as an expert in several international teacher education development projects.

Nico Verloop, Ph.D., was appointed as a Professor of Education in 1991 and served was director of ICLON Graduate School of Teaching from 1995 to 2010. He was the President of the Dutch Educational Research Association and is on the Editorial Board of six international journals. His main research interests are teacher learning, teachers' practical knowledge and teacher evaluation.

Xiaohong Yang is a Professor of English Literature and Language at Hangzhou Normal University, China. He graduated from Shanghai International Studies University in 1989. He has spent more than ten years in transforming his own classroom from the test-orientation prevalent in China to an orientation toward the growth of students. He is currently interested in and working toward digitalizing student-centered learning strategies to reach greater audiences.

Issa Danjun Ying, Ph.D., is an Instructor in the Centre for Language in Education, the Hong Kong Institute of Education, Hong Kong. Her research interests are primarily in the areas of teacher development, teacher identity, professional learning community, and discourse studies in education. She has been an ISATT member since 2007 and is currently the ISATT National Representative for Hong Kong. She enjoys the learning opportunities provided by ISATT.

Michal Zellermayer, Ph.D., is a Professor of Teacher Education at Levinsky College of Education in Tel Aviv, Israel. She is the head of the Graduate

School at the college and the leader of the Action Research SIG at the MOFET institute (the national intercollegial center for the research and development of programs in teacher education and teaching in the colleges) in Israel. She served as a co-coordinator of the Teaching and Teacher Education Special Interest Group at the European Association for Research on Learning and Instruction and was a member of the Editorial Board of the Educational Research Review as well as Teachers and Teaching: Theory and Practice. She has published numerous papers on writing instruction, developing rich communicative environments, teacher learning, and action research.